Why Do You Need this New Edition?

5 good reasons why you should buy this new edition of Rockin' Out!

1. The first major overhaul since the book was first published in 1997. Overall, the text has been reduced by 15 percent even as whole new sections have been added.

2. The book has been revised and updated throughout—reflecting the incorporation of new research and more current literature—to create a clearer, more streamlined focus on the story being told.

3. The introduction now goes back to minstrelsy, new sections on jazz have been added to chapters 1 and 2, and new discussions of Latin music and musicians have been incorporated throughout.

4. Now available with MyMusicKit, including timeline, documentaries, chapter questions and summaries, and links to NPR features on rock.

5. Full iTunes lists, with links, are given for all listening.

PEARSON

FIFTH EDITION

Rockin' Out

Popular Music in the USA

Reebee Garofalo

University of Massachusetts, Boston

Prentice Hall

Boston   Columbus   Indianapolis   New York   San Francisco   Upper Saddle River
Amsterdam   Cape Town   Dubai   London   Madrid   Milan   Munich   Paris   Montreal   Toronto
Delhi   Mexico City   São Paulo   Sydney   Hong Kong   Seoul   Singapore   Taipei   Tokyo

Editorial Director: Craig Campanella
Editor in Chief: Sarah Touborg
Executive Editor: Richard Carlin
Editorial Assistant: Tricia Murphy
Vice President of Marketing: Brandy Dawson
Executive Marketing Manager:
  Kate Stewart Mitchell
Senior Managing Editor: Ann Marie McCarthy
Assistant Managing Editor: Melissa Feimer
Project Manager: Marlene Gassler
Senior Manufacturing and Operations Manager:
  Nick Sklitsis
Senior Operations Specialist: Brian Mackey

Senior Art Director: Pat Smythe
Cover Designer: Joseph DePinho
Cover Photo Credit: Getty Images, Inc./Win McNamee/Staff
Manager, Visual Research: Beth Brenzel
Image Permission Coordinator: Nancy Seise
Manager, Cover Visual Research & Permissions:
  Karen Sanatar
Senior Media Editor: David Alick
Full-Service Project Management: Karpagam Jagadeesan,
  PreMediaGlobal
Composition: PreMediaGlobal
Printer/Binder: Edwards Brothers
Cover Printer: Lehigh-Phoenix Color/Hagerstown

Library of Congress Cataloging-in-Publication Data

Garofalo, Reebee.
  Rockin' out : popular music in the USA / Reebee Garofalo. — 5th ed.
    p. cm.
  Includes bibliographical references and index.
  ISBN-13: 978-0-205-76378-8
  ISBN-10: 0-205-76378-2
 1. Popular music—United States—History and criticism. I. Title. II. Title: Rocking out.
  ML3477.G37 2010
  781.640973—dc22

                                          2010005346

10 9 8 7 6 5 4 3 2 1

Prentice Hall
is an imprint of

PEARSON

www.pearsonhighered.com

ISBN 10: 0-205-76378-2
ISBN 13: 978-0-205-76378-8
Exam Copy ISBN 10: 0-205-76379-0
ISBN 13: 978-0-205-76379-5

Contents

3 "Good Rockin' Tonight": The Rise of Rhythm and Blues   58

4 Crossing Cultures: The Eruption of Rock 'n' Roll   80

5   The Empire Strikes Back: The Reaction to Rock 'n' Roll   125

6   Popular Music and Political Culture: The Sixties   151

7 Music Versus Markets: The Fragmentation of Pop   201

8 Punk and Disco: The Poles of Pop   252

9   Are We the World? Music Videos, Superstars, and Mega-Events   292

10   Rap and Metal: The Voices of Youth Culture   325

Preface

The fifth edition of *Rockin' Out: Popular Music in the U.S.A.* represents its first major overhaul since the book was first published in 1997. Overall, the text has been reduced by 15 percent even as whole new sections have been added. The book has been revised and updated throughout—reflecting the incorporation of new research and more current literature—to create a clearer, more streamlined focus on the story being told. The result, I think, is a richer, more nuanced history. I have taken the introduction back to minstrelsy, added new sections on jazz in Chapters 1 and 2, and incorporated new discussions of Latin music and musicians throughout. The analysis of mega-events has been extended, discussions of the structure of the music industry have been consolidated, and the book concludes with a consideration of the long tail effect as we envision the future of music. Finally, a number of the user-friendly tables that appeared in the fourth edition have been moved to the Web and now include audio links for your listening pleasure.

As I have said in previous editions of *Rockin' Out*, popular music—playing it, listening to it, learning from it, teaching others what I know—has been one of the organizing principles of my life ever since I can remember. It still energizes me, provides the sound track for significant moments in my life, and helps me to navigate the world around me. In the society at large, discussions of its significance can be found everywhere, from family dinners and Saturday night parties to corporate boardrooms and congressional chambers. There has also been an increasing interest in popular music courses on college and university campuses. The fact that popular music has been a source of pleasure for millions of people all over the world is reason enough for listening to it. But popular music is also a social and political indicator that mirrors and influences the society in which we live. This is the reason for studying it. *Rockin' Out* offers one good way to do that.

Successive editions of *Rockin' Out* have not only updated popular music history with new research into current trends, but they have also added features designed to make the text more user-friendly. The second edition of the book, for example, saw the addition of a song index, which made *Rockin' Out* more useful as a source book. That edition also included the conversion of a number of artist and song lists from the text into easy-to-understand tables that gave the reader a graphic sense of historical patterns and preserved the narrative for more important analytic points. The third edition included an accompanying compilation CD of songs selected to enhance the historical narrative. In the fourth edition, the CD was replaced by two iTunes playlists, constructed by Richard Kassel, that made nearly 200 songs from the book readily available for convenient download. The fourth edition also added a number of carefully selected listening guides to deepen the analysis of musical elements and further enhance the narrative. Angela Mariani-Smith deserves major credit, along with Chris Smith, for contributing the listening guides. This fifth edition is accompanied by a much more feature-rich website that includes additional music tables and listening guides with direct links to musical selections, chapter outlines, and discussion questions, as well as pointers to regularly updated supplementary resources and other interactive features.

(((● HEAR MORE
Download the iMix playlists on MyMusicKit

Naturally, a book of the scope of *Rockin' Out* does not fall from the sky. Although my name graces the cover, *Rockin' Out* is a work that involves countless others. In addition to drawing on original research and a wealth of primary and secondary source material, *Rockin' Out* has been shaped by discussions over the years with Bill Adler, William Barlow, Marcus Breen, Iain Chambers, Jannette Dates, Kai Fikentscher, Murray Forman, Simon Frith, Donna Gaines, Andrew Goodwin, Herman Gray, Larry Grossberg, Charles Hamm, Dave Harker, Simon Jones, Steve Jones, Anahid Kassabian, Charlie Keil, George Lipsitz, Dick Lourie, Portia Maultsby, Susan McClary, Keith Negus, Deborah Pacini Hernandez, Richard Peterson, Tricia Rose, Danny Schechter, Larry Shore, Philip Tagg, Robert Walser, Peter Wicke, and many others too numerous to mention.

Dave Sanjek has demonstrated over and over that he is one of the most knowledgeable and forthcoming researchers in the field. Now professor of music at Salford University, he also deserves special mention in his former position of BMI archivist for helping to enhance these pages with a treasure trove of photographs. The late Rick Dutka still occupies a special place in my heart and mind as someone whose knowledge of and love for popular music were as boundless as his political energy and activist spirit.

Brad Martin worked as my research assistant for the first edition, contributing everything from footnote corrections to substantive commentary. In preparation for the second edition, Craig Morrison offered challenging comments and a detailed review of the entire first edition. Students from my History of Rock 'n' Roll class at Tufts University contributed to the research for the second edition, including Ana Garnecho and Christina Lembo (teen pop), Lisa Wichter (women), Elise Podell (MP3), Matthew Baron (r&b), Mark Scholnick (rap), Laura Horstmann and Zach Berge (turntablism), Allie Schwartz and Alison Clarke (swing), and Suzanne Szwarc (Latin pop). More recent conversations with Kai Fikentscher, Murray Forman, and Deborah Pacini Hernandez have helped me to better understand electronic dance music, contemporary hip hop, and Latin(o) popular music, respectively. Marcus Breen gave the final chapter for the third edition a useful critical read. I am indebted to Andrew Ryan, my research assistant from UMass Boston, for his research contributions to the fourth edition, particularly in the area of hip hop. Raquel Z. Rivera, Wayne Marshall, and Deborah Pacini Hernandez were invaluable in shaping my understanding of reggaeton.

As to my own previous work, echoes of *Rock 'n' Roll Is Here to Pay,* the book with which I was first identified, can certainly be detected in *Rockin' Out.* In this instance, I owe a major debt of gratitude to senior author Steve Chapple, whose pioneering contributions to popular music studies helped define the field and pushed me to formulate my own views. My chapter on the history of black popular music that appeared in *Split Image,* edited by Jannette Dates and William Barlow, informed the discussions of r&b, soul, and rap that appear in these pages. An earlier version of the discussion of popular music and the civil rights movement was published in *Radical America* and reprinted in my own *Rockin' the Boat.* More detailed versions of my research on mega-events have appeared in *Reimaging America,* edited by Mark O'Brien and Craig Little; *Technoculture,* edited by Constance Penley and Andrew Ross; and *Rockin' the Boat.* My research on censorship has been published in greater detail in the *Journal of Popular Music Studies.* It was originally funded by a grant from the Massachusetts Foundation for the Humanities and the Massachusetts Cultural Council, neither of which bear any responsibility for my opinions on the subject. My research for the chapter on Internet music in *Policing Pop,* edited by Martin Cloonan and me, provided the basis for earlier discussions of peer-to-peer file-sharing networks. This work has been regularly revised and updated in *Rockin' Out*. A version of my post-9/11 research was published in *Music in the Post-9/11 World*, edited by Jonathan Ritter and J. Martin Daughtry.

The story of *Rockin' Out* has been an interesting one for me. I continue to be indebted to Susannah Brabant for bringing the original book proposal to the attention of Bill Barke at Allyn and Bacon, who published the first edition. Subsequent editions have been published by Prentice Hall. (Those corporate mergers I write about are not limited to the music industry.) Copyright was transferred to me for the fourth edition, and the editorial baton was passed to Richard Carlin, who came to Prentice Hall as a seasoned editor with a wealth of valuable experience, a congenial style, and a willingness to think outside the box, all of which have been most appreciated. I would like to acknowledge the following reviewers: Clifford Adams, College-Conservatory of Music, Univ. of Cincinnati; Carey Fleiner, University of Delaware; Guy Capuzzo, University of North Carolina, Greensboro; Danilo Lozano, Whittier College; Kai Fikentscher, Ramapo College of New Jersey; Scott D. Shinbara, University of Arizona; Douglas G. Weeks, WPI; Joseph Kotarba, University of Houston.

For the fifth edition, Richard assembled a new crack team of professionals. Leslie Cohen was brought on board as developmental editor. Her assistance in editing, reorganizing, and developing the book has been invaluable in bringing the fifth edition to fruition, and her insight, astute analyses, and friendship have gone well beyond anything that could possibly have been specified in her scope of work. The actual production process was coordinated expertly by production manager Marlene Gassler and, halfway around the world, production editor Karpagam Jagadeesan, along with the able colleagues who comprise their staffs.

As for me, I am in my thirty-first year at the College of Public and Community Service (CPCS) at UMass Boston, and I continue to enjoy my affiliation with the American Studies Program. CPCS and public higher education generally are still in rough shape. To keep my sanity, I play drums and sing in two bands. The Blue Suede Boppers, a fifties rock 'n' roll band, has been delivering hot sounds from the cold war for some 22 years now. In 2007, I joined a New Orleans–style marching band called the Second Line Social Aid and Pleasure Society Brass Band. SLSAPS is an activist street band, devoted to inclusion, community building, and social justice. How cool is that? Every year, we host the HONK! Festival (check it out at honkfest.org).

Then there is my family. Deborah Pacini Hernandez is not just my partner for life but also a colleague whose knowledge of popular music has added immeasurably to my own. Since the beginning of our relationship, she has offered perspective, insight, and criticism that have been incredibly valuable, and love and emotional support I can't imagine living without. The family that I inherited from her, which includes daughter Radha and son Tai, continues to be a source of great joy and incredibly eclectic musical tastes. The fact that I still have my brother Gary and his family in my life eases the loss of our father in 1999 and our mother in 2004. Between those losses I was blessed with a granddaughter, Radha's daughter Soleil. Now seven years old, she continues to fill me with a sense of wonderment in the present and hope for the future.

Reebee Garofalo
December 2009

Introduction: Definitions, Themes, and Issues

In my view, popular music cannot be fully understood simply as a stand-alone musical text and then measured against some abstract aesthetic notion of quality. Although it is important to explore the specificities of the music itself, it is equally important to recognize that the text is as much a product of its social and political context as any individual's creativity or talent. Because the economics of popularity matters, I attach a certain amount of importance to sales data. *Rockin' Out: Popular Music in the U.S.A.* is peppered with popularity chart listings and references to "gold" and "platinum" records (the sale of 500,000 and 1 million album units, respectively). At the same time, I am aware that commercially successful artists and records may or may not be the most influential or culturally important. Qualitative indicators such as historical accounts, musical analyses, critical reviews, and audience reactions must also play a role in the analysis.

Because the enslavement and oppression of African Americans and resulting cultural interactions have had such a profound effect on the development of our popular music, my inclination is to view popular music first through the lens of race and racism. Accordingly, *Rockin' Out* begins with a discussion of blackface minstrelsy and its controversial appropriation of African American culture for the primary benefit of a largely European American market. In minstrelsy, we see the development of a troubling, yet defining aspect of the early popular music business that carried forward into the Tin Pan Alley era of popular music in the twentieth century. There are also important patterns based on other crucial demographic variables, such as age, gender, and ethnicity. Technological advances and the political economy of the industry have also been important in shaping the development of popular music. Finally, popular music invariably develops in relation to the prevailing political climate in a given era. These, then, are the themes that run throughout this book.

While this book covers well over one hundred years of popular music history, its primary focus begins in the second half of the twentieth century. The pivotal moment in this history was the emergence of rock 'n' roll in the 1950s, as the transition from Tin Pan Alley pop to rock 'n' roll revealed important social and cultural shifts in U.S. society. If the music of Tin Pan Alley was lighthearted and urbane, the rock 'n' roll of the 1950s was heavy-handed and urban. While Tin Pan Alley appealed to middle-class sensibilities, rock 'n' roll was decidedly working class in its orientation. Whereas Tin Pan Alley made no particular age distinctions among its listeners, rock 'n' roll was targeted at youth. Tin Pan Alley was identified with sheet music in the same way that rock 'n' roll was associated with records, and this difference signified the beginning of an inextricable connection between popular music and advanced recording technology. Finally, the music of Tin Pan Alley evolved according to a European American paradigm of music making, even when it incorporated other cultural influences. In contrast, rock 'n' roll turned dramatically toward African American conventions. In short, the rock 'n' roll that emerged in the 1950s combined all the elements that would define the broad parameters of popular music in the United States for at least the next forty years.

In short, the rock 'n' roll that emerged in the 1950s combined all the elements that would define the broad parameters of popular music in the United States for at least the next forty years.

Into the Twentieth Century: Popular Music and Mass Culture

In its association with sheet music, Tin Pan Alley can be seen as a descendant of a popular culture that dates back to the invention of the printing press in fifteenth-century Europe.[1] When the music of Tin Pan Alley emerged, popular music was distinguished from both folk music and folk culture on the one hand, and classical or art music and high culture on the other. These distinctions were part of our inheritance that came with European colonization.

Prior to the advent of popular culture in Europe, European societies were characterized by a two-tiered system of culture that was composed of *folk culture* and *high culture.* Ample evidence suggests that there was considerable interaction between the two, but at the time, these different levels of culture were officially considered separate and distinct. Historically, folk culture has been associated with the poor and those lacking formal education—in European feudal societies, with the peasantry; after the Industrial Revolution, with agricultural workers and the urban proletariat. It was a collective and participatory culture, shared by a particular community of people. The music arising from it was comparatively simple in form and structure, performed by nonprofessionals, and passed along, usually anonymously, in oral tradition. Its production and consumption were noncommercial. At the other end of the European cultural spectrum was high culture, which was associated with the ruling classes—the feudal aristocracy, the capitalist bourgeoisie. Its music was more complicated in form and structure and was composed by paid professionals who were commissioned through a system of patronage. Because this music was notated (written down), it required a certain literacy and training for its performance. High culture thus imposed a separation between artists and consumers that was unknown in folk culture.

What was a community in folk culture was an audience in high culture. As the official culture of court and church, high culture was considered to be superior to folk culture.

Popular culture insinuated itself between folk culture and high culture as a third cultural category, a hybrid that was distinguishable from both but borrowed freely from each as needed. Tin Pan Alley provides an excellent example of these contradictory tendencies. In attempting to cater exclusively to popular (albeit narrow mainstream) tastes, Tin Pan Alley writers consciously sought to construct an alternative to the cultural dominance of European art music. In the process, these writers incorporated influences, however superficially, from a wide range of sources, including a number of African American genres. At the same time, however, these writers often took their cues from classical music and high culture. For example, the 1941 melody of "Tonight We Love," a popular song by Ray Austin and Bobby Worth, was lifted almost note for note from the first movement of Tchaikovsky's *Piano Concerto No. 1.* In leaning heavily on upper-middle-class themes and images—dining at the Ritz, performing in black tie and tails—Tin Pan Alley writers further (and perhaps unwittingly) allied themselves with the high culture they sought to displace.

The invention of new mass communication technologies—records, radio, film, and eventually television—inserted yet another distinction into the cultural lexicon, namely, the concept of *mass culture.* The new term indicated cultural dissemination on a scale that increased by orders of magnitude. The question of scale had important implications for qualitative judgments about mass culture. Prior to its advent, it was possible to consider popular culture as historically continuous with folk culture, either slowly replacing folk cultures as the next stage of development following the Industrial Revolution or as coexisting with rural or industrial folk cultures in the modern era. When viewed in this way, popular culture, like folk culture, was a culture of the people. With the introduction of the mass media, however, the idea of a continuing historical progression came to an abrupt halt. In the eyes of most observers, the emergence of mass culture was accompanied by a subtle but important shift in orientation from a culture *of* the people to a culture *for* the masses. In this deceptively simple change, there was a profound transformation of meaning. Mass culture was not seen as the lived culture of an identifiable group of people, which reflected their values and aspirations. Instead, it was a commodified culture produced by a centralized, corporate culture industry for privatized, passive consumption by an alienated, undifferentiated mass.[2] Thus, although the terms *mass culture* and *popular culture* are often used interchangeably today, most observers tended to distinguish between the two in language that was pejorative and/or politically charged until well into the 1960s. In 1959, for example, Oscar Handlin, among others, argued forcefully against "the misconception that the 'mass culture' of the present is but an extension of the popular culture of the past."[3] Indeed, as late as 1965, Stuart Hall and Paddy Whannel maintained that "the typical 'art' of the mass media today is not a continuity from, but a *corruption of,* popular art."[4]

Rock 'n' roll, of course, could be numbered among the victims of this largely false distinction. As an unabashedly commercial product clearly intended for mass consumption, most critics dismissed the music as inferior and unworthy of serious consideration. To avoid the mass culture stigma, critics and historians in the 1960s who became invested in the cultural importance

> *In the eyes of most observers, the emergence of mass culture was accompanied by a subtle but important shift in orientation from a culture of the people to a culture for the masses.*

of rock as the mature form of rock 'n' roll tended to characterize the music as something other than what it was. Historian Carl Belz, for example, argued that "rock is a part of the long tradition of folk art in the United States and throughout the world."[5] As the music took a turn toward greater sophistication, this characterization underwent further change. Discussions of Bob Dylan's lyrics as poetry and the Beatles' *Sgt. Pepper's Lonely Hearts Club Band* as art reflected an attempt by some to "elevate" rock from folk music to art, thereby allying it with high culture. At the time, these efforts to categorize rock represented genuine attempts to understand the place of popular music in the hierarchy of cultural practices. Ultimately, however, there was no getting around the fact that rock was both a popular music and a mass cultural form. In 1981, music sociologist Simon Frith, among others, dismissed both earlier positions of rock as folk and rock as art. "Rock is a commercially made mass music," he asserted, "and this must be the starting point for its celebration as well as its dismissal."[6] Since then, musical practices have been discussed more in terms of the death throes of the modern era and its uneasy segue into postmodernism, a period characterized by, among other things, the collapse of all cultural categories.

Rock 'N' Roll: The Birth of a New Era

The straightforward commercialism and mass appeal of rock 'n' roll did not set it apart from other popular music. What made rock 'n' roll different was its urban orientation, focus on youth culture, appeal to working-class sensibilities, and relationship to technology and African American musical influences and performance styles. As Charlie Gillett argued in his classic study *The Sound of the City,* rock 'n' roll was the first popular genre to incorporate the relentless pulse and sheer volume of urban life into the music itself. In his words, "Rock and Roll was perhaps the first form of popular culture to celebrate without reservation characteristics of city life that had been among the most criticized."[7] Here Gillett was referring to urban sounds that were perceived as "brutal and oppressive." In this world of droning machines, post–World War II adolescents "staked out their freedom . . . inspired and reassured by the rock and roll beat."[8]

Gillett's conflation of adolescence and rock 'n' roll highlights the fact that the emergence of the music as a genre coincided with the beginnings of youth culture as a phenomenon. Due to the convergence of a number of social forces in the 1950s, including postwar affluence and a demographic shift in the population toward youth, teenagers became an identifiable consumer group and one that possessed an ample amount of disposable income. The music industry learned, albeit not without considerable resistance, that targeting the musical tastes of this generation could be quite lucrative. As Simon Frith noted:

> The young had always had idols—film stars, sportsmen, singers like Frank Sinatra and Johnny Ray; the novelty of rock 'n' roll was that its performers were the same age as their audience, came from similar backgrounds, had similar interests; and the rise of rock 'n' roll meant a generation gap . . . . Rock 'n' roll records and radio shows were aimed exclusively at the young, . . . and by the end of the 1950s most pop records were being bought by the young.[9]

Following the eruption of rock 'n' roll, the music industry identified young people as the primary audience for popular music. This new marketing strategy was later complicated by the fact that the baby boomers who comprised the initial rock 'n' roll audience kept on buying records well into their thirties and forties. Indeed, different generational preferences can be seen as a partial explanation for the fragmentation of popular genres in the 1970s. In the 1980s and 1990s, clear generational differences resurfaced as rap, metal, and alternative became the cutting-edge statements of youth culture. In response, many baby boomers have adopted the same critical tone toward this new music that their parents directed at early rock 'n' roll.

If rock 'n' roll was different from other forms of popular music in its unique relationship to youth, its connection to technology was also different. Different media have their own internal logic for elements such as composition, chronology, pacing, gesture, tone, inflection, and so forth. The power of filmmaking, for example, does not lie in the simple reproduction and transmission of an existing written work; rather, it is in exploiting the particular characteristics of the medium—camera angles, lighting, editing—that filmmaking becomes an art form in its own right. The same logic extends to the relationship between music and recording. However, while the artistic possibilities of filmmaking were recognized fairly early in the development of the medium, the incorporation of recording technology into the creation of music—as opposed to its simple reproduction—was slower to take hold. Initially, recording was thought of as a documentary process that sought only to preserve the quality of a live performance. Thus, while the success of popular music—even the music of Tin Pan Alley—depended to a large extent on mass communication technologies, these technologies were used in the dissemination of the music rather than its creation.

Unlike earlier forms of popular music, rock 'n' roll incorporated the capabilities of advanced technology into the creative process itself. Far from valuing the purity of the live performance, rock 'n' roll records consciously used the technical features of echo, editing, overdubbing, and multitracking to distort the reality of the perform-

> **U**nlike earlier forms of popular music, rock 'n' roll incorporated the capabilities of advanced technology into the creative process itself.

ance. "Technical processes," as musicologist Peter Wicke has said, "became musical opportunities."[10] Thus, the emergence of rock 'n' roll was characterized by a progressively more intimate relationship with the technologies used in its production and dissemination. This relationship continued as rock ventured toward art in the 1960s. Following the release of *Sgt. Pepper,* an album so dependent on studio technology that it couldn't be performed live, rock groups spent untold hours in the studio experimenting with technological gimmickry, overdubbing and adding special effects, and mixing each cut to perfection. Disco was further immersed in technological wizardry, becoming almost completely a product of the studio. In live performance, the use of feedback and distortion pioneered by Jimi Hendrix has become institutionalized in heavy metal through the use of voltage regulators, special effects boxes, and vocal distortion devices. Rap has pushed the envelope still further, first by using dual turntables as musical instruments, and then by using samplers, sequencers, and programmable drum machines as essential tools of the trade. To the extent that these creative uses of technology have been accepted as artistically valid, they have pushed the very definition of popular music beyond a traditional European conception of music as a pattern of *notes* toward a conception of music as organized *sound.*

Beginning with early rock 'n' roll, advanced technologies were married to musical elements that in themselves separated the music from earlier forms of mainstream popular music along lines of class and race. The prominence of rhythm, immoderate volume, slurred notes, grainy vocals, aggressive attack, and vernacular speech that characterized rock 'n' roll tended to place the music outside the reach of middle-class culture and beyond the purview of musicological investigation. Because the field of musicology derives its main categories of investigation from the "notated" tradition of European art music, there has been a tendency to dismiss most working-class forms of popular music (and certainly rock 'n' roll) as "formulaic" and therefore insignificant. Within the parameters valued by official tastemakers—melody, harmony, structure—rock 'n' roll was found wanting. However, as Richard Middleton has pointed out:

> *The formulaic processes operate within parameters relatively highly valued by traditional musicology: harmony, melodic shape, basic rhythm pattern. Variant processes, on the other hand, often take place in parameters little valued by traditional musicology (and much harder to notate): slight pitch inflection or rhythmic variation, timbre and timbre changes, accent, and attack.* [11]

The subtlety and sophistication of rock 'n' roll, then, were to be found in features of the music that were outside the frame of reference of the cultural elite.

Analyses of structure, melody, and chord progressions, of course, are not without value. They can offer important insights into the differences existing between popular music and other forms of music, as well as differences among popular genres themselves. Rock 'n' roll and Tin Pan Alley pop, for example, can be distinguished in these terms. However, a surface analysis of these elements alone cannot adequately capture the disjuncture that characterized the transition between the two. To get to this level of analysis, it is necessary to examine the full range of cultural practices and performance styles that comprised these respective musical eras. The ascendancy of Tin Pan Alley coincided with the emergence of a number of African American genres and subgenres, including ragtime, blues, boogie woogie, and jazz. Certain aspects of these African American sounds were appropriated by Tin Pan Alley songwriters who were somewhat open to outside influences. From ragtime to swing, one can find a hint of syncopation here, a blue note there. But while grassroots blues and jazz lured listeners toward Africa, mainstream pop interpretations of these genres quickly pulled them back to Europe. Tin Pan Alley appropriations were, by and large, superficial adaptations—what musicologist Charles Hamm has called "a touch of exotic seasoning"[12]—that were incorporated into an aesthetic framework defined by the European tradition. This, of course, was reassuring to some. It preserved the centrality of Western civilization and kept upstart African American artists in check. Conservative culture critic H. F. Mooney, for example, considered it fortunate that the influence of African American music was "limited by compromises with middle class conventions" and delighted in the fact that it was "'polished' . . . so as to conform to the standards of European rendition."[13] Revealing his bias further, Mooney noted, "The highest compliment most of the public could pay to big-band jazz between 1928 and 1950 was 'symphonic' or 'advanced.'"[14] He went on to describe the pressures on African American artists to toe the line:

> *Middle-class Negroes who desired to "come up," as they put it, during the 1930s and the 1940s responded to the smoothly harmonized arrangements of a white Jimmy Dorsey's watered-down jazz. Duke Ellington himself was influenced by Guy Lombardo's "sweetest music this side of heaven," and*

brought something of the sound of the Roosevelt Hotel ballroom to Harlem. Commercial orchestras of the period around 1920–50 followed more or less the "safe bet"—the aesthetic aspirations of the middle-class market—as did, indeed, most of the big Negro bands.[15]

Rock 'n' roll, however, turned this situation on its head. By all accounts, the eruption of rock 'n' roll entailed a profound shift in cultural values on the part of mainstream youth, a shift away from European American sensibilities and toward African American ones. The most important feature of this shift was an increased emphasis on rhythm. In the words of Christopher Small, "Rhythm is to the African musician what harmony is to the European—the central organizing principle of the art."[16] Although in the slave cultures of the Americas, this African tradition was complicated by considerable pressure to adopt European ways of music making (indeed the history of African American music is fraught with this tension), rock 'n' roll is clearly descended from the tradition of organizing musical elements around a recurring rhythmic structure. In its early years, rock 'n' roll was often referred to as the Big Beat. With the ascent of rock 'n' roll, this "central organizing principle" came to define mainstream popular music in a way that it never had before.

*B*y all accounts, the eruption of rock 'n' roll entailed a profound shift in cultural values on the part of mainstream youth, a shift away from European American sensibilities and toward African American ones.

The orientation toward an African American aesthetic also affected musical elements such as structure, chord patterns, and scales, as well as the more subtle features mentioned earlier. As music historian Iain Chambers has written:

> *While the thirty-two bar format is the musical cornerstone of Tin Pan Alley, in the Afro-American tradition it is the twelve bar blues: three chords alternating in a fixed pattern. From the perspective of European classical harmony, this offers an even more rigid and correspondingly "poorer" musical frame than that used by the white popular music industry. The "blues scale" is also sparse: consisting of five rather than the seven notes of the official European scale. This produces a telling disorientation for our ears as the blues singer stretches and slides over those intervals ("blue notes") we are accustomed to expect. Such a sensation of "foreignness" is the most recognisable aural trait of the blues and Afro-American music in pop—the slides, slurs, bent, "dirty" and uncertain notes in the voice, guitar, saxophone and bass. It remains the irreducible testimony of the clash between a legitimised white European-derived tradition and a barely recognised Afro-American one.*[17]

While there had been an awareness of African American influences among white jazz musicians and Tin Pan Alley composers, rock 'n' roll pushed performers toward the wholesale adoption of an African American orientation. As Peter Wicke has stated:

> *Elvis Presley or Bill Haley were no longer merely taking set pieces from blues and rhythm & blues and imposing them as superficial effects on quite different musical categories. Their popularity was founded precisely on the fact that they were copying Afro-American music with all its characteristic features, including the performance style of black musicians, as closely as possible. What was happening was a complete reversal of the earlier situation. Whereas before white musicians had adapted elements of the Afro-American musical tradition to their own aesthetic ideas, now they were trying to suit their performances to the aesthetics of Afro-American music.*[18]

If rock 'n' roll tipped the cultural balance toward an African American aesthetic, it was also a music defined by its hybridity. While Elvis Presley clearly drew on African American performance styles, he adopted the instrumentation of country music and was also driven by pop tendencies that were entirely consistent with Tin Pan Alley values. Chuck Berry and Sam Cooke, as well as many doo wop groups, enunciated clearly enough to pass muster with the harshest diction teacher. Indeed, doo wop harmonies and vocal styles defy any attempt to analyze rock 'n' roll solely in terms of race. In short, European cultural standards were never abandoned altogether; rock 'n' roll simply imposed a new cultural formula that favored African American values.

Since the advent of rock 'n' roll, there has been a continuing debate regarding the relative proportions of African American and European American influences in popular music. It was considered a mark of distinction by some critics that many of the San Francisco groups of the late 1960s did not sound like they were emulating African American performance styles. Art rock made its musical statement by looking to classical European influences. The concept of instrumental virtuosity in heavy metal derived from the same source. Punk, which ironically was formed in reaction to the excesses of art rock, stripped the music of whatever African American influences remained. Even disco, in the United States, was marked by the tension between funk and soft soul influences on the one hand, and the influence of Eurodisco on the other. Popular music has been re-Africanized in rap and hip hop culture, which has concentrated primarily on heavy beats and spoken word rhymes, eschewing melody almost completely. In fact, there has been considerable debate about whether hip hop represents a new paradigm that has superseded rock.

Marketing and the Politics of Race, Language, and Gender

If rock 'n' roll represented the triumph of African American culture, it did not automatically follow that African Americans would be the main beneficiaries of the victory. The way in which music actually unfolds as a social practice does not necessarily determine the way in which it reaches the ears of its audience. By the time a creative urge has been fed through the star-making machinery of the culture industry, all the biases of class, race, and gender have been brought to bear. Although rock 'n' roll proceeded from an aesthetic impulse that viewed cultural borrowing as both natural and desirable, it developed in a commercial context where the natural process of cultural borrowing can become theft, and artists can be categorized incorrectly or excluded from the marketplace altogether for reasons that have little to do with talent or musical style.

If rock 'n' roll represented the triumph of African American culture, it did not automatically follow that African Americans would be the main beneficiaries of the victory.

The marketing categories of the music industry have often classified performers as much by race as by musical style. The beginnings of this practice date back to the 1920s, when the music industry organized popular music into three categories: "race" (African American popular music); "hillbilly" (white working-class rural styles); and "popular" (mainstream pop of the type produced by Tin Pan Alley).[19] Initially, *Billboard,* the leading music industry trade magazine, published popularity charts for only that music classified as "popular" by the industry.

However, when *Your Hit Parade,* a radio program based on (and shaped by) listener preferences, became one of the most popular programs in the country in 1935, it became apparent that the commercial interests of the industry were not being served by only one chart. Thus, by the end of the decade, *Billboard* had inaugurated a popularity chart for hillbilly music and in 1942 added a chart titled "The Harlem Hit Parade." Three years later, the magazine changed this title to "Race Music."

Each marketing category was presumed to be a distinct musical style with its own audience. "The assumed mainstream pop audience," according to David Brackett, "was northern, urban, middle or upper class, and also white. The charts for the marginal musics also assumed an audience—African American for race and r&b [rhythm and blues], rural southern white for hillbilly, folk, and country and western (as these charts were variously designated during the 1940s)."[20] Initially, there was little overlap among the categories, which lent credence to the industry's assumption that these were separate, distinct styles. Indeed, these styles did develop regionally in a country that was segregated and wracked by class divisions. In fact, the social and cultural changes associated with World War II began to render the barriers between marketing categories a bit more porous. As the categories "race" and "hillbilly" began to come to the attention of the mainstream audience, these styles were said to cross over.

The term *crossover* refers to that process whereby an artist or a recording from a secondary or specialty marketing category, such as country and western (c&w) or rhythm and blues (r&b), achieves hit status in the mainstream market. Although recently the term has been used simply to indicate multiple chart listings in any direction, historically it connoted movement from a marginal category to the mainstream. In writing of the golden years of r&b, music historian Arnold Shaw has noted:

> *The crossover concept was inherent in R&B from the start. In fact, acceptance by the pop market of an R&B disk (Cecil Gant's "I Wonder") generated the first mushrooming of R&B record companies. While these labels produced disks basically for ghetto consumption, they always hoped that the larger white market might be receptive.[21]*

The greater acceptance of African Americans in the mainstream market after World War II not only prompted some changes in music charting practices but also put the industry on the horns of a racial dilemma that has been the subject of heated debate ever since.

As late as 1949, most of the music by African American artists could be found under the heading *Race Music* in record company catalogues. As this music began to cross over to the white market, however, it was decided that a more palatable term was needed. Record companies toyed with labels like *ebony* and *sepia* for a while, but these too were obviously distinctions of color, not musical style. Eventually *rhythm and blues* (reportedly coined by Jerry Wexler at *Billboard*) became the accepted term, and from 1949 until 1963, *Billboard* charted the music as such. *Billboard* discontinued its r&b charts from the end of 1963 until the beginning of 1965, presumably because the pop charts were becoming increasingly integrated. During this time, however, the number of African American artists on the pop charts actually declined. Accordingly, the r&b charts were reinstated by the magazine, and in 1969, r&b was replaced with the term *soul.* The industry came full circle in 1982 when the soul charts were renamed *black* music. *Billboard* later offered the explanation that "'soul' was too limited a term to define the diversity of musical styles appearing on the chart, and that 'black' was a better tribute to the music's cultural origins."[22] Ultimately, however, this term was as vulnerable to criticism as the term *race music* had been four decades earlier. Thus in 1990, *Billboard* reinstated the r&b category, explaining that it was "becoming less acceptable to identify music in racial terms."[23] And the beat goes on. . . .

Were it not for this artificial separation of the races, popular music history might read quite differently. When Syd Nathan, the founder of King Records, encouraged his r&b and c&w artists to record different versions of the same songs, he understood intuitively that pieces of music do not automatically have a genre, that they can be interpreted in many idioms. Still, in keeping with prevailing industry practices, he marketed his r&b releases only to black audiences and his country records only to white audiences. While Nathan was not limited in his choice of artists or material, he, like many others, accepted the notion that a separation of the races was "the way things were."

These same prevailing industry practices may have led Leonard Chess, head of Chess Records, to add "the rock beat of the Chicago blues" to Chuck Berry's more country-oriented audition performance of "Ida Red" ("Maybellene").[24] Chess was quite aware of the difficulties of marketing a black man as a country singer. Were it not for that reality, Chuck Berry might well have had a very different career trajectory. R&b artist Jimmy Witherspoon once argued, "Chuck Berry is a country singer. People put everybody in categories, black, white, this. Now if Chuck Berry was white, with the lyrics he writes, he would be the top country star in the world."[25] There have been any number of country-oriented versions of Chuck Berry songs, from Hoyt Axton's "Maybellene" to Freddy Weller's "Too Much Monkey Business" and "Promised Land," Waylon Jennings's "Brown-Eyed Handsome Man," Buck Owen's "Johnny B. Goode," Linda Rondstadt's "Back in the U.S.A.," Emmy Lou Harris's "You Never Can Tell," and Johnny Rivers's "Memphis," but all of them have been performed by whites.

Such music marketing practices were briefly challenged when Ray Charles recorded *Modern Sounds in Country and Western Music* (Volume I) and *Modern Sounds in Country and Western Music* (Volume II) for ABC-Paramount in 1962. Through these recordings, Charles proved that an artist does not have to be limited to a single performance style and that a song can have more than one genre. He had long felt connections between the blues and country that rendered the rigid separation of markets suspect from a musical point of view. "I really thought that it was somethin' about country music, even as a youngster," Charles once remarked. "I always . . . felt the closest music, really, to the blues [was country and western]. They'd make them steel guitars cry and whine, and it really attracted me."[26] These long-playing records (LPs) turned out to be the two best-selling albums of his career. Volume I made the pop charts for fifty-nine weeks and was firmly ensconced in the number one slot for fourteen of them. The album also contained a recording of his best-selling single—Don Gibson's "I Can't Stop Loving You"—which went to number one on all three charts, perhaps the only record by an African American artist ever to do so. Even so, it was not until the end of the decade that another African American artist—Charlie Pride—made the country charts.

The identification of music with race, which has tended to exclude African American artists and others from certain marketing structures in the music industry, makes the task of unearthing an accurate history of U.S. popular music quite difficult and encourages serious underestimates of the degree of cross-cultural collaboration that has taken place. For example, rockabilly, the country strain of rock 'n' roll in the 1950s, was a legitimate musical movement that integrated blues with country and western styles. It had its own identity, and in singers such as Elvis Presley, Carl Perkins, and Jerry Lee Lewis, performers of real originality and talent. But because rockabilly was one strand of a musical transformation that was most heavily indebted to African American culture, it is impossible to separate its popularity from a racist pattern in which styles pioneered by black artists are popularized, dominated, and even defined by whites as if they were the originators. This pattern is apparent in the history of popular music in the United States, from ragtime to jazz, to swing. Rock 'n' roll was neither an exception—Presley was not simply crowned the King of Rockabilly—nor the end of the line. As a result, styles are often described (and defended) in terms that are clearly racial rather than musical. In 1984, Nick Tosches insisted that "rockabilly is hillbilly rock-and-roll. It was not a usurpation of black music by whites because its soul, its pneuma, was white, full of the redneck ethos."[27] Arnold Shaw had acknowledged a decade earlier that "it was that to a degree," but he went on to say that "it would probably be more accurate to describe [rockabilly] as the sound of young, white Southerners imitating black bluesmen."[28] The late 1960s were marked by endless debates over whether whites could sing the blues. The relative absence of African Americans in heavy metal and whites in rap suggests that racial divisions are still powerful determinants in social and cultural relations.

No Hablamos Español: The Language Barrier

Because of this country's history of slavery, there is a tendency to think of racism, whether in the music industry or society as a whole, as a black/white issue. It should be recognized, however, that discriminatory practices have not been limited to African Americans alone. In many ways, the language barrier has proven to be even more intractable than the race barrier. Latin music, for instance, has always been an important influence in U.S. popular music. In the 1950s, a series of mambos, rumbas, and cha-chas were popular. Indeed, from Ritchie Valens to Santana, to Los Lobos, there has always been a strong

In many ways, the language barrier has proven to be even more intractable than the race barrier.

Latino presence in rock and a recognizable Latin influence in dance styles, from disco to hip hop. But even with the reggaeton boom in the mid-2000s, the number of Top Forty pop hits sung in Spanish in the United States could probably be counted on one hand. "La Bamba" (by Ritchie Valens and Los Lobos) and Santana's "Oye Como Va" readily come to mind, and more recently, Daddy Yankee's "Gasolina," but precious few others.

One could probably tally all of the non-English Top Forty pop hits on two hands. Four versions of "Volare" appeared on the charts, as did "Dominique" by the Singing Nun. Kyu Sakamoto's "Sukiyaki" was covered by Taste of Honey during the disco era. While one might quibble about whether to include Ray Barretto's "El Watusi" or Manu Dibango's "Soul Makossa" (both of which are primarily instrumental), the point is clear. Non-English hits in the United States are rare. As a result, artists who might sing in other languages feel compelled to record in English when they approach the U.S. market. In the late 1970s and early 1980s, Spanish balladeer Julio Iglesias, a resident of the United States, was among the best-selling recording artists in the world, but he had never had a hit in this country. The only way he could break into the U.S. market was with two English duets—one with Willie Nelson ("To All the Girls I've Loved Before") and one with Diana Ross ("All of You"), both in 1984. Linda Ronstadt, who achieved U.S. superstardom singing in English, provides an example of this logic in reverse. In 1988, Ronstadt, who is part Mexican, returned to her roots to record *Cancions de mi Padre.* The album never reached the U.S. pop Top Forty, even though it received the 1988 Grammy for Best Mexican/American Performance. Cuban-born Gloria Estefan's Top Ten pop album *Cuts Both Ways* (1989) included Spanish and English versions of "Don't Wanna Lose You" and "Here We Are," but only the English versions became Top Ten pop hits. The Swedish group ABBA charted fourteen Top Forty hits in the United States in the 1970s and 1980s, but all were sung in English. Norway's A-Ha broke into the U.S. market with "Take on Me," a cut with spectacular video animation and sung in English. When French Canadian Celine Dion, a veteran of the Quebec music scene, made a bid for international stardom in 1990, she did so on the basis of her first all-English LP, *Unison.* In 1993, she scored her first number one pop hit in the United States with "The Power of Love," which was, of course, sung in English.

For the moment, language barriers in popular music remain strong. Ricky Martin did include a dominant Spanish phrase in his blockbuster pop hit "Livin' La Vida Loca" (1999). And reggaeton has managed to achieve some measure of mainstream acceptance, with albums by artists such as Daddy Yankee and Don Omar peaking in the pop Top Forty. This status has thus far eluded individual songs sung in Spanish. But with the increasing diversity of the U.S. population, this situation is bound to change.

The Long, Hard Climb: Gender Discrimination

Historically, the images of women in popular songs—from angel and baby to earth mother and sex goddess, to bitch and "ho"—have been limiting or belittling, if not flat-out offensive and degrading.

The barriers that women face in the music industry are equally formidable. Historically, the images of women in popular songs—from angel and baby to earth mother and sex goddess, to bitch and "ho"—have been limiting or belittling, if not flat-out offensive and degrading. Women performers have often been pressured by the industry to assume personas based on these stereotypes. The existence of a double standard regarding intimacy and sexual practices in the United States has made the social dynamics of life on the road more complicated and alienating for women than for men. As if these difficulties were not enough, women have had to overcome the obstacles that stand between them and control over the creative processes. Technical processes such as record producing, engineering, mixing, and mastering are still overwhelmingly male-dominated.

While some women were able to achieve a certain status as vocalists in the decades preceding the emergence of rock 'n' roll, no woman ever achieved the status of an Al Jolson, Bing Crosby, or Frank Sinatra, and women almost never became successful as instrumentalists. Whatever status could be achieved disappeared rapidly with the advent of rock 'n' roll. Indeed, rock 'n' roll actually reduced the presence of women in popular music. In the early 1960s, the women who were marketed as folk madonnas were channeled toward softer vocal styles, which were usually linked only to acoustic instruments. This trend continued among the female singer/songwriters of the

1970s, Bonnie Raitt being a notable exception. Even harder rocking women in the 1960s—from the Crystals and the Ronettes to Grace Slick, Janis Joplin, and Aretha Franklin—were promoted as vocalists who never touched electric instruments. While there were certain breakthroughs for women when the punk movement rewrote the rules of access, these gains were offset to some degree in the next decade by the misogyny displayed in rap and heavy metal.

By the late 1980s, women were fairly well represented in most styles (with the exception of heavy metal), and in the early 1990s, they had finally begun to compete on a roughly equal footing with men for lucrative recording contracts. As they have achieved greater acceptance in the popular market, however, they have had to confront an industry infrastructure that is fully owned and operated by men whose ideas about career development frequently push them to conform to male stereotypes of how female performers should act and sound. In other words, like African Americans and other people of color, women performers must confront norms and social practices that limit their development and chances for success.

Regulating Popular Music

Because popular music always interacts with its social environment, it often serves as a lightning rod for the political controversies that invariably accompany change. The Tin Pan Alley pop that dominated the first half of the twentieth century, for example, was marked by a purposeful blandness and a studied inoffensiveness that, in retrospect, makes it difficult to imagine that anything about it, except its saccharine sweetness, could upset anyone. Still, the moral guardians of the early twentieth century felt that even Tin Pan Alley pop was too depraved for mainstream consumption, let alone the jazz that developed concurrently. As early as 1913, the well-known violinist Maud Powell told the National Federation of Music Clubs that the music of the United States had been

> thrown into disrepute through the unspeakably depraved modern popular song, . . . which consists of brazenly suggestive words to a catchy rag-time accompaniment.
>
> Its effect on young folk is shocking. The vicious song is allowed in the home by parents, who, no doubt, have not troubled themselves to look at the words. As a result the suggestive meanings are allowed to play upon immature minds at the dangerous age. It is from the popular song that the popular suggestive dance sprang. Together and apart they are a menace to the social fabric.[29]

Powell went on to state that she was "heartily in favor of a board of censorship for the popular song."[30] Imagine the horror she would have felt had she been exposed to the rumblings of blues or country music, which surveyed more personal themes in a far more vernacular tone.

Throughout the second half of the twentieth century, popular music was connected quite explicitly with social change and political controversy. As millions of adults left the intensity of urban life in the 1950s for the new and expansive sprawl called suburbia, rock 'n' roll pulled their offspring back to the sounds of the city. While postwar youth may have found the new sound exciting and engaging, adults found it threatening and levied criticisms far more damning than Powell's condemnations of Tin Pan Alley pop. Indeed in the late 1950s, a conservative reaction against rock 'n' roll sought to turn back the musical clock by imposing rigid guidelines on radio.

A variation of this same social drama was played out in the 1980s and 1990s, when the custodians of culture became convinced that rap and heavy metal had gone too far and tried to regulate popular music through tactics ranging from a demand for warning labels on sound recordings to outright censorship. A more aggressive suppression of popular music was undertaken after the attacks on the World Trade Center and the Pentagon on September 11, 2001, in the name of national security. In fact, given the pronouncements of a whole range of public figures and elected officials on this topic, a compelling case can be made that popular culture—particularly popular music—has become the ideological battlefield on which struggles for power, values, and identity take place. Clearly then, popular music is potent cultural capital—aesthetically, economically, and politically. Unraveling and analyzing the complexities of its often contradictory social functions is the subject matter of *Rockin' Out*.

> **A** *compelling case can be made that popular culture—particularly popular music—has become the ideological battlefield on which struggles for power, values, and identity take place.*

Constructing Tin Pan Alley: From Minstrelsy to Mass Culture

The institution of slavery has been such a defining feature of U.S. history that it is hardly surprising to find the roots of our popular music embedded in this tortured legacy. Indeed, the first indigenous U.S. popular music to capture the imagination of a broad public, at home and abroad, was blackface minstrelsy, a cultural form involving mostly Northern whites in blackened faces, parodying their perceptions of African American culture. Minstrelsy appeared at a time when songwriting and music publishing were dispersed throughout the country and sound recording had not yet been invented. During this period, there was an important geographical pattern in the way music circulated. Concert music by foreign composers intended for elite U.S. audiences generally played in New York City first and then in other major cities. In

> *The institution of slavery has been such a defining feature of U.S. history that it is hardly surprising to find the roots of our popular music embedded in this tortured legacy.*

contrast, domestic popular music, including minstrel music, was first tested in smaller towns, then went to larger urban areas, and entered New York only after success elsewhere. Songwriting and music publishing were similarly dispersed. New York did not become the nerve center for indigenous popular music until later in the nineteenth century, when the previously scattered conglomeration of songwriters and publishers began to converge on the Broadway and 28th Street section of the city, in an area that came to be called Tin Pan Alley after the tinny output of its upright pianos. These talented songwriters and indefatigable publishers, who would go on to dominate mainstream popular music until the post–World War II period, were attuned to every nuance of cultural variation the United States had to offer. And during their reign, they would encounter all of the new technologies—sound recording, talking films, radio, and television—that would come to define mass culture.

LEARN MORE
Learning objectives on MyMusicKit

Minstrelsy: The Making of Mainstream U.S. Culture

EXPLORE MORE
Timeline on
MyMusicKit

When blackface minstrelsy first appeared in the early nineteenth century, U.S. popular music existed in the shadow of European opera, which enjoyed considerable popular support. As the class hierarchy in the United States became more clearly delineated, opera came to be increasingly identified with the cultural elite, while those lower down the socioeconomic scale gravitated more toward ethnic Scottish and Irish melodies, Italian bel canto, and the soon to be dominant homegrown songs of minstrelsy. As the complexity of U.S. society increased, it led to greater segregation of audiences—not only by class, but by race and gender as well. Accordingly, the initial audiences for blackface minstrelsy tended to be white, working class, and male. Minstrelsy established a vexing and recurring pattern of uneven musical exchange in which white interpretations and appropriations of African American culture would receive disproportionate credit in defining mainstream popular culture, while the original black sources would recede into the background of their own history.

> **W**hite interpretations and appropriations of African American culture would receive disproportionate credit in defining mainstream popular culture, while the original black sources would recede into the background of their own history.

At a superficial level, minstrelsy's assertive rhythms and vigorous dancing, coupled with singing and dialogue that combined biting wit and social commentary, were not inconsistent with the cultural patterns of enslaved Africans. Still, with relatively little understanding of or sensitivity toward African American culture, the curiosity and enthusiasm with which these white entertainers approached it were matched only by the distortions and virulence with which they reproduced it. In minstrelsy, we find both the centrality of African American contributions to our popular culture and the uneasy blending of fascination and fear, delight and disdain, respect and rebuke—indeed, love and hate—that typified the posture of most U.S. whites toward African Americans and their culture.

Blackface masking did not begin with minstrelsy, nor was it inevitably race-related. The practice dates back at least to the middle ages in Britain and Europe in certain ritual dramas such as morris dancing and mummer's plays. The performers, often called "guisers," sometimes masked their faces with chimney soot or grease to disguise the true identity of their characters and heighten the sense of mystery and danger in the performance. Callithumpian bands—agitators who had been known to disrupt parliamentary elections in Britain and Ireland—also blackened their faces at times. In the United States, they roamed the streets of New York, Philadelphia, and Boston from the 1820s onward and were described in the *Philadelphia Sunday Dispatch* as "men who render the night hideous by their yelling, drum-beatings, and horn-toutings, and the day disgusting by their outrageous masking and foul disguises."[1] In these so-called "rituals of inversion," masking was used as a way of hiding one's identity and symbolically inverting social roles to disrupt the normal flow and power relations of daily life. The available evidence indicates that, in most instances, these actors were not attempting to represent persons of African descent. There were also rituals of West African origin involving parading, reveling, and grotesque masking that worked their way to the "New World" during the slave trade. In the Jonkonnu festivals that traveled from West Africa to the Caribbean and up the Eastern seaboard of the United States, actors of African descent masked their faces with ash to perform similar role inversions.

In the slaveholding United States, of course, associations between blackface and race were more likely intentional and, in any case, inevitable. The parodic humor of minstrel songs was most often hostile and degrading; minstrel lyrics were invariably written and sung in a caricatured black dialect and routinely referred to African Americans as "niggers," "darkies," and "coons." Still, the immediate acceptance of minstrelsy suggests that it might not have been received as a totally new cultural form, but rather a form that was already familiar, albeit one that was laden with new meaning in its new context. It is also worth noting that in minstrelsy, a performance was no longer a time-bound, seasonal ritual, but now a defining popular art.

Though Thomas Dartmouth Rice was not the first U.S. entertainer to blacken his face with burnt cork to impersonate a black person, he is most often credited with institutionalizing the practice. As cultural lore would have it, Rice, an aspiring young actor, was in Cincinnati when he happened upon a black street performer dressed in tatters singing a song called "Jim Crow" while performing a dance, often described as grotesque, in which he "jumped Jim Crow." It is tempting to imagine, as Dale Cockrell does, that the performer Rice encountered was a Jonkonnu,[2] but with no clear evidence to support the claim, it is easier to fall back on the oft-told story that the man was in some way disabled. In any case, Rice saw this combination of elements as his ticket to the future and set about creating a version of "Jim Crow" as a slow-witted, lackadaisical plantation slave that could be performed "behind the footlights." In addition to Cincinnati, Rice "jumped Jim Crow" in Louisville, Philadelphia, Washington, and Baltimore for enthusiastic crowds before appearing in New York in 1832. He eventually parlayed his fame into a well-received yearlong tour of the British Isles in 1836, thereby introducing foreign audiences to the first form of popular music that was considered distinctly "American." Jim Crow, the character and the song, remained a mainstay of Rice's stage act throughout his career and, as a testament to the staying power of this negative stereotype, it was the unofficial name given to the legislation that was used to deprive African Americans of their civil rights in the latter half of the nineteenth century.

As early minstrelsy developed, it was dominated by two characters—both demeaning. If Jim Crow was the rural archetype, at the other end of the spectrum was the urban dandy—a northern city slicker who went variously by names like Zip Coon, Jim Dandy, and others; he was fashionably dressed, streetwise, and at times given to violence. The song "Zip Coon," was performed in the early 1930s by George Washington Dixon and others, and it lives on as "Turkey in the Straw," a perennial favorite among country fiddlers. At this time, minstrel performance was a solo art that might take place in a theater, the street, or someone's kitchen, and minstrel performances in public venues were sandwiched between all other kinds of entertainment, from legitimate theater to circus acts.

It wasn't until the appearance of Dan Emmett and the Virginia Minstrels in the early 1840s that the genre began to take shape as a self-contained ensemble performance of its own. Like Rice, the Virginia Minstrels followed U.S. success with a tour of the British Isles, where the group disbanded. During this period, Emmett composed one of the most popular and enduring "plantation songs" of minstrelsy, "Dixie Land," about a freed slave who longs for the simple pleasures of plantation life. During the Civil War, "Dixie" became the unofficial anthem of the Confederacy, and the word became a synonym for the southern United States. By the time Emmett returned to the United States, he was pleased to find a minstrel troupe in just

In "Jim Crow," Thomas Dartmouth Rice created a character that was a grotesque impression of an enslaved African American.

about every city in the country. In addition to groups named after their founders or places of origin, there were attempts to capture the supposed ethnic origins of the genre with names like the African Melodists, the Congo Minstrels, and the Ethiopian Band. The popular Christy Minstrels billed themselves as the "original and far famed band of Ethiopian Minstrels."[3] In minstrel music, however, the influence of spirited English or Irish folk music was as strong as the African or African American styles it sought to mimic.

In its standard form, the minstrel show included ensemble singing, dances and marches, stump speeches, and comic sketches, "strung together with witticisms, ripostes, shouts, puns, and other attempts at Negro impersonation."[4] Instrumentation consisted of strings such as violin and banjo for melody, and a rhythm section comprising the two "endmen"—Mr. Tambo (on tambourine) and Mr. Bones (who played bones or castanets). As minstrelsy matured, the show was divided into three parts: the opening segment was devoted to the Northern dandy, while the closing centered on a skit involving the Southern plantation slave. A later middle section, the olio, included mock lectures and speeches. Over time, the endmen gained in importance, as the addition of a third character, Mr. Interlocutor, provided a target for their witty repartee.

Although racial oppression and nostalgic views of slavery persisted after Emancipation, minstrelsy generally moved toward a more sympathetic treatment of African Americans. No one was more identified with this trajectory than Stephen Foster, perhaps the best-known U.S. songwriter of the nineteenth century. There is some evidence that Foster's development may have been influenced by exposure to the abolitionist movement. But if Foster humanized minstrelsy, he did so without directly challenging black stereotypes or the institution of slavery. One of his first and most popular minstrel songs, "Oh! Susanna" (1848), portrayed African Americans as good natured but simple-minded, and it is still taught in primary schools as an innocent novelty song. The term *nigger* was liberally sprinkled throughout "Old Uncle Ned," written the same year, but by song's end the slave master genuinely mourns Ned's passing. One year later, "Nelly Was a Lady" depicted a loving relationship among African Americans in a respectful tone. In some of his next compositions—"Old Folks at Home," "My Old Kentucky Home"—Foster began to downplay the exaggerated black dialect and achieved "a lament for lost home, friends, and youth, cutting across racial and ethnic lines. . . ."[5] But even as late as 1860, "Old Black Joe," which borrowed respectfully from the "Negro spiritual" tradition, could be criticized for its racial condescension. Foster's songs were sufficiently popular—some selling in the range of

100,000 copies—that he became the first U.S. composer to eke out a living from songwriting alone. Still, never having received his due from publishers, he died with thirty-eight cents in his pocket.

By the postbellum period, minstrelsy had become so overpowering that even African Americans composed minstrel songs and joined minstrel troupes, complete with blackface performances. Among the most famous was James Bland, who dropped out of Howard University to pursue a career in minstrelsy and later joined Sprague's Georgia Minstrels. Bland became the first commercially successful African American songwriter, writing over 700 songs, including plantation songs such as "Carry Me Back to Old Virginny," which actually became the Virginia state song in 1940, even though many found the well-worn trope of the nostalgic ex-slave and the language of "massa" and "darkey" to be offensive. In the end, Bland's music was no more indebted to black culture than that of his white minstrel counterparts. At that moment, minstrelsy offered black entertainers the most lucrative opportunity available to them; they may have felt that they had no better alternative than to imitate the white performers imitating them.

Sheet Music, Sound Recording, and the Sounds of Music

Between the Civil War and the turn of the twentieth century, minstrelsy was gradually supplanted by vaudeville, a variety show format that marked the beginning of popular entertainment as big business. From its modest beginnings at Tony Pastor's Opera House in New York City's Bowery, vaudeville had evolved by the turn of the century into a national network of hundreds of venues dominated by the Keith-Albee theater chain in the East and the Orpheum circuit in the West. Because popular songs were a staple of vaudeville, Tin Pan Alley publishers were regular visitors to the gala shows produced in New York by the likes of F. F. Proctor, Oscar Hammerstein, and Flo Ziegfeld. "They made fifty or sixty visits a week," Russell Sanjek has noted, "to boost their newest publications."[6] Their "persuasion tactics," according to Charles Hamm, might include "out-and-out payment by the publisher—a flat fee, or in some cases a promise of a percentage of profits from sales of sheet music."[7] The practice of "paying for play"—legal at the time and considered a form of intelligent marketing rather than a shady business practice— eventually came to be known as "payola." For the publishers, such investments in vaudeville stars were often returned many times in sheet music sales.

The practice of "paying for play"— legal at the time and considered a form of intelligent marketing rather than a shady business practice— eventually came to be known as "payola."

Because middle-class home entertainment at this time centered around the piano, sheet music was the main vehicle for the mass dissemination of music, and publishing firms were at the center of the music business. In 1880, some 45,000 pianos were manufactured in the United States.[8] Over the next thirty years, annual production increased eightfold. Sheet music retailed for thirty to forty cents a copy; for the major publishers, sales were known to reach millions of copies. Charles K. Harris's "After the Ball," written and published in 1892, "quickly reached sales of $25,000 a week" and "sold more than 2,000,000 copies in only several years, eventually achieving a sale of some five million."[9] With potential sales such as these, it is not surprising that music publishers were not particularly interested in the cylinder phonograph that Thomas Edison had invented in 1877. They were far too preoccupied with the sale of sheet music—their primary source of revenue—to bother about records.

When Edison first conceived of sound recording, he felt that its greatest potential lay in reproducing speech and hailed his invention as a "talking machine." Still, he decided to introduce it to the public by exploiting its musical properties. In countless demonstrations in lecture halls and vaudeville houses, scores of local vocalists, whistlers, and instrumentalists were invited to try their hand at recording. Although brass reproduced reasonably well, the poor sound quality of early cylinders severely hampered their commercial value. Once awed by its potential, Edison momentarily dismissed his phonograph as "a mere toy, which has no commercial value," and turned his attention to the invention of the electric light before once again returning to recording.[10]

The next steps in recording were undertaken by Charles Sumner Tainter and Chichester Bell in the Volta Laboratory of Edison's fellow inventor, Alexander Graham Bell. Five years of research yielded the graphophone, whose floating stylus and wax-coated cardboard cylinder produced better sound quality than Edison's machine. In the late 1880s, the Edison patents and the national sales rights to the graphophone were consolidated into the North American Phonograph Company, which originally intended to sell the recording devices as dictating machines. Their District of Columbia franchise—the Columbia Phonograph Company—would go on to become the oldest trademark in the recording business. Because at this time recording was a mechanical process rather than an electromechanical one, it was called *acoustic recording* and it would soon be devoted almost exclusively to music.

In 1889, Louis Glass pointed the way to the future of the phonograph. Glass had equipped some of his dictating machines with a patented, coin-activated mechanism and four sets of stethoscopic listening tubes, and he placed them in the Palais Royal Saloon in San Francisco. For a nickel per listener per play, patrons could avail themselves of the sounds of a prerecorded "entertainment" cylinder. These "nickel-in-the-slot" machines were so successful that, within a year, Glass had placed machines in eighteen other locations, some of which began bringing in as much as $1,200 annually. The enterprise won for Glass the title of Father of the Juke Box. Pay phonographs proved to be very popular in a wide range of venues, from amusement parks and drug stores to saloons and train stations. However, because phonographs retailed for almost $150 and cylinders could not be mass-produced economically, a home entertainment market for prerecorded music was not yet feasible.

Among the early cylinders that caught on were those featuring brass bands, instrumental solos, comic Irish tales, and so-called coon songs, novelty songs exploiting negative stereotypes of African Americans in caricatured black dialect. As the number of locations for coin-operated phonographs increased, so did the demand for prerecorded cylinders. However, three factors stood in the way of a natural alliance between Tin Pan Alley and the new cylinder-recording companies: because of their limited sound quality, cylinders tended to favor spoken-word and instrumental selections; publishers did not receive royalties from the sale or

John Philip Sousa, famous for his military marches, led the U.S. Marine Band to popular success during an era when the limitations of recording technology favored the reproduction of brass bands. In the 1890s, Columbia catalogues listed scores of recordings by the Marine Band.

use of recorded music; and the demand for prerecorded cylinders could not compete with the demand for sheet music. Thus, the companies manufacturing prerecorded cylinders grew independently of Tin Pan Alley.

The Columbia Phonograph Company quickly distinguished itself as the leading producer of quality entertainment cylinders. Among the company's earliest popular cylinders were marches, waltzes, and popular Irish favorites such as "Little Annie Rooney" and "Down Went McGinty," as well as about one hundred recordings of the U.S. Marine Band. Meanwhile, new developments in recording technology had rekindled Edison's interest in the field. During the early 1890s, improvements in sound reproduction came quickly, and within a few years, both Columbia and Edison had introduced affordable phonographs, leading to the creation of a home entertainment market for prerecorded cylinders.

By 1896, Columbia's catalogue of prerecorded cylinders listed thousands of titles. Edison boasted George Washington Johnson—if not the first, then certainly the most successful black recording artist at the time—who achieved fame and fortune with two hits, "The Whistling Coon" and "The Laughing Song." Competition between the two companies was fierce; in fact, they spent so much time fighting each other that they paid little attention to the development of disc recording, an innovation that eventually consigned cylinders to the dustbin of history.

Emile Berliner, a German immigrant, developed the flat recording disc that became the industry standard. In 1888, Berliner unveiled his gramophone and, at its first demonstration, prophesied the ability to make an unlimited number of copies from a single master, the use of discs for home entertainment on a mass scale, and a system of royalty payments to artists derived from the sale of discs. In short, Berliner was the first to envision the contours of the modern music industry.

Berliner delivered on his first prophecy when he made negative discs, called "stampers," which were then pressed into ebonite rubber biscuits to produce an exact duplicate, or "record," of the master. A later improvement replaced the rubber discs with shellac-based, 78 revolutions per minute (rpm) pressings, which became the industry standard until the late 1940s. To realize his second prophecy, the use of discs for home entertainment, Berliner recruited Fred Gaisberg. Gaisberg had been coordinating talent and recording at Columbia, and Berliner made him, in effect, the first artist and repertoire (a&r) man in the infant industry.

Berliner hired Eldridge R. Johnson to manufacture the gramophones. Adding improvements of his own, Johnson soon began turning out machines by the hundreds. In 1901, the two men consolidated their interests into the Victor Talking Machine Company, with Johnson as the senior partner. They adopted as the company logo the famous Little Nipper (the pup listening attentively to his master's voice emanating from a record horn). Shortly afterward, the major recording companies—Edison, Columbia, and Victor—pooled their patents and set about the business of making better records and machines.[11] From this point until the advent of commercial radio following World War I, acoustic recording enjoyed its golden era.

Because exclusive recording contracts were not yet the industry standard, artists were not tied to a single company. Gaisberg was soon recording Columbia's top artists for Victor and, through its British partner, the Gramophone Company, those in every music capital in Europe. The British Gramophone catalogue contained songs and arias in every European language and many Oriental languages that were considered culturally superior to most recordings. Victor

((•● **HEAR MORE**
"Happy Birthday Phonograph" on MyMusicKit

imported these higher-priced Red Seal classical recordings for sale in the United States and then began a domestic Red Label series of its own, featuring stars of New York's Metropolitan Opera.[12] Italian tenor Enrico Caruso became the jewel in the crown of the new series when he signed an exclusive Victor contract offering him the unprecedented provision of a royalty on records sold—thereby fulfilling the last of Berliner's 1888 prophecies. Victor's Red Label series was clearly intended for the wealthy "carriage trade." Columbia also featured a grand opera series of its own. However, by 1910, as Ian Whitcomb points out in his inimitable style, "It was quite clear to the record companies that the classics only brought in prestige and that the steady income was to be made from sales to the 'Cracker-Barrel Trade,' to the 'Good Old Coon Song–Sousa–Monologue–Sentimental Ballad–Bunch.'"[13]

If the choice of recorded material was an indicator of class differences, the choice of format revealed a rural–urban split. "By the middle of the first decade of the twentieth century," writes C. A. Schicke, "the disc had distinctly succeeded in capturing the buying power of the upper and middle classes and the urban population. The cylinder's stronghold—and mostly Edison cylinders at that—was the poorer, rural market."[14] In both instances, however, the selection of recording artists was made with only the white population in mind. With the exception of George W. Johnson and the great black vaudevillian Bert Williams, even so-called coon songs, a staple of the recording companies from the beginning, were almost invariably sung by whites. Indeed, prior to World War I, only one African American ensemble had landed a recording contract—the Syncopated Society Orchestra led by James Reese Europe (see below).

While the golden age of acoustic recording drew on and preserved a broad range of musical styles, it also established some of the most troubling aspects of the contemporary music industry, the first being the fragmentation of the audience not only along class lines but also along geographic and, of course, racial lines. It was also claimed that the existing technology favored lower (i.e., male) voices. Ada Jones was not simply the "First Lady of Phonograph Records," she was one of the *only* ladies of phonograph records. In addition, the technological advances of the late nineteenth and early twentieth centuries introduced what later critics of mass culture would see as the historical schism that marked the transition from active music making to passive music consumption. In the popular image of a family gathered around the living-room piano, music is "consumed" through the active participation of all concerned. With the invention of recording, it was no longer necessary to have any musical ability whatsoever to re-create the sound of music. In playing to the earlier image of "family entertainment," the Tin Pan Alley publishing houses were naturally at odds with the record companies.

In its formative stages, then, the "music industry" could in no way be considered synonymous with the "recording industry," as it has been more recently.

In its formative stages, then, the "music industry" could in no way be considered synonymous with the "recording industry," as it has been more recently; it was, if anything, songwriting and music publishing. Of course, the writers of Tin Pan Alley, from Charles K. Harris, Paul Dresser, and Harry Von Tilzer to George Gershwin, Jerome Kern, and Irving Berlin, took notice of records and eventually pushed record companies to record their songs, but for a variety of reasons—practical, technical, legal, aesthetic, and economic—Tin Pan Alley never embraced records. Thus, while Tin Pan Alley and the recording industry intersected at many points and with increasing frequency over the years, in many ways they developed as separate industries. Even as records promised to become the dominant medium for the mass reproduction of music, Tin Pan Alley continued to identify itself primarily with the "literate" Broadway–Hollywood axis of popular music—a fact that helps account for the disjuncture that marked the emergence of rock 'n' roll, a product that was identified with record labels. Just as record companies would come to replace publishing houses as the center of the music industry, rock 'n' roll would push aside Tin Pan Alley pop as the dominant style of popular music. But not until midcentury.

Tin Pan Alley Creates Musical Tradition

Tin Pan Alley centralized the U.S. popular music business during the ascendancy of vaudeville, at a time when European opera was still the hallmark of (upper-class) taste. Although songwriters in the United States often took their cues from European high culture, they soon came to realize that the key to profitability lay in catering to popular tastes. Unlike older, more traditional music publishing houses that issued a broad range of material, the song factories of Tin Pan Alley produced only popular songs; in so doing, "Tin Pan Alley songwriters soon reached a stylistic plateau, a much more homogeneous style than had ever before been the case in the history of song in America."[15] Indeed, Tin Pan Alley availed itself of a much narrower range of material than did the record companies and parlayed the undertaking into an overwhelming—and distinctly "American"—success. "Tin Pan Alley did not draw on traditional music," musicologist Charles Hamm has said, "it created traditional music."[16]

> *U*nlike older, more traditional music publishing houses that issued a broad range of material, the song factories of Tin Pan Alley produced only popular songs.

Typical of early Tin Pan Alley fare were graceful waltzes and spirited marches. Familiar waltzes included Harry Von Tilzer's "Bird in a Gilded Cage" (1900), "In the Good Old Summer Time" by George Evans (1902), and Egbert Van Alstyne's "In the Shade of the Old Apple Tree" (1905). All sold millions. The marches of John Philip Sousa and the Marine Band were perhaps best echoed in popular song by the multitalented George M. Cohan. From "Give My Regards to Broadway" in 1904 to his World War I rally tune, "Over There," in 1917, Cohan's up-tempo, lightly syncopated numbers won him enduring popularity.

Ironically, for all its definitive American-ness, Tin Pan Alley was dominated by Jewish Americans, at a time when Jewish immigrants were considered racially different by many. If one had to choose a single artist who epitomized the Tin Pan Alley ethos, it would be Irving Berlin, about whom the *Literary Digest,* after praising his work, remarked with surprise: "And Berlin belongs to the Jewish race."[17] Berlin (Israel Baline) was four years old in 1892 when he and his family came to the United States after escaping Russian pogroms. Like many Jewish immigrants of the period, they settled in New York's Lower East Side, where they lived in abject poverty. "At fourteen, he was a singing waiter in the honky tonks of Chinatown and the Bowery, absorbing the rich sounds and rhythms of the musical melting pot."[18] Two years later, Berlin landed his first Tin Pan Alley job. There, he wrote classics such as "A Pretty Girl Is Like a Melody" (1919), "Puttin' on the Ritz" (1929), "Easter Parade" (1933), and "God Bless America" (1939), which captured the hearts and minds of generations and made Berlin a household name. Until he was unseated by Paul McCartney, Berlin was easily the most successful songwriter in history. "The range of his songs, in content and mood, if not in form,"

Irving Berlin lived to be 101 years old and became one of the most prolific songwriters of the twentieth century. Because he could play piano in only one key, he compensated by using a piano with a moveable keyboard that could transpose into other keys.

Hamm has said, "is enormous. . . . Some take on a bit of the flavor of ragtime, of the blues, of country-western, Latin-American, or jazz."[19] His appropriations of multicultural sounds and rhythms—particularly those of ragtime and jazz—speak volumes about his uncanny ability to interpret diverse influences for the mainstream audience and the systematic cultural distortions that accompanied mainstream popularization.

Incorporating Ragtime, Blues, and Jazz

The rise of Tin Pan Alley paralleled the emergence of ragtime, and the connections between the two reveal the inequitable pattern of cultural borrowing and economic reward between black and white artists that has characterized much of the history of popular music in this country. This pattern is central to understanding the advent of rock 'n' roll. Ragtime—as opposed to ragtime songs, which were creations of Tin Pan Alley—began as a syncopated, African American music with structural ties to European marches. It employed, in the words of Gunther Schuller, "the polymetric . . . approach of the African native forced into the simple 2/4 pattern of European marches."[20] It evolved from a dance called the cakewalk, which involved blacks imitating the grand entrance of whites to society balls. In the hands of its most famous practitioner, the African American pianist and composer Scott Joplin, ragtime was a self-conscious art form, a composed music. Joplin himself, Whitcomb has noted, "presented the New Negro,"[21] a polished composer well-versed in musical notation. His "Maple Leaf Rag" (1899) remains one of the best-known ragtime compositions.[22]

For Tin Pan Alley, ragtime was a craze to be incorporated into popular song. As such, it is often difficult to separate ragtime songs from other Tin Pan Alley pop. In their affinity for slow march tempos, for example, ragtime songs tended to resemble George M. Cohan's most successful musical theater numbers. It can also be argued that there is a historical and stylistic continuity from "coon" songs to the ragtime songs of Tin Pan Alley, although the latter were clearly less offensive. Irving Berlin turned out dozens of ragtime songs, including "Play Some Ragtime" in 1909; "Stop That Rag," "Dat Draggy Rag," and "Oh, That Beautiful Rag" in 1910; and "Ragtime Violin" and his best-known "Alexander's Ragtime Band" in 1911. Although this last song did not marry syncopation and the march tradition the way Joplin might have, the catchy, well-crafted tune, which balanced "dash and energy" with a "bow to negro music," as

((•● **HEAR MORE**
"Alexander's Ragtime Band" on MyMusicKit

"Alexander's Ragtime Band"

Artist: Bessie Smith
Music/Lyrics by Irving Berlin (published 1911)
Label: Columbia (1927)

As was the case with her stature (over 6 feet), weight (over 200 pounds), appetite for food and sex, and enormous voice, Bessie Smith's talent was so great that anything she sang—from Tin Pan Alley to Mississippi Delta songs—became the blues. She is one of the most influential singers of the early twentieth century, but like many of her musical contemporaries, her career could not recover from the economic downturn of the Great Depression. In 1937, she was severely injured in a car accident on Mississippi's notorious Highway 61 and died within hours.

Musical Style Notes

"Alexander's Ragtime Band" (1911) was a relic of an earlier age, when Tin Pan Alley songwriters explored the rhythmic possibilities and the pop hooks implicit in ragtime. These "ragtime songs" did not employ the multistrain form of true ragtime, but the incorporation of its syncopation (accents on the off-beats) and pentatonic (five-note) melodies made for enormously effective pop music.

Like many Irving Berlin standards, "Alexander's Ragtime Band" was constructed of multiple verses with a repeating chorus. On this recording, however, we hear only the first verse, which is then followed by three repetitions of the chorus: vocal, instrumental, and then vocal again. Smith has also changed some of the words, replacing some of Berlin's 1911 imitation "black dialect" with more natural-sounding lyrics: "Oh, honey" instead of "Oh, ma honey," and "the best-est band in the land" rather than "the best-est band what am in the land."

Bessie Smith sings in a classic blues style, but many of her instrumentalists on this track are jazz players (Joe Smith, trumpet; Coleman Hawkins, clarinet; Jimmy Harrison, trombone; Fletcher Henderson, piano; Charlie Dixon, banjo). They play in ragtime-inspired rhythms, and the trumpet, clarinet, and trombone are all improvising over the melody at the same time, New Orleans style (although the trumpet is featured and is most prominent in the mix).

Musical "Road Map"

TIMINGS	COMMENTS	LYRICS
0:00–0:07	Instrumental introduction	
0:07–0:31	Verse 1	*Oh, honey, . . . let's go down there . . .*
0:31–0:56	Chorus (1st section)	*Come on and hear . . .*
0:56–1:19	(second section—same melody, different words)	*Alexander's rag-time band . . .*
1:19–2:08	Chorus repeated instrumentally, with trumpet, clarinet, and trombone improvising	
2:08–2:22	Repeat of chorus (1st section)	*. . . Alexander's rag-time band . . .*
2:33–2:59	Chorus pauses for brief trumpet "break"	*[Smith says "Listen to the bugle call!" and the music stops except for the trumpet.]*
2:59	(second section—same melody, different words)	*Come on along, . . .*
	Chorus ends; track fades out abruptly	

Gilbert Seldes noted in 1924,[23] proved to be so popular that Berlin was subsequently billed as the Father of Ragtime. Charles Hamm described this process as one that "skimmed off superficial stylistic elements of a type of music originating among black musicians, and used these to give a somewhat different, exotic flavor to white music."[24]

A similar, but far more complicated pattern characterized Tin Pan Alley's use of blues and jazz. The blues appeared at about the same time as ragtime. "But, unlike ragtime," Gunther Schuller has noted, "the blues were improvised and as such were more successful in preserving the original and melodic patterns of African music."[25] Using, as writer Amiri Baraka (a.k.a. Leroi Jones) has pointed out, a "three-line verse form [that] springs from no readily apparent Western source"[26] and other African retentions, such as the call-and-response style and the flatted thirds and sevenths ("blue notes") that typify the singing of many West African tribes, the blues are clearly part of the African American musical tradition. This, however, is not the impression one would have gotten if one followed the pattern of published and recorded blues songs comprising the "blues craze" that swept the country in the second decade of the twentieth century.

In 1912, three blues compositions were published: Hart Wand's "Dallas Blues," Arthur Seals's "Baby Seals' Blues," and "Memphis Blues" by W. C. Handy. There has been considerable debate about whether such compositions fit the strict definition of the blues. In 1959, blues historian Samuel Charters took the narrow view: "Both Handy and Arthur Seals were Negroes, but the music that they titled 'blues' is more or less derived from the standard popular musical styles of the 'coon song' and 'cake walk' type. It is ironic that the first published piece in the Negro 'blues' idiom, 'Dallas Blues,' was written by a white man, Hart Wand."[27] Others have tended to grant more latitude in defining the blues, acknowledging Handy's claim to being the Father of the Blues.

Handy was a trained composer who was as conversant with African American folkloric idioms as he was with musical notation. During this period, he published some of his most memorable compositions, including "St. Louis Blues" (1914), "Joe Turner Blues" (1916), and "Beale Street Blues" (1917). Accordingly, Baraka has argued that, "W. C. Handy, with the publication of his various 'blues compositions,' invented [the blues] for a great many Americans and also showed that there was money to be made from it."[28] Handy's success alerted Tin Pan Alley writers, who turned out a rash of so-called blues songs during this period.[29] Given record company practices at the time, these songs were invariably recorded by white singers. As Robert Palmer has said, "The idea of making recordings by and for blacks hadn't occurred to anyone in a position to do

W. C. Handy was one of the first songwriters to bring a feel for the blues into the world of popular composition. Also a successful businessman, Handy established his own publishing house and record label with his partner Harry Pace.

anything about it when the so-called blues craze hit around 1914–15, so [W. C.] Handy's 'blues' and the blues of other popular tunesmiths, black and white, were recorded by whites, many of them specialists in Negro dialect material."[30] Some like Al Bernard and Marion Harris had a better feel for the music than most and were heartily endorsed by Handy himself. Others could be more easily dismissed as holdovers from minstrelsy.[31] This situation would have defined most people's understanding of the blues in the 1910s, before the onslaught of blues recordings by scores of African Americans in the 1920s (see Chapter 2).

Early appropriations of jazz created the impression among mainstream listeners that jazz was the product of "polite society" white dance bands, like that of Paul Whiteman, whom the media crowned the King of Jazz. Actually, by the time the term *jazz* had come into popular usage, the style had been fed by a number of musical tributaries (minstrelsy, spirituals, ragtime, and blues, as well as European classical music and Tin Pan Alley pop) that contained African as well as European

> *Early appropriations of jazz created the impression among mainstream listeners that jazz was the product of "polite society" white dance bands, like that of Paul Whiteman, whom the media crowned the King of Jazz.*

elements. Indeed, many African American jazz musicians were well versed in the European classics as well as the current Tin Pan Alley hits. Still, there is an important—though not absolute—distinction to be made between the oral tradition of improvisational, "hot" jazz and the written tradition of "sweet" dance music that defined white society orchestras like Paul Whiteman's. Because high-society whites and middle-class blacks tended to shun the rough, hard-driving styles played in honky-tonks and brothels, the jazz showcased in upscale venues aspired to a smoothness and cosmopolitanism that was less important in other places. As a result, most mainstream listeners associated jazz with sweet dance music, even though, by the time of Whiteman's success, most jazz musicians, including African Americans, were playing scored arrangements that combined sweet and hot styles; some, like Fletcher Henderson and Duke Ellington, had improved on the model, creating the space for hot improvised solos within innovatively structured arrangements.

Patterns of racial exclusion in the recording industry and later in broadcast radio skewed public perceptions of jazz even more. In 1917, for example, when Victor decided to take a chance on the new sound, the band it ended up recording was the all-white Original Dixieland Jazz Band.[32] Similarly, with few exceptions, radio broadcasts excluded black performers as a matter of policy. To most mainstream listeners, then, jazz—which was what just about all dance music was called at this time—was the music played by white dance bands.

The Tin Pan Alley songwriter who had the closest association with jazz in reality was George Gershwin. Thoroughly conversant with the European classics as well as with popular styles, Gershwin sought to bridge the gap between art music and popular music. He had a genuine affinity for and personal interest in the music of African Americans. One of the earliest and most familiar fruits of this interest was his *Rhapsody in Blue,* written for "jazz band and piano" and originally performed at Aeolian Hall in New York in 1924 by Paul Whiteman's orchestra, with Gershwin at the piano. While *Rhapsody* is an extraordinary piece of music for its time, it is much more a symphonic piece than a jazz composition. Still, Gershwin was more sensitive to and respectful of the subtle nuances of African American music than most of his contemporaries. His music found wide acceptance among black as well as white audiences. His "Summertime," originally written for the opera *Porgy and Bess* in 1935, quickly passed into the realm of a jazz classic. Indeed, it was the rare black jazz band that did not include a Gershwin tune in its repertoire.

Gershwin's identification with jazz is all the more incredible given the isolationist stance of Tin Pan Alley as a whole. Like his colleagues, Gershwin had little contact with musical developments outside New York City. The fact that he was able to assimilate African American influences in a way that resonated across racial lines says more about his musical instincts and talent than it does about the openness of the industry or society as a whole.

Dance Crazes, Latin Influences, Musical Theater, and Records

As early as 1909, records were a force to be reckoned with. According to Russell Sanjek, "In 1909, more than 27 million phonograph records and cylinders were manufactured, having a wholesale value of nearly $12 million."[33] While the larger proportion of their revenues would derive from the sale of sheet music for years to come, publishers and a growing number of popular artists felt that additional revenue from record sales couldn't hurt. Thus, Victor Herbert, a successful composer, and John Philip Sousa led the charge to revise the copyright laws. The resulting Copyright Act of 1909 mandated a royalty of two cents for each cylinder, record, or piano roll manufactured, in addition to the royalties already derived from live performances. Shortly after the passage of the act, the recording industry and Tin Pan Alley began to cross paths regularly, beginning with the dance fever that swept the country from 1910 to World War I and continuing with the growth of musical theater.

Tin Pan Alley hits such as Irving Berlin's "Everybody's Doin' It" and "Alexander's Ragtime Band" and Gilbert and Muir's "Waiting for the Robert E. Lee" were well suited to new social dances like the one-step, two-step, and turkey trot, and records made it easier for couples to practice at home. The dancing public was most eager to follow in the footsteps of the cosmopolitan husband-and-wife dance team of Vernon and Irene Castle, who popularized these new dances with the able assistance of the African American bandleader and composer, James Reese Europe, whom they hired as their music director. The Castles pushed the envelope further after returning from Paris with the Argentine tango, which marked the beginnings of what John Storm Roberts has called the "Latin tinge" in mainstream popular music.[34] This being the ragtime era, Tin Pan Alley was quick to issue a number of "ragtime tangos" with titles like "Tango Rag" and "Everybody Tango." The tango also had an effect on the African American music that became popular in the mainstream; it can be heard most prominently on the tango introduction to W. C. Handy's "St. Louis Blues." The Castles made the tango an enduring classic and helped demonstrate the value of dance music on record. In addition to their string of successful Castle House dance studios and lucrative public appearances, the Castles had a deal with Victor to produce a series of dance records. Europe supervised the project, providing opportunities for dozens of African American musicians to participate in (and shape) mainstream culture, and also contributing to the Latin tinge by adding Puerto Rican musicians to the mix.

Europe had organized the Clef Club in New York as a black musicians' union of sorts that could furnish dance orchestras of almost any size, like the 145-piece orchestra—fifty-eight banjos, mandolins, and bandores; ten pianos; five drum kits, and more—he assembled for a 1912 Carnegie Hall concert, which was a first for a black orchestra and the first concert to showcase popular tunes in the hallowed hall.[35] Because of his association with the Castles, Europe's Syncopated Society Orchestra was signed to Victor in 1914—another first for an African

The Clef Club, organized by James Reese Europe, was an African American musicians' union that could supply orchestras of varying sizes on request. In 1914, Europe's own Syncopated Society Orchestra was signed to Victor, becoming the first African American ensemble to secure a recording contract.

American ensemble. They produced eight dance records for Victor that remained profitable for years. After the outbreak of World War I, Europe joined an all-black regiment where he was asked to organize "the best damn brass band in the United States Army."[36] Simultaneously, the Jones Act of 1917 made all Puerto Ricans citizens of the United States. Thus, while his partner Noble Sissle auditioned musicians in Harlem, Europe recruited an additional eighteen darker-skinned Puerto Ricans from the island and formed the 369th Infantry Regiment Hell Fighters Band. After months of trench warfare and reportedly spectacular concerts throughout France, the Hell Fighters returned home to a hero's welcome (including a parade up Fifth Avenue to Harlem), and toured the United States, recording 24 sides of ragtime and jazz for the French Pathé label.

In addition to dance music, musical theater became another force linking Tin Pan Alley and the record companies; its value became apparent during World War I, when British Gramophone made successful recordings of the songs from *Business As Usual* and two of Irving

Berlin's shows, *Watch Your Step* and *Cheep*. Afterward, Victor—followed by Columbia and Edison—emulated the success of its British partner by recording the best-known stage entertainers in the United States. The singer who created the strongest bridge between Tin Pan Alley and the world of records was Al Jolson. His 1919 Columbia recording of Gershwin's "Swanee," which he usually performed live in blackface and white gloves, sold over 2 million records. This figure was equaled by the 1920 Victor recordings of "Whispering" and "The Japanese Sandman," two Tin Pan Alley favorites performed by the Paul Whiteman Orchestra. Following these hits, popular stage entertainers like George M. Cohan, Al Jolson, Nora Bays, and Sophie Tucker soon found themselves pushing Tin Pan Alley songs on records.

The Tin Pan Alley songsters organized the American Society of Composers, Authors, and Publishers (ASCAP) in 1914 to recover royalties on performances of their copyrighted music. This is done by issuing a blanket license for the use of any selection in the catalogue to live-performance venues such as hotels and nightclubs (and later radio and television) and then distributing these royalties to writers and publishers. Membership in ASCAP was skewed toward writers of show tunes and semiserious works, and included Richard Rodgers, Lorenz Hart, Cole Porter, George Gershwin, Irving Berlin, and George M. Cohan. Of the society's 170 charter members, only six were black: Harry Burleigh, Will Marion Cook, J. Rosamond, James Weldon Johnson, Cecil Mack, and Will Tyers.[37] While other black writers and composers who were schooled in musical notation (W. C. Handy, Duke Ellington) were able to gain entrance to ASCAP, the vast majority of black artists were routinely excluded from the society and thereby systematically denied the full benefit of copyright protection. Until 1939, when a rival organization was formed, ASCAP was a closed society with a near monopoly on all copyrighted music. As proprietor of its members' compositions, ASCAP controlled the use of any selection in its catalogue, thereby exercising considerable power in shaping public taste.

> **M**embership in ASCAP was skewed toward writers of show tunes and semiserious works; The vast majority of black artists were routinely excluded from the society and thereby systematically denied the full benefit of copyright protection.

Commercial Broadcasting: A Very Private Enterprise

At the beginning of the 1920s, the outlook for records was rosy. While gross revenues hit an all-time high of $106 million in 1921, however, shrewd observers might have noticed a cloud on the horizon—radio. Two years after the advent of commercial radio broadcasting in 1920, annual record revenues showed a decline. By 1933, the height of the Great Depression, they had plummeted to an unprecedented low of $6 million.

The scientific properties of radio waves had been known since the latter half of the nineteenth century. In 1886, Guglielmo Marconi developed the first practical application of wireless communication. He secured a British patent in 1896 and, a year later, established the Wireless Telegraph and Signal Company. In 1899, he founded American Marconi in the United States and set his sights on nothing short of a worldwide monopoly on wireless communication. In its formative stages, wireless communication was used primarily for telegraphy. The man usually credited with transforming the wireless into a technology for *telephony*—the basis of radio broadcasting—is

Lee de Forest, inventor of the audion, an early version of the vacuum tube that could generate, modulate, amplify, and detect radio energy. Reginald Fessenden, who worked with Edison, made the first long-distance telephonic transmission in 1906. While this can be considered the birth of broadcasting, his transmissions were far less dramatic than de Forest's 1908 broadcasts of phonograph music from the Eiffel Tower or his 1910 broadcast of Caruso from the Metropolitan Opera in New York. As a result, it is de Forest who is known as the Father of Radio.

The Growth of Network Radio

During World War I, there were tremendous advances in radio because competing companies suspended their patent disputes for the war effort. Seeing international communication as a key element in the balance of world power after the war ended, President Woodrow Wilson noted that British-domination of radio—represented by Marconi's company—would not be satisfactory. In 1919, the president of American Marconi was forced to tell his stockholders: "We have found that there exists on the part of the officials of the [U.S.] Government a very strong and irremovable objection to [American Marconi] because of the stock interest held therein by the British Company."[38] Harnessing patriotism to the profit motive, General Electric (GE) engineered a "solution," with the active support of the U.S. government. When all was said and done, the operations and assets of American Marconi were transferred to a new entity—the Radio Corporation of America (RCA). RCA was set up as a holding company for the major radio patent holders in the United States. Its stock was divided among GE and Westinghouse, which would manufacture radio equipment; American Telephone and Telegraph (AT&T), which would manufacture transmitters and control telephonic communication; and the former stockholders of American Marconi.

Harnessing patriotism to the profit motive, the operations and assets of American Marconi were transferred to a new entity—the Radio Corporation of America (RCA).

With the future of North American radio firmly in U.S. hands, a regular schedule of broadcasting began in the United States. In November 1920, Westinghouse's KDKA went on the air from the roof of the company's Pittsburgh factory to broadcast the results of the Harding/Cox presidential election. Within two to three years, and with few precedents to guide their development, nearly 600 stations across the country were licensed to operate. Existing legislation, designed primarily to govern maritime telegraphy, did not anticipate the impact of commercialized telephonic broadcasting. Issues such as programming, financing, organization, ownership, networking, interference, and advertising were worked out in practice and over time.

By the mid-1920s, the structures and practices that would dominate radio for the next two decades were already in place. RCA formed the National Broadcasting Company (NBC), a twenty-five-station network, extending from New York to Kansas City, that went on the air with a most ambitious program, featuring the New York Symphony Orchestra at the Grand Ballroom of the Waldorf-Astoria, and a number of remote feeds, including the dance bands of Vincent Lopez, Ben Bernie, George Olsen, and B. A. Rolfe; the Metropolitan Opera star Titta Ruffo; the comedy team of Webber and Fields; and a Will Rogers monologue. By 1926, NBC was operating two semiautonomous networks out of New York—the more powerful Red Network offering news, semiserious works, and light opera, and the Blue Network, broadcasting more popular fare. These networks were headed by David Sarnoff; Sarnoff had distinguished himself in 1912 as an American Marconi telegraph operator who had been in constant contact with the sinking Titanic. Called "wonder boy of the radio," Sarnoff had envisioned consumer broadcasting as early as 1916. "I have in mind a plan of development which would make radio a 'household utility,' in the same sense as the piano or phonograph," he wrote in a memo to his superiors. "The idea is to bring music into the home by wireless."[39] Sarnoff became president of RCA in 1930, the year the company was severed from GE in a government-led antitrust suit, and was the chair of its board from 1947 until he retired in 1969.

In 1927, Arthur Judson, a violinist turned artist manager, began the Columbia Phonograph Broadcasting System, with financial backing from the Columbia Phonograph Company, which eventually withdrew from the project. The fledgling network received an influx of cash from one of its main advertisers, the owner of La Palina cigars—whose son, William S. Paley, was installed as the network's new president in 1928. At this time, the name of the network was shortened to the Columbia Broadcasting System (CBS). Within months, CBS was NBC's major competitor, and coast-to-coast broadcasting was a reality. Paley and Sarnoff would be the dominant figures in broadcasting for years, each controlling vast media empires.

Although radio developed with little government interference, it was closely monitored by the National Alliance of Broadcasters (NAB), which recommended an extension of government regulatory powers. These recommendations were codified in the Radio Act of 1927 and expanded in the Communications Act of 1934, which created the Federal Communications Commission (FCC). Still, the law lagged behind technological advances and ownership patterns embodied in the predominance of network broadcasting. By 1938, the networks were using 98 percent of the available nighttime wattage, and NBC and CBS had already locked up fifty of the fifty-two clear channels—special frequencies allocated to stations with large transmitters positioned to broadcast over great distances with minimal interference—as well as 75 percent of the most powerful regional stations. In terms of ownership patterns, radio had developed as a very private enterprise indeed. Programming, however, was another matter entirely.

The Advertisers Versus the Programmers

Until World War II, radio was dominated by four national networks that viewed the market as one monolithic listening audience. Their strategy was to pull in as broad a slice of this total listenership as possible—hence the term *broadcasting*. Early radio pioneers felt that the new medium should nourish the spirit and raise the nation's cultural level through programs of news, literature, drama, and concert music. While this belief did little for either the fortunes of Tin Pan Alley or the cultural preferences of huge segments of the U.S. public, it did affect the programming decisions of commercial station owners, who demanded propriety and "good taste" in everything from program content to advertising. Direct advertising of a product was permitted only during business hours; at night, only a discreet mention of a program sponsor's name was allowed. When it appeared that such principles might somehow be compromised, "cultured" industry stalwarts like Lee de Forest

> *lost no opportunity to cry out in earnest protest against the crass commercialism, the etheric vandalism of the vulger hucksters, agencies, advertisers, station owners—who lacking awareness of their*

grand opportunities and moral responsibilities to make of radio an uplifting experience, continue to enslave and sell for quick cash the grandest medium which has yet been given to man to help upward his struggling spirit.[40]

As the twenties roared past most nineteenth-century conventions, the old guard of broadcasting often found itself locking horns with a new breed of unabashedly commercial advertisers. In many ways, Sarnoff and Paley personified the two camps. As a visionary corporate executive, Sarnoff was immersed in the public service aspects of the medium. He viewed radio as an "electronic library" that brought useful information, uplifting literature, and tasteful music into the home. (Of course, as an equally good businessman, he was not oblivious to the fact that such services would sell millions of the radio receivers his company manufactured.) Paley, on the other hand, came to radio as the advertising manager of his father's cigar factory. His product needed a harder sell, the kind that was considered crass by the old guard. Fortunately for popular music, advertisers like Paley, who catered to "vulgar" popular tastes as a matter of necessity, ended up playing the major role in determining the course of radio programming.

> **F**ortunately for popular music, advertisers like Paley, who catered to "vulgar" popular tastes as a matter of necessity, ended up playing the major role in determining the course of radio programming.

Consistent with radio's educational mission, news had always been a staple of radio programming. Drama also added to radio's aura of respectability. The bulk of radio programming, however, was music. Ever vigilant concerning the economic self-interest of its members, ASCAP notified radio early of its intention to include musical broadcasts among its sources of copyright royalties. Commercial advertising had placed musical broadcasts within the "public performance for profit" provision of the 1909 Copyright Act. By the end of 1924, Sanjek notes, "ASCAP income from 199 radio licenses was $130,000, up from the previous year's $35,000 but far from the million predicted when the drive to collect from broadcasters began in the summer of 1922."[41] Dissatisfied with its share, ASCAP complained that radio had not simply killed records and vaudeville, it had killed popular music itself. Publishers and broadcasters thus began an adversarial relationship that continued well into the 1960s.

In 1934, ASCAP's radio royalties were $850,000—still not the sought-after $1 million. By 1937, however, its radio royalties had jumped to $5.9 million, thanks to advertisers. To draw listeners—and thus increase sales—the advertisers supported "dialect" comedy and popular song programs rather than dramatic series or concerts of classical or semiclassical music. Pepsodent toothpaste, in this sense, turned Freeman Gosden and Charles Correll, the white creators of the "blackface" comedy series *Amos 'n' Andy,* into the highest paid entertainers in broadcasting. (As usual, racial parody could be counted on to turn a profit.) Advertisers also provided the listening audience with "live" musical entertainment—and, at the same time, skirted the stringent advertising code by promoting artists with the sponsoring corporation in their group name: the A&P supermarket chain sponsored the A&P Gypsies; Ipana toothpaste, the Ipana Troubadours; and Cliquot Club soft drinks, the Cliquot Club Eskimos.

One of the most interesting national prime-time experiments in popular music was sponsored on NBC by the American Tobacco Company, maker of Lucky Strike cigarettes. Company president George Washington Hill directed B. A. Rolfe and his thirty-five-piece orchestra to play only popular dance music with "no extravagant, bizarre, involved arrangements," and invited listeners to send in their song preferences. With Hill's advertising budget of $20 million, even staid NBC executives "suffered his brash, boorish behavior and joined him at Sunday-morning rehearsals to test the 'foxtrotability' of every selection programmed."[42] The show evolved into the famous *Your Hit Parade*, one of the most popular shows to hit network radio. In focusing solely on musical selections that were popular among the listening audience, *Your Hit Parade* conferred a measure of power in determining public taste on the consumer. The show's admittedly flawed and probably rigged rankings foreshadowed the more "scientific" methods of rating that determine programming formats today.

The tension between "culture" and straight commercial entertainment in radio programming continued until the economic imperatives of the Great Depression put the advertisers in a position to determine the tone of radio more than the programmers. During the depression, as Erik Barnouw has written, "Destitute families that had to give up an icebox or furniture or bedding still clung to the radio as to a last link with humanity."[43] Such loyalty tipped the balance of power in programming to the side of the advertisers. As a result, radio has tended to follow the popular tastes of consumers. This tendency had quite surprising consequences when rock 'n' roll arrived in the early 1950s.

Tin Pan Alley Goes Hollywood . . . and Latin

If radio never quite measured up to ASCAP's musical or financial expectations, the creation of another new medium—talking films—held out the promise of even greener pastures for Tin Pan Alley composers. A number of processes were developed for adding sound to film. In 1924, AT&T's Western Electric developed the vitaphone process of synchronizing disc recordings with film, and it was purchased by Warner Brothers. Warner's classic 1927 film, *The Jazz Singer* starring Al Jolson, often remembered as the first talkie, was in fact a silent film with songs. GE had developed a process for photographing sound onto film in 1922; and in 1928, David Sarnoff organized RCA Photophone to exploit the process. Sarnoff then developed a theater chain, Radio-Keith-Orpheum (RKO), which controlled about 12 percent of all first-run outlets in the United States. By 1930, sound had been installed in 83 percent of the country's theaters.

The runaway success of Metro-Goldwyn-Mayer's (MGM's) Broadway Melody, released in 1929, made it clear that mainstream popular music (i.e., Tin Pan Alley compositions) would play a major role in talking films.

The runaway success of Metro-Goldwyn-Mayer's (MGM's) *Broadway Melody,* released in 1929, made it clear that mainstream popular music (i.e., Tin Pan Alley compositions) would play a major role in talking films. Record companies rushed to record dance and vocal versions of the film's hit songs, including "Give My Regards to Broadway" and the title song. The major motion picture companies—Warner, United Artists, Fox, Paramount, Universal, and MGM—all planned musicals. To secure entertainers with guaranteed appeal, they raided the most popular entertainment medium available to them—network radio. Accordingly, *The Big Broadcast* (1932), a film about radio, numbered among its artists Kate Smith, the Boswell Sisters, and the Mills Brothers, making it one of the few early Hollywood musicals to use African American talent. Also staring in the film was Bing Crosby, who would set the standard for pop vocals until World War II.

Originally steeped in minstrelsy (he actually appeared on film in blackface), Crosby began his singing career in 1926 as one of the Rhythm Boys in the Paul Whiteman band. In 1931, he

launched his solo recording career and landed his first radio show. He recorded with everyone from Al Jolson and Louis Armstrong, to Paul Whiteman, and Duke Ellington. Crosby pioneered a style of singing called "crooning," a laid back, more personal approach that allowed for greater vocal nuance and feelings of intimacy between artist and audience. Crooning was made possible when the microphone replaced the acoustic megaphone and singers no longer had to project their voices to the far reaches of a nightclub or concert hall to be heard. In addition, hits like "Sweet Leilani" (1937), a pseudo-Hawaiian number from the Oscar-winning film *Waikiki Wedding*, and "San Antonio Rose" (1940), a western swing song penned by Bob Wills, fed the mainstream attraction for exotic cultural influences. Crosby went on to star in over sixty musical films. His recording of Irving Berlin's "White Christmas" from the 1942 film *Holiday Inn* sold more than 30 million copies and entered the pop charts eighteen years in a row.[44]

HEAR MORE
"Bing Crosby" on MyMusicKit

Fox was the first major Hollywood studio to ally itself with a Tin Pan Alley publishing house: De Sylva, Brown, and Henderson, which turned out a string of hit musical comedies, including *Good News, Three Cheers, Hold Everything,* and *Sunny Side Up*. In turn, Warner Brothers acquired a dozen New York publishing houses. The studio used the songwriting team of Harry Warren and Al Dubin to score most of Busby Berkeley's choreographic extravaganzas such as *42nd Street, Gold Diggers,* and *Footlight Parade* in 1933. Family-oriented Broadway musicals, such as Jerome Kern's *Babes in Toyland* and *The Merry Widow* by Rodgers and Hart, were reproduced for the silver screen in 1934. The indefatigable Irving Berlin, whose fee for a musical film score was $75,000 plus a percentage of gross receipts, contributed hit songs to films like *Puttin' on the Ritz* (1930), *Top Hat* (1935), *Follow the Fleet* (1936), and *On the Avenue* (1937). By 1937, the music publishing houses associated with Hollywood shared 65 percent of ASCAP's publisher dividends and continued to do so for the next decade.[45]

Another aspect of the connection between Hollywood musicals and mainstream culture bears mentioning. In the buildup to World War II, the United States, concerned about hemispheric solidarity, instituted the Good Neighbor policy toward Latin America. This policy went into high gear in the late 1930s and was embraced by Hollywood, which flooded the United States and international markets with films featuring Latin American themes, stories, images, music, and locations.[46] Many of these films were big-budget musical comedies, with U.S. stars appearing alongside well-known Latin American entertainers. They were intended to avoid the despicable stereotypes of earlier Latin-themed films in their attempts to distinguish among the national characteristics, geographical boundaries, and cultural differences of various Latin American countries. Even with good intentions, however, Hollywood could conflate Buenos Aires, Rio de Janeiro, and Havana as easily as Tin Pan Alley could confuse a tango, a samba, and a rumba.

All the major Hollywood studios participated in this exercise. Indeed, some Latin-themed films that fit the above description predated the Good Neighbor policy, such as *Cuban Love Song* (1931), which starred Jimmy Durante, Lawrence Tibbett, and Lupe Velez and featured Ernesto Lecuona's Orchestra performing "The Peanut Vendor," and *Flying Down To Rio* (1933), which first paired Fred Astaire and Ginger Rogers and featured Vincent Youman's "Carioca." By the late 1930s, Fox led the pack with Brazilian singer and dancer Carmen Miranda, whose riveting performance of "South American Way" in the Broadway revue *The Streets of Paris* (1939) captivated the U.S. audience and led to a string of musical films, including *Down Argentine Way* (1940), *Weekend in Havana* and *That Night in Rio* (1941), and Busby Berkeley's *The Gangs All Here* (1943) in which she performed the "Uncle Sam-ba." Typically performing in carnivalesque outfits and a headdress piled high with tropical fruit, the excess that defined Miranda's image could easily be taken as a demeaning caricature of all things Latin. Still, her signature performances and nonthreatening sexuality turned her into one of the highest paid actors in Hollywood.

The Good Neighbor period coincided with the appearance of a new song type in the U.S. cultural landscape that Gustavo Pérez Firmat has referred to as the "latune"—"a tune with a Latin beat and an English language lyric."[47] Coupled with the influx of new Latin American immigrants, this new type of song created the conditions under which "genuine and imitation Latin songs both competed and reinforced each other."[48] In *Cuban Love Song* "The Peanut Vendor" was performed alongside the title song, which was considered by Firmat to be the first Anglophone *bolero*. "Cuban Love Song" was straight Tin Pan Alley pop in a Latin-themed film. But "The Peanut Vendor" was originally "*El Manisero*," a Cuban composition that was marketed as a *rumba* (spelled rhumba in

Carmen Miranda was a major star in Brazil before coming to the attention of Hollywood. Narrowly stereotyped as the feisty Latina, she was nevertheless instrumental in popularizing Latin music and culture throughout the Americas.

the United States). For the U.S. market, the song was fitted with English lyrics; it sold over 1 million copies of sheet music for E. B. Marks (which listed 600 Latin music tunes in its catalogue) and may well have been the first million-selling Latin music record, too. It has since been recorded over 160 times.

The Tin Pan Alley writers who contributed to the "latune songbook" included luminaries such as George Gershwin and Irving Berlin. Veteran songwriters Harry Warren and Mack Gordon penned all the "Latin" material for Carmen Miranda's musicals, including "I Yi Yi Yi Yi," "Chica Chica Boom Chic," and "They Met in Rio." Though a broad range of Latin American sources were appropriated, Cuban rhythms proved to be the most popular. Cole Porter classics such as "In the Still of the Night," "Night and Day," "I've Got You under My Skin," and "Begin the Beguine" reflect his fascination with Cuban sounds, and, like latunes in general, they have been criticized for trivializing vibrant Latin music. In this climate, Ernesto Lecuona's "Andalucia" could easily be morphed into the decidedly un-Latin "The Breeze and I" with enough momentum to reach number one on *Your Hit Parade*. At the same time, original Latin selections like "Siboney" and "Perfidia" passed into the realm of "American standards."

The Good Neighbor years brought to the fore performers like Xavier Cugot and Desi Arnaz, who could negotiate the demands of the pop market with just enough Latin-ness to thrive. But they also created the space for groups like Machito's Afro-Cubans, who played a "high-octane rumba style" generally for darker-skinned audiences that could "rattle the fenders off a jeep."[49] If African American and

> **T**he Good Neighbor years brought to the fore performers like Xavier Cugot and Desi Arnaz, who could negotiate the demands of the pop market with just enough Latin-ness to thrive.

European influences continued to vie for what would become the dominant force in the U.S. popular culture dialectic, it was clear that Latin music had become the primary source for further rhythmic innovation and exotic seasoning.

In the early twentieth century, established Tin Pan Alley publishing houses consolidated their interests across popular music genres and in every medium used to disseminate popular music—sheet music, radio, Broadway plays, Hollywood films, and (to a lesser extent) records. At times, Tin Pan Alley's relationship with the recording industry conflicted with its other interests. Radio and movies, for example, netted Tin Pan Alley a hefty sum but hurt the recording industry. After all, the consumer did not have to buy a record to hear the latest hit; he or she needed only to turn on the radio. Movie music remained in demand for only as long as the film was in circulation. "When Hollywood created a glut of as many as six or eight songs in a single production, it led to a superabundance of recorded movie music, which sold pictures but not recordings. A Hollywood-connected publisher could no longer assure record makers that a specific song in a forthcoming film would be the plugged hit."[50] Therefore, what were profitable ventures for Tin Pan Alley songwriters and publishers may not have been equally lucrative for recording companies. During the 1920s and 1930s, record companies had to look elsewhere to realize the financial potential of their product. It may not be purely coincidental that they exploited the markets for blues and country music at precisely the moment that record sales began to decline.

LEARN MORE
Chapter Test
on MyMusicKit

Blues, Jazz, and Country: The Segregation of Popular Music

LEARN MORE
Learning objectives on MyMusicKit

In the creation of their distinctive brand of popular music, the most creative Tin Pan Alley songwriters absorbed outside influences like aural sponges. For all their incredible breadth of influences, however, they were in many ways narrowly provincial, products of the urban Northeast and Hollywood. Charles Hamm, among others, has argued that "Tin Pan Alley songs were for white, urban, literate, middle- and upper-class Americans," but it is less certain, as Hamm continues, that this immensely popular music "remained practically unknown to large segments of American society, including most blacks . . . and the millions of poor, white, rural Americans . . . in the South and scattered across the lower Midwest."[1] The available evidence suggests a significant degree of cross-cultural awareness and mixing. When Hamm adds that blacks and poor whites "had their own distinctive types of . . . oral-tradition music," he is calling attention to what we would identify today as blues, jazz, and country music. At the time, record companies categorized this "oral-tradition" music using terms like *race* and *hillbilly music*, reserving what came to be known as the more general "pop" category for mainstream styles. We are thus forced to grapple with the question of how one addresses a history of widespread cultural crossover in a society stratified by class and segregated by race.

Prior to recording, the music business hadn't given that much thought to targeted marketing strategies or to categorizing music by style. Tin Pan Alley songsters knew only too well that songs do not automatically belong to a genre. The whole point of plugging a song

Prior to recording, the music business hadn't given that much thought to targeted marketing strategies or to categorizing music by style.

was to get as many people as possible to buy the sheet music and perform the music in any way they wanted to. As Elijah Wald reminds us, " 'After the Ball' was performed by amateur parlor players, string quartets, brass bands, Appalachian fiddlers, African-American guitarists, black-face minstrels, and vaudeville sopranos."[2] In this sense, the market for sheet music was treated like an undifferentiated mass, albeit one with an imagined white middle class at its core. Initially records were treated the same way. Particular songs were important and it mattered less who recorded them. As concert stars and well-known bands began to make recording more a part of their careers and records became more popular, audiences began to appreciate what was distinctive and exciting about a particular artist's version of a song. From this point on, songs started to be identified by who recorded them rather than who wrote them. In many ways, the history of blues, jazz, and country is the history of these musics on record. And that history has been shaped as much by what record companies and folklorists wanted to present to the public as by what these musicians actually played. Searching for ways to direct audiences to records that would be appropriate for them, record companies chose categories that mirrored the social divisions of U.S. society. As a result, musics that enjoyed considerable overlap in cultural terms have been documented and discussed as if they had separate histories.

Blues, Jazz, and Country: More Equal Than Separate

It is difficult to trace the cultural inputs that went into the creation of grassroots music in the first decades of the twentieth century. At street level, of course, considerable cross-cultural contact occurred; it was part of everyday life. To offer but one example: Polk Brockman owned a furniture store in Atlanta, Georgia. His customers cut across racial lines. In the early 1920s, Brockman, like other furniture store owners, expanded his business to include phonographs. Being attuned to the musical tastes of his diverse clientele, Brockman and others like him—Sam Price in Dallas and Henry C. Speir in Jackson—often served as local talent scouts for record companies.[3] In fact, Brockman had a very lucrative sideline supplying both black and white talent to the OKeh Record Company, where black artists were assigned to the label's 14000 race series and white artists to its 15000 hillbilly series. As marketing categories, designations like *race* and *hillbilly* intentionally separated artists along racial lines and conveyed the impression that their music came from different sources. Nothing could have been further from the truth. Across the social divide of segregation, these artists were aware of and influenced by each other's work. In cultural terms, blues, jazz, and country were far more equal than they were separate.

As marketing categories, designations like **race** and **hillbilly** *intentionally separated artists along racial lines and conveyed the impression that their music came from different sources.*

The United States can be justifiably proud of the melding of African and European conventions that produced the blues, if not the circumstances of the music's creation. Originally, the term *blues* was not a racially coded reference. As the description of a mood or feeling, it dates back to sixteenth-century England. "In the nineteenth century, it was a common expression in the United States," Samuel Charters has reported. "The word was used occasionally in song titles, but as a slang expression, without reference to any Negro musical style."[4]

The evolution of the blues as a fundamentally African American musical genre can be traced back to the shouts, field hollers, and work songs of slavery, which followed the call-and-response style of, say, a foreman, who set the pace of work by uttering a phrase answered in rhythm by the laborers. From these pre-blues forms, which were largely improvised and unaccompanied, with no particular musical structure, a crude blues form developed that would evolve into what came to be known as *country blues*.[5] Gradually, instrumental and harmonic accompaniment were added, reflecting increasing cross-cultural contact. The "Ethiopian airs" of early minstrelsy "with strange modal harmonies and sharply rhythmic dissonance"[6] and the "Negro spirituals" popularized later in the nineteenth century by the Fisk Jubilee Singers, who presented "spirituals in choral versions that were greatly influenced by white singing societies,"[7] were early codifications of this evolution.

One of the more compelling—if oversimplified—stories about the birth of jazz traces its origins to the tripartite division of New Orleans society into black, white, and Creole social circles. Until New Orleans adopted a set of Jim Crow laws that reclassified Creoles of mixed French and African descent as black, they had enjoyed many of the privileges of white society, among them formal musical training and membership in white brass and string bands. "The emergence of jazz," according to jazz scholar Ingrid Monson, "has often been explained as the meeting of the uptown African American brass and string band tradition of blues-drenched aurally transmitted music, with the downtown Creole band tradition of instrumental virtuosity, musical literacy, and training in classical music."[8] The resulting sound combined improvisatory blues styles with the notated tradition of syncopated rags. Indeed, for a time, the line separating ragtime dance music from jazz was not entirely clear; many critics used the terms interchangeably. New Orleans jazz pioneer, Sidney Bechet claimed that white northerners changed the name to describe the music of the white dance bands who were catching on to the style. "In this sense," Wald has argued, "jazz was like rock 'n' roll, a new name that signified white dancers catching up with black styles, rather than a new music."[9]

Country music was also shaped by multicultural influences. In the words of country music historian Bill C. Malone:

> *The folk music of the South was a blending of cultural strains, British at its core, but overlain and intermingled with the musical contributions of other ethnic and racial groups . . . the Germans of the Great Valley of Virginia; the Indians of the backcountry; Spanish, French, and mixed-breed elements in the Mississippi Valley; the Mexicans of South Texas; and, of course, blacks everywhere.*[10]

As country music evolved into a commercial enterprise, one could add to Malone's list the influence of German and Swiss yodelers, Italian mandolin players, and Hawaiian string bands.

The instrumentation in blues, jazz, and country music likewise revealed considerable overlap. Of the two most common instruments in early country music—the fiddle and the banjo—the fiddle was from Europe and the banjo was most probably of African origin. While the fiddle undoubtedly arrived with the earliest colonists, it was soon mastered by others. Black fiddlers, for example, were well represented in the antebellum South. From the 1920s on, country fiddlers borrowed heavily from blues and jazz, using syncopated rhythms, improvisational styles, and call-and-response patterns. An early form of the banjo—a four-stringed instrument with a long neck and a skin stretched over a hollow body, referred to as a *banza,* a *banshaw,* a *banjil,*[11] a *banjor,*[12] or a *banjar*[13]—was brought over from West Africa in the late seventeenth century. A fifth string and a fretted neck were added in the 1800s to produce the instrument that became a staple of country music, but banjos of various types were routinely used in blues accompaniment and in early jazz ensembles, too.

The guitar—also common in blues, jazz, and country music—had been in this country since the colonial period, when it was considered a classical instrument. It found its way into country string bands through white musicians' fascination with black artists' elaborate finger-picking, characteristic of West African techniques but unknown in European folk music. Like the guitar, the mandolin, brought by Italian immigrants and concert musicians, was initially regarded as an upper-class instrument that found its way to the working class through mail-order catalogues. The ukulele and steel guitar were introduced to the United States by Hawaiian string bands that toured the country after Hawaii became a U.S. territory in 1900. The wail of the steel guitar in country music at that time echoed the sounds produced by black guitarists fretting their instruments with knife blades, bottlenecks, and other devices.

Neither vocal style nor choice of material was limited by race. For instance, yodeling, most readily identified with country music, has a more complicated history than one might suspect. Certain pre-blues shouts and hollers were described in John W. Work's *American Negro Songs* as a "fragmentary bit of a yodel, half sung, half yelled."[14] Yodeling became part of American minstrelsy early on. Although Jimmie Rodgers popularized it on record, black musicians had also learned the technique. Blues artists contemporary with Rodgers, such as Stovepipe Johnson ("Devilish Blues," 1928) and Tampa Red ("Worried Devil Blues," 1934), can be heard yodeling on record.[15]

Folkloric characters also cut across racial lines. In his book *Country,* Nick Tosches argues that the ballad "Frankie and Johnny," with a tragic theme common in blues and country, was written by a black singer named Mammy Lou. The tale of Casey Jones, recorded by both blues and country artists in the 1920s, was also written by an African American, Wallace Saunders. At the same time, black musicians were drawn to folk tales of British origin. Tosches refers to a black version of "Barbara Allen" in which the Scottish lady is a black boy named Boberick Allen. Black versions exist of "The Maid Freed from the Gallows," "Lord Lovel," and "Lady Isabel and Elf-Knight," three more British ballads that traveled to the United States in the eighteenth century.[16]

Even when race and hillbilly recordings were segregated in record company catalogues in the 1920s and 1930s, anomalies were not uncommon, cross-pollination was routine, and artists were sometimes listed in the "wrong" category. While most black jazz bands were listed in the race catalogues of record labels, those with more polished, orchestrated arrangements were often issued alongside white dance orchestras. As sidemen for countless blues singers, Fletcher Henderson and his musicians made numerous records for the more limited race market, but his jazz band's recordings competed favorably with the most popular white dance orchestras in the mainstream market, including Paul Whiteman's. Papa Charlie Jackson was marketed as a blues singer, yet his most memorable recording was "Salty Dog Blues," which became a standard in the country repertoire. Concludes Wald, "[I]f our usual views of music history were not so deeply colored

Even when race and hillbilly recordings were segregated in record company catalogues, anomalies were not uncommon, cross-pollination was routine, and artists were sometimes listed in the "wrong" category.

by race, Jackson might be considered a pioneering 'hillbilly' performer as much as a blues singer."[17] One of the white acts that recorded a version of "Salty Dog Blues" for Columbia's hillbilly series was the Allen Brothers. For their second outing, which paired "Chattanooga Blues" and "Laughin' and Cryin' Blues," however, someone in Columbia's New York office thought the duo was black and listed them in the 14000 race series. Whether they were personally offended or simply troubled that the mistake could affect their bookings on the segregated white vaudeville circuit, the Allens sued Columbia and eventually left the label. Because racial separation has been so prominent in U.S. social relations, the histories of blues, jazz, and country have often treated these styles as separate and distinct, using designations such as race and hillbilly to stress difference.

Race Music: The Popular Sounds of Black America

Once one understands that so-called genres in popular music are more often marketing categories than musical distinctions, one is less surprised at just how arbitrary designations like *blues* and *jazz* can be. New Orleans jazz incorporated blues and ragtime. The blues queens of the 1920s regularly performed with jazz bands. Countless jazz tunes have the word *blues* in their titles. These styles are briefly discussed separately here only because this is the way they have been presented for public consumption.

The Birth of the Blues

Although all of what is now called *blues* was categorized as *race music* in the 1920s and 1930s, many historians have distinguished between *country blues* (also referred to as *down home* or *rural blues* or, in a more specific context, *Delta blues*) and *city,* or *classic, blues* (also known as *urban blues* or *vaudeville blues*). "Classic blues was entertainment," Amiri Baraka (a.k.a Leroi Jones) has said, "and country blues, folklore."[18] Country blues was intensely personal, highly improvised, and quite irregular in form. It was usually performed by a single male vocalist with only banjo or guitar accompaniment, if any. In the cities, the myriad of blues styles were codified into eight- and sixteen-bar patterns, as well as the twelve-bar form that became the standard for classic blues. Classic blues follows a 1, 4, 5 (tonic, subdominant, dominant) chord progression and is constructed so that each verse of the aab rhyme scheme leaves space for a vocal or instrumental response. In this call-and-response pattern, there is considerable room for improvisation, but within a standardized musical framework. This is the structure that came to dominate the blues in the 1920s and 1930s—albeit with some significant exceptions—and is the structure upon which a good deal of rhythm and blues and rock 'n' roll was built.

Despite a rash of so-called blues recordings by white entertainers in the 1910s, it wasn't until 1920—and then quite by accident—that recording companies "discovered" a significant African American market for classic blues recordings by black artists. When a recording session with the popular white artist Sophie Tucker had to be canceled, the enterprising black producer and songwriter, Perry Bradford, convinced OKeh executives to let him record a black contralto named Mamie Smith. Smith's recording of Bradford's "Crazy Blues" sold 8,000 copies a week,

"Crazy Blues"

Artist: Mamie Smith (1883–1946)
Music/Lyrics: Perry Bradford
Label: OKeh (1920)

The first recordings of classic, urban blues were made in 1920, when vaudeville singer/songwriter Perry "Mule" Bradford convinced the OKeh label to record Mamie Smith. She was the star of a musical revue called *Maid of Harlem*, in which she sang some of his tunes. Bradford backed up Smith with a band, the Jazz Hounds. The result was "Crazy Blues," a blockbuster hit, which demonstrated that the African American listening audience was an untapped market for the recording industry. This inspired OKeh (and other labels) to produce more recordings of African American artists, which were called race records.

Mamie Smith's singing style actually owes more to theater and vaudeville than it does to blues. Her stage show with the Jazz Hounds was a theatrical extravaganza and, like vaudeville, incorporated dance, humorous skits, and other nonmusical entertainment.

Musical Style Notes

A blues song generally consists of a certain number of measures, or bars (see sidebar). Each verse of the song generally contains this same number of measures. There are sixteen-bar blues, eight-bar blues, and—the most common—twelve-bar blues. "Crazy Blues" is in fact a "crazy blues," with the verses alternating between a sixteen-bar and a twelve-bar structure (see road map below) in an unpredictable pattern.

As the name of Smith's band suggests, the instrumentation (cornet, trombone, violin, piano) is much more commonly associated with jazz, and the style of simultaneous improvisation employed by the players gives the piece a ragtime feel that places the piece squarely in the late 1910s and early 1920s.

Music Terminology Demystified What Is a Bar?

Most types of Western music feature a repeated succession of rhythmic pulses, or beats. By placing emphasis on certain beats in a recurrent pattern, we can group these beats into rhythmic units. There can be units of two (like a march), three (like a waltz), four (like many rock and blues styles), or even more. One of these rhythmic units is called a measure or, in idiomatic American music terminology, a bar.

Musical "Road Map"

TIMINGS	COMMENTS	LYRICS
0:0–0:09	Introduction (4 bars) Instrumental entrance, featuring simultaneous improvisation and sliding instrumental attacks characteristic of a ragtime style.	
0:10–0:45	First verse (16 bars) Notice the way in which the trombone "walks" the bass notes (descending down the musical scale in stepwise motion), both during the verse and in playing transitions from one verse to another.	*I can't sleep at night . . .*
0:46–1:13	Second verse (12 bars)	*There's a change in the ocean . . .*
1:14–1:48	Third verse (16 bars)	*Now I've got the crazy blues . . .*
1:49–2:15	Fourth verse (12 bars) Notice how the bass instruments begin to double the singer's melody at the beginning of this verse.	*Now I can read his letter . . .*
2:16–2:40	Fifth verse (12 bars)	*I went to the railroad . . .*
2:41–3:13	Sixth verse (16 bars)	*Now I've got the crazy blues . . .*
3:14	Tag at the end	*. . . Those blues.*

mostly to black buyers.[19] OKeh thus became the first beneficiary of a large, previously untapped market of African American consumers. Ralph Peer, the presiding OKeh recording director, dubbed these recordings "race records."[20] The label remained the designation for black music by black artists for a black audience until 1949.

While Smith's singing style "was more in the tradition of the vaudeville stage than it was 'bluesy,' "[21] her overwhelming success ushered in an era of classic blues recordings made almost invariably by African American women: Ida Cox, Chippie Hill, Sarah Martin, Clara Smith, Trixie Smith, Victoria Spivey, Ethel Waters, and Sippie Wallace, among others. Taking their cue from the style of Gertrude (Ma) Rainey, called Mother of the Blues, these women formed "the link between the earlier, less polished blues styles and the smoother theatrical style of the later urban blues singers."[22] All were veterans of traveling tent shows and later the black-oriented Theater Owners Booking Association (TOBA) theater circuit. In contrast to (usually male) country blues singers, these classic blues women were typically accompanied by "a red hot jazz band" or a "scintillating master of the keyboard."[23] As a group, they projected a polish hitherto unknown in the blues. The bulk of their material—"upwards of seventy-five percent" according to one estimate—was sung from the point of view of women.[24]

> *In contrast to (usually male) country blues singers, these classic blues women were typically accompanied by "a red hot jazz band" or a "scintillating master of the keyboard."*

Easily the most famous classic blues singer of her time was Bessie Smith, the Empress of the Blues. A protégé of Ma Rainey, she spent years on the road perfecting her craft. Her singing style "combined the emotional fervor of country blues with the vigorous appeal of jazz."[25] Eventually, she developed her own Liberty Belles revue and became a vaudeville headliner with her own show, *Harlem Frolics.* Smith performed with some of the best jazz bands of the era, including Louis Armstrong's and Fletcher Henderson's. Signed to a failing Columbia in 1923, she recorded scores of sides over the next decade. Her records sold so well—her "Down-hearted Blues" (1923), for example, reportedly sold 780,000 copies in six months—that she was said to have saved the company from bankruptcy. One of the high points of her career was the title role in the 1929 film *St. Louis Blues,* based on the W. C. Handy composition of the same name. That same year she

The flamboyant and talented Bessie Smith rose to the pinnacle of classic blues success during the 1920s. Her career crashed along with the stock market at the end of the decade.

recorded "Nobody Knows You When You're Down and Out," her last big hit before the Great Depression wrecked her career.

The initial success of various blues recordings encouraged the formation of a handful of black-owned, independent labels such as Black Swan, Sunshine, Merritt, and Black Patti. W. C. Handy and his publishing partner, Harry Pace, started Black Swan in 1921. Mayo "Ink" Williams, head of the race series for Paramount (a company owned by the Wisconsin Chair Company, which entered the record business to sell phonographs), formed his own company, Black Patti, in 1927. However, because these companies lacked sufficient resources for national promotion and distribution, they were either bought up by the major labels or forced out of the industry. Not a single black-owned label survived the 1920s intact.

Following the initial surge of classic blues recordings, record companies began to test the boundaries of the African American market and discovered a considerable demand for country blues, particularly among southern blacks who had left the largely rural South for northern industrial jobs. At first, these companies brought country blues performers to northern studios to record in the more sophisticated styles associated with the city blues. Later, venturing south to record local singers, they became the unwitting folklorists of U.S. culture.

In 1924, Paramount began country blues recordings, with its race series under the direction of Ink Williams. Its first release was Papa Charlie Jackson's "Lawdy Lawdy Blues," followed by releases from Arthur "Blind" Blake and Blind Lemon Jefferson, perhaps the most popular country blues singer of the decade. A native of Wortham, Texas, Jefferson was born blind but with a gift for music. While he led a chaotic and dissolute life as an itinerant bluesman, his style influenced almost every country blues artist of the 1920s. Jefferson made seventy-nine recordings for Paramount in four years, including "Black Snake Blues." His "Match Box Blues" was covered by rockers from Carl Perkins to the Beatles. As Charters has noted, many of his recordings "were direct reworkings of old field cries and work songs. He shouted the melody in a long, free rhythmic pattern, and the guitar sang behind the voice in a subtle counterpoint."[26]

Throughout the 1920s and 1930s, OKeh, Columbia, Victor, and Vocalion (a small, independent label) engaged in extensive field recording, documenting a crucial period in the development of

African American music. The person most associated with commercial field recordings was Ralph Peer, who had coined the term *race records* at OKeh. In the 1930s, the Library of Congress began field recording through the efforts of John Lomax and his son Alan. As a result of all these

Blind Lemon Jefferson was one of the first musicians to codify the country blues and was the most successful artist to record in the style. Although he was credited as the writer of many of his songs, he was probably paid a flat fee for most of his recording sessions, leaving his producer and record company to reap most of the profits.

forays, commercial and noncommercial, dozens of country blues artists—among them, Skip James, Mississippi John Hurt, Sleepy John Estes, Blind Willie McTell, Son House, Charlie Patton, Lead Belly, and Robert Johnson—were brought to wider public attention.

Robert Johnson, later to be known as the King of the Delta Blues Singers, lead a life shrouded in myth and mystery. Even after he allegedly sold his soul to the devil to enhance his talent and career, he remained a relatively minor player on the blues stage of his time. His entire recorded output comprised 29 songs (plus alternate takes) made in two sessions in 1936 and 1937. For anyone who was listening, it revealed the genius of his ability to "sing and play cross-rhythms on the guitar, relating the parts in . . . complex syncopations."[27] Still, it wasn't until Columbia released *King of the Delta Blues Singers* (1961), a compilation of Johnson's recordings, that British rockers discovered and popularized his material and Johnson became the towering blues figure that he is remembered as today. His material has been covered by notable contemporary rockers, including the Rolling Stones, Bob Dylan, Led Zeppelin, and Jeff Beck, and especially Eric Clapton ("32-20 Blues," "Come on in My Kitchen," "Love in Vain," "Malted Milk," "Ramblin' on My Mind," and "Walkin' Blues"). Clapton's inspired vocal and guitar work made Cream's live version of Johnson's "Crossroads" one of the standout blues recordings of the rock era.

The formative influence of blues artists on rock 'n' roll has been undeniable. Their diverse, idiosyncratic styles ultimately evolved into a more classic mold with standardized structures, tunes, and even guitar breaks. Just as the pioneering guitar work of Blind Lemon Jefferson is echoed in the playing of Lightnin' Hopkins, Aaron "T-Bone" Walker, and ultimately B. B. King, a similar stylistic connection can be traced from blues artists of the Mississippi Delta, especially Robert Johnson, to John Lee Hooker, Muddy Waters, and Howlin' Wolf. It is fitting, therefore, that Ma Rainey, Bessie Smith, Lead Belly, Robert Johnson, and Howlin' Wolf have been inducted into the Rock 'n' Roll Hall of Fame as "early influences." B. B. King, John Lee Hooker, and Muddy Waters have been admitted as rock 'n' roll artists in their own right.

All That Jazz

The New Orleans fusion of blues, ragtime, and brass band marches, characterized by ensemble playing, improvised solos, and syncopated rhythms, that began with Buddy Bolden at the turn of the century, was certainly a defining moment in the history of jazz. In 1908, Freddy Keppard's Original Creole Band toured the country from New York to Los Angeles, spreading the New Orleans style across the nation. From hot instrumentalists like Joe "King" Oliver and Louis "Satchmo" Armstrong to composer/pianists like Jelly Roll Morton, one major point to be made is that these musicians were playing the music that people danced to. Well before *jazz* became the accepted term for such music, bands all over the country were playing some brand of syncopated dance music. The music spread that much quicker because depressed economic conditions in the South encouraged people to migrate north from World War I on. In the case of New Orleans musicians, they left because in 1917 the Department of the Navy shuttered Storyville, the red light district that had served as the music's birthing center.

Chicago became a primary destination for New Orleans musicians. King Oliver made his way there in 1918 and by 1920, he had taken over the Creole Jazz Band from bassist Bill Johnson.

> **T**he New Orleans fusion of blues, ragtime, and brass band marches, characterized by ensemble playing, improvised solos, and syncopated rhythms, that began with Buddy Bolden at the turn of the century, was certainly a defining moment in the history of jazz.

Less than two years later, he sent for his protégé, Louis Armstrong, to join the band. Oliver's journey to Chicago was preceded by two white New Orleans dance bands. Tom Brown's Dixieland Jas Band had taken up residency in Chicago in 1915, and in 1916, Nick LaRocca's Original Dixieland Jass Band (ODJB) had its first national booking in the city. ODJB then headed for New York, where they made the first jazz recordings of "Livery Stable Blues" and "The Dixieland Jass Band One-Step," which turned them (and, perhaps, the term *jazz* itself) into a national sensation.

By the early 1920s, New York was becoming more prominent as a center for jazz. One musician who can be seen as pivotal to early New York jazz is Fletcher Henderson. Henderson inherited the mantle of large ensembles, unorthodox instrumentation, and precise arrangements from James Reese Europe, along with a less bluesy feeling than New Orleans. Of course, Henderson encountered the blues routinely as the recording manager for W. C. Handy's Black Swan label, where he toured with Ethel Waters. When his jazz orchestra grew to sixteen players for an extended stay at the Roseland Ballroom beginning in 1924, Henderson was credited with inaugurating the "big band" era of jazz. He was also the first black jazz musician to combine composing, arranging, and performing with an unmatched recording career. In addition to the countless blues recordings he made as a sideman for Handy's company, Fletcher Henderson and His Orchestra made approximately 100 recordings for various labels from 1923–1924, including "Copenhagen" and "King Porter Stomp," placing him on a par with the most prolific white orchestras of the day. While his blues recordings were issued as race records, the record companies directed his orchestra's material toward a crossover audience that included white enthusiasts like those who comprised the audience at the Roseland Ballroom.

When King Oliver turned down a 1927 invitation to appear at the recently opened Cotton Club in Harlem (as white audiences were beginning to move uptown clubs), the offer was accepted by an up and coming bandleader/pianist from Washington, D. C.—Edward Kennedy "Duke" Ellington. Ellington's unique style incorporated everything from the exuberance of New Orleans to the sweet jazz of the white society orchestras. The growling trumpet solos of Bubber Miley provided Ellington's band with its fabled "jungle sound," which could be heard on "East St. Louis Toodle-oo" and "Black and Tan Fantasy." Ellington's piano playing was influenced by the Harlem "stride" pianists such as James P. Johnson, Willie-the-Lion Smith, Luckey Roberts, and Fats Waller, who also influenced the piano styles of early rock 'n' roll artists such as Fats Domino, Little Richard, Huey "Piano" Smith, and Jerry Lee Lewis. Ellington's talent as a composer and arranger, however, won him early acclaim as the country's greatest composer. According to Eileen Southern, "his genius led him to create an orchestra style marked by rich and daring harmonies, by subtle contrastings of color and timbres, and by an ingenious handling of solo and ensemble relationships."[28] He not only developed his arrangements collectively with the band, he also envisioned parts for specific players, rather than just particular instruments. Over the course of his career, he composed and/or arranged more than 2,000 songs, many of which live on as jazz classics, from "Black and Tan Fantasy" and "I'm Beginning to See the Light" to "Satin Doll" and (with co-composer Billy Strayhorn) "Take the 'A' Train."

If Fletcher Henderson's arrangements sometimes felt stiff or awkward, the Ellington band was said to "swing." In 1932, the Duke wrote "It Don't Mean a Thing, If It Ain't Got That Swing," giving a name to the jazz era that followed. Although regular national radio broadcasts from the Cotton Club turned the Ellington band into a household name, swing came to be associated with the white dance bands of Tommy and Jimmy Dorsey, Artie Shaw,

SEE MORE
Duke Ellington documentary on MyMusicKit

Glenn Miller, and Benny Goodman. Goodman, in particular, could swing more than most; he hired Fletcher Henderson, among other African Americans, as his arrangers, and he made jazz history when he added black pianist Teddy Wilson to his band in 1935.

As *jazz moved in the direction of more symphonic orchestrations and becoming an art music in the 1940s, it lost its connection to the more accessible dance styles that would drive rhythm and blues and rock 'n' roll.*

As jazz moved in the direction of more symphonic orchestrations and becoming an art music in the 1940s, it lost its connection to the more accessible dance styles that would drive rhythm and blues and rock 'n' roll. One group that maintained a connection to dance-oriented blues styles was the Count Basie Orchestra. In 1927, Basie found himself stranded in Kansas City when the vaudeville company with which he was touring went bankrupt. He decided to stay, eventually joining Benny Moten's band. By 1935, he was fronting his own band and broadcasting from the Reno Club. As a major junction for rail and riverboat traffic, Kansas City was a regular stopping place for touring musicians, who often gathered for competitive jam sessions. Given the need for a familiar musical structure with plenty of room for improvisation, the twelve-bar blues often served as the basis for these sessions. The Basie band carried this sense of excitement forward in material such as "Boogie Woogie," "One O'Clock Jump," and " Jumpin' at the Woodside." In addition, Joe Jones's propulsive drumming foreshadowed the rhythms that would come to dominate rhythm and blues. It is not surprising, then, that two of the vocalists who performed with the Basie Orchestra, Kansas City blues shouters Jimmy Rushing and Big Joe Turner, blurred the line between jazz and blues and had no trouble maintaining vibrant careers through the ascendancy of rhythm and blues, even after the heyday of the big bands.

The Count Basie orchestra maintained a connection to the blues as they helped chart the course for jazz.

Hillbilly: The Music of the White Working Class

The first recordings of country musicians were as accidental as the classic blues and, once again, it was Ralph Peer who opened the market for the music. In 1923, when Peer visited Atlanta in search of new black artists, Polk Brockman persuaded him to record a man who had been a mainstay of the North Georgia folk scene for forty years, Fiddlin' John Carson. Although Carson had won the Atlanta Old Time Fiddler's Convention numerous times, Peer was unimpressed with his "Little Old Log Cabin in the Lane" and "The Old Hen Cackled and the Rooster's Going to Crow." The recordings' sales figures were what convinced Peer of the music's value.

At the time, this music was never referred to as country music. Record catalogues used labels such as "old time music" (OKeh), "old familiar tunes" (Columbia), and "songs from Dixie" (Brunswick).[29] The word *hillbilly* had been used since the turn of the century as a catchall (and pejorative) term for southern backwoods culture. In 1925, a string band headed by Al Hopkins recorded six songs for Ralph Peer. Asked the group's name, Hopkins responded: "Call the band anything you want. We are nothing but a bunch of hillbillies from North Carolina and Virginia anyway."[30] Peer listed the band as the "Hill Billies"—which soon became the generic term for commercial country music. Just like the term *race music,* it was laden with contradictory meanings. According to Bill C. Malone,

> Like the South itself, hillbilly music suffered and profited from a conflicting set of images held by Americans that ranged from stability and enchantment to decadence and cultural degeneracy. . . . To many people hillbilly music was just one more example, along with Ku Kluxism, Prohibition, sharecropping, racial violence, and religious bigotry, of the South's retarded and degenerate culture. On the other hand, many people no doubt responded positively to the South as a bastion of traditional values and orthodox religion in a nation given over to rapid and bewildering change.[31]

In the early period of commercial country music, white string bands like the Hill Billies predominated. Among the finest were Charlie Poole and his North Carolina Ramblers, and Gil Tanner's Skillet Lickers. At first, these bands' repertoires consisted of traditional, anonymous folk tunes, surprisingly few of which were of British origin.[32] Then professional songwriters began to appear. By the time the Skillet Lickers started recording for Columbia in 1926, their selections included "everything from traditional ballads, breakdowns, and rural 'dramas' (humorous skits) to the latest popular hits from Tin Pan Alley."[33] The North Carolina Ramblers included popular songs such as "Goodbye Sweet Liza Jane" and "Milwaukee Blues." A number of interracial string bands also recorded hillbilly music, such as the the Kentucky Boys and the Georgia Yellowhammers, both of which used black fiddlers. All-black string bands like the Mississippi Sheiks could handle country material as well as anyone, but the record companies pushed them toward their blues repertoire in the studio.[34] These artists drew on a broad range of sources that they incorporated into regional styles that were intensely familiar to their audiences.

Most early commercial performers were working people who played music in their off-hours. A few, like Charlie Poole, toured regularly on the vaudeville circuit, but it was rare for a hillbilly performer to have a show business career that paid the rent. One such performer, Vernon Dalhart (who took his name from Vernon and Dalhart, Texas, where he had worked as

The Carter Family (from left, Maybelle, Sara, and A. P.) represented "family values" in country music even after Sara and A. P. divorced. Their traditional image corresponded with the treasure trove of traditional songs they helped to preserve.

a cowboy), entered the business via vaudeville and light opera. A graduate of the Dallas Conservatory of Music, Dalhart began recording for Edison in 1916, specializing in so-called coon songs. In 1924, Victor recorded his "Wreck of the Old 97" and "The Prisoner's Song," the first country music recordings to sell in the millions. By 1933, when his career ended, he had sold an estimated 75 million records.

In 1927, two of country music's most influential acts—Jimmie Rodgers and the Carter Family—were first recorded within days of each other by the tireless Ralph Peer, now at Victor. Rodgers represented the archetypal "ramblin' man"; the Carter Family projected stability. (These two polar—and equally marketable—images were well represented among country musicians for years to come.) While Rodgers roamed through vaudeville and the blues, the Carter Family explored the traditional folkloric component of country music. Any number of their songs, including "The Wabash Cannonball," "Wildwood Flower," and "Will the Circle Be Unbroken," have become country music classics, but they exerted relatively less influence on the future of pop. That's where Jimmie Rodgers came in.

Jimmie Rodgers, the "Singing Brakeman," was the first real star of country music. As a boy, he often accompanied his father, a rail crew foreman, on extended journeys to different cities in the South, learning the language and culture of the railroad men he would later immortalize in song. In 1925, he joined a minstrel troupe and toured the South and Midwest as a blackface entertainer. He first recorded for Ralph Peer in 1927, singing two sentimental, traditional songs. Victor executives then invited Rodgers to their New Jersey studios, where he recorded the first of his twelve blue yodels, so-called because they incorporated yodeling into the blues. Popularly known as "T for Texas," this recording took

((• HEAR MORE
Jimmie Rodgers
on MyMusicKit

Jimmie Rodgers played the "ramblin' man" to the Carters' stable family image. If the Carters stayed close to home musically, Rodgers' travels encouraged him to incorporate a greater diversity of influences into his music than any other country artist at the time.

"Blue Yodel #9 (Standin' on the Corner)"

Artist: Jimmie Rodgers
Music/Lyrics: Jimmie Rodgers
Label: RCA Victor (1931)

If you were searching for one artist who incorporated the widest range of American roots music in the early twentieth century, you couldn't go wrong with Jimmie Rodgers. While considered the first true country music star, Rodgers's songs incorporated blues, country, jazz, and even Hawaiian guitar. Rodgers wrote twelve blues–country hybrid Blue Yodel #9, recorded on September 11, 1931, is listed as number 23 in the Rock 'n' Roll Hall of Fame's "500 Songs That Shaped Rock and Roll."

Musical Style Notes

"Blue Yodel #9" is a blues song with elements of country and jazz. The song features typical blues chord progressions but an irregular form. It's basically an eight-bar blues (eight bars of four beats each), but Rodgers adds some two-beat bars here and there, and not all the verses have exactly the same structure. (At 1:07 and 1:16, you can hear the pianist changing chords quickly; she is concentrating intensely on following Rodgers as he varies the eight-bar form.) Each verse also ends with Rodgers's signature yodel, which gives this blues song a country twist. To further add to the stylistic mix, the song features the New Orleans–style improvisations of jazz trumpeter Louis Armstrong; the pianist is his wife Lillian Armstrong.

Musical "Road Map"

TIMINGS	COMMENTS	LYRICS
0:00–0:14	Introduction; trumpet and piano	
0:14–0:32	Verse 1	*Standin' on . . .*
0:32–0:53 @0:47	Verse 2 Trademark yodel at 0:47	*It was . . .* (yodel)
0:53–1:01	Verse 3	*I said . . .*
1:01–1:06	(Brief trumpet interlude between verses)	
1:07–1:27 1:22	Verse 4 Yodel at 1:22, leading into instrumental solo	*Listen . . .* (yodel)
1:27–1:54	Instrumental verse; trumpet solos	
1:54–2:11	Verse 5	*My good . . .*
2:11–2:37 2:27–2:37	Verse 6 Yodel, leading into final trumpet phrase (Notice this is the first time you can really hear the guitar—the slow strum right at the end!)	*She come . . .*

the country by storm and became Rodgers's only million seller. Though he usually performed solo, Rodgers used a broad range of players and instruments in his recordings, including fiddles, banjos, ukuleles, pianos, and guitars, as well as brass and the one instrument that became a defining characteristic of certain strains of country music—the steel guitar. His steel guitarists included Joe Kaipo, a Hawaiian, and he recorded with the (black) Louisville Jug Band. On "Blue Yodel No. 9," Rodgers was joined by Louis Armstrong on trumpet and Lillian Hardin on piano. Rodgers's blue yodels showcased the cultural diversity that informed his music and influenced generations of musicians. Nothing corresponding to this combination of elements had ever before appeared in country music or the blues. Like some of his blues contemporaries, Rodgers was inducted as an early influence into the Rock 'n' Roll Hall of Fame.

> **R**odgers's blue yodels showcased the cultural diversity that informed his music and influenced generations of musicians. Nothing corresponding to this combination of elements had ever before appeared in country music or the blues.

Rodgers's influence on country music was incalculable. Following his success, groups like Roy Hall's Blue Ridge Entertainers and Roy Acuff's Smoky Mountain Boys established the steel guitar as a staple in country music. With the rise of Texas hillbillies such as Ernest Tubb, Lefty Frizzell, and Bob Wills, all of whom considered Rodgers their inspiration, country music took a turn to the West, especially benefitting Gene Autry, the Singing Cowboy, who began his career as a Jimmie Rodgers imitator. Bob Wills and His Texas Playboys, however, popularized a brand of music called western swing, which became a formative influence on early rock 'n' roll. An unorthodox bandleader with eclectic taste in music, Wills and his group performed daily on KVOO in Tulsa, Oklahoma, from 1934 to 1942. In its various incarnations, the Texas Playboys included brass, reeds, drums, and electric guitars, all frowned upon in country music at the time. By the end of the 1930s, Wills and his group could play anything from fiddle music to big band jazz. In 1939, his "San Antonio Rose" became a certified million seller for the group and a national sensation when it was recorded by Bing Crosby the following year.

Neither Rodgers nor the Carter Family toured extensively—the Carters because of their complicated family dynamics, which included separation and divorce; Rodgers due to a running battle with tuberculosis, which eventually took his life. Their careers were propelled in large measure by their recordings and radio appearances. Although radio had devastating effects on the recording industry as a whole, early country musicians seem to have benefited from a complementary relationship between radio appearances and record sales.

Gene Autry was not only the most famous singing cowboy on film, but he also made a successful transition to television with his own weekly series in the early 1950s.

Disseminating Blues, Jazz, and Country: More Separate Than Equal

While significant markets existed for jazz and blues records, African American artists rarely performed on radio or in film. Following Bessie Smith's starring role in *St. Louis Blues* in 1929, the film's director, Dudley Murphy, made *Black and Tan Fantasy,* a movie built around Duke Ellington's composition. In 1933, Murphy filmed an operatic version of Eugene O'Neill's *Emperor Jones* with the incomparable Paul Robeson in the title role. But the Great Depression shut most independent black-oriented films out of the business, leaving Hollywood firmly in control—and Hollywood seldom cast African Americans in anything but subservient and/or degrading roles.

The situation was even worse on radio. The blues—particularly country blues—were seldom heard on the airwaves. "Radio broadcasts," as Nelson George has noted, "were rarely used to promote the grittier forms of music."[35] In 1932, however, Fats Waller played a series titled *Fats Waller's Rhythm Club* over WLW in Cincinnati, Ohio. Two other blues performers, Sonny Boy Williamson (Rice Miller), a singer and harmonica player, and Robert Lockwood, a guitarist, were featured on the King Biscuit Flour Company's *King Biscuit Time,* broadcast from Helena, Arkansas, in the early 1940s. Radio made a few short-lived attempts to feature well-known African American talent on network shows. The *Ethel Waters Show,* sponsored by Amoco on NBC, was quickly canceled when the network's southern affiliates threatened to boycott the program. Fleischman Yeast sponsored the *Louis Armstrong Show* on CBS in 1937, but by then Armstrong was doing comedy and singing Tin Pan Alley pop. Scheduled opposite NBC's popular *Jack Benny Show*, the program lasted only thirteen weeks. African American jazz bands, if aired at all, were usually relegated to late-night broadcasts from popular nightspots—Duke Ellington at the Cotton Club, Chick Webb at the Savoy in Harlem, Earl (Fatha) Hines from Chicago's Grand Terrace. "Significantly, these broadcasts weren't aimed at blacks. Broadcasters and advertisers were simply meeting America's demand for big-band music. These bands just happened to be black and popular."[36]

Occasionally, an extremely talented African American musician, like William Grant Still, could find work in radio as a composer or arranger. Still had studied at the New England Conservatory as well as with avant-garde composer Edgar Varése. At one point, he worked at W. C. Handy's publishing house and at the Black Swan record company; during the Great Depression, he worked as an arranger and staff composer at both WCBS and WNBC in New York. He received commissions from Artie Shaw, Sophie Tucker, and Paul Whiteman, among others, and became the first African American conductor of a white radio orchestra. The employment of African Americans in radio, however, was contingent on their ability to relate to European conventions and mainstream tastes.

In contrast, broadcasters and film producers gave country music a considerable boost. Since the dawn of commercial radio in the early twenties, stations throughout the South and Midwest had broadcast country music. The barn dance format quickly became the most popular showcase for country talent. The first such program of note was *National Barn Dance,* introduced in 1924 by the Sears Roebuck station, WLS in Chicago. Combining country and folk material with older pop standards, the program had a broader appeal than most country-oriented shows.

Of course, the *Grand Ole Opry* eventually overshadowed all other country broadcasts. It was the brainchild of George D. Hay, a columnist for the *Memphis Commercial-Appeal* and a veteran announcer on WLS. In 1925, Hay became the station manager for WSM in Nashville, owned by the National Life and Accident Insurance Company. Bypassing the cultural biases of the station owners and the Nashville elite, Hay launched *Barn Dance,* later renamed the *Grand Ole Opry*. At first, the program emphasized instrumental music. Its first major singing star was Uncle Dave Macon, a gifted and unpretentious banjo player with a vast storehouse of folkloric material. The program also introduced one of the first black stars of country music (and radio), Deford Bailey, a country harmonica player who proved to be one of the show's most popular

> *The* Grand Ole Opry *eventually became the longest-running show on U.S. radio, a clear indicator of the commercial potential of country music.*

artists. In 1928, Bailey made twice as many *Opry* appearances as any other performer. The *Grand Ole Opry* eventually became the longest-running show on U.S. radio, a clear indicator of the commercial potential of country music.

Opry's biggest star was Roy Acuff. A singer and fiddler raised on a tenant farm in the Smoky Mountains, Acuff achieved worldwide fame playing traditional mountain music. In 1932, he toured with Doc Hauer's Medicine Show, hawking Moc-A-Tan Compound in blackface. Later, he appeared with different groups on stations WROL and WNOX in Knoxville, Tennessee. His first recording session, in 1936, yielded two of his biggest hits, "Great Speckled Bird" and "Wabash Cannonball," which became a million seller. Joining the *Grand Ole Opry* in 1938, Acuff soon established the singer, rather than the string band, as the show's main attraction.

As country music began to incorporate western themes, radio and film helped to popularize the so-called singing cowboys. Tex Ritter, a native of Murvaul, Texas, who attended the University of Texas and Northeastern Law School, began singing western and mountain songs on KPRC in Houston in 1929. He moved to WOR's *Lone Star Rangers* in 1932, one of the first western radio shows to originate in New York. The Sons of the Pioneers—which included Roy Rogers, the King of the Cowboys—had an early-morning radio program on KFWB in Hollywood. Gene Autry got his start as the Oklahoma Yodeling Cowboy on KVOO in Tulsa, Oklahoma. Sometime after recording on the Sears Conqueror label, Autry landed his own radio show, *Conqueror Record Time,* on WLS, where he became one of the most popular entertainers in the station's history. The singing cowboys were also popularized in scores of Hollywood movies. Autry starred in more than 100 cowboy movies, most produced by Republic, the home of countless B-movie westerns. Autry's success was rivaled only by that of Roy Rogers, who signed with Republic in 1937.

The cowboy image became so prevalent in country music that even performers who did not perform western-related material began to dress in garish western-style garb. For a time, the term *western* even became an alternative to the *hillbilly* designation for country music but, as usual, the label obscured the diversity of cultural inputs in the music. As Bill C. Malone has pointed out,

> *The "western" music which became fashionable in the mid-thirties came from . . . southern traditional and gospel music, popular music, commercial recordings of all kinds (including blues and jazz), and, crucially, black music. Southwesterners could draw additionally on Mexican, Cajun,*

German, and what generally was described as "Bohemian" music (that is, the polka-derived styles of people who emigrated to South-Central Texas from what is now Czechoslovakia). [37]

Country music would make its contribution to the eruption of rock 'n' roll with this kind of cultural mixing.

The Long Road Back for Records

The Great Depression decimated the ranks of small independent blues, jazz, and country music labels, and things were not much rosier for the majors. Paramount had acquired the Black Swan catalogue in 1924 (before the depression), and Columbia had absorbed OKeh in 1926, only to be bought by the American Record Company for a mere $70,000 during the depression. Edison ceased production in 1930; Warner Brothers acquired Brunswick to promote its film stars. In 1929, David Sarnoff, as vice president of RCA, engineered a merger between RCA and Victor records, becoming president of the new company. RCA Victor was one of the only record companies still holding its own.

For the record industry, the long road back to prosperity began with a machine that had been laid to rest more than two decades earlier—the jukebox. The 1908 nickel-in-the-slot phonograph had quickly fallen into disuse when phonographs and records moved into homes. A new incarnation of the coin-operated record player appeared in 1927, when the Automatic Musical Instrument Company introduced its Selective Phonograph. Once Prohibition was repealed in 1933, thousands of newly (re)opened bars and cocktail lounges, looking for low-cost entertainment and additional sources of revenue, were happy to consider the jukebox. A number of other companies, including Wurlitzer, Rockola, and Seburg, soon entered the business. By 1935, 150,000 jukeboxes operated in the United States, accounting for 40 percent of the record trade.

Jukeboxes included a much broader range of music than most radio stations. They provided a guaranteed market for record companies and a promotional vehicle for recording artists. As with *Your Hit Parade*, the jukebox enabled the mass audience to play a powerful role in determining public taste. Following the dramatic growth of jukeboxes, *Billboard* and *Variety*, the major entertainment industry trade magazines, began charting jukebox hits. Once this happened, radio producers used the charts to shape live programming, and song-pluggers paid more attention to records.

As with Your Hit Parade, *the jukebox enabled the mass audience to play a powerful role in determining public taste.*

Other technological advances also increased the desirability of records. In the mid-1920s, broadcast technology led to electronic recording, which used microphones, vacuum-tube amplifiers, and an electromagnetic cutting stylus to make records. No longer did musicians have to crowd around a single recording horn; recording studios became expansive, able to accommodate whole orchestras. The better frequency response of the new technology created a more lifelike sound. By 1925, both Victor and Columbia were issuing electrically recorded discs. But with record sales falling, it did not seem practical to market expensive new electric record players. In 1932, Ted Wallerstein, of RCA Victor, solved the cost problem when he offered the Duo, Jr.—an electric turntable with no tubes or speakers, which could be jacked into a radio—for a list price of $16.50. Then in 1934, Decca, a new U.S. label that was formed when British Decca bought Brunswick from Warner Brothers, slashed the price of a record from seventy-five cents to thirty-five cents, contributing not only to its own success but to the revival of the record business as a whole.

After delivering the Duo, Jr. to RCA Victor, Wallerstein prepared to jump ship to CBS. Until this time, CBS had been operating without a record division. In 1938, Wallerstein convinced William Paley to purchase the American Record Company, which owned Columbia Records, Victor's main rival, for the seemingly outrageous price of $700,000, ten times its purchase price of a few years earlier. Wallerstein had judged correctly that CBS would benefit from acquiring an established trademark, a pressing plant, and the rights to British Columbia's U.S. recordings. Abandoning RCA Victor to become head of the new CBS record division, Wallerstein lured talent such as Benny Goodman, Duke Ellington, and Count Basie to the Columbia label.

One of the key players in the talent raids that brought Goodman and Basie to Columbia was John Hammond, a wealthy Vanderbilt on his mother's side, a staunch civil rights activist, an aficionado of African American music, and soon to become Benny Goodman's brother-in-law. Hammond had produced Bessie Smith's final recording session and Billie Holiday's first session within months of each other in 1933. In 1939, he became a full-time producer at Columbia; his years at the label spanned generations and influenced the careers of artists as diverse as Aretha Franklin, Bob Dylan, and Bruce Springsteen. Hammond was widely respected among African American musicians (and widely considered to be a wealthy eccentric, if not an outright communist, in the music industry) for his attempts to break down racial barriers. It was Hammond who convinced Benny Goodman to add Teddy Wilson to his band. In 1938, he produced *From Spirituals to Swing,* a landmark concert at Carnegie Hall showcasing the history of African American music (and repeated this success a year later). In his autobiography, he argued for a "lessening of differences between country and popular music, between folk, rock, jazz, gospel, and other categories."[38] He was clearly more attuned than most to the sounds that would eventually transform the character of popular music.

LEARN MORE
Chapter Test on MyMusicKit

With the advent of commercial radio and talkies after World War I, record companies found their sales slipping and they looked for new markets. In the process, they discovered a sizable African American market for blues recordings by black artists as well as an untapped market for so-called hillbilly music. While new labels, such as OKeh, Black Swan, and Black Patti, came into existence, most of these were forced out of business or absorbed by larger companies as record sales continued to fall. Radio remained the focus of home entertainment throughout the Great Depression, but it provided far more access to pop and country music than to blues or jazz. It was not until the rebirth of the jukebox, which gave the mass audience more of a voice in public taste, that the record companies made a real financial comeback. Cheaper records and playback equipment certainly helped grow the consumer market. By the end of the depression, Columbia, Victor, and Decca had emerged as the big three in recording. Although they faced almost no competition, they saw no harm in protecting themselves from the possibility that small new companies would find new grassroots musics. Thus, each company established a less expensive subsidiary to cover the grassroots. Victor created Bluebird for its so-called race and hillbilly artists. In 1940, Columbia revitalized OKeh as its specialty label. The more recently formed Decca acquired Gennett, an old-time label, in the late 1930s. By this time, jazz had morphed into swing, the hottest trend in popular music. This, then, was the situation as the United States prepared for its entrance into World War II.

"Good Rockin' Tonight": The Rise of Rhythm and Blues

The military buildup that preceded the United States' entry into World War II greatly enhanced the country's prospects for a complete economic recovery from the Great Depression. The nation's involvement in the war led, in turn, to profound social changes, including the successful challenging of policies and practices concerning race and gender relations. As the country approached full employment, most citizens' improved financial status contrasted sharply with the hardship of the Great Depression. In the cultural arena, these changes and others associated with the war, such as population migrations, material shortages, and technological advances, played major roles in determining the course of popular music.

As the military buildup began, thousands of southern blacks and whites abandoned the oppressive conditions of sharecropping and tenant farming to find better-paying jobs elsewhere. Naturally, they took their music with them. At the same time, countless eastern and midwestern soldiers were put through basic training in southern military bases, where they heard musical styles that had not achieved mainstream popularity in the North. In this way, blues and country music received unprecedented exposure. By the early 1940s, hundreds of stations across the country were broadcasting country music. Detroit jukebox operators reported that country music records were the selections played the most, and in Europe, the Armed Forces Radio Network voted Roy Acuff more popular than Frank Sinatra. It seemed even the enemy recognized his importance: A widely reported war story held that Japanese troops went into battle shouting: "To hell with Roosevelt, Babe Ruth, and Roy Acuff."[1]

Unlike country music, the blues, as a rule, had been excluded from radio in earlier years, but the war-era exodus of over 1 million African Americans from the South helped to loosen these restrictive programming policies. Wartime prosperity made them an identifiable and desirable consumer group. Gradually, in areas with high concentrations of African

LEARN MORE
Learning objectives
on MyMusicKit

Americans, some black-oriented programs, usually slotted late at night, appeared on a few stations. Such programming began to tear down the walls of the so-called race market toward the end of the decade.

In the music industry, economic recovery led to bitter and prolonged power struggles that revolved around a single question: Who should benefit, and in what proportion, from the profits derived from the use and sale of intellectual property? The music business in the 1940s had expanded far beyond the legal and organizational machinery that determined how to allocate the fruits of the market. The sweeping commodification of music that accompanied the development of recording and broadcasting had created possibilities for financial gain unimaginable prior to the advent of mass culture. Neither the Copyright Act of 1909 nor the Communications Act of 1934 anticipated the complex interrelationships that had now developed among the major interests in the music business—writers, publishers, performers, broadcasters, and record companies—let alone the relationships between these groups and consumers. As a result, these parties often found themselves in the midst of shifting alliances, competing interests, and dramatic cultural changes.

> *The sweeping commodification of music that accompanied the development of recording and broadcasting had created possibilities for financial gain unimaginable prior to the advent of mass culture.*

The Publishers and the Broadcasters: ASCAP Versus BMI

Publishers and broadcasters had been at odds ever since the American Society of Composers, Authors, and Publishers' (ASCAP's) members made their first demand for a $5-a-day royalty fee in 1922, and radio formed the National Association of Broadcasters (NAB) in reaction. Throughout the first two decades of radio broadcasting, the major publishers had complained about declining profits . . . all the way to the bank. In the 1930s, according to Russell Sanjek, "ASCAP income from radio, of which the networks paid about 20 percent, had risen from $757,450 in 1932 to . . . $4.3 million, in 1939."[2] Representing about two-thirds of ASCAP's total income, radio revenues were clearly substantial, and their potential at the start of the 1940s was even greater.

As it had before, the prospect of windfall profits brought out the greed in ASCAP's 1,250 members who controlled the performing rights to almost all of the best-known songs in the country. ASCAP's fee for a blanket license (permission to broadcast any selection in the ASCAP catalogue) was 5 percent of the total receipts from all sponsored programs, including talk shows and sports broadcasts that did not use music. Such terms naturally exacerbated the tension between ASCAP and the broadcasters. Their already strained relationship began to disintegrate in the summer of 1940, when ASCAP mailed out a new contract that would have doubled its revenues when the existing contract expired on 31 December 1940. Designed to divide the broadcasters, it included a sliding-scale fee that ranged from 3 percent for smaller stations to 7.5 percent for the networks. ASCAP's divide-and-conquer strategy did not work; instead, the broadcasters closed ranks.

The year before, the NAB, representing some 600 radio stations, had decided to challenge ASCAP's monopoly by forming a performing rights organization of its own. Some 256 stations raised close to $1.5 million to capitalize Broadcast Music Incorporated (BMI), launched on 13 October 1939. "Taking advantage of ASCAP's stringent membership requirements, as well as its relative indifference to the popular and folk music being produced outside of New York and Hollywood," Nat Shapiro has written, "BMI sought out and acquired its support from the 'have not' publishers and writers in the grassroots areas."[3] Blues and country music songwriters and publishers found in BMI an inviting home for their work. By the end of 1940, BMI had become a sizable operation, registering about 30 songs a month and acquiring a number of existing catalogues, including Ralph Peer's Southern Music Publishing Company.[4]

The broadcasters responded to ASCAP's demands by boycotting the entire ASCAP catalogue. ASCAP had assumed that public demand for the likes of Irving Berlin, Cole Porter, and George Gershwin would soon bring the NAB back into the fold. But as NAB president Neville Miller opined somewhat cynically: "The music the people like is the music people hear. It is likely that no one will notice the difference in character and quality of programs on and after January 1, 1941."[5] For about ten months in 1941, ASCAP music on radio was replaced by authentic regional music and some international styles, supplemented by melodies in the public domain. As the broadcasters had predicted, no public protest arose. Some key acquisitions by BMI contributed measurably to the boycott's success. Ralph Peer, now in the international market, offered a catalogue of Latin popular music; Roy Acuff and Fred Rose (ASCAP members since 1928) offered Acuff-Rose Music, the first all-country catalogue; and E. B. Marks, a major Tin Pan Alley firm, offered the familiar pop fare required for network broadcasts. Broadcasters and publishers came to terms in 1941, but only after a federally initiated antitrust action forced ASCAP into a consent decree regulating its dealings.

At first, BMI came up with few songs of lasting significance. Still, by the end of 1941, its catalogue contained 36,000 copyrights from fifty-two publishers.[6] What was originally envisioned as a throwaway bargaining tool emerged as a valuable source of music and ASCAP's primary competition. For the first time, the Tin Pan Alley/Broadway/Hollywood monopoly on public taste had been challenged. As writers from grassroots areas received encouragement from BMI, songwriting itself became more decentralized. By the end of the decade, BMI writers like Huddie Ledbetter (Lead Belly), Hank Snow, Arthur "Big Boy" Crudup, Roy Brown, Ivory Joe Hunter, Hank Williams, Ernest Tubb, Johnny Otis, Fats Domino, and Wynonie Harris had begun to play a major role in redefining popular music.

Enter the Deejay: The Broadcasters Versus the AFM

Less than a year after the settlement of its dispute with ASCAP, the NAB found itself embroiled in another controversy, this time with the American Federation of Musicians (AFM). As a rule, the music heard on radio was performed live, often in formal concert settings with audiences in attendance. Searching desperately for less expensive programming during the Great Depression, some radio stations had begun to use records as an alternative. Records, however, were a direct challenge to the primacy of live music and one that would change the face of popular music.

Records were played by a new figure in broadcasting, the disc jockey, a term that came to be defined as a person who was "jockeying or riding a record toward success."[7] Until the advent of the disc jockey, or deejay, radio had simply been a vehicle for transmitting the substance of other media—newspapers, religious pulpits, concert halls, vaudeville, and theater. The deejay's show was unique in its combination of live announcing and "canned" (prerecorded) music. The earliest deejays appeared even before the stock market crash in 1929. Three stations in Los Angeles programmed records almost exclusively. The powerful X stations (those with X in their call letters), which broadcast from across the Mexican border and were exempt from U.S. wattage regulations, also relied heavily on records. "Doc" Brinkley, the first country deejay, beamed country music into millions of U.S. homes from the 100,000-watt XER in Mexico. The first black deejay, Jack L. Cooper, sold an incredible amount of Tip Top Bread in the 1930s while spinning "jump, jam, and jive" records on his pioneering show, *The Negro Hour,* broadcast from WSBC on the south side of Chicago. The first woman deejay on a commercially licensed station was Miss Halloween Martin, featured on Marshall Field and Company's *Musical Clock,* a wakeup show on KYW in Chicago.

Until the advent of the disc jockey, or deejay, radio had simply been a vehicle for transmitting the substance of other media—newspapers, religious pulpits, concert halls, vaudeville, and theater.

The archetypal deejay show appeared in 1935 when the smooth-talking Martin Block began his show *Make Believe Ballroom* on WNEW in New York. Block, "whose facile tongue soon successfully defeated all record hiss or needle noise and made the time between records exciting with spellbinding monologues and irresistible advertising pitches," copied the concept for his program from a Los Angeles deejay, Al Jarvis.[8] Within months, 4 million listeners were tuning in to Block's two-and-a-half-hour daily broadcasts. Focusing systematically on the most recent releases, Block and Jarvis introduced the beginnings of formula radio.

As deejays became more common, the practice of programming only live music on radio became harder to maintain. Indeed, after the formation of Capitol Records by record-store owner Glenn Wallichs, songwriter Johnny Mercer, and Paramount Pictures executive Buddy De Sylva in 1942, many programs and record companies pushed recorded music. In a 1969 interview, Wallichs recalled the special consideration Capitol Records offered to deejays: "We typed special labels with their names on both sides, pressed them on expensive lightweights, unbreakable vinylite compound, and then had our limited employee force drive around and distribute each personally. It was a service that created a sensation. We made the jock a Big Man, an Important Guy, VIP in the industry."[9]

It fell to James C. Petrillo, the president of the AFM, who had risen through the ranks of the Chicago local during Prohibition, to declare war on canned music. Reasoning correctly that records would put live radio musicians out of work, Petrillo had tried for years to deal with the problem. He had unsuccessfully lobbied the Roosevelt administration to ban records on radio. Then he forced Chicago radio stations to employ union musicians to operate turntables. Because neither musicians nor record companies received royalties from record broadcasts, Petrillo had also convinced record manufacturers to print a warning against airing commercial discs on record labels.[10] In 1940, however, a lower court decision restraining WNEW from broadcasting Paul Whiteman's records was reversed on appeal. Judge Learned Hand opined that "the common-law property of orchestra leader and corporation manufacturing phonograph records ended with sale of record, so that radio broadcasting company could not be restrained from using records in broadcasts."[11] Nevertheless, Petrillo decided to step up his campaign.

Not one to get overly bogged down in legalities or past alliances, Petrillo turned his wrath on the record companies in 1942. If no records were produced, Petrillo reasoned, recorded music could not be broadcast. He warned the record companies that unless they could prevent radio stations and jukebox operators from playing records, his organization would strike the recording studios—a strategy intended to hurt record production and, at the same time, keep musicians working on radio. When the record companies did not comply, Petrillo ordered a ban on recording. No musicians were to enter recording studios in Canada or the United States until the AFM's demands were met.

Anticipating the strike, the record companies had stockpiled unreleased masters.[12] They finished the year in reasonably good shape, but the musicians lost millions of dollars. As the demand for new releases grew, however, the musicians began to prevail. Decca, now severed from its British parent, capitulated after thirteen months; Victor and Columbia held out for about two years. The strike ended when the record companies agreed to pay a royalty on record sales, which was used to finance a fund for out-of-work musicians. Petrillo couldn't force radio to stop playing records, but at least somebody would pay for the privilege. By 1950, when WINS in New York announced plans to program records exclusively, the era of live music network radio had clearly come to an end.

It is not surprising that the musicians held out for as long as they did in their struggle to preserve radio as a live performance medium. Radio had provided steady work during a period when the vast bulk of most musicians' income came from live performances. Of course, at that time, live music on radio had meant music performed by white musicians for the most part. The AFM itself failed to extend protection to all musicians equally. In 1944, as Arnold Shaw has pointed out, the "NAACP [National Association for the Advancement of Colored People] noted that of [AFM's] 673 locals, 32 were 'colored.' . . . [O]nly 2 locals, those in Detroit and New York, admitted Negroes to full membership."[13]

> **I**t is not surprising that the musicians held out for as long as they did in their struggle to preserve radio as a live performance medium. Radio had provided steady work during a period when the vast bulk of most musicians' income came from live performances.

Another group of artists that were not part of the AFM were vocalists. They were covered by a different union—currently called the American Federation of Television and Radio Artists (AFTRA)— which didn't join the strike. Throughout the strike, vocalists recorded a cappella. By the time the musicians returned to the studios, the vocalists were in charge. Although the AFM strike probably was not a causal factor, it did mark a turning point in the rise of the solo vocalist and the decline of the big bands.

From Big Bands to Solo Singers

Initially, dance music was primarily an instrumental music. As swing (a danceable amalgam of blues, jazz, and Tin Pan Alley pop) grew in popularity in the mid-1930s, nearly all the big bands had begun to perform with vocalists. Paid less than other members of the band, vocalists were often limited to one chorus of a tune and were sometimes used simply to give instrumental soloists a rest. Audiences enjoyed the vocal numbers, however, and singers eventually became popular enough to begin solo careers. Bing Crosby, of course, was the most successful vocalist of the era, totaling more than 300 hits between 1931 and 1954.

Several female singers who worked with big bands also had successful solo careers. Mildred Bailey predated Crosby as a vocalist with the Whiteman band. Ella Fitzgerald started her career with Chick Webb; "A-Tisket, A-Tasket" (1938) made her a pop star. Peggy Lee sang with Benny Goodman and Duke Ellington and then moved into songwriting and acting. Beginning as a country singer, Kay Starr launched a solo pop career after a stint with Charlie Barnet. Jo Stafford began with Tommy Dorsey and went on to record numerous pop hits that included folk and country material. Anita O'Day graduated from the Max Miller combo to the Gene Krupa and Stan Kenton bands and then to solo stardom.

The first pop vocalist to engender hysteria among fans was an Italian American who refused to anglicize his name—Frank Sinatra, the Sultan of Swoon. A song stylist with an unmistakable baritone, Sinatra won the *Major Bowes Amateur Hour* with the Hoboken Four in 1935 and then toured with Bowes for two years. In 1939, an appearance on WNEW's *Dance Parade* led to engagements with the Harry James and the Tommy Dorsey bands. According to legend, his 1942 appearance at the Paramount Theater with Benny Goodman unleashed a veritable teen frenzy. At his return engagement two years later, 25,000 screaming bobby-soxers blocked the street in what was referred to as the Columbus Day Riot. From 1943 to 1945, Sinatra was the top vocalist on NBC's *Your Hit Parade.*

Sinatra was also unique among the pop vocalists of the day because he was socially engaged. He supported Roosevelt for president and spoke out against racial and religious intolerance, even excising the word *darky* from his recording of Jerome Kern's and Oscar Hammerstein's "Ol' Man River." In the late 1940s, when he was accused of having both communist and Mafia ties, his career faltered; it was revitalized by his Oscar-winning performance as Maggio in the 1954 film *From Here to Eternity*, a role he allegedly landed through Mafia influence. During this period, he also became a vicious opponent of rock 'n' roll.

Sinatra's early success is perhaps the strongest indicator of the rise of the solo vocalist. His buyout of his contract with Tommy Dorsey in 1942, the same year as the AFM strike, marked the transition from big bands fronted by singers to vocalists backed up by big bands. As rock 'n' roll historian Charlie Gillett has noted, "Records by the big bands dominated the best selling lists in 1937 to 1941. During this period band recordings accounted for twenty-nine of the forty-three records that sold over a million copies each."[14] With the rise of the vocalists, however, the pop market was taken over by figures such as Bing Crosby ("Swingin' on a Star"), Dinah Shore ("I'll Walk Alone," "Anniversary Song," "Buttons and Bows"), and Vaughn Monroe ("Rum and Coca Cola," "Let It Snow, Let It Snow, Let It Snow").

Although a number of pop-sounding black vocal acts scored major hits in the pop market in the postwar era—Nat "King" Cole ("For Sentimental Reasons"), Ella Fitzgerald ("My Happiness"), the Mills Brothers ("Across the Valley from the Alamo"), and the Ink Spots ("The Gypsy")—the period was dominated by Italian American men. In addition to Sinatra, there was Perry Como ("Long Ago and Far Away"), Frankie Laine ("That's My Desire," "Mule Train"), Vic Damone ("You're Breaking My Heart"), and later Al Martino ("Here in My Heart"),

((• HEAR MORE
Frank Sinatra on MyMusicKit

Dean Martin ("That's Amore"), and Tony Bennett ("Because of You," "Rags to Riches," "Stranger in Paradise").[15] The rich tradition of heart-wrenching emotionality that had long been part of Italian popular song seemed quite well suited to American popular styles in the 1940s and 1950s.

Returning troops looking to start families reclaimed the well-paying jobs that women had taken during the war, which effectively forced women back into the domestic sphere and replaced weekend rituals like dancing with more family-oriented activities.

If the rise of the solo vocalist pushed the big bands into the background, they were only one piece of a much larger cultural shift. The removal of World War II price ceilings on items like gasoline made it more difficult to keep large orchestras on the road. Returning troops looking to start families reclaimed the well-paying jobs that women had taken during the war, which effectively forced women back into the domestic sphere and replaced weekend rituals like dancing with more family-oriented activities. As the audience that had supported the ballroom circuit dwindled, the big bands closed shop. As Ian Whitcomb has written:

> [Glenn] Miller died in a wartime plane crash, but Herman, James, and Dorsey had folded their original bands in late 1946, together with Benny Goodman and many others. The straighter, less jazzy bands like Lawrence Welk's and Guy Lombardo's survived (for a specialist and aging public) but the Big Band Era, just over a decade, was finished.[16]

While the better-known black bands, conspicuous in Whitcomb's account by their absence, could count on an occasional hit record, such as Basie's "Open the Door, Richard" (1947), it was clear that an era had ended, especially for the hotter bands. Between 1947 and 1949, record sales dropped more than $50 million, over 20 percent of the dollar volume of the industry. The passing of the big bands created something of a void in popular music that contributed to the rise of rhythm and blues and, to a lesser extent, country and western.

The Major Labels Reclaim Country Music

The population migrations that had begun with the pre–World War II military buildup had opened the possibility of nationwide markets for specialty music. During the war, the major record companies were unable to exploit this market because materials shortages significantly reduced the number of records that could be manufactured. (At the height of the shortage, often a person wanting to buy a new record had to return an old one first.) Because the mainstream audience alone could absorb almost all the records made, the major companies concentrated their efforts on the mainstream market. The specialty fields—country, to some extent, but especially blues, jazz, and gospel—bore the brunt of the cutbacks.

Although record shortages had seriously limited the supply of specialty music, cross-cultural contact had increased the demand for it. After the war, the major labels thought about regaining their control over the specialty fields. Naturally, company executives, concerned about their declining bottom lines, were intrigued by the possibility of nationwide markets for regional musics. In the postwar context, however, the categories *race* and *hillbilly* seemed inappropriate, if not downright offensive. In 1949, *rhythm and blues* became the official designation for what was once called *race music*. A few years earlier, the industry had begun to use *country and western*, or *country*, for what was once called *hillbilly*.

The strategies of the major companies for reclaiming country and western proved to be remarkably effective, if somewhat dispiriting in retrospect. According to Gillett,

> *[T]he companies responded by heavily promoting various songs performed in versions of country and western styles. One tactic was to promote the strong southern accent of most country and western singers as a "novelty," as Capitol did successfully with Tex Williams' "Smoke That Cigarette" in 1947, and as Columbia did for several years with various Gene Autry songs, including "Rudolph, the Red-Nosed Reindeer" (1950). Alternatively, the country and western songs that were closest to the melodramatic or sentimental modes of conventional popular songs were promoted as popular songs—or, more frequently, recorded by popular singers in a style that was halfway between country and pop.*[17]

By marketing recordings like Frankie Laine's "Mule Train" and "High Noon" as Gillett suggests, country and western music was soon firmly back in the hands of the major companies. The one exception to this rule was King Records in Cincinnati, Ohio, which boasted a strong roster of country and western artists like Cowboy Copas, Hawkshaw Hawkins, and Moon Mullican, who, as we shall see, came into regular contact with rhythm and blues and were heavily influenced by the western end of the country music spectrum.

The entry of two new major companies into the music industry during this period contributed to the majors' hold on country and western music. The first was MGM Records, formed originally in 1946 as an outlet for the film company's movie soundtracks but soon expanded into other kinds of music. The second entry was Mercury, which began in Chicago in 1947 as a specialty label focusing primarily on polka and rhythm and blues. Mercury operated with the flair of an independent, but its ownership of both a record-pressing plant and its own distribution system defined it as a major label. In 1947, it signed Frankie Laine, whose million-seller hits, "Mule Train" (1949) and "Cry of the Wild Goose" (1950), were in the ersatz country mold. It was MGM, however, that picked up Hank Williams, the biggest country and western star since Jimmie Rodgers.

A veteran of life on the road, Hank Williams continued along the path pioneered by Jimmie Rodgers. His honky tonk swagger brought country music one step closer to rockabilly.

"Hey Good Lookin'"

Artist: Hank Williams

Music/Lyrics by Hank Williams

Label: MGM (1951)

Some artists seem to embody the myths associated with their particular style of music: Robert Johnson with Delta blues, Charlie Parker with bebop jazz, Tupac with hip hop. The high-lonesome, alcohol-drenched image of honky-tonk country was embodied in Hank Williams, singer-songwriter extra-ordinaire. His songs were perfectly crafted gems, simple in structure but deep in feeling, intensely personal, and universally accessible. Dead before his time at age 29, Hank Williams's long and celebrated shadow loomed over practically every country songwriter for the next two generations.

"Hey, Good Lookin'" was recorded in March 1951 during the same recording session as his equally famous song "I Can't Help It If I'm Still in Love with You." The other instrumental parts were provided by Hank's Driftin' Cowboys band, beefed up with a few studio musicians: Don Helms, steel guitar; Jerry Rivers, fiddle; Sammy Pruett, electric guitar; Jack Shook, rhythm guitar; Ernie Newton and Howard Watts, bass; and pianists Owen Bradley and Fred Rose.

Musical Style Notes

In contrast to the sad, soulful ballad style of "I'm So Lonesome I Could Cry" or "Your Cheatin' Heart," "Hey Good Lookin'" is one of Hank Williams's up-tempo, honky-tonk songs with its backbeat (accents on beats 2 and 4) and tasty steel guitar licks. The structure of the song is fairly straightforward: Each verse has an aaba form, where a is one melody that repeats several times with different lyrics and b is a contrasting melody. The instrumental in the middle of the song follows the same melodic form but gives the steel guitarist (Don Helms) and the fiddler (Jerry Rivers) a chance to show off their improvisational skills.

Musical "Road Map"

TIMINGS	COMMENTS	LYRICS
0:00–0:07	Introduction, played by pedal (lap?) steel	
0:07–0:21	Verse 1(a)	*Hey, good lookin' . . .*
0:21–0:34	Verse 1(a)	*Hey, sweet baby . . .*
0:34–0:48	Verse 1(b)	*I got . . .*
0:48–1:02	Verse 1(a)	*Hey, good lookin' . . .*
1:02–1:29	Instrumental verse with solos 2 × (a) = lap steel solo	
1:29–1:42	(b) = fiddle solo	
1:42–1:56	(a) = lap steel returns with (a) melody	
1:56–2:10	Verse 2(a)	*I'm free . . .*
2:10–2:23	Verse 2(a)	*No more lookin' . . .*
2:23–2:37	Verse 2(b)	*I'm gonna . . .*
2:37–2:50	Verse 2(a)	*Hey, good lookin' . . .*
2:50–2:53	Last chord, fades	

Williams began his singing career at the age of thirteen on KSFA in Montgomery, Alabama, and worked in roadhouses and honky-tonks for years. With Fred Rose as his manager, he registered his original compositions with Acuff-Rose in Nashville. He first recorded for the independent Sterling label in 1946 but switched to MGM in 1947 with assistance from Rose. Between 1949 and 1953, the year he died, eleven of his songs for MGM sold more than 1 million copies each. Rose also plugged Williams's songs to pop producers, and numerous popular artists recorded the tunes as pop country hits, including Frankie Laine, who recorded "Your Cheatin' Heart" and "Tonight We're Settin' the Woods on Fire" as solo vocals and "Hey Good Lookin'" as a duet with Jo Stafford, who did a solo version of "Jambalaya." Tony Bennett recorded "There'll Be No Teardrops Tonight" and hit pop number one with "Cold, Cold Heart." Guy Mitchell did "I Can't Help It," and Rosemary Clooney scored with "Half as Much."

Altogether, Williams, who credited as his inspiration a black street singer nicknamed Tee Tot (Rufus Payne), penned about 125 songs. His honest, straightforward lyrics and catchy, well-crafted tunes lent his music to a variety of interpretations and established him as something of a folk poet. His honky-tonk swagger, working-class sympathies, use of backbeat (accents on the second and fourth beats of a measure), and hot live performances made him a vital link in the musical chain that joined Jimmie Rodgers and Texas hillbillies like Bob Wills and Ernest Tubb to Elvis Presley. Like Rodgers before him, Williams was inducted into the Rock 'n' Roll Hall of Fame as an "early influence" in 1987.

The Independents Promote Rhythm and Blues

The major labels were able to bring country and western music firmly into their fold, and new developments in African American music seemed less desirable to them. During the big band era, the majors had contented themselves with connections to the most prominent black innovators of the big band sound and had lost touch with other developments in the rich and constantly evolving African American music culture. A number of African American musicians were now developing styles closer to the blues. As the swing era declined, rhythm and blues (r&b) came to the fore in working-class black communities. Amiri Baraka (a.k.a. Leroi Jones) described it as "huge rhythm units smashing away behind screaming blues singers."[18] Because of its insistent rhythms, uncontrolled energy, and suggestive content, the majors viewed r&b as unsuitable for mainstream consumption, so they decided to pass on the sound that would soon transform the very concept of popular music.

Because of its insistent rhythms, uncontrolled energy, and suggestive content, the majors viewed r&b as unsuitable for mainstream consumption, so they decided to pass on the sound that would soon transform the very concept of popular music.

If there was one artist who signified the transition from the controlled energy and smooth delivery of the big bands to the unbridled emotion of rhythm and blues, it was Louis Jordan. Signed to Decca in 1939, Jordan and his group, the Tympani Five, anticipated the decline of the big bands and helped to define the instrumentation for the r&b combos that followed. With a much smaller horn section, rhythm became more

Louis Jordan was a pivotal musician in the development of rhythm and blues. He and his group, the Tympani Five, brought African American working-class sensibilities into the mainstream with polish and humor. Film clips of their engaging performances were shown in movie theaters between features.

pronounced. While Jordan's material was composed and arranged, selections like "Saturday Night Fishfry," "Honey Chile," and "Ain't Nobody Here But Us Chickens" evoked blues images not found in most black pop. "Chickens," for example, told the story of a farmer duped by a fox in his henhouse. "Those lyrics," according to George Lipsitz, "had their origins in the culture of . . . slavery. African legends about 'trickster-hero buffoons' provided the basis for slave stories in which animals or lesser gods outwitted stronger opponents."[19] At the same time, Jordan's performances were exceptionally engaging, a factor that measurably increased his mainstream acceptance.

Between 1944 and 1949, Jordan furnished Decca with nineteen pop hits. His "G. I. Jive," backed with "Is You Is or Is You Ain't My Baby?" (1944), sold 1 million copies, as did "Choo Choo Ch'Boogie" (1946). The shuffle boogie beat that he used is one of the elements that followed r&b into rock 'n' roll. Like Jordan, whose music was described as "jumpin' the blues," most r&b artists of the late 1940s screeched, honked, and shouted their way to success. This raucous music—of artists such as Wynonie Harris ("Good Rockin' Tonight"), John Lee Hooker ("Boogie Chillen"), Eddie "Cleanhead" Vinson ("I'm Weak but I'm Willing"), Bullmoose Jackson ("I Want a Bow-Legged Woman"), Joe Liggins and the Honeydrippers ("Honeydripper"), saxophonist Big Jay McNeely ("Deacon's Hop"), drummer Roy Milton ("The Hucklebuck"), and pianist Amos Milburn ("Bad, Bad Whiskey")—was a harbinger of sounds to come.

The success of these artists speaks to what Nelson George has referred to as "an aesthetic schism between high-brow, more assimilated black styles and working-class, grass-roots sounds" that had existed in the black community for a long time.[20] A number of writers, notably Baraka, have written at length about class differences between jazz and blues. While jazz was an immensely popular and influential crossover music that introduced elements of the African American tradition into the mainstream, in some ways it was also a product of the black middle class. Many of its most prominent practitioners—Coleman Hawkins, Don Redman, and Fletcher Henderson, among others—attended college. By the 1930s, jazz was a music that had "moved away from the older *lowdown* forms of blues . . . [It was] a music that still relied on older Afro-American musical tradition, but one that had begun to utilize still greater amounts of popular American music as well as certain formal European traditions."[21]

The pioneer r&b artists of the 1940s were still close to their blues roots. While they often retained some semblance of the big band sound, their popularity in the black community in many ways represented a resuscitation of the blues, or race, market of the 1920s and 1930s. "While the term 'jazz' gave Whiteman equal weight with Ellington, and Bix Beiderbecke comparable standing with Louis Armstrong," George has written, "the term 'race' was applied to forms of black music—primarily blues—that whites and . . . the black elite disdained."[22] In the glow of postwar affluence, the African American working class imposed its tastes on black popular music and the results were electrifying (and electrified).

> *Suddenly it was as if a great deal of the Euro-American humanist facade Afro-American music had taken on had been washed away by the war. Rhythm & blues singers literally had to shout to be heard above the clanging and strumming of the various electrified instruments and the churning rhythm sections. And somehow the louder the instrumental accompaniment and the more harshly screamed the singing, the more expressive the music was.[23]*

Because of the demand for r&b, several hundred independent labels were able to enter the business. By the early 1950s, more than 100 of these labels were still in operation. The most important were Aladdin, Modern, Specialty, and Imperial in Los Angeles; Atlantic in New York; Savoy in Newark, New Jersey; King in Cincinnati, Ohio; Chess in Chicago; and black-owned Duke/Peacock in Houston. While some of them produced country and western music, all of them produced r&b. These companies, along with other important independents founded later—Herald/Ember and several others in New York, black-owned Vee Jay in Chicago, and Sun in Memphis—produced r&b first for the black community and, with the aid of jukeboxes and independent deejays, brought the music to the attention of a national audience. Indeed, companies like these produced the bulk of the repertoire that constituted the foundation of rock 'n' roll. Perhaps the best indication of their success in popularizing r&b can be seen in *Billboard*'s 1949 decision to drop the term *race music* in favor of the more descriptive *rhythm and blues*.

King Records could be distinguished by its ability to produce r&b and country and western with equal success. No doubt, the fact that the city of Cincinnati offered significant outlets for blues, jazz, and country music contributed measurably to King's good fortune. While African Americans had less access to the airwaves in Cincinnati than other performers—Fats Waller's WLW broadcasts in 1932 stand out as a notable exception—the entertainment needs of the city's sizable black population were addressed in live music venues, especially Cincinnati's Cotton Club. The bands of Lucky Millinder, Todd Rhodes, and Tiny Bradshaw were among those that toured the region regularly.

The man who brought the city's divergent musical tendencies together under one recording roof was Syd Nathan, who started King Records in 1945. From the beginning, he was eclectic in his musical acquisitions and astute, if ruthless, in his business decisions. Nathan signed the Delmore Brothers, Grandpa Jones, and Hank Penny, as well as the next generation of country singers, including Cowboy Copas, Moon Mullican, Hawkshaw Hawkins, and Wayne Raney. Mullican, the King of the Hillbilly Piano Players, was a pioneer of country boogie. His influence on early rock 'n' roll can be heard in the piano playing of Jerry Lee Lewis and others.

Initially, most of King's r&b artists were issued on Nathan's Queen label, established to separate r&b releases from country releases. An innovative wrinkle to this separation added measurably to the company's profit margin. Nathan, largely for reasons of economic self-interest, encouraged his black artists and white artists to record each other's material.

King was perhaps the only independent record company that had equally strong rosters of r&b and c&w artists. As King's African American producer Henry Glover once told Arnold Shaw:

> *King Records was covering R&B with country singers almost from the beginning of my work with Syd Nathan. . . . We were more successful in doing the reverse—covering C&W hits with R&B singers. In '49 . . . Bullmoose Jackson's hit "Why Don't You Haul Off and Love Me" was a cover of a Wayne Raney country hit. And Wynonie Harris' "Bloodshot Eyes"—on R&B charts in '51— was originally a Hank Penny country record . . . when a song happened in one field, Syd Nathan wanted it moved into the other.*
>
> *You see it was a matter of Cincinnati's population. You couldn't sell Wynonie Harris to country folk, and black folk weren't buying Hank Penny. But black folk might buy Wynonie Harris doing a country tune. And since Syd published most of the tunes we recorded, he was also augmenting his publishing income and building important copyrights. He was a smart businessman and he didn't miss a trick.*[24]

Whatever Nathan's motivation, his actions produced a far greater cultural mix than might otherwise have occurred. Of course, the key to the company's success in these crossover ventures was the free hand that Nathan gave Glover in recording both r&b and c&w acts. No producer spanned the two fields more successfully. The fact that Glover wrote and/or produced many of King's r&b hits marked him as successful. The fact that he consciously sought out country artists with whom to accomplish the same success moves him closer to the status of legendary. Under Glover's musical direction, the King empire not only maintained a foothold in country music but became one of the premiere r&b labels as well.

The fact that Glover wrote and/or produced many of King's r&b hits marked him as successful. The fact that he consciously sought out country artists with whom to accomplish the same success moves him closer to the status of legendary.

Like King Records, Chess Records in Chicago was another instance of successful collaboration between Jewish businessmen and black producers. Brothers Leonard and Phil Chess were Jewish immigrants from Poland who had settled in Chicago in 1928. In the 1940s, they owned and operated the Macomba, a night club that presented talent such as Louis Armstrong, Lionel Hampton, Billy Eckstine, and Ella Fitzgerald. Struck by the lack of adequate recording facilities in Chicago, the brothers took over Aristocrat Records in 1949 and changed its name to Chess, eventually establishing three subsidiaries, Checker, Cadet, and Argo. With a small studio in the back room of its storefront record company, Chess, like other indies, was a quintessential shoestring operation, distributing records from the trunks of the owners' cars and using recording techniques such as hanging a mike in a tiny toilet to add echo.[25] Even so, Chess Records managed to turn out some of the most significant urban blues recordings and eventually to become one of the most important rock 'n' roll labels in the country.

One key to Chess's success was Willie Dixon, a Mississippian who had been associated with the label as a singer, composer, bassist, talent scout, and producer since its days as Aristocrat. Leonard Chess thought of Dixon as "his right arm." Among the 200 or so songs written by Dixon were "Hoochie Coochie Man," "I Just Want to Make Love to You," "Little Red Rooster," and "Seventh Son." He contributed in other capacities to any number of hits by Chess artists, including Muddy Waters and Howlin' Wolf.

((•⎪• **HEAR MORE**
Chess Records
on MyMusicKit

Mississippi Delta–born Muddy Waters (née McKinley Morganfield) was one of Chess's earliest discoveries. A master of slide guitar, Waters had been recorded for the Library of Congress by Alan Lomax and John Work in 1943; he switched to electric guitar after moving to Chicago. Waters followed the Chess brothers from Aristocrat, where he had recorded "I Can't Be Satisfied" and "I Feel Like Goin' Home," to Chess, where he followed up with one of his first hits, the immortal "Rolling Stone." Subsequent recordings included "Mannish Boy" (1955), "Got My Mojo Working" (1957), and "Baby Please Don't Go" (1958). Most of the next generation of Chicago blues musicians, including Buddy Guy, Junior Wells, and James Cotton, passed through Waters's band. Waters was a major inspiration for the white blues revival of the 1960s, which featured artists such as Paul Butterfield, Nick Gravenites, and Mike Bloomfield. When the Rolling Stones took their name from Waters's early Chess hit, he remarked: "They stole my music, but they gave me my name."[26]

((• HEAR MORE
Muddy Waters
on MyMusicKit

Perhaps the most important of all the new independent labels was Atlantic Records, founded in 1947 by Ahmet Ertegun, the son of a prominent Turkish diplomat, and Herb Abramson, the former recording director for National Records. Jerry Wexler, a reviewer for *Billboard*, who is said to have coined the term *rhythm and blues*, joined the company in 1953 and went on to become head of artist and repertoire. In 1956, Ertegun's brother, Nesuhi, set up what would become a distinguished jazz division. Both brothers were avid jazz and blues collectors, with some 30,000 records in their private collection. Perhaps their privileged position and their love of the music gave them an advantage over entrepreneurs who entered the business solely as a commercial gambit because the Erteguns attracted outstanding talent. Ahmet, in particular, enjoyed a reputation for honesty and integrity particularly in his treatment of black artists, which was unmatched at the time but challenged years later when several Atlantic artists successfully sued the company for unpaid back royalties.

The company first hit r&b pay dirt in 1949 with Stick McGhee's "Drinkin' Wine Spo-dee-o-dee." Its first star was Ruth Brown, whose 1949 debut release, "So Long," was a Top Ten hit. She turned out ten more Top Ten r&b hits over the next five years, including "Teardrops from My Eyes" (1950), "5-10-15 Hours" (1952), "Mama, He Treats Your Daughter Mean" (1953), and "Oh, What a Dream" (1954). She was rewarded with a contract that guaranteed her $100,000 over five years. For a time, Atlantic was known as "The house that Ruth built." Big Joe Turner, signed after Ahmet Ertegun heard him perform with the Basie band at the Apollo, also turned out a series of block-buster r&b hits for Atlantic—"Chains of Love" (1951), "Sweet Sixteen" (1952), and "Honey Hush" (1953). By the early 1950s, Atlantic was the most important r&b label in the country, with a talent roster that also included LaVern Baker, Ray Charles, the

Ruth Brown began singing in church. The lure of rhythm and blues, however, led her to Atlantic Records, where she became the fledgling label's first big star. Although Atlantic was among the most reputable companies and Brown had a decent contract, years later she sued the label for back royalties and won.

"(Mama) He Treats Your Daughter Mean"

Artist: Ruth Brown

Music/Lyrics by Herb Lance, John Wallace, and Charlie Singleton

Label: Atlantic (1953)

"(Mama) He Treats Your Daughter Mean" was a big hit in 1953 for Ruth Brown and Atlantic. In terms of its driving dance rhythms, instrumentation, and sixteen-bar blues structure, and its slightly suggestive lyrics, it's a classic example of 1950s rhythm and blues style.

Musical Style Notes

"(Mama) He Treats Your Daughter Mean" has a typical r&b text and rhythmic pattern. It begins with a pickup (if you were counting "And-a one, and-a two," the "and-a" is a pickup). The overall rhythmic pattern is subdivided into four-beat units, or measures:

(and-a)	1	2	3	4

In r&b, the primary accents fall on 2 and 4. The r&b "swing" feeling comes partly from the fact that each one of those four beats is subdivided into three equal parts, called triplets.

Major beats in the measure	and-a	1	2	3	4
Subdivision of beat into triplets	1 2 3	1 2 3	1 2 3	1 2 3	1 2 3

The drumbeats can be shown, with a slash representing an accented strike and a dash representing an unaccented strike, as follows:

Major beats in the measure	and-a	1	2	3	4
Subdivision of beat into triplets	1 2 3	1 2 3	1 2 3	1 2 3	1 2 3
Drum strikes here	/ –	/	/ – /	/ – /	/ –

In other words, the drummer actually hits the drum a fraction of a second after the ear expects the next downbeat, yielding a looser, more relaxed feeling to the rhythm. Meanwhile, the other instruments and the singer may put rhythmic accents in different places. For example, when Ruth Brown begins singing, the text accents fall on beats 1 and 3:

(and-a)	1	2	3	4	1	2	3	4
1 2 3	1 2 3	1 2 3	1 2 3	1 2 3	1 2 3	1 2 3	1 2 3	1 2 3
/ –	/	/ – /	/ – /	/ – /	/ – /	/ – /	/ – /	/ –
	Mama	- - -	- - -	- - he	treats	your	daugh-	ter mean

This use of layers of different rhythms, or *polyrhythms,* is one of the most prominent characteristics of African American music styles.

The song begins with the refrain, which then repeats after each verse. The melody of the verse is different from the melody of the refrain, although both are characterized by short melodic units that repeat several times and then are varied at the end. For instrumentation, the track uses drums, electric guitar, acoustic piano, and a horn section—in this case, simply a saxophone and a trumpet.

Musical "Road Map"

TIMINGS	COMMENTS	LYRICS
0:00–0:05	Drum introduction, 2 measures	
0:05–0:12	Introduction continues; saxophones and guitar join. Notice that they don't play exactly the same rhythmic accents as the drum. The saxes, for example, put the accent on the 3 in the triplet, which creates a *syncopation* with the drums. The guitar is emphasizing the triplet division of the beat.	
0:12–0:43	Refrain Notice the vocal technique of "sliding" the pitch up in the second syllable of "Mama."	*Mama, he treats . . .*
0:17	Piano enters, also emphasizing the triplet division of the beat.	
0:36–0:37	Note how Brown "bends the pitch" on the word *meanest*, wringing a great deal of expression from this one word!	
0:43–1:16	Verse 1 The actual 16-bar pattern begins on the word *treats*.	*Mama, he treats . . .*
1:07	The melody changes on the last line, "All of my friends say they don't understand—what's the matter with this man?" Note that the horn section plays more sparsely on the verse. This helps to highlight the singer's part and differentiates the verse from the refrain.	
1:17–1:46	Refrain	
1:20	Full horn section enters here, providing sonic contrast with first refrain.	*Mama, he treats . . .*
1:47–2:21	Verse 2 The actual 16-bar pattern begins on the word *man*.	*Mama, this man . . .*
2:12	As in verse 1, the melody changes on the last line, "I've stood for all that I can stand—what's the matter with this man?	
2:21–2:55	Refrain	*Mama, he treats . . .*
2:47–2:55	Ruth Brown varies the melody just slightly at the end, elongating the words *I've ever seen*, to signal the end of the song. The band responds with an ending phrase that is almost a cliché in r&b: the ascending scale followed by a strongly accented keynote (tonic). Over that last sustained note, you can hear the keyboard add one last rhythmic lick—another characteristic of blues and rhythm and blues.	

Clovers, and the Drifters. By 1954, its releases
began to cross over to the pop charts. Hits such as
the Chords' "Sh-Boom," Baker's "Tra La La" and
"Jim Dandy," Joe Turner's "Shake, Rattle, and
Roll," and Brown's "Lucky Lips" made an unmistakable imprint on rock 'n' roll.

Mass Technology and Popular Taste

If the abandonment of certain specialty fields by the major labels allowed independents to
enter the business, technological advances helped them to survive and even to gain ground.
Television, because of its devastating impact on network radio, helped to clear the airwaves for
local, independent broadcasting. Increasingly, the growth of independent record companies and
of independent radio stations made it possible for consumers to hear the music so many were
hungry to hear—rhythm and blues.

High Fidelity/Low Overhead

The first technical advance that had a marked impact on independent production was magnetic tape recording, "liberated" from the Nazis during World War II. Using a plastic tape
coated with iron oxide as its recording medium, the advantages of the German magneto-
phone were obvious. Magnetic tape could be edited and spliced; it was more durable, more
portable, and less expensive, with better sound reproduction, than the wire recording it
replaced. After the technology was smuggled back into the United States, the Minnesota
Mining and Manufacturing Company (3M) came up with a tape that surpassed the sound
quality of the German product. At the same time, tape recorder manufacturers reduced
recording speeds from 30 inches per second (ips) to 15 ips, and then to 7.5 ips, without seriously compromising sound quality, thus quadrupling the amount of material that could be
recorded on a standard tape. Recording companies and radio stations immediately invested
in the technology.

The transistor, introduced by Bell Laboratories in 1948, was a welcome companion to the
new recording technology. By incorporating all the functions of the vacuum tube into a solid
state environment, devices using transistors could be made smaller, less power hungry, and

more durable than the cumbersome tube amplifiers used in electronic recorders and radio receivers. Smaller, more affordable, longer-lasting recording equipment aided independent production. The transistor made truly portable radio receivers possible for the first time. With the advent of portable transistor radios, teenagers, soon to become an identifiable consumer group, could explore their developing musical tastes in complete privacy.

With the advent of portable transistor radios, teenagers, soon to become an identifiable consumer group, could explore their developing musical tastes in complete privacy.

In 1948, the same year that the transistor was unveiled, scientists at CBS laboratories, working under the leadership of Dr. Peter Goldmark and William Bachman, invented high fidelity. This breakthrough yielded the microgroove, or long-playing (LP), 33 revolutions per minute (rpm) record (the LP), which increased the number of grooves per inch on a standard record from 85 to 300. Years later, Goldmark described the challenge the creation of the LP had presented to the group:

> *First of all, to provide more playing time, it was necessary to change the number of grooves—which then necessitated changing the speed—which, in turn, required offsetting the resulting distortion— which then required offsetting the limitation of frequency response which would have occurred. . . . So we had to change the radius of the stylus. We went from sapphire to diamond. But, in order for the tiny radii not to chew up the record, we had to reduce the pressure. . . . Then you had wonderful sound quality, but you didn't have a microphone capable of creating wonderful sounds. . . . We . . . had to . . . develop a new kind of microphone, which turned out to be the condenser microphone . . . [that] the Germans already had invented.*[27]

"In other words," Goldmark concluded, "we had to develop a whole new science."[28]

Hoping to make the LP the industry standard, Columbia's Ted Wallerstein demonstrated it to David Sarnoff and other RCA executives. When the record played for twenty-three minutes without stopping, the RCA executives realized that Columbia had pulled off a major coup. Sarnoff responded with polite approval and promptly directed his technical staff to come up with a record that could play at a different speed. In what was to become known as the "battle of the speeds"—pitting Columbia's LP against RCA's newly developed 45 rpm record—the two firms produced "unbreakable" vinylite discs with excellent sound quality and maximum durability. The size of the 45 caught the fancy of jukebox manufacturers and soon became the preferred configuration for singles, while the LP became the industry standard for albums.

Because of these technological advances, records emerged as a relatively inexpensive medium compared to radio, film, and television, which all required huge sums of money for production, elaborate systems for transmission, and/or complex bureaucratic arrangements. For this reason, in part, small independent labels were able to challenge the giants that monopolized the music business. Records soon became the staple of all radio programming and the dominant product of the music industry as a whole. By the early 1950s, record companies were replacing publishing houses as the power centers of the music industry, and radio had established its primacy over the jukebox as the number one hit maker.

By the early 1950s, record companies were replacing publishing houses as the power centers of the music industry, and radio had established its primacy over the jukebox as the number one hit maker.

Television and the Suppression of FM Broadcasting

In the late 1940s, the entry of frequency modulation (FM) broadcasting into the marketplace was intentionally, if temporarily, suppressed because it conflicted with the development of television. Ironically, the advent of television then opened the door to independent radio—and thus to greater dissemination of r&b.

Messages can be sent over the airwaves either by modulating, or varying, their amplitude (size) or by modulating their frequency (rate of propagation). Early technical limitations favored the development of amplitude modulation (AM), as opposed to FM.[29] Although AM broadcasting became the standard in the United States, static interference from stations on adjacent frequencies presented a major problem. It had driven David Sarnoff to wish out loud for "a little black box to eliminate [radio] static."[30] Intrigued by the wish, inventor Edwin H. Armstrong spent the next ten years developing a new patented transmission system using an FM signal in the very-high-frequency (VHF) range of the electromagnetic spectrum. Sarnoff was so impressed that he moved Armstrong's operation to the RCA facilities atop the Empire State Building. In 1935, however, Sarnoff reneged on his commitment to Armstrong's invention, announcing instead a $1 million RCA research initiative to develop television. Both television and FM transmission operated best in the VHF range. Sarnoff, understanding even then that television would replace radio as the primary entertainment fixture in the home, decided to back the visual medium.

The outbreak of World War II stalled the further development of television and FM because RCA diverted its resources toward the advance of radar, and Armstrong contributed his personal services and the use of his FM patents to the war effort. After the war, the Federal Communications Commission (FCC) assigned FM radio to the frequency band between television channels 6 and 7 (88 to 108 megacycles), where FM later thrived. At the time, however, the ruling was devastating; it placed FM into a band for which neither transmitters nor receivers existed. Investors in FM promptly withdrew their money, and pending applications for FM licenses fell victim to bureaucratic shuffling. The public demand for radio was met through the manufacture of 6.5 million new AM receivers in 1946, as opposed to only 80,000 FM receivers, even though the latter produced better sound.

Television became a viable consumer item in the late 1940s. By 1951, nearly 16 million televisions were in operation in the United States, luring most of the national advertising away from network radio. Independent radio, on the other hand, emerged as an effective medium for local advertisers because stations doubled to 2,000 between 1946 and 1948. Eventually, the most successful independent radio outlets pushed aside the more staid network stations and cemented a reciprocal arrangement with record companies that has defined the music industry ever since: inexpensive programming in return for free promotion. At the time, these technological advances set the stage for the explosive popularity of independent deejays spinning r&b discs.

Independent Radio: Deejays in Your Face

With the devastation of network radio by television, local radio became the primary vehicle for popularizing the music produced by independent record companies and licensed to BMI, which—technically—the broadcasters owned. And as national programming gave way to hundreds of locally programmed stations, each appealing to its own audience, the flawless, even-toned, accent-free radio voice of the typical announcer soon went the way of studio orchestras. Fast-talking deejays—personality jocks—took over, and their stock in trade was their own eccentricity. These deejays enjoyed a personal involvement with their listeners. "We were the stars in our hometown," said deejay Diggie Doo. "We went to the churches, we went to the clubs, to the schools, the little kids knew us."[31] They not only talked to their fans, they talked *like* their fans. From his late night slot on WOV in New York, Jocko Henderson held forth in classic jive: "Eeeee tiddilee yok. Ho, this is the Jock. I'm back on the scene with the record machine. Saying goo bop-a doo, how do you do."[32] Hardly the King's English of an earlier generation of announcers, Jocko's rhymes are often cited as one of the formative influences in rap.

> **A**s national programming gave way to hundreds of locally programmed stations, each appealing to its own audience, the flawless, even-toned, accent-free radio voice of the typical announcer soon went the way of studio orchestras.

Replacing the live entertainment personalities who had dominated national radio, these independent deejays became, for a time, pivotal figures in the music industry. Record companies routinely supplied them with free new releases, hoping they could turn them into hits. Relying on their own inventiveness for popularity, independent deejays often experimented with specialty music and, in most cases, the key to their success turned out to be r&b.

R&b radio represented a considerable departure from standard radio practices. Up to this point, not much black music had been broadcast and few African American announcers had been used. As late as 1947, *Ebony* magazine had reported that, out of an estimated 3,000 deejays around the country, only sixteen were black.[33] What deejays there were usually followed the example of Jack L. Cooper, a veteran black announcer from the 1930s who had eschewed all traces of black dialect. According to Nelson George, Cooper's successors "tended to be conservative in their programming choices, leaning as heavily on Count Basie and Sarah Vaughan as on their vowels."[34] In r&b radio, however, black deejays and white deejays existed from the start. While pay scales usually favored white personnel, the new breed of black deejays set the tone.

> [B]lack disk jockeys were a much more colorful group of platter-spinners than their white brethren, whose main concern seemed to be with dignity, decorum, and the King's English. Black jockeys tended to take over the manners and mannerisms of black preachers. They were showmen rather than announcers. Their job was to entertain, not just to introduce records. By the early '50s, there were quite a number who had made names for themselves on ghetto stations.[35]

At first, the South was the major center for r&b radio. There were pioneer black r&b deejays as well as popular white r&b deejays who modeled themselves after these "preacher-emcees."[36] By the early 1950s, a number of so-called Negro stations in the South had proven to be quite successful. In St. Louis, Spider Burks addressed himself to the city's 328,000 African Americans over station KXLW. WDIA in Memphis, the country's only 50,000-watt black-oriented station, could broadcast to nearly 10 percent of the country's 12 million African Americans. WSOK in Nashville claimed to have several black stockholders. And, in 1951, WERD in Atlanta became the first totally black-owned radio outlet in the country.

Of course, r&b radio was not limited to the South. It also flourished in those major cities of the North and West that had large concentrations of African Americans. There was a black r&b deejay named Willie Mays on KSAN in San Francisco, and two white r&b jocks in Berkeley—"Jumpin'" George Oxford in Oakland and Phil McKernan (father of the late Pigpen of Grateful Dead fame). In Los Angeles, a white deejay named Hunter Hancock remained among the city's top-rated r&b deejays for twenty years.

In Chicago, Delta bluesman Muddy Waters held forth on WOPA before going on to record for Chess records. There was also a white r&b deejay on WOPA, Big Bill Hill, who sang the blues and sold Cadillacs in his version of highly stylized black speech: "Ah doan ca' if you got gahnashees on yo' gahnashees, ah cain p'choo in a big bread box by fo' o'clock dis aftanoon!"[37] However, Chicago's premiere r&b deejay in the late 1940s was Al Benson, "Yo' Ol' Swingmaster," an African American. At the peak of his popularity, Benson hosted five shows on a number of stations and earned as much as $100,000 a year. "Benson killed the King's English," recalled one of Benson's young Milwaukee colleagues. "He wasn't pretending to be white. He sounded black . . . and most of us were proud of the fact."[38] He made something of a splash in 1956 when "[h]e hired two white men (because he feared violence to himself) to shower five thousand copies of the Constitution on Jackson, Mississippi, to emphasize the Supreme Court's antisegregation ruling."[39]

New York and its environs were, of course, the center for r&b radio in the Northeast. In addition to a number of white deejays—George "Hound Dog" Lorenz in Buffalo, Danny "Cat Man" Stiles in Newark, "Symphony Sid" Torin at WMCA in New York City—the city also had a raucous contingent of black announcers/entertainers. Willie Bryant, "the Mayor of Harlem," and Ray Carroll broadcast their program *After Hours Swing Session* on WHOM, a foreign-language station by day. Jack Walker, "the Pear-Shaped Talker," appeared on foreign-language outlet WOV. Joe Bostic, who started at WBNX, held down a late-night slot for his program *Harlem Music Shop* on WINS. Tommy Smalls broadcast from WWRL, and Phil "Dr. Jive" Gordon broadcast from WLIB.

Unlike dance halls, record stores, and jukeboxes, the airwaves could not be segregated. If white teenagers wanted to turn their radio dials to the local r&b station, they were free to do so, and apparently that is exactly what they did.

Unlike dance halls, record stores, and jukeboxes, the airwaves could not be segregated. If white teenagers wanted to turn their radio dials to the local r&b station, they were free to do so, and apparently that is exactly what they did. As early as 1952, Dolphin's Hollywood Record Shop, a black retail outlet in Los Angeles, reported that, because of independent deejays spinning r&b records, its business was suddenly 40 percent white. Not yet a widespread practice, a change in popular music tastes was emerging as listeners across racial lines began calling into radio stations (not yet a widespread practice) to request Fats Domino's "The Fat Man" (1950); Jackie Brenston's "Rocket 88" (1951); Lloyd Price's "Lawdy Miss Clawdy" (1952); and Joe Turner's "Chains of Love" (1951), "Sweet Sixteen" (1952), and "Honey Hush" (1953)—all on independent labels.

Alan Freed was a reluctant convert to rhythm and blues, but, once convinced, he embraced the music with a fervor that became part of his own undoing. Because of his crucial role in popularizing rock 'n' roll, Freed became the sacrificial lamb in the government investigations that robbed him of his livelihood and eventually ended his life.

The most famous of all the r&b deejays was a white classically trained trombonist from Ohio named Alan Freed, who had fronted a jazz band called the Sultans of Swing in high school. When his career as a deejay on WAKR in Akron stalled in the late 1940s, he drank heavily and blamed the music he was playing, saying that jazz had become too abstract and intellectualized to be "the people's music" and that "the run-of-the-mill, country-affected, pop-hit sound didn't do anything for him."[40] Then in 1951, Leo Mintz, a record store owner in Cleveland who sponsored WJW's *Record Rendezvous* program, invited Freed to watch white customers buying up r&b records. Mintz convinced Freed to take over the radio show and devote it to r&b. Freed bayed like a hound over Todd Rhodes's "Blues for Moon Dog" to introduce the show that became *The Moon Dog House Rock 'n' Roll Party.* His gravelly voice and colorful announcing style were well suited to his new material. Freed's show proved so popular that he was hired by WINS in New York, which he turned into the number one popular music station in the city.

Freed is often remembered as the Father of Rock 'n' Roll. He even claimed to have invented the term *rock 'n' roll.* While ample evidence suggests that he was the first to use the expression on radio, the phrase had been around the African American community for years. What is beyond dispute, however, is that the trajectory of Freed's career paralleled the rise and fall of this exciting new trend in popular music almost perfectly. "Anyone who says rock 'n' roll is a passing fad or flash-in-the-pan trend along the music road," Freed once said, "has rocks in his head, Dad!"[41] How right he was. Early in 1956, *Billboard* ran a retrospective piece on popular music trends for the previous year under the headline, "1955—THE YEAR R&B TOOK OVER POP FIELD."

In the 1940s, all the forces that would unleash rock 'n' roll were set in motion. The tension between ASCAP and radio set the stage for the structural realignments that affected the very character of popular music. There were subsequent struggles between radio and the musicians' union and within the radio establishment itself (between network and independent stations). The death throes of swing created a void that signaled a culture in flux. Technological advances favoring decentralization allowed small independent record companies and flamboyant local deejays to become major players in the music business. Rivalries among giant record companies and competition between major and independent labels provided the corporate backdrop for the cultural developments that led to the rise of rhythm and blues in the late 1940s and the eruption of rock 'n' roll in the next decade.

LEARN MORE
Chapter Test
on MyMusicKit

Crossing Cultures:
The Eruption of
Rock 'n' Roll

Trying to pinpoint the beginning of rock 'n' roll is like trying to isolate the first drop of rain in a hurricane. The uninitiated may claim it began in 1955 when "Rock Around the Clock" by Bill Haley and His Comets became the best-selling record of the year. Others may want to date the phenomenon from the first rock 'n' roll record to make the pop charts, but no one agrees on which record that was. Charlie Gillett has said it was Bill Haley's "Crazy Man Crazy" in 1953.[1] Nick Tosches has argued for "Sixty Minute Man," recorded by the Dominoes in 1951.[2] Writer Jim Dawson and deejay Steve Propes decided "to pick out the [records] which have elements of rock 'n' roll in them—and which influenced the music that followed" and ended up debating among fifty contenders.[3]

Of course, part of the problem in determining the beginning of rock 'n' roll is that rock 'n' roll evolved over time; it was not a one-time event. There is also an issue of definition. There is rock 'n' roll, the musical genre unto itself; rock 'n' roll, the seemingly more acceptable term for rhythm and blues (r&b); and rock 'n' roll, the sexual metaphor. While Haley's "Crazy Man Crazy" fits the first definition well enough, the Dominoes' "Sixty Minute Man" highlights all three. "Sixty Minute Man" was a popular r&b release that crossed over to the mainstream audience; such r&b crossovers were often called rock 'n' roll to obscure their origins. The song's hero is a legendary lover who "rocks" and "rolls" his partners "all night long," leaving little doubt as to the sexual connotation of the term.

It is ironic that the term *rock 'n' roll,* eventually used by many white r&b deejays to give rhythm and blues a more wholesome veneer, had been common in African American music for years as a slang term for the sexual act. Thus, one might date the start of rock 'n' roll from earlier releases that used the phrase in this way—Li'l Son Jackson's "Rockin' and Rollin'" in 1950 or John Lee Hooker's "Rock 'n' Roll" in

LEARN MORE
Learning objectives
on MyMusicKit

It is ironic that the term rock 'n' roll, eventually used by many white r&b deejays to give rhythm and blues a more wholesome veneer, had been common in African American music for years as a slang term for the sexual act.

the same year; Wynonie Harris's hit recording of Roy Brown's "Good Rockin' Tonight" in 1948 or Sister Rosetta Tharpe's "Rock Me" (with the Lucky Millinder Orchestra) in 1942. For that matter, one could go back to Trixie Smith's 1922 recording of "My Daddy Rocks Me (With One Steady Roll)." Tosches, taking the exercise to the extreme, has traced the sexual origins of the phrase back to medieval times.[4] Suffice it to say (lest we get lost in history), that the music that came to be called rock 'n' roll began in the 1950s, as diverse and seldom-heard segments of the population achieved a dominant voice in mainstream culture and transformed the very concept of what was popular music.

Cultural Diversity: The Roots of Rock 'n' Roll

In an age in which the virtues of multiculturalism challenge the limitations of a narrowly Eurocentric worldview, it is fashionable to focus self-righteously on the culturally diverse influences that gave birth to rock 'n' roll. Unquestionably, rock 'n' roll was profoundly multicultural, but any serious analysis of its characteristics should attempt to apportion fairly the influence of various cultures. Unfortunately, the origins of rock 'n' roll are often described in a way that could be represented by an algebraic formula: r&b + c&w = r&r. The formula is elegant in its simplicity and not without an element of truth—rhythm and blues and country and western (c&w) *were* the primary styles that gave birth to rock 'n' roll—but it suffers from a number of shortcomings that can easily distort the contributions of participating groups. The limited focus on broad marketing categories, coded as black and white, avoids crucial issues of class, ethnicity, and gender and also ignores the myriad of influences that comprise rhythm and blues and country and western themselves, as well as other stylistic elements that exist outside these categories. In such a narrow formulation, Latinos, for example, can easily be erased from rock 'n' roll history, even though almost all descriptions of the music, including those cited below, mention Latin influences prominently.

Clearly, rock 'n' roll resulted from a complex interplay of social and cultural forces that cannot be reduced to a simple formula. As Robert Palmer has noted:

> The cliché is that rock & roll was a melding of country music and blues, and if you are talking about, say, Chuck Berry or Elvis Presley, the description, though simplistic, does fit. But the black inner-city vocal-group sound . . . had little to do with either blues or country music in their purer forms.
>
> The Bo Diddley beat . . . was Afro-Caribbean in derivation. The most durable . . . bass riff in Fifties rock & roll . . . had been pinched . . . from a Cuban son record. The screaming, athletic saxophone playing . . . was straight out of Forties big-band swing. . . . Traditional Mexican rhythms entered the rock & roll arena through Chicano artists. . . . Rock & roll proved an All-American, multi-ethnic hybrid, its sources and developing substyles too various to be explained away by "blues plus country" or any other reductionist formula.[5]

Attempting to avoid this reductionism, George Lipsitz has located rock 'n' roll at the intersection of urbanization, multiculturalism, and class:

> Workers drawn to cities by the manpower needs of American industry retained elements from their traditional cultures, but also combined with others to form a polyglot, urban, working-class culture.

The social meanings previously conveyed in isolation by blues, country, polka, zydeco, and Latin musics found new expression as they blended in an urban setting. . . . Rock and Roll music accelerated and intensified the interactions among ethnic groups, becoming the most visible expression of the increasing commonality of working-class experience.[6]

A final limitation of the algebraic formula: From it, one might infer that r&b and c&w contributed equally to the new genre. Such an inference invariably undervalues the African American contribution. When rock 'n' roll erupted full-blown in the national pop market in 1956, it presented itself as an integrated phenomenon with performers such as Bill Haley and Elvis Presley sharing the stage equally with artists like Fats Domino, Little Richard, and Chuck Berry. Accordingly, Steve Perry painted the early history of rock 'n' roll in racially glowing terms: "From 1955–1958, the roster of popular rock 'n' rollers was more racially equal than at any time before or since. Chuck Berry, Little Richard, the Coasters, the Platters, Fats Domino, Lloyd Price—major stars all, and on a rough par with the likes of Bill Haley, Jerry Lee Lewis, and Buddy Holly."[7] But this only happened after it had begun to expand to disruptive proportions among mainstream fans. As Greil Marcus correctly points out: "Most of the first rock 'n' roll styles were variations on black forms that had taken shape before the white audience moved in."[8]

The athletic, honking saxophone, reminiscent of Illinois Jacquet ("Flying Home") and Big Jay McNeely, found its way into rock 'n' roll through Jackie Brenston's spirited solo on "Rocket 88" in 1951. That classic sound was soon echoed on countless rock 'n' roll records by towering figures such as Lee Allen and Herb Hardesty in New Orleans and King Curtis and Sam Taylor in New York. T-Bone Walker ("Call It Stormy Monday") practically invented electric blues guitar playing in the 1940s.[9] His picking style, which Robert Palmer has described as "clean, with a terse, dry tone, and minimal vibrato and sustain," had an obvious effect on Memphis-based B. B. King ("Three O'Clock Blues," "The Thrill Is Gone"), whose bent notes and single string runs influenced generations of rock guitarists.[10] By merging T-Bone Walker's playing with jazz and pop influences, Chuck Berry created the definitive rock 'n' roll guitar style and mixed in universal odes to teenage life: "School Day," "Rock 'n' Roll Music," "Sweet Little Sixteen," and "Johnny B. Goode." This list of influences does not even include Muddy Waters ("Got My Mojo Working"), who had "electrified" country blues in Chicago so he could be heard above the din in noisy honky-tonks and juke joints. Shortly thereafter, Bo Diddley ("Bo Diddley," "Say Man"), another Delta-born Chicago transplant, crossed over into the pop market as a rock 'n' roll star with a distinctive Afro-Caribbean variant of the style. New Orleans boogie pianist Professor Longhair, who described his own playing as a "combination of offbeat Spanish beats and calypso downbeats" and "a mixture of rumba, mambo and calypso," was a major influence on Fats Domino, whose successful r&b career was transformed into rock 'n' roll legend with hits such as "Ain't That a Shame," "I'm in Love Again," and "Blueberry Hill."[11]

On the vocal front, the assertiveness of r&b performers such as Joe Turner, Ruth Brown, and LaVern Baker helped to create the rock 'n' roll style. The emotional intensity of Roy Brown ("Good Rockin' Tonight"), for example, was carried to an extreme in the outrageous antics of archetypal rock 'n' roll screamer Little Richard ("Tutti-Frutti," "Long Tall Sally," "Rip It Up"). The jazz/gospel fusions of Ray Charles ("Hallelujah, I Love Her So," "I Got a Woman") and the more pop-oriented gospel stylings of vocalists like Clyde McPhatter ("Treasure of Love,"

"A Lover's Question") and Sam Cooke ("You Send Me") brought the traditions of the black church into the secular world of rock 'n' roll. The elegant harmonies of urban vocal harmony groups like the Orioles ("Crying in the Chapel"), the Crows ("Gee"), the Chords ("Sh-Boom"), and the Penguins ("Earth Angel") ushered in a whole subgenre of rock 'n' roll known as *doo wop.*

Thus, in the well-intentioned and largely accurate celebration of rock 'n' roll's mongrel character, it is important not to lose sight of the fact that most of its formative influences, as well as almost all of its early innovators, were African American. Among the artists who could have been considered rock 'n' roll musicians prior to 1955, there was only one white act that made a national impact—Bill Haley and His Comets.

Perhaps the most disturbing thing about the revolution that was rock 'n' roll was that it just about eliminated women from the ranks of the best-selling recording artists. In the years immediately preceding rock 'n' roll, female vocalists had accounted for up to one-third of the best-selling singles in a given year. Of course, these were women in the pop Tin Pan Alley mold who performed suitably inoffensive material—Patti Page ("Doggie in the Window," 1953), Kitty Kallen ("Little Things Mean a Lot," 1954), Rosemary Clooney ("Hey There," 1954), Doris Day ("Secret Love," 1954), and so forth. By 1957, however, only two women appeared on *Cashbox*'s list of the twenty-five best-selling records of the year: Debbie Reynolds ("Tammy") and Jane Morgan ("Fascination"), and none of the eighteen or so rock 'n' roll records on the list was by a woman. The breakdown for the following year was exactly the same, unless Connie Francis's recording of "Who's Sorry Now" is counted as rock 'n' roll. Occasionally, female performers did penetrate the weekly best-seller lists with rock 'n' roll material—LaVern Baker's "Tweedlee Dee" in 1955 and "Jim Dandy" in 1957 and Ruth Brown's "Lucky Lips" in 1957—but a pattern of overwhelming male domination prevailed.

Clearly, the sexuality that characterized rock 'n' roll's initial burst of energy was male sexuality. Women did not sing; they were sung about, most often as babies—"Since I met you baby," "Honeycomb, won't you be my baby," "Be Bop a Lula, she's my baby," and so forth. Young male rock 'n' rollers were caught between the macho posturing of the "Sixty Minute Man" with his "Great Balls of Fire" and passionate, even vulnerable, declarations of unconditional romantic love, delivered in teenage idiom. Accordingly, a woman could be portrayed as a "Party Doll," a promiscuous "Butterfly," or a "Devil in Disguise," or, alternatively, as a heavenly goddess, "Venus" or "Diana," a "Dream Lover" with "Angel Eyes" sent to Earth by a "Little Star" or a "Blue Moon." At best, women were treated as totally dependent creatures or ideal, unreal apparitions, perched high atop celestial pedestals. Rarely were they seen as normal human beings or "real" people.

> **P**erhaps the most disturbing thing about the revolution that was rock 'n' roll was that it just about eliminated women from the ranks of the best-selling recording artists.

Structural Changes in the Music Industry

Whatever else may be said about rock 'n' roll, in the early 1950s, the appearance in the mainstream market of African American artists recording rhythm and blues for independent labels turned all the music industry rules upside down—especially those concerning artist and repertoire, recording techniques, marketing strategies, national distribution, and consumer preference.

After Sonny Til and the Orioles crossed over into the mainstream market in 1953, the floodgates opened for African American artists produced by independent labels. This new trend in popular music took the established powers of the music industry totally by surprise.

In 1953, for example, the Orioles, a black group originally from Baltimore, recorded "Crying in the Chapel," a sentimental country song, for Jubilee, an independent record label. Although three other versions of the song were on various best-seller lists at the time, the Orioles' release, with its sparse accompaniment, a slight gospel tinge, and wordless falsetto swoops in the background, went to number one on the r&b charts and then crossed over to the pop market. According to Charlie Gillett:

> Lead singer Sonny Til's wavering tenor and the sighs and cries of the group were familiar to the black audience, but sounded appealingly strange to the popular music audience. Perhaps aided by the fact that Til didn't sound very "black," the record broke into the white popular music market, thereby establishing a precedent for independently produced records featuring black singers.[12]

Marketing categories were simple, narrow, and limiting: pop for the national market, country and western for the regional market, and rhythm and blues for the African American market. In one blow, rock 'n' roll swept away this conventional wisdom.

Prior to this, the major labels had dominated the mainstream market. Estimates indicate that in 1948 and 1949, RCA, CBS, Decca, and Capitol released more than 80 percent of all the weekly Top Ten hits.[13] Marketing categories were simple, narrow, and limiting: pop for the national market, country and western for the regional market, and rhythm and blues for the African American market. In one blow, rock 'n' roll swept away this conventional wisdom.

The major labels had been able to keep their hold on the market in part because they controlled the entire production process—from songwriting to pressing to distribution, and in some cases, retail sales; these were in-house functions performed under a strict division of labor. Independent labels born in the 1940s and 1950s had far less-organized systems, but two events permitted them to compete successfully. First, several poorly capitalized independent radio stations, desperate for inexpensive programming, were brought into being as the Federal Communications Commission (FCC) cleared away its backlog of World War II–era license applications. Second was the development of the 45 rpm record. In 1945, Jack Gutshall had set up the first nationwide independent distribution system, but independent labels found shipping 78 rpm records prohibitively expensive because of their weight and fragility. With the introduction of light, "unbreakable" 45s, national distribution became a viable and cost-effective option for independent companies. These labels began to supply independent radio stations with their records, thus introducing specialty music to the mainstream market.

Following the decline of network radio in the early 1950s, ownership patterns in independent broadcasting began to change from individual stations to "chains"—individually programmed stations under one corporate roof. Chain owners were businesspeople for whom radio was just another investment. Said George Storer, the president of Storer Broadcasting,

> *If the legend still persists that a radio station is some kind of art center, a technical museum, or a little piece of Hollywood transplanted strangely to your home town, then the first official act of the second quarter century [of commercial broadcasting] should be to list it along with the local dairies, laundries, banks, restaurants, and filling stations.*[14]

Of course, these businesspeople expected their investments to be profitable; thus, programming not only had to be inexpensive but also had to appeal to a wide range of listeners. In addition to the specialty markets that the personality jocks had tapped, the tastes of the mainstream audience could not be discounted, and there was now a burgeoning youth market to consider. Todd Storz and Gordon McLendon, both chain owners, found the solution to this dilemma in a new format, which placed the forty best-selling records in constant rotation all day long. This was Top Forty radio.

Numerous stories exist about how Top Forty came into being. One has its origin as a cost-cutting measure at Storz's WTIX in New Orleans in 1953, with McLendon's KLIF in Dallas following soon after.[15] A more dramatic story has the format's birth in Omaha, Nebraska, when Storz and Bill Stewart, his program director at KOWH, noticed that bar patrons played the same jukebox song over and over. When a cocktail waitress—subjected to the song all day—selected it yet again at closing time, a new format was born. The Top Forty format was essentially an on-air jukebox, *Your Hit Parade,* programmed daily and with records. As a total "sound," Top Forty radio integrated jingles, special effects, promotional gimmicks, and hourly news broadcasts into the music program. The format proved so successful that it soon dominated pop radio.

With Top Forty radio, the deejay became a replaceable element in a total sound formula. Naturally the personality jocks railed against the increasing rationalization. George "Hound Dog" Lorenz, the most popular deejay in Buffalo, left WKBW because, he said, "[t]his concept of radio programming is helping to kill the single-record business, is lowering radio listenership, and is decreasing a new artist's chances of making it."[16] To many, the inescapable conclusion was that the new format would restrict audience access to new music. While this became true over time, ample evidence suggests that, paradoxically, in its initial stages, the format had precisely the opposite effect. According to Richard Peterson, "[b]ecause the charts were based not only on radio airplay but also on jukebox play and record sales, many r&b records as well as some country music records charted. Thus, for the first time, these sorts of records began to receive wide exposure via the radio."[17]

Network radio programming had not kept pace with popular taste. The Top Forty format, based on public appeal, at first broadened the range of a station's musical offerings. Imagine hearing Little Richard's "Long Tall Sally," Patti Page's "Allegheny Moon," Carl

Perkins's "Blue Suede Shoes," and Morris Stoloff's "Moonglow and Theme from Picnic," all on the same radio station—indeed, on the same show. It was possible in June 1956, when all four recordings were in the Top Forty simultaneously. In the heyday of rock 'n' roll, a greater diversity of music was heard on the radio than ever before.

Sounds of the Cities

The music that became rock 'n' roll issued from cities in just about every region of the country. While it is always tempting to trace the roots of rock 'n' roll to the South, perhaps because of the r&b + c&w formula, this analysis does not do justice to the geographical dispersion of the music or the variety of cultural inputs. In fact, there is no wholly satisfactory way to chart the course of the music. The one thing that can be said with certainty is that rock 'n' roll was an urban sound. Beyond that, the music often owed its characteristic sound to the magical ingredients of some bewitching musical brew—the distinctiveness of a particular region or city; the exceptional quality of a specific recording studio or record company; a unique vocal or instrumental style; even the creative genius of a particular writer, performer, producer, and/or engineer.

Rock 'n' roll often owed its characteristic sound to the magical ingredients of some bewitching musical brew—the distinctiveness of a particular region or city; the exceptional quality of a specific recording studio or record company; a unique vocal or instrumental style; even the creative genius of a particular writer, performer, producer, and/or engineer.

New Orleans: The Fertile Crescent of Rock 'n' Roll

New Orleans was one of those places where diverse musical elements really gelled. The Crescent City had been home to people from widely varied backgrounds—French, Spanish, African, English, Native American, Cajun, and Creole—for many years before it was purchased by the United States in 1803. The resulting cultural blend, born of conflict and accommodation, gave the city a distinctive cuisine, language, architecture, and musical culture. Known in legend as the birthplace of jazz, New Orleans was the site of a thriving r&b scene in the late 1940s and early 1950s. Thus, as Langdon Winner has noted:

> *Rock and roll performers nurtured in this fertile environment had a wealth of musical sources upon which to draw. The fabulous ensemble playing of the black funeral bands, the syncopated "second line" rhythms of Mardi Gras parades, the rugged country blues from the surrounding Mississippi delta, the raucous chords of barrelhouse piano players, the elegant styles of jazz improvisation—all became underlying elements of New Orleans rock.*[18]

An Italian American jukebox operator named Cosimo Matassa, co-owner and chief engineer of J&M Studio, was a key figure in the construction of the New Orleans sound. From the 1940s until the late 1960s, almost every r&b record cut in New Orleans was recorded in one of his studios. Matassa's productions had no overdubbing, multitracking, or electronic embellishments. His style was simple: He set the knobs at the desired level and let the band play. With this elementary philosophy, as well as brilliant sidemen, unique room acoustics, and some well-placed microphones, Matassa created classic New Orleans rock 'n' roll—heavy on bass and drums, light on horns and piano, with a strong vocal lead—that had independent labels flocking to New Orleans to record.

The first label to use Matassa's studio, in 1947, was De Luxe from New Jersey. Roy Brown's recording for De Luxe of "Good Rockin' Tonight" (a rock 'n' roll classic) was outsold by Wynonie Harris's that same year, but Brown's record turned the industry spotlight on New Orleans. Brown became a significant influence on the vocal styles of artists from B. B. King and Bobby Bland to Jackie Wilson, the young James Brown, and even Little Richard.

Fats Domino's laid-back New Orleans r&b style brought him a devoted rock 'n' roll following even after he was well into his thirties. With the exception of Elvis Presley (and Pat Boone), he charted more Top Forty pop hits than any other rock 'n' roller.

The city's fine array of session musicians was another essential ingredient in the creation of the New Orleans sound. At the center of this pool of talented sidemen was writer, producer, manager, arranger, trumpet player, and bandleader Dave Bartholomew. The son of a respected Dixieland tuba player and one-time trumpet player with Duke Ellington, Bartholomew started his own band/organization in New Orleans in the late 1940s. From that point on, he maintained a stable of first-rate musicians that included drummers Charles Williams and Earl Palmer, whose syncopated bass-drum style helped define rock 'n' roll drumming, and saxophonists Herb Hardesty, Red Tyler, and Lee Allen, who was also a mainstay in the band of Paul Gayten, another noteworthy New Orleans bandleader and session musician.

Bartholomew and his band enjoyed steady live work, but their most influential performances were as the house band at Matassa's studio. They can be heard as backup on Lloyd Price's "Lawdy Miss Clawdy" (1952); Shirley and Lee's "I'm Gone" (1952); the Spiders' "I Didn't Want to Do It" (1954); and Smiley Lewis's "I Hear You Knocking" (1955), with Huey "Piano" Smith on piano. Bartholomew's biggest successes were with Fats Domino, for whom he acted as mentor, manager, co-writer, arranger, and producer.

Antoine "Fats" Domino was born in New Orleans in 1928. Taught to play piano by his brother-in-law, Domino quit school at fourteen to work in a bedspring factory and to play in clubs at night, which is how he met Dave Bartholomew. Domino's music can be identified by his warm, inviting French Creole accent; Bartholomew's clear, well-constructed arrangements; and that steady boogie-woogie piano, which dates back to Albert Ammons, Meade Lux Lewis, and Pete Johnson, but was influenced most immediately by Professor Longhair.

Domino began recording at Matassa's studio in 1949. His rock 'n' roll breakthrough came in 1955 when Pat Boone's version of "Ain't That a Shame" went to number one on the pop charts and Domino's original followed it to number ten, establishing him as a full-fledged rock 'n' roll star with no change in his r&b style. From then on, Domino outdistanced almost all the competition. From 1955 to 1963, well into his thirties, Domino charted thirty-six Top Forty pop hits, more than any other rock 'n' roll artist except Elvis Presley (unless Boone, with thirty-eight, is included). In total, nine of Domino's records entered the Top Ten, including "I'm in Love Again"

Never a sex symbol or a musical iconoclast, Domino managed to transcend, to a great degree, the racism that cheated so many other African American artists and the ageism that plagued Bill Haley's career.

and "Blueberry Hill" (1956), "Blue Monday" (1957), and "Walking to New Orleans" (1960). Never a sex symbol or a musical iconoclast, Domino managed to transcend, to a great degree, the racism that cheated so many other African American artists and the ageism that plagued Bill Haley's career.

> *Somehow he was rock 'n' roll's safety valve, and all he was putting down was good time New Orleans music. . . . Fats' music had not changed in any way to meet his increased popularity. He was still a rhythm and blues singer whose music just happened to be the roots of rock 'n' roll. What he had in abundance was a natural, mellow infectiousness which was instantly recognizable whether the songs were happy frolics or merely plaintive ballads. Relaxed good humor permeated his records, everything was so simple and danceable.* [19]

All of Domino's hits, with the possible exception of "I'm Walkin'," were recorded in Matassa's studio; all were produced and arranged, and most co-written, by Bartholomew; and all used some combination of the same session musicians.

Interestingly, nobody consolidated the New Orleans sound into a successful New Orleans record label in the 1950s. Matassa founded Rex Records in 1958, but the company barely made a ripple outside New Orleans. The prodigious output of Matassa's studio was licensed to out-of-state independent labels. It wasn't until Bartholomew passed the creative baton to a second generation of producers, best exemplified by Allen Toussaint at Minit Records in the early 1960s, that New Orleans had even a fleeting success with a homegrown label.

The closest thing New Orleans had to a local label in the initial surge of rock 'n' roll was Ace Records, headquartered in Jackson, Mississippi, but centered in New Orleans. Founded in 1955 by Johnny Vincent (Vincent Imbragulio), who had been an artist and repertoire man for Specialty, the company had an immediate success with Earl King's "Those Lonely, Lonely Nights." King's second release, "Well-O, Well-O, Well-O, Baby," had that rocking New Orleans piano groove made famous by Huey "Piano" Smith. Smith and his band, the Clowns, provided Ace with its first pop hit—"(I Got the) Rockin' Pneumonia and the Boogie-Woogie Flu" (1957)—with Bobby Marchan as lead vocalist. In 1958, the Clowns hit the pop Top Ten with "Don't You Just Know It." Following that, their biggest success was as Frankie Ford's session band on "Sea Cruise." As Langdon Winner has pointed out, with this 1959 hit, "all of the elements of a sound which had been evolving for a decade are carried to their logical extremes. The New Orleans horns finally cook like their lives depend on it. The piano prances along, reaching the very essence of boogie-woogie. The lead vocal finally achieves the perfect mix of pure joke and pure hysteria." [20]

Ace's original recording had featured Bobby Marchan's vocal, but the company used Frankie Ford in the final release in an attempt to find a teen idol who could compete with white rock 'n' rollers such as Elvis Presley and Ricky Nelson. This practice was all too common in rock 'n' roll at the time. To Ford's credit, he had a genuine feel for r&b, and he delivered the song in a style heavily indebted to Marchan. Ace also recorded Jimmy Clanton, another white New Orleans rocker who produced a string of pop hits between 1958 and 1962, including three that made the Top Ten: "Just a Dream," "Go, Jimmy, Go," and "Venus in Blue Jeans." These three, especially the last one, removed him from his New Orleans roots and placed him in the company of ersatz rockers such as Fabian, Frankie Avalon, and Bobby Rydell.

The rest of the music recorded at Matassa's studio by New Orleans musicians was issued by more distant labels. Clarence "The Frogman" Henry's "Ain't Got No Home," "But I Do," and "You Always Hurt the One You Love" were issued by Argo, a subsidiary of Chess in Chicago, but the bulk of the material went to Los Angeles–based labels, primarily Aladdin, Specialty, and Imperial. Aladdin signed Shirley and Lee (Shirley Goodman and Leonard Lee), whose "Let the Good Times Roll" reached number twenty on the pop charts in 1956. Imperial had Smiley Lewis ("I Hear You Knockin'") and the Spiders ("I Didn't Want to Do It"). Imperial's founder, Lew Chudd, also signed Fats Domino, who turned the label into one of the most successful independents in the country.

Art Rupe, the owner of Specialty, was so impressed with Domino that he went to New Orleans in 1952 to find someone who could sing like him. He found seventeen-year-old Lloyd Price, at a public audition at Matassa's studio. Taken by Price's rendition of "Lawdy Miss Clawdy," Rupe put together a band to record it; Bartholomew rounded up the usual sidemen, including Fats Domino on piano. The record went to number one on the r&b charts and was followed by two more Top Ten r&b hits—"Restless Heart" (1952) and "Ain't That a Shame" (1953). Before Price could hit his stride, however, he was drafted into the army. After his service, he switched to ABC-Paramount and delivered nine Top Forty pop hits, including "Stagger Lee," "Personality," and "I'm Gonna Get Married," numbers one, two, and three, respectively, in 1959.

Rupe found two new artists to replace Price—Little Richard and Larry Williams, both examples of the New Orleans–Los Angeles connection. Williams came to Rupe's attention when he was Lloyd Price's valet. Recording in Los Angeles with New Orleans session musicians, Williams turned out three pop hits, "Short Fat Fanny" and "Bony Maronie" in 1957 and "Dizzy Miss Lizzy" in 1958, then faded from the scene. By this time, however, Little Richard had become the most colorful figure in rock 'n' roll.

Little Richard (née Richard Penniman) hailed from Macon, Georgia, where he sang and learned to play piano in the Pentecostal church, before being forced to leave home because of

alleged homosexual activity. In 1951, he landed a recording contract with RCA Victor, which failed to ignite his career, much like his next contract with Peacock. Later, Art Rupe bought out his contract from Peacock for $600 and sent Richard and producer Bumps Blackwell to New Orleans to record for Specialty. Naturally, they went to Matassa's studio and used Bartholomew's sidemen. Toward the end of the session, Richard

Perhaps more than any other artist, Little Richard unleashed the energy of early rock 'n' roll. On a number of occasions Richard left the world of music to pursue a higher calling. Fortunately for rock 'n' roll, however, his uncontrollable style and irrepressible spirit always won out in the end.

"Tutti Frutti"

Artist: Little Richard
Music/Lyrics by Little Richard
(and Dorothy La Bostrie)
Label: Specialty (1956)

Little Richard's first hits were recorded in Cosimo Matassa's famous studio in New Orleans with Dave Bartholomew's band, the same musicians who can be heard on recordings of Fats Domino and other New Orleans luminaries. "Tutti Frutti" hadn't been on the docket for that particular recording session, but Richard started singing it during a break:

> A wop-bop-a-loo-mop, a good goddamn,
>
> Tutti frutti . . . good booty . . .

Producer Bumps Blackwell decided that it would make a great single, once the lyrics were cleaned up (in addition to the obvious, *tutti frutti* was a contemporary slang term for a gay man). The task of rewriting the lyrics was given to Dorothy La Bostrie, an aspiring young New Orleans songwriter. The result was the now-famous "*A wop-bop-a-loo-mop, a lop bam boom, Tutti Frutti—oh Rootie. . . .*" "Tutti Frutti" was the first big hit for Richard and reached the Top Ten on both the r&b charts and the pop charts.

Musical Style Notes

"Tutti Frutti" is a classic 12-bar blues structure. The last 4 bars of each verse are generally played as a *stop time chorus*: The band hits only the downbeat of each bar, highlighting the singer's lines. The last 2 bars of each verse feature the "*wop-bop-a-loo-mop, a lop bam boom*" line.

Vocal *cues* are an important part of Little Richard's style. If you listen to several of Richard's songs in a row, you'll notice that there's a particular "scream" that always cues in an instrumental solo verse.

In some ways, Little Richard is Fats Domino's alter ego: Both played piano; both artists' records featured the same New Orleans–style instrumental combination, with its emphasis on sax and boogie-influenced piano rather than guitar; and both artists wrote accessible, catchy pop tunes. However, Fats's elegant New Orleans' gentleman persona and smooth vocals were the polar opposite of Richard's outrageous stage presence and his manic yips and howls.

Musical "Road Map"

TIMINGS	COMMENTS	LYRICS
0:00–0:03	Begins with Little Richard's famous nonsense-syllable refrain, unaccompanied. The band stops each time this refrain is sung throughout the song, except for the lead into the sax solo (see below).	*"A wop-bop-a-loo-mop,"*
0:03–0:19	"Tutti frutti" verse 12 bar blues form, the last 2 bars of which are the *"wop-bop-a-loo-mop"* Note drum "pickup" to next verse—in other words, the drummer anticipates the next verse by starting a beat before the verse begins.	*Tutti . . .*
0:19–0:34	Verse 1 12 bar blues form; last 4 measures are a "stop-time" chorus.	*Sue . . .*
0:35–0:50 0:37–0:39	"Tutti frutti" verse, as before Richard's trademark squeal and high-pitched "wooo"	*Tutti . . .*
0:50–1:05	Verse 2, same form as Verse 1	*Daisy . . .*
1:05–1:20 1:18	"Tutti frutti" verse, as before, with one exception: Listen to the way the drummer plays "A wop-bop-a-loo-mop" with Richard, then does a drum roll to lead into the sax solo. Richard also leads into the sax solo with a scream, one of his favorite cueing techniques.	*Tutti . . .*
1:20–1:36	Sax solo over the 12-bar blues form of a verse. Listen to the drummer "ride" the high-hat cymbal; you won't hear this in Pat Boone's version.	
1:36–1:51	"Tutti frutti" verse	*Tutti . . .*
1:51–2:07	Verse 2, same form as Verse 1	*Daisy . . .*
2:07–2:23 2:11	"Tutti frutti" verse Richard's trademark high-pitched "wooo" (copied later by Paul McCartney) Song ends with Richard's unaccompanied *A wop-bop-a-loo-mop, alop bam boom."*	*Tutti . . .*

began fooling around with a reportedly obscene song called "Wop Bop Aloo Bop." Blackwell quickly brought in Dorothy La Bostrie, a local songwriter, to clean up the lyrics, and with fifteen minutes of studio time left, "Tutti Frutti" was recorded. It hit number twenty-one on the pop charts in 1956 and established Little Richard as the most outrageous rock 'n' roller of them all.

Little Richard turned out eight other Top Forty pop hits for Specialty, including "Long Tall Sally" and "Slippin' and Slidin'" (1956), "Lucille" and "Keep a Knockin'" (1957), and "Good Golly, Miss Molly" (1958). Each was as unrestrained as the one before it. Richard's outrageous personal appearance was the perfect complement to his uninhibited stage act. The eye-popping costumes, exaggerated pompadour, and heavy mascara defined a rock 'n' roll image with which few could compete. His stage antics would later be rivaled only by Jerry Lee Lewis; his fashion statement (minus the eye makeup) only by Elvis Presley. If Fats Domino was rock 'n' roll's safety valve, Little Richard was the steam that made it blow. In describing the difference between the two, Arnold Shaw has also noted the versatility of the New Orleans sound itself.

> *Fats had a friendly baritone and Little Richard's sound was strident and slam-bam. Fats' Cajun-inflected speech had an appealing musicality; Little Richard was a shouter. For Fats, the band played New Orleans jazz with an after beat while he boogied and barrelhoused at the piano. With Little Richard's crashing piano triplets, the band picked up drive and went "a-womp-bomp-a-loo-bomp a-lomp bomp boom" and "bama lama bama loo."*[21]

Little Richard's career came to an abrupt halt in 1958 when he unexpectedly quit the business to join the ministry. A few not very convincing explanations have been offered for his sudden change in profession. Rupe blamed the first Russian satellite. "He thought that the Sputnik was a sign from heaven. That was it."[22] According to another tale, the engine of an airplane Richard was on caught fire and he promised God he would leave the devil's music if he could be saved. Some have suggested more cynically that he thought ministers did not pay income taxes. In any case, while on tour in Australia, Richard plucked $8,000 worth of rings from his fingers and tossed them into the sea. "If you want to live with the Lord," he told a reporter, "you can't rock 'n' roll it, too. God doesn't like it."[23] Whatever the reason for Little Richard's conversion, it was one of a number of fateful occurrences in the late 1950s that signaled the decline of rock 'n' roll.

Los Angeles: From Jump Blues to Chicano Rock

The independent labels in Los Angeles in the late 1940s sought to satisfy the cultural needs of the poor white, black, and Chicano migrants who had come to work in the shipyards and airplane manufacturing plants. Many artists who first recorded for these labels were pioneers in the transition from big band jazz to various styles of r&b. The first-wave artists—Roy Milton, Amos Milburn, T-Bone Walker, and Charles Brown, among others—came from Texas. In Los Angeles, they encountered local jazz–turned r&b musicians like Joe Liggins and Johnny Otis, who helped to shape their sound. As a new wave of immigrants arrived from southern Louisiana, Los Angeles' independent labels began to explore the music of New Orleans.

If Fats Domino was rock 'n' roll's safety valve, Little Richard was the steam that made it blow.

Perhaps they did so because New Orleans' early jazz sound, steeped in the blues, resonated well with the transition from jazz to rhythm and blues that was then occurring. As Johnny Otis once noted,

> [i]n the early 40's a hybrid form of music developed on the West Coast. . . . [T]he people who were there, like myself and Roy Milton, T-Bone Walker, and Joe Liggins and the Honeydrippers, we all had big band experience. We all thought in terms of big bands, but when it became impossible to maintain a big band, . . . we didn't break down to just a guitar and a rhythm section. We still tried to maintain some of that sound of the jazz bands. We kept maybe a trumpet, a trombone, and saxes—this was a semblance of brass and reeds, and they continued to play the bop and swing riffs. And this superimposed on the country blues and boogie structure began to become rhythm and blues. And out of rhythm and blues grew rock 'n' roll.[24]

Even before Fats Domino and Little Richard recorded with some semblance of the big band sound, as Otis called it, Roy Milton (Specialty), T-Bone Walker (Imperial), Amos Milburn (Aladdin), and Joe Liggins and the Honeydrippers (Exclusive) had developed distinctive regional variants of Louis Jordan's jump blues. Charles Brown, the lead singer for Johnny Moore's Three Blazers, developed a smooth r&b style that was heavily influenced by Nat "King" Cole and Leroy Carr in "Driftin' Blues" (Aladdin, 1948) and "Merry Christmas, Baby" (Modern, 1949).

Only Johnny Otis, however, was able to make the successful transition to rock 'n' roll. After moving to Los Angeles in the early 1940s, he started his own big band, whose first hit, "Harlem Nocturne" (1945), was on Excelsior, a subsidiary of Exclusive, then one of the only black-owned labels in Los Angeles. Otis was also part owner of the Barrel House, an r&b club in Los Angeles, and had a daily radio show and a weekly television show. The Johnny Otis Show, a traveling "rhythm and blues caravan," as he called it, featured vocalists Little Esther and Mel Walker. He is credited with discovering Hank Ballard, Little Willie John, Jackie Wilson, and Etta James. He also produced Johnny Ace[25] ("Pledging My Love," 1955), as well as Willie Mae "Big Mama" Thornton, for whom he claimed he co-wrote the original version of "Hound Dog" with Jerry Leiber and Mike Stoller. Otis hit rock 'n' roll pay dirt with "Willie and the Hand Jive" (1958), a novelty song played to the "Bo Diddley" beat, an Afro-Caribbean clavé rhythm that Otis said he had learned twenty years earlier.

Otis was such an important catalyst for African American culture and talent that people are sometimes surprised to learn that he is white. Otis identifies himself as "black by persuasion." When speaking of African Americans, he uses the pronoun *we* and does so with credibility. "My friend, Johnny Otis, is genetically white, but in all other respects completely black," wrote black musician Preston Love in the preface to *Listen to the Lambs,* a book Otis wrote after the Watts rebellion in 1965. "His life has been that of a black man joined with other black men to combat the outside—the hostile and unjust white establishment."[26]

Robert Byrd was one of the musicians at the Barrel House; he recorded as Bobby Day, Bobby Garrett (lead singer for the Hollywood Flames [a.k.a. the Satellites]), and Bob of Bob and Earl (who was Earl Nelson of the Flames). In 1957, Byrd (as Bobby Day) wrote and recorded "Little Bitty Pretty One" for the Class label, owned by Otis and Leon René. Aladdin put out a nearly identical version of the song, with Thurston Harris, which Dick Clark selected for *American Bandstand.* It outsold Day's original, four to one. The following year, René, who had written "When the Swallows Come Back to Capistrano" as the B-side of Day's record, wrote another "bird" song for Day. "Rockin' Robin" (1958) went to number two on the pop charts and became one of the all-time classic rock 'n' roll records.

As of 1958, Los Angeles had produced a number of distinctive performers but never a specific sound that was identified with the city. Given the historic presence of its Chicano residents, it was only a matter of time until Los Angeles musicians began incorporating the sounds of Mexico and the Southwest into rock 'n' roll. Johnny Otis anticipated this move when he presented Li'l Julian Herrera at the El Monte Legion Stadium in 1956. Herrera was actually Hungarian born but raised by Chicano parents. He had a major local hit with "Lonely, Lonely Nights," co-written with Otis. "It's an elegant and beautiful doo wop ballad, very much in the black style," Rubén Geuvara has written, "but something about it—the accent, the voice, the *attitude*—made it different. It was Chicano *rock*."[27] In the hands of the Champs ("Tequila") and Ritchie Valens ("La Bamba"), the sound of Chicano rock would extend to up-tempo rock 'n' roll by the end of the decade and develop further in the years to come. (It is dealt with in more detail in the section on Latin influences in this chapter and the section on Chicano rock in Chapter 6.)

> **G**iven the historic presence of its Chicano residents, it was only a matter of time until Los Angeles musicians began incorporating the sounds of Mexico and the Southwest into rock 'n' roll.

Chicago: The Blues Electrified

Chicago was one of the main watering holes for urbanized blues musicians from the Mississippi Delta, including Big Bill Broonzy, Sonny Boy Williamson, Willie Mabon, Jimmy Reed, John Lee Hooker, Muddy Waters, and Howlin' Wolf. All of them, except Broonzy, recorded for Chicago's two main independent record labels, Chess (Williamson, Mabon, Waters, and Wolf) and Vee Jay (Reed and Hooker).

According to legend, many of the Chicago blues greats simply walked into Chess Records off the street. Leonard Chess, however, was not one to sit and wait for talent to come to him. He made regular trips to the South to find bluesmen. On one trip, he recorded Howlin' Wolf with Ike Turner on piano and James Cotton on harp. On another, in 1951, Chess acquired Jackie Brenston's recording of "Rocket 88," with Turner's band and Brenston playing sax and singing lead, from Sam Phillips, who later founded Sun Records. The song rocketed to the top of the r&b charts and inspired Bill Haley to move in an r&b direction. Indeed, "Rocket 88" is sometimes cited as one of the first rock 'n' roll records. Chess's pioneering role in advancing rock 'n' roll was even more apparent in the label's next two major performers—Bo Diddley and Chuck Berry.

Like the early bluesmen who recorded for Chess, Bo Diddley came from Mississippi. Diddley moved to Chicago in 1934 but did not record for Chess until 1955. He is distinguishable from his blues contemporaries because he studied the violin—not the fiddle, but the classical instrument—before switching to guitar. Between 1955 and 1959, he turned out eight r&b hits, including the classic "Bo Diddley" (1955) backed with "I'm a Man." In 1959, "Say Man" crossed over to the pop market, and "Crackin' Up" made the pop charts but not the r&b charts, reflecting the beginning of the separation of rock 'n' roll from rhythm and blues. Diddley was more influential than his chart entries indicate. His rhythmic signature—an

Afro-Latin, three-against-two clavé-influenced rhythm (also known as the Bo Diddley beat and often misidentified as the shave-and-a-haircut beat)—was copied by numerous rock 'n' rollers. However, his importance at Chess, and in rock 'n' roll generally, was overshadowed by the label's biggest star and possibly the greatest rock 'n' roller of them all—Chuck Berry.

Were it not for the dynamics of racism in U.S. society, Chuck Berry probably would have been crowned king of rock 'n' roll. When Berry, the son of a middle-class contractor from St. Louis, Missouri, walked into the offices of Chess Records on the recommendation of Muddy Waters, his demo of "Ida Red" (backed with "Wee Wee Hours," a blues number) had already been turned down by both Capitol and Mercury because it sounded "too country" for a black man. On the advice of Leonard Chess, Berry gave the tune a bigger beat and changed the title to "Maybellene," a name he took from a hair creme. Said Chess a few weeks before he died:

> I liked it, thought it was something new. . . . I took a dub to Alan [Freed] and said "Play this." . . . By the time I got back to Chicago, Freed had called a dozen times, saying it was his biggest record ever. History, the rest, y' know? Sure, "Wee Wee Hour," that was on the back side of the release, was a good tune too, but the kids wanted the big beat, cars, and young love.[28]

For his part in popularizing the song, Freed and another deejay, Russ Fratto, were credited as co-writers of the song, a practice that eventually contributed to the undoing of rock 'n' roll.

The country-tinged "Maybellene" went to number five on the pop charts in 1955, but some of Berry's songs were too socially relevant for pop. As Charlie Gillett has written:

> [Berry's] next four singles, performed in a blues style and presenting . . . some strong criticisms . . . of American life, showed his interests much more obviously. Judges and courts in "Thirty Days," credit and car salesmen in "No Money Down," high culture in "Roll Over Beethoven," and all these and more in "Too Much Monkey Business" were cause for complaint. Since these records were performed in a strong "blues" voice, the songs . . . received relatively little attention from disc jockeys.[29]

HEAR MORE
Chuck Berry
on MyMusicKit

"Too Much Monkey Business" was actually a two-sided r&b hit, backed with "Brown-Eyed Handsome Man," a thinlyveiled comment on race. Berry is best remembered for the simpler, teen-directed but socially relevant recordings that came later—"School Day" and "Rock & Roll Music" in 1957, and "Sweet Little Sixteen" and "Johnny B. Goode" in 1958. All reached the Top Ten on the pop charts. In his

Chuck Berry had it all: sex appeal, talent, wit, stage presence, and an incredible ability to relate to teen culture. Had this country been more tolerant of racial differences, this "brown-eyed handsome man" would probably have been crowned the "King of Rock 'n' Roll."

"Rock and Roll Music"

Artist: Chuck Berry

Music/Lyrics by Chuck Berry

Label: Chess (1958)

Chuck Berry's 1950s singles represent what are in some ways the clearest combination of cross-cultural influences of early rock 'n' roll: the forms, harmonies, and pounding backbeats of rhythm and blues, and the twangy, clear-toned guitar solos of "hot country." Chuck Berry's music very much represents the musical *and* cultural boundary-crossing that went on in the music underworlds of Memphis and St. Louis.

Though he played the blues in East St. Louis clubs, Berry had clearly listened extensively to country artists as well—as can be heard on some of the sides he recorded in Chicago. While the rhythm section holds down a solid, behind-the-beat, triplet-laden blues shuffle ("tri-pl-et tri-pl-et tri-pl-et tri-pl-et"), Berry's twangy guitar solos are in rock-hard straight-eighths ("dunka-DUNKA-dunka-DUNKA"). He never varied from this formula, and there was no reason to: He was the first rock guitar hero, and his twangy solos are the foundation of every young wannabe guitarist's first education.

Musical Style Notes

The strong drum backbeat, Berry's repeating guitar riff, and the boogie-woogie piano sound are all typical of 1950s rock 'n' roll style, as is the prominent echo effect. "Rock and Roll Music" begins as a typical 12-bar blues form, but only the chorus maintains that structure; the verse is actually 8 bars long. The lyric verses of "Rock and Roll Music" also form an interesting structural overlap with the music. The first line of the verse is actually sung over the last bar (measure) of the chorus's 12-bar blues form. Likewise, the last line of the verse ("That's why I go for that—") could be considered the first line of the chorus rather than the words "rock and roll music," which occur on the downbeat of the first bar of the chorus's 12-bar blues form.

Chorus, bar 11				Chorus, bar 12				Verse, bar 1			
1	2	3	4	1	2	3	4	1	2	3	4
if you	wanna	dance	with me	—I	got no	kick a-	gainst	mo-	dern jazz . . .		

The overall effect is a very seamless progression through the song; notice that there is no instrumental solo verse to interrupt the flow of the words.

Musical "Road Map"

TIMINGS	COMMENTS	LYRICS
0:00–0:25	Four quick guitar strums, directly into 12-bar chorus. The lyrics over the last measure are actually the first line of the verse.	*Just let me . . .* *I have no*
0:25–0:37	Verse 1 The last line of each verse, which occurs on the last measure, is actually a lead-in to the first line of the chorus.	*modern jazz . . .* *That's why*
0:37–0:57	Chorus	*rock and roll . . .* *I took my*
0:57–1:09	Verse 2	*cross the tracks . . .* *That's why*
1:09–1:28	Chorus	*rock and roll . . .* *Way down*
1:28–1:41	Verse 3	*jubilee . . .* *And started playing*
1:41–2:00	Chorus	*rock and roll . . .*
2:00–2:13	Verse 4 Listen to the way that the drums and percussion change style here, from the rock backbeat to a Latin percussion beat; they're "commenting" on the reference to "tango" and "mambo" in the lyrics.	*Don't care . . .* *So I can*
2:13–2:33	Chorus Rhythmic "tag" at the end—"cha-cha CHA" beat	*rock and roll . . .* *If you want*

writing, Berry had the uncanny ability to relate r&b to white teen culture without disowning his blackness. His "duck walk" and other guitar gymnastics—indeed, his comedic yet cool stage demeanor in general—added tremendous visual appeal to his performances without demeaning the substance of his music. "As rock & roll's first guitar hero," Nelson George has written: "Berry, along with various rockabilly musicians, made that instrument the genre's dominant musical element, supplanting the sax of previous black stars."[30]

In 1959, Berry was arrested for a violation of the Mann Act (transporting a minor across state lines for immoral purposes). The impulse to discredit rock 'n' roll was shown in a headline of the time: ROCK 'N' ROLL SINGER LURED ME TO ST. LOUIS, SAYS 14 YEAR OLD.[31] It took two trials to convict him. The first was vacated because of the blatant racism of the judge, who referred to Berry as "this Negro." The second, which ended in 1962, landed him in jail for nearly two years. Despite this, Berry's songs continued to sell well in 1964 and 1965, but his career slipped in the late 1960s. He staged a comeback in 1972 with a song as commercially successful as it was puerile—"My Ding-a-Ling," his first and only number one pop hit. Although other heroes of rock 'n' roll may have had more and bigger hits than Chuck Berry, none matched his influence in defining its style.

Chicago's other main independent label was formed in the early 1950s by an African American couple, Vivian Carter and James Bracken; hence its name, Vee Jay. Carter was one of the few women deejays at the time; Bracken owned and operated a record store. Vivian's brother, Calvin Carter, was their producer. Vee Jay began as a gospel label. Its artists included the Swan Silvertones, the Harmonizing Four, the Highway QCs, and the Staple Singers. The company experienced some early success in doo wop, recording both the Spaniels and the El Dorados. However, its best-selling artist in the 1950s was Delta bluesman Jimmy Reed. Signed to the label in 1955, Reed produced thirteen r&b hits over the next six years, including "Honest I Do" (1957) and "Baby What You Want Me to Do" (1960), which crossed over to the pop Top Forty. John Lee Hooker joined Vee Jay in 1955. Although a more versatile performer, Hooker was less successful than Reed as an r&b artist. He became better known later because of his Newport Folk Festival appearances and recordings, which were influential in the blues revival of the 1960s.

Vee Jay seemed destined for major success when it signed the Impressions. The original Impressions included Jerry Butler and Curtis Mayfield, who had met when they joined the same gospel choir. In 1957, they joined forces with the core of a group called the Roosters to form the Impressions. The group's 1958 audition at Vee Jay yielded "For Your Precious Love," which became a Top Twenty pop hit but contributed to the destruction of the group because it was inadvertently credited to Jerry Butler *and* the Impressions. Butler stayed with Vee Jay as a solo artist, with Mayfield as a writer and arranger; but as recording artists, Mayfield and the rest of the Impressions switched to ABC-Paramount, where Mayfield penned a series of gospel-influenced "sermon songs" (rightfully belonging to the era of the civil rights movement, discussed in Chapter 6). Vee Jay made its mark on rock 'n' roll with hits by Dee Clark ("Hey Little Girl," 1959, and "Raindrops," 1961), Gene Chandler ("Duke of Earl," 1962), and Betty Everett ("The Shoop Shoop Song [It's in His Kiss]," 1964).

In terms of offering career direction to African American artists and crossing black music over to a white audience, Vee Jay could have been what Motown became. Unfortunately, the company seemed to have a knack for losing many of its best acts. Gene Chandler, for example, signed with Constellation shortly after "Duke of Earl" ran its course. While Vee Jay introduced a number of name artists—including the Four Seasons, Gladys Knight and the Pips, and the Dells—many had their biggest successes after switching to other labels. Even the Beatles were first issued on Vee Jay in the United States, when Capitol initially passed on them. In 1966, the company unexpectedly folded amidst rumors of fiscal mismanagement.

In terms of offering career direction to African American artists and crossing black music over to a white audience, Vee Jay could have been what Motown became. Unfortunately, the company seemed to have a knack for losing many of its best acts.

Cincinnati: The Crossroads of Blues and Country

As a major rail stop situated along the Ohio River, Cincinnati had served for years as a gateway to northern iron and steel mills for blacks and whites from the South. As such, it was a crossroads for blues and country music. As noted in Chapter 3, Syd Nathan's King Records consolidated these influences into a diverse musical enterprise. Under the able direction of producer Henry Glover, Nathan's policy of encouraging his artists—country and western and rhythm and blues—to record each other's songs provided early examples of the cultural cross-pollination that would yield rock 'n' roll.

Among King's country artists, the Delmore Brothers had first recorded blues-based country hits ("I've Got the Big River Blues") when they were with RCA. Glover continued their development with a wealth of blues-influenced material that culminated in the 1949 country hit "Blues Stay Away from Me." Glover's biggest country breakthroughs, however, were with Moon Mullican, who scored unorthodox country hits early on with "Shoot the Moon" and an updated version of the Cajun classic "New Jole Blon" (1947). Mullican was comfortable with a broad range of material, but his biggest influence was in the realm of country boogie. "[U]nder Glover's influence," according to historian John W. Rumble, "Mullican expressed his fascination with black music on levels that few country artists had ever attained."[32] By the time of his biggest hit, "Cherokee Boogie" (1951), he was a star of the Grand Ole Opry and formative influence on the young Jerry Lee Lewis.

Ivory Joe Hunter was an African American artist who moved in the other direction. Hunter had recorded a number of early r&b hits for King in the late 1940s, such as "Landlord Blues" and "I Quit My Pretty Mama." He achieved pop crossover success with his biggest hit, "Since I Met You Baby" in 1956, after leaving King for Atlantic and became one of the few African American artists ever to become a regular on the *Grand Ole Opry*.

King Records eventually made a direct impact on the rock 'n' roll market with three acts: the Charms ("Hearts of Stone," 1954), Bill Doggett's combo ("Honky Tonk," 1956), and Little Willie John ("Fever," 1956). However, King's greatest influence on rock 'n' roll was through its subsidiary, Federal, set up in the early 1950s with producer Ralph Bass. Bass established a personality for the new label with gospel-influenced vocal harmony groups, including Billy Ward and the Dominoes, the "5" Royales, Hank Ballard and the Midnighters, and the Famous

Flames. These groups, along with others, challenged the perceived morality gap between gospel music and rhythm and blues and contributed one of the major strands to the style of rock 'n' roll known as doo wop.

R&B Sanctified: The Gospel Connection

In the late 1940s, as r&b grew in popularity, gospel music was also being recorded. In the Northeast, New York's Apollo label had Mahalia Jackson, Savoy in Newark had James Cleveland, and Gotham in Philadelphia had the Famous Ward Singers. Three other well-known groups—the Dixie Hummingbirds, the Silver Echoes, and the Skylight Singers—recorded for various labels in New York City. In the West, the best-known gospel talent, including the Pilgrim Travelers and the Soul Stirrers, appeared on Specialty. Black-owned Peacock Records, founded by Don Robey in Houston, recorded the Five Blind Boys of Mississippi and the Bells of Joy, among others.[33]

At the time, there was a sharp distinction between gospel and rhythm and blues in the African American community. Rhythm and blues artists did not perform in church, and gospel singers were expected to steer clear of "the devil's music."

At the time, there was a sharp distinction between gospel and rhythm and blues in the African American community. "[R]hythm and blues was felt to be degrading, low," said Robey, "and not to be heard by respectable people."[34] Rhythm and blues artists did not perform in church, and gospel singers were expected to steer clear of "the devil's music." In the early 1950s, however, some gospel-trained singers began to move into the secular world of rhythm and blues, retaining a gospel tinge in their use of organs, soaring vocals, background choruses, and the call-and-response style. The first such group was the Dominoes, founded in 1950 by the multitalented Billy Ward. In 1951, the group had three r&b successes on the Federal label—"Do Something for Me," "I Am with You," and "Sixty Minute Man" (featuring Bill Brown's bass), which became a crossover classic whose sexual lyrics caused no small stir in the gospel community. Two later gospel-flavored releases were the Orioles' "Crying in the Chapel" and "Shake a Hand" by Faye Adams. Both were released in r&b and country versions, and both lent themselves to various interpretations. "Here for the first time you were not sure exactly what ground you were on," r&b historian Peter Guralnick has written. "Were these love songs or devotionals? Was the second person singular you or You? It was an intentional ambivalence that was to persist."[35]

The Dominoes' early successes were due in large measure to the incredible leads of gospel-trained Clyde McPhatter. In 1952, McPhatter capped his stay with the group with "Have Mercy Baby," a number one r&b hit. The following year he formed his own group, the Drifters. The equally talented Jackie Wilson took McPhatter's place with the Dominoes; when Wilson went solo in 1957, Billy Ward became lead vocalist. The Dominoes had two Top Twenty pop hits that year with "Star Dust" and "Deep Purple."

Between 1953 and 1956, the Drifters—all of whom had a gospel background—delivered six Top Ten r&b hits for Atlantic, including "Money Honey" and the double-sided hit "Such a Night"/"Lucille." After McPhatter was drafted in 1955, the group eventually disbanded, later re-forming with new personnel and a totally new sound. McPhatter continued with Atlantic after his service, becoming an r&b and pop sensation with hits such as "Treasure of Love"

(1956) and "A Lover's Question" (1958), number six on the pop charts. He continued producing hits well into the 1960s.

Atlantic also produced the most influential gospel-tinged vocalist of all—Ray Charles Robinson, a.k.a. Ray Charles, a.k.a. "the Genius." Blinded by glaucoma as a youth, Charles attended the St. Augustine School for the Deaf and the Blind in Florida (where he learned to compose and arrange in Braille), then moved to Seattle. The influences on his music were absolutely catholic, ranging from the Five Blind Boys of Mississippi to Chopin, to legendary jazz pianist Art Tatum, to jazz pianist–turned pop vocal stylist Nat "King" Cole. In Florida, Charles had even joined a hillbilly band and learned to yodel. After cutting some forty sides (including a few r&b hits) for Swingtime Records in the late 1940s and early 1950s, he signed with Atlantic in 1952.

((•● **HEAR MORE**
Ray Charles
on MyMusicKit

Charles saw no contradiction between gospel and r&b. "Now I'd been singing spirituals since I was three," he said in his autobiography, "and I'd been hearing the blues for just as long. So what could be more natural than to combine them?"[36] The Genius began to hit his stride with a string of original r&b hits in 1954—"Don't You Know," "Come Back Baby," and the gospel-inflected "Hallelujah, I Just Love Her So." Often he mined the gospel repertory directly for new material: "Talkin' 'Bout Jesus" became "Talkin' 'Bout You"; "This Little Light of Mine" became "This Little Girl of Mine"; "How Jesus Died" became "Lonely Avenue." All the elements of his revolutionary jazz-gospel-r&b fusion were present by the time he released "I Got a Woman" (1954), one of his most influential and, to some, apocalyptic records. "The very strategem of adapting a traditional gospel song, putting secular lyrics to it, and then delivering it with all the attendant fanfare of a Pentecostal service was, simply, staggering," Peter Guralnick has said. "It was like a blinding flash of light in which the millennium, all of a sudden and unannounced, had arrived."[37] The style reached its logical conclusion with the release of Charles's Top Ten classic "What'd I Say" (1959), "a culmination of the gospel blues style

that Ray Charles had virtually created, an altogether secular evocation of an actual church service, complete with moaning, groaning, and speaking in tongues, a joyous celebration of an utterly profane love."[38]

By this time, Jackie Wilson had left the Dominoes to pursue a solo career at Brunswick. His first six hits, including "Reet Petite" (1957), "Lonely

With musical tastes ranging from Chopin to Nat "King" Cole, Ray Charles was a pioneer of the r&b/gospel fusion that has come to be known as rhythm and gospel. *For many, his spirited live performances were, indeed, a religious experience.*

Teardrops" (1958), and "That's Why (I Love You So)" (1959), were co-written by Berry Gordy, the founder of Motown. Wilson demonstrated his incredible versatility and operatic vocal range in 1960 on "Alone at Last" and "Night," both of which hit the Top Ten. As he remarked at the time, "Now they knew I wasn't just a screamer."[39] In 1967, he was still straddling the narrow line that separated gospel from rhythm and blues. His last Top Ten pop hit, "(Your Love Keeps Lifting Me) Higher and Higher," projected the same sexual/spiritual ambiguity that made the fusion so exciting in the first place.[40]

Perhaps the most profound gospel desertion was Sam Cooke's. Son of a Chicago Baptist minister, Cooke was in the choir before he was ten. He joined the Soul Stirrers in 1950 and quickly became, according to gospel historian Tony Heilbut, "the greatest sex symbol in gospel history."[41] In 1956, Bumps Blackwell, Little Richard's producer at Specialty, offered to "cut" Sam Cooke "pop." His first session yielded eight sides, one of which was "Lovable," released under the name of Dale Cook in a fairly transparent attempt to avoid the wrath of the gospel community. Sam Cooke agonized over what musical direction to take, but in the end the decision was made for him, as his outraged gospel followers forced him to leave the Soul Stirrers in 1957.

Sam Cooke agonized over what musical direction to take, but in the end the decision was made for him, as his outraged gospel followers forced him to leave the Soul Stirrers in 1957.

Fearing reprisals from his gospel constituency, Art Rupe, owner of Specialty, released both Cooke and Blackwell from the label and gave them Cooke's masters in return for back royalties. Cooke and Blackwell teamed up with Bob Keene, who had just launched the Keen label. Cooke's first Keen release, "You Send Me" (1957), climbed straight to pop number one; seven more entered the Top Forty over the next three years. Cooke's pop appeal seemed as effortless as the gospel-influenced melismas he used to embellish his vocals. In 1960, RCA, a label with almost no African American artists, was looking for an answer to the black-velvet tones of Columbia's Johnny Mathis and signed Cooke. He scored nineteen more Top Forty hits, of which "Chain Gang" (1960), "Twistin' the Night Away" (1962), "Another Saturday Night" (1963), and "Shake" (1964) entered the Top Ten.

In 1959, Cooke took the rare step of forming his own publishing company, Kags Music, with his mentor J. W. Alexander, tenor vocalist for the Pilgrim Travelers. Kags's audit of Keen's royalty statements bankrupted the label and ended

Like many African American singers who learned their trade in the church, Sam Cooke abandoned gospel for the secular world of commercial pop. He went on to become a major hit maker and a business institution with his own record label and publishing and management companies.

Cooke's relationship with Bumps Blackwell. Cooke and Alexander used their Kags earnings to finance a production company, an artists' management company, and SAR (Sam and Alex Records)—arguably the first soul label—for which Cooke wrote and produced. SAR issued straight gospel recordings by the Soul Stirrers and more soul-oriented material by Johnny Taylor (later of disco fame); the Sims Twins; and the Valentinos, featuring Bobby Womack, all of whom were gospel artists who had embraced r&b.

Meanwhile, a number of full-fledged gospel groups moved into r&b. These groups joined the King subsidiary Federal, second only to Atlantic in the successful production of "rhythm and gospel." The Gospel Starlighters became the Famous Flames, James Brown's backup group. Echoes of the group's gospel past could be heard on "Please, Please, Please" (1956), an eventual million seller. The Royal Sons emerged as the "5" Royales; after recording two Top Ten r&b hits ("Baby Don't Do It" and "Help Me Somebody") for Apollo in 1953, they moved to King and recorded "Think" (1957) and "Dedicated to the One I Love" (1958). (The latter became a Top Ten pop hit for the Shirelles in 1961 and The Mamas and The Papas in 1967.) To avoid confusion with the "5" Royales, the Royals became the Midnighters; their "Work with Me Annie" (1954) launched the erotic Annie series that shocked the nation and rocked the gospel world to its foundations.

The Midnighters' lead singer, Hank Ballard, heavily influenced by gospel as a boy, imbued the song with tremendous suggestiveness. Any doubt about the sexual connotation of the verb *work* was laid to rest in the two follow-up songs, "Sexy Ways" and "Annie Had a Baby," also released in 1954. All three were heavily censored, and all three were million sellers. The success of the trilogy spurred a number of decreasingly successful answer songs.[42] One answer song that was incredibly popular was Etta James's "Wallflower" (1955), popularly known as "Roll with Me Henry" (a reference to Hank Ballard). When pop singer Georgia Gibbs tried to eliminate all traces of eroticism by redoing James's song as "Dance with Me Henry," the Midnighters responded with "Henry's Got Flat Feet (Can't Dance No More)"—effectively ending the two-year affair.

Doo Wop: The Intersection of Gospel, Jazz, and Pop

To the average listener, gospel-oriented vocal groups were nearly indistinguishable from groups that employed a rock 'n' roll style known as *doo wop.* Doo wop was the product of urban vocal harmony groups—mostly black and almost invariably male—and owed as much to gospel, jazz, and pop as it did to the blues. Typical of the genre was a melodramatic, often gospel-inflected lead tenor bracketed by a distinctive bass and a soaring falsetto. Background vocals usually consisted of nonsense syllables such as "Sha-na-na-na sha-na-na-na-na" and "Oodly-pop-a-cow pop-a-cow pop-a-cow cow." *Doo* and

> **D**oo wop was the product of urban vocal harmony groups—mostly black and almost invariably male—and owed as much to gospel, jazz, and pop as it did to the blues.

wop were syllables used to name the music, but not until well after the style had been established. In terms of output, doo wop was the largest single subgenre of rock 'n' roll to come into existence; according to Greil Marcus, "it was the first form of rock & roll to take shape, to define itself as something people recognized as new, different, strange, *theirs.*"[43] Doo wop came from just about every region in the country. While there were a few dozen groups who dominated the genre, some with one or two hits, hundreds more were destined only for obscurity. Among these were countless "bird groups": the Ravens, the Orioles, the Larks, the Robins, the Swallows, the Flamingos, the Crows, the Cardinals, the Falcons, the Penguins, the Pelicans, the Jayhawks, and (stretching the concept) the Feathers. And there were slightly fewer "car groups": the Cadillacs, the El Dorados, the Fleetwoods, the Continentals, the Impalas, the Imperials, even the Edsels.

In addition to its gospel roots, doo wop could be traced back to two black pop/jazz vocal harmony groups that had achieved mainstream success in the 1930s and 1940s—the Mills Brothers and, to an even greater degree, the Ink Spots, who turned out nearly fifty hits for Decca between 1939 and 1951. Both groups used close barbershop harmonies and light rhythms. The Ink Spots' "If I Didn't Care" and "My Prayer" (1939), featuring lead singer Bill Kenny's high tenor and "Hoppy" Jones' talking bass, are, by almost any measure, proto doo wop.

In the late 1940s, a number of young black groups—among them, the Ravens, the Four Tunes, the Four Knights, and the Orioles—tried to emulate, with some innovations and varying degrees of success, the style of these groups. The Ravens pioneered the use of the bass lead on "Old Man River" (1946), which sold 2 million copies. Over the next several years, the group turned out a string of r&b hits, including "I Don't Have to Ride No More" (1950) and "Rock Me All Night Long" (1952), both of which achieved Top Ten r&b status.

When the Orioles—originally called the Vibranaires—came to the attention of Deborah Chessler, an astute manager-songwriter, in Baltimore, Maryland, Greil Marcus has said, "They made their piece of history—a young Jewish woman and five black men in an utterly segregated American city. . . . Together they found the new sound."[44] After a booking on Arthur Godfrey's talent show in 1948, Jubilee Records signed the group and renamed them the Orioles. Their first recording, Chessler's "It's Too Soon to Know," went Top Ten r&b in 1948 and has been named by Marcus as a contender for "first rock 'n' roll record." The Orioles followed with a string of r&b classics, including "Forgive and Forget" (1950), "Baby Please Don't Go" (1952), and their biggest hit, "Crying in the Chapel" (1953). Jubilee also had the Four Tunes, a group that had r&b hits with "Marie" and "I Understand" in 1954, and the Cadillacs, who crossed over to the pop charts with the up-tempo "Speedo" in 1956. Other groups that tried to duplicate the Orioles' "cool" sound included the Larks ("My Reverie," 1951) and the Five Keys ("Glory of Love," 1951; "Ling Ting Tong," 1954; "Out of Sight, Out of Mind," 1956; and "Wisdom of a Fool," 1957).

> **D**oo wop hit makers were spread across every region of the country. One noticeable pattern among them was the dazzling array of "one hit wonders"—groups that disappeared after only one (or two) pop hits.

Doo wop hit makers were spread across every region of the country. One noticeable pattern among them was the dazzling array of "one hit wonders"—groups that disappeared after only one (or two) pop hits. This pattern was more a reflection of how the record companies treated these artists than of the groups' talent. The sheer number of these groups was rivaled only by the number of places they came from and the number of labels for which they recorded. Other, more successful, groups—for example, the Harptones ("Sunday Kind of Love" [1953, Bruce], "Life Is but a Dream" [1954, Paradise], and "What Will I Tell My Heart?" [1961, Companion])—bounced from label to label before fading from the scene.

The most interesting thing about these groups is that, in many instances, their individual and unrelated recordings gave doo wop its overall character. As a result, the history of doo wop

(((• **HEAR MORE**
Audio Links for a list of One Hit Wonders on MyMusicKit

often reads like a record catalogue. But what a remarkable catalogue it is. The sounds that helped define this era include the Crows' fluid dance rhythm on "Gee," Carl Feaster's jazz scatting on the Chord's "Sh'Boom," Cleveland Duncan's plaintive cry on "Earth Angel," the elegant balladry of Fred Parris on "Still of the Night" and Lee Andrews on "Tear Drops," the playful macho posturing of Mr. Earl (Carroll) on "Speedo," Little Joe Cook's screeching falsetto on "Peanuts," Fred Johnson's staccato bass on "Blue Moon," and the subtle Latin blush of the Elegants' "Little Star" and the Mystics' "Hushabye."

If the doo wop style had a center, however, it was New York City. A greater number of groups and labels were found in and around New York than any other region. Herald/Ember, founded by Al Silver in 1952, generally recorded out-of-state talent: the Nutmegs and the Five Satins from Connecticut and the Turbans and the Silhouettes from Pennsylvania. In 1952, Rama's founder, George Goldner, began recruiting directly from New York's streets. He launched a subsidiary, Gee, that had hits with the Mello-Tones, the Cleftones, and Frankie Lymon and the Teenagers ("Why Do Fools Fall in Love" and "I Want You to Be My Girl" in 1956; "Goody Goody" in 1957). In 1957, Goldner formed two other labels, Gone and End, with deejay Alan Freed listed as producer. Freed changed the Chesters' name to Little Anthony and the Imperials; their "Tears on My Pillow" was a Top Ten pop hit in 1959 on End. After re-forming in the mid-1960s, they scored two more Top Ten hits (on DCP)—"Goin' Out of My Head" (1964) and "Hurts So Bad" (1965).

The New York label that had the most luck with vocal harmony groups was Atlantic. Its first successful group was the Clovers from Washington, D.C. From 1951 to 1954, the group had thirteen consecutive Top Ten r&b hits, including "Don't You Know I Love You," "Fool,

"Sh'Boom"

Artist: The Chords
Music/Lyrics by James Keyes, Carl Feaster, Claude Feaster, Floyd McRae, and Ricky Edwards
Label: Cat (1954)

"Sh'Boom" was an early doo wop hit by a South Bronx group called The Chords: Jimmy Keyes, Carl Feaster, Claude Feaster, Floyd "Buddy" McRae, and Ricky Edwards, who supposedly wrote the song together while sitting in a Cadillac convertible.

Many record company executives in the 1950s believed that the *song* is what sold and not the singer(s) or the particular performance. This belief fueled the unfortunate practice of re-recording an African American group's r&b hit with a new version by a white vocal group that would have been, in the 1950s, more attractive to white teenage listeners, the major market for this music.

The Chords' "Sh'Boom" is a famous and oft-cited example of this phenomenon. After reaching number 5 on the pop charts, it was trounced by a cover version that a white group called the Crew Cuts recorded for Mercury. But the story of "Sh'Boom" is actually a bit more complex. Ironically, the Chords' version had originally been the B-side of a single, the A-side of which was a cover of Patti Page's tune "Cross over the Bridge." Disc jockeys preferred "Sh'Boom," which became a huge hit, going to number 5 on the pop charts. Patti Page's label, Mercury, then released the Crew Cuts' watered-down but highly successful version of "Sh'Boom," whereupon Atlantic, the parent label of Cat, rereleased the Chords' "Sh'Boom" with a different flip side, dumping the Patti Page cover. The bottom line? The Chords still lost out; "Sh'Boom" was their only big hit. It has become a beloved classic, however, of the early doo wop era.

Musical Style Notes

Like many doo wop songs, the structure of "Sh'Boom" is loosely based on the tried-and-true template of verse-verse-bridge-verse: two initial verses, both sung to the same melody, which are followed by a bridge section with a new melody, which then leads back into another verse with the original melody. This aaba form, as it's sometimes called, is one of the most common popular song forms, from Tin Pan Alley to doo wop, to Beatles songs. However, the Chords vary it somewhat, adding short verses in which singer Carl Feaster scats (a term taken from jazz), or sings on nonsense syllables leading into a repetition of the "Life could be a dream" lyric. There is also an instrumental break over the chords of the verse, with a sax solo by Sam Taylor in the great, gritty r&b style sometimes called dirty sax.

Musical "Road Map"

TIMINGS	COMMENTS	LYRICS
0:00–0:04	A capella voices begin in harmony.	*Life could be . . .*
0:04–0:08	Instruments enter.	*doo doot . . .*
0:08–0:23	Verse 1 Background vocals add nonsense syllables, "Sh'boom."	*if I could . . .*
0:23–0:29	Singer Carl Feaster "scats" (sings on nonsense syllables).	
0:29–0:44	Verse 2	*if only . . .*
0:44–0:58	Bridge section; different melody, sung by bass Ricky Edwards; guitar plays fills; background vocals on "ahh."	*Every time I look . . .*
0:58–1:12	Verse 3 All voices sing lyrics in harmony.	*sh'boom . . .*
1:12–1:22 1:18	Singer Carl Feaster "scats" (sings on nonsense syllables); background harmonies. All sing.	*life could be*
1:22–1:53	Sam Taylor plays sax solo over the chords of the verse, twice through.	
1:53–2:08	Verse 3 repeats, beginning with unison "wooooo. . . ." All voices sing lyrics in harmony.	*sh'boom . . .*
2:08–2:26	Singer Carl Feaster "scats" (sings on nonsense syllables); background harmonies. Vocals reenter.	*doo, doot doot.*

Fool, Fool," "One Mint Julep," "Ting-a-Ling," and the original rock 'n' roll versions of "Blue Velvet" and "Devil or Angel." They crossed over to pop with "Love, Love, Love" (1956). Their last hit was their best—"Love Potion No. 9" (1959), a rock 'n' roll classic, written and produced by Jerry Leiber and Mike Stoller for United Artists after the group had left Atlantic.

Two other Atlantic vocal groups achieved greatness working with Leiber and Stoller—the Coasters and the Drifters. The Coasters had begun in Los Angeles as the Robins, whose "Double Crossing Blues" (1950) was a number one r&b hit. Atlantic was sufficiently impressed with songs such as "Smokey Joe's Cafe" and "Riot in Cell Block No. 9" that it bought the Robins' catalogue and hired Leiber and Stoller as independent producers to work with them. The Coasters' first six releases—"Searchin'" and "Young Blood" (1957), "Yakety Yak" (1958), and "Charlie Brown," "Along Came Jones," and "Poison Ivy" (1959), all written and produced by Leiber and Stoller and punctuated instrumentally by the "yakety sax" of King Curtis—made the pop Top Ten. The Coasters remained major hit-makers until 1961.

After the original Drifters broke up, their manager, George Treadwell, persuaded the Five Crowns (with Ben E. King on lead) to take their name. Produced by Leiber and Stoller, who merged r&b and gospel with a decided Latin tinge, the new Drifters had immediate success with hits such as "There Goes My Baby" and "Dance with Me" in 1959 and "This Magic Moment" and "Save the Last Dance for Me" in 1960. When King left the group in 1960, gospel-trained

Under the tutelage of producers Leiber and Stoller, the Drifters took the vocal harmonies of doo wop to new heights and provided a gateway to the more produced r&b sounds of the early 1960s.

Rudy Lewis replaced him, singing lead on "Up on the Roof" (1962) and "On Broadway" (1963). Sadly, Lewis died just before the group recorded their classic "Under the Boardwalk" (1964).

The productions of Leiber and Stoller were so elaborate—often involving dozens of takes, complex arrangements, and significant editing to achieve the desired effect—that they must be seen as the moment of transition from the innocence and spontaneity (and amateurishness) of classic doo wop to the calculated products of the producer as an artist in his own right. This difference separates the early doo wop groups from the vocal harmony groups (chiefly, the "girl groups") of the 1960s.

The productions of Leiber and Stoller were so elaborate that they must be seen as the moment of transition from the innocence and spontaneity (and amateurishness) of classic doo wop to the calculated products of the producer as an artist in his own right.

Of course, New York City was not the only place that produced doo wop. Both the Spaniels ("Baby It's You," 1953) and the Flamingos ("Golden Teardrops," 1953) started with Chance Records in Chicago. The Spaniels moved to Vee Jay, where they recorded their biggest hit, "Goodnight, It's Time to Go," in 1954. The Flamingos broke through to the pop market on the End label with "Lovers Never Say Goodbye" (1957). Their biggest hits were "I Only Have Eyes for You" (1959) and "Nobody Loves Me Like You" (1960). Chicago's Chess label had the Moonglows, founded in Cleveland by Harvey Fuqua (later a Motown writer/producer) in 1951. The group scored three Top Thirty hits—"Sincerely" (1955), "See Saw" (1956), and "Ten Commandments of Love" (1958)—in the classic doo wop mold.

In Cincinnati, King Records had the Charms ("Gum Drop" and "Hearts of Stone," 1954; "Ling Ting Tong," 1955; "Ivory Tower," 1956) on its De Luxe label, bought in 1953. King lost the group that went on to become the most successful of all the vocal harmony groups—the Platters. Originally signed to King's Federal label, they were often used as backup. When Buck Ram, their coach/manager, insisted on $100 a session for background vocals, Federal released them. Ram got them signed to Mercury, a major label, in 1955, where they scored twenty Top Forty pop hits over the next seven years.

More than any other group, the Platters carried the torch lit by the Ink Spots two decades earlier. Their first two releases for Mercury were Ram tunes: "Only You" went to number five in 1955 and "The Great Pretender" hit number one in 1956. "My Prayer" (1956), with Tony Williams on lead vocal, was a number one pop hit and a virtual remake of the Ink Spots' 1939 original. "Twilight Time," a number one hit in 1958, had been co-written by Ram in 1938 for the Three Suns. In the same year, the Platters went to number one with Jerome Kern's "Smoke Gets in Your Eyes." The group's last Top Ten hit, "Harbor Lights" (1960), had been popularized by Rudy Vallee in 1937. Although the Platters, in fact, sounded more pop than doo wop, their music was accepted as rock 'n' roll.

Pioneering black doo wop groups were followed by white or integrated groups. Among the white groups, Italian Americans predominated.[45] The most popular Italian American doo wop group, from Belmont Avenue in the Bronx, called themselves Dion (DiMucci) and the Belmonts. Performed in classic doo wop style, "I Wonder Why," the group's first of many releases on Laurie, became a Top Twenty pop hit in 1958. "A Teenager in Love" and "Where or When," the Rodgers and Hart classic, made the Top Ten in 1959 and 1960, respectively. In 1960, Dion left the group to go solo. By 1963, he had acquired thirteen Top Forty pop hits, a new wife (the inspiration for "Runaround Sue," recorded with the uncredited

Dion and the Belmonts were one of the first white groups to pick up the torch of doo wop and carry it beyond the 1950s. Italian Americans all, they were true to the style and a testament to the hybridity of the music.

Del-Satins), and a drug problem that forced him out of the business for the next five years. The Belmonts had two more hits—"Tell Me Why" (1961) and "Come On Little Angel" (1962)—then faded from view.

The Dell-Vikings, who met in the service, were the first racially integrated doo wop group (originally, three black and two white singers) to hit the pop charts. "Come Go With Me" and "Whispering Bells" both entered the Top Ten in 1957. Johnny Maestro and the Crests included an Italian American lead (John Mastrangelo) and a background vocal group of color. They recorded five Top Thirty hits, the best being the first—"Sixteen Candles" (1958). Maestro resurfaced in the 1960s as the lead singer for the Brooklyn Bridge ("The Worst Thing That Could Happen," 1967).

Second in rarity to racial integration was gender balance. While some doo wop groups added women essentially for show,[46] a few boasted strong female leads. There were also some all-female groups, whose songs defined male–female relationships in ways that prefigured the arrival of the early 1960s "girl groups." (See the chart below.) The producer most associated with the girl group phenomenon, Phil Spector, got his first big break as part of a vocal trio with a female lead. The Teddy Bears' "To Know Him Is to Love Him," a song Spector fashioned from the inscription on his father's tombstone, featured Annette Kleinbard's lead and went to number one in 1958. Spector duplicated the soothing vocal sound with the Paris Sisters ("I Love How You Love Me") in 1961 before his production style became completely devoted to his legendary "wall of sound." Taking that soothing vocal sound still further, the Fleetwoods, a trio of one man and two women, used soft, elegant harmonies built around an almost seamless male–female blend that moved vocal harmony groups further away from doo wop style.

Doo wop was a 1950s phenomenon that spilled over somewhat into the next decade.[47] The Four Seasons' musical roots, for example, could be traced to doo wop. Their "Sherry" (1962, Vee Jay), a number one pop hit, received significant play on black radio before a live appearance on *American Bandstand* revealed a white Italian American vocal harmony group. The group, featuring the three-octave range of lead singer Frankie Valli (born Francis Castelluccio), had twenty-nine chart singles over the next fifteen years, in addition to Valli's nine solo hits.

GROUPS/SONGS WITH FEMALE LEADS	SONGS, LEAD SINGER	YEAR
Six Teens	"A Casual Look" (Trudy Willaims)	1956
The Tune Weavers	"Happy, Happy Birthday, Baby" (Margo Sylvia)	1957
The Aquatones	"You" (Barbara Lee)	1958
The Teddy Bears	"To Know Him Is to Love Him" (Annette Kleinbard)	1958
The Innocents	"A Thousand Stars" (Kathy Young)	1960
The Fleetwoods	"Come Softly to Me"	1959
	"Mr. Blue"	1959
	"Tragedy"	1961

ALL-FEMALE GROUPS	SONG TITLE	YEAR
The Teen Queens	"Eddie, My Love"	1956
The Bobbettes	"Mr. Lee"	1957
The Shepherd Sisters	"Alone"	1957
The Poni-Tails	"Born Too Late"	1958
The Quintones	"Down the Isle of Love"	1958
The Chantels	"Maybe"	1958
The Paris Sisters	"I Love How You Love Me"	1961

((•● **HEAR MORE**
Audio Links on
MyMusicKit

Still, as a phenomenon, doo wop was over in 1961. As if to signal the end of the era, Little Caesar and the Romans released "Those Oldies but Goodies" that same year. The song went to number nine on the pop charts, and the designation "oldies but goodies" was immediately applied to songs released in the previous decade, including some that had been hits a year earlier.

Latin Music Rocks

Although U.S. popular music can be described as profoundly hybrid, drawing on multiple sources, its history is most often recounted in terms of black and white—black culture versus the mainstream. Individuals and groups that do not fit neatly into this black–white binary have tended to be rendered invisible or simply assigned to one or the other group. Frankie Lymon and the Teenagers, for example, were identified as a black group, even though two of its members, Joe Negroni and Herman Santiago, were Puerto Rican. The Harptones and the Vocaleers were similarly "integrated." Latino Harold Torres rounded out the background vocals of Johnny Maestro and the Crests, even though the Crests were identified as black. In the 1950s, if Latinos looked black, they were assumed to be African American, whether or not their own primary identification was racial. Conversely, when Ritchie Valens was riding the popularity of his pop-sounding

In the 1950s, if Latinos looked black, they were assumed to be African American, whether or not their own primary identification was racial.

number two hit "Donna," prior to the ascendancy of its B-side "La Bamba," most of his white fans simply assumed he was white.

Further confusions arose from the fact that perceptions of Latin Americans were sometimes conflated with those of Mediterranean immigrants whose languages had Latin roots. The "Latin lover" stereotype, for example, applied equally well to people of Italian or Latin American descent (as did the more negative term *greaser*). Given such cultural confusion, it was not surprising to see mid-1950s Tin Pan Alley hits such as Rosemary Clooney's "Mambo Italiano" or Perry Como's "Papa Loves Mambo." This situation has to be unraveled to engage in a reasonable discussion of Latin(o) music and musicians as a major influence on U.S. popular music.

In the 1950s, the U.S. Latino population comprised mainly Chicanos in the Southwest and a large influx of Puerto Ricans (and a smattering of Cubans) along the eastern seaboard. At this time, Cuban musics such as rumba, mambo, and cha cha cha invariably generated national dance crazes in the United States. For this music, there were hot Latin bands like those of Machito, Tito Rodriguez, and Tito Puente, which entertained a hard-core Latino audience, and others like Perez Prado and Xavier Cugat, which catered to a more upscale Anglo clientele. When Tin Pan Alley incorporated these influences into popular song, it was generally for their novelty value. The 1924 Tin Pan Alley classic "Tea For Two" thus became "Tea for Two Cha Cha" in 1958 and a Top Ten hit for the Tommy Dorsey Orchestra. But we have already seen how Tin Pan Alley embraced Latin influences; the point here is that rock 'n' roll was no exception.

Countless rock 'n' roll songs, crossing lines of race, ethnicity, and style, appropriated Latin rhythms, some with more success and credibility than others. The A-side of the Penguins surprise 1954 hit "Earth Angel" was the Latin-inspired "Hey Senorita." Ruth Brown's "Mambo Baby" hit number one on the r&b charts in 1954. Even as Bill Haley was "rocking around the clock" in 1955, he cracked the Top Twenty with "Mambo Rock." The Ventures scored a number fifteen pop hit with a rock 'n' roll version of the Latin classic "Perfidia." Doo wop abounded with Latin-inflected releases, such as the Turbans' "When You Dance," the Gladiolas' "Little Darlin'," the Elegants' "Little Star," and the Mystics' "Hushabye." There were the compelling bongo riffs on Bobbie Freeman's "Do You Wanna Dance." Examples from the teen idols include Paul Anka's "Diana" and Bobby Darren's "Dream Lover." From rhythm and gospel, Jackie Wilson had a number of Latin-tinged hits such as "Reet Petite" and "Lonely Teardrops." The apex of Ray Charles's rhythm and gospel fusion was his 1959 hit "What'd I Say," played to a rumba beat.

At times, Latin influences found their way into rock 'n' roll through producers who straddled both worlds. George Goldner, who started the Rama, Gee, Gone, and End labels in New York (home to the Crows and Frankie Lyman and the Teenagers, among others), began his music career as the owner and head producer of Tico Records, New York's most important independent Latin label (and home to Tito Rodriguez and Tito Puente). Before the Crows had a bona fide rock 'n' roll hit with "Gee" in 1954, Goldner had released a mambo version of the song on Tico. He even convinced the Crows to record the novelty "Mambo Shevitz" after their initial success.

Nowhere was the incorporation of Spanish Caribbean influences more integrated or better executed than in the work of writer/producers Jerry Leiber and Mike Stoller with African American vocal harmony group, the Drifters. The story of Leiber and Stoller is usually discussed in terms of two young white Jewish writers/producers sufficiently immersed in African American culture to achieve credibility. There is certainly merit to this story, but there's more. After moving to Los Angeles with his family in 1949, Stoller became heavily involved with young, working-class Mexican American hipsters known as *pachucos*, who were into cutting-edge r&b and current Spanish Caribbean styles. Stoller even claimed to have "learned the pachuco dances and joined a pachuco social club."[48] He got his start as a musician playing piano with the Blas Vasquez band, which of course influenced his songwriting. After being paired with the Drifters in New York, Leiber and Stoller combined lavish strings and orchestral arrangements with sensuous Latin rhythms to produce countless hits such as "Dance with Me," "This Magic Moment," "Save the Last Dance for Me," and "Up on the Roof." Leiber then added content to Latin musical influences when he teamed up with Phil Spector in 1960 to write "Spanish Harlem"—which provided vocalist Ben E. King with his first solo hit after leaving the Drifters.

By the late 1950s, Los Angeles' rock 'n' rollers began to move toward styles that drew on Mexican sounds. The Champs' "Tequila" went to number one on the pop charts for five weeks in 1958. It was followed with "El Rancho Rock," a rocked-up version of the 1934 Mexican ballad "Alla en El Rancho Grande," which had been a hit for Bing Crosby. It is often noted that the Champs included, at various times, Jim Seals and Dash Crofts (later Seals and Crofts) and Glen Campbell on guitar. Less often mentioned is the fact that "Tequila" was written by the Champs' Chicano sax player Danny Flores, who performed as Chuck Rio.[49]

One artist who might have developed this sound further was Ritchie Valens (Richard Valenzuela), the first Chicano rock 'n' roll star. While his biggest hit, "Donna," sounded like it could have been one more classic rock 'n' roll ballad by another white rocker, Valens revealed a different persona on the record's B-side and challenged the conventional wisdom of the music industry, not simply by recording a rock 'n' roll version of a traditional Mexican song—the Champs had already done that—but by recording it in Spanish. "La Bamba" may have only reached number twenty-two, but its influence on popular music has been incalculable. All of the other hits were sung in English ("C'mon, Let's Go," "That's My Little Susie," "Little Girl"), but there is evidence to suggest that he had broader plans, including a rock 'n' roll version of Ernesto Lecuona's "Malaguena." Unfortunately, Valens was killed in the 3 February 1959 plane crash that took the lives of Buddy Holly and the Big Bopper, which has been eulogized as "the day the music died." But his legacy lived on in the Chicano rock groups of the 1960s (covered in Chapter 6) and in the rock/Mexican fusions of Los Lobos in the 1970s and beyond.

Ritchie Valens drew on his Chicano heritage to add another cultural source to the musical brew that was rock 'n' roll. Who knows how much further he might have taken that sound had he not been killed in a plane crash three months before his eighteenth birthday?

Rockabilly: The Country Strain

It was only a matter of time until some entrepreneur figured out that white artists who could merge r&b and c&w with credibility would have enormous sales potential.

As rock 'n' roll developed, it was only a matter of time until some entrepreneur figured out that white artists who could merge r&b and c&w with credibility would have enormous sales potential. The person usually credited with this discovery is Sam Phillips, who founded Sun Records in Memphis, Tennessee, in 1953. According to Marion Keisker, Phillips's secretary, Phillips once said, "If I could find a white man who had the Negro sound and the Negro feel, I could make a billion dollars."[50] The answer to his prayers was, needless to say, Elvis Presley, crowned the King of Rock 'n' Roll. The rest, as rock 'n' roll lore would have it, is history—or at least a serviceable version of it.

In fact, Bill Haley and His Comets, not Presley, were the first major white rock 'n' roll act to reach the mainstream market with a fusion of r&b and c&w. Haley is often distinguished from Presley because of differences in musical style and public image. The music that Presley and the Sun artists who followed him played was called "rockabilly," after its amalgam of rocking African American and so-called hillbilly styles. According to Charlie Gillett, rockabilly differs from Haley's fusion because it has "much looser rhythms, no saxophones, nor any chorus singing."[51] Haley's music, in contrast, sounds more arranged, more calculated. Haley related to his country roots through the instrumentation of a western swing combo; Presley's early Sun sides did not even include drums.

Bill Haley and His Comets drew their inspiration from sources as disparate as Bob Wills and the Texas Playboys and Louis Jordan and The Tympani Five in constructing their country/r&b fusion. Adding outrageous stage antics to the mix, they earned a memorable niche in rock 'n' roll history.

The differences between Haley's public persona and that of the rockabilly artists are even more significant. In the mythology of rockabilly, there has always been something appealing about white southern performers, roughly the same age as their fans, who recorded with pronounced regional accents for independent labels. Presley was the archetype even after he no longer fit the image. Bill Haley's celebrity was quite different. Balding and looking somewhat middle-aged by the time his career took off, he was a most unlikely candidate to become a rock 'n' roll sensation. Born in Highland Park, Michigan, and singing with no distinguishable accent, Haley's celebrity seems all the more improbable because he was signed by a major label, Decca, and his best-selling record, "Rock Around the Clock," was written by two Tin Pan Alley veterans (Max Freedman and Jimmy DeKnight).

Haley experimented with various styles for ten years before he hit the mainstream; he once described his early sound as "a combination of country and western, Dixieland, and the old style rhythm and blues."[52] His heroes were Bob Wills and His Texas Playboys, who played western swing, and his band approximated the pivotal sound of Louis Jordan. Haley's producer, Milt Gabler (Jordan's producer in the 1940s), told Arnold Shaw that he had consciously modeled Haley's sound after Jordan's jump beat. "We'd begin with Jordan's shuffle rhythm," said Gabler. "You know, dotted eighth notes and sixteenths, and we'd build on it. I'd sing Jordan riffs to the group that would be picked up by the electric guitars and tenor sax. . . . They got a sound that had the drive of The Tympani Five and the color of country and western."[53]

In the early 1950s, Haley decided that r&b-flavored dance music was the key to his future. He signed with Decca in 1953 and, with Gabler as his producer, enjoyed his biggest hits, including "Dim, Dim the Lights" (1954), "Burn That Candle" (1955), and "See You Later, Alligator" (1956). With its lyrics cleaned up, his 1954 version of Big Joe Turner's "Shake, Rattle, and Roll" became a classic rock 'n' roll recording and his first million seller.

When "Rock Around the Clock" was first released in 1954, it fizzled. Because of its Tin Pan Alley parentage, however, it was selected as the theme for the Hollywood film *Blackboard Jungle*.[54] Within weeks of the film's 1955 release, the song went to number one on the pop charts and stayed there for eight weeks, eventually becoming one of the biggest-selling rock 'n' roll records in history, with sales of nearly 17 million copies. By the time Elvis Presley hit the pop charts, over a year after "Rock Around the Clock" was released, Haley was in his thirties and over the hill by teenage standards. His star was soon supplanted by younger rockabilly artists from Memphis—Carl Perkins, Johnny Cash, Jerry Lee Lewis, and, of course, Presley himself.

Sam Phillips had a definite strategy when he launched the careers of these younger artists. While Syd Nathan at King Records encouraged his c&w artists to record country versions of r&b hits, and vice versa, Nathan was not trying to break down racial barriers. He was simply trying to maximize his publishing income. With a similar economic motivation, Phillips tried a different tack; he deliberately sought to filter the black experience through white performers to make it more accessible to the mainstream audience. As Peter Guralnick has noted, "With Elvis, Phillips apparently found the key

Phillips deliberately sought to filter the black experience through white performers, to make it more accessible to the mainstream audience.

because following Elvis' success he had a succession of rockabillies who did just that. All of his major artists were poor whites who had not only lived in constant contact with black people all their lives but had obviously absorbed a great deal of their culture."[55] Phillips's strategy earned

Sun Records a place of mythic proportions in the history of rock 'n' roll, but it also begged questions about rip-offs and racism.

Phillips started the Memphis Recording Service in 1950. For $2 a side, anyone could walk in and make a record. His was the only convenient studio for the Delta bluesmen who played the nearby Beale Street clubs. In the days when out-of-town producers were scouring the South for new talent, Phillips was already recording Howlin' Wolf, B. B. King, Bobby Bland, James Cotton, Little Walter, Little Junior Parker, Elmore James, Walter Horton, and Rufus Thomas, among others. At first, he leased all his masters to Modern and Chess, but after producing notable r&b hits such as Jackie Brenston's "Rocket 88" and Little Walter's "Juke," for Chess and Checker, respectively, Phillips decided in 1952 to launch his own label—Sun Records. The following year, a young truck driver stopped in to cut two songs for his mother's birthday. Four dollars and a little more than a year later, Elvis Presley had changed the face of popular music forever.

Presley also altered the operations of Sun Records profoundly. As Rufus Thomas once said, "When Elvis and Carl Perkins and Johnny Cash come along, just like he catered to black, Phillips cut it off and went to white. No more blacks did he pick up at all."[56] Most of the white artists who gravitated toward Sun had grown up dirt poor and in close proximity to African Americans and their culture. Jerry Lee Lewis explained how he "used to hang around Haney's Big House, that was a colored establishment where they had dances and such. . . . I saw a lot of 'em there, all those blues players."[57] Carl Perkins noted that he was

> raised on a plantation in the flatlands of Lake Country, Tennessee, and we were about the only white people on it. . . . Working in the cotton fields in the sun, music was the only escape. The coloured people would sing, and I'd join in, just a little kid, and that was coloured rhythm and blues, got named rock 'n' roll, got named that in 1956, but the same music was there years before, and it was my music.[58]

Elvis Aron Presley was born in Tupelo, Mississippi, the only child (a twin brother was born dead) of Vernon and Gladys Presley, on 8 January 1935. When he was ten years old, he was placed fifth in a talent contest, singing "Old Shep," a sentimental country tune. He learned to play the guitar a year later. As a teenager in Memphis, where his family had moved, Presley attended Pentecostal church services and, in a more secular vein, was introduced to the Delta bluesmen.

> I'd play along with the radio or phonograph, and taught myself the chord positions. We were a religious family, going round together to sing at camp meetings and revivals, and I'd take my guitar with us when I could. I also dug the real low-down Mississippi singers, mostly Big Bill Broonzy and Big Boy Crudup, although they would scold me at home for listening to them.
> "Sinful music," the townsfolk in Memphis said it was. Which never bothered me, I guess.[59]

It took Phillips more than a year to record Presley commercially. According to one story, Phillips intended to work on sentimental ballads like the ones Presley had cut for his mother. When nothing gelled, Presley and session musicians Scotty Moore (guitar) and Bill Black (bass) started fooling around with Big Boy Crudup's "That's All Right." According to Presley, however, the song was Phillips's suggestion. Either way, that song, backed with Bill Monroe's classic bluegrass tune "Blue Moon of Kentucky," set in motion a chain reaction that ultimately transformed the pop landscape. A dub of the recording was sent to Dewey Phillips (no relation),

By any measure, Elvis Presley—the rock 'n' roller who was crowned king—was a monster talent, albeit one who sometimes applied his considerable gifts to material that was of questionable value. He is pictured in a scene from Jailhouse Rock, *one of his better movies.*

a Memphis deejay, who liked it so much that he played it thirty times in one night. By the time Sun pressed the record, it had orders for 5,000 copies.

From the beginning, Presley presented a marketing dilemma. No one knew exactly what to make of this "hillbilly cat," as he was described by one early billing that managed to capture the tension of his down-home, yet wildly cool persona. "I recall one jockey telling me that Elvis was so country he shouldn't be played after 5 A.M.," said Sam Phillips. "And others said he was too black for them."[60] When Dewey Phillips interviewed Presley on the air, he made it a point to establish that Elvis had attended the all-white Humes High School "because a lot of people listening had thought he was colored."[61] Though Presley's first release combined r&b and c&w (as did all his subsequent Sun releases), he was marketed as country. The record, which was a local hit, appeared only on the Memphis c&w charts.

The professional reaction to Presley's unorthodox style was mixed. After his debut at the *Grand Ole Opry,* he was told to go back to truck driving. He had better luck at the *Louisiana Hayride,* where he became a regular. Invariably, his live performances were electrifying, as country singer Bob Luman recalled.

> *This cat came out in red pants and a green coat and a pink shirt and socks, and had this sneer on his face and he stood behind the mike for five minutes, I'll bet, before he made a move. Then he hit his guitar a lick, and he broke two strings. I'd been playing ten years, and I hadn't broken a total of two strings. So there he was, these two strings dangling, and he hadn't done anything yet, and these high school girls were screaming and fainting and running up to the stage, and then he started to move his hips real slow like he had a thing for his guitar. That was Elvis Presley when he was about 19, playing Kilgore, Texas.*[62]

Presley recorded a total of ten sides for Sun. Each of the five records had an r&b song backed with a c&w song. In their innocence and seeming spontaneity, these recordings helped shape the Presley legend, and in their unique blend of cultural influences, they contributed to the

*I*t was not until the heavy-handed Colonel Tom Parker replaced deejay Bob Neal as Presley's manager in 1955 that his career was transformed into the stuff of myth.

definition of the rockabilly style. Although each record sold better than the one before it, Presley never reached a mass popular music audience through them. It was not until the heavy-handed Colonel Tom Parker replaced deejay Bob Neal as Presley's manager in 1955 that his career was transformed into the stuff of myth.

Parker engineered the sale of Presley's contract to RCA-Victor for the then unheard-of sum of $35,000 plus $5,000 in back royalties, which Presley used to purchase his fabled pink Cadillac. His first RCA release, "Heartbreak Hotel" (1956), with Chet Atkins on guitar and Floyd Cramer on piano, was number one on the pop charts for eight weeks. That same year, "Hound Dog"/"Don't Be Cruel," a double-sided hit, reached number one on the pop charts, the r&b charts, and the c&w charts simultaneously, perhaps the first record ever to do so. From then on, Presley had multiple Top Forty pop hits every year until the day he died. Parker's practice of allowing his star to record only songs with publishing rights assigned to Presley Music (BMI) or Gladys Music (ASCAP) restricted Presley's choice of material in later years but added significantly to his income. "When I first knew Elvis," Parker once said with pride, "he had a million dollars' worth of talent. Now he has a million dollars."[63]

Following television appearances on the shows of Milton Berle, the Dorsey Brothers, and Steve Allen, Presley landed a coveted $50,000 series of slots on *The Ed Sullivan Show*. Anticipating the objections of his family audience, Sullivan had Presley filmed only from the waist up. However, nothing could contain the sex appeal of Elvis the Pelvis, as his detractors called him. Presley used one of his Sullivan appearances to debut the title song from his first film, *Love Me Tender*. The song became a number one pop hit, and the film catapulted Presley to stardom in yet another medium.

Presley recorded some quality material before his 1958–1960 stint in the army. "Hound Dog" writers Leiber and Stoller were brought in to write "Don't" and "Jailhouse Rock," the title song for his third and best movie. Writer Otis Blackwell followed up "Don't Be Cruel" with "All Shook Up" in 1957. In 1958, "One Night" came close to recapturing the excitement of his Sun

*A*t RCA Presley's clear tenor, the stripped-down energy of early rockabilly, and the simplicity and straightforwardness of the Sun sound were overshadowed by vocal swoops from the higher to the lower register, bloated productions (supervised by Chet Atkins), and syrupy background choruses by the Jordanaires

recordings. At RCA, however, Presley's clear tenor, the stripped-down energy of early rockabilly, and the simplicity and straightforwardness of the Sun sound were overshadowed by vocal swoops from the higher to the lower register, bloated productions (supervised by Chet Atkins), and syrupy background choruses by the Jordanaires—encouraging Presley to indulge the pop tendencies that had always been part of his musical aesthetic. The blues and country aura of the Presley myth never adequately captured the range of styles that shaped the singer. The songs he cut for his mother in 1953, "My Happiness" and "That's When Your Heartaches Begin," had been popular hits for the Ink Spots. At the time he made his first commercial recordings, his singing idol was Dean Martin. Following military service, he reentered popular music through a television special with Frank Sinatra. His inclination toward pop conventions was evident in his ardent gushing on "Love Me Tender." It emerged full-blown in a number of releases he made after the army, such as "Are You Lonesome Tonight," written in 1926; "Surrender," adapted from "Come Back to Sorrento"; and reputedly his own favorite, "It's Now or Never," a

"Hound Dog"

Artist: Elvis Presley
Music/Lyrics by Jerry Lieber and Mike Stoller (and possibly Big Mama Thornton)
Label: RCA (1956)

In 1953, Willie Mae "Big Mama" Thornton had a hit on the r&b charts with the song "Hound Dog," delivered with fearsome, gritty conviction by Thornton's huge voice, Johnny Otis's band, and the smoking guitar work of Pete Lewis. The song was written by the well-known r&b songwriters Jerry Lieber and Mike Stoller (although both Otis and Thornton have claimed the actual songwriting credit). Sometime after that, Elvis Presley heard the song performed by a Las Vegas lounge musician named Freddie Bell. It was Bell's version, with its adapted lyrics, that Presley recorded for RCA in 1956 (as the B-side of the single "Don't Be Cruel").

It was common for white musicians to cover an African American musician's r&b hit, often replacing suggestive lyrics with more conservative fare that the major labels deemed more palatable for the white listening audience. (On Elvis's recording, the original lyrics, which were much more interesting and made more sense, are replaced with two verses that he alternates repeatedly throughout the song.) The financial success of white performers' versions of popular r&b tunes also frequently overshadowed the success of the original—an oft-repeated story in the history of American popular music, especially in the 1950s and 1960s. While it was said that Elvis consciously avoided covering r&b tunes that were still "on the charts," he recorded dozens of cover versions. After all, Elvis was not a songwriter, and his fame came from lending his own personal performance style to other people's music. "Hound Dog" was a huge hit for Elvis, staying at number one on the pop charts for eleven weeks in the summer of 1956.

Musical Style Notes

"Hound Dog" is a 12-bar blues song with the stepped-up tempo; slapping bass; and percussive, "twangy" guitar sound characteristic of the rockabilly style associated with Sun Records. However, Elvis had left Sun by the time he recorded "Hound Dog" and was now with RCA. With this change, we hear an important departure from Sun Records' rockabilly sound: the use of the drum set. Sam Phillips's early Sun recordings didn't emphasize drum-set percussion, but now, drummer D. J. Fontana is right up front in the mix, especially in the drum "roll" that you hear in the transition between verses. (You can also hear hand-claps in the background during the sung verses.) Along with bass player Bill Black, the rhythm section provides a great foundation for the famous high-energy guitar solos Scotty Moore created for this track.

Musical "Road Map"

TIMINGS	COMMENTS	LYRICS
0:00–0:17	Verse 1 (12-bar blues form) As in Big Mama Thornton's original, Elvis starts singing a cappella (no instruments); the instruments come in on the downbeat at the words "hound dog." Note hand-claps. Strong, foregrounded drum sound	*You ain't nothing . . .* *You ain't . . .*
0:18–0:33	Verse 2	*When they said . . .*
0:34–0:50	Verse 1 repeats.	*You ain't nothing . . .*
0:50–1:06	Scotty Moore's guitar solo, over the verse form (Note background vocals singing "ah.")	
1:06–1:22	Verse 2 repeats. Hand-claps return.	*When they said . . .*
1:22–1:38	Another Scotty Moore guitar solo over verse form (Return of background vocals singing "ah.")	
1:38–1:54	Verse 2 repeats. Hand-claps return.	*When they said . . .*
1:54–2:09	Verse 1 repeats.	*You ain't nothing . . .*
2:09–2:13	"Tag" (short phrase and final chord)	

pop-oriented, Latin-flavored number, based loosely on "O Sole Mio" by Mario Lanza, Presley's favorite opera star.

HEAR MORE
"Hound Dog" on MyMusicKit

There has never been another career quite like that of Elvis Presley's. He charted 149 Top Forty hits on *Billboard*'s Hot 100 and 92 long-playing records (LPs) on the album charts—all this with some of the most insipid material ever recorded. His soundtrack albums—from some of the worst (though profitable) films imaginable—almost invariably entered the Top Forty. "The fact is, I think, that Elvis was too well suited to success," Peter Guralnick has said. "He was intelligent, adaptable, ambitious, and sure of his goals. . . . He soon settled in fact on a fairly comfortable and formulaic approach that took advantage of his wide-ranging musical background, facility in a number of styles, real talent as a quick study, and almost total lack of taste."[64] He briefly redeemed himself as the quintessential rock 'n' roller in a 1968 television special. "If you're looking for trouble," sneered Elvis into the camera, completely outfitted in black leather and looking his greased-back best, "you've come to the right place." In addition to the obligatory big production numbers, he was joined on stage by old musical friends such as Scotty Moore and drummer D. J. Fontana. In those moments, he recaptured the "young Elvis" pictured on his 1992 memorial postage stamp.[65]

When Sam Phillips sold Presley's contract to RCA—making what, in retrospect, appears to have been a miscalculation of monumental proportions—he thought he had another artist who would be bigger than Elvis. In 1956, Carl Perkins' "Blue Suede Shoes" climbed to number two on the pop charts, making it Sun's best-selling record to date; the number one pop song, tellingly, was "Heartbreak Hotel," Presley's debut release on RCA. "Blue Suede Shoes" is considered a contender as the first rock 'n' roll record because of its cross-over success in all markets.[66] Perkins's early rockabilly recordings, such as "Gone, Gone, Gone," hinted at a fusion of blues and country. "That's what rockabilly music is," he once said, "a country man's song with a black man's rhythm."[67] Just as Perkins was about to take off commercially after the success of "Blue Suede Shoes," he was nearly killed in a car crash. Perkins never entered the Top Forty again, and his career never regained its momentum. Still, his influence on rock 'n' roll is undeniable. In 1964, the Beatles invited him to a session where they recorded three of his songs—"Honey Don't," "Everybody's Trying to Be My Baby," and his adaptation of an old Blind Lemon Jefferson song, "Matchbox."

The uncontrollable Jerry Lee Lewis—inspired by a long line of hard-rocking piano men, including boogie woogie greats on the r&b side and artists like Moon Mullican on the country side—was the rock 'n' roller who did the most to keep Sun in the black. Typical of rockabillies, Lewis grew up poor amid that convoluted southern mixture of music and religion, sin and depravity. Nicknamed the Killer in his adolescence, Lewis had a personal life peppered with debauchery and violence (two of his six wives died under mysterious circumstances). He quit high school after logging a record twenty-nine Fs and was expelled from Bible school. Once forced to take second billing to Chuck Berry, Lewis reportedly closed his set with a frenzied rendition of "Whole Lotta Shakin' Goin' On" as he set fire to the piano. With the crowd boosted to fever pitch, he walked off stage and calmly said to Berry: "Follow *that,* Nigger."[68]

With his boogie-powered "pumping piano," as his instrument was billed, Lewis turned out three Top Ten pop hits in a row for Sun—"Whole Lotta Shakin' Goin' On" (1956), "Great Balls of Fire" (1957), and "Breathless" (1958). "Whole Lotta Shakin'" not only went to number three on the pop charts, it topped the c&w and the r&b charts as well. Shortly after "Breathless," Lewis left his second wife and, without divorcing her, married his thirteen-year-old cousin, Myra, whose father played bass in his band. The press had a field day with Lewis, who was on tour in Great Britain. The remaining concerts were canceled and Lewis returned to a career in shambles. He hit the pop charts three more times but was never again a pop headliner.

Other white southern artists also passed through Sun. Warren Smith recorded the memorable (and racist) "Ubangi Stomp" and "So Long, I'm Gone," a minor pop hit, before his short-lived country career on Liberty. Charlie Rich began as a session musician at Sun and had a pop hit with "Lonely Weekends" in 1960. He became a major country star a decade later. Conway Twitty recorded for Sun under his real name, Harold Jenkins, but none of his recordings were released. Roy Orbison cut a version of "Ooby Dooby" at Sun before switching to Monument. Johnny Cash started at Sun in 1955; after a few country hits (including "Folsom Prison Blues"), his "I Walk the Line" went pop Top Twenty in 1956. Cash switched to Columbia in 1958 and embarked on a career that included gold and platinum albums, films, and even his own television show. Perkins did the same, though less successfully.

The sound Sam Phillips had created—soulful white singers from the grassroots, embellished by tape-delay echo and backed by instrumentation (slap bass, electric guitar, pumping piano) that straddled c&w and r&b perfectly—defined one of the major strands of rock 'n' roll and set the stage for other white rock 'n' rollers who could be marketed as rockabillies. Impressed by RCA's success with Presley, Capitol signed Gene Vincent (Vincent Eugene Craddock) from Norfolk, Virginia. On Vincent's first release, "Be-Bop-A-Lula" (1956), Capitol engineers pumped up his naturally gentle voice with "flutter echo" to achieve "a perverse, gothic performance."[69] Vincent intended the song to be the B-side of the record, but "Woman Love" on the flip side was an "overtly sexual record, full of glottal twitches and orgasmic pantings" that was judged hardly suitable for mainstream airplay.[70] Of nineteen Vincent releases, only two more made the Top Forty in the United States—"Lotta Lovin' " (1957) and "Dance to the Bop" (1958)—but he was revered in Great Britain. Eddie Cochran ("Summertime Blues," 1958), another would-be Elvis, joined Vincent for a British tour in 1960, but he was killed in a car accident on the way to the airport after the tour. Vincent, also injured in the crash, never recovered from the incident.

Buddy Holly was another artist who enjoyed greater success in Great Britain than in the United States. Indeed, some of Holly's hits in Great Britain—"It's So Easy," for example—did not even chart on this side of the Atlantic. One of a number of Texas-born rockabillies to reach the pop audience, Holly was probably positioned better than anyone to follow in Presley's footsteps. After a few missteps on Decca, Holly was released from the label. He returned to his native Lubbock, Texas, formed the Crickets, then headed to Clovis, New Mexico, to record with producer Norman Petty, a collaboration that proved to be worthwhile for all concerned. Their first release, "That'll Be the Day" (1957)—a revved-up, heavily electrified version of a number Holly had cut for Decca—turned out to be their best and most successful recording. At the time, however, it was turned down by Roulette, Atlantic, Columbia, and RCA, before being released on Brunswick where it shot straight to number one and then remained in the Top

> *The sound Sam Phillips had created—soulful white singers from the grassroots, embellished by tape-delay echo and backed by instrumentation (slap bass, electric guitar, pumping piano) that straddled c&w and r&b perfectly—defined one of the major strands of rock 'n' roll.*

The fact that Buddy Holly did not fit the description of a teen idol did not prevent him from becoming a rock 'n' roll legend. He and his group, the Crickets, were regular hit makers on the pop and r&b charts. Interestingly, they never had a country hit.

Forty for sixteen weeks. Ironically, Bob Thiele, a Decca producer, had engineered a contract for the Crickets on Brunswick and a solo deal for Holly on Coral, both Decca subsidiaries, after Holly's relationship with Decca was terminated. Holly and the Crickets recorded fifteen more songs in Petty's studio. "Peggy Sue" backed with "Everyday" (1957), on Coral, was credited only to Buddy Holly. A month later, "Oh Boy!" backed with "Not Fade Away," on Brunswick, was credited to the Crickets. Other Coral releases, credited only to Holly, included "Early in the Morning" (recorded without the Crickets) and "Rave On."

In retrospect, it seems difficult to imagine that anyone could mistake Buddy Holly and the Crickets for a black r&b act. In the 1950s, however, rock 'n' roll was an expression of cultural upheaval that was rife with racial ambiguities. As country as "That'll Be the Day" may sound today, it was an r&b hit in 1957. In fact, Holly was the only major rockabilly act who never had a country hit. Holly and the Crickets were booked, sight unseen, into the Apollo Theater. "I knew his records," recalled singer Leslie Uggams, who saw that performance. "You thought, 'Hey, another brother out there doing his number.' Then this white guy comes out and everybody says, 'Oh, that's Buddy Holly!' . . . You know, here comes this guy with these glasses and funny-looking suit and stuff. I said, 'He's white, isn't he?' But he was terrific."[71] Crossing personal racial barriers as well, Holly married Maria Elena Santiago, a Puerto Rican receptionist at Peer-Southern Music in New York. A new wife and the lure of New York precipitated a split for Holly, the Crickets, and Petty. Holly's last Top Forty hit with the group was "It Doesn't Matter Anymore" (1959), a pop-oriented Paul Anka tune that reached the pop charts one month after Holly's untimely death in 1959.

Holly was not the only Texas rockabilly to make it. Petty had already had a notable rock 'n' roll success with another Texas group, the Rhythm Orchids, for whom he produced "Party Doll" and "I'm Stickin' with You." Roulette Records bought the masters and released the cuts separately as "Party Doll" by Buddy Knox and "I'm Stickin' with You" by Jimmy Bowen with the Rhythm Orchids. "Stickin'" went to number fourteen and "Party Doll" hit number one. Roy Orbison was another Texas rockabilly who first recorded in Petty's studio, then quickly moved to Sun, RCA, and finally to Monument, where he made his biggest hits. "Only the Lonely" (1960), his first Top Ten pop hit, featured a heart-wrenching vocal in a call-and-response style with a hint of Latin flavor; it embodied the diverse cultural influences of rock 'n' roll in classic style. Orbison's amazing vocal range and crystal-clear upper register lent a distinctive sound to the releases that followed—"Blue Angel" (1960), "Running Scared" and "Crying" (1961), and "Dream Baby" (1962). Perhaps because of his unique vocal talents, Orbison was among the few rockabilly artists to ride out the British Invasion. His biggest hit, "Oh, Pretty Woman" (1964), became number one at a time when the U.S. pop charts were dominated by the Beatles and a host of other British groups.

Somewhat outside the Sun orbit, but well within the boundaries of rockabilly, were the Everly Brothers among the most successful of the country-influenced rock 'n' rollers. Their close harmonies were characteristic of country music, but their syncopated guitar riffs, positioned as instrumental responses to their vocal leads, suggested possible African American influences. In the early 1950s, brothers Don and Phil went to Nashville to sing and write songs for Acuff-Rose. When "Bye Bye Love" (1957) went to number two on the pop charts, they gave Nashville a new profile in rock 'n' roll and launched a career that included twenty-six Top Forty pop hits, including four that went to number one: "Wake Up Little Susie" (1957), "All I Have to Do Is Dream" and "Bird Dog" (1958), and "Cathy's Clown" (1960).

The appeal of country-influenced rock 'n' roll enabled a number of major label country acts to experience success in the pop market. Columbia's Guy Mitchell recorded "Singing the Blues" (1956) and "Heartaches by the Number" (1959), which both went to number one; his "Rock-A-Billy" (1957) hit the Top Ten. Marty Robbins, also with Columbia, broke the Top Three three times with "A White Sport Coat (and a Pink Carnation)" (1957), "El Paso" (1959), and "Don't Worry" (1961). Capitol had Sonny James ("Young Love"), Tommy Sands ("Teen-Age Crush"), and Ferlin Husky ("Gone"), all of whom had their biggest hits in 1957. Patsy Cline ("Walking After Midnight," "I Fall to Pieces," "Crazy"), signed by Decca, was a straight country artist who crossed over to the pop market on the heels of country rock. Conway Twitty on MGM made the Top Ten three times with "It's Only Make Believe" (1958), "Danny Boy" (1959), and "Lonely Blue Boy" (1960). Don Gibson hit the Top Ten with "Oh, Lonesome Me" for RCA in 1958.

Rockabilly was no kinder to women than was the rest of rock 'n' roll, and it wasn't because women couldn't sing rockabilly. Charlene Arthur and Janis Martin (the Female Elvis) on RCA, Rose Maddox on Capitol, and Barbara Pittman and Jean Chapel (a.k.a. Mattie O'neill) on Sun could deliver the goods, but a lack of interest in these artists, a dearth of good material, weak promotion, and/or outright male hostility kept them from the attention of the mainstream public.[72] Except for Capitol's hard-rocking Wanda Jackson, who edged into the Top Forty three times beginning with "Let's Have a Party" (1960), only one other nationally successful woman could be included in a discussion of rockabilly—the diminutive Brenda Mae Tarpley (a.k.a. Brenda Lee). Signed by Decca at eleven, she turned out twenty-nine Top Forty hits between 1960 and 1967, including the suggestive "Sweet Nothin's" and two number one ballads, "I'm Sorry" and "I Want to Be Wanted." Like Orbison, she rode out the British onslaught with dignity (and hits), then returned to more traditional country roots for the remainder of her career.

> **R**ockabilly was no kinder to women than was the rest of rock 'n' roll, and it wasn't because women couldn't sing rockabilly. A lack of interest in these artists, a dearth of good material, weak promotion, and/or outright male hostility kept them from the attention of the mainstream public.

The energy of early rock 'n' roll had crossed lines of age, class, race, and culture in a country that seldom takes kindly to social upheaval and certainly didn't during the conservative 1950s. The music was ubiquitous, issuing from every region in the country. As soon as rock 'n' roll captured the hearts, minds, and bodies of teenagers across all demographics, some people linked it with every perceived social ill from juvenile delinquency and miscegenation to atheism and communism.

LEARN MORE

Chapter Test on
MyMusicKit

Asa Carter, executive secretary of the Alabama White Citizens Council, put the threat into stark words when he said in 1956, "[T]he obscenity and vulgarity of the rock 'n' roll music is obviously a means by which the white man and his children can be driven to the level with a 'nigra'. . . . If we choose to call it the Communist ideology, I think we hit it fairly on the head."[73] While Carter's position was extreme, rhetoric like this pushed all the emotional buttons of white middle-class parents concerned about the new sound. If some variant of rock 'n' roll was "here to stay," as Danny and the Juniors had prophesied in 1958, nowhere was it written that social pressures could not alter its character.

Sam Phillips may have been the first rock 'n' roll producer to look for "a white man with the Negro sound," but he was not the only one. Ace Records tried with Frankie Ford and Atlantic with Bobby Darin. To their credit, these artists had at least some musical connection to the styles they interpreted. Unfortunately, the same cannot be said of the next generation of white rockers, who mustered little more than boy-next-door good looks and a feeble Elvis sneer. They had few, if any, identifiable links to previous rock 'n' roll styles, but youthful attractiveness and some semblance of rhythm enabled them to be successfully marketed as rock 'n' roll singers. Such a musical development, though possibly inevitable, served the purposes of those who were terrified by the cultural implications of rock 'n' roll. The rock 'n' roll facelift of the late 1950s, as we shall see, was but the most visible manifestation of a much broader reaction to the music.

The Empire Strikes Back: The Reaction to Rock 'n' Roll

By the late 1950s, rock 'n' roll had changed the popular music landscape irrevocably and, in so doing, was signaling the coming of still broader social change. The prospect of such change precipitated unbridled enthusiasm and vicious backlash in equal proportions. Economically, the music had enhanced the fortunes of what seemed, to some, to be untutored writers and artists, upstart independent record companies, and wildly eccentric deejays. In essence, rock 'n' roll had turned the structure of the music business on its head. Aesthetically, it had encouraged a tilt toward African American sensibilities and working-class styles. Thus, to some, it challenged the existing canons of cultural value and public taste. Socially, the music had threatened to upset the separation of races and classes that had guided not just the operations of the music industry but the dynamics of all social interaction to date. Depending on how one felt about these issues, rock 'n' roll was either celebrated as a true democratization of culture or decried as the destruction of Western civilization.

LEARN MORE
Learning Objectives
on MyMusicKit

Given its impact and the conservative political climate in which it developed, it is not terribly surprising that rock 'n' roll became a target for repression. As surely as the 1950s are remembered musically as the decade of rock 'n' roll, they are remembered politically as the Eisenhower era. Two, more diametrically opposed images would be hard to find. General, and then President, Dwight D. Eisenhower was as old-fashioned, conventional, bland, polite, and conserva-

Eisenhower was as old-fashioned, conventional, bland, polite, and conservative as rock 'n' roll was youthful, innovative, wild, intrusive, and rebellious.

tive as rock 'n' roll was youthful, innovative, wild, intrusive, and rebellious. Eisenhower became president in 1953 while U.S. troops were fighting communists in Korea and while Senator Joe McCarthy was feverishly inventing them at home. Eisenhower's vice president, Richard M. Nixon, began pushing to contain communism in Vietnam, eventually precipitating cataclysmic political reverberations in the United States and around the world in the next decade.

As if culture could be similarly contained, the following middle-of-the-road releases appeared in *Billboard* as the ten best-selling records for 1953, the year Eisenhower took office:

1. Song from Moulin Rouge—Percy Faith
2. Vaya Con Dios—Les Paul and Mary Ford
3. Doggie in the Window—Patti Page
4. I'm Walking Behind You—Eddie Fisher
5. You, You, You—Ames Brothers
6. Till I Waltz Again with You—Teresa Brewer
7. April in Portugal—Les Baxter
8. No Other Love—Perry Como
9. Don't Let the Stars Get in Your Eyes—Perry Como
10. I Believe—Frankie Laine

((•• **HEAR MORE**

Audio links for this 1953 Top Ten List on MyMusicKit

Uninspiring political leaders and insipid popular music ran in tandem with another aspect of U.S. life in the 1950s—mind-numbing conformity. Battle-weary veterans, seeking to forget the ravages of war, sought peace, quiet, and prosperity in a new place—suburbia. Entrance to this tranquil environment did not come without a price. The white middle-class men of David Reisman's "lonely crowd" commuted to work daily, where they became "organization men," mere cogs in the machine of the expanding U.S. economy; their wives stayed at home, even lonelier and more isolated. Teens had to endure the regimentation of school. In its essential features—compartmentalization of knowledge, passive reception of information, pressure to achieve, competition for grades, and regulation of behavior—school was preparation for work.

Unfortunately, rigidity and conformity, so desirable in the workplace, conflicted sharply with the demands of the new consumer economy. The successful conversion to a peacetime economy depended in large part on creating an increased demand for consumer items. The single most important strategy in this effort was (and remains) the pleasure principle: If it makes you feel good, buy it. The most obvious application of this principle was the use of sexuality to sell products. Thus, a contradiction existed: The traits encouraged in the Protestant work ethic—discipline, frugality, asceticism, and abstinence—are best represented in a rather rigid, authoritarian, and sexually repressed personality. The ideal consumer, on the other hand, is an impulsive hedonist, given to boundless extravagance and instant gratification—that is to say, sexually more liberated. For teenagers in the 1950s, this tension was experienced as a conflict between the official values of school, family, and church and the reality of their leisure-time activities.[1]

Postwar prosperity made teenagers an identifiable consumer group, and manufacturers began to produce products specifically for a youth market. Buying rock 'n' roll records, for example, prepared teens to be good consumers, and the music has been used effectively to sell other products. At the same time, full entrance into adulthood and financial independence was delayed as more and more teenagers completed high school and college. As teens sought escape from school and parents, leisure became their alternative world and rock 'n' roll its major port of entry. For many adults, however, the message of "rocking around the clock," not to mention rocking and rolling "all night long" in "sixty minute" intervals, undermined the values of work, a necessary condition for consumption. Indeed, rock 'n' roll represented everything that white, middle-class parents feared: It was urban, it was sexual, and most of it was black. As a result, this music was frequently denounced by adults as the "devil's music," as a National Association for the Advancement of Colored People (NAACP) strategy for recruiting young whites, or as a communist plot to undermine the moral fiber of the younger generation.

The Established Powers Fight Back

The fortunes of the music industry as a whole nearly tripled during the vintage rock 'n' roll years: Revenues from record sales climbed from $213 million in 1954 to $603 million in 1959. The question is: How much of this expansion can be attributed to rock 'n' roll?

While market-share data broken out by musical style is difficult to come by, Charlie Gillett has offered some indication of relative proportions. In 1955, of the fifty-one records to make the pop Top Ten, only eight were rock 'n' roll—or 15.7 percent. In contrast, in 1959, thirty-eight of the eighty-nine Top Ten records were rock 'n' roll—42.7 percent. In this same five-year span, Top Ten pop hits by major record companies *decreased* from forty to thirty, while those by independent companies *increased* from eleven to fifty-nine. In other words, in that time period, independent record companies went from a 21.6 percent share of the pop market to a 66.3 percent share of a pop market that had grown roughly three times larger.[2]

The major labels had only themselves to blame for this situation. In the late 1940s and early 1950s, when countless independent labels sprang up to cash in on the growing demand for rhythm and blues (r&b), ideological blinders prevented the mainstream music industry from operating in its own economic self-interest. After it was clear that rock 'n' roll was here to stay, the industry giants responded with strategies that ranged from ostrich-like stances to some talent buying, to the widespread practice of cover records (making new versions of original releases), to promoting alternative styles of music. When these efforts failed, the established industry powers—artists, labels, and (most prominently) the American Society of Composers, Authors, and Publishers (ASCAP)—joined forces with the U.S. government to suppress the music in a campaign that Russell Sanjek has labeled the "War on Rock."[3]

In the late 1940s and early 1950s, when countless independent labels sprang up to cash in on the growing demand for rhythm and blues (r&b), ideological blinders prevented the mainstream music industry from operating in its own economic self-interest.

Given Columbia's historical connection to African American music (its vaults contained some of the best recordings of Bessie Smith, Robert Johnson, Louis Armstrong, Fletcher Henderson, Duke Ellington, and Count Basie), the label's comparatively lukewarm response to rock 'n' roll is somewhat surprising (although the label did sign Johnny Cash and Carl Perkins in 1958). Mitch Miller, Columbia's artist and repertoire chief, reportedly despised rock 'n' roll personally but, to his credit, he never joined the chorus of industry malcontents who publicly denounced it. At one point in 1955, he defended the crossover of rhythm and blues in the *New York Times* as part of "a steady—and healthy—breaking down of color barriers."[4] At Columbia, he devoted his time and energy to perfecting the pop production techniques used with artists like Frankie Laine, Jo Stafford, Rosemary Clooney, and Doris Day. These techniques had made Columbia the most successful label in the country.[5]

Early in the 1950s, the emotionally unhinged Johnny Ray could have provided Columbia with a way into rock 'n' roll. Following the phenomenal success of his heart-wrenching, tear-jerking, shirt-ripping performance of "Cry"—number one on the pop charts for eleven weeks—Ray was switched from the OKeh subsidiary to the parent Columbia label. However, after ASCAP had Ray's successful cover of the Drifters' "Such a Night" banned from the airwaves in 1954 for sexual suggestiveness, Columbia may have thought that a deeper commitment to the performer would be more trouble than it was worth. Still, he turned out a few more hits before his career ran out of steam. Except for a brief and inexplicable flirtation with the outrageous Screamin' Jay Hawkins ("I Put a Spell on You," 1956) on OKeh, the closest Columbia came to rock 'n' roll prior to 1958 was the silken balladry of Johnny Mathis ("It's Not for Me to Say," "Chances Are," "The Twelfth of Never"). With decidedly pop material, the African American baritone was young enough and hip enough to appeal to the rock 'n' roll audience.

At the Radio Corporation of America (RCA), Hugo Winterhalter was no better than Miller at producing rock 'n' roll, and artists like Vaughn Monroe, Dinah Shore, and Eddie Fisher were certainly no better at performing it than Columbia's artists.[6] However, in the Sarnoff tradition of covering all bases, RCA's strategy for dealing with the new sound was simply to buy the most promising rock 'n' roll star it could—Elvis Presley. It was the smartest move the company ever made. Presley carried the faltering record division for years. Impressed by RCA's success, other major labels searched for the "new Elvis." Capitol found Gene Vincent. Conway Twitty landed at Metro-Goldwyn-Mayer (MGM), where his country background enabled him to create that delicate balance of country and pop that found acceptance as rock 'n' roll. His biggest hit, "It's Only Make Believe," "was one of the many records of 1958 that succeeded in absorbing elements of rock 'n' roll into the tradition of melodramatic ballads that popular music arrangers enjoyed working with."[7]

It is not surprising that MGM turned to Twitty. The major labels often gravitated toward pop-oriented, country-influenced singers and material on their first forays into rock 'n' roll territory. This was a music to which they still had some connection and, given the racial fears that rock 'n' roll conjured up, it was probably considered a safer move. Decca had set the example by signing Bill Haley in 1953, eighteen months ahead of the other major labels, but it failed to replicate the pattern when it turned down Buddy Holly and the Crickets in 1957. As noted in Chapter 4, however, Holly and company were signed to two of Decca's subsidiaries, Coral and Brunswick. Coral, founded in 1949 as an r&b label, was, ironically, one of the labels in the early 1950s that issued cover records in a systematic attempt to blunt the crossover appeal of early rock 'n' roll.

Covering the Bases

There was nothing new about recording multiple versions of a song by various artists in different styles. What was new in the 1950s was using this strategy to sanitize a particular style of music. In the vast majority of (though not all) cases, black artists recording for independent labels were covered by white artists on major labels.[8] Cover records were often released during the expected chart life of the original and, because of the superior distribution channels and promotional powers of the majors, frequently outsold the original. They altered stylistic elements and often doctored lyrics. Bill Haley's 1954 cover of Joe Turner's "Shake, Rattle, and Roll," for example, cleaned up the original version by replacing sexual phrases with fashion statements and moving the action from the bedroom to the kitchen.

The practice began in earnest in 1953 when June Valli recorded "Crying in the Chapel" for RCA. At its release, three other versions of the song—two country and one r&b—were also out. The r&b release by Sonny Til and the Orioles had crossed over to the pop market and was enjoying considerable success until it was eclipsed by the Valli cover, which became one of the best-selling records of the year. RCA scored another coup with Perry Como's cover of "Ko Ko Mo," a lively novelty song originally recorded by Gene and Eunice for Combo in 1954, then rerecorded by the same group for Aladdin. This rerecording became an r&b hit. Rare for the time, it was covered by two independent labels using black acts—Parrot, with the Flamingos, and Modern, with Marvin and Johnny. Their efforts were thwarted when three major labels also covered the song. Columbia used Tony Bennett, and Mercury had a hit with the Crew Cuts' version, but RCA's release by Perry Como became the most popular.

Of the major companies, Decca and Mercury had the best luck with covers. Bill Haley's "Shake, Rattle, and Roll" cover for Decca became the artist's first gold record. Theresa Brewer and the McGuire Sisters, on Decca's Coral subsidiary, also made successful cover records. Brewer's 1956 cover of Fats Domino's "Bo Weevil" went to number seventeen; Domino's original reached only thirty-five. The McGuire Sisters' cover of "Sincerely" by the Moonglows hit number one on the pop charts and became the seventh best-selling pop single of 1955.

Mercury used Georgia Gibbs to cover Etta James's "Wallflower" (a.k.a. "Roll with Me, Henry") with a cleaned-up version, "Dance with Me, Henry." James's version sold 400,000 copies for Modern, but the Gibbs cover hit the 1 million mark. This was only the beginning for Mercury, which cashed in with two Canadian groups, the Diamonds and the Crew Cuts. The Crew Cuts systematically pillaged the r&b charts after their cover of the Chords' "Sh'Boom" (originally on Atlantic's Cat label) became the fifth best-selling song of 1954. In addition to "Ko Ko Mo," the group covered the Penguins' "Earth Angel" (Dootone), Nappy Brown's "Don't Be Angry" (Savoy), and the Charms' "Gum Drop" (De Luxe). Between 1956 and 1961, the Diamonds had hits with covers of Frankie Lymon and the Teenagers' "Why Do Fools Fall in Love," the Gladiolas' "Little Darlin'," the G-Clef's "Ka-Ding-Dong," and the Danleers' "One Summer Night."

The label that really worked the cover market was Dot Records, launched by Randy Wood in Gallatin, Tennessee, in 1951.[9] Two of Dot's female acts were quite successful covering a wide variety of rock 'n' roll. The Fontane Sisters recorded "Seventeen" by Boyd Bennett and the Rockets, "Eddie My Love" by the Teen Queens, and "I'm in Love Again" by Fats Domino. They also hit pop number one with "Hearts of Stone," outselling a version by the Charms (who had covered the original by the Jewels). Gale Storm had Top Ten hits with Frankie Lymon and the Teenagers' "Why Do Fools Fall in Love," Smiley Lewis's "I Hear You Knocking," and the Charms' "Ivory Tower," among others. The company also had on its roster the singer who most often serves as the whipping boy for cultural theft—Pat Boone.

HEAR MORE

Pat Boone on
MyMusicKit

Pat Boone has been the lightning rod for criticism about covering other artists, not because he did it more than anyone else but because he seemed to be more out of his element than most. His antiseptic versions of Little Richard's "Tutti Frutti" and "Long Tall Sally" alone would be enough to make the point. For many, the white buck shoes that became his signature only reinforced the racist implications of his white-bread delivery. Boone's cover of Fats Domino's "Ain't That a Shame" (1955) became his first number one pop single; his second number one single, though not strictly speaking a cover record, was "I Almost Lost My Mind" (1956), originally recorded years earlier by Ivory Joe Hunter. He also cleaned up the El Dorados' "At My Front Door" and the Flamingos' "I'll Be Home." Once he was firmly established in the rock 'n' roll market, Boone segued into mainstream pop balladry ("Love Letters in the Sand," "April Love," and "Moody River") and scored thirty-eight Top Forty hits. He was rewarded in 1957 with his own television show. That Pat Boone built his career on early rock 'n' roll is indisputable; that he did so more successfully than anyone except Elvis continues to gall his detractors. To be fair, however, a comparison of "Love Letters in the Sand" with Presley's "Love Me Tender" would yield very few stylistic differences. In the end, we are left to ponder why some of Boone's recordings, including "Love Letters in the Sand," sold to black buyers and why some of his covers remain better known than the originals.

All record companies act in contradictory ways that are as likely to involve idiosyncratic choices and dumb luck as carefully crafted business plans or scientific market analyses.

All record companies act in contradictory ways that are as likely to involve idiosyncratic choices and dumb luck as carefully crafted business plans or scientific market analyses. The appearance of Haley on Decca and Presley on RCA, let alone Lloyd Price on ABC-Paramount, certainly complicates the mythology of major record companies as defenders of the musical status quo and independents as selfless promoters of grassroots music. Given Columbia's aversion to rock 'n' roll, why did it take a chance on Screamin' Jay Hawkins, whose stage act included rising from a burning coffin in full voodoo regalia? Capitol nurtured an equally outrageous performer named Esquerita. Toward the end of the 1950s, MGM signed two black rock 'n' roll acts—the Impalas ("Sorry [I Ran All the Way Home]," 1959) and Jimmy Jones ("Handy Man" and "Good Timin'," 1960)—to its Cub subsidiary. These are not the acts of companies that are trying to hold the cultural line. By the same token, few, if any, independents entered the business solely for artistic reasons; they had a progressive impact because they were smart enough and flexible enough to respond to a consumer demand that would have required a considerable shift in orientation for the majors. Even Dot, the most systematic purveyor of cover records, was sufficiently attuned to the music to sign the Dell-Vikings, whose "Come Go with Me" and "Whispering Bells" (1957) are regarded as vocal harmony classics. In any case, as teenagers became more adept at distinguishing originals from covers, covers became less valuable to the majors as a strategy for dealing with rock 'n' roll.

Pat Boone has served as the lightning rod for all the race-related criticism associated with the practice of cover records. This dimension of his questionable contribution to rock 'n' roll has prevented him from being inducted into the Rock 'n' Roll Hall of Fame.

"Tutti Frutti"

Artist: Pat Boone
Music/Lyrics by Little Richard
(and Dorothy La Bostrie)
Label: Dot (1956)

Musical Style Notes

Boone's smooth, mellifluous vocal style was part of his great appeal and owes more to pop crooners Bing Crosby or Perry Como than to Little Richard or Fats Domino. In terms of musical structure, tempo, and length, Boone's cover of "Tutti Frutti" is almost an exact copy of Little Richard's, but the vocal style and the clearly enunciated lyrics are utterly different from Richard's growling, high-tenor, powerhouse style.

Some of the lyrics have been changed here (even though Little Richard's had already been "cleaned up" for his recording). Richard's "She rocks to the east, she rocks to the west" was changed to "I've been to the east, I've been to the west."

One curious departure from the original comes at the end. Whereas Little Richard's version ends with Richard singing the "wop-bop-a-loo-mop" line by himself, the sax has the last word on Boone's version, punctuating the last line with one final note at the end.

Musical "Road Map"

TIMINGS	COMMENTS	LYRICS
0:00–0:02	Begins directly with a stop-time chord hit by the band and Boone singing the famous nonsense-syllable refrain.	A-wop-bop-a-loo-mop . . .
0:02–0:18	Refrain (12-bar blues—last 2 measures wop bop)	Tutti . . .
0:18–0:33	Verse 2 (12-bar blues form—last 4 measures stop-time)	Sue . . .
0:33–0:49	Refrain (12-bar blues—last 2 measures wop bop)	Tutti . . .
0:49–1:04	Verse 1 (12-bar blues form—last 4 measures stop-time)	Daisy . . .
1:04–1:19	Refrain (12-bar blues—last 2 measures wop bop)	Tutti frutti . . .
1:19–1:34	Sax solo over the 12-bar blues form of a verse	
1:35–1:50	Refrain (12-bar blues—last 2 measures wop bop)	Tutti . . .
1:50–2:06	Verse 2 (again, 12-bar blues form—last 4 measures stop-time)	
2:06–2:22	Refrain (12-bar blues—last 2 measures wop bop) Note the one solitary sax note right at the end!	

Pop Diversions: From Kingston Town to the Kingston Trio

The majors could rely on their catalogues or subsidies from other corporate divisions to carry them through a slump or a craze they thought faddish like rock 'n' roll. For a brief time, it appeared as though they might have other strategies for dealing with the new music market. Chief among these was an attempt to divert popular tastes away from rock 'n' roll by promoting calypso and popularized folk music from the top down.

Beginning in late 1956, RCA and Columbia began promoting U.S. interpretations of calypso. As Gillett has pointed out, this strategy had a certain logic.

> *Given the way major record companies seemed to think and operate, calypso no doubt seemed to them a logical and clever answer to the dilemma of needing to divert their audience's attention from a product that the independent companies were best able to supply. Calypso was a black people's music, as jazz and rhythm and blues before it had been. Further, it had a Latin beat, which had always seemed to fit nicely into North American popular music. . . . Best of all, there were enough novelty songs in calypso with no sensual implications for the companies to escape having to deal with the disturbing content of rhythm and blues.* [10]

Had Trinidadian calypsonians like Lord Kitchener and the Mighty Sparrow been able to achieve mainstream success in the United States, the major labels might well have found they had a tiger by the tail. In its original Trinidadian form, calypso had long been a highly politicized music based on topical social commentary and often lewd depictions of male–female relations. As it happened, the task of representing West Indian culture fell primarily to New York born Harry Belafonte. The multitalented Belafonte started his singing career as a straight pop vocalist for Jubilee in 1949. In 1955, he was signed by RCA as a folk singer, recording material like "Scarlet Ribbons" and "Shenandoah." In 1956, he made the transition to what passed for calypso in the United States with the long-playing record (LP) *Calypso,* the first million-selling LP by a solo artist, which charted for eighty-four weeks and was firmly ensconced at number one for thirty-one of them. This was an unprecedented chart run. Two hit singles from the album, "Jamaica Farewell" and "Banana Boat" (a.k.a. "Day-O"), established the tone and content of U.S. calypso: The sexual innuendo and pointed social commentary of Caribbean calypso was discarded and the novelty

Beginning his career as a straight pop vocalist, it fell to Harry Belafonte to interpret a depoliticized version of Trinidadian calypso for the U.S. audience. Never one to be a pawn of the music industry, he soon took his considerable talent and progressive political views to the world stage, where he continues to champion humanitarian causes.

value of the sound was emphasized. The result was well-crafted pop arrangements with a Latin rhythmic flavor. In retrospect, such apolitical pop calypso appears to be an ironic career choice for Belafonte, a leading civil rights activist and outspoken critic of injustice.

There were a few other so-called calypso hits such as the Tarriers' "The Banana Boat Song" (1956) and Terry Gilkyson and the Easy Riders' "Marianne" (1957). As it turned out, however, U.S. calypso, not rock 'n' roll, was the fad. Within two years, the sound had segued into popular folk music. When the Kingston Trio unleashed their repertoire of popular folk sounds, the music industry realized the potential power of such material. The Kingston Trio came up through the San Francisco folk scene but managed to avoid the left-wing taint that had haunted most folk artists since the McCarthy era. Perhaps their clean-cut image, brightly colored matching shirts, and upscale college humor made it difficult to think of them as politically subversive. No other folk artists had ever matched their success. Signed to Capitol in 1957, they released eighteen albums that made the Top Twenty, a number of these charting for a year or more; five hit the number one spot. Some of their LPs generated hit pop singles. "Tom Dooley," for example, went to number one, which was almost unheard of for folk material.

Soon other, largely forgettable, folk-oriented groups, including the Limeliters, the Highwaymen, and the Journeymen, tried their hand at the pop market. Columbia had moderate success with the Brothers Four ("Greenfields," 1960). During this period, college campuses became fertile grounds for talent scouts (and political activists). By the time the folk revival of the 1960s got into full swing, it was a bottom-up phenomenon with another roster of talent, and it was allied with the burgeoning civil rights movement. This time the music industry really did have a tiger by the tail.

With coordinated preppy attire and college-oriented humor, the Kingston Trio swept the country with a pop folk repertoire that only hinted at the power of the folk revival yet to come.

"Schlock Rock": Enter the White Middle Class

By the late 1950s, the initial rush of rock 'n' roll excitement was over. The music by then had been sufficiently absorbed into the collective unconscious that singers, songwriters, and producers with no particular feel for the music's roots or subtleties could still turn out commercially viable approximations. This new reality brought forth a new generation of white, middle-class teen idols—Fabian, Frankie Avalon, Bobby Rydell, and others—whose roots barely scratched the surface of pop. Along with many others, they ushered in a style of music my colleague Steve Chapple and I have referred to elsewhere as "schlock rock."[11]

In the rise of schlock rock, little separated the majors from the independents save for market superiority. For every Tommy Sands ("Teen-Age Crush"), Connie Francis ("Who's Sorry Now"), and Sonny James ("Young Love") who recorded for a major label, there was a Charlie Gracie ("Butterfly"), Annette ("Tall Paul"), and Tab Hunter ("Young Love") who recorded for an independent. Warner and Colpix, new Hollywood-related labels, contributed Connie Stevens ("Sixteen Reasons") and James Darren ("Goodbye Cruel World"), respectively. Whatever higher morality or artistic integrity might have been attributed to the independents in the early days of rock 'n' roll had given way to a singular commercial pop orientation.

The major hub for this commercial activity was Philadelphia, home of three pivotal independent labels—Chancellor, Cameo/Parkway, and Swan. These three labels transformed local teenage singers into archetypal teen idols. Chancellor offered Fabian and Frankie Avalon; Cameo had Bobby Rydell; and Swan signed Freddy Cannon (from Lynn, Massachusetts, but contractually and aesthetically Philadelphian). "The focus in Philadelphia in particular was on image," Gillett has noted. "The unsophisticated white southern singers, and the unfashionable black ones, were supplanted by kids who could be the boy-next-door, whose visual appeal was more important than their musical ability."[12]

In this regard, Chancellor led the pack. According to critic Ed Ward, co-owner Bob Marcucci told *Billboard* in the late 1950s:

> *We now run a school where we indoctrinate artists into show business. We may sign them and spend three months schooling them before they cut their first record. We teach them how to walk, how to talk, and how to act onstage when they're performing. We worked with Frankie Avalon for three months before making "Dede Dinah."*
>
> *It was Frankie who introduced me to Fabian, a sixteen-year-old high school kid who likes to play football. Somehow I sensed that here was a kid who could go. He looks a little bit like both Presley and Ricky Nelson. I figured he was a natural. It's true that he couldn't sing. He knew it and I knew it.[13]*

Frankie Avalon was one of a number of teen idols who turned boy-next-door good looks and a modicum of talent into a full-fledged rock 'n' roll career.

By the time the rest of the world found out, however, Fabian had racked up eight Top Forty hits. In a few short years, rock 'n' roll had degenerated from Sam Phillips's dream of a white man who could sing black to a white high-school kid who couldn't sing at all.

"Showing a perverse wish to return to the standards of pre–rock 'n' roll days," Gillett has written, "the operators of the new independents scoured the same streets that had spawned the crooners who had been the core of major company rosters."[14] They, like the majors, assembled a roster of vocalists who were, for the most part, pale imitations of the pop mainstays of the late 1940s and early 1950s. Once again, they were predominantly of Italian descent—Fabian (Fabiano Forte), Frankie Avalon (Francis Avalone), Bobby Rydell (Robert Ridarelli), Freddy Cannon (Frederick Picariello), Bobby Darin (Walden Robert Cassotto), Annette (Funicello), Connie Francis (Concetta Franconero), James Darren (James Ercolani), and Connie Stevens (Concetta Ingolia). Perhaps this is not surprising because entertainment and sports (as black artists and athletes knew only too well) have often offered "ethnic Americans" their most promising avenues for upward mobility. Still, it is noteworthy that all of these performers felt compelled to anglicize their names.

As in the 1940s, there was an obvious, if narrow, connection between Italian American cultural tendencies and pop/rock crooning. Connie Francis toted up thirty-five Top Forty singles for MGM, but her two albums of *Italian Favorites* far outdistanced her two *Greatest Hits* LPs. One of Bobby Rydell's best-selling singles was "Volare" (1960). Rydell, discovered at the age of nine by bandleader Paul Whiteman, also hit pay dirt with "That Old Black Magic" (1961), a Johnny Mercer/Harold Arlen tune from the 1940s. Bobby Darin can also be included here because when he changed his singing style to record Kurt Weill's "Mack the Knife" (1959), his first number one single, he was aspiring to be the next Frank Sinatra, not the next Elvis Presley. Still, Darin is in something of a class by himself, as the first white artist signed to Atlantic subsidiary Atco in 1957, which had been promoting black artists exclusively. Two of his earliest releases, "Splish Splash" and "Queen of the Hop," hit the Top Ten on both the pop and r&b charts in 1958.

The new pop orientation in rock 'n' roll could not be reduced to a particular ethnic affiliation. By the 1960s, a second generation of heartthrobs and teen queens across white ethnic lines with varying degrees of talent had come to the fore. Del Shannon ("Runaway," "Hats Off to Larry") evidenced musical roots in the country sound of Hank Williams. Gene Pitney delivered some powerful, if pop-oriented, vocals on hits such as "(The Man Who Shot) Liberty Valence," "Only Love Can Break a Heart," and "It Hurts to Be in Love." He also distinguished himself as a writer of considerable note, penning classics such as "Hello Mary Lou" for Ricky Nelson and "He's a Rebel" for the Crystals. Paul Anka and Neil Sedaka, also in this group, achieved success as songwriters for other artists in the 1960s. Leslie Gore is positioned here, although she recorded one of the first feminist songs, "You Don't Own Me" (1963).

Schlock Rock's Greatest Hits, Volume I

Paul Anka "Diana," "You Are My Destiny," "Lonely Boy," "Put Your Head on My Shoulder," "Puppy Love"

Frankie Avalon "Dede Dinah," "Ginger Bread," "Venus," "Bobby Sox to Stockings"

Annette "Tall Paul," "O Dio Mio"

Fabian "Turn Me Loose," "Tiger," "Hound Dog Man"

Bobby Rydell "We Got Love," "Wild One," "Swinging School"

Connie Francis "Who's Sorry Now," "My Happiness," "Lipstick on Your Collar," "Everybody's Somebody's Fool"

Freddy Cannon "Tallahassee Lassie," "Way Down Yonder in New Orleans," "Palisades Park"

Neil Sedaka "Oh! Carol," "Stairway to Heaven," "Calendar Girl," "Happy Birthday Sweet Sixteen," "Breaking Up Is Hard to Do"

((• HEAR MORE Audio links on MyMusicKit

In the end, an oversupply of artists, both male and female, contributed to what I would call "Schlock Rock's Greatest Hits, Volumes I and II" (see the boxes). Individual differences and notable exceptions aside, the overwhelming social function of these artists as a group was to put a bland, white, middle-class face on rock 'n' roll. Gradually, but decisively, strong regional accents gave way to neutral, unlocalized voices. Raucous improvised riffs and solos on sax, guitar, or piano were overtaken by lavish strings and orchestral arrangements. The sexual double entendre was replaced by a highly romanticized vision of teenage love and/or angst.

> **G**radually, but decisively, strong regional accents gave way to neutral, unlocalized voices. Raucous improvised riffs and solos on sax, guitar, or piano were overtaken by lavish strings and orchestral arrangements. The sexual double entendre was replaced by a highly romanticized vision of teenage love and/or angst.

While the second generation of schlock was overwhelmingly white, one black superstar emerged—Chubby Checker. His recording of "The Twist" launched the first of a series of dance crazes that swept the country in the early 1960s. The funkier, original version by Hank Ballard and the Midnighters had sold extremely well in the r&b market, but there was little crossover into pop. Unlike Ballard, Checker was a pop phenomenon, created as an image act in the corporate offices of Cameo/Parkway Records in Philadelphia. At the suggestion of Dick Clark's wife, Ernest Evans took the name "Chubby Checker," linguistically paralleling "Fats Domino." Checker's "The Twist" reached number one on the pop charts twice (1960 and 1962). In fact, it was the best-selling single of all time well into the 1970s.

Attempting to cash in on the craze the twist had set in motion, Cameo/Parkway concocted a seemingly endless series of new dance records, made by both black and white artists: Checker—"The Hucklebuck," "Pony Time," "The Fly," and "Limbo Rock"; Bobby Rydell—"The Fish"; The Orlons—"The Wah Watusi"; The Dovells—"Bristol Stomp" and the "Hully Gully"; Dee Dee Sharp—"Mashed Potato Time" and "Do the Bird." Sharp was offered "The Loco-Motion" by Gerry Goffin and Carole King, but when her label passed on the song, the writers released a version by their babysitter on the Dimension label. Eva Narcissus Boyd became Little Eva and "The Loco-Motion" became a number one hit.

In its historical context, the twist craze was socially ambiguous. The dance was welcomed enthusiastically into conservative white suburban America even though its leading exponent was African American. Certainly, it anticipated more openly sexual dances like the monkey, the jerk, and the Philly dog. For a brief period, it served as an alternative entry into the pop market for African American artists, even as mainstream forces sought to turn back rock 'n' roll. In 1962 alone, Sam Cooke's "Twistin' the Night Away" and Gary "U.S." Bonds' "Dear Lady Twist" and "Twist, Twist Senora" broke into the Top Ten; the Isley Brothers followed their classic "Shout" with "Twist and Shout"; and Atlantic Records reissued an album of old Ray Charles material as *Do the Twist with Ray Charles*, which hit number eleven on the album charts. In the long run, however, Cameo/Parkway's faddish

Schlock Rock's Greatest Hits, Volume II

Bobby Vee "Devil or Angel," "Rubber Ball," "Take Good Care of My Baby," "Run to Him," "The Night Has a Thousand Eyes"

Brian Hyland "Itsy Bitsy Teenie Weenie Yellow Polkadot Bikini," "Sealed with a Kiss"

Johnny Tillotson "Poetry in Motion," "Without You," "It Keeps Right on A-Hurtin'," "Talk Back Trembling Lips"

Bobby Vinton "Roses Are Red," "Blue on Blue," "Blue Velvet," "There I've Said It Again," "My Heart Belongs to Only You," "Mr. Lonely"

Jay and the Americans "She Cried," "Only in America," "Come a Little Bit Closer," "Cara Mia"

Sue Thompson "Norman"

Little Peggy March "I Will Follow Him"

Leslie Gore "It's My Party," "Judy's Turn to Cry," "She's a Fool"

Paul and Paula "Hey Paula"

((• HEAR MORE Audio links on MyMusicKit

The biggest African American star to emerge from the Philadelphia scene of the late 1950s, Chubby Checker generated contradictory impulses in mainstream culture. His version of "The Twist" kicked off a national dance craze that the whole family could enjoy even as it anticipated more openly sexual dances.

dance crazes tended to reduce rock 'n' roll to a novelty. The company also had a close association with *American Bandstand*, the televised dance party that was primarily responsible for promoting the new teen idols.

Television's Greatest Hits

Bandstand, as it was called in 1952, was a local Philadelphia dance party broadcast on ABC affiliate WFIL-TV. The show's first host, Bob Horn, was fired after he was arrested for drunk driving. In 1956, the station asked Dick Clark, a news announcer there since 1952, to take over. Although Clark, "the perpetual teenager," was twenty-seven years old, he looked as young as the teenagers who danced on the show, but carried himself more like a big brother. Under his leadership, *Bandstand* quickly became one of the most important promotional vehicles in the music industry. By 1957, the show had been picked up by ABC-TV for national broadcast and renamed *American Bandstand*. As Russell Sanjek has noted, "Within two years, it was being broadcast by 101 affiliates to an audience of 20 million. . . . Because of program policy, [the performers on *Bandstand*] were invariably white in the early years."[15] As a result, "Dick Clark, the youthful, debonair host with the Dentyne smile," was remembered by Arnold Shaw "as the ballast to Alan Freed, representing cool, white rock as Freed was the avatar of hot black rock."[16] Clark has maintained that associating him with only white rock is a cheap shot. "To write that the music we presented was all white bread is a fallacious premise. It's an easy angle," he has said. "It happens to be wrong."[17]

While it may be true, as Clark pointed out in 1990, "that over two-thirds of the people who've been initiated into the Rock & Roll Hall of Fame had their television debuts on *American Bandstand*,"[18] the show's Philadelphia location undoubtedly placed the local independents in a particularly good position to display their wares. Fabian, Frankie Avalon, Bobby Rydell, and Freddy Cannon made regular appearances; it seems likely that such exposure helped increase their popularity. It is equally clear that Clark positioned himself to benefit from such successes. By the end of the decade, he was financially involved in thirty-three music-related corporations,

In rock 'n' roll lore, Dick Clark is usually positioned as counterpoint to Alan Freed, promoting white middle-class schlock in opposition to Freed's penchant for black rhythm and blues. While too simplistic to hold up under scrutiny, such dichotomies helped Clark survive the official attacks on rock 'n' roll that destroyed Freed

((• HEAR MORE
Dick Clark on
MyMusicKit

including three record companies, a management firm, and a pressing plant. His publishing company held the copyright on 162 songs, many of which his show had helped to popularize. Clark's financial entanglements often led him to the borders of ethical practice, as his handling of Duane Eddy illustrates.

Born in Corning, New York, Eddy moved to Phoenix when he was seventeen years old to work with producer Lee Hazelwood to create the "twangy" guitar sound that became Eddy's signature. From 1958 to 1963, Eddy and his group, the Rebels, charted fifteen Top Forty hits, the best known of which are "Rebel Rouser" (1958), "Forty Miles of Bad Road" (1959), and "Because They're Young" (1960). Between 1958 and 1961, Clark played eleven of Eddy's hits some 240 times on *Bandstand*. While Clark has claimed that the show simply followed national trends, his promotion unquestionably helped to propel songs to hit status. Throughout this period, Eddy recorded for Clark's Jaime label, he toured under the auspices of Clark's management company, and all of his copyrights were owned by Clark's publishing company. Given this, it is not difficult to imagine how Clark's private business holdings could have come into conflict with the promotional aspects of *American Bandstand.*

Of course, television had long been used as a promotional vehicle for all kinds of music, including, on occasion, rock 'n' roll. Elvis Presley, Chuck Berry, Carl Perkins, Jerry Lee Lewis, Buddy Holly, and Bo Diddley, for example, had all appeared, albeit infrequently, on TV variety shows. However, they did not appear on national television until their musical abilities were proven. In the new pop mentality, visual appeal itself became the basis for launching a musical career.

American Bandstand was not the only culprit in this area. Annette Funicello had been the *Mickey Mouse Club*'s most popular mouseketeer since 1955. Connie Stevens, from the television series *Hawaiian Eye,* teamed up with Ed "Kookie" Byrnes, the ultra-cool parking attendant on *77 Sunset Strip* who wowed millions of viewers with his hair-combing technique, for a duet titled, naturally, "Kookie, Kookie (Lend Me Your Comb)." The Top Ten single launched short-lived singing careers for both actors. Tommy Sands starred in *The Singing Idol,* a TV play based loosely on Elvis Presley's life. Sands's first hit, "Teen-Age Crush," came from the telecast.

Although most of the teen idols were cast in something of an Elvis Presley mold, they seldom measured up.

Although most of the teen idols were cast in something of an Elvis Presley mold, they seldom measured up. One television artist managed to project at least some continuity with his rockabilly forebears—the soft-spoken, soft-rocking Ricky Nelson. Starring with his real-life family, Nelson played himself on the television sit-com *The Adventures of Ozzie and Harriet,* a show about a so-called normal middle-class suburban family in the 1950s. In 1957, Verve records hit on the idea of recording Nelson singing on the show. His mediocre cover of Fats Domino's "I'm Walking" broke into the Top Twenty, while the flip side, "A Teenager's Romance," unexpectedly went to number two. Imperial (Domino's label) bought Nelson's contract and began promoting him as a respectable alternative to Presley. Over the next seven years, Nelson released twenty-five Top Forty hits, including "Be-Bop Baby" (1957), "Poor Little Fool" (1958), "It's Late" (1959), and "Travelin' Man" backed with "Hello Mary Lou" (1961), and a few more on Decca before he was swamped by the British wave in the mid-1960s.

Nelson's clean-cut image and popular television series figured heavily in his success, but he was not simply a media creation. His father was a multitalented big band leader in the 1930s with nearly forty hit records to his credit; his mother was the band's vocalist. His backup band included guitarist James Burton, who went on to join Presley, and most of his own early hits were written by Dorsey and/or Johnny Burnette, two over-the-top rockabilly artists. Furthermore, he had the capacity to grow as a singer. After his untimely death in 1985, Nelson was eulogized as a country rock singer of some stature. Still, it is impossible to separate his early career from the white middle-class makeover of rock 'n' roll.

The Brill Building: The New Tin Pan Alley

As rock 'n' roll became too popular for the established music industry to ignore, it attracted a new breed of professional—songwriters with a respect for the Tin Pan Alley tradition who could write (and sometimes sing) in teenage idiom. Paul Anka, a Canadian of Middle Eastern descent, aspired to a career as a professional songwriter and was convinced he could sing as well. While in Los Angeles, he pitched some tunes to Don Costa, a record executive at ABC-

Paramount. Costa signed him and produced Anka's first record, the Latin-inflected "Diana" (1957), written for an older babysitter from his childhood years. The song became a number one hit single. With Costa arranging and conducting, Anka continued to do well in the pop market until the British Invasion in 1964 swept away all the reigning popular styles. Undaunted, he segued into the role of adult songwriter, penning "Johnny's Theme" for the *Tonight Show* and the lyrics to "My Way" for Sinatra.

Neil Sedaka was a concert pianist who studied at Julliard. Like Anka, he began his career as a professional songwriter, working in collaboration with Howard Greenfield, his high-school friend. Sedaka and Greenfield displayed a versatility and a breadth—ranging from "Stupid Cupid" and "Frankie" for Connie Francis to "Since You've Been Gone" for Clyde McPhatter and "I Waited Too Long" for LaVern Baker—that defy easy categorization. His

Paul Anka was one teen idol who got more gratification from being a songwriter. He was part of a stable of young writers who found a home near the Brill Building, the Tin Pan Alley of rock 'n' roll.

own singing career was defined by trivial, teen-oriented songs. Sedaka and Greenfield, like Anka, turned toward adult pop following the British Invasion, writing for Peggy Lee, Johnny Mathis, and the Fifth Dimension, among others.

It is easy to associate writers like Anka and Sedaka and Greenfield with the death of rock 'n' roll—they wrote plenty of anemic material and effortlessly transitioned to adult songwriting. At the same time, they were part of an effort to professionalize rock 'n' roll by restoring a Tin Pan Alley approach to popular music, in which writers wrote songs, singers sang them, and artist and repertoire staff brought the two together. In this model, corporate executives could feel reasonably assured that the appropriate artist would be matched with a professionally written song. The physical and spiritual center of this new enterprise was the Brill Building at 1619 Broadway, the Manhattan location for a new Tin Pan Alley. In cramped quarters, songwriting teams like Gerry Goffin and Carole King, Barry Mann and Cynthia Weil, Greenfield and Sedaka, Jeff Barry and Ellie Greenwich, and Doc Pomus and Mort Shuman pounded out new melodies as their Tin Pan Alley forebears had decades earlier. This latest generation of composers was to rock 'n' roll what Richard Rodgers and Lorenz Hart and George and Ira Gershwin were to the popular music of an earlier time. The results were mixed.

Aldon's young writers displayed consummate skill, real innovation, and genuine sensitivity one minute and a truly incredible flair for the insipid the next.

Sedaka and Greenfield went to work at Aldon Music, the flagship company of Brill Building pop. Like Sedaka and Greenfield, Aldon's other young writers (including Goffin/King, Mann/Weil, and even Bobby Darin) displayed consummate skill, real innovation, and genuine sensitivity one minute and a truly incredible flair for the insipid the next. It is difficult to believe that the same Goffin and King who wrote "Up on the Roof" for the Drifters and "Natural Woman" for Aretha Franklin also wrote "Her Royal Majesty" for James Darren. How could Mann/Weil have turned out both "You've Lost That Lovin' Feeling" for the Righteous Brothers and "Blame It on the Bossa Nova" for Edie Gorme? In short, the Brill Building writers produced some of best rock 'n' roll of the era as well as some of the worst schlock imaginable (as we shall see in more detail in Chapter 6).

The War on Rock 'n' Roll

By the mid-1950s, rock 'n' roll had become the focal point for society's fears of miscegenation, sexuality, violence, juvenile delinquency, and general moral decline. In the eyes of many, a paramount danger was that this music was no longer contained on "the other side of the tracks." Rock 'n' roll's biggest sin was to bring styles of music once considered class- and race-specific into the mainstream and, in so doing, to redefine our conception of popular music.

The opening salvo of organized opposition began in late 1954, even before the term *rock 'n' roll* had come into widespread usage. Opining that the sexual double entendres entering the mainstream primarily through r&b crossovers were in poor taste, entertainment trade papers—most notably, a three-part series in *Variety* on what they termed "leer-ics"—called on the industry to police itself lest other forces do it for them. These articles generated a considerable public response. Fearing reprisals, record companies and radio stations—including prominent black-oriented outlets like WDIA in Memphis—announced campaigns to weed out suggestive lyrics.

Catholic youth organizations in Boston, Chicago, and Minneapolis, and fundamentalist religious groups all over the South supplied lists of objectionable records. As one might expect, such songs as "Sixty Minute Man" and "Work with Me Annie" made all the lists, but even the Everly Brothers' "Wake Up Little Susie" managed to get banned in Boston. Municipalities set up review boards to screen new releases. When all else failed, police confiscated offensive records and jukeboxes.

Finding their offensive against "smutty" lyrics did not stop the music, opponents changed their tactics. After 1955, according to Linda Martin and Kerry Segrave,

> the anti-rock advocates moved into broader attacks on the music. Attacking with just a sexual brush could only "tar" a few songs. By moving into wider areas of attack the opposition hoped to tar the full spectrum of rock 'n' roll. Henceforth attacks would center more on the poor and abysmal quality of rock music, its supposed effect in creating juvenile delinquency, and the lewdness of performers themselves.[19]

The industry was not of one mind on these matters. "American pop music today, despite the attacks upon it, is in its most vital period," editorialized the outspoken Paul Ackerman in *Billboard*. "It most broadly reflects the diverse elements making up musical America. It is rich and fresh in sound and content."[20] Still, attacks on rock 'n' roll encouraged more official interventions, which took the form of a loosely coordinated series of government investigations and legislative actions culminating in the infamous "payola hearings" of 1959 and 1960. As noted in Chapter 1, payola—the practice of "paying for play," that is, offering financial, sexual, or other personal inducements in return for promotion—was hardly a newcomer to the music business. Song plugging, as the practice was called earlier in the century, had been the lynchpin of industry marketing since the heyday of Tin Pan Alley. As early as World War I, it was estimated that about $400,000 per year was paid to singers for the express purpose of pushing certain songs. Indeed, similar practices have characterized the development of most industries in their formative stages. In the 1950s, however, the focus on payola in the music industry became the operative strategy for neutralizing rock 'n' roll.

By initially ignoring rock 'n' roll as a passing fad, society's established powers had allowed it to gather a momentum that could not be stopped. As it mushroomed, rock 'n' roll had engendered changes in the way popular music was produced and disseminated and that had made the music even more difficult to contain. Mainstream pop had been produced by the major record companies according to a fairly precise division of labor and with fairly clear lines of power and authority. In contrast, rock 'n' roll's low-cost, independent, and often disorganized production and distribution—in part the result of technological advances—precipitated shifts that tended to democratize and decentralize the production of popular music. As illustrated in a *Billboard* study comparing production in 1939 and 1959:

> Whereas the publishers of Top Ten songs in '39 were all located in New York, in '59 they were distributed in eight states. The songwriters now came from eighteen states instead of three. In '39 Top Ten disks were made by only three companies; in '59 by thirty-nine companies. And these companies, instead of all being located in New York, were distributed in ten states.
>
> The conclusion was inescapable: music business had broken out of Broadway, and Tin Pan Alley was gone as a shaper of trends and styles.[21]

Acting in concert, if not conspiracy, ASCAP and some of its most notable publishers, the major record companies and some of their biggest stars, and the U.S. government and some of its most tiresome elected officials waged a protracted public battle for a return to "good music."

Although the established industry powers wanted to eliminate rock 'n' roll, they were never sure, given the anarchy of its production, where or how to intervene. Acting in concert, if not conspiracy, ASCAP and some of its most notable publishers, the major record companies and some of their biggest stars, and the U.S. government and some of its most tiresome elected officials waged a protracted public battle for a return to "good music." Because most rock 'n' roll material was written by Broadcast Music Incorporated (BMI) writers, ASCAP happily joined in the attack. For ASCAP, the offensive against rock 'n' roll was simply an escalation of its efforts since 1939 to put BMI out of business. For the major labels, the fight was an attempt to halt the market expansion of the independents. (Forty of the seventy Top Ten records in 1957, for example, were produced by independent labels.[22]) To conservative elected officials, jumping on the bandwagon with the likes of Frank Sinatra, Bing Crosby, Steve Allen, Ira Gershwin, and Oscar Hammerstein to hold back the floodgates of social change may have seemed like a sure way of grabbing some quick and memorable headlines. Beneath all the high-toned rhetoric, then, lay a massive accumulation of ignorance and racism and a fair amount of unabashed economic and political self-interest.

ASCAP—in effect, the organizational agent of Tin Pan Alley—led the charge. In 1953, thirty-three ASCAP members filed a $150 million antitrust suit against BMI, charging it with a conspiracy to dominate the market by keeping ASCAP music off the radio. Sydney M. Kaye, chair of BMI, pointed out that none of the radio stations that owned stock in BMI had ever received a dividend and that "all broadcasters have so-called blanket licenses from both ASCAP and BMI. . . . They cannot save one penny if they play more BMI and less ASCAP music. Broadcasters have, therefore, no incentive to discriminate against ASCAP music."[23] Stanley Adams, president of ASCAP, could not identify a single station or network that had discriminated against ASCAP. Still, ASCAP continued to attack.

In 1956, under pressure from the Songwriters of America, a group of some 700 ASCAP writers, the Antitrust Subcommittee of the House Judiciary Committee, chaired by Congressman Emanuel Celler, initiated a probe into BMI. Officially, the committee was to investigate whether the relationship between BMI and radio had any influence on the music that was aired. However, Congressman Celler made clear the racial undertones of the investigation when he said: "Well, rock and roll has its place. There is no question about it. It's given great impetus to talent, particularly among the colored people. It's a natural expression of their emotions and feelings."[24] The committee heard testimony from a parade of influential ASCAP writers but could find no evidence of wrongdoing by BMI and referred the matter to the Justice Department.

The next battle occurred in 1958. ASCAP had a Senate bill introduced to prevent broadcasters from owning BMI stock. To gather support for the bill, no less a figure than Frank Sinatra wrote:

> *My only sorrow is the unrelenting insistence of recording and motion picture companies upon purveying the most brutal, ugly, degenerate, vicious form of expression it has been my misfortune to hear—naturally, I refer to the bulk of rock 'n' roll.*
>
> *It fosters almost totally negative and destructive reactions in young people. It smells phony and false. It is sung, played and written for the most part by cretinous goons and by means of its almost imbecilic reiterations and sly—lewd—in plain fact, dirty—lyrics, and as I said before, it*

manages to be the martial music of every sideburned delinquent on the face of the earth. This rancid aphrodisiac I deplore.[25]

Once again, a chorus of ASCAP sympathizers held forth. The Songwriters Protective Association, made up of ASCAP members, testified before the Communications Subcommittee of the Senate Committee on Interstate and Foreign Commerce, charged with gathering information relevant to the bill. Social critic Vance Packard, appearing as a paid witness, declared that rock 'n' roll "was inspired by what had been called race music modified to stir the animal instinct in modern teenagers."[26] Even with 1,200 pages of such testimony, however, the bill died in committee.

In 1959, rock 'n' roll's opponents came closer to hitting its nerve center when ASCAP convinced the Legislative Oversight Subcommittee of the House Committee on Interstate and Foreign Commerce to launch a new probe into payola. Rock 'n' roll's opponents reasoned correctly that curtailing the freedom of (largely unregulated) deejays could go a long way toward stopping the flow of rock 'n' roll music. While the committee, chaired by Arkansas Democrat Oren Harris, was to investigate abuses at all levels of the recording industry, deejays became the main targets of its hearings.

Ignoring all previous evidence of the music's popularity, the payola hearings proceeded on the assumption that no deejay would play music as inferior and tasteless as rock 'n' roll unless he was handsomely rewarded for it. The most damning indictment in the payola hearings was that against Alan Freed. While other deejays also fell victim to the probe, Freed was the most visible symbol of everything that many found threatening about the music and thus the most obvious target. He had played a major role in popularizing r&b among white teenagers and had continued to push original black recordings during the cover-record period. He had also refused to sign a statement saying that he had never received money or gifts to promote records. Freed had run afoul of the law when a concert he staged in 1952 at the Cleveland Arena was oversold and had to be canceled. Although he was charged with fraud (charges were eventually dropped), the real issue had been that the crowd was racially integrated at a time when Cleveland was a segregated city. In Boston in 1958, a concert he staged at the Boston Arena degenerated into violence outside the building. This time Freed was indicted on two charges of inciting a riot. One week after the concert, he was no longer a WINS deejay. He moved to a slot at WABC radio and also began hosting a dance party on WNEW-TV. In November 1959, after one of his Boston indictments had been dropped and he had pleaded no contest to the other, he was fired from WABC. Two days later, he lost his job at WNEW as well. By the time the payola hearings really took off, Freed's career was already on the ropes. In 1960, he was arrested for accepting $30,000 in payola and two years later was fined and given a suspended sentence. Unemployed and penniless, he was indicted again in 1964 for income tax evasion. He died of uremia the following year, a broken man.

Dick Clark, in contrast, came through the hearings with his reputation intact, if not strengthened. Clark represented a respectability that Freed did not. He was also toting up some $12 million in annual billings for ABC, compared to Freed's $250,000. As a result, ABC-TV issued a statement in support of Clark even after its radio division had fired Freed. Having voluntarily divested himself of the companies most likely to show conflicts of interest, Clark was pronounced "a fine young man" by chair Oren Harris.

The number of deejays who felt compelled to come forward, confess their
sins, and name others was reminiscent
of the worst aspects of the McCarthy
era witch hunts.

When all was said and done, the committee had identified a
paltry $263,245 in payola to deejays, but with no hard evidence to
support even this figure. It was not even comparable to World War I
levels of abuse, so one could not help but wonder what all the fuss
was about. Still, the number of deejays who felt compelled to come
forward, confess their sins, and name others was reminiscent of the
worst aspects of the McCarthy era witch hunts. Reams of such public testimony and extensive
media coverage helped to create a climate that encouraged the pop-oriented makeover of "down
and dirty" rock 'n' roll. Of course, by this time, many of the most prominent rock 'n' roll pioneers had already been neutralized in one way or another. Presley had been drafted in early
1958; by the time he came home from Germany in 1960, his influence in shaping the genre had
ended. Little Richard had quit rock 'n' roll in the late fifties to join the ministry. Jerry Lee
Lewis's career had self-destructed in 1958 when he married his thirteen-year-old cousin. Buddy
Holly had died in a plane crash, which also took the lives of Ritchie Valens and the Big Bopper,
in 1959—the same year the committee began its hearings. Later that year, Chuck Berry's arrest
for a violation of the Mann Act effectively removed him as a hit-maker on the rock 'n' roll scene.

In the end, a bill passed that outlawed payola. Its most immediate effect was to impose
on radio a tighter, more hierarchical structure that rendered popular music easier to control.[27]
Thus, in effect, radio was caught between a rock and a hard place. Severely chastised by the
committee, which had delivered its racial message in no uncertain terms, and fearful of Federal
Communications Commission (FCC) reprisals that could affect licensing, rock-oriented radio
became skittish about programming too many black artists. However, listeners still demanded
the music, so these stations could not afford to ignore it completely. In general, they responded
by playing as few black artists as they could without losing their listenership.

Surf's Up!

In the early 1960s, as the second generation of schlock rockers pitted their uneven talents
against the phenomenon of the girl groups and the emergence of Motown (see Chapter 6), surf
music emerged with vocal and instrumental variants. Its trajectory was remarkably short,
essentially rising and falling from 1962 to 1964.

While surf music was part of the continuing trend that made rock 'n' roll both white and
middle class, it was also a more complex phenomenon. In the early 1960s, surfing became the
central metaphor for an easygoing lifestyle based on the unabashed celebration of consumption. Nowhere was the image of white middle-class America more on display than in surf music.
Its themes dealt primarily with affluence—fast cars, attractive women and men at leisure on
the beach, and, of course, the sport itself. Still, unlike schlock, which offered rock 'n' roll little
more than a backward look to pop song stylists of an earlier era, surf music provided something
of a gateway to the 1960s. It offered a vibrant, driving sound worthy of the name *rock 'n' roll*. As
Steve Chapple and I have argued elsewhere:

> The surfing music that appeared in the early sixties should not be seen as just another fad that soft-
> ened rock 'n' roll. Rather it was a precursor to the psychedelic and underground progressive rock of

the sixties. Several of the important people involved in surfing music—especially the Beach Boys . . . and Lou Adler, one of the first producers of Jan and Dean, became central figures in sixties rock. Surfing music represented an authentic West Coast rock 'n' roll culture that differed in one important way from earlier rock 'n' roll produced by urban blacks and Southern rockabillies: it was made by middle-class whites.[28]

Surf music should not be confused with the drivel that issued from Hollywood "beach party" movies, beginning in 1959 with *Gidget* (Sandra Dee and James Darren) and culminating in 1963 with *Beach Party* (Annette Funicello and Frankie Avalon). They transformed the southern California surf cult into a national fad, but they trivialized the sport with their focus on bikinis and middle-class teen dilemmas. They do represent, however, one instance in which Hollywood beat the record companies to the punch.

Surf music should not be confused with the drivel that issued from Hollywood "beach party" movies, beginning in 1959 with **Gidget** and culminating in 1963 with **Beach Party.**

HEAR MORE
Dick Dale on
MyMusicKit

The prototypical surf music group was Dick Dale and the Del-tones from southern California. Working closely with Leo Fender, creator of the first solid-body electric guitars, Dale helped to develop the amplification and reverberation equipment that gave much of surf music its distinctive sound. He and his group were a powerhouse live combo with a dedicated following that had a local hit with "Let's Go Trippin'" in 1961. On the strength of the group's live shows, Capitol signed them in 1963, but the group failed to deliver any hits. By this time, their strong bass lines, sax-based instrumentals, and Dale's harsh vocal style—indeed, the very name of the band—seemed almost anachronistic in the national market. It would be left to other groups, primarily from southern California, to establish the style nationally.

A number of these groups were instrumental ensembles. First out of the gate were the Marketts, who released "Surfer's Stomp" in 1962. That same year a British group, the Tornadoes, effected a surf sound on "Telstar," a number one hit. Instrumental surf peaked in 1963 with the release of "Pipeline" by the Chantays, "Wipe Out" by the Surfaris, and "The Lonely Surfer" by session musician Jack Nitzsche. The Pyramids scored with "Penetration" in 1964 and, by this time, other groups from across the country, such as the Astronauts from Denver and the Trashmen from Minnesota ("Surfin' Bird," 1964) had found their way into the pop market through the surf tag. But 1964 was really the swan song for surf as the British Invasion effectively washed away the entire genre.

In its short life, instrumental surf music was part of a venerable tradition of instrumental rock 'n' roll that began with talented musicians like organist Bill Doggett ("Honky Tonk," 1956), alto sax player Bill Justis ("Raunchy," 1957), and Bill Black, Elvis Presley's original bass player, who recorded eight Top Thirty instrumental hits with his own combo. Initially, instrumental rock 'n' roll drew on a wide range of sources. The Champs' "Tequila" echoed the Chicano rhythms of the Southwest. Jazz drummer Cozy Cole broke into the rock 'n' roll market in 1958 with "Topsy Part II"—a Basie tune from the late 1930s—followed by "Topsy Part I" and "Turvy Part II" in 1958. In 1959, Santo and Johnny Farina had a number one hit with "Sleep Walk," featuring a lilting Hawaiian steel guitar. In 1960, the Viscounts resurrected the jazz classic "Harlem Nocturne" with enough tremolo and echo to qualify it as pure rock 'n' roll.

Instrumental rock 'n' roll had its greatest successes, however, as novelty music. In 1959, Johnny and the Hurricanes hit number five with "Red River Rock," a rock 'n' roll version of the traditional "Red River Valley." It was followed quickly by "Reveille Rock" (1959), an adaptation of the Army bugle call, and "Beatnik Fly" (1960), a remake of Burl Ives's "Blue Tail Fly." Kokomo pillaged a Grieg piano concerto to turn "Asia Minor" into a Top Ten rock 'n' roll hit in 1961. That same year, B. Bumble and the Stingers turned "The Flight of the Bumble Bee" into a boogie-woogie piano hit called "Bumble Boogie." The group followed up in 1962 with "Nut Rocker," a rock 'n' roll version of the march from Tchaikovsky's *Nutcracker*. The subtlety and polish of Cozy Cole gave way to the novelty drumming of Sandy Nelson, whose adolescent pounding on "Teen Beat" (1959) and "Let There Be Drums" (1961) anticipated the classic surf drum solo that appeared on "Wipe Out" two years later.

Two groups dominated the guitar-based sound that eventually came to define instrumental rock 'n' roll—Duane Eddy and the Rebels, and the Ventures. Eddy and the Rebels were the most successful, but the Ventures were the most influential. The Ventures, the pride of Seattle, established the instrumentation of the classic rock 'n' roll quartet—electric lead, rhythm, and bass guitars, and drums—no horns, no keyboards; just electricity and rhythm. On their debut single, "Walk—Don't Run" (1960), the group evidenced polish, technical precision, and versatility without sacrificing excitement and drive. Overall, they enjoyed a longevity rare for an instrumental group, recording more than fifty albums, sixteen of which made the Top Forty. As rock writer Greg Shaw has noted, however, "[s]urf music was the last hurrah for instrumental rock as a popular genre; after the British Invasion of 1964, vocals again assumed primacy in white rock."[29] By then, surf itself had become a vocally dominant music, with hits such as the Hondells "Little Honda," Ronny & the Daytonas' "G.T.O.," and the Rip Chords' "Hey Little Cobra."

The Beach Boys became the definitive surf group. The group was a family affair. In the early 1960s, brothers Brian (keyboards, bass), Carl (guitar), and Dennis Wilson (drums) teamed up with their cousin Mike Love (lead vocals) and their Hawthorne, California, neighbor Al Jardine (guitar, bass) to form the most popular self-contained vocal/instrumental combo in town. Dennis, the only surfer in the group, convinced Brian and Mike to write songs that elevated the sport to a metaphor for the American Dream. Their images, like surf music in general, were bound to a kind of affluence available only to a narrow segment of the population.

The Beach Boys constructed teen anthems in much the same way that Chuck Berry did. Their sophisticated close harmonies and elegant counterpoint created a sound that was unique among white U.S. rock groups.

Seemingly oblivious to their own privilege or the social currents around them, such as the growing civil rights movement, the Beach Boys were hardly apologetic for their music. "We're white and we sing white," the group said.[30] Despite this comment, they copped (with attribution) the tune for "Surfin' U.S.A.," their first Top Ten single, from Chuck Berry's "Sweet Little Sixteen." In many ways, it was fitting that the group should "collaborate" with Berry. Barring the suburban focus and a West Coast orientation, the Beach Boys constructed teen anthems in much the same way that Chuck Berry did. Their sophisticated close harmonies and elegant counterpoint created a sound that was unique among white U.S. rock groups.

The Beach Boys came to national attention in 1962 when their first release, "Surfin'," reached number seventy-five on the national pop charts. Signed to Capitol that year, the group hit number fourteen with "Surfin' Safari." Their biggest year was 1963, which was also the peak of the surfing fad. "Surfin' U.S.A."/"Shut Down," "Surfer Girl"/"Little Deuce Coup," and "Be True to Your School"/"In My Room" all hit the charts between April and November. By

"Surfin' U.S.A."

Artist: The Beach Boys
Music / Lyrics by Brian Wilson
and Chuck Berry
Label: Capitol (1963)

The Beach Boys' music is distinguished from the many "surf and sun" bands of the 1960s by the innovative production skills of leader/songwriter Brian Wilson. His methods of complex, multi-sectioned musical structures ("Good Vibrations"), multiple layers of overdubbed vocal harmonies, and sophisticated production techniques were emulated by many of the Beach Boys' contemporaries. The Beatles have often cited the influence of the Beach Boys' *Pet Sounds* LP on *Sgt. Pepper's Lonely Hearts Club Band*. "Surfin' U.S.A." is notable for having been included in the Rock and Roll Hall of Fame's list of *50 Songs That Shaped Rock and Roll*.

Musical Style Notes

The musical style of "Surfin' U.S.A." has three major elements: the influence of Chuck Berry, the musical conventions of "surf" music, and the Beach Boys' signature multiple vocal harmonies.

- The opening guitar riff, the chord progressions, and the refrain all borrow heavily from Chuck Berry's song "Sweet Little Sixteen"—so heavily, in fact, that Brian Wilson had to give Berry a songwriting credit on the LP in order to avoid a lawsuit.
- The "surf music" influence, which is obvious in the lyrics, can be heard in the instrumentation: through the high, treble-dominated, and reverb-heavy guitar tone reminiscent of surf music king Dick Dale, and the relentless, pounding, quarter-note pulse of the bass drum (meaning one drum hit per beat).
- On the refrain "Everybody's gone surfin'," we hear the Beach Boys' impeccable multiple vocal harmonies, with their wide range (from bass to falsetto). This refrain is a good example of a skill shared by both Brian Wilson and Chuck Berry: the ability to write a musical "hook," one of those phrases that gets stuck in your brain for the rest of the day.

Musical "Road Map"

TIMINGS	COMMENTS	LYRICS
0:00–0:02	Introduction—electric guitar riff, borrowed directly from Chuck Berry.	
0:02–0:25	Verse 1 Note the vocal background harmony parts, singing on "oo" syllable.	*If everybody . . .*
0:25–0:49 0:44	Verse 2 Vocal harmony parts acquire their own lyrics: "Inside, outside, USA." Harmony parts join refrain: "Everybody's gone surfin'. . . ."	*You'd catch . . .*
0:50–1:13 1:13	Verse 3 Vocal background harmony parts, singing again on "oo" syllable. Typical surf-style drum "kick" into fourth verse.	*We're gonna . . .*
1:14–1:37 1:32	Verse 4 Vocal harmony parts repeat lyrics from verse 2: "Inside, outside, USA." Harmony parts join refrain: "Everybody's gone surfin' . . . ."	*Pacific Palisades . . .*
1:38–1:51	Keyboard (organ) solo and guitar solo over form of the verse. Guitar comes in.	
1:57–2:26	Harmony parts join refrain: "Everybody's gone surfin' . . . ." Refrain repeats five times (fades during fifth repeat).	

The Beach Boys made no bones about infusing rock 'n' roll with white middle-class themes and images. They managed to merge the squeaky cleanliness of Philadelphia schlock with the unbridled energy of a high-school garage band.

1964, the group's boldly conceived ideology of "Fun, Fun, Fun" was well established, if not quite believable. In pursuit of this ideology, the lyrics of the group's songs "shut down" all challengers on the dragstrip, defended the honor of their high school, and wished aloud that all (attractive) women could be "California Girls."

Clearly, the group is vulnerable to the criticism that their songs offered primarily male-oriented, sexist imagery. At the same time, however, they were capable of expressing doubt ("When I Grow Up [To Be a Man]"), even insecurity ("Don't Worry Baby"), and they invested even the most tired clichés with a certain freshness and vitality. Although the group's songs were never quite cynical, they managed to convey the sense that propping up false myths was a task that could not be taken too seriously. In this spirit, they delivered all the raunchiness of a high-school garage band but still managed to sound as squeaky clean as the Philadelphia crowd. The job of managing these contradictions—transforming them into hits—fell mostly to Brian Wilson, a largely self-taught musical genius and an increasingly tortured soul.

Brian had emerged as the group's main writer, arranger, and producer (a rarity at major labels) following the extraordinary success of the group's second album, *Surfin' U.S.A.* He became determined to perfect the oceanic version of his idol Phil Spector's "wall of sound" (see Chapter 6) based on the Beach Boys' harmonic virtuosity. Starting with the complicated arrangement and unorthodox harmonies on "I Get Around" (1964), Brian began to push the limits of pop convention. By the time the style was fully developed on "California Girls"

(1965), he had also begun testing the limits of his own consciousness with mind-altering drugs. The Beach Boys' *Pet Sounds* LP (1966) experimented with advanced studio techniques well before the Beatles' *Sgt. Pepper* album. After the success of the fully "psychedelic" million-seller "Good Vibrations" in 1966, Brian embarked on what was supposed to be his crowning achievement—a concept LP tentatively titled *Smile.* A short time into the project, however, his behavior became erratic. After he allegedly destroyed many of the album's vocal tracks in a fit of paranoia, the project became irrevocably stalled. The release of *Sgt. Pepper* was the final blow. Brian suffered a complete breakdown and withdrew from the group. The remaining members released a hastily assembled substitute LP, *Smiley Smile,* which included some fine cuts but failed to reach the Top Forty. Although the group continued to produce hits, it never regained the magic of Brian's peak years.

The only other act that came within striking distance of the surf crown was Jan and Dean. Jan Berry, Dean Torrence, and Arnie Ginsburg (not to be confused with the deejay of the same name) had been active since 1959, when "Jennie Lee"—released as "Jan and Arnie" because Dean was in the army at the time—became a Top Ten hit. A year later, Jan and Dean, no longer with Arnie, scored another Top Ten hit, "Baby Talk." In 1963, "Surf City," written by Jan and Brian Wilson, went to number one, establishing Jan and Dean as a surf act. The two rode that marketing label to chart success with "Drag City" (1963) and "Dead Man's Curve" and "The Little Old Lady (From Pasadena)" (1964), among others. In 1966, Jan hit a parked vehicle at 65 miles per hour, killing three passengers and sustaining brain damage. The tragedy effectively ended the career of Jan and Dean, but only after the genre itself had already self-destructed.

Because it opened a new chapter in the social relations of class, age, and race (but not gender), rock 'n' roll became a target of attack by those who feared the changes the music signaled. Behind every attack—from cover records to government investigations—was an attempt to reclaim mainstream cultural space for white middle-class values, themes, and images. This attempt was at least in part successful as the characteristics that had defined rock 'n' roll in the first place—strong regional accents, hot instrumental solos, and suggestive lyrics—gradually fell by the wayside. In all these changes, the connections between rock 'n' roll and its r&b heritage became more strained, which separated two genres that had been nearly indistinguishable.

Prior to 1959, rock 'n' roll had effected an extraordinary degree of overlap between the pop charts and the r&b charts. Not only had black artists gained unprecedented access to the popular market through rock 'n' roll, but white artists had sold to the black record-buying public in unprecedented numbers. In 1958, for example, more than half the records to make the r&b Top Ten were by white artists.[31] From 1959 on, however, bland white vocalists like Fabian, Frankie Avalon, and Bobby Rydell were marketed as rock 'n' rollers. Although they achieved considerable success as such, their styles were inappropriate for r&b radio and, as a result, white artists' penetration of the r&b market declined sharply. Somewhat paradoxically, the separation of rock 'n' roll and r&b contributed to a resurgence of rhythm and blues as a separate style with crossover potential. After 1959, artists like Wilbert Harrison ("Kansas City"), Barrett Strong ("Money"), Jimmy Jones

LEARN MORE
Chapter Test on
MyMusicKit

("Handy Man," "Good Timin'"), the Shirelles ("Will You Love Me Tomorrow," "Dedicated to the One I Love"), Gary "U.S." Bonds ("New Orleans," "Quarter to Three," "School Is Out"), the Crystals ("He's a Rebel"), Gene Chandler ("Duke of Earl"), and the Marvelettes ("Please Mr. Postman") provided a welcome change of pace (and race) in the popular market.

The percentage of black artists crossing over into the popular market remained uncommonly high until the onslaught of British performers in 1964. Seen in this light, not even the Beatles—the very musicians who breathed new life into the music—can be considered apart from the racist patterns that shaped rock 'n' roll. In fact, it is impossible to understand the magnitude and immediacy of their acceptance in this country without some reference to the theme of race. At the same time, it would be a gross distortion of history to underplay their unique contribution to the music and the culture of the 1960s. The Beatles were refreshing and talented, and they were the harbingers of broad cultural and political change.

Popular Music and Political Culture: The Sixties

The conservative hegemony and control that rock 'n' roll challenged implicitly in the 1950s gave way to open social and political upheaval in the 1960s. Just as the Beatles marked the decade musically, a myriad of grassroots social and political movements—civil rights; antiwar; black power; student power; the counterculture; and later, women's liberation; among other movements—signified a dramatic shift in the political center of gravity toward the left. These changes arose from contradictions that had been bubbling just beneath the surface of American life for quite some time.

In the 1950s, it was expected that each generation of Americans would be heir to a higher standard of living than the generation before it. However, significant paradoxes co-existed in this picture. First and perhaps foremost was the "race problem," brought into bold relief by the historic U.S. Supreme Court school desegregation decision of 1954, *Brown v. Board of Education*. Second, while Madison Avenue encouraged disciplined workers to become hedonistic consumers, an almost Victorian attitude toward sexuality still existed throughout the country. In some ways, rock 'n' roll represented an initial (and partial) response to this contradiction. Finally, even while the country had entered a period of unprecedented affluence, some segments of the population still experienced widespread poverty nationwide.

LEARN MORE
Learning Objectives
on MyMusicKit

The Soviet Union launched *Sputnik*, the first orbiting space satellite, in 1957, forcing Americans to question U.S. superiority in everything from national defense to scientific research. An educated workforce was seized upon as the key to continued U.S. dominance, and a tremendous nationwide expansion of the university system ensued. Higher education, once the province of the economic and intellectual elite, became available on a mass scale.

Thus, as the 1960s dawned, the United States was in the process of reinventing itself. The search for a new image led to the election of one of the youngest presidents in U.S. history,

John F. Kennedy. He assembled "the best and the brightest" to address the country's problems and asked Americans to give unselfishly of themselves in the restructuring of American values. The momentum of his vision; the political acumen of Lyndon Johnson, his vice president and then successor; and the organized moral and political force of the civil rights movement yielded landmark legislation and social programs. In this context, young men and women of all classes, races, and ethnic backgrounds entered college in record numbers. The participation of these young people—indeed, their leadership—in rethinking America produced the movements and the tumultuousness that defined the 1960s.

The Civil Rights Movement and Popular Music

The link between the civil rights movement (the movement from which all other movements took their cue) and music was first forged through early union songs and spirituals, such as "Which Side Are You On," "This Little Light of Mine," "Keep Your Eyes on the Prize," "This Land Is Your Land," "Down by the Riverside," and, of course, "We Shall Overcome." In the words of Bernice Johnson Reagon, these were the "songs that moved the movement."[1] Given that rock 'n' roll crossed the lines of class, race, and age, it is ironic, in retrospect, that civil rights activists tended to avoid the music initially because its commercial bent seemed antithetical to the goals of the struggle.[2] Still, while civil rights activists may have avoided rock 'n' roll, one can analyze the movement's influence on the national consciousness by charting the trajectory of popular music during this period.

Given that rock 'n' roll crossed the lines of class, race, and age, it is ironic, in retrospect, that civil rights activists tended to avoid the music initially because its commercial bent seemed antithetical to the goals of the struggle.

Consider, for example, the mid-1950s. An activist southern black clergy, led by the Reverend Martin Luther King, Jr., began to ally with secular organizations such as the National Association for the Advancement of Colored People (NAACP), the Congress on Racial Equality (CORE), and later the Student Non-Violent Coordinating Committee (SNCC). At the same time, as Nelson George has noted, "The music world was witnessing the breaking of a longstanding taboo, as gospel began to fuse with rhythm and blues."[3] Thus, in popular music, as in the struggle for civil rights, the black church became a force to be reckoned with. As regional civil rights struggles, erupting primarily in the South, came to national attention, early rock 'n' roll, based on southern rhythm and blues (r&b) styles, found a national audience. In Montgomery, Alabama, in 1955, Rosa Parks's defiance struck a blow for racial equality at the same time that Fats Domino, Little Richard, and Chuck Berry began to conquer the mainstream market as rock 'n' roll heroes. The rebellious tone of early rock 'n' roll mirrored the growing demand for political change in the black community.

The strategy of the early civil rights movement was integrationist; even at its most militant—the lunch-counter sit-ins of 1960 and the freedom rides of 1961—the demand was for social equality. Issues like institutionalized racism, white skin privilege, and black self-determination were not yet prominent on the political agenda. Paralleling this integrationist ideal, Chuck Berry chronicled a typical "School Day" in 1957 without mentioning race—even as President Eisenhower sent federal troops to Little Rock, Arkansas, to enforce the Supreme Court's school desegregation edict. As Berry would later state, "I said: 'Why can't I do as Pat Boone does and play good music for the white people and sell as well there as I could in the neighborhood? And that's what I shot for writing 'School Day.'"[4] During this period, then, the influence of the civil rights movement on rock 'n' roll was not apparent in its lyrics but in the ascendancy of black producers and black-owned record labels and in the appearance of black female vocal groups. There can be no question that the growing civil rights movement provided a climate that encouraged these developments.

Girl Groups, Male Producers, and Brill Building Pop

In the early 1960s, as civil rights activity heated up, r&b moved *uptown,* to use the term Charlie Gillett coined to describe the new, more polished, distinctly urban production style. Uptown r&b had been prefigured in Jerry Leiber and Mike Stoller's pioneering work with the Drifters ("There Goes My Baby," "Dance with Me," "This Magic Moment," "Save the Last Dance for Me") in 1959 and 1960, and its crossover potential was immediately apparent. Using combinations of elaborate instrumentation, lavish studio production, and advanced recording techniques, the next generation of independent r&b producers (Luther Dixon, Phil Spector, Berry Gordy) were able to deliver the forcefulness and emotional impact of rhythm and blues to the mainstream market. In the process, they rekindled the spirit of early rock 'n' roll and brought to the forefront for the first time a score of black female vocal groups, known collectively as the girl groups, who became overwhelmingly popular until disappearing under the onslaught of the mid-1960s British Invasion.

In 1962, thanks primarily to the girl groups, more black artists appeared on the year-end singles charts than at any time in history. Between 1962 and 1963 alone, for example, the best-selling singles lists included the Crystals ("He's a Rebel," "Da Doo Ron Ron," "Then He Kissed Me"), the Sensations ("Let Me In"), the Chiffons ("He's So Fine," "One Fine Day"), the Essex ("Easier Said Than Done"), the Ronettes ("Be My Baby"), Ruby and the Romantics ("Our Day Will Come"), and the Motown groups Martha and the Vandellas ("Come and Get These Memories," "Heat Wave," "Quicksand") and the Marvelettes ("Please Mr. Postman," "Playboy"). By 1964, Motown's Supremes had come into their own; they turned out fifteen hit singles in a row over the next few years. The Orlons ("The Wah Watusi," "Don't Hang Up," "South Street") are often included in these lists, even though they had one male vocalist.

The only significant girl groups that were white were the Angels ("My Boyfriend's Back") and the Shangri-Las ("Leader of the Pack"). Still, as talented as these groups were, it is almost impossible to separate their artistry from the genius of the producers who molded their sound.

The Shirelles, from Passaic, New Jersey, were the prototypical girl group. They first recorded for the independent Tiara label

Phil Spector is often regarded as the genius behind some of the most important "girl groups." The "wall of sound" he created for them produced the perfect marriage of technology and rhythm and blues. It remains one of the defining sounds of the early 1960s.

formed by Florence Greenberg, one of the few women to own her own record company. The Shirelles' first hit, "I Met Him on a Sunday," was written by the group; it sold so well locally that Decca picked it up for national distribution in 1958. Decca had no faith in the group, however, and their next records appeared on Greenberg's Scepter label, produced by Luther Dixon. Combining a plaintive gospel call-and-response style with the urban sensibilities of uptown r&b, Dixon shepherded the Shirelles through a string of hits from 1960 to 1962 that are now considered rock 'n' roll classics: "Will You Still Love Me Tomorrow," "Dedicated to the One I Love," "Mama Said," "Baby It's You," and "Soldier Boy." By this time, the commercial appeal of female vocal groups had been proven, and Dixon's production techniques, developed simultaneously by Phil Spector and Berry Gordy, had become nearly a science.

((·• **HEAR MORE**
Phil Spector on
MyMusicKit

Phil Spector, who worked with two of the most important groups, the Crystals and the Ronettes, is the producer most readily associated with the girl group phenomenon. Like Leiber and Stoller, whom he apprenticed, Spector was a white man whose vision was to harness the wizardry of studio production and the precision of a professionally written song to the energy and vitality of rhythm and blues. Certainly, no better cultural milieu existed to nurture such a vision than the integrationist stance of the early civil rights movement. Indeed, "Spanish Harlem" (one of Spector's first hits) and "Black Pearl" (his last) seem to underscore this connection. As David Hinckley has written: "That Spector helped bring to life a rose that was Spanish and a pearl that was Black reflects a human rainbow pop music did not always acknowledge so sympathetically."[5]

The Ronettes belted out some of the most memorable songs of the early 1960s. Often, however, a consideration of their talent seemed to be overshadowed by a focus on their sexuality. Too bad the two could not have been appreciated equally.

Spector's artistic vision and genius for production were matched only by his egotism and paranoia. As to his control of every aspect of production, Tom Wolfe noted:

Spector does the whole thing. He writes the words and the music, scouts and signs up the talent. He takes them out to a recording studio in Los Angeles and runs the recording session himself. He puts them through hours and days of recording to get the two or three minutes he wants. Two or three minutes out of the whole struggle. He handles the control dials like an electronic maestro, tuning various instruments or sound up, down, out, every which way, using things like two pianos, a harpsichord and three guitars on one record; then re-recording the whole thing with esoteric dubbing and overdubbing effects—reinforcing instruments or voices—coming out with what is known throughout the industry as "the Spector sound."[6]

While other companies issued multiple releases simultaneously, Spector labored over and thoroughly promoted only a few records per year. This singular devotion to his recordings contributed greatly to the perception of Spector as a Svengali-like producer who treated his artists as one more element in the creation of a total sound—a view that encouraged the notion of girl group singers as interchangeable entities on the pop assembly line.

This singular devotion to his recordings contributed greatly to the perception of Spector as a Svengali-like producer who treated his artists as one more element in the creation of a total sound—a view that encouraged the notion of girl group singers as interchangeable entities on the pop assembly line.

To offer but one example, Darlene Love recorded only two Top Forty hits (both with Spector in 1963) under her own name: "(Today I Met) The Boy I'm Gonna Marry" and "Wait Til' My Bobby Gets Home." However, she was part of the Blossoms, a group Spector used for background vocals, and a member of Bob B. Soxx & the Blue Jeans, another Spector group with two Top Forty hits: "Zip-A-Dee Doo-Dah" (1962) and "Why Do Lovers Break Each Other's Hearts" (1963). She also sang lead on two of the Crystals' biggest hits in 1962—"He's a Rebel" and "He's Sure the Boy I Love"—though she was never listed as a member of the group. In short, a substantial Darlene Love legacy has been compromised by the shoddy practice of crediting recordings incorrectly and the more general tendency to submerge the noteworthy talents of these women singers beneath a consideration of their producers' overall sound.[7]

Spector formed Philles Records (with Lester Sill) and soon became the best customer of some of the Brill Building's best songwriting teams: Gerry Goffin and Carole King, Barry Mann and Cynthia Weil, and Ellie Greenwich and Jeff Barry. While they turned out their share of schlock (see Chapter 5), they also accomplished culturally, in microcosm, one political dream of the early civil rights movement: an integrated, productive society. Together, white songwriters and black vocalists incorporated the excitement and urgency of rhythm and blues into the mainstream tradition of professional pop. Nowhere was this marriage better executed than in the classic hits of the girl groups (see the table).

Mining more gold from the Brill Building in his work with the Righteous Brothers—Bob Hatfield and Bill Medley, a white male pop/r&b duo—Spector wrote their first and biggest hit, "You've Lost That Lovin' Feelin'" (1964), with Mann and Weil, and their second release, "Just Once in My Life" (1965), with Goffin and King. The sound that Spector created for the Righteous Brothers was so successful that it commanded a new marketing category of its own, *blue-eyed soul,* which included the Young Rascals ("Good Lovin',"

Selected Brill Building Girl Group Classics

SONGWRITERS	SONG	ARTIST
Gerry Goffin and Carole King	"One Fine Day"	Chiffons
	"Chains"	Cookies
	"Don't Say Nothin' Bad About My Baby"	Cookies
	"Will You Love Me Tomorrow"	Shirelles
	"He Hit Me (It Felt Like a Kiss)"	Crystals
(with Phil Spector)	"Is This What I Get for Loving You?"	Ronettes
Barry Mann and Cynthia Weil	"Uptown"	Crystals
	"He's Sure the Boy I Love"	Crystals
(with Phil Spector)	"Walking in the Rain"	Ronettes
Gene Pitney	"He's a Rebel"	Crystals
Ellie Greenwich and Jeff Barry		
(with Phil Spector)	"Da Doo Ron Ron"	Crystals
(with Phil Spector)	"Then He Kissed Me"	Crystals
(with Phil Spector)	"Chapel of Love"	Dixie Cups
(with Phil Spector)	"Be My Baby"	Ronettes
(with Phil Spector)	"Baby I Love You"	Ronettes
(with Phil Spector)	"Wait til' My Bobby Gets Home"	Darlene Love
(with Phil Spector)	"Not Too Young to Get Married"	Bob B. Soxx & the Blue Jeans
(with Tony Powers)	"Today I Met the Boy I'm Gonna Marry"	Darlene Love
(with Tony Powers)	"Why Do Lovers Break Each Others' Hearts"	Bob B. Soxx & the Blue Jeans
(with Shadow Morton)	"Leader of the Pack"	Shangri-Las

(((• HEAR MORE
Audio links on
MyMusicKit

"Groovin'") and Mitch Ryder and the Detroit Wheels ("Sock It to Me, Baby"). In these instances, the color-blindness of the early civil rights movement was reinforced, for here was black-sounding music written by whites, produced by whites, and performed by whites that was accepted by blacks.

Brill Building writers also figured prominently in the success of the Shangri-Las, a white girl group. When producer George "Shadow" Morton discovered the Shangri-Las, he called on his friends Greenwich and Barry to help him write "Leader of the Pack" (1964), the group's best-selling single. The song—whose tragic story ends with a motorcycle accident—was recorded with the sound of a real motorcycle and a horrifying crash as if to emphasize the power of the music. In these days before feminism, the Shangri-Las, like the other girl groups, were confined to singing about their relationships with men and were marketed as much for sexual appeal as for musical abilities.

Gender issues notwithstanding, the best rock 'n' roll of the era was being composed by Brill Building songwriters, who often wrote with intelligence and even wit but, with few exceptions, an utter lack of substance. Nowhere was this clearer than in the pop/soul alliance between Brill Building writer/producers Burt Bacharach and Hal David and song stylist Dionne Warwick, who recorded for Scepter Records. Warwick's soulful delivery of the writers' well-crafted tunes transformed lyric fluff into works of beauty. From 1963 to 1970, Warwick recorded twenty-two Top Forty hits ("Anyone Who Had a Heart," "Walk on By," "I Say a Little Prayer") that never broached a topical issue.

Gender issues notwithstanding, the best rock 'n' roll of the era was being composed by Brill Building songwriters, who often wrote with intelligence and even wit but, with few exceptions, an utter lack of substance.

The girl groups were a short-lived phenomenon for several reasons. Despite their talent and sophisticated production, these artists simply faced too many obstacles: They were, in many ways, a throwback to a 1950s style, they were women, and they were black. After the British Invasion, only two girl group releases reached the Top Ten, the Shangri-Las' "I Can Never Go Home Anymore" (1965) and the Chiffons' "Sweet Talkin' Guy" (1966). Motown's female acts that survived and thrived did so because they transcended the girl group label; they were able to do so because Berry Gordy did not just produce great records, he built long-term careers.

Motown: The Integration of Pop

Motown developed and defined itself in the context of the early civil rights movement, where assimilation into the mainstream of American life was seen as desirable. The company soon integrated the pop market with a success unmatched in the history of the music industry. Until its 1988 purchase by MCA and subsequent mergers with other industry giants, Motown was the largest black-owned corporation in the United States. Its founder, Berry Gordy, was a tough, black, middle-class jazz buff from Detroit, who preferred the world of music to life in the Ford Motor Company. A regular at local jazz clubs, Gordy ran a small jazz record store in the mid-1950s. He was also a prizefighter with a number of wins to his credit. His association with Jackie Wilson, a Golden Gloves champion and r&b star, brought these two strands of his life together. In the late 1950s, Gordy wrote Wilson's biggest hits, including "Reet Petite," "Lonely Teardrops," "That's Why (I Love You So)," and "I'll Be Satisfied." During this period, Gordy met Smokey Robinson of the Miracles. After Gordy wrote and produced a Top Thirty hit for Barrett Strong ("Money," 1960), Robinson convinced him to start his own company. This was the beginning of the Motown empire.

With few exceptions, Motown's creative personnel—artists, writers, producers, and session musicians—were African American and all were groomed for long careers (if not paid accordingly). One of the few white employees was Barney Ales, vice president for distribution, whose relationships with mainstream distributors were crucial to the label's financial health. It was Gordy's job to produce the records that would satisfy their pop needs. As secretive a company as there ever was, Motown was a completely in-house operation under the total control of Gordy. It included not only the Motown and Tamla labels but also the Hitsville USA studio, Jobete Publishing, and International Talent Management (ITM). ITM provided personal

((•● **HEAR MORE**
Motown on MyMusicKit

Beginning with a modest studio in Detroit, Berry Gordy built his Motown empire into the largest black-owned corporation in the United States. It opened a new chapter in the treatment of African American artists in the music industry.

management, including choreographic training by industry veteran Cholly Atkins, lessons on etiquette from local beauty-school owner Maxine Powell, and tour bookings.

Like Spector, Gordy evolved a production technique aimed at maximum crossover. Working closely with Smokey Robinson on the label's early releases, he multitracked compelling leads and rich gospel harmonies over strong rhythm and horn tracks and the signature bass lines of the legendary James Jamerson. In doing this, Gordy came up with a musical formula that was the perfect metaphor for the early civil rights era: upbeat black pop that was irresistibly danceable and threatening to no one in tone or content. This was the Motown Sound or, as the Motown label logo boasted, "The Sound of Young America." Gordy would later comment that any successful Motown hit sold at least 70 percent to white audiences.

> **G**ordy came up with a musical formula that was the perfect metaphor for the early civil rights era: upbeat black pop that was irresistibly danceable and threatening to no one in tone or content. This was the Motown Sound or, as the Motown label logo boasted, "The Sound of Young America."

To his credit, Gordy built all of his acts from the ground up; he did not simply bleed them for one or two hits, an all-too-common experience for black artists in the past. As a result, first-generation Motown artists—the Miracles ("Shop Around"), the Marvelettes ("Please Mr. Postman"), Martha and the Vandellas ("Dancing in the Streets"), the Temptations ("My Girl"), the Four Tops ("I Can't Help Myself"), Marvin Gaye ("Pride and Joy"), and Stevie Wonder ("Fingertips—Part 2"), among others—enjoyed a longevity almost unheard of for black artists in the pop market. While other labels may have treated particularly successful groups with such care, Motown approached its whole roster in these terms. From 1961 to 1971, the company placed well over 100 singles in the pop Top Ten, not to mention scores of lesser hits.

Motown hit its stride in 1964 when the Supremes were assigned to the writer/producer team of Eddie Holland, Lamont Dozier, and Brian Holland. The trio of Florence Ballard, Mary Wilson, and Diana Ross quickly became the crown jewel of the Motown empire. Beginning with "Where Did Our Love Go," the Supremes turned out five number one singles in a row,

HEAR MORE
Audio links of selected Motown Top Ten Hits on MyMusicKit

Motown groomed its artists to look as presentable as possible without compromising the infectious dance music that defined the label. The Supremes, shown here performing "Stop! In the Name of Love," were considered the height of elegance in 1965.

including "Baby Love," "Come See About Me," "Stop! In the Name of Love," and "Back in My Arms Again"—no mean achievement for an African American act during the first wave of the British Invasion. By the time Cindy Birdsong (formerly of Patti LaBelle and the Blue Belles) replaced Ballard in 1967, the group had turned out five more number one hits.

Motown's understanding of the Top Forty radio format, as well as its outstanding artists and production, enabled the company to produce countless hits. On Top Forty radio, records were squeezed in between commercials and fast-talking deejays. Understanding these constraints, Smokey Robinson sought to exercise maximum creativity in a two- to three-minute timeframe. In his own words: "My theory of writing is to write a song that has a complete idea and tells a story in the time allotted for a record. . . . I've just geared myself to radio time. The shorter a record is nowadays, the more it's gonna be played."[8] While such a formula may have structured a song, it could not substitute for creativity. With songwriters like Eddie Holland, Lamont Dozier, and Brian Holland ("Where Did Our Love Go"), Norman Whitfield ("Pride and Joy"), and Nick Ashford and Valerie Simpson ("Ain't No Mountain High Enough"), Motown boasted an in-house staff that could rival the best of the Brill Building writers.

In his quest for a mainstream audience, Gordy adopted the Brill Building aesthetic that controversial issues had no place in Motown songs. "[W]hen it came to lyrics," as Gerri Hershey has said, Berry Gordy "had a larger constituency to consider. . . . Gordy's demographics could countenance no overt militancy."[9] It should not be surprising, then, that socially relevant themes and images were no more prevalent in early Motown lyrics than in any other genre of pop, rock, or rhythm and blues. Stevie Wonder's 1966

HEAR MORE
Audio links of selected Motown Staff Writers' Hits on MyMusicKit

In his quest for a mainstream audience, Gordy adopted the Brill Building aesthetic that controversial issues had no place in Motown songs.

"Stop! In the Name of Love"

Artist: The Supremes
Music/Lyrics by Eddie Holland, Lamont Dozier, and Brian Holland
Label: Motown (1965)

The Supremes (Diana Ross, Florence Ballard, and Mary Wilson) were Motown's most successful girl group, part of a roster that also included the Marvelettes and Martha and the Vandellas. Berry Gordy employed a whole team of music coaches, choreographers, fashion consultants, and modeling coaches for his artists in order to create the sleek, elegant image exemplified by the Supremes. Their sound, which took America by storm, was the combined result of their beautifully blended voices, Motown's roster of great recording session players and arrangers, and songwriters such as Smokey Robinson and the team of Eddie Holland, Lamont Dozier, and Brian Holland, who wrote "Stop! In the Name of Love."

"Stop! In the Name of Love" garnered a Grammy nomination in 1966. Gordy's formula for crossover appeal was bearing fruit in many ways: "Stop! In the Name of Love" was nominated in the "Best Contemporary Rock and Roll Group Vocal Performance" category and *not* the "Rhythm and Blues" category, as the Supreme's "Baby Love" had been a year before.

Musical Style Notes

Motown's songwriters were masters of the Top Forty pop song: a simple, familiar musical structure consisting of short verses and catchy, uptempo refrains, usually with one brief solo improvisation over an instrumental verse. Brevity was another consideration; few pop singles were over 3 minutes long. "Stop! In the Name of Love" is a classic example of this kind of structure and also features a signature Motown combination: a strong lead singer plus doo wop–influenced background vocals, combined with slick, tightly arranged instrumental parts provided by a roster of virtuoso studio musicians known as the Funk Brothers. The Funk Brothers' roster included a long list of distinguished players, including the unmistakable Motown rhythm section of drummer Benny Benjamin and bass player James Jamerson.

Musical "Road Map"

TIMINGS	COMMENTS	LYRICS
0:00–0:10	Electronic organ glissando (rapid slide up through several notes) leads into refrain.	*Stop, . . .*
0:10–0:19	Instrumental interlude between refrain and verse.	
0:19–0:51	Verse 1	*Baby baby . . .*
0:28	Background vocals begin.	
0:43	Background vocals: "Think it over" (using same melody as refrain's last phrase).	
0:51–1:17	Refrain (repeated twice) (no instrumental interlude here)	*Stop,*
1:17–1:51	Verse 2	*I've known . . .*
1:26	Background vocals begin.	
1:42	Background vocals: "Think it over" (using same melody as refrain's last phrase).	
1:51–2:16	Refrain (repeated twice)	*Stop,*
2:16–2:33	Verse 3	*I've tried . . .*
2:24	Background vocals begin. ("Think it over" phrase omitted in this verse—instead, they proceed directly into the refrain.)	
2:33–2:54	Refrain (repeated twice)	*Stop,*

cover of "Blowin' in the Wind"—six years after the founding of the label and well past the initial surge of the civil rights movement—was easily Motown's most prominent "topical" release to date. Thus, while the climate of the early civil rights movement encouraged the success of Motown, the company never became a voice for the cause. During this period, social commentary could be found primarily in the folk arena and, to a lesser extent, in jazz.

Folk Music: The Voice of Civil Rights

It is impossible to analyze the 1960s folk revival without mentioning Woodie Guthrie and Pete Seeger, avowed left-wing activists since the 1930s. Guthrie was an Okie—someone who traveled to California with other Oklahomans during the Dust Bowl era, learning folk and blues along the way and writing songs about his experiences. Radicalized by his experiences of the Great Depression and his associations with left-wing activists in California and then New York, Guthrie wrote some of this country's most enduring folk songs, including "This Land Is Your Land," "So Long, It's Been Good to Know You," and "This Train Is Bound for Glory." Indeed, he helped to create the association between folk music and leftist politics that was reflected in the statement displayed on his guitar: "This machine kills fascists." Seeger was a college-educated, New York radical who saw music as a means to mobilize a mass movement. Guthrie and Seeger formed the Almanac Singers in 1941 and promoted their progressive political message throughout the country. In the early 1950s, Seeger recorded million-selling records as a member of the Weavers. His dis-affection with pop success and the specter of McCarthyism, however, forced his career into the background. By this time, Guthrie was seriously debilitated by Huntington's chorea. From the 1950s until his death in 1967, he was bedridden; among his visitors was the young Bob Dylan, who described himself as something of a Woody Guthrie jukebox.

The civil rights movement was a natural outlet for Pete Seeger's creative and political energies. More than anyone else, Seeger tirelessly popularized the movement's anthem, "We Shall Overcome," to a global audience. While he was a folk purist who railed against commer-cialism in music and seldom basked in the limelight himself, his guiding hand was never far from view. "If I Had a Hammer," a song he had written in 1949 with Lee Hays, became a Top Ten hit in 1962 for Peter, Paul, and Mary and again in 1963 for Trini Lopez. The Kingston Trio scored in 1962 with his "Where Have All the Flowers Gone." And the Byrds had a number one folk-rock hit with his "Turn! Turn! Turn!" in 1965, although Seeger hadn't yet come to grips with his misgivings about the marriage of folk and rock.

In folk circles at the time, there was a fiercely argued distinction between performers con-sidered "authentic" and those considered "commercial." For most, Seeger defined authenticity; while the Kingston Trio and the groups that garnered Top Forty hits from popularized folk material—the Rooftop Singers ("Walk Right In," 1963), the New Christy Minstrels ("Green, Green," 1963), and the Serendipity Singers ("Don't Let the Rain Come Down," 1964)—were clearly commercial. The distinction, of course, was riddled with inconsistency. Eric Darling, leader of the Rooftop Singers, had been a member of the Weavers with Seeger. Joan Baez was considered authentic even though she charted twelve Top Forty long-playing records (LPs), six of which were certified gold albums. As activist liberals with commercial success, Peter, Paul, and Mary straddled the fence.

After sitting at the feet of an ailing Woody Guthrie, the freewheeling Bob Dylan shrouded his past in mystery and set about building his own myth as a Guthrie-style folksinger. The early civil rights movement gave him the perfect springboard for success.

(((• HEAR MORE
Bob Dylan on
MyMusicKit

The artist who openly challenged the distinction and ultimately rendered it useless was a newcomer—the enigmatic Bob Dylan. Born Robert Zimmerman into a middle-class Jewish family, Dylan grew up in Hibbing, Minnesota, listening to a 1950s mixture of rhythm and blues, country and western, rock 'n' roll, and pop. One of his boyhood dreams was to play in Little Richard's band. After attending college for a while and reading Guthrie's autobiography, *Bound for Glory,* Zimmerman moved to New York, where he began building his own myth as a Guthrie-style folk singer. He also legalized his newly acquired surname and shrouded his earlier life in mystery. He was signed by John Hammond to Columbia in 1962 and, over the next two years, issued three albums of highly unorthodox, mostly self-accompanied acoustic folk to critical raves.

With selections like "Oxford Town" (about racism in a Mississippi town) from his second album, *The Freewheelin' Bob Dylan* (1963) and "The Lonesome Death of Hattie Carroll" (the true story of the killing of a black woman) from his third, *The Times They Are A-Changin'* (1964), Dylan was early proclaimed a leader in the civil rights movement. In 1963, he performed "Only a Pawn in Their Game," a song about the murder of civil rights leader Medgar Evers, at the March on Washington, where he stood next to Martin Luther King, Jr., and shared the stage with folk luminaries such as Pete Seeger, Joan Baez, and Peter, Paul, and Mary. (That same year, Peter, Paul, and Mary had Top Ten pop hits with Dylan's "Blowin' in the Wind" and "Don't Think Twice, It's Alright.") In three short years, then, Dylan was well along the road to transforming, almost singlehandedly, the lyric content of popular music. At this point, he made a musical decision that cost him his authenticity but brought him a mass audience.

In 1965, Dylan appeared at the Newport Folk Festival playing an electric guitar (a classic rock Fender Stratocaster, no less), backed by an electric band (the Paul Butterfield Blues Band), and tried to perform some material from his new album, *Bringing It All Back Home.* Seeger was livid, and Dylan was booed off the stage. But as the song says, "the times they are a-changin'," which Dylan knew better than his critics. Dylan released his first album in 1962 as Tom Hayden and other radical students were writing "The Port Huron Statement," the manifesto of Students for a Democratic Society (SDS). In a world of increasing student activism folk offered an alternative to rock 'n' roll's lyric vacuity, but it could never supplant the more primal urges that rhythm and blues and

Folk offered an alternative to rock 'n' roll's lyric vacuity, but it could never supplant the more primal urges that rhythm and blues and rock 'n' roll had turned loose. Bridging that gap was Dylan's particular genius.

"The Times They Are A-Changin'"

Artist: Bob Dylan
Music/Lyrics by Bob Dylan
Label: Columbia (1964)

"The Times They Are A-Changin'" (1964), like the LP that shares its name, represents the Bob Dylan that became, perhaps somewhat reluctantly, a political and social spokesperson for his generation. Dylan captured in his lyrics a time when the youth movement was growing in strength, when the civil rights movement was making sea changes in the cultural landscape of America, and when we still thought that music might change the world.

Musical Style Notes

"The Times They Are A-Changin'" features a relatively short, repeated-verse structure with a simple acoustic guitar accompaniment. The occasional harmonica comment adds some color to the arrangement and strengthens the listener's association with the American folk music tradition of Woody Guthrie and Pete Seeger. The time-honored combination of solo voice with one accompanying instrument played in a relatively simple manner serves to foreground the lyrics, an effective combination for any genre that prioritizes lyric content over musical complexity.

Musical "Road Map"

TIMINGS	COMMENTS	LYRICS
0:0–0:3	Introduction; acoustic guitar	
0:3–0:32	Verse 1	*Come gather . . .*
0:33–0:40	Harmonica bridge to second verse	
0:40–1:07	Verse 2	*Come writers . . .*
1:08–1:18	Harmonica bridge to third verse	
1:19–1:45	Verse 3	*Come senators, . . .*
1:46–1:52	Harmonica bridge to fourth verse	
1:53–2:19	Verse 4	*Come mothers . . .*
2:20–2:37	Harmonica bridge to fifth verse	
2:37–3:04	Verse 5	*The line . . .*
3:04–3:11	Harmonica fades to end of song	

rock 'n' roll had turned loose. For this reason, folk could never capture a mass audience. Bridging that gap was Dylan's particular genius.

Bringing It All Back Home contained one acoustic side and one side of electric music with uncommonly substantive lyrics held up by a hard-driving, straight-ahead rock 'n' roll beat. As one reviewer has noted: "This is the point where Dylan eclipses any conventional sense of folk and rewrites the rules of rock, making it safe for personal expression and poetry."[10] "Subterranean Homesick Blues," the first cut on the electric side, became his first Top Forty pop hit, and a roar of outrage arose from the folk community. Was Dylan the true seer the folkies had once thought he was or the consummate opportunist they now criticized? It depended on who was asked. Amid charges that he had sold out not just the civil rights movement but the entire American left, Dylan took his own advice about following leaders and turned his back on politics. In this change of direction, he was often contrasted with Phil Ochs, whose songs such as "Here's to the State of Mississippi" and "I Ain't Marching Anymore" from his second album, remained true to the folk protest ideal. Ostracized by the true believers, Dylan soon left his detractors in the dust as he ushered in the era of folk rock. Ochs, in contrast, was tortured by his inability to become "the first left-wing star," a torment that eventually pushed him to take his own life in 1976.

The debate over commercial versus authentic performers tended to obscure a far more important issue at the time. From old-timers like Pete Seeger to newcomers like Joan Baez, Bob Dylan, and Peter, Paul, and Mary, the best-known artists in folk music were white. Seeger, to his credit, included African Americans (for example, Odetta, Sonny Terry, and Brownie McGhee) in his concerts and on his albums; gradually, these artists became prominent voices of the civil rights movement. During the initial surge of the folk revival, however, artists of color who performed folkloric material, from Lead Belly to Josh White, seldom became well known outside folk circles.

Harry Belafonte, an outspoken activist and a director of Martin Luther King's Southern Christian Leadership Conference (SCLC), was an obvious exception. In 1960, he recorded a second million-selling live album at Carnegie Hall, this one including Odetta, Miriam Makeba, and the Chad Mitchell Trio. But Belafonte was already a pop star; his music and his acting and television career seemed curiously separate from his political choices. Trini Lopez was also something of an exception. Like Ritchie Valens before him, the Tex-Mex pop singer included Mexican and American popular and folk material in his repertoire. His best-selling "Lemon Tree" (1965) was adapted from the traditional Latin song "Hojita de Lemon." Buffy Sainte-Marie (a Cree Indian from Canada) wrote original compositions such as "Now That the Buffalo's Gone" and "My Country 'Tis of Thy People You're Dying" that offered her limited audience a profoundly different view of Native Americans than that expressed by pop fare such as Johnny Preston's "Running Bear" or Larry Verne's "Mr. Custer."

Not until the mid-1960s was the social consciousness of folk music linked to the popular appeal of the gospel/r&b fusion. The center for this innovation was Chicago and the often underappreciated Curtis Mayfield. Like fellow Chicagoan Sam Cooke, Mayfield had left the gospel choir for the secular world of popular music in the 1950s. After hits with the Impressions—"For Your Precious Love" (1958), "Gypsy Woman" (1961), and "It's All Right" (1963)—Mayfield "got religion" once again. He penned a series of successful folk-sounding but

Curtis Mayfield started as a talented writer and singer who effected a successful pop gospel fusion in the 1950s with his group the Impressions. The civil rights movement provided the inspiration for some of his best music. He went on to become a producer, label chief, and solo artist, scoring Superfly, *one of the most successful so-called blaxploitation films of the early 1970s.*

pop-produced "sermon songs" for the group, including "Keep on Pushing" and "Amen" in 1964 and "People Get Ready" in 1965. Through these songs, he became, in the words of Nelson George, "black music's most unflagging civil rights champion."[11]

Mayfield's fusion had been anticipated by the Staple Singers, a family gospel group that started in a Chicago Baptist church in 1950. In the late 1950s, they recorded gospel for Vee Jay with Pop Staples's understated guitar and daughter Mavis's compelling lead vocals. In the early 1960s, the group demonstrated Mayfield's pop feel for the material, recording spiritual classics such as "Will the Circle Be Unbroken?" "Amazing Grace," and "We Shall Overcome" with electric guitar and drums. When they signed with Stax in the 1970s, they made the charts with gospel-tinged songs "I'll Take You There," "If You're Ready (Come Go with Me)," and "Touch a Hand, Make a Friend" prominent among their hits.

Another note about Sam Cooke's career completes this look at Chicago's musical connections to the civil rights struggle. Cooke had made a mild but successful foray into social commentary as early as 1960 when "Chain Gang" went to number two on the pop charts. Still, it was not until he heard Dylan's "Blowin' in the Wind" that he felt compelled to relate to the civil rights movement more directly. In late 1964, he attempted a pop/folk fusion with "A Change Is Gonna Come." By the time the record was released, however, Cooke had been shot to death under unsavory circumstances. When his friend Malcolm X was assassinated only two months later, on 21 February 1965, "A Change Is Gonna Come" was moving up the charts to Top Forty status. It stands as Cooke's monument to civil rights.

The British Invasion Occupies the Pop Charts

The promise of President John F. Kennedy's New Frontier, as his blueprint for America was called, was dealt a crushing blow when he was assassinated on 22 November 1963. In the aftermath of his death, the national mood was one of defeat and depression. It is noteworthy that in the six months between Kennedy's assassination and the passage of the Civil Rights Act of 1964, the Beatles' upbeat sound captured the cultural life of the nation. "In retrospect," as critic Lester Bangs has written, "it seems obvious that this elevation of our mood had to come from outside the parameters of America's own musical culture, if only because

SEE MORE
The Beatles documentary on MyMusicKit

The Beatles were not what they appeared to be. After paying their dues in the rough-and-tumble nightclubs of Hamburg, manager Brian Epstein dressed them up in suits and ties and went to great pains to present them as clean-cut entertainers.

the folk music which then dominated American pop was so tied to the crushed dreams of the New Frontier."[12]

The Beatles transformed popular music just as the issue of civil rights became permanently imprinted on the national consciousness. For both the Beatles and the civil rights movement, the time was right; for both, the results were profound. So dramatic was the Beatles' impact that, from a cultural point of view, there is a tendency to think that the sixties (that is, the cultural era) began in 1964, the year the group hit the U.S. pop charts. It was as if the country had simply been marking time for four years, waiting for their arrival.

So *dramatic was the Beatles' impact that, from a cultural point of view, there is a tendency to think that the sixties (that is, the cultural era) began in 1964, the year the group hit the U.S. pop charts.*

There were many reasons for this perception. First, the Beatles made their American debut at a time when the U.S. music industry was stagnating. While the industry had more than doubled in size between 1955 and 1959, record sales had fallen by 5 percent (to $600 million) in 1960. By 1963, sales were up by only 1.6 percent from the previous year. After 1964, the industry had double-digit growth every year until the end of the decade and, including tape sales, more than doubled its revenues (to about $1.6 billion). The Beatles, of course, did not rejuvenate the music business singlehandedly, but other artists paled in the face of their impressive statistics and fresh sound. When the Beatles first hit the U.S. pop charts in January 1964, their records were issued on six different labels (because EMI's U.S. partner Capitol initially passed on their contract). By February, they had become the country's hottest act, although they had yet to step foot on U.S. soil. In mid-April they had twelve singles in the *Billboard Hot 100,* including the top five positions. In 1964 alone, they charted thirty singles and released six best-selling albums. *Billboard* reported that, for a period of about three weeks, the Beatles accounted for nearly 60 percent of all singles sold. From 1963 to 1968, the group sold an estimated $154 million worth of records worldwide.[13] Not even Elvis in his heyday could compete with numbers like these.

Second, the Beatles eclipsed all other talent so quickly and so completely that many lost sight of the fact that, prior to their arrival, the most exciting developments in popular music had been in African American music. Indeed, the Beatles' first album in the United States, *Introducing . . . The Beatles,* which included five Top Ten singles, was released on the black-owned Vee Jay label. The early sound of the Beatles, the Animals, and the Rolling Stones, among others, was hard-driving rock 'n' roll—and much of its inspiration came directly from African American blues and r&b artists. Indeed, this was the expected repertoire of any successful club band in the venues where these groups got their start. Many of the Beatles' early recordings were nearly note-for-note reproductions of African American rock 'n' roll classics. This is not to suggest that the Beatles could, in any way, be reduced to mere cover artists. The group broke new ground in untold ways and changed the course of popular music. Their motivation in rerecording so many African American hits was less to cash in on black culture than to pay tribute to their musical forebears. The Beatles openly credited Chuck Berry, the Miracles, Chuck Jackson, and Ben E. King as formative influences, introducing (along with the Animals, the Rolling Stones, and to a lesser extent the Dave Clark Five) a generation of white, middle-class Americans to the rich tradition of African American music that had always existed within earshot. Still, it was a fact of American life that, though repeatedly acknowledging their debt to African American music and touring with early rock 'n' roll greats like Little Richard, the Beatles and other English groups were more marketable than the African American artists they admired.

In the two years following the Beatles' arrival, no fewer than two dozen British groups appeared on the U.S. pop charts. The previous year there had been none. But if the British Invasion dominated the U.S. pop charts generally, there was another development that was particularly devastating for black artists. In keeping with the integrationist impulse of the early civil rights movement, the r&b charts were briefly discontinued from the end of 1963 until the beginning of 1965. If the separate and unequal r&b market was problematic, "integration" proved to be more so. In 1962, 42 percent of the songs on the year-end singles charts were by African Americans. In 1966, this figure declined to 22 percent, the lowest point since the initial surge of rock 'n' roll. Only three of the top fifty albums for the years 1964 and 1965 were by black artists. In contrast, nearly one-third of the Top Ten releases for 1964 belonged to British acts.

Among African American artists, Motown acts survived the first wave of the British Invasion better than most, not only because of the freshness of the Motown sound but also because Berry Gordy purposefully forged alliances with popular British groups. It was no coincidence that the Supremes' third album, *A Bit of Liverpool* (1964), showcased cover tunes from British groups, especially the Beatles. In two important telecasts, *T.A.M.I.* (1964) and *TNT* (1965), the Supremes, Smokey Robinson and the Miracles, and Marvin Gaye appeared with the British groups Gerry and the Pacemakers and the Rolling Stones.[14] *Ready Steady Go!,*

HEAR MORE
Audio links for British Invasion Blues/R&B Recordings on MyMusicKit

a television pop music variety show in Great Britain, devoted an entire episode to the Motown sound in 1965. When Motown launched a tour of Britain featuring a number of the company's best-selling artists that year, everybody gushed. The Beatles lauded the music at every opportunity. If there had been any misconceptions about where Berry Gordy sought to position Motown on the pop music continuum, his remarks laid them to rest: "We are very honored the Beatles should have said what they did. . . . They're creating the same type of music as we are and we're part of the same stream."[15]

At its best, the British Invasion recalled the enthusiasm of early rock 'n' roll and pointed the way to numerous future developments in popular music. At its worst, the taste for anything British became so indiscriminate that British acts like Chad and Jeremy ("Yesterday's Gone") and Ian Whitcomb ("You Turn Me On") had Top Ten pop hits in the United States while remaining completely unknown at home. The groups identified with the first wave of the British Invasion came from throughout the British Commonwealth. The Zombies ("She's Not There") hailed from Hertfordshire; the Moody Blues ("Go Now!"), from Birmingham; Peter and Gordon ("A World Without Love"), from Scotland; Them ("Here Comes the Night," "Gloria"), from Ireland; the Seekers ("I'll Never Find Another You"), from Australia; the Nashville Teens, ("Tobacco Road") from Surrey. The Animals ("House of the Rising Sun," 1964), from Newcastle, were an influential blues-based group that was steeped in African American music. Lead singer Eric Burdon's hard, bluesy delivery over Alan Price's soulful organ riffs prompted *Ebony* magazine to devote five pages to Burdon and his group's funky sound, rare coverage for a white singer, even one as obsessed with blackness as Burdon.[16] Mostly, however, the British Invasion came from three cities—Liverpool, Manchester, and London.

The Beatles, of course, came from Liverpool, as did the Searchers ("Needles and Pins"), Gerry and the Pacemakers ("Don't Let the Sun Catch You Crying," "Ferry Cross the Mersey"), Billy J. Kramer and the Dakotas ("Little Children"), Cilla Black ("You're My World"), and the Swinging Blue Jeans ("Hippy Hippy Shake"). Although Liverpool was a dreary, gray, industrial seaport town, a rock 'n' roll culture had flourished among its working-class residents due to the steady stream of U.S. merchant marines who brought records over. Once absorbed, rock 'n' roll mingled with British folk styles and achieved pop status in a type of music known as *skiffle*. Skiffle was fleetingly exposed to American audiences in Lonnie Donegan's "Rock Island Line" (1956) and "Does Your Chewing Gum Lose Its Flavor (on the Bedpost over Night)," (1961). John Lennon, Paul McCartney, George Harrison, and Stuart Sutcliffe (who later died of a brain hemorrhage) played skiffle as the Quarrymen. This was the musical amalgam that shaped the Beatles, but they paid their dues playing rock 'n' roll in the rough-and-tumble nightclubs of the German port city of Hamburg.

Hamburg was the crucible that forged the future Beatles' professionalism. By the time they played there, the Quarrymen had metamorphosed to Johnny and the Moondogs, then to the Silver Beatles, and at last to simply the Beatles, with Pete Best on drums. When they returned home, they were showcased with the best-known Liverpudlian groups at a dingy basement club called the Cavern, where they first came to the attention of Brian Epstein, record-store owner turned manager. Like all beat groups, the Beatles had mastered a standard rock 'n' roll repertoire of Chuck Berry, Little Richard, Elvis Presley, and Buddy Holly, as well as numerous r&b crossover classics. Unlike many of the groups, however, Lennon and McCartney wrote original songs right from the beginning.

Once under the brilliant tutelage of Epstein, the group, which had been turned down at other labels, was signed by producer George Martin to EMI. Their first single, "Love Me Do" (with Ringo Starr replacing Best on drums), went Top Twenty in Great Britain in 1962. In 1963, "Please, Please Me" hit number two there and "From Me to You" went all the way to number one. All three of these hits were Lennon–McCartney tunes. When another Lennon–McCartney original, "She Loves You," became the best-selling single in British history in late 1963, Epstein decided the group was ready to take on the United States. The "fab four" arrived in New York on 7 February 1964, when "I Want to Hold Your Hand" was the number one single in the United States. For the next six months, they occupied the number one slot on the U.S. pop charts. Eight of their nine Top Ten hits during this period were Lennon–McCartney tunes. Their first movie, *A Hard Day's Night,* a black-and-white film by director Richard Lester about a day in the life of the group, opened in August to rave reviews. The soundtrack album yielded two Top Ten singles—the title song and "Can't Buy Me Love." Beatlemania, as the frenzied reaction to the group was called, had taken hold in the United States as it had in England. In a few short months, the Beatles had established an impregnable beachhead for the British Invasion.

The city of Manchester turned out some of the most mindless drivel ever associated with the British Invasion, as well as the notable sounds of Wayne Fontana and the Mindbenders— who spent one glorious week at number one with "The Game of Love" (1965)—and the Hollies, whose close harmonies set them apart from other Manchester groups, even if their biggest hit of the 1960s was the insipid "Bus Stop" (1966). (Graham Nash left the group in 1968 to "make records that say something" with David Crosby and Stephen Stills in Los Angeles.) Herman's Hermits ("Mrs. Brown, You've Got a Lovely Daughter," "I'm Henry VIII, I Am") presented a version of the rock 'n' roll/skiffle fusion that showed how low a pop interpretation of the British music hall tradition could sink. Even so, between 1964 and 1970, Herman's Hermits charted eighteen Top Forty singles and ten albums in the United States. Freddie and the Dreamers ("I'm Telling You Now," 1965) elevated vacuity to an art form, as Freddie Garrity's stage act of flapping both arms while lifting each leg out to the side—a set of moves requiring no skill and less grace—became a dance craze that guaranteed another hit, "Do the Freddie."

London featured a far more eclectic mix of artists than either Liverpool or Manchester: the jazz-influenced Manfred Mann ("Doo Wah Diddy Diddy"); the soulful Dusty Springfield ("I Only Want to Be with You," "You Don't Have to Say You Love Me") and pop-oriented Petula Clark ("Downtown," "I Know a Place"), two woman who held their own throughout the decade; the Dave Clack Five ("Glad All Over"), whose pneumatic drumming, raspy vocals, and r&b covers pointed the way to success; and, finally, the hard-rocking Kinks and the Rolling Stones, the band that outlasted them all.

Under the leadership of writer/vocalist/guitarist Ray Davies, the Kinks took the United States by storm in late 1964 with three original Top Ten hard rockers ("You Really Got Me," "All Day and All of the Night," and "Tired of Waiting for You"). After these releases, the group seemed to stall. Whether due to the union problems they encountered on their first U.S. tour, or the lack of an effective promotional apparatus, or because their follow-up hits ("A Well Respected Man" and "Dedicated Follower of Fashion") were so distinctly British as to be lost on U.S. audiences, the Kinks never attained the stature that should have been their due.

The London musicians who had the most influence on U.S. music were the white blues revivalists, most of whom got their start with Alexis Korner's Blues Incorporated or John Mayall's Bluesbreakers. Among the musicians who passed through these ensembles were Mick Fleetwood, John McVie, and Peter Green of Fleetwood Mac; Eric Clapton, Jack Bruce, and Ginger Baker, who went on to become Cream; Ray Davies of Kinks fame; future members of Pentangle, Free, and Led Zeppelin; and four founders of the Rolling Stones—lead singer Mick Jagger, guitarists Keith Richards and Brian Jones, and drummer Charlie Watts.

Like most British rockers at the time, the Rolling Stones included a good deal of African American music in their repertoire. Even when pushed by their manager to write original material ("It's All Over Now," "The Last Time"), it was clear that the tradition they wished to explore, the musical statement they wanted to make, was based in the blues. It was down and dirty, replete with exaggerated aggressiveness and overt sexuality. It almost demanded a tough, streetwise, working-class image. But if anything, the Stones were bohemians; while they displayed the typical British fascination with African American culture, they had a sufficient distance on it that Jagger could pull off his self-mocking delivery of African American styles with ironic detachment. They took longer to arrive in the United States than the Beatles, but when they did, they were embraced as the menacing, street-toughened alternative to the playful mop-tops. In fact, a comparison of the two groups' marketing strategies reveals a study in image construction.

> **T**he Stones were bohemians; while they displayed the typical British fascination with African American culture, they had a sufficient distance on it that Jagger could pull off his self-mocking delivery of African American styles with ironic detachment.

The Rolling Stones arrive in New York for the first time in 1964 with Brian Jones (second from left) as rhythm guitarist. In retrospect, the bad boys of sixties rock look more youthful than tough. They have gone on to become one of the longest-running self-contained rock acts in the business.

Issues of class and culture played themselves out in tensions between the Beatles and the Rolling Stones. As revolutionary as the Beatles' music may have sounded, Brian Epstein took great pains to present the group as middle-class family entertainment. Their first U.S. appearance was on the *Ed Sullivan Show*. The press marveled at their wit. Even parents liked them—they were "cute." They wanted only "to hold your hand." Andrew Loog Oldham, the Stones' manager and former Epstein employee, cultivated precisely the opposite image for his group. The Stones wanted to "spend the night together." Their music was full of disdain (mostly for women). The Stones scowled at the camera; they were surly. After they played the *Ed Sullivan Show,* Sullivan vowed that they would never return.

SEE MORE
The Rolling Stones documentary on MyMusicKit

Of course, neither the Beatles nor the Rolling Stones were quite what they appeared to be. Though John had attended art school (and hated it), the Beatles were more solidly working class than the Stones; they had played Hamburg in slicked-back hair and black leather jackets before Epstein scrubbed them clean and dressed them up in suits and ties. Only two of the Stones—Bill Wyman and Charlie Watts—came from working-class backgrounds. Brian Jones, the Stones' first rhythm guitarist (who drowned in 1969), was an upper-middle-class dropout. Keith Richards attended art school, and Mick Jagger remained a student at the London School of Economics until the group became a going concern. They were no more "street-fighting men" than the Beatles were wholesome and carefree. The images of each group were based on strategic career choices and the musical terrain each group had staked out. Certainly, the Beatles were as well-schooled in contemporary African American music as the Stones, but the group's equally strong affinity for skiffle and the British music hall tradition resonated more with another musical phenomenon that was beginning to bloom in the United States—folk rock.

Breaking the Sounds of Silence: New Voices in the Music

Given the folk revival's stringent requirements for authenticity, it would have been difficult for Bob Dylan to trumpet his admiration for the Beatles in 1964, but his attraction for the group started him thinking more seriously about recording with other musicians and moving in a rock 'n' roll direction. As he later confessed to Anthony Scaduto, his first serious biographer:

> I had heard the Beatles in New York when they first hit. Then, when we were driving through Colorado we had the radio on and eight of the ten top songs were Beatles songs. In Colorado! I Wanna Hold Your Hand, *all those early ones.*
>
> They were doing these things nobody was doing. Their chords were outrageous, just outrageous, and their harmonies made it all valid. You could only do that with other musicians. Even if you're playing your own chords you had to have other people playing with you. That was obvious. And it started me thinking about other people.
>
> But I just kept it to myself that I really dug them. Everybody else thought they were for the teenyboppers, that they were gonna pass right away. But it was obvious to me that they had staying power. I knew they were pointing the direction where music had to go.[17]

When Dylan toured England in May 1964, the Beatles, as well as the Rolling Stones and Eric Burdon, went to see him. According to popular music lore, two important things happened. First, Dylan allegedly turned the Beatles on to marijuana.[18] Hallucinogenic drugs had an obvious influence on their future musical development, and therefore on the rest of popular music. Second, Dylan heard the Animals' "House of the Rising Sun" before it was released in the United States. It knocked him out. "My God, ya oughtta hear what's going down over there," he told a friend. "Eric Burdon, the Animals, ya know? Well, he's doing *House of the Rising Sun* in rock. *Rock*! It's fuckin' *wild*! Blew my mind."[19] The Animals had, in fact, mined Dylan's first album for their first two recordings, redoing "Baby Let Me Follow You Down" as "Baby, Let Me Take You Home" and then transforming "House" into electric, transatlantic magic. Dylan appreciated its significance immediately. "You see, there was a lot of hypocrisy all around," he told Scaduto, "people saying it had to be folk or rock. But I knew it didn't have to be like that."[20]

Folk Rock: Adding Substance to Form

Dylan credited the Animals with concocting the alloy that would yield folk rock, though he might have looked to the earlier model of Ritchie Valens's "La Bamba." Still, it was the Byrds who turned it into a full-fledged genre (marketing category). The Animals had come at folk material from a rock and blues direction. The Byrds were folkies who, like Dylan, embraced rock. Leader Jim (later, Roger) McGuinn had arrived in Los Angeles through the Chicago folk circuit; guitarist and vocalist David Crosby was a California-bred folk singer; Chris Hillman picked up the electric bass after laying down his bluegrass mandolin. Together, they evolved a

The Byrds showed how rock could transform folk. They are pictured in an airport about to begin the journey that would take them eight miles high.

self-conscious sound (defined by McGuinn's electric twelve-string Rickenbacker) based in a rock aesthetic. Like Dylan's Newport 1965 debacle, the Byrds' sonic conception challenged a number of orthodoxies, as Lillian Roxon has pointed out:

> *Until the Byrds, the very notion of a group of folk singers strengthening their sound with rock devices was unthinkable. Folk was highminded, pure and untouched by sordid commercial values. Rock was something you played for a quick buck. The most important thing the Byrds ever did was to recognize that rock could revitalize folk—with a finished product that was considerably more than the sum of its parts.*[21]

At the beginning of their career, the Byrds drank heavily from the well of Dylan's creativity, recording rock versions of four of his songs on their first album. When the group's version of "Mr. Tambourine Man," the title song from their debut album, became a number one pop hit in 1965, folk rock became a "thing." Lovin' Spoonful ("Do You Believe in Magic"), Barry McGuire ("Eve of Destruction"), Sonny and Cher ("I Got You Babe"), and Simon and Garfunkel ("Sounds of Silence") all debuted in 1965. Donovan also came into his own that year with "Sunshine Superman." The Turtles' rendering of Dylan's "It Ain't Me Babe" quickly followed the Byrds' "Tambourine Man" up the charts. Cher even offered Dylan to the teenyboppers in 1965 with her version of "All I Really Want to Do," which was also a hit for the Byrds that year.

After 1965, the electrification of folk in the rock market was more or less taken for granted. Almost everyone understood that, in the mainstream market, the social consciousness that folk brought to the table would be folded into a commercialized rock aesthetic, not the other way around. Lillian Roxon correctly chastised *Newsweek* for referring to the Byrds as "Dylanized Beatles when the whole point was that they were Beatlized Dylans."[22] In the marriage of folk and rock, rock was in control, with all the contradictions that such a statement implied. For those artists who could not reconcile themselves to these contradictions, the results could be disastrous, as the suicide of Phil Ochs indicated. Others expressed their uneasiness in their music. Peter, Paul, and Mary's tentative ode to rock, "I Dig Rock and Roll Music" (1967), revealed both their musical discomfort with the genre and their political distrust of its unabashedly commercial bent.

At the time, folk rockers were usually considered to be "thinking musicians," which was considered a contradiction in terms in the rock market until the Beatles. Certainly topical songs had existed in rock 'n' roll—from Chuck Berry's "Brown-Eyed Handsome Man" to the Crystals' "Uptown," rock 'n' roll had occasionally flirted with the notion of something more. But folk rock offered a steady diet of such material, be it about personal relationships ("All I Really Want to Do") or social commentary ("Sounds of Silence"). In this way, folk rock pointed the way for the singer/songwriters who would go on to capture one strand of the fragmented audience of the 1970s (see Chapter 7). Perhaps nothing illustrates the transition from one era to the other better than the career of Simon and Garfunkel.

Paul Simon and Art Garfunkel first performed in the late 1950s as Tom and Jerry. Eight years later, when their producer Tom Wilson added drums and electric backing to an acoustic recording of "Sounds of Silence" (1965) without their permission, their careers took off. The song shot to number one and established them (now using their real names) as a folk rock act. After racking up

> *Almost everyone understood that, in the mainstream market, the social consciousness that folk brought to the table would be folded into a commercialized rock aesthetic, not the other way around.*

five gold or platinum albums and ten Top Thirty singles (including "Mrs. Robinson," their number one hit from the film *The Graduate*), the duo entered the 1970s with the moving, if sentimental, social commentary of "Bridge Over Troubled Water" from their Grammy Award–winning album of the same name. When they broke up over artistic differences around 1972, both men segued easily into solo soft rock careers, with Simon eventually leaving his former song mate far behind.

In addition to the social consciousness embedded in its songs, folk rock held out the elusive possibility of rock protest. Rock 'n' roll's energy had always been identified with rebels but never with a cause. Folk rock was a mainstream music that could be used explicitly in the service of thoughtful protest and creative opposition. Folk rock thus brought to a mainstream audience not only folk music's poetry but also folk's predominantly left-wing political leanings. In its earliest and most didactic form, there was Barry McGuire's raspy "Eve of Destruction" (1965), which rose to the top of the pop charts. Such doomsday fears, however, were met with rejoinders. Within six months, "Ballads of the Green Berets" by Sgt. Barry Sadler, himself a Green Beret, had also risen to the top of the charts.[23] The battle lines that would soon separate hippies from hard hats were already being drawn.

Oddly enough, given the times and its folk roots, a good deal of folk rock had an uncommonly sunny disposition, even while President Johnson was irrevocably committing U.S. forces to Vietnam. Two groups in particular—the Lovin' Spoonful and the Mamas and the Papas—seemed to offer as large a dose of good old Tin Pan Alley escapism as they did folk protest. John Sebastian, Zal Yanovsky, Cass Elliot, and Dennis Doherty had been the Mugwumps (the name was taken from a group of nineteenth-century liberal reformers). When the group split up after one forgettable LP, Sebastian and Yanovsky formed the Lovin' Spoonful and Elliot and Doherty joined John and Michelle Phillips to become the Mamas and the Papas. The Mamas and the Papas launched their career in 1966 with the cheerful-sounding "California Dreamin'," while the Lovin' Spoonful began with two unbelievably lighthearted singles, "Do You Believe in Magic?" and "You Didn't Have to Be So Nice" and continued the trend with "Daydream" (1966). Even the respective distrustfulness and cynicism of the Mamas and the Papas' "Monday, Monday" and their "Words of Love" were delivered congenially. About the closest either group came to rock grittiness was the Spoonful's "Summer in the City" (1966), recorded with street sounds and a real jackhammer to give it a convincingly urban sound.

Even groups more given to social commentary sounded fairly lighthearted. Compare, for example, the Byrds' "Chimes of Freedom" with Dylan's original. Dylan's half-spoken/half-sung delivery, with sparse acoustic accompaniment, sounds almost ominous when contrasted with the brightness of McGuinn's electric twelve string and the Byrds' upbeat falsetto harmonies. For all its folkiness, folk rock never lost sight of the sheer delight of rock entertainment—or perhaps its spirit emanated from those innocent "years of hope," as Todd Gitlin has said, before they turned to "days of rage."[24]

Black (Music) Is Beautiful

If 1965 was a pivotal year for folk rock, it was even more so for the civil rights movement. Sam Cooke's posthumous tribute to the early phase of that movement, "A Change Is Gonna Come," ironically coincided with the assassination of Malcolm X; the passage of the Voting Rights Act;

the march from Selma to Montgomery, Alabama, to protest racial discrimination; and the Watts rebellion in Los Angeles, signaling an era of urban unrest. The phrase *black power*—coined by Stokely Carmichael (a.k.a. Kwame Ture) that year and invested with new meaning by the Black Panther Party, formed a year later—would soon occupy a prominent place in the American political lexicon. Nina Simone captured the tenor of the times with "Mississippi Goddam" (1964), which foreshadowed the coming militancy, just as her "Backlash Blues" (1967) anticipated the reaction to it. This transformation in the tenor of the times was reflected in changes in the form, tone, production style, and eventually lyrics of black popular music.

As the themes of black pride and black self-determination gradually supplanted the call for integration, Motown's hegemony over black pop was successfully challenged by a resurgence of closer-to-the-roots, hard-driving rhythm and blues recorded in the South. Chiefly responsible for the popularization of southern soul, as this grittier r&b was called, was a highly successful collaboration between Atlantic Records and a number of southern studios, most notably Stax-Volt in Memphis, Tennessee, and Fame in Muscle Shoals, Alabama. The fruits of this collaboration captured the spirit of the emerging black militancy in tone rather than content. From 1965 on, artists like Otis Redding ("I've Been Loving You Too Long"), Wilson Pickett ("In the Midnight Hour"), Sam and Dave ("Soul Man"), Arthur Conley ("Sweet Soul Music"), and Percy Sledge ("When a Man Loves a Woman") were the new chart toppers. Their recordings were raw, basic, almost angry, and much less "produced" than the cleaner, brighter Motown sound.

Stax-Volt, Motown's chief competitor, was founded around 1960, about the same time as Motown. It was as open and disorganized as Motown was opaque and tightly controlled. Originally, Stax was a white-owned company, named after its founders, Jim Stewart and Estelle Axton. With integrated units like Booker T. and the MGs and the Memphis Horns as session musicians, creative functions were as likely to be handled by whites as by blacks. The "Memphis sound" that these musicians spawned was almost invariably the product of cross-racial teamwork. Initially, the credits on all Stax recordings read simply: "produced by the Stax staff." While Motown, a haven for black talent, is remembered by Nelson George as being "totally committed to reaching white audiences," Stax aimed its recordings "at r&b fans first, the pop market second."[25]

In many ways, the simplicity and straightforwardness of southern soul production gave the music its claim to authenticity. Motown's lavish use of multitrack studio production to achieve a more pop sound seemed out of sync with the black-pride search for African roots. Commenting on the difference in style between Stax-Volt and Motown, Otis Redding said:

> *Motown does a lot of overdubbing. It's mechanically done. At Stax the rule is: whatever you feel, play it. We cut together, horns, rhythms, and vocal. We'll do it three or four times and listen to the results and pick the best one. If somebody doesn't like a line in the song we'll go back and cut the whole song over. Until last year [1967], we didn't even have a four track tape recorder. You can't overdub on a one track machine.*[26]

Ironically, this largely integrated effort came to signify black power at its most militant. When southern soul crossed over to the pop market, it was not because the music had changed—it was because black pride

When southern soul crossed over to the pop market, it was not because the music had changed—it was because black pride had created a cultural space in which unrefined r&b could find mainstream acceptance on its own terms.

had created a cultural space in which unrefined r&b could find mainstream acceptance on its own terms.

Between 1965 and 1967, the Stax roster grew from a dozen or so acts to about 100, with a concomitant expansion in sales. A good deal of the credit for sales growth has to go to Al Bell, a former deejay and Stax's first black executive. Hired as head of sales in 1965, Bell opened promotional doors Stax did not know existed. In his outgoing, flamboyant style, he was the perfect foil to Jim Stewart's inherent conservatism. "To most of the blacks in the company," music historian Peter Guralnick has said, "Al Bell was a kind of secret hero, the 'Jesse Jackson' of in-house politics."[27] The internal tensions that would eventually prove to be Stax's undoing were not apparent in 1966 when Al Bell toted up sales of 8 million records. At that moment, all was right with the world, and Al Bell was on everybody's A-list at Stax.

Of the many artists who passed through Stax on their way to fame, Wilson Pickett is perhaps most illustrative of the magic of Stax's marriage with Atlantic Records. Signed to Atlantic in the early 1960s, Pickett was sent by producer Jerry Wexler to Memphis to record with Booker T. and the MGs. The results were immediate. "In the Midnight Hour" (co-written in typical cross-racial Stax fashion by Pickett and guitarist Steve Cropper) went to number one on the r&b charts in 1965 and also achieved significant crossover to the pop market. Pickett's next song, "634-5789," replicated that success one year later. When relations between Atlantic and Stax became strained in 1966, Wexler simply sent Pickett over to Fame studios in Muscle Shoals, with the same results. Over the next few years, Pickett tallied a couple of dozen more pop hits, reaching the Top Ten with "Land of 1000 Dances" in 1966 and "Funky Broadway" in 1967. Pickett's hits were straight-ahead dance tunes. While the coarse grain of his voice and the rhythmic insistence of southern soul signified the forcefulness of the new black militancy, it would be left to others to combine southern soul's passion with explicit social consciousness.

Aretha Franklin was one artist who did just that. After floundering at Columbia for years, she was signed to Atlantic in January 1967 by Jerry Wexler and taken immediately to Muscle Shoals, where, after one legendary session, she found her sound. The resulting single, "I Never Loved a Man (The Way I Love You)," became her first of many Top Ten releases for Atlantic. Later that spring, she

HEAR MORE
"Respect" on MyMusicKit

Aretha Franklin earned the title "Lady Soul" as she took the fusion of gospel and r&b to new heights. Her music was as powerful and uplifting as the civil rights movement at its best.

James Brown's performances were unparalleled and got him billing as "the hardest working man in show business." By the late 1960s, his stripped-down, rhythmically charged proto-funk echoed the forcefulness of the black power movement.

cut a version of Otis Redding's signature tune. "Respect" went straight to number one and was instantly "transformed from a demand for conjugal rights into a soaring cry of freedom."[28] Shortly thereafter, she was crowned Lady Soul. Aretha herself projected a presence that embodied the slogan "black is beautiful." The vocal and emotional range of her early Atlantic releases ("Baby, I Love You," "Natural Woman," "Chain of Fools," and "Think," to name a few) express the fervor of the era dramatically. As Hettie Jones once remarked,

> Aretha did not pray like Mahalia for the endurance to make it on through, nor make you believe her pain as Billie Holiday had. The statement black artists wished to make had changed, the blues had been transfigured by anger and pride. Aretha's music was a celebration, she was "earthmother" exhorting, preacher woman denouncing, militant demanding, forgotten woman wailing. She was black, she was beautiful, and she was the best. Someone called that time in 1967 the summer of "Retha, Rap, and revolt."[29]

An even more dramatic parallel to the trajectory of black politics can be found in the career of another southern soul artist—James Brown. In the 1950s, Brown was an ambitious and headstrong r&b artist whose music was intended for, and in many ways confined to, the black audience. His first Top Ten crossover single was in 1965, "Papa's Got a Brand New Bag"; by 1968, he was Soul Brother No. 1. When he came to the attention of the white audience, he did so without compromise. His string of Top Ten pop hits ("I Got You," "It's a Man's Man's Man's World," "Cold Sweat," "I Got the Feelin'") made fewer concessions to mainstream sensibilities than any music in the pop market. Critic Robert Palmer has described it as follows:

> With no chord changes and precious little melodic variety to sustain listener interest, rhythm became everything. Brown and his musicians and arrangers began to treat every instrument and voice in the group as if each were a drum. The horns played single-note bursts that were often sprung against the downbeats. The bass lines were broken up into choppy two- or three-note patterns, a procedure common in Latin music but rare in r&b. Brown's rhythm guitarist choked his guitar strings against the instrument's neck so hard that his playing began to sound like a jagged tin can being scraped with a pocketknife. Only occasionally were the horns, organ or backing vocalists allowed to provide a harmonic continuum by holding a chord.[30]

"(I Got You) I Feel Good"

Artist: James Brown
Music/Lyrics by James Brown
Label: King (1965)

James Brown was the most influential African American bandleader between Duke Ellington and Prince and, like them, he understood what makes great dance music: focus, discipline, and precision. James developed a complex, polyrhythmic ensemble approach in which all instruments—basses and drums, guitars, horns, and vocals—functioned as parts of a percussive whole. Rooted in the tap-dancing and gospel singing of Brown's childhood, his musical approach evolved swiftly and radically, putting ever more attention on the rhythmic "groove," his show-stopping stage theatrics, and the complex improvised interactions between himself and the band.

Brown's genius was a particularly minimalist one: He stripped the rhythmic grooves of r&b, blues, and gospel down to their barest bones. With a succession of great rhythm sections, including most notably the great bass player Bootsy Collins and horn soloist Maceo Parker, Brown developed the layered, double-timed rhythmic interaction that was the basic foundation of funk.

Musical Style Notes

"(I Got You) I Feel Good" has all the elements of soul: the strong backbeat (accent on the second and fourth beats of the bar), emotional intensity, the "wailing" call-and-response vocals of gospel, impeccable horn arrangements, and rhythmic drive that just won't quit. In its percussive bass line, and the way the horns "punctuate" the musical line with short, precise phrases, it also foreshadows funk. Brown was a master of vocal "cues"—in other words, vocalizations that would cue the stopping and starting of phrases by the instrumentalists. Brown's cues help the musicians execute these "breaks" with razor-sharp precision:

> "So good"—(bomp bomp)
>
> "So good"—(bomp)
>
> "I got you"—(bomp-bomp-*bomp-bomp*-BOMP)

In Brown's live performances, you can see that many of his wails and screams are accompanied by certain physical gestures that serve as further cues for the band. This ensemble precision was a signature part of James Brown's style.

Musical "Road Map"

TIMINGS	COMMENTS	LYRICS
0:00–0:20	Song starts with one of Brown's signature vocal screams: "Wow! I feel good—" Verse 1 Note call and response between voice and horn section at the end of the verse.	*I feel good*
0:20–0:40	Verse 2 Again, note call and response.	*I feel . . . nice*

TIMINGS	COMMENTS	LYRICS
0:40–0:47	Saxophone break (transitional musical phrase leading into bridge)	
0:47–0:59	Bridge Note how the instruments stop completely when Brown sings, "My love won't do me no harm—" This cues the next verse.	*. . . my love*
0:59–1:20	Verse 2 repeats. Call and response between voice and horn section at the end of the verse	*So nice — —*
1:20–1:26	Reprise of saxophone break leading into bridge	
1:26–1:39	Bridge Instruments stop again at 1:36—"my love can't do me no harm."	*my love*
1:39–1:59	Verse 2 repeats.	*So nice — —*
1:59–2:19	Verse 1 repeats.	*So good — —*
2:19–2:30	Reprise last line twice. Horns play extended line, then stop.	*So good — —*
2:30	Brown screams, "Hey!" (This vocalization is Brown cueing the band for the last chord.) Band hits last chord.	*Hey!*

Brown's music was prototypical funk. In taking every instrument to the limit of its rhythmic capabilities, Brown carried the Africanization of popular music to its logical extreme. It was a musical statement that strongly echoed the cultural nationalism developing in some segments of the African American community. If, by chance, a listener missed the political significance of Brown's music, it became explicit in the lyrics of his 1968 hit single, "Say It Loud—I'm Black and I'm Proud," which became an anthem in the struggle for black liberation.

> *In taking every instrument to the limit of its rhythmic capabilities, Brown carried the Africanization of popular music to its logical extreme. It was a musical statement that strongly echoed the cultural nationalism developing in some segments of the African American community.*

Latino Rock 'n' Roll: From the Southwest to the Spanish Caribbean

Latinos were among those groups whose popular music practices were profoundly affected by political currents in the United States. In the 1950s and 1960s, there were two main groups—Chicanos in the Southwest (especially Los Angeles) and Puerto Ricans in the Northeast (mostly in New York City). Chicanos didn't exactly migrate to the United States initially; they became a part of it when the United States annexed California after the Mexican-American War in 1848. Puerto Ricans, in contrast, became U.S. citizens, albeit with limited rights, in 1917, two decades after the island became a U.S. commonwealth in the Spanish-American War of 1898. Chicanos and Puerto Ricans have lived in segregated neighborhoods adjacent to African American enclaves, absorbing elements of their neighbors' culture. Both groups engaged rock 'n' roll in the 1950s, especially doo wop, because these romantic ballads resonated with similar traditions in Mexican and Spanish Caribbean music. Engagement with the rock and soul styles of the 1960s, however, was different for different segments of the Latino community.

Because most early Puerto Rican migrants came from Afro-Caribbean backgrounds, when they moved beyond their own ethnic enclave, they were more likely to gravitate toward African American culture than to engage directly with the mainstream. Indeed, until the 1960s, Spanish Caribbean sounds defined such a vibrant Latin music scene in the United States that Puerto Rican musicians seldom had to look beyond their own Spanish-speaking subindustry to find gainful employment. Even those who became fully established in the United States still identified with Puerto Rico—in effect, a Spanish-speaking island colony—as their homeland. In contrast, Chicanos, who are more likely to be *mestizo* (of mixed European-Amerindian ancestry), have lived for over 150 years in a territory they have historically considered their own, which has conferred on them a greater sense of cultural belonging. When Chicanos have experimented with non-Latino musical forms, in addition to displaying deep affinities with African American culture, they have felt relatively little hesitation in adopting mainstream styles or the English language, in addition to displaying deep affinities with African American culture.[31]

> *When Chicanos have experimented with non-Latino musical forms, in addition to displaying deep affinities with African American culture, they have felt relatively little hesitation in adopting mainstream styles or the English language, in addition to displaying deep affinities with African American culture.*

Following the success of Ritchie Valens and the Champs in the late 1950s, Herb Alpert and the Tijuana Brass were so successful in tapping another strand of Mexican music (which they popularized as *Ameriachi*) that Alpert was able to form his own record label with partner Jerry Moss—A&M records. One of their first big stars was Chris Montez, a protégé of Ritchie Valens, who had a Top Ten hit with "Let's Dance" in 1962; he was signed to A&M and scored four more Top Forty hits in 1966. Another Chicano act from Los Angeles, Cannibal and the Headhunters, released the defining arrangement of "Land of 1000 Dances" in 1965, a year before Wilson Pickett had a Top Ten hit with the same song. Among the best-known Chicano rock acts in Los Angeles were the Premiers ("Farmer John," 1964); The Blendells ("La La La La," 1964); and the hottest local group of them all, Thee Midnighters, whose "Whittier Boulevard" (1965)—named after Chicanos' preferred avenue for cruising—bore more than a faint resemblance to the Rolling Stones' "2120 South Michigan Ave," which was the address of Chess records.

The center for this music was Los Angeles (where it was dubbed the "East Side Sound"), but Chicano rock also issued from other locales. A Chicano group from Detroit, ? & the Mysterians (as in Question Mark, rendered with the punctuation sign), hit number one with "96 Tears" in 1966. From 1965 to 1967, Sam the Sham & the Pharaohs, from Dallas, Texas, turned out six Top Forty hits, including "Wooly Bully" (1965) and "Lil' Red Riding Hood" (1966). However, the craving for British acts overshadowed the impact of this music to such an extent that another rock band influenced by Tex-Mex, the Sir Douglas Quintet ("She's About a Mover," 1965), led by a white local, Doug Sahm, from San Antonio, Texas, was promoted as a new British group.

On the East Coast, the trade embargo imposed on Cuba following the Revolution of 1959 restricted the flow of Cuba's rich cultural resources. Brazilian *bossa nova* experienced limited mainstream success as Cuban music went into decline. In 1966, the closing of New York's Palladium, the central gathering place for fans of Spanish Caribbean music—black, white, and Latino—marked both the end of the mambo era and the coming out of boogaloo (*bugalú*), a transitional Latin/r&b hybrid described by René Lopez as "the first Nuyorican music"[32] and by John Storm Roberts as "the first, and only, uptown Latin form to use largely English lyrics."[33] Boogaloo was embraced by younger musicians and fans but was immediately shunned by established Latin musicians for being off-clave—the complex 3-against-2 rhythm that underpinned much of Cuban music. Boogaloo retained the horn-based sound of most Latin music and the full range of Latin percussion but added English (or bilingual) lyrics, electric guitars, trap drums, and the 4/4 rhythms and heavy backbeat characteristic of early rock 'n' roll and r&b.

This marriage of Latin music and r&b was announced to the mainstream public in 1966 with the pop success of Joe Cuba's "Bang, Bang." Obvious nods to black culture could be heard in the repeated lyric exhortation "cornbread, hog maw, and chitlins." Other notable boogaloo hits that same year included Pete Rodríguez's "I Like It Like That" and Johnny Colon's "Boogaloo Blues." The style was anticipated earlier in the decade in Mongo Santamaría's "Watermelon Man" and Ray Barretto's "El Watusi," both of which "involved an inflection of Latin traditions in the direction of African American r&b and soul sounds."[34] Like the watusi before it, the boogaloo became the hottest dance craze of 1965–1966. By 1969, however, it had all but disappeared, submerged beneath the political currents that swept the Puerto Rican community.

By the late 1960s the cultural nationalism that had taken hold in the African American community also affected Latinos, albeit in different ways. Chicanos were able to express their ethnic consciousness without ever abandoning the rock and r&b styles that had become so

"Oye Como Va"

Artist: Santana
Music/Lyrics by Tito Puente
Label: Columbia (1970), from the LP *Abraxas*

Composed by New York–based salsa percussionist Tito Puente, "Oye Como Va" is, quite literally, a song about rhythm. Its text celebrates the great dances of Afro-Cuban music, and its music is based on a distinctive Afro-Cuban "cha-cha" rhythm. "Oye Como Va" was made famous among Anglo audiences in this particular 1970 version by Santana, which married a traditional Afro-Cuban percussion section (timbales, congas, guiro) to the slightly "distorted" sound of the Hammond organ and the singing, bent-note guitar solos of late 1960s rock. In this performance, guitarist and bandleader Carlos Santana, the offspring of Mexico-born parents, illustrated that he did not need to invent Latin roots for rock music: They had been there all along, in jazz, r&b, and (eventually) disco and hip hop.

The players on the *Abraxas* LP were Carlos Santana, guitar and vocals; Rico Reyes, percussion; Mike Carabello, percussion and conga; José Chepitó Areas, percussion, conga, and timbales; Michael Shrieve, drums; Alberto Gianquinto, piano; David Brown, bass and guitar; and Gregg Rolie, keyboards and vocals.

Musical Style Notes

"Oye Como Va" is a good example of a piece that is constructed of several repetitive melodic and rhythmic formulas over which improvisation can happen. Harmonically, it is simple: Two chords are played over and over again. The complexity lies in the layering of musical elements: Over those two chords, we hear the percussion section playing Latin polyrhythms (multiple rhythms layered over each other and played simultaneously), to which are added improvisations by the guitar and organ.

The Afro-Cuban rhythm is a very important part of the stylistic footprint of "Oye Como Va." The beginning consists of a vamp (a short musical phrase, usually with a distinct rhythm, that repeats a number of times, sometimes through an entire song). The vamp begins right at the introduction. Here's the rhythm the organ plays:

1 + 2 + 3 + 4 +	1 + 2 + 3 + 4 +
/ / / /	/ /

Overlaid with this, you can then hear the distinctive "cha-cha" rhythm in the *sheee-yuk-shuk-shuk shee-yuk-shuk-shuk* sound of the guiro, a grooved percussion instrument played with a stick:

1 + 2 + 3 + 4 +	1 + 2 + 3 + 4 +
/ /// //	/ /// //

Transitions between musical sections are marked by a short, percussive phrase played in rhythmic unison. This has been indicated in the musical road map as "rhythmic transition."

Musical "Road Map"

TIMINGS	COMMENTS	LYRICS
0:00–0:06	Hammond organ "vamp"	
0:06–0:15	Percussion enters. Guiro enters at 0:08.	
0:15–0:30	Guitar enters, layered over organ, bass, percussion; guitar plays the same phrase four times.	
0:30–0:37	Rhythmic transition (short, percussive phrase played in rhythmic unison)	
0:38–0:53	Verse	Oye como va . . .
0:53–0:57	Rhythmic transition	
0:57–1:45	Guitar solo (based on opening phrase)	
1:45–1:53	Rhythmic introduction "vamp" returns as transitional passage.	
1:53–2:08	Volume drops; organ plays repetitive riff; section ends with another unison passage played with percussive rhythm, forming transition to organ solo.	
02:08–2:48	Hammond organ solo	
2:48–3:00	Rhythmic "vamp" (as in introduction)	
3:00–3:14	Verse	Oye como va . . .
3:14–3:22	Rhythmic transition	
3:22–4:06	Guitar solo	
4:06–4:14	Rhythmic transition, ending with vocal "huh!" and final chord	

much a part of their music. The VIPs, a group whose sound roamed from the British Invasion to southern soul, for example, changed their name to the more ethnic-sounding El Chicano in 1969 and added newer material like "Viva Tirado" to their repertoire. For Puerto Rican cultural nationalists, authenticity meant a return to clave-based Spanish Caribbean roots, as guitar-based rock became the music of the enemy, and *salsa* came to the fore, reestablishing a cultural continuity with Latin bands of an earlier generation. "Salsa drew on multiple contemporary musical sources . . .," Deborah Pacini Hernandez has noted, "but at its core it reinvigorated and celebrated the Spanish Caribbean musical aesthetics that had flourished in New York in the 1940s and 1950s."[35] Issued primarily by Fania Records in New York, salsa remained a product of the Latino community, with relatively little crossover to the mainstream. The only "Nuyoricans" who crossed over at this time were José Feliciano ("Light My Fire," 1968), and Tony Orlando ("Knock Three Times," 1970), with scant connection to Latin music of any kind.

It fell to a West Coast Chicano rock group to interpret contemporary Spanish Caribbean rhythmic sensibilities for the rock audience.

It fell to a West Coast Chicano rock group to interpret contemporary Spanish Caribbean rhythmic sensibilities for the rock audience. Carlos Santana was born in Mexico and migrated to San Francisco. He started his band, Santana, as a blues band in 1967. Their self-titled 1969 debut album rose to number four and included Latin-influenced versions of Olatunji's "Jingo" and Willie Bobo's "Evil Ways." Their next album, *Abraxas* (1970), went to number one and acquainted the national audience with a Latin rock version of Peter Green's "Black Magic Woman" and a stunning interpretation of Tito Puente's "Oye Como Va." Santana's band was a model for other Latin rock groups such as Malo and Azteca, and his ethereal guitar playing found a welcome home amid the psychedelic sounds of the counterculture.

Rock and Revolution: The Counterculture

As black power groups like the Black Panthers became more militant, record numbers of white youth (as well as some youth of color) began to experiment with alternatives to middle-class life.

The counterculture, as this movement was called, was based on the rejection of a competitive, achievement-oriented society in favor of free-living, free-loving lifestyles and shared communities.

The counterculture, as this movement was called, was based on the rejection of a competitive, achievement-oriented society in favor of free-living, free-loving lifestyles and shared communities. Its citizens were called *hippies,* a play on *hipster,* a black term from the 1940s and 1950s for urban outsiders. If the Panthers felt that "power comes from the barrel of a gun," hippies leaned more toward nonviolence. Indeed, *flower power* became the hippie analog to *black power.* Several philosophical tendencies and political developments framed the counterculture: a Christian belief in "loving thy neighbor" and a fascination with Eastern religions and music, the mass availability of reliable birth control (the Pill), and the escalation of the war in Vietnam. One unifying element was the widespread use of mind-expanding drugs.

By the mid-1960s, drug references could be found (or imagined) most anywhere: the Beatles' "Yellow Submarine" was a submarine-shaped barbiturate known as a "yellow jacket"; Peter, Paul, and Mary's "Puff the Magic Dragon" was a drug song because *puff* was a verb; "Mary" in the Association's "Along Comes Mary" was code for marijuana. Still, when the Byrds flew "Eight Miles High" in 1966, none of the radio stations that banned the song thought it referred to an airplane ride. A year later, Jefferson Airplane's "White Rabbit," which openly referred to mind-altering pills, and Jimi Hendrix's "Purple Haze" were both part of the "Journey to the Center of the Mind" (Amboy Dukes, 1968). Not all the drug songs were in favor of drugs. Paul Revere and the Raiders released the first Top Ten antidrug song "Kicks" in 1966, when they were the house band for Dick Clark's television program *Where the Action Is*. Donovan, whose "Mellow Yellow" (1966) had unintentionally initiated a banana-smoking craze, may have bewildered his fans when he suddenly denounced drug use in 1967, although they might have gotten a hint from "Sunshine Superman." In that same year, the Rolling Stones' "Mother's Little Helper" criticized middle-class prescription drug abuse. Merle Haggard's "Okie from Muskogee" (1969), a number one country hit that crossed over to pop, chided marijuana-smoking hippies for their anti-American values while extolling the virtues of "white lightning." Later, the Stones' "Sister Morphine" and James Brown's "King Heroin" would capture the downside of inner-city addictions, a theme taken up in the 1980s and 1990s. For the counterculture, the focus on mind-expanding drugs seemed to offer the possibility of greater self-awareness and consciousness, which in turn would lead to a world without war, competition, or regimentation.

Blues on Acid: Psychedelic Rock

By the late 1960s, a number of musical strands—folk rock, a home-grown blues revival, and the second wave of the British Invasion—seemed emblematic of the cultural changes associated with the counterculture. Blues-based rock in particular enjoyed a surge among white rockers across the country and was soon folded into the psychedelic experience, where it morphed into the music that framed the counterculture—acid rock.

The blues revival had its beginnings in Chicago in the early 1960s, where white teenager Paul Butterfield served as the U.S. counterpart to Britain's Alexis Korner. Butterfield jammed with blues greats like Muddy Waters, Howlin' Wolf, and others, eventually forming his own integrated blues band in 1963 with Mike Bloomfield on guitar. By 1965, New York folk-blues artists Danny Kalb, Tommy Flanders, Steve Katz, and Al Kooper had followed suit and formed The Blues Project. Both groups recorded reasonably successful LPs. In Los Angeles, Canned Heat began in 1965 but did not get off the ground until "On the Road Again" hit the Top Twenty in 1968. (By then, Butterfield had added horns to his group, thus anticipating Katz and Kooper's formation of Blood, Sweat, and Tears.) At first, the music these groups played was largely derivative. It was the British group Cream that married the simplicity of the blues to the extravagance of the new rock aesthetic.

Cream was the first power trio, bringing together drummer Ginger Baker, bassist Jack Bruce, and virtuoso blues guitarist Eric Clapton, who had recently left the Yardbirds (Jeff Beck replaced him) as the blatantly commercial "For Your Love" (1965) hit number six. Cream provided its members with more room to move than they had ever enjoyed before. In live performance, all three soloed extensively at deafening volumes; through all the calculated distortion, their musicianship was impeccable. The group combined psychedelics and the blues at the production level, defying listeners to figure out how many times Clapton had overdubbed himself. The layers of sound on the group's first LP, *Fresh Cream* (1966) added a new dimension to the

Janis Joplin gave her life to rock 'n' roll—literally. The intensity of her bluesy performances mirrored the tumultuousness of her life. In the end, hers was a flame that burned out all too soon.

((• HEAR MORE
Janis Joplin on
MyMusicKit

music, and yet somehow Delta bluesman Skip James's "I'm So Glad" could still be related to its originator. The group's second album, *Disraeli Gears* (1967) yielded a Top Ten single, "Sunshine of Your Love." *Wheels of Fire* went to number one on the album charts before the group disbanded in 1968. Although other British blues groups followed—most notably the Jeff Beck Group, which included Rod Stewart and Ron Wood; and Traffic, which featured Steve Winwood—Cream set the standard to which all others had to measure up.

San Francisco attracted white blues enthusiasts as well. Steve Miller, a veteran of the Chicago blues scene, was lured to San Francisco by the prospect of lucrative recording contracts. His band, formed in 1967, included fellow Chicagoan Boz Scaggs. Mike Bloomfield also left Chicago for San Francisco, where he teamed up with drummer Buddy Miles to form the Electric Flag in 1967. Janis Joplin, conspicuous as one of the few white female blues singers, came to the city from Port Arthur, Texas. Paired with Big Brother and the Holding Company, Joplin covered Big Mama Thornton's "Ball and Chain" and Irma Franklin's "Piece of My Heart" in 1968. Joplin poured everything she had into every performance, and the intensity of her performances and her lifestyle took its toll. Having become a symbol of rebellion for millions of white middle-class youth, she died of a heroin overdose in 1970. The following year, her last album *Pearl,* released posthumously, and its hit single "Me and Bobby McGee" rose to the top of the pop charts.

By the mid-1960s, San Francisco was widely acknowledged to be the spiritual Mecca of the counterculture. Hardly limited to blues rockers, San Francisco was the site of a broader rock scene, boasting groups such as the Charlatans, Country Joe and the Fish, Quicksilver Messenger Service, Moby Grape, Sopwith Camel, Sly and the Family Stone, and, of course, the Jefferson Airplane and the Grateful Dead. San Francisco was also the site of a burgeoning drug culture, which encouraged experimentation with mind-altering drugs—particularly lysergic acid diethylamide (LSD, or acid). The music that emerged from these psychedelic experiences came to be known, logically enough, as *acid rock.* Efforts to reproduce these experiences naturally led to swirling poster and album cover art and light shows in which colorful pulsating images became an integral part of the live music.

The music that emerged from these psychedelic experiences came to be known, logically enough, as acid rock. Efforts to reproduce these experiences naturally led to swirling poster and album cover art and light shows in which colorful pulsating images became an integral part of the live music.

Indeed, these extramusical elements alone were often enough to categorize the music as acid rock. As Lillian Roxon has noted, "Much of the San Francisco music of that period came out of the blues, but because of the whole psychedelic coloring of that culture, it moved out of blues into the wider realms of acid rock."[36]

The Jefferson Airplane was the only San Francisco group to have Top Ten singles in the 1960s. In 1967, primarily because of the powerful vocals of Grace Slick, "Somebody to Love" and "White Rabbit" moved into the upper reaches of the pop charts. Even before Slick replaced Signe Andersen as lead singer of the group, the Jefferson Airplane was the first San Francisco band to get a major label contract. Still, it was the Grateful Dead—with no Top Ten album or single until 1987—that most embodied the sense of community and spirit of experimentation that defined the counterculture.

The Grateful Dead lived in the Haight-Ashbury district, the heart of the hippie scene. Musically, they came from a smorgasbord of influences. Leader Jerry Garcia had played folk and bluegrass. Ron "Pigpen" McKernan, the son of a white r&b deejay, brought his blues background to bear in his keyboard and harmonica playing. Bassist Phil Lesh had studied classical music. The group's sound was rounded out by Bill Kreutzmann on drums, Bob Weir on guitar, and the later addition of eclectic percussionist Mickey Hart. Originally called the Warlocks, the Grateful Dead were part of a larger social circle that included novelist (and former state wrestling champion) Ken Kesey and the LSD-evangelizing Merry Pranksters. Together they organized a number of public LSD gatherings, chronicled by Tom Wolfe in *The Electric Kool-Aid Acid Test.* The band's first album, *The Grateful Dead* (1967), was a straightforward rock album

The sense of community that the Grateful Dead created was easily as important as the music they played. From the beginning, they were first among equals in giving of themselves to the counterculture.

with a distinctly r&b flavor. Ever open to the beckoning of psychedelia, the Grateful Dead went on to become one of the most experimental and improvisatory bands in rock, while continuing to perform "more free concerts than any band in the history of music."[37] While the Grateful Dead tried to maintain their integrity throughout their career, the counterculture, like most social movements, was vulnerable to cooptation.

Commercializing the Counterculture: *Sgt. Pepper* and Monterey Pop

After the first Human Be-In Festival drew 20,000 fans to San Francisco's Golden Gate Park in January 1967, some hip capitalist rock entrepreneurs from Los Angeles booked the Monterey fairgrounds for the weekend of June 16–18 and the Monterey International Pop Festival was born. Throughout this period, the Beatles had been in the studio recording the masterpiece that would change popular music forever. *Sgt. Pepper's Lonely Hearts Club Band* was released on June 1, 1967, three weeks before the Monterey Pop Festival. Together, these two landmark events ushered in the amorphous call to celebrate peace, love, and good vibes that came to be known as the Summer of Love.

Eight months in the making, *Sgt. Pepper* epitomized all the creativity (and excesses) of the counterculture. As the first concept LP (an album designed as a coherent whole, with each song segueing seamlessly into the next), *Sgt. Pepper* established a new plateau in record production: It was an album conceived as a single; it required hundreds of hours of studio time; it utilized special effects so sophisticated the music could not be performed live. Certain aspects of *Sgt. Pepper* had been foreshadowed in earlier releases. *Rubber Soul* (1965) showed a new level of maturity in Lennon and McCartney's songwriting (even as "Nowhere Man" hinted at Lennon's frustration with the group's lack of political engagement). Harrison pioneered the use of the sitar in rock on "Norwegian Wood," introducing a sound that would become more familiar in the psychedelic era. George Martin, now called the "fifth Beatle," went from being an excellent producer to being an indispensable creative force. *Revolver* (1966), an even more experimental album, continued these trends. Harrison developed his sitar playing further under the tutelage of Ravi Shankar, and Martin polished every layer of sound to perfection. Both sides of the 1967 single "Penny Lane/Strawberry Fields" once again confirmed the Beatles' artistry and prefigured the sound of things to come.

But all of these releases merely hinted at the impact that *Sgt. Pepper* would have as the connection between music and psychedelics came to full fruition. It was not just transparent drug references like "Lucy in the Sky with Diamonds" or "With a Little Help from My Friends" or the cannabis plants tucked away on the album cover art; it was in the integrated sonic presentation of the entire album—from the hurdy-gurdy organ effects on "Mr. Kite" to the seemingly interminable decay of the final mesmerizing chord on "A Day in the Life"—that *Sgt. Pepper* offered an artful and engaging foray into new musical terrain and represented for many an alternative way of life. Because *Sgt. Pepper* quickly rose to number one, where it remained for fifteen weeks, it also demonstrated the commercial possibilities of the counterculture.

Originally conceived as a straight commercial concert, John Phillips of the Mamas and the Papas, and his manager, Lou Adler, convinced the organizers of Monterey Pop to turn it into an artist-run, nonprofit (but still very commercial) event. With a decidedly West Coast orientation, about half of the two dozen or so artists came from Los Angeles (the Byrds, Buffalo Springfield, the Mamas and the Papas, Canned Heat, Scott McKenzie) and San Francisco (Jefferson Airplane; Country Joe and the Fish; the Grateful Dead; Big Brother and the Holding Company, which featured Janis Joplin; Quicksilver Messenger Service; Steve Miller). New York singer/songwriters were represented by Laura Nyro and Simon and Garfunkel. The Animals and the Who advanced the British Invasion. (The Beatles had declined an invitation and the Stones couldn't perform because of their recent drug bust.) Even though Smokey Robinson sat on the festival board, not a single Motown act materialized. Perhaps not surprisingly, few black artists were on the program; those who performed included Lou Rawls, Hugh Masekela, a pumped-up Otis Redding, and an outrageous Jimi Hendrix.

Whatever its shortcomings, the Monterey Pop Festival was a landmark event. As the first huge rock festival (30,000 in attendance), it pointed the way for all others. It was patronized by the "hip-eoisie" of the counterculture and by the elite of the recording industry, both of whom took it extremely seriously. It provided Otis Redding with a springboard for crossover success, which ended tragically when he died in a plane crash later in the year, just three days after recording "(Sittin' On) The Dock of the Bay." This song was his only number one pop single. Janis Joplin emerged from the festival as nothing short of a white blues goddess and was promptly signed to a lucrative contract by Clive Davis, president of CBS Records. The festival propelled the Who into the U.S. mainstream following their blistering performance of "My Generation." The flowering San Francisco scene had already earned the Grateful Dead and

Jefferson Airplane contracts with Warner and RCA, respectively, and Vanguard had picked up Country Joe and the Fish. Later, Capitol signed both Quicksilver Messenger Service and the Steve Miller Band, reportedly for the then unheard-of sum of $40,000 in advances. Perhaps most important, Monterey Pop made Jimi Hendrix an icon because he took Pete Townshend's guitar-smashing routine to a whole new level.

Hendrix, who appeared at the urging of Paul McCartney, a

Jimi Hendrix hovered above most other musicians. With his group, the Jimi Hendrix Experience, he elevated rock to new highs.

"A Day in the Life"

Artist: The Beatles

Music/Lyrics by John Lennon and Paul McCartney

Label: Parlophone, England; Capitol, U.S.A. (1967), from the LP *Sgt. Pepper's Lonely Hearts Club Band*

"A Day in the Life" is the grand finale of the Beatles' celebrated concept album. It turns a narration on the morning paper, a recently viewed film, and a morning's work commute into a surreal vision of the nature of daily life. The song's refrain caused a controversy because of its use of drug-related slang ("I'd love to turn you on," heard at 1:39 and 3:45), and it was initially banned by the British Broadcasting Corporation (BBC).

Musical Style Notes

"A Day in the Life" features use of multiple-track recording and tape manipulation, the use of an orchestra as a key part of the musical composition rather than simple background color, and diverse sections of simple musical forms combined into more complex musical structures. It begins as a simple rock ballad, written by John Lennon, with acoustic guitar and piano, drums, and Lennon's solo vocal. At the end of the third verse, we hear the refrain "I'd love to turn you on," the orchestra enters, and a huge crescendo (increase in volume) begins. In fact, the orchestra had been recorded separately, and this tape was played backward and overlaid on multiple tracks.

At the crescendo's climax, the orchestra abruptly ends, and Lennon's lyric reflections are replaced by an uptempo bridge section (written by Paul McCartney, originally as a separate song). Notice the style change: The bridge shows McCartney's music-hall influence and sounds more like a show tune than a rock ballad. When he arrives at the words "And I went into a dream," a transitional dream sequence occurs, featuring a heavily processed reverberant vocal on the syllable "ah" and orchestral accompaniment. Taking advantage of the relatively new technology of stereo recording, producer George Martin also pans the voice from one speaker to another, creating the illusion of movement. This section ends abruptly, transitioning into a reprise of the opening verse's musical texture and melody and Lennon's fourth verse. At the end of the fourth and final verse and the refrain "I'd love to turn you on," the backward orchestra passage begins again, increasing in volume until it ends abruptly, followed by the enormous crash of a full-orchestra chord, which fades very slowly to the end of the recording.

Musical "Road Map"

TIMINGS	COMMENTS	LYRICS
0:00–0:12	Introduction: acoustic guitar, piano, bass	
0:12–0:44	Verse 1—the vocalist is John Lennon.	*I read*
0:44–1:05	Verse 2—drums are added.	*He blew . . .*
1:05–1:11	Slight melodic variation at the end of verse: "*Nobody was really sure . . .*"	
1:11–1:39	Verse 3	*I saw . . .*
1:39–2:16	Infamous tag line "*I'd love to turn you on . . .*" Note the tremolo in the pitch of the voice. The sound of the orchestra fades in (see musical style notes above). Notice that the bass continues its steady beat and does so right into the next section. The backward orchestral track continues and ends abruptly at 2:16, providing a transition to the bridge section.	*I'd love . . .*
2:16–2:34 2:18 2:33	Bridge section, Verse 1 Instrumentation: bass, drums, and piano The vocalist is now McCartney. Sound effects: alarm clock Sound effects: hurried "panting"	*Woke up, . . .*
2:35–2:48	Bridge section, Verse 2	*Found my coat*
2:48–3:18	Musical dream sequence (see musical style notes above) Instrumentation: orchestra added to texture. Vocals are panned (the sound moves from one speaker to another, creating the illusion of movement). End of dream sequence provides transition back to original verse form.	"*ahhhh . . .*"
3:18–3:44	Verse 4 Instrumentation: bass, drums, guitar, piano, maracas The vocalist is now Lennon.	*I read . . .*
3:44–4:21	Reprise of "I'd love to turn you on . . . " lyric, with backwards orchestral track Orchestra rises in pitch and creates large crescendo (increase in volume), then stops abruptly at climactic point, followed by . . .	*I'd love . . .*
4:21	The orchestra strikes a huge, full chord, which fades until 5:04.	

festival board member, was an African American virtuoso guitarist from Seattle who started in his teens as a sideman for Little Richard and the Isley Brothers. After being lured to London by ex-Animal Chas Chandler, dressed up in mod gear, and paired with Noel Redding on bass and Mitch Mitchell on drums, he proceeded to dazzle British audiences with his technical ability and his image, which Lillian Roxon has described as "the Wild Man of Borneo . . . crossed with all the languid, silken, jeweled elegance of a Carnaby Street fop."[38] After the Jimi Hendrix Experience hit the British Top Ten early in 1967 with their first single, "Hey Joe," Hendrix brought the group to the United States, where their debut album, *Are You Experienced*, promptly climbed to number five on the charts following their performance at Monterey Pop.

HEAR MORE
Jimi Hendrix on MyMusicKit

Hendrix, who died unexpectedly from drug complications in 1970, never attracted a substantial black U.S. audience to his music during his lifetime, but he was considerably more important to music than his commercial, psychedelic, oversexed black man image indicated. He was a fine writer. He pioneered the incorporation of distortion and feedback into the language of popular music. His interpretation of Dylan's "All Along the Watchtower," his only single to break the U.S. Top Twenty, was praised by Dylan himself. However, the commercial interests surrounding him kept him tied to the formula that had made him a star. The pressures of the situation drove him not only to chemical excesses but also to his Electric Ladyland studios, where he logged some 800 hours of tape exploring fusions of jazz, rhythm and blues, and contemporary rock styles with Miles Davis, John McLaughlin, and other avant-garde jazz notables. None of these tapes was released during Hendrix's lifetime, and it is only recently that black artists and audiences have begun to recover the music with which he was identified during his life.

Monterey Pop both confirmed the counterculture's creeping commercialization and provided a platform for its anti-establishment views, both political and cultural. The festival was, in fact, peppered with artists who had taken anti-establishment stances in their music for some time. David Crosby introduced the Byrds' "He Was a Friend of Mine," a song about the Kennedy assassination; he challenged the Warren Commission's official version of the story[39] and waxed eloquent about the joys of acid. (Crosby also sat in with Buffalo Springfield, which included Stephen Stills and Neil Young, laying the groundwork for the supergroup configurations of Crosby, Stills, & Nash, and Crosby, Stills, Nash, & Young.) Earlier in the year, Buffalo Springfield had scored a Top Ten hit with "For What It's Worth (Stop, Hey What's That Sound)," a Stephen Stills song protesting the brutal police treatment of peaceful demonstrators. The Animals' "We Gotta Get Out of This Place" had already become an anthem protesting the constraints of urban life. The Who's "My Generation" emphasized the generation gap.

Lyric content was not the only source of anti-establishment sentiment at the festival. One look at a stoned Mama Cass drinking in Janis Joplin with her eyes made it abundantly clear that applying the label *acid rock* to music required little more than music . . . and acid. Indeed, throughout the weekend, a range of anti-establishment impulses were on display, from the violent spectacle of the Who smashing their equipment to the curious sexuality of Jimi Hendrix making love to his guitar as he set it ablaze. At Monterey (as in the counterculture generally), psychedelia was the common thread that bound these disparate artists together.

Riding the Storm: Radicals, Riots, and Revolutions

If the Beatles brought out the optimistic, upbeat spirit of the counterculture, the Doors represented its darker side. Doors leader Jim Morrison embraced madness and terror in both his art and his life. Morrison had met keyboardist Ray Manzarek when they were University of California—Los Angeles (UCLA) students, and Manzarek had then recruited guitarist Robby Krieger and drummer John Densmore from the headquarters of Maharishi Mahesh Yogi, where they practiced transcendental meditation. The group took its name from Aldous Huxley's *The Doors of Perception,* a book about the liberating aspects of drug use. After playing rock in underground Los Angeles clubs for a while, the group came to the attention of Jac Holzman, who signed them to his Elektra label in 1967. Their self-titled debut LP was an immediate smash. "Break on Through (To the Other Side)," the album's hard-rocking first single, defined the group's music and captured their image perfectly. The final cut, "The End," was an Oedipal fantasy that ran eleven minutes and forty-one seconds. By the time "Light My Fire" rocketed to the top of the charts in 1967, spreads in teenage magazines that cast Morrison as a teen idol were juxtaposed against a dramatic onstage, sex-related bust in New Haven, Connecticut, and warrants for "lewd and lascivious behavior" in Miami. The Doors' success spoke volumes about 1950s sexual repression coming undone in strange ways.

Throughout the late 1960s, as the group's next five albums made the Top Ten, the Doors remained one of the rock acts most in demand. Even Ed Sullivan felt compelled to book them, a move he regretted when they defied his censors and included a reference to getting "higher" in their performance of "Light My Fire." Although Morrison's constant brushes with the law served to bolster the group's outlaw image, the intensity of his lifestyle took its toll on all

Led by poet/vocalist Jim Morrison, the Doors explored the darker side of rock, made headlines for their sex- and drug-related escapades, and, much to the dismay of parents, became teen idols in the process.

concerned. In 1971, he left the band for a sabbatical in Paris, where he died on July 3, most probably from a drug-induced heart attack. Three weeks later, the Doors' final hit single, "Riders on the Storm," began its ascent into the Top Twenty.

For observers of the American scene, the storm had begun several years earlier. In 1968, the Tet Offensive in Vietnam had shattered all hopes of a short war. At home, the war's unpopularity forced President Johnson to abandon his reelection campaign. On April 4, shortly after the Kerner Commission on Civil Disorders warned that the country was "moving toward two societies, one black, one white—separate and unequal," Martin Luther King, Jr., was assassinated. His death provoked violent reactions in over 100 American cities. That day, James Brown was scheduled to perform at the Boston Garden. Faced with a potentially uncontrollable outburst of sorrow and rage, the city made arrangements to broadcast the show on public television, which kept Boston cool, at least for one evening. Brown was later flown to Washington, D.C., to appeal to rioting youth there. On June 6, Robert Kennedy was murdered as he was about to wrap up the Democratic nomination for the presidency. (That night, David Crosby wrote "Long Time Coming" lamenting his death.) Later that summer, the shocking, nationally televised violence at the Democratic Convention in Chicago left the nation profoundly shaken. To some, it seemed that revolution was just around the corner.

Artists of all styles and personal backgrounds responded to race-related tensions in their own ways. Releases like "Abraham, Martin, and John" (1968) by Dion and "Everyday People" by Sly and the Family Stone (1969) picked up the "black and white together" theme of the early civil rights movement. The difficulties of interracial relationships had been explored in Janis Ian's "Society's Child," in 1967, and the Rascals had taken antiracist stances even before their 1968 "People Got to Be Free," reportedly refusing a slot on the *Ed Sullivan Show* when Sullivan refused to book a black opening act. Curtis Mayfield and the Impressions continued a series of socially conscious "sermon songs" with "We're a Winner" and "This Is My Country" in 1968 and "Choice of Colors" in 1969. Even Elvis Presley's "In the Ghetto" (1969) went to number three on the pop charts. The Temptations' "Ball of Confusion (That's What the World Is Today)" (1969) captured the bewilderment of the era and the state of the civil rights movement after King's death. "The civil-rights struggle was not dead," Nelson George has written, "but its energy was increasingly scattered. The Black Panthers embraced communism. Ron Karenga's U.S. organization advocated an Afrocentric cultural nationalism. . . . Black Power came to mean whatever its user needed it to . . . the assimilationists pressed on."[40]

In 1971, the movement's entropy was reflected in popular music. John Lennon's exhortation "Power to the People" and the Chi-Lites' "(For God's Sake) Give More Power to the People" recalled the heyday of the Black Panthers, while Bob Dylan's "George Jackson"—a tribute to the slain black leader—made clear that the radical elements in the black liberation struggle had already been neutralized. The disillusionment of the period was best expressed in Marvin Gaye's "What's Goin' On" and "Inner City Blues." At the same time, Aretha Franklin's stirring recording of Nina Simone's "Young, Gifted, and Black" captured the spirit of a community that had weathered a torrent of urban violence and provided the musical capstone for a decade of civil rights struggle.

Aretha Franklin's stirring recording of Nina Simone's "Young, Gifted, and Black" captured the spirit of a community that had weathered a torrent of urban violence and provided the musical capstone for a decade of civil rights struggle.

Meanwhile, the new social and political consciousness found its way into an increasingly broad range of concerns, from sexual liberation to fundamental social change. The Beatles' 1964 willingness just to "hold your hand" had, by 1967, escalated to the Rolling Stones' open call to "spend the night together" (though they agreed to change the lyric to "spend some *time* together" for their appearance on the *Ed Sullivan Show*). In that year, the social complexity of Janis Ian's conception of interracial intimacy in "Society's Child" gave way to the Beatles' simpler maxim "All You Need Is Love." Even teenyboppers were included in the new sexual freedom, as they "tumbled to the ground" embracing each other in Tommy James and the Shondells' "I Think We're Alone Now" (1967). There was little doubt about what was going on in "Itchycoo Park" in 1968. One year later, even the Beatles wondered aloud: "Why Don't We Do It in the Road."

While the sexual revolution was real enough, it did not liberate men and women equally. Many of the Stones' songs—"Stupid Girl," "Under My Thumb," and later "Honky-Tonk Women" and "Brown Sugar"—were downright nasty toward women. Despite the rising women's consciousness—the National Organization for Women (NOW) was founded in 1966—Sandy Posey's defeatist "Born a Woman" and Nancy Sinatra's more aggressive "These Boots Are Made for Walkin'" were among the few musical signs of women speaking up for themselves. Even when Helen Reddy roared "I Am Woman" in 1972, it was less than ferocious, although it was explicitly feminist. Janis Joplin and Grace Slick held out to their listeners the possibility of a stronger voice for women, but only Aretha Franklin demanded respect. As a group, women declined on the year-end singles charts from an all-time high of 32 percent in 1963 to 6 percent in 1969.

The call for social change split white youth into two dominant groups: those who favored a strategy of militant political action and those who favored one of individual consciousness raising. The popular slogan "The revolution is in your head" reflected the counterculture's preoccupation with self-awareness and consciousness expansion, which sometimes intermingled the call for social change with spiritual transcendence. For some, revolution was an act of self-development, not the overthrow of one political system by another. The Beatles' "Revolution" (1968) rose to number twelve as the flip side of "Hey Jude," the group's best-selling single; it represented a rejection of militant political action in favor of consciousness-raising, which would make everything "all right." Lennon made a highly significant change in the song's slower version on the so-called *White Album* (1968). Where the single had spoken of "destruction," Lennon had said "count me out"; on the album cut, however, he added "in," which was then sung as "count me out/in." Confronted with a real dilemma about the value of violent political action, Lennon could only leave the choice up to the listener. After the Beatles broke up, Lennon tried to connect to grassroots political movements and to assume, in his own way, a more activist stance. There were, for example, the bed-ins he staged with Yoko Ono to protest the war in Vietnam, and his anthems "Give Peace a Chance" and "Power to the People," which were clearly intended for mass participation. Beautifully expressed in "Imagine" (1971) with the Plastic Ono Band, Lennon's vision was ultimately utopian. For radical activists, the Doors' "Five to One" (1968), referring to the notion that *our* "numbers" were more powerful than *their* "guns," or the Jefferson Airplane's "We Can Be Together" (1969), calling together those who were "outlaws" in their country's eyes, had more appeal.

In the summer of 1968, radical leaders—later dubbed the Chicago Eight after they were tried, and acquitted, for inciting a riot—eyed Chicago, the site of the Democratic National Convention, as the occasion to embarrass the government for its repressive policies at home and abroad. Todd Gitlin recalls thinking of Chicago as a "grand fusion between radical politics and counterculture—drugs, sex, rock 'n' roll, smash the State."[41] Antiwar protestors, conscientious objectors, student radicals, yippies, and Black Panthers—joined by Phil Ochs and the MC5 ("Kick Out The Jams")—descended on Chicago for the protest. The theme music for the event could have been the Rolling Stones' just released "Street Fighting Man" (despite its own disclaimers), if most of the Chicago rock stations had not refused to play it. The ensuing "police riot" against demonstrators, media, and bystanders shocked the nation and further undermined an atomized Democratic Party, leading to the election of Richard Nixon.

Chicago 1968 was a watershed event. Some on the left withdrew from politics altogether; others became more radicalized. Bitter factionalism came to a head at the 1969 SDS National Convention. The meeting was already torn by rifts between the Progressive Labor Party and the Revolutionary Youth Movement–Weatherman faction. Finally, when a Black Panther attending the SDS Convention announced that the only position for a woman in the revolution was "prone," the voice of feminism rose to a deafening roar. In the end, SDS, the largest and most visionary organization of the New Left, was irrevocably shattered.

Woodstock and Altamont: The Highs and the Lows

Just as the Weathermen were gearing up to "bring the war home" during the "days of rage," Woodstock offered—in August 1969—a fleeting pastoral approximation of the countercultural utopia. A short five months later, this vision was wiped away by the events of another concert at the Altamont Speedway.

The Woodstock Music and Art Fair took place in August 1969 on Max Yasgur's 600-acre farm in Bethel, New York. Despite a solid financial base and considerable advanced planning, the festival was a prime example of Murphy's law—everything that could possibly go wrong did so. The crowd was expected to number 50,000 or so. Seven or eight times that number showed up.

Roads were obstructed for miles; there was insufficient food and water, and dreadfully inadequate medical and sanitary facilities. And then it began to rain. For all of this, Woodstock was the counterculture's finest hour.

Roads were obstructed for miles; there was insufficient food and water, and dreadfully inadequate medical and sanitary facilities. And then it began to rain. For all of this, Woodstock was the counterculture's finest hour. A spirit of cooperation infused the entire event. Three accidental deaths did occur—and three births. Bad acid to be avoided was announced from the stage. Wavy Gravy and the Hog Farm Commune offered practical guidance and makeshift medical attention and even managed to stretch the food supply to provide "breakfast in bed for 400,000," as Gravy described it. On the last day of the festival, Yasgur was moved to tell "the largest group of people ever assembled in one place" that "you have proven something to the world . . . that half a million kids can get together and have three days of fun and music and have nothing *but* fun and music."[42] Here, then, was the counterculture made real—the spontaneous temporary community later lionized by Abbie Hoffman, one of the Chicago Eight, as the Woodstock Nation.

Woodstock summed up an era of rock styles as it capped the counterculture. Creedence Clearwater Revival and The Band represented good old American rock 'n' roll. Arriving from England, the Who began with "Touch me, feel me . . ." from its groundbreaking rock opera, *Tommy,* and then burst into a memorable performance of "Summertime Blues." Ten Years After also represented the second wave of British bands, as did Joe Cocker, whose first LP, *With a Little Help from My Friends* (which included Jimmy Page and Steve Winwood), had just been released. San Francisco offered the Jefferson Airplane, Country Joe and the Fish, and Santana, whose performance of "Soul Sacrifice" earned them a Columbia recording contract. The Jefferson Airplane delivered some of the more political material from their *Volunteers* album. Country Joe and the Fish introduced "I-Feel-Like-I'm-Fixin'-to-Die-Rag" with a rousing version of the "Fish Cheer."

The festival also had the expected deficiencies. Aside from Melanie, Grace Slick, and Janis Joplin (none of whom were included in the original film), there was only one other female headliner—Joan Baez. Performing "Joe Hill," a song about the martyred labor organizer, Baez introduced a new generation of rock fans to the music of the labor movement. There were also only three African American acts for three days of morning-to-evening performances—Richie Havens, Jimi Hendrix, and Sly and the Family Stone. Havens, a black folkie and as much an anomaly as Hendrix, opened the festival. Asked to stall until the next act was ready, he improvised an astonishing version of "Freedom," a song that captured the ethos of the day. Hendrix also delivered a political message of sorts. His searing performance of "The Star-Spangled Banner," which replicated the sounds of "bombs bursting in air" on the guitar, turned the national anthem into an antiwar song.

Sly and the Family Stone was the only act with a substantial following in the African American community. Comprised of women and men, both black and white, the San

👁 **SEE MORE**
Woodstock documentary on MyMusicKit

Sly (second from left) and the Family Stone created socially relevant music that crossed the boundaries of r&b, jazz, and psychedelic rock as boldly as the group transcended the divisions of race and gender. It was an ambitious project for the late 1960s, and, for a while, they pulled it off better than anyone else.

Francisco–based group married funk and rock cultures as no other artists had been able to. Between 1968 and 1971, they recorded Top Ten pop hits—"Dance to the Music" (1968), "Everyday People" and "Hot Fun in the Summertime" (1969), "Thank You (Falletinme Be Mice Elf Agin)" (1970), and "Family Affair" (1971)—that transcended the confines of established musical styles. Their 1969 album *Stand!* contained the number one single "Everyday People" and the provocative "Don't Call Me Nigger, Whitey." The group's 1971 album, *There's a Riot Goin' On,* was even more controversial, but by this time Sly's growing militance was overshadowed by his drug-induced unreliability. Following a number of personnel changes, the group slowly disintegrated.

Crosby, Stills & Nash—David Crosby (from the Byrds), Stephen Stills (Buffalo Springfield), and Graham Nash (the Hollies)—signed with Atlantic in 1968. Their self-titled debut album showcased their writing ability, elegant harmonies, penchant for social commentary, and seasoned professionalism. Heralded by critics as the best LP of the year, the album included the seven-minute single they performed at Woodstock, "Suite: Judy Blue Eyes," as well as "Marrakesh Express," Crosby's "Long Time Coming," and "Wooden Ships," written by Crosby, Stills, and Paul Kantner of the Jefferson Airplane about the horrors of nuclear war. Neil Young (also from Buffalo Springfield) was recruited for their second effort; the number one *Déjà Vu* (1970), which included "Woodstock," a song that Joni Mitchell had written about the festival, was received even more warmly. That year, when the National Guard opened fire on antiwar demonstrators at Kent State University in Ohio, killing four students and wounding nine others, the group responded with "Ohio," naming Nixon as the guilty party. The single was released within weeks of the shooting and quickly became a Top Twenty hit. Each member of Crosby, Stills, Nash & Young turned out quality solo projects throughout the life of the group, often using topical material, as in Young's "Southern Man," Crosby and Nash's "Immigration Man," and Nash's "Chicago," about the 1968 convention. Individually and as a group, Crosby, Stills, Nash & Young represented the creativity and positive political impulses of the 1960s as well as the commercial potential of topical material.

In the five months between Woodstock and Altamont, it seemed like the apocalypse was approaching. Having promised "days of rage," the Weathermen tore up Chicago's upscale Gold

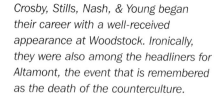

Crosby, Stills, Nash, & Young began their career with a well-received appearance at Woodstock. Ironically, they were also among the headliners for Altamont, the event that is remembered as the death of the counterculture.

Coast in October. In Washington, D.C., at the Vietnam Moratorium on November 15, Pete Seeger led three-quarters of a million antiwar activists in a chorus of John Lennon's "Give Peace a Chance." On December 4, Chicago police shot Black Panther Fred Hampton dead in his bed. Two days later, there was Altamont.

Altamont was a free concert that the Rolling Stones had planned as the climax to their 1969 U.S. tour promoting their *Let It Bleed* album. Held just outside San Francisco, the concert was captured in gory detail in a documentary titled *Gimme Shelter.* There were similarities between Woodstock and Altamont—hundreds of thousands in attendance; inadequate food, water, and toilets; last-minute shifts in sites; traffic jams; equal numbers of deaths and births. Altamont might well have turned into a Woodstock-like miracle save for two key differences. First, the concert was held in an area a fraction of the size of Max Yasgur's farm. Second, the San Francisco chapter of the Hell's Angels was hired to do security for $500 worth of beer.

> **A**ltamont might well have turned into a Woodstock-like miracle save for two key differences. First, the concert was held in an area a fraction of the size of Max Yasgur's farm. Second, the San Francisco chapter of the Hell's Angels was hired to do security for $500 worth of beer.

The concert, originally slated for Golden Gate Park in San Francisco, was shifted to the Sears Point Raceway. After all the logistical planning and construction were completed, final negotiations with the raceway owners broke down. Attorneys quickly negotiated a deal with the Altamont Speedway, which meant that all the logistics had to be redone and all the staging torn down and reassembled. The idea of hiring Hell's Angels to do security was accepted by the Stones for a number of reasons. One was that the British Hell's Angels had done security without incident for the Stones' free concert in London's Hyde Park for 300,000 the previous summer. Another reason was that the Grateful Dead—however naively, optimistically, or stupidly—had advised the Stones that it would be "cool" to use the group. The romantic outlaw-biker image in mid-to-late 1960s films from *Wild Angels* to *Easy Rider* fascinated Americans, and the Stones probably felt that the Angels would complement their own outlaw image. However, the British Hell's Angels were pale imitations of their U.S. counterparts, who came with knives and lead-filled pool cues, which they wielded freely.

From the beginning, the concert was marred by bad drug trips and violence. Instructed to keep people off the stage, Hell's Angels treated the area as a military stronghold. Marty Balin, the Jefferson Airplane's lead singer, was punched unconscious by a Hell's Angel during the group's performance of "Somebody to Love" when Balin was caught between the Angels and some fans who had climbed onto the stage. The violence continued throughout the day, reaching its apex when a black student, Meredith Hunter, was murdered. Hunter, brandishing a pistol, was stabbed several times by an Angel and then clubbed to death during the Stones' performance of "Under My Thumb." Mick Jagger made feeble attempts to calm the crowd, but it was clear who were the real street-fighting men and who were the rock 'n' roll pretenders, and it was all captured on film.[43]

The violence at Altamont in 1969 reflected the deterioration of political movements and served notice of the counterculture's impending demise. Within months, New York City construction workers would attack antiwar activists and hippies in the street with the tacit approval of the Nixon administration. With hundreds of Panthers already dead or in jail, Bobby Seale, having just weathered the Chicago Eight trial, would find himself on trial for murder. In 1970, the U.S. military would bomb Cambodia illegally, and repression of the anti-war movement would reach a pinnacle with the killing of student demonstrators at Kent State and, shortly thereafter, at Jackson State in Mississippi. Their deaths would have the same chilling effect on direct political action that the deaths of Hendrix and Joplin that year and later Morrison's would have on popular music.

LEARN MORE
Chapter Test
on MyMusicKit

If the trajectory of the civil rights movement affected the course of black popular music, its reverberations were felt throughout the culture. Other constituencies (radical students, antiwar activists, Latinos and, later, feminists, environmentalists, and gay rights advocates) began to use it as a model for airing their own grievances. It was an era in which rock was infused with the lyric substance of folk music and the insistent rhythms of southern soul called attention to a more demanding black community. In 1970, Motown made a rare sortie into social commentary when it released Edwin Starr's "War." "War," bellowed Starr, was worth "absolutely nothing." Starr's recording and his follow-up hit, "Stop the War" (1971), echoed the sentiments of millions of Americans, while the war continued unabated, even expanding into Cambodia and Laos. An era of enormous potential was coming to an unsettled and troubling end, with a forced decline in urban violence but no alleviation of its root causes, and a fragmentation of the popular music audience that paralleled the disintegration of the decade's social movements.

Music Versus Markets: The Fragmentation of Pop

The 1960s rolled into the 1970s, leaving behind a series of unresolved issues. As a result, the 1970s are often viewed as a decade of retreat. While it is true that the two great movements of the previous decade—the civil rights movement and the antiwar movement— were in decline, lasting social and cultural (if not structural) changes did occur during the 1970s. Society was not radically transformed in the manner that the New Left wanted, but neither did conservatives reestablish the cultural and political hegemony that they had enjoyed in the early 1950s. There were advances in environmental politics and particularly in the women's movement. The oppression of poor people, people of color, and women would not disappear, but these constituencies would never again be silent or invisible. Finally, the 1970s called into question all traditional notions of masculinity and femininity.

While popular music was used to fuel every impulse, from explorations of awakened sexuality and flights of psychedelic fantasy to furious discharges of political spleen, the music industry never lost its footing as an enduring capitalist enterprise. Any internal tensions the industry felt were expressed, predictably, in terms of culture versus commerce, music versus markets—the electric version of the authentic versus commercial debate of the folk revival. The more astute observers of the scene understood that this contradiction had always been inherent in rock 'n' roll. "From the start," Michael Lydon said in 1970, "rock has been commercial in its very essence . . . it was never an art form that just happened to make money, nor a commercial undertaking that sometimes became art. Its

> **W**hile popular music was used to fuel every impulse, from explorations of awakened sexuality and flights of psychedelic fantasy to furious discharges of political spleen, the music industry never lost its footing as an enduring capitalist enterprise.

art was synonymous with its business."[1] Popular music was bound to the capitalist interests that produced it. Thus, to understand the trajectory of popular music in the 1970s, it is necessary to explore the commercial (and technological) developments that began in the music industry in the late 1960s.

LEARN MORE
Learning Objectives
on MyMusicKit

As popular music in the late 1960s began to incorporate blues, jazz, classical, East Indian, and electronic sounds, the boundaries separating audiences became somewhat murky. The technical development of FM rock radio led to short-lived experiments in free-form programming, in which it was not uncommon to hear the Beatles, Stevie Wonder, Janis Joplin, Jimi Hendrix, Pink Floyd, and the Grateful Dead on the same radio program nor to find them in the same record collection. All these artists were included in the umbrella category of progressive rock, which presumably distinguished them from less interesting formulaic pop. A few years later, however, as the industry tried to rationalize production, artists would be spread over a number of more discrete, less overlapping audiences. For this reason, *Rolling Stone*'s Steve Pond remembers the 1970s as a time when rock

> *became diffuse, scattered and unfocused, fragmenting into little genres whose fans paid less and less attention to other little genres. In the Seventies, rock had a hundred different focal points: Elton John for popsters; Led Zeppelin for hard rockers; Emerson, Lake and Palmer for the art rockers; Joni Mitchell for the singer/songwriter contingent; David Bowie in the glam rock corner; Stevie Wonder for soul aficionados. Instead of a center, rock had a batch of radio formats.*[2]

Reflecting its capitalistic roots, the music industry moved to a strategy of trying to target fans with the most disposable income. Thus, the art of marketing became more and more tied to the science of demographics.

The Music Industry: A Sound Investment

By 1973, the music business had become a $2-billion-a-year industry, about as large as the sports and film industries combined. Having learned from their rock 'n' roll mistakes, major record companies no longer resisted the creative impulses of offbeat artists or upstart independent labels. Instead, they happily signed acts directly, made label deals, entered into joint ventures, or contracted for distribution. When the Jefferson Airplane left RCA to set up Grunt records, the group looked to its old label for distribution. Capitol contracted with the Beach Boys to distribute Brother Records. Frank Zappa's Bizarre label, which was distributed by Warner, developed new talent. When Zappa directed Alice Cooper to Warner in the early 1970s, the company was smart enough to listen, and the outrageous metal ensemble became one of the label's best-selling acts. Warner also entered into a lucrative distribution deal with Chrysalis, which had Jethro Tull and Procol Harum. At the same time, distribution deals with Stax and Philadelphia International provided CBS Records with a profitable entree to the soul market. What had begun in the late 1960s as a period of political awakening with a cultural flourish for the rock 'n' roll audience was, for the music industry, a period of commercial expansion and corporate consolidation.

Merger Mania

Wall Street soon came to view the music industry as a sound investment, and a period of unprecedented merger activity ensued—not just large record companies gobbling up smaller ones, but huge conglomerates, unrelated to music, acquiring properties in the music industry. RCA, CBS, Capitol-EMI, and their related labels, which had long been divisions of multinational electronics firms, simply expanded their holdings. Phillips, the Dutch electronics conglomerate, acquired Mercury and MGM. Gulf and Western bought Paramount. GRT, the tape company, purchased Chess. Omega Equities bought Roulette.[3]

By far the most interesting merger was the one that created the Warner Communications empire. Warner Brothers Records had been a rather lackluster label that was created in 1958 as a division of the film company. In 1963, the label bought Frank Sinatra's Reprise label, only to be acquired itself by the smaller Seven Arts film company in a 1967 deal that also included Atlantic Records. Next came entrepreneur Steve Ross, who parlayed his Kinney Corporation parking lot interests into an entertainment conglomerate that included the Warner–Seven Arts labels and Elektra Records, adding David Geffen's Asylum Records in 1973. Now reorganized as Warner Communications, the corporation and its affiliated labels represented the Grateful Dead, Aretha Franklin, Cream, Led Zeppelin, Deep Purple, Black Sabbath, the Faces, Crosby, Stills & Nash, Neil Young, Arlo Guthrie, Gordon Lightfoot, Van Morrison, Joni Mitchell, the Eagles, Jackson Browne, James Taylor, Randy Newman, and the Mothers of Invention, and it owned extensive holdings in film and television, *Mad* magazine, sixty-three comic books, and a piece of *Ms.* magazine.

By 1973–1974, structural realignments had produced a level of concentration in the music industry that had not been witnessed since the postwar 1940s. The top four record corporations accounted for over 50 percent of all records and tapes sold; CBS and Warner Communications alone took in about 40 percent of the total. The industry had also consolidated vertically. In addition to its own labels, recording studios, pressing plants, national distribution, and publishing division, CBS, Inc., for example, owned the Columbia Record and Tape Club, Pacific Stereo and the Discount Records chain, Fender Guitars, Leslie Speakers, Rhodes Pianos, and Rogers Drums. EMI in Great Britain had an analogous set of holdings.

Because of the predominance of electronics corporations in the field, there was a wrinkle to this corporate structure that seemed particularly antithetical to the ideology of popular music at the time: the unexpected connection between music and the military. Ever since the invention of the wireless, electronic communication had developed according to its military applications. "Audio is a fairly obscure backwater of electronics," producer Peter Williams has explained. "When people do go out to design a new chip they're not thinking how many recording studios can we sell it to. They're thinking how many missiles can we stick this in. Most electronic development is highly military."[4] The connection between music and the military was driven home dramatically to Keith Richards when he discovered that Decca, the Stones' label, had diverted the profits it made from the sale of Rolling Stones records to precisely this kind of research and development.

> **W**all Street soon came to view the music industry as a sound investment, and a period of unprecedented merger activity ensued—not just large record companies gobbling up smaller ones, but huge conglomerates, unrelated to music, acquiring properties in the music industry.

We found out, and it wasn't years till we did, that all the bread we made for Decca was going into making little black boxes that go into American Air Force bombers to bomb fucking North Vietnam. They took the bread we made for them and put it into the radar section of their business. When we found that out, it blew our minds. That was it. Goddamn, you find you've helped to kill God knows how many thousands of people without even knowing it. I'd rather the Mafia than Decca.[5]

In the headiness of the late 1960s and early 1970s, such connections were not always apparent. This was the time when rock became art, when it became progressive, indeed, revolutionary. The industry rose willingly to the challenge of accommodating the new aesthetic.

Expanding the Infrastructure: Counterculture as Commodity

Developments in recording technology had a dramatic impact on the production of music. By the late 1960s and early 1970s, high-fidelity stereo records had become the industry standard (with various tape configurations vying for acceptance) and had increased the public's desire for high-quality sound. In the search for better sound, the two four-track tape machines that had been used to record *Sgt. Pepper* in 1967 were rendered obsolete by the appearance of eight- and sixteen-track studios. Multi-track recording had immediate consequences for the social relations of musical production. No longer was it necessary for musicians to perform together to make a record. Indeed, a single musician could now play all the instruments. Overdubbing, layering, mixing, and the addition of special effects such as reverb, equalization, and compression removed increasingly important aspects of the creative process from the studio performance and located them in the control room, elevating the producer to an artistic status equal to that of the musicians he produced. As a result, the term *production* in the music industry, as Peter Wicke has astutely pointed out, came to have two related but distinct definitions: "the production of music and the manufacture of records."[6]

By the early 1970s, the major record labels had narrowed their focus essentially to the manufacture and sale of records. Almost all of the creative aspects of music making were contracted out.

By the early 1970s, the major record labels had narrowed their focus essentially to the manufacture and sale of records. Almost all of the creative aspects of music making were contracted out. "The mechanics of a record company are just that—the mechanics," said Joe Smith in 1974.[7] On the creative end, record companies were involved primarily in talent acquisition, marketing, and promotion. And promote they did. The record companies were quick to pick up on the anti-establishment fervor of the late 1960s and early 1970s in promoting some of the more creative strands of rock that were being labeled *progressive rock,* a term that resonated nicely with the radical rhetoric of the era. In 1968, CBS introduced an ad campaign that promoted some of its rock acts as "The Revolutionaries." Advertisements were headlined with slogans like "The Man can't bust our music." Warner released a compilation long-playing record (LP) called *The People's Album,* which was largely a repository for their singer/songwriters and soft rock acts. The album cover art, however, had lettering intended to look like Chinese characters and depicted heroic, banner-waving protesters in Mao jackets, thus suggesting an association with the cultural revolution occurring halfway around the world.

The appearance of a whole new industry infrastructure greatly enhanced the promotional power of the record companies. Once experimentation with psychedelic drugs introduced a new visual dimension to live rock performances, a touring circuit of ballrooms and small clubs opened up to showcase the new progressive rock acts. Taking their cue from promoter Bill Graham's Fillmore Auditorium in San Francisco, clubs like the Electric Circus in New York, the Boston Tea Party, the Electric Factory in Philadelphia, the Grande Ballroom in Detroit, and the Kinetic Playground in Chicago embellished rock performances with strobe effects and undulating, amoeba-like light patterns that pulsated to the beat of the music. The psychedelic clubs and ballrooms folded after only a few years, largely because the progressive rock market had outgrown such small venues. Established promoters simply moved into arena or stadium-size venues and huge outdoor festivals; advances in sound reinforcement technology had opened up the possibility of mass audience events on the scale of Woodstock. By the early 1970s, the Grateful Dead were touring with enough power to provide electricity for a small neighborhood. Traveling with thirty-two tons of equipment, Emerson, Lake, and Palmer brought new meaning to the term "power trio."

A burgeoning rock press and the advent of FM rock radio completed the picture of the music industry's growing infrastructure. As Smokey Robinson at Motown recognized early on, the unit of pop production for AM Top Forty was the three-minute single. By the mid-1960s, this fast-paced format had been perfected by programmer Bill Drake, who taught his "boss jocks" to eliminate "dead air." However, the format did not readily lend itself to the new lyric substance that the folk revival of the early 1960s had brought to popular music, nor to extended singles or concept LPs like *Sgt. Pepper*. FM rock radio opened up to accommodate this new musical style.

In the 1960s, two Federal Communications Commission (FCC) rulings transformed the importance of FM for rock. In 1961, the FCC authorized FM "multiplexing," a process of broadcasting two signals simultaneously on a single channel; this is the process that makes possible a stereo broadcast. The second FCC decision, in 1965, married FM and rock: It ruled that FM programming in cities with a population greater than 100,000 had to differ from AM programming at least 50 percent of the time. Station owners promptly decided to use FM to explore new styles of music. Progressive FM rock began more or less simultaneously on the East and West coasts around 1967, although a number of college stations had used the format even earlier. One of its commercial pioneers was "Big Daddy" Tom Donahue, who initiated a laid-back, "free form" music show on station KMPX in San Francisco and, within months, was programming the whole station. He described the format as one that "embraces the best of today's rock and roll, folk, traditional and city blues, raga, electronic music, and some jazz and classical selections."[8] By 1970, there were 668 FM outlets in the United States, and a good number of them—WBCN in Boston, WABC and WNEW in New York, WBBM in Chicago, WKNR in Detroit, KSAN in San Francisco, and KMET in Los Angeles, among others—were playing rock.

Born of the counterculture, progressive FM rock radio exhibited a unique blend of culture and politics in its formative stages. Within a few years, the better FM stations even rivaled some AM outlets in commercial success, but as soon as they did, they fell victim to the same corporate pressures toward homogenization that affected AM radio. *Rolling Stone*'s Ben Fong-Torres, who did some moonlighting as a deejay, detailed the process in 1973:

> *The typical FM station goes on with waves of good vibes, building an audience of loyal listeners by playing album cuts unheard on AM, by talking with, instead of to, listeners, and by opening up the station to the community. As the audience builds, however, the ratings, "the numbers," climb, and*

the station owners suddenly have a marketable commodity. Suddenly the air is filled with increasingly uptight advertisers, administration takes over, and everything is sterilized. Suddenly there are playlists; certain records have to be banned. No more interviews—can't stop the flow of music. No politicizing—remember the Fairness Doctrine. Got to have that license in order to do your thing, you know. Suddenly there's no community out there, but a "share" of the "quarter hour audience." And in the end, FM rock stands naked. It is, after all, just another commercial radio station.[9]

The rock press followed much the same trajectory. The existing trade magazines—*Billboard, Cash Box, Record World*—shared AM radio's inability to incorporate new developments in music. It is hardly surprising, then, that dozens of alternative magazines began appearing around 1966 to fill the void. *Crawdaddy!* in Boston was the proving ground for Jon Landau, Peter Guralnick, and Ed Ward. Robert Christgau, Ellen Willis, and Richard Goldstein cut their journalistic teeth at *Cheetah* in New York. Most of the alternative rags, such as San Francisco's *Mojo-Navigator R&R News,* were completely disorganized and folded within months. Some, such as *Creem,* watering hole for Dave Marsh and Lester Bangs, published sporadically but with considerable impact. On 18 October 1967, Jann Wenner launched the magazine that would outlast them all—*Rolling Stone.* From its very beginnings, it ran counter to the antibusiness culture of rock.

Wenner, whom Robert Draper has described as a dedicated and driven journalist, an unabashed and insecure social climber, a fawning stargazer, and a ruthless businessman "who cut a multitude of ethical corners," was a Berkeley dropout and rock 'n' roll fanatic who found himself immersed in the eruptions of mid-1960s San Francisco.[10] Through the efforts of his friend and mentor, Ralph Gleason, the *San Francisco Chronicle's* music critic, Wenner landed a job as entertainment editor for the radical *Sunday Ramparts.* He then joined a group that, by his standards, was taking an interminably long time to start a counterculture magazine called *Straight Arrow.* After attending a few meetings, Wenner stole the group's mailing list and started his own magazine. Cofounder Ralph Gleason christened the magazine *Rolling Stone,* and it was published by Wenner's own company, which he named Straight Arrow.

Gleason gave the magazine legitimacy in progressive rock circles. He had been a tireless advocate of the alternative rock scene at a time when few established critics ventured out onto that limb. With Gleason's name on its masthead, musicians were willing to grant interviews to the magazine, and record companies were willing to buy ads. Taking both rock and journalism seriously, Wenner attracted a formidable first-generation stable of writers, including Michael Lydon, Jon Landau, Greil Marcus, Langdon Winner, and Jim Miller.

In the first issue of *Rolling Stone* (which pictured John Lennon in an army uniform on the cover), Wenner told his readers, "*Rolling Stone* is not just about music, but also about the things and attitudes that the music embraces."[11] This hint of a connection to politics seemed to be borne out in Ralph Gleason's piece on racism in television and

When Jann Wenner launched Rolling Stone, he was responding to the tenor of the times. Although he evidenced little tolerance for countercultural inefficiency or movement politics, he genuinely sought to develop a serious journalism for the music he loved.

Michael Lydon's exposé of the Monterey Pop Festival, which he criticized as being "done for a cost plus songs, not for a song plus costs."[12] *Rolling Stone* soon became required reading in the music industry. At the same time, Wenner clearly separated himself from the more radical political tendencies of his generation when he condemned the yippie protest at the 1968 Democratic National Convention in Chicago for "using methods and means as corrupt as the political machine it hopes to disrupt" and said, to the outrage of the New Left, "Rock and roll is the *only* way in which the vast but formless power of youth is structured, the only way in which it can be defined or inspected."[13] For the New Left, this kind of mystification of rock was precisely what was wrong with the counterculture. As Robert Draper has said,

> *While the nation buried Martin Luther King, Jr.,* Rolling Stone *published an obituary of . . . Frankie Lymon; while America cried for Robert F. Kennedy, Jann Wenner fired bullets at the new Cream album.* Rolling Stone *responded to the rapid escalation of the Vietnam War with an article showing how soldiers were smoking good weed overseas. Nixon's election—a brutal blow to the counterculture—did not warrant a mention, as the magazine was preoccupied with John Lennon's foreskin.*[14]

By the magazine's fourth anniversary in 1971, Wenner had embraced the term *capitalist,* trying to invest it with a positive spin. "As long as there are bills to pay, writers who want to earn a living by their craft, people who pay for their groceries, want to raise children and have their own homes," he editorialized, "*Rolling Stone* will be a capitalistic operation."[15] After all, music had always been *Rolling Stone*'s primary mission, and Wenner had reasoned early on that, to realize his vision, the magazine would have to be built on a solid economic foundation, even if that meant distancing it from the political upheaval that provided its context. What was important to Jann Wenner was the surety that the music he loved was taken seriously and that there was a place for him in the scene.

Creativity and Commerce: Rock as Art

In the new music industry, rock enjoyed a privileged position. Technological advances and journalistic seriousness had invested it with the status of art. The signal event for this development had been, of course, the 1967 release of the Beatles' *Sgt. Pepper* album. With 900 hours of studio time required for completion at the then unheard of price of $100,000, *Sgt. Pepper* became the Sistine ceiling of rock and George Martin, its Michelangelo. Meticulous attention had been paid to every detail of composition, balance, and technical execution. It was, in the modest opinion of guitarist Lenny Kaye, "an artistic statement in a music that was never regarded as art before."[16] Even established academics stood up and took notice. Renowned musicologist Wilfred Mellers called it "the most distinctive event in pop's brief history."[17] Clearly, the days when the Beatles, or any other rock group, could release six best-selling albums in one year were gone forever. Rock artists now labored over every cut, experimenting with new sounds, adding special effects, and overdubbing to perfection. Warner label head Joe Smith told a story of how the Grateful Dead said they wanted to "record thirty minutes of air in the summertime, when it's hot and smoggy. Thirty minutes of heavy air. Then we could go to the desert and record thirty minutes of clean air. Then mix the two together, get a good sound, and record over it."[18]

As social movements and the counterculture that accompanied them deteriorated in the early 1970s, rock increasingly found refuge in its newly acquired standing as art. If rock-as-counterculture had existed outside market relations, then rock-as-art hovered above them.

The Grateful Dead were not alone in the search for perfection. As social movements and the counterculture that accompanied them deteriorated in the early 1970s, rock increasingly found refuge in its newly acquired standing as art. If rock-as-counterculture had existed outside market relations, then rock-as-art hovered above them. This was, of course, a hopelessly contradictory belief, but it echoed the anticommercialism of the period and made musicians central to the creative process. Critics friendly to the music began to construct their own versions of *auteur* theory in popular music. "The criterion of art in rock," said Jon Landau, "is the capacity of the musician to create a personal, almost private, universe and to express it fully."[19] This focus tended to carry rock in the direction of European art music, drawing on classical influences, delving into opera, exploring the possibilities of orchestration, and stressing the technical aspects of musicianship. George Martin's training as a classical oboist had doubtless played more than a small role in the appearance of cellos, piccolo trumpets, and classical string quartets on Beatles' records. *Sgt. Pepper* "marked the turning point," Wilfred Mellers has said, "when the Beatles stopped being ritual dance music and became music to be listened to."[20] In this sense, then, rock was said to be the mature form of rock 'n' roll. However, that construction was laden with extramusical baggage.

In the context of U.S. race relations, rock's artistic explorations were not simply neutral forays into a broader musical terrain; they mirrored the separation of the races that had begun in the late 1960s. "No one who can hear today," proclaimed *Rolling Stone* editor Ralph Gleason in January 1968, "can possibly find any way in which the Beatles imitate Black musicians."[21] In May of that year, Gleason extolled the virtues of the San Francisco groups for much the same reason:

> One of the most encouraging things about the whole hippie scene and rock music in San Francisco which grew out of it is that no one is really trying to be anything other than what he is. The white sons of middle class America who are in this thing are not ashamed of being white. They are the first American musicians, aside from the country and western players, who are not trying to sound black.[22]

These sentiments were later echoed by Eric Clapton, who built his career covering B. B. King guitar licks. "My whole attitude has changed," said Clapton. "I listen to the same sounds and records but with a different ear. I'm no longer trying to play anything but like a white man."[23] Such comments devalued the contributions that black artists made, placing them outside the definition of progressive music and therefore beneath the critical attention of the rock press. Progressive rockers headed off in new artistic directions, relating to black music as a touchstone of historical significance rather than a continuing source of artistic inspiration. Black music had provided the foundation; now progressive rock would construct the edifice. By 1971, Motown chronicler Dave Morse was able to observe, rather bitterly,

Progressive rockers headed off in new artistic directions, relating to black music as a touchstone of historical significance rather than a continuing source of artistic inspiration. Black music had provided the foundation; now progressive rock would construct the edifice.

"Black musicians are now implicitly regarded as precursors who, having taught the white men all they know, must gradually recede into the distance as white progressive music, the simple lessons mastered, advances irresistibly into the future."[24] Jon Landau argued that black music "provides rock with the continuity which allows developments like the rise of San Francisco to take place."[25]

San Francisco's psychedelic clubs, of course, were some of the places where rock began its advance toward art. When George Hunter formed the Charlatans, one of the progenitors of the San Francisco scene, he was studying electronic music and staging "happenings" at San Francisco State College. The Charlatans' good-time electric folk had less of an impact than the group's vintage gold-rush cowboy fashions and innovative poster art, inspired by turn-of-the-century illustrator Maxfield Parrish. These images found a ready home in the city's psychedelic clubs where designers, sculptors, visual artists, and electronics experts were as important to the "total environment" as the music itself. A more systematic impetus for combining these elements came from British art schools, which had long been a haven for bohemian students who went on to become rock stars. As Peter Wicke has pointed out, a remarkable number of British rock musicians took this path to stardom:

John Lennon was registered at the Liverpool College of Art from 1957 to 1959; Pete Townshend studied at London's Ealing Art College at the same time as Ron Wood, later a member of the Rolling Stones, and Freddie Mercury of Queen; Ray Davies of the Kinks was from London's Hornsey Art College; Jeff Beck, guitarist with the Yardbirds, and Eric Clapton were both educated at London's Wimbleton College of Art; and even David Bowie and Adam Ant were art school graduates, from St. Martin's School of Art and Hornsey Art College respectively.[26]

In their engaging study *Art Into Pop*, Simon Frith and Howard Horne noted that British art schools promoted a nineteenth-century Romantic notion of (high) art as an autonomous, personal statement operating within (and sometimes resisting) the shifting demands of capitalist culture. The schools thus encouraged an atmosphere of experimentation and self-indulgence that enabled would-be musicians to bring "into music-making attitudes that could never have been fostered under the pressures of professional entertainment."[27] Alongside

The Who were the first pop art band. From Pete Townshend's Union Jack jacket to the use of real radio ads and jingles on record, they pioneered the use of popular signs and symbols as an artistic statement in music.

fine arts courses, classes in industrial and fashion design and photography allowed students to investigate image and style within modern mass media.

For those who were interested and talented, rock offered the potential for bringing all of these elements together in a single, total experience (and held out the possibility of earning a living from it). Pete Townshend, for example, applied what he had learned about theater, poetry, and film to the Who's stage act, treating it as performance art. In this spirit, the Who experimented with noise and destroyed instruments and sound systems. Pop artist Peter Blake (who designed the *Sgt. Pepper* cover) played a key role in determining the image of the Who (badges, medals, targets, the Union Jack on Townshend's jacket), which established the group as the first pop art band. The Who's release of the first rock opera, *Tommy,* in 1969, placed them in an artistic realm that would have been considered a contradiction in terms a few years earlier.

Andy Warhol, perhaps pop art's most famous practitioner, became directly involved in rock through his tutelage of the Velvet Underground, a group with a discomforting sound that would become influential in the void that yielded punk. He saw "commercial art as real art and real art as commercial art."[28] While his position displayed both disturbing cynicism and considerable insight, it also addressed the needs of the music industry.

> By the end of the 1960s LP sleeve designers were roaming across the history of modern art, film and fashion as knowingly (and for much the same reason) as advertising agencies—the sleeves, like the rock posters and group images, at first glimpse the most obvious sign of a high art presence in rock, were, in fact, designed to sell the product.[29]

All told, Warhol created over 50 album covers during his career.

For a time, the move to elevate rock to art was balanced by a sense of humor. When the Beatles acknowledged the Mothers of Invention's *Freak Out* as one of the inspirations for *Sgt. Pepper,* Frank Zappa returned the favor with a complete send-up of *Sgt. Pepper*'s cover art on an album entitled *We're Only in It for the Money.* The Who followed with the tongue-in-cheek *The Who Sell Out,* which simulated a commercial radio broadcast and included ads and jingles, some made up and some real. As the 1960s turned into the 1970s, however, a new generation of British art rockers brought artistic "seriousness" to full fruition and the music abandoned its sense of humor. "It was the abstract chimera of 'art' surrounding the music of such groups as Yes, Jethro Tull, Genesis, Emerson, Lake & Palmer, and the Moody Blues," contends Iain Chambers, "that continued to exert a disproportional influence on the direction and sense of much pop music, distributing judgment and dividing the musical field into frequently quite rigid divisions."[30]

As the 1960s turned into the 1970s, a new generation of British art rockers brought artistic "seriousness" to full fruition and the music abandoned its sense of humor.

At this point, art rock emerged as a new marketing category that distinguished these groups from other progressive rock acts. There was perhaps a greater tendency to "dignify" the music with classical references in Britain, where class distinctions are more sharply felt than in the United States. The Moody Blues kicked off this trend when the group's *Days of Future Past,* which was recorded with the London Festival Orchestra, reached number three on the charts in 1968. They followed up with six gold LPs in a row. With keyboardist John Lord's *Concerto for Group and Orchestra* in 1970, recorded at the Royal Albert Hall, Deep Purple was headed in the same direction until guitarist Ritchie Blackmore intervened and changed it. At their worst,

musicologist Rob Walser has said, these classical appropriations reeked of upper-class preten-
sion. In this regard, he has been particularly critical of Emerson, Lake & Palmer:

> [N]eoclassical extravaganzas, such as their rendering of Mussorgsky's Pictures at an Exhibition
> (1972), were intended as elevations of public taste and expressions of advanced musicianship. Keith
> Emerson's attraction to classical resources was unabashedly elitist; he considered ordinary popular
> music degraded and took on the mission of raising the artistic level of rock.[31]

Despite these criticisms, it has to be acknowledged that this music worked artistically
and commercially. Indeed, it worked beyond the wildest fantasies of the record companies.
"Emerson, Lake & Palmer have no faults," said the Cash Box review of the group's first New
York City appearance in 1971.[32] Apparently fans concurred; all of the albums the group
released in the 1970s were certified gold.

Emerson, Lake & Palmer was a supergroup that had drawn its members from existing rock
bands: keyboardist Keith Emerson from the Nice, an earlier rock/classical fusion group, guitarist
Greg Lake from King Crimson, drummer Carl Palmer from the Crazy World of Arthur Brown.
Lake's and Palmer's blues orientation provided the group with a hard rock base, but Emerson
was the group's guiding force. As a boy he had taken classical piano lessons, which had introduced him to the percussive piano sound of Béla Bartok. Indeed, Bartok's influence colored
their self-titled debut album. As the group matured, Emerson took the concept to new heights,
typically rushing around amidst a bank of keyboards (at one point a piano, a Moog synthesizer,
two electric organs, and other unnamed sound-producing devices), stabbing at them with staccato thirty-second-note runs. Four of the group's next five albums reached the Top Ten. By the
second half of the 1970s, however, disco was making far more efficient use of the synthesizer,

*Emerson, Lake & Palmer were among the groups who felt that there was
no incompatibility between rank and serious art. Among their defining
characteristics were the use of synthesizers and the incorporation of
classical influences in their music.*

"Roundabout"

Artist: Yes
Music/Lyrics by Jon Anderson and Steve Howe
Label: Atlantic (1971), from the LP *Fragile*

Art or progressive rock was identified with large musical structures, layers of overdubbed sound, experimentation with instrumentation and electronic effects, and compositional techniques borrowed from classical music. These musical elements were often paired with poetic, philosophical, weighty, or somewhat surreal lyrics. The English group Yes, with its team of virtuoso players and production wizard Eddie Offord, was a classic English "prog" rock band, and "Roundabout" is a classic example of the style.

Musical Style Notes

One of the hallmarks of Yes's style lay in their collaborative compositional method. The members all contributed to compositions and arrangements, which partly accounts for the "sectional" sound of a lot of their music. Yes's guitarist Steve Howe once noted that another one of the group's "secret ingredients" was the "intensity of the color," referring to the use of tone and timbre (the quality of the sound) to create vivid sonic effects. This is illustrated beautifully in "Roundabout" because the different sections of the piece are marked by changes in tone and timbre as well as rhythm.

Another important aspect of Yes's style is the focus on multiple layers of beautifully executed harmony vocals, as precise in live performance as they were on record. The lyrics to "Roundabout" were written during a drive from Aberdeen to Glasgow in Scotland ("Roundabout" is the British name for a traffic circle), and much of the imagery is literally taken from the countryside ("mountains come out of the sky"; "in and around the lake," which happened to be Loch Ness).

Yes's lineup on the *Fragile* LP was Jon Anderson, vocals; Steve Howe, guitar and vocals; Chris Squire, bass and vocals; Rick Wakeman, keyboards; and Bill Bruford, drums.

Musical "Road Map"

TIMINGS	COMMENTS	LYRICS
0:00–0:07	Introduction: sound effect created by reversing a recording of a grand piano.	
0:07	Free-rhythm introduction on guitar, beginning with "harmonics," created by lightly touching the sixth, third, second, and first strings of the acoustic guitar at the twelfth fret.	
0:40	Descending acoustic guitar line, providing a transition into the first verse.	
0:44	Verse 1—melody A; instruments begin.	
0:58	Vocal enters.	*I'll be . . .*
1:18–1:44 1:25	Verse 2—melody A Vocal enters (lyrics begin at 1:25). Note how additional vocals are layered in.	*The music . . .*
1:44–2:15	Transitional or bridge verse—melody B	*In and around . . .*

TIMINGS	COMMENTS	LYRICS
2:15–3:21	Verse 3—melody A Instrumental beginning is extended in length.	*I will remember . . .*
2:34	Vocal enters.	
3:21–4:57	Instrumental section, featuring a repeating bass and guitar riff over a complex, polyrhythmic drum part (several different rhythms being played simultaneously)	
3:40	Vocals in multiple harmonies are layered over the bass, guitar, and drum riff.	*Along the*
4:36	Melody A returns, also sung over the bass, guitar, and drum riff.	
4:57–	Return of acoustic guitar introduction, played over a repeated, very fast synthesizer riff; sonic texture is much more sparse.	*In and around . . .*
5:33	Keyboard riff continues, while vocal enters with truncated version bridge B melody—last vocal line cues following instrumental section.	
5:50–6:16	Instrumental section: blues-style organ solo, while bass, guitar, and drums play the instrumental lines from the transitional bridge.	
6:16–7:05	Another instrumental section; solos traded between organ and guitar. Instruments cue the return to the verse with a passage that ascends up the scale.	
7:05–7:25	Verse 1—melody A returns.	*I'll be . . .*
7:25–7:53	Transitional or bridge verse—melody B	*In and around . . .*
7:53–8:21	Multiple harmony vocals enter over an acoustic rhythm guitar part, singing "da-da-da" syllables. The harmonies are layered in two groups: The first sings a simple, repetitive melody; the second enters with a short countermelody (the first three notes of "Three Blind Mice").	
8:21–8:29	Return of the descending acoustic guitar line from the end of the song's introduction, ending on a single chord.	

and punk had stripped rock down to its bare essentials. Art rock extravagance—such as the seventy-piece orchestra the group had assembled for a 1977 tour—seemed bloated by comparison. Emerson, Lake & Palmer disbanded in 1979, only to regroup at the end of the next decade.

Another art rock group, Yes, had actually begun recording for Atlantic in 1968, before Emerson, Lake & Palmer formed. After some personnel changes, they edged into the U.S. Top Forty by the time their third LP, *The Yes Album,* was released. But they didn't hit their stride until keyboardist Tony Kaye was replaced by Rick Wakeman, a classically trained pianist from the Royal Academy. The next album, *Fragile* (1972), hit the Top Ten and yielded one of the group's only successful singles of the decade, "Roundabout." From *Fragile* on, every Yes album reached the Top Twenty.

Pink Floyd was more eclectic in its influences than Emerson, Lake & Palmer or Yes. From 1965 to 1968, the group was dominated by writer/guitarist Syd Barrett, a Camberwell Art School student with an unusual flair for combining kinky imagery with all the psychedelic trappings of San Francisco. "Arnold Layne," the group's debut single about a transvestite, was banned by the British Broadcasting Corporation (BBC). By 1968, Barrett had succumbed to the psychic perils of lysergic acid diethylamide (LSD) experimentation and had been replaced by David Gilmour. *A Saucerful of Secrets,* released that year, marked the ascendancy of bassist Roger Waters as the spiritual center of the group. Under Waters's leadership, the group eschewed Barrett's three-minute forays into psychedelia in favor of long-winded, spacy sonic voyages often based on a single chord. This tendency earned them equal measures of critical praise as the quintessence of art in rock and out-of-hand dismissal as purveyors of psychedelic muzak. The group reached its zenith in 1973 with the release of *Dark Side of the Moon,* one of the darkest and best-selling rock albums ever. Some 566 weeks and 10 million copies after its release, the album still registered on the pop charts. During this period, the group began playing "concert halls to audiences as hushed as if they were at a classical event."[33] They continued in this vein throughout the punk era, crowning the decade with *The Wall* (1979), a number one album that yielded their only number one single, the anthemic critique of traditional education, "Another Brick in the Wall."

Ultimately, the canon of art rock that emerged was a social construct. Inclusion in the art rock category was linked to art school training, to the appropriation of classical and other esoteric resources, even to being British. Using these criteria, Procol Harum, with its nod toward Bach on "A Whiter Shade of Pale" in 1967, was an easy entry. The Bach influence was also enough to place Deep Purple in the art rock category at least for a while, even though the group was bordering on the emerging and much less prestigious category of heavy metal. Led Zeppelin, despite its broad range of influences, was excluded from the art rock category, in part because hip critics could not find a constructive way of relating to the group's ultra-macho presentation. Concept LPs and theatrical stage shows that were more intelligent than most allowed Genesis to be categorized as art rock. Ian Anderson's spirited flute playing and religious musings propelled Jethro Tull into the category. The release of the Who's second rock opera, *Quadrophenia,* was enough to continue the group's association with art. On the other hand, few U.S. groups seemed to meet the criteria. Nobody, for example, thought of Chicago as an art rock group, even though several of its members had studied in conservatories or had majored in music at college. Perhaps, in the eyes of the critics, the group had too many Top Forty hits to be considered serious or perhaps a horn-based group sounded too much like jazz, which was a different kind of art.

In fact, a jazz rock, or fusion, category emerged in the early 1970s after Miles Davis's *Bitches Brew* (1970) reached number thirty-five on the pop charts. At the time, a gold jazz album was almost unthinkable. A full-page ad in *Rolling Stone* boasted: "Critics agree Miles Davis has found a new audience. Or is it that Rock has just found Miles Davis."[34] Jazz rockers differed from art rockers because they were jazz musicians enjoying a brief flirtation with the mainstream audience rather than rock musicians who were drawn to jazz influences; jazz rock was almost invariably a repository for black or racially integrated groups, while art rock remained the exclusive province of white men. There was almost no overlap between the two categories. John McLaughlin, who played guitar on *Bitches Brew*, reached the mainstream audience with his Mahavishnu Orchestra on *Inner Mounting Flame* (1971) and *Birds of Fire* (1973). He also teamed up with fellow Sri Chimnoy devotee Carlos Santana for *Love Devotion Surrender* in 1973. Another Davis alumnus, Herbie Hancock, scored with the platinum *Headhunters* in 1974 and finished the decade with three more Top Forty albums. While jazz artists like George Benson and Chuck Mangione achieved mainstream success in the late 1970s, their sound is better described as pop jazz rather than jazz rock.

Art rock was also separate from other forms of black music in significant ways. At a time when most black music was still built around the hit single, art rock focused on extended compositions and LP suites. Typically, art rockers sold far more albums than singles. Among the most successful, Emerson, Lake & Palmer, Yes, Jethro Tull, Pink Floyd, and the Moody Blues routinely tallied Top Ten album entries and gold record certifications, but only one of these groups ever had a Top Ten single in the 1970s (the Moody Blues' "Nights in White Satin" hit number two in 1972) and only two had a Top Ten single in the 1980s (Pink Floyd and Yes). By the late 1960s, revenues from LPs had surpassed those from singles. By the early 1970s, about 80 percent of the sales dollars—and therefore the lion's share of promotional budgets—was in albums. Thus, black music was marginalized financially.

This financial separation also had an aesthetic/social dimension. Art rock was often a music of ponderous introspection; it underscored the connection between rock and hallucinogenic drugs. At its most ethereal, it was called "head" music. Clearly, this was a music of the mind, not a music of the body. Nourishment for the body—the "ritual dance music" that drew on ever more distant African resources—was devalued accordingly. In addition to racist homologies suggesting the superiority of European/art/mind over African/entertainment/body, the marginalization of black music pushed stylized partner dancing to the periphery, until it resurfaced with a vengeance during the disco craze. In the interim, it was replaced by the broadly interpretative and highly individualized free-form swirling that sometimes accompanied "journeys to the center of the mind."

> *In addition to racist homologies suggesting the superiority of European/art/mind over African/entertainment/body, the marginalization of black music pushed stylized partner dancing to the periphery, until it resurfaced with a vengeance during the disco craze.*

Sweeter Soul Music

In the late 1960s, the music press often decried the commercialism of black popular music while praising the artistry of rock, even r&b-based rock. "The soul and R & B strains of Janis Joplin, Rod Stewart, Joe Cocker, and Van Morrison were praised," Iain Chambers has said, "while Ray

Charles and Aretha Franklin, not to mention the unredeemable Tamla Motown stable (with the precise exception of the 'progressive' Stevie Wonder), were accused of decaying in the swamps of a commercial jungle."[35] If the music press tended to deprecate black music, mainstream radio tended to ignore it entirely. Jerry Wexler, Atlantic's primary rhythm and blues producer, has said that, by 1971, radio stations did not want to "burden" their listeners "with the sound of breaking glass in Watts or the sirens coming from Detroit, which is what r&b music meant at the time, . . . so they took most of it off the radio."[36] Hardly above criticism itself, Atlantic responded to this situation by changing direction to focus primarily on its British rock acts, just as its former soul partner, Stax, was about to begin its long and torturous descent into bankruptcy.

Wexler's comment suggests that there was a connection between the decline of rhythm and blues on the radio and the political shift that marked the end of the tumultuousness associated with the 1960s. Certainly by the early 1970s, the civil rights movement appeared to have run its course, and civil rights themes declined in popular music. While War scored with "The World Is a Ghetto" in 1972, by 1973, only the Spinners' "Ghetto Child" and Stevie Wonder's "Living for the City" were noticeable in the pop singles market. There was a corresponding decline in the popularity of southern soul, the militant-sounding strain of r&b from the Deep South. Arthur Conley, Percy Sledge, and Sam and Dave disappeared from the Top Forty after 1968 and, by then, Otis Redding had died. Wilson Pickett lasted until 1972 and then faded from pop view. That same year, Ike and Tina Turner had their last Top Ten hit of the decade. Soul music had not disappeared completely; instead, outside social forces had altered its character.

As radicalism in the black community was repressed either by the cooptation of key leaders or by the more sinister effectiveness of the FBI's Counter-Intelligence Program (COINTELPRO) operation, there was a fleeting attempt to embrace black capitalism within the music industry as a solution to racism and its attendant ills. The music industry was quite aware of discrimination within its own ranks. At the 1969 convention of the National Association of Television and Radio Announcers (NATRA), Stan Gortikov, then president of Capitol, had accused the industry of being "too damn white."[37] Earlier that year, at a conference held by the Recording Industry Association of America (RIAA), New York senator Jacob Javits had expressed the "hope that the industry . . . will move forward . . . by striking a resounding note for black capitalism."[38]

The flurry of rhetoric and action that ensued over the next few years produced some interesting, if paradoxical, results. Having declined on the singles charts from 34 percent in 1968 to 24 percent in 1971, artists of color then accounted for an all-time high of 44 percent of the best-selling singles in 1972. From just 12 percent on the album charts in 1971, they rebounded to 24 percent one year later. During this time, there had been a short-lived and highly controversial breakthrough of sorts for African Americans in Hollywood in the form of black-oriented movies like *Shaft, Superfly,* and *Troubleman* (the so-called blaxploitation films). The soundtracks for these movies were scored by Isaac Hayes, Curtis Mayfield, and Marvin Gaye, respectively. Still, soundtrack albums alone do not account for the substantial presence of African Americans on the pop charts in 1972. Two other developments come closer to explaining these increases: the emergence of a number of African American artists as album-oriented acts and the popularization of softer soul sounds that would provide one of the building blocks for disco.

If there was a dominant black sound that reflected the seemingly quieter mood of the early 1970s, it was Philadelphia soft soul, or Philly soft soul, pioneered by the writer-producer team of Kenny Gamble and Leon Huff and producer-arranger Thom Bell, who joined forces with Sigma Sound Studios. The three men collaborated in the tripartite administration of Mighty Three Music, the publishing company they formed for their music. Having come of age in Philadelphia in the early 1960s, they were no strangers to a predominantly white music scene. Gamble had sessioned for Leiber and Stoller in New York and had helped to produce Danny and the Juniors' "At the Hop." When he returned to Philadelphia, he formed the Romeos, with Thom Bell on keyboards. After Bell was replaced by Huff, Gamble and Huff free-lanced for Atlantic and other labels. The two scored their first Top Ten hit with the blue-eyed Soul Survivors' "Expressway to Your Heart" on Crimson. Bell worked at Cameo and later moved to Philly Groove with the Delfonics, producing the group's blockbuster hit, "La La Means I Love You." Gamble and Huff quickly followed suit with novelty songs for the Intruders, "Cowboys to Girls" and "(Love Is Like a) Baseball Game." After these, they resuscitated the flagging career of Jerry Butler with a new persona—The Iceman—and smoothed out the rough edges of soul on his "Only the Strong Survive," "Moody Woman," and "What's the Use of Breaking Up." In doing so, they perfected the production style that would be described in *Rolling Stone* as "not as bluesy as the Memphis/Muscle Shoals stuff, not as pop as Detroit."[39]

HEAR MORE
Gamble and Huff
on MyMusicKit

In a five-year period, Gamble and Huff produced thirty million-selling singles, with twenty-two records on the charts in 1968 alone; in 1970, the duo grossed over $1 million. Even so, they did not hit their stride until 1971, when they formed Philadelphia International Records (PIR) and made a distribution deal with CBS Records. The deal offered economic self-sufficiency and was also important to Gamble personally. Gamble was a nationalist with inclinations toward Islam. He saw PIR as a platform for pushing messages; thus, in the words of Nelson George, "Gamble and Huff contemplated slavery (the O'Jays' mini-epic 'Ship A'Hoy'), ecology ('The Air I Breathe'), spiritual enlightenment ('Wake Up Everybody'), corruption ('Bad Luck'), and the male-dominated nuclear family ('Family Reunion')."[40] In the context of the increasingly conservative Nixon–Ford era, certain aspects of nationalism (economic self-sufficiency, for example) resonated as well with Nixon's call for black capitalism as with the development of a strong opposition movement. Ironically, rather than rejuvenating the civil rights movement with a message of black liberation, Gamble and Huff were far more successful at infusing the market with romantic ballads and stylish dance music.

Ironically, rather than rejuvenating the civil rights movement with a message of black liberation, Gamble and Huff were far more successful at infusing the market with romantic ballads and stylish dance music.

Gamble and Huff's two biggest groups—Harold Melvin and the Blue Notes ("If You Don't Know Me by Now," "The Love I Lost") and the O'Jays ("Back Stabbers," "Love Train," "I Love Music," "Use Ta Be My Girl")—were produced throughout the 1970s with what critic Jim Miller called an "urbane glossiness."[41] During the same time, Thom Bell drew on his classical training to provide lush orchestral arrangements over a polite rhythmic pulse for the Stylistics ("Betcha by Golly, Wow," "Break Up to Make Up," "You Make Me Feel Brand New") and the Spinners ("I'll Be Around," "Could It Be I'm Falling in Love," "The Rubberband Man," "Working My Way Back to You"/"Forgive Me, Girl"). By the mid-1970s, MFSB (Mother Father Sister Brother, the massive, integrated house band at Sigma Studios, and its backup vocal trio, The Three Degrees, had become hit-makers in their own right. In 1974, their recordings of "TSOP (The Sound of Philadelphia)" and "When Will I See You Again" were numbers one and two, respectively, on the

"You Make Me Feel Brand New"

Artist: Stylistics
Music/Lyrics by Thom Bell
and Linda Creed
Label: Avco (1973), from
the LP *Rockin' Roll, Baby*

"You Make Me Feel Brand New," with its lush vocal harmonies, string arrangements, smooth production, and relaxed rhythmic feel, is a perfect example of Philadelphia soft soul. It was a huge hit for the Stylistics, reaching number two on the pop charts in 1974. An important part of the Stylistics' sound was the work of producer Thom Bell, who had also enjoyed great career success producing the Delfonics. The song was written by Linda Creed, a well-known songwriter who worked extensively with Bell and wrote hits for a number of pop and soul artists before her untimely death from breast cancer in 1986.

While an important development in the history of African American soul music, Philly soft soul was a style that crossed over into a number of markets. A song like "You Make Me Feel Brand New," a hit on the pop and soul charts, was as likely to be heard on Adult Contemporary radio or found in the Easy Listening section of a record store. The widespread popularity of this particular single can also be illustrated by its frequent use in the early 1970s as a wedding song by couples of all creeds and colors.

Musical Style Notes

The beautifully crafted musical and lyrical structure of "You Make Me Feel Brand New" was a variation on popular songs' typical verse-chorus pattern, and it became a model for subsequent ballads. The verse itself is divided into two sections, which are marked on the musical road map below as A and B. Each has a different melody and features a different vocalist: Airrion Love on the A section and the Stylistics' lead singer Russell Thompkins Jr. on the B section and chorus (the other members of the group are James Dunn, Herbie Murrell, and James Smith). The instrumental texture is dominated by keyboards (electric and acoustic piano and synthesizers), with the typical Philly soft soul string orchestra layered in at various points.

Musical "Road Map"

TIMINGS	COMMENTS	LYRICS
0:00–0:13	Introduction: synthesizers and keyboards, with sitarlike synth sound	
0:13–0:26	At the whoosh of the cymbal, tremolo strings enter.	
0:26–0:37 0:37–1:29	Entrance of full string orchestra Verse 1, section A, with vocal by Airrion Love Instrumental texture reduced to just keyboards, bass, synthesizer, basic percussion.	*My love. . .*
1:29–1:55	Verse 1, section B Lead vocal switches to Russell Thompkins Jr.	*Only you. . .*
1:55–2:34	Chorus (multiple voices in wide harmony; Thompkins's vocal most prominent) Synth orchestra enters right at the "God Bless You."	*God Bless You. . .*
2:34–2:44	Transitional instrumental passage. Note glockenspiel sound at transition.	
2:44–3:54	Verse 2, section A Airrion Love vocal. Note that this verse is instrumentally much thicker than verse 1—strings, synthesizer, additional keyboards.	*My love. . .*
3:54–4:04	Verse 2, section B Russell Thompkins's vocal.	*Without you*
4:04–4:37	Chorus (multiple voices in wide harmony; Thompkins's vocal most prominent) Synth orchestra continues through chorus.	*God Bless You. . .*
4:37–4:47	Track fades.	

The Spinners started in 1957 as Harvey Fuqua's backup group, the Moonglows, but didn't achieve major success on their own until the 1970s. In that decade, they straddled the fence between soft soul and disco.

charts. Together, these groups set the standard in black popular music for the first half of the decade and anticipated one strand of the disco craze that was about to erupt.

Other artists quickly tuned into the new soft soul sound—in Chicago, the Chi-Lites ("Oh Girl") and the ever-changing Isley Brothers ("That Lady"). Even southern soul yielded the velvety smooth Al Green ("Let's Stay Together," "I'm Still in Love with You"). One of the most striking features about the soft soul groups is how long many of them had been together. The Chi-Lites had formed in 1961. The Isley Brothers had their first hit in 1959. The Spinners had begun in 1957 as Harvey Fuqua's backup group, the Moonglows, then became the Spinners in the early 1960s on Fuqua's Tri-Phi label; personnel changes and moves to Motown and VIP eventually led to their 1970s configuration and five gold albums on Atlantic. The O'Jays had begun in Canton, Ohio, as the Triumphs in 1958. The group changed its name in the early 1960s to honor Eddie O'Jay, the Cleveland deejay who showed them the ropes. They had been signed by Imperial, Bell, and Minit before recording six gold and three platinum LPs for PIR in the 1970s.[42] The fact that it took so many years for these groups to peak says something about their perseverance and about the strength of the forces arrayed against them.

Clearly, the heyday of vintage Motown had ended. The Supremes were performing without Diana Ross; the Miracles, without Smokey Robinson. David Ruffin and Eddie Kendricks had left the Temptations (in 1968 and 1971, respectively). The Marvelettes and Martha and the Vandellas were already groups of the past. After a $22-million lawsuit, Holland-Dozier-Holland, Motown's top writer/producer team, left the label to form their own Invictus imprint.

The Four Tops followed them to the new label in 1971. Two years later, Gladys Knight and the Pips moved to Buddah, where they recorded some of their biggest hits, including their only number one single, "Midnight Train to Georgia."

Still, while Motown may have been down, it was not out, thanks to the Jackson 5. Their first four releases on the label—"I Want You Back," "ABC," "The Love You Save," and "I'll Be There"—all rose to number one on the pop charts in 1970. Their next two—"Mamma's Pearl" and "Never Can Say Goodbye"—went to number two in 1971. This kind of success with debut releases was almost unheard of. From Berry Gordy's perspective, the success of the Jackson 5 proved that his upbeat pop orientation still worked; to some critics, however, such releases appeared to be a throwback to Motown formula production. For many of the label's veterans, Gordy's centralized control, once necessary to the survival of the organization, was artistic constraint. Gordy would have to be dragged, kicking and screaming, toward a new point of view. It was Stevie Wonder and Marvin Gaye, two important exceptions to the initial talent drain at Motown, who accomplished this feat.

When he turned twenty-one in 1972, Stevie Wonder demanded the royalty payments that Gordy had held in trust for him since he was a child. Wonder spent about $250,000 of this money to produce *Music of My Mind* (1972), which reintroduced him to the white audience as a progressive act. At about the same time, he gained control of his own publishing—the first Motown artist to do so. Subsequent progressive albums—*Talking Book* (1972), *Innervisions* (1973), *Fulfillingness' First Finale* (1974), and *Songs in the Key of Life* (1976)—were all top five albums and confirmed his position as a crossover star. Gaye spent years trying to convince Gordy to back him as an album artist. He finally succeeded in 1971 when *What's Goin' On* was released; it was followed by *Let's Get It On* (1973). Both albums went Top Ten. Although Motown released smash hit singles by the Jackson 5, the new Temptations, and the solo Diana Ross throughout the 1970s, it was Stevie Wonder and Marvin Gaye who introduced the company to the financial joys of independent production and album-oriented releases.

Other black artists' album-oriented releases also did well. War—initially Eric Burdon's backup band—released eight albums of their own in the 1970s; four made the Top Ten and all were certified gold or platinum. United Artists tried to take credit for the group's success, pointing to the label's policy of promoting black acts no differently from white acts. Jerry Wexler, however, had a different explanation: "The old myth used

Stevie Wonder began his career as a multitalented twelve-year-old musical genius with the prefix "Little" attached to his name. By the early 1970s, he had secured his own publishing rights, successfully challenged Motown's formula mentality, and was well on his way to becoming an international superstar.

to be that an r&b record could sell maybe 200,000 copies and, in order to get any real muscle in sales, [it] had to sell pop (to whites). But now I think millions of sales are possible on 'secret service' hits—records that whites may not really be familiar with."[43] Whatever the truth, War's mellow grooves, which tended toward a laid-back rhythmic base with a funky r&b feel ("Slippin' into Darkness," "The Cisco Kid"), seemed consonant with the tenor of the new times.

HEAR MORE
James Brown on MyMusicKit

James Brown adapted to the new political era by singing a new political tune. While the streetwise artist had always projected a clear sense of where his anti-establishment sympathies lay, in 1972, his loyalties changed. That year Brown endorsed Nixon for reelection, a move that compromised his credibility in the traditionally Democratic black community. Soul Brother No. 1 became, in the eyes of his detractors, Sold Brother No. 1. He had his last pop hits of the decade in 1974, the year Nixon resigned, and did not return to the Top Forty until the film *Rocky IV* propelled "Living in America" to number four in 1986. Aretha Franklin also faded from pop view. She hit the Top Ten for the last time in the 1970s in 1974 with "Until You Come Back to Me (That's What I'm Gonna Do)" and did not achieve that position again until 1985 with "Freeway of Love," a duet with Annie Lennox of Eurythmics.

James Brown adapted to the new political era by singing a new political tune. Brown endorsed Nixon for reelection, a move that compromised his credibility in the traditionally Democratic black community. Soul Brother No. 1 became, in the eyes of his detractors, Sold Brother No. 1.

In the early 1970s, great black popular music was still being produced, but it no longer had the insistence of southern soul. The operatic Roberta Flack hit the number one slot three times in three years for Atlantic, with singles as soothing as they were beautiful—"The First Time Ever I Saw Your Face" (1972), "Killing Me Softly with His Song" (1973), and "Feel Like Makin' Love" (1974). Her duets with Donny Hathaway were equally delicious. Taking romantic sincerity all the way to self-parody, Barry White, backed by his Love Unlimited female trio and the forty-piece, string-laden Love Unlimited Orchestra, produced hits such as "I'm Gonna Love You Just a Little More Baby" and "Never, Never Gonna Give Ya Up" (1973), and "Can't Get Enough of Your Love, Babe" and "You're the First, the Last, My Everything" (1974). Both Flack and White joined the ranks of successful album artists: Flack had eight gold records to her credit; White had five gold and two platinum. White's saccharine grunting and groaning had actually been anticipated by Isaac Hayes's *Hot Buttered Soul,* released on Stax's Enterprise label in 1969. Hayes's eighteen-minute version of "By the Time I Get to Phoenix," with its extended spoken-word introduction of murmured declarations of love, made the album the best-selling LP in Stax's history.

By the start of the 1970s, Stax had become a multimillion-dollar corporation. Under the leadership of Al Bell, the company had entered a new period of political engagement, with ties to Richard Prior and the Reverend Jesse Jackson. Sales were fine, and a new distribution deal with CBS provided the company with $6 million in capital advances. In 1972, the label undertook its most ambitious project, Wattstax, a spectacular benefit concert in Los Angeles to commemorate the 1965 Watts uprising. The concert featured all the Stax stars and, in many ways, it was a success, resulting in a feature-length film, a six-sided album, and almost $100,000 in contributions for charitable black organizations. Without question, the concert underscored the connection between southern soul and black power. At the same time, however, it revealed identity problems and political tensions within the company. Why was Stax promoting a benefit in Los Angeles? What had they done for hometown Memphis? As these questions were being raised within the company, the Internal Revenue Service (IRS) launched an investigation into the company's business operations—and of Al Bell in particular. By the time Bell was cleared of all charges in 1976, Stax had closed its doors. Jim Stewart, Stax's conservative white founder, defended his partner's honesty, adding that Bell "got too involved in politics and not enough in the record business."[44] It was clear that the times demanded a new cultural orientation. Philadelphia provided soft soul sounds; white singer/songwriters provided soft rock.

Singer/Songwriters, Soft Rock, and More

The singer/songwriters of the 1970s wrote songs that were intensely personal—at times intimate, at times introspective, at times confessional. In the aspirations of rock toward art, they represented an attempt to apply lyric poetry to semi-autobiographical themes. As a trend in popular music, they were born of the 1960s and edged toward a break with that same era. In them, the introspection of the drug culture manifested itself in a level of self-disclosure that, a decade before, would have been revealed only to a psychiatrist. This turning inward signaled a retreat from—or was it a reevaluation of—the political engagement of the 1960s.

In the radical movements of the 1960s, personal concerns were often treated as psychological inadequacies that got in the way of revolutionary transformation. Eventually, the articulation of the powerfully simple feminist maxim "the personal is political" rendered all such thinking invalid. Now power relations had to be considered at all levels. Vulnerability was no longer a sign of political or psychological weakness; it was an essential ingredient in any trusting relationship. For radicals, of course, this maxim posed a dilemma: While personal openness tended toward equalizing power, at least among individuals, it could also undermine revolutionary discipline. In certain circles, such an outcome would have been considered "soft." And soft was not the stuff that revolutions were made of.

Soft was also not the stuff that rock was about at the turn of the decade. Indeed, until the appearance of the singer/songwriters, the words *soft* and *rock* would not have appeared in the same sentence. Surprisingly, at a time when most rock was rough, this new music was gentle; when most rock was deafening, its amplification was modest; while rock sought to let it all hang out, the tone of soft rock was reserved. At the time, hard rock was perceived as male in its loud, aggressive tone and phallocentric connection to instruments; soft rock represented the female side of the equation. The results were mixed. On the plus side, soft rock was the first style since the advent of rock 'n' roll that allowed women to sing in their own voices and encouraged men to try on new personas. On the minus side, its gentleness could sound mousy and its self-revelations could approach masochism or cliché.

Hard rock was perceived as male in its loud, aggressive tone and phallocentric connection to instruments; soft rock represented the female side of the equation.

If an appearance of vulnerability defined soft rock, then singer/songwriter Joni Mitchell led the pack. Her romantic involvements (with David Crosby, producer of her first album *Songs to a Seagull* [1967], Graham Nash, the inspiration for "Willy" on *Clouds* [1969], and James Taylor, "My Old Man" on *Blue* [1971]) were more widely noted than her music and frequently submerged consideration of her artistry. Mitchell bore some responsibility for the situation because she devoted much of her considerable talent—a near three-octave range, intricate melodies and instrumentation, and elegant lyrics—to exploring the exquisite pain of her amorous ups and downs. On her intensely personal album, *Blue*, she combined all these elements. In his review, Christgau saw evidence of feminism at work, even if Mitchell didn't.

> *Like her voice, Joni Mitchell's lyrics have always suggested emotional life with startling highs and lows and an attenuated middle. Just because she knows herself, she reveals how dangerous and attractive such a life can be, especially for women. . . . In a male performer such intense self-concern would be an egotistic cop-out. In a woman it is an act of defiance.*
> *Not that Mitchell herself has always perceived it that way.*[45]

Signed to Reprise in 1967, Mitchell had her first big break in 1968 when Judy Collins scored a Top Ten hit with Mitchell's "Both Sides Now." In 1970, she released *Ladies of the Canyon*, which included her anthemic "Woodstock," a hit for Crosby, Stills, Nash & Young. As her career progressed, she moved from acoustic accompaniment to a soft rock band and switched to Asylum, While she generated a handful of Top Forty hits—"Big Yellow Taxi," "You Turn Me On, I'm a Radio," "Help Me"—she was first and foremost an album artist. After turning out eight gold or platinum LPs in the 1970s, she turned briefly toward jazz, then returned to more accessible material in the 1980s, switching labels to Geffen.

Second only to Mitchell self-absorption, James Taylor was strikingly mellow, somewhat wooden, and always polite—the antithesis of in-your-face 1960s rockers. To the trained observer, his overly laid-back demeanor may have suggested his frequent bouts of depression as a teen or the heroin addiction that marred his career in his early twenties. Following his success, some critics spewed venom. Christgau said the late Lester Bangs wanted to run Taylor through "with a broken-off Ripple bottle," and went on to say, "Me, I only took the poster from his third album and ripped it into four or five pieces. Then I hung the face on my wall and scrawled upon it slogans from imaginary Maoist comic books, e.g.: 'Eat felt-tipped death, capitalist pig!'"[46]

Of course, these responses to Taylor would not have been so virulent had he not become so famous. Originally signed to the Beatles' Apple label by Peter Asher, Taylor's self-titled debut album caused little stir even with the appearance of Paul McCartney and George Harrison. When he returned to the United States with Asher as his new manager and switched to Warner, his star began to rise. His first album for the company, *Sweet Baby James* (1970), became one of the defining sounds of the soft rock genre and went platinum to boot. For the next eleven years, Taylor enjoyed nothing less than gold album sales. His 1972 marriage to Carly Simon simply heightened his visibility. Despite Taylor's skill as a songwriter ("Fire and Rain," "Country Road"), most of his hit singles were covers of other artists' material—Carole King's "You've Got a Friend" (1971), Marvin Gaye's "How Sweet It Is (To Be Loved By You)" (1975), and Jimmy Jones's "Handy Man" (1977). Taylor joined Simon and Garfunkel on

James Taylor's soft rock career was one of the most successful of the 1970s. In part because he was so famous, Taylor became a target for those who felt that soft rock represented a retreat from the engagement of the 1960s.

Sam Cooke's "What a Wonderful World" and hit number five with Carly Simon on Charlie and Inez Foxx's "Mockingbird" in 1974.

Carly Simon had tried to launch a career as a recording artist in the 1960s, but when differences with manager Albert Grossman (also Dylan's manager) scuttled a 1966 Columbia recording session, she spent the next few years regrouping. She signed with Elektra in 1970 and hit the Top Thirty with her self-titled debut album in 1971. The LP's hit single, "That's the Way I've Always Heard It Should Be," hinted at a feminist influence in its exploration of the deadening effects of marriage. The following year, her number one single, "You're So Vain," released just after her marriage to James Taylor, prompted endless queries about whether Mick Jagger (who sang backup vocals) or Warren Beatty (a rumored earlier affair) was the subject of the song. If nothing else, the queries placed her squarely in the middle of the rock aristocracy that framed her experience. In the end, the independence that Simon projected was more a function of economic privilege—she was an heir to the Simon and Schuster publishing empire—than political choice.

In the end, the independence that Simon projected was more a function of economic privilege—she was an heir to the Simon and Schuster publishing empire—than political choice.

Carole King was neither consumed by politics nor driven to share the intimate details of her private life. And she never tried to become either "one of the boys" or a sex kitten. She seemed at home with herself—forthright, genuine, and content. She wrote with a personal touch, sang in a conversational tone, and in 1971 outsold everyone in the music business. King had been in the business much longer than most of her contemporaries. By 1961, before she was out of her teens, she and Gerry Goffin, her lyricist husband, were already collecting royalties on their first major hit, the Shirelles' "Will You Love Me Tomorrow." In 1962, she had her

Carole King began her career as a Brill Building songwriter in 1960. As a singer/songwriter, she projected the quiet confidence of someone who had already been successful for more than a decade.

"You've Got a Friend"

Artist: Carole King
Music/Lyrics by Carole King
Label: Ode (1971), from the
LP *Tapestry*

The early 1970s saw a trend away from lyrics that focused on social and political commentary toward those that expressed the highly individual emotions of the singer/songwriter. Carole King is a master of the songwriting craft; in the 1960s, she and her then-husband Gerry Goffin were churning out number one hits for other artists as a member of the songwriting staff at Aldon Music (known collectively as the Brill Building songwriters after the New York building that housed Aldon).

King's ability to write songs that were simultaneously universal and deeply personal made her one of the era's most beloved singer/songwriters, and *Tapestry* was one of the most popular recordings of the early 1970s (it was seemed to be required listening in women's dorms at colleges across the United States). The musical cast featured the cream of the crop of Los Angeles session musicians (including drummer Russ Kunkel and guitarist Danny "Kootch" Kortchmar) and a team of backup singers that included James Taylor and Joni Mitchell. It swept the Grammy Awards for 1971. These accolades were a fitting tribute to a songwriter who had provided classic hits for so many artists (her own versions of two of her former hits, Aretha Franklin's "You Make Me Feel Like a Natural Woman" and the Shirelles' "Will You Love Me Tomorrow," are also included on *Tapestry*).

Musical Style Notes

The style of "You've Got a Friend" is dominated by Carole King's clear and beautifully understated vocals and her tasteful and soulful piano style. Producer Lou Adler's addition of a touch of string orchestra heightens the sentimentality without overpowering the sound texture. The song has several classic elements of a popular hit: the honest, forthright emotions of the lyrics; a simple verse-and-chorus structure; and a chorus that has one of those hooks ("Winter, spring, summer, or fall . . . ") that remains on replay in your mind for the rest of the day.

Musical "Road Map"

TIMINGS	COMMENTS	LYRICS
0:00–0:10	Piano introduction	
0:10–0:58	Verse 1	*When you're down . . .*
0:58–1:38	Chorus	*You just call . . .*
1:20		*Winter, spring, summer, or fall. . .*
1:38–1:48	Piano interlude (same as introduction)	
1:48–2:34	Verse 2 (Note entrance of string orchestra to sound texture.)	*If the sky . . .*
2:34–3:13 2:56	Chorus	*Winter, spring, summer, or fall. . .*
3:13–3:42	Bridge (new melody)	*Now ain't it good*
3:42–4:25 4:05	Chorus	*Winter, spring, summer, or fall. . .*
4:25–5:04	Last line of chorus, "You've got a friend," followed by King's vocal improvisations over this line, which continue until the end of the song.	

own pop hit as a solo vocalist, "It Might as Well Rain until September." After she and Goffin divorced, she and their two daughters moved to the West Coast, where she continued to write songs. A contract with Lou Adler's Ode Records launched her career as a full-fledged singer/songwriter. Her first outing, *Carole King: Writer* (1970), failed to crack the Top Forty, but her second, *Tapestry* (1971), broke all existing records.

((•● **HEAR MORE**
Carole King on
MyMusicKit

Tapestry contained its share of sentimentality, but it was never disingenuous. On an artistic level, all of its elements worked in synergy—King's genius as a songwriter, the understated sensuality of her lightly r&b-inflected piano playing, the warm and friendly voice you could believe in. Another key ingredient was Adler's uncluttered production. *Tapestry* "was a very naked sounding album," Adler said. "I wanted it to sound like she was in the room playing piano for you."[47] In its first year, *Tapestry* ended up in 5 million homes. It remained in the Top Forty for sixty-eight weeks and was number one for fifteen of them. Within five years, it had sold 13 million copies, becoming the best-selling record of all time. It also garnered an impressive four Grammies: Album of the Year, Song of the Year ("You've Got a Friend"), Record of the Year ("It's Too Late"), and Best Female Pop Vocalist.

Tapestry was such an outstanding achievement—"a triumph of mass culture," said Christgau—that it would be difficult to fault King for not repeating its success. The album allowed her to withdraw from touring almost completely. She adopted a strict no-interview policy, becoming, in the words of Katherine Orloff, "a housewife who writes songs."[48] While she turned out seven more Top Forty albums before the decade was out, by the late 1970s she had moved to Idaho and had limited her live performances to occasional appearances at benefits.

Australian-born Helen Reddy is seldom classified as a singer/songwriter because she was essentially a nightclub singer who introduced material by singer/songwriters into her act. However, she also co-wrote "I Am Woman" (with Ray Burton), which announced feminism to the mainstream audience in 1972, and caused Reddy to take heat from all sides. Its obvious connection to feminism angered conservatives, prompting mainstream radio to demur from playing it; the easy-listening, pop feel of the song made it odious to radicals. In her own way, Reddy was committed to the women's movement (she even started her own Hollywood Hills consciousness-raising group), but she never strayed far from its more centrist tendencies. "I am first and foremost a singer," she told historian Gillian Gaar. "That's how I earn my living. I don't earn my living as a feminist."[49] All the same, Reddy would be the first to admit that the women's movement had a palpable effect on her career, as it did on the other female performers of the era.

In the early 1970s, all the women—and a good many men—in rock were affected by the women's movement to some degree. Whether they were singer/songwriters or not, the women rockers who came into their own during this era—among them, Maria Muldaur, Melissa Manchester, Bonnie Raitt, and Linda Ronstadt—took a soft rock approach in their music. Maria Muldaur knocked around the acoustic folk scene for years with her husband Jeff (of Jim Kweskin's Jug Band) before she achieved solo success with the balmy "Midnight at the Oasis" in 1974. Melissa Manchester studied under Paul Simon at the High School of Performing Arts in New York before moving on to middle-level soft rock success on her own. Bonnie Raitt always seemed destined for superstardom, but at the beginning of the 1970s, it was still nearly two decades away. Her love of blues and her proficiency on electric slide guitar—as well as her Quaker upbringing and political activism—set her apart from most of her contemporaries, as did the fact that her father was Broadway singer John Raitt. Linda Ronstadt found a pop niche much earlier. After major success as the lead singer for the Stone Poneys ("Different Drummer," 1967), she went solo at the end of the 1960s, steadily built her career, and achieved number one status with *Heart Like a Wheel* and its hit single, "You're No Good," both released in 1974. Ronstadt became one of the most successful solo female vocalists of the decade, with nothing but gold and platinum albums to her credit, including two more that were number one—*Simple Dreams* (1977) and *Living in the USA* (1978).

All of these women were aware of themselves as female performers, wrestled with the contradictions of life on the road, and grappled publicly with the difficulties of expressing their sexuality comfortably. And they all turned toward soft rock. To the extent that soft rock offered a vehicle for more personal communication, it was progressive for women. But to the extent that it looked to acoustic folk as its model, it was regressive in form, and not just for women but for rock as a whole. Many of the men categorized as soft rockers or singer/songwriters— from major stars like James Taylor and Paul Simon to lesser known artists like Jonathan Edwards, Jim Croce, Harry Chapin, and Mac Davis—were identified with a retreat from rock. "[James] Taylor is leading a retreat," said Christgau in 1972, "and the reason why us rock and rollers are so mad at him is simply because the retreat has been so successful."[50] Artists like British-born Cat Stevens and Canadian Gordon Lightfoot, who both began recording in the mid-1960s, added to the perception of regression. Influenced by the hippie mysticism of Donovan, Stevens, described by one reviewer as "the English James Taylor," came to the attention of the U.S. market in 1971 with *Tea for the Tillerman,* which included the hit single "Wild World." As critic Stephen Holden has noted, "Although his records were pretty, they were quite vacuous."[51] Nine Top Forty albums later, Stevens began to tire of the music business; after his 1979 conversion to Islam, he withdrew from the business completely. Lightfoot was a folkie who had written songs for Peter, Paul, and Mary, Marty Robbins, and others in the mid-1960s. His seven Top Forty albums between 1971 and 1978, including the number one *Sundown* (1974), set him up for a comfortable recording career in the 1980s, even though his music seemed to be a throwback to an earlier time. Similarly, (Jim) Seals and (Dash) Crofts ("Summer Breeze," 1972) sounded far more reserved than they had when they first started playing with the Champs in 1958. Nevertheless, six gold albums established them as a solid soft rock act. Even more successful were folk-rockers America ("A Horse with No Name," 1972), who had eight Top Forty albums to their credit.

The singer/songwriter category included some variation, particularly among the critics' choices for the "next Dylan"—David Bromberg, Loudon Wainwright III, John Prine, Steve Goodman, even the early Bruce Springsteen,[52] and a range of cult-figure types, including Leonard Cohen, the poet, Tom Waits, the beatnik barfly who claimed to have slept through the 1960s, and Randy Newman, whose wry humor more than balanced the earnestness of most others in the field. Many of Newman's compositions were clever dramatic narratives that dealt with issues such as racism and other forms of discrimination ("Sail Away," "Rednecks," "Short People"), but often from the point of view of the perpetrators, which left the listener to grapple with the uncomfortable ambiguity.

There were several reasons for promoting Bruce Springsteen as the new Dylan. He was signed to Columbia by the same John Hammond who had brought Dylan himself to the label.

Bruce Springsteen combined working-class roots and social consciousness with riveting live performances. Even as a superstar in the age of video, he remained essentially a live artist who could project working-class solidarity with credibility.

On his first two albums—*Greetings From Asbury Park, N.J.* (1973) and *The Wild, the Innocent, and the E Street Shuffle* (1974)—he exhibited Dylan's tendency to fill a song with more words than a line could hold. At the same time, Springsteen could evoke images of everyday working-class lives that were as powerful as they were sympathetic. His live shows were raw, brash, and full of energy, often extending to the three-hour range. Songs like "Rosalita" from his second album were absolute showstoppers. More than any other performer, Springsteen demonstrated that singer/songwriters did not have to be hamstrung by the parameters of soft rock. To his followers, he was a legend even before Jon Landau wrote in 1974, "I saw rock and roll's future and its name is Bruce Springsteen."[53]

> **S**pringsteen could evoke images of everyday working-class lives that were as powerful as they were sympathetic. More than any other performer, Springsteen demonstrated that singer/songwriters did not have to be hamstrung by the parameters of soft rock.

Born to Run (1975), co-produced by Springsteen, his manager Mike Appel, and Landau, provided Springsteen with the creative and commercial breakthroughs he needed to crack the Top Ten. "Thunder Road," and "Jungleland" became instant rock classics. On its release, the album was hailed as a rock masterpiece; it hit number three and propelled Springsteen to national fame. In October of that year, both *Time* and *Newsweek* pictured him on their covers. At about this time, Springsteen began to part ways with Appel. When he insisted on using Landau as the producer for his next album, Appel refused. The ensuing lawsuits kept Springsteen tied up in court for the next year. By the time *Darkness on the Edge of Town* was released in 1978, a number of its cuts, including the title track, "Badlands," and "The Promised Land," were already live performance favorites. Throughout the remainder of the 1970s, Springsteen matured musically and politically. He pared down his music, unleashed the fury of his guitar, and created ever more vivid images. In 1979, he took a step that moved him closer to the activism that would characterize his career in the 1980s, headlining two shows for No Nukes, a weeklong series of concerts protesting the construction of nuclear power plants. (The only sellout nights in the No Nukes series were the nights that Springsteen played.)

The antinuclear movement tapped the creativity and activism of a number of artists at the softer end of the spectrum in the 1970s. Among those participating in No Nukes (Bonnie Raitt, James Taylor, Carly Simon, Sweet Honey in the Rock, Chaka Khan, Tom Petty, the

((⸱• HEAR MORE
Born to Run on MyMusicKit

Doobie Brothers, and Crosby, Stills & Nash) were John Hall, Jackson Browne, and Gil Scott-Heron. Hall, formerly of Orleans ("Dance with Me," "Still the One") provided the movement with its anthem "Power." Browne had come into his own as a solo vocalist with "Doctor My Eyes" in 1972. In the latter half of the decade, *The Pretender* (produced by Landau) and *Running on Empty* moved him into the Top Ten. As a singer/songwriter, he was as self-confessional as any of them, but he had an activist spirit. Scott-Heron, a political singer/songwriter if there ever was one, was a poet and novelist before collaborating with musician Brian Jackson. He is perhaps best known for his anti-apartheid "Johannesburg" from the album *From South Africa to South Carolina* (1975). "South Carolina" referred to the song "South Carolina (Barnwell)," protesting plans to build a reprocessing plant for nuclear waste in Barnwell. Two years later, Scott-Heron raised the issue even more forcefully in "We Almost Lost Detroit."

The California Alliance for Survival was even more successful in recruiting musicians to their cause. It staged over fifty shows that included Joan Baez, Peter, Paul, and Mary, Bob Dylan, Gil Scott-Heron, Bruce Springsteen, Jackson Browne, Minnie Ripperton, Bette Midler, and Stevie Wonder. The artists who worked on these benefits can claim some share of the credit for helping to make the antinuclear power plant movement one of the more successful protest movements of that time. By 1982, Robin Denselow has noted, "every single [nuclear power] station ordered in the USA since 1974 had either been canceled completely or indefinitely postponed."[54]

The connection between songwriting and activist politics was made most forcefully in a concert that was staged in Harvard Stadium on 21 July 1979. Amandla: Festival of Unity, was a benefit concert for the liberation organizations in southern Africa. It was headlined by Bob Marley and the Wailers and featured Patty Labelle, Eddie Palmieri, and Olatunji, among others, with Dick Gregory as emcee. Bob Marley had already distinguished himself in his native Jamaica as a songwriter and performing artist of genuine talent, moral authority, and political principle by the time Chris Blackwell signed him to Island Records in 1971. Marley and the Wailers broke into the U.S. Top Thirty with two albums—*Rastaman Vibration* (1976) and *Exodus* (1977). By 1979, Marley had become the first black international superstar. For Amandla, he demonstrated the power of his political convictions, performing songs such as "Slave Driver," "Get Up, Stand Up," "No Woman, No Cry," and a stirring rendition of "War/We Don't Need No Trouble."

Women's Music: The Feminist Alternative

Throughout the 1970s, the sexist nature of rock was openly debated in the feminist press. Those who felt that rock was irrevocably sexist gravitated toward softer styles. There were some, however, who felt that rock could be a valuable cultural asset for them. Feminist critic Ellen Willis wrote:

> *Music that boldly and aggressively laid out what the singer wanted, loved, hated—as good rock-and-roll did—challenged me to do the same, and so, even when the content was antiwoman, antisexual, in a sense antihuman, the form encouraged my struggle for liberation. Similarly, timid music made me feel timid, whatever its ostensible politics.*[55]

In 1972, in an attempt to harness the energy of rock in the service of feminism, the Chicago Women's Liberation Rock Band and its East Coast counterpart, the New Haven Women's Liberation Rock Band, recorded *Mountain Moving Day* for Rounder Records, an independent label. While the creation of the record was an overtly political act, even in circles that were less political, women began to venture into territory that had been exclusively male. A number of regionally known, all-female rock bands—including Eyes, the Enchanted Forest, Ace of Cups, and Isis—came and went. Goldie and the Gingerbreads, popular in Great Britain since the early 1960s, never made a dent in the U.S. market. The Deadly Nightshade recorded *The Deadly Nightshade* (1975) and *Funky and Western* (1976) for RCA and then folded. A mixed-gender group from Berkeley—Joy of Cooking—showed promise. Two women led the band, electric guitarist Terry Garthwaite and electric keyboardist Toni Brown. Garthwaite and Brown's music was not political in the narrow sense, but it compellingly reflected the experiences of women. With two well-received albums to their credit by 1971 (*Joy of Cooking* and *Closer to the Ground*), it looked as if the group might be the beginning of a nonsexist tradition in commercial rock. Christgau opined: "Many vaguely feminist women have no special connection to rock not out of ideology but simply because it has never really spoken to them. Joy of Cooking can end that."[56] However, after a disappointing third album, *Castles* (1972), the group dissolved. Brown and Garthwaite recorded *Cross Country* (as Toni and Terry) in Nashville before embarking on solo careers.

Fanny, started by two sisters from the Philippines, June and Jean Millington, was the first self-contained, all-female rock band to be signed to a major label and the only one of its generation to hit the Top Forty. Signed to Reprise in 1969 by Richard Perry, the band faced an almost impossible situation. Within the women's movement, their impolitic name and double-entendre album titles such as *Charity Ball* (1971) and *Fanny Hill* (1972) made them something

of an embarrassment. A promotional campaign that included "Get Behind Fanny" bumper stickers did not help. In the music business, the band was seen as a novelty group; when their concerts were well received, the sentiment was "not bad—for chicks." The fact that the title cut from *Charity Ball* reached the Top Forty was remarkable.

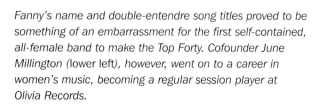

Fanny's name and double-entendre song titles proved to be something of an embarrassment for the first self-contained, all-female band to make the Top Forty. Cofounder June Millington (lower left), however, went on to a career in women's music, becoming a regular session player at Olivia Records.

Fanny was caught between rock and a hard place: It had entered a sector of the music business that had no female referents, let alone a support network. Feminism "was such a dirty word!" said June Millington.[57] She came to resent the fact that the quality of Fanny's music was measured by the group's ability to play like men. "You had to prove that you could play like a guy, or play as good as a guy," Millington later recalled. "That's really all there was. The whole attitude, what you wore, the way that you projected, every note that you played, was male territory."[58] In such a milieu, the women's movement could never have presented itself as a refuge. For the members of Fanny, becoming a rock band and developing a feminist consciousness were mutually exclusive choices. The group chose to become a rock band and, in so doing, helped women gain access to electric instruments—one of the biggest obstacles facing women in popular music.

> **F**or the members of Fanny, becoming a rock band and developing a feminist consciousness were mutually exclusive choices. The group chose to become a rock band and, in so doing, helped women gain access to electric instruments—one of the biggest obstacles facing women in popular music.

Fanny was the model for the Runaways, another all-female rock band made up of four southern California teenagers. As with Fanny, male handlers sought to promote the Runaways' sexuality more than their musicianship with releases like "Cherry Bomb" and the group eventually broke up. Still, the band was the proving ground for Joan Jett and Lita Ford, who went on to achieve some measure of solo hard rock success in the 1980s. The group's one-time vocalist, Micki Steele, later surfaced as one of the Bangles. Suzi Quatro, the group's fourth member, also ventured into hard rock with some success, which was somewhat trivialized by her role as Leather Tuscadero on the television series Happy Days.

The failure of all-female rock bands and the hostility of the music industry toward women in mixed bands led to the development of explicitly feminist, mostly folk-oriented, alternative music. For the most part, it was music Ellen Willis would have found timid. Women's music, as this new sound came to be called, was institutionalized in 1973 when a group of politically active women from Washington, D.C., started Olivia Records at the suggestion of singer Cris Williamson. Olivia's first release was a single that featured Williamson's "If It Weren't for the Music" backed by Meg Christian's rendition of "Lady" by Carole King/Gerry Goffin. The single sold 5,000 copies through mail order. The revenue it generated was used to relocate the operation to San Francisco and to finance the label's first album, Meg Christian's *I Know You Know* (1975), which sold 70,000 copies. Olivia's second album, Cris Williamson's *The Changer and the Changed*, sold over 250,000 copies—revealing the existence of an untapped feminist market.

Seeking to avoid the mainstream music industry completely, women's music formed its own subindustry. Olivia established a network of volunteers to distribute its records at concerts, in feminist bookstores, and door to door. As other women's music labels came into existence—Margie Adam launched Pleiades and Kay Gardner founded Wide Woman/Urana—Olivia's volunteers formed a network called Women's Independent Labels Distributors (WILD), which distributed these labels as well as Olivia. Women's music festivals began to attract thousands of feminists annually. In 1978, Roadwork, Inc., a national booking agency, was created to coordinate tour bookings.

Women's music was originally conceived as music by women, for women, and about women. It was, for all intents and purposes, lesbian music. However, the term *women's music* was used because it was less threatening to the public as a whole. "Women were less likely to be harassed for listening to or performing 'women's music' than 'lesbian music,'" said feminist music historian Cynthia Lont.[59] Because of the women's movement, there was a tendency to think of women's music in separatist terms, and a separatist orientation was probably necessary, at least in the short run. The male-dominated music industry was sufficiently exclusionary that there were no career paths to positions of power for women. As a way of life, however, separatism limited the audience for the music and led to damaging internal tensions within the movement. The experience of Holly Near and Redwood Records is a case in point. In political circles, Near was originally known as an antiwar activist. She started Redwood Records as an outlet for political material after visiting North Vietnam in 1973. Because of her involvement with the women's movement, however, and when she came out as a lesbian in 1978 on *Imagine My Surprise* (1978), she was criticized by some separatists for using Jeff Langley, her long-time piano player, on the album. Political differences of this sort sapped an inordinate amount of time and energy from women's music.

In this instance, the marketplace served as the final arbiter. By the 1980s, the market for women's music had become saturated, leaving the alternative industry with no choice but to expand its audience or die. "Ironically," Gillian Gaar wrote, "Olivia now found itself trying to break out of the 'women's music' genre they worked so hard to create."[60] The label responded to market problems by launching Second Wave to diversify its roster. While this move did compromise one of Olivia's original principles—that of using only female musicians—it allowed Olivia to help create a cultural space for postpunk feminists, from Tracy Chapman to Two Nice Girls. Ultimately unable to maintain its recording business, Olivia morphed into a lesbian cruise operator in 1988.

From Country Rock to Southern Boogie

In the late 1960s, *country rock* became yet another term in the growing lexicon of hyphenated rock styles. Country music had long been a significant influence in popular music. Rockabilly, a major strand of rock 'n' roll in the 1950s, was carried into the 1960s by artists like Roy Orbison and Brenda Lee. Ray Charles's two volumes of pop country and western tunes were his best-selling albums. The late 1960s brought down-home, traditional Nashville sounds into the rock idiom. The artist who kicked off this trend in 1968 used clean, unfettered production, accompaniment that was laid back and spare, and sang in an uncharacteristically throaty voice. On first hearing, it would have been difficult to tell that it was Bob Dylan.

At a time when rock was immersed in technological overindulgence, Dylan's John Wesley Harding was as spartan as his earlier acoustic efforts. At a time when the counterculture was free-spirited and anti-establishment, John Wesley Harding was recorded in Nashville, a bastion of traditional values. Dylan had, once again, thrown his fans a curve.

Dylan had been on hiatus since *Blonde on Blonde* had been released following his 1966 motorcycle accident. In the interim, Columbia had issued a greatest hits album. By 1968, then, Dylan's new album had been long awaited. When it came, it was totally unlike anything anyone had been expecting. At a time when rock was immersed in technological overindulgence, Dylan's *John Wesley Harding* was as spartan as his earlier acoustic efforts. At a time when the counterculture was free-spirited and anti-establishment, *John Wesley Harding* was recorded in Nashville, a bastion of traditional values. Dylan had, once again, thrown his fans a curve. *John Wesley Harding* rose to number two on the album charts, Dylan's highest position to date. If any doubts existed about the seriousness of his new artistic direction, he laid them to rest with the release of *Nashville Skyline* in 1969, which included the Top Ten hit single "Lay Lady Lay" and a duet with country legend Johnny Cash on "Girl from the North Country." As Bill Malone has written, "Dylan lent respectability to a musical form, and to a body of musicians, that had been perceived as 'corny' or old fashioned."[61]

Nashville soon became the hot "new" recording center, and country rock became a new trend. The top session players in the country music capital, those "Nashville Cats" the Lovin' Spoonful sang about, began getting so much work that they started their own performing ensemble, Area Code 615. Over the next few years, folk and rock musicians, from Buffy Sainte-Marie to the Nitty Gritty Dirt Band, to the Byrds, followed Dylan into country, thus putting an end to its association with socially regressive values. Sainte-Marie journeyed to Nashville to record *I'm Gonna Be a Country Girl Again,* whose title song became a hit single in 1972. That same year, the Nitty Gritty Dirt Band recruited country greats Roy Acuff, Doc Watson, Merle Travis, Maybelle Carter, and Earl Scruggs, among others, for a three-record album, *Will the Circle Be Unbroken.* Because the artists who traveled to Nashville treated country and western music without condescension, they began to soften the negative view that Acuff and other country performers had of hippies.

Most prominent among Dylan's fellow travelers on the road to country rock at the end of the 1960s were four Canadians and one "good ole boy" from Arkansas, known collectively as the Band. Guitarist Robbie Robertson, organist Garth Hudson, bassist Rick Danko, and pianist Rich Manuel had been fans of country music from childhood, though they were born and raised in Canada. Drummer Levon Helm from Marvell, Arkansas, could not have avoided country music if he wanted to. One by one, beginning in the late 1950s, these players joined the Hawks, the backup band for rockabilly artist Ronnie Hawkins, with whom they toured for years, honing their craft. "There were only three kinds of rock then: rhythm and blues, corny white rock, and rockabilly," said Robertson. "We played rockabilly."[62] They met Dylan through folk blues guitarist John Hammond, Jr., the son of Dylan's producer; at the time, Dylan was moving toward electric music. Hired as the backup band for his 1965 tour, they withdrew with him to Woodstock, New York, after his accident. There they collaborated—jammed, really—on rock's first significant bootleg, later released by Columbia as *The Basement Tapes.* The Band's official debut album, *Music from Big Pink* (1968), a reference to their Woodstock home, and their second release, *The Band* (1969), introduced a number of country rock classics, including Dylan's "I Shall Be Released," and Robertson's "Up on Cripple Creek," "Rag, Mama, Rag," "Across the Great Divide," and "The Night They Drove Old Dixie Down." (This last song became a Top Ten hit for Joan Baez in 1971.) Their third (and again critically acclaimed) album, *Stage Fright,* continued in the country rock mold.

In 1973, Dylan and the Band recorded their first official album together. *Planet Waves* was recorded in three days and rose to number one on the album charts almost as fast. They then embarked on Dylan's first full tour in eight years. The tour was captured on the two-disc LP *Before the Flood.* Because Dylan's contract with Columbia was in limbo at this time, both albums

The Band started as a rockabilly outfit and became Bob Dylan's backup band for his first electric tour. Their breakup on Thanksgiving Day, 1976, was immortalized in The Last Waltz, *directed by Martin Scorsese, one of the best concert films ever made.*

came out on Asylum, a major coup for David Geffen. However, Dylan returned to Columbia for *Blood on the Tracks* (1975) and *Desire* (1976). Both of these albums, which went to number one, would have been introspective enough to land Dylan back in the singer/songwriter category had it not been for the hit single "Hurricane," a political protest song dedicated to boxer Rubin "Hurricane" Carter, whom Dylan believed had been wrongly convicted of murder.

Several groups, mostly from southern California, picked up on Dylan's turn toward country. The Byrds, who transformed Dylan's acoustic material into folk rock earlier in the decade, again followed his lead. By this time, the group had recruited Gram Parsons, a Harvard Divinity School dropout, who became a pioneer of country rock. His influence on the Byrds' *Sweethearts of the Rodeo* (recorded in Nashville) helped them become the first rock band to play the Grand Ole Opry. Parsons soon left the Byrds and, with Byrds' alumni Chris Hillman and Gene Clarke, formed the Flying Burrito Brothers.[63] On *Last of the Red Hot Burritos,* they merged rock and country as no other group had done and they performed in striking sequined Nudie suits embroidered with marijuana leaves instead of the cactus plants and wagon wheels selected by most country artists.

When Stills and Young left the Buffalo Springfield (to form Crosby, Stills, Nash, and Young), two of the group's remaining members, Richie Furay and Jim Messina, made up the nucleus of another country rock ensemble, Poco. The band never matched their solid performances with comparable record sales. By the time Poco's best-selling album, *Legend,* was released in 1979, none of the original members were still in the group. Furay had fallen on hard times with the intended supergroup configuration of Souther, Hillman, and Furay. Messina had become the second half of Loggins and Messina, a country-inflected pop rock act best known for the light rocker, "Your Mama Don't Dance" (1972); both went solo in the late 1970s, with Kenny Loggins recording five best-selling solo albums.

The Eagles, the group that would come to dominate country rock in the 1970s, was composed of accomplished writers and vocalists—as attested to by sixteen Top Forty singles and four number one albums in a row. Bassist Randy Meisner had been a founding member of Poco and guitarist Bernie Leadon had played with the Burritos. Both, along with drummer Don Henley and guitarist Glenn Frey—the main writers when Meisner and Leadon departed—had backed up Linda Ronstadt. Something about the group was unsettling, however. When rockers like Creedence Clearwater Revival or the New Riders of the Purple Sage or the Grateful Dead or Neil Young performed country-flavored material, they sang with a certain southern ethos, a down-home earthiness. The Eagles were slicker, more polished. They were certainly talented enough to replicate the sound of country music, but they brought it out of the backwoods and into the big city. The word that most readily comes to mind in describing them is *corporate*. Somehow, the Eagles placed country rock in a new social context. With *John Wesley Harding*, Dylan had reclaimed the music of the heartland for rock 'n' roll. The Eagles were different. From their signature song, "Take It Easy" (cowritten by Jackson Browne in 1972), about the joys of an unencumbered life on the road, to the music on *Hotel California* (1976), their seminal statement about the California good life, they used country rock as a vehicle for embracing the hedonism of the 1970s. "The Eagles are the ultimate in California dreaming," said Christgau, "a fantasy of fulfillment that has been made real only in the hip upper-middle-class suburbs of Marin County and the Los Angeles canyons."[64]

The Eagles were certainly talented enough to replicate the sound of country music, but they brought it out of the backwoods and into the big city. The word that most readily comes to mind in describing them is **corporate**.

The Eagles were consummate musicians and canny self-promoters. In the mid-1970s, they came to dominate country rock with music (and a lifestyle) that was as hedonistic as it was successful.

The Eagles were not unaware of politics. Once Linda Ronstadt started dating Jerry Brown, who was then governor of California, she pulled them into the electoral arena and, later, Jackson Browne imparted an awareness of environmental issues. The very fact that the group took its name from Native American folklore suggested political awareness of some kind. But in the context of the early 1970s—Nixon's final years, and the culmination of the Vietnam War—the eagle was as likely to represent a bird of prey as a symbol of liberation. Still, the group was politically astute enough to know that with a name like the Eagles, it should have a major album out in 1976, the bicentennial year. *Hotel California,* musically their best effort, commercially their biggest success (fifteen million copies in U.S. sales), was the pinnacle of their success. By this time, guitarists Don Felder and Joe Walsh had replaced Leadon in the group, and Meissner was soon to depart. Eventually, the years of "Life in the Fast Lane," as the Eagles termed it, took their toll on the group. "I think the underbelly of success is the burden of having to follow things up," Frey told an interviewer. "We started to run out of gas. Don [Henley] sort of blew his literary nut on *Hotel California.*"[65] The result was the nightmarish three-year effort it took to produce the group's final studio LP, ironically titled *The Long Run.* Still, this ordeal did not prevent *Their Greatest Hits (1971–1975)* from becoming the best-selling album of all time.

The success of country rock paralleled that of its pop/country variants. Glen Campbell and John Denver were the biggest beneficiaries of this trend. Campbell parlayed songs such as "Wichita Lineman" and "Galveston" into major pop stardom in the late 1960s. Between 1968 and 1978, he tallied eleven gold albums, which brought him his own television program. Denver scored fifteen Top Forty albums and placed thirty-two singles in the Hot 100 between 1971 and 1982. A number of his biggest singles—"Take Me Home, Country Roads," "Rocky Mountain High," "Thank God I'm a Country Boy," and "Sunshine on My Shoulder"—suggested country themes, which his jeans-and-flannel image reinforced. Other artists cashed in, too. Canadian Anne Murray placed "Snowbird" in the pop and country Top Ten in 1970, kicking off an eleven-year run as a hit-maker.

As rock artists made a move toward country, a number of country artists were drawn to rock. At the center of this movement were a number of country artists who sought to challenge the conservative hegemony of Nashville. For their insolence, they came to be known collectively as "the outlaws." They wore the label proudly and marketed it to their advantage, as well as RCA's. In 1976, the label released *Wanted: The Outlaws,* a compilation LP with songs by Willie Nelson, Waylon Jennings, Tompall Glaser, and Jessi Colter. The album became the first certified platinum country album.

Nelson and Jennings were the most famous of the so-called outlaws. By the time he began to tire of Nashville's slickness in the mid-1960s, Willie Nelson had toed the country mark for over a decade, achieving great success as both a writer—he wrote "Crazy," Patsy Cline's biggest hit—and a performer. Before the 1960s ended, he had more than a dozen albums to his credit. When he moved back to Texas in the early 1970s, he changed his image, growing his hair long and discarding his western suits and ties in favor of jeans and T-shirts. His new look suited both his laid-back, conversational singing style and his refusal to be pigeonholed for commercial reasons. He first came to the attention of the rock press with *Shotgun Willie* and *Phases and Stages,* which he recorded in the early 1970s. He crossed over to the pop market with *Red Headed Stranger* in 1975, his first of more than thirty albums to make the pop charts. In 1978, he recorded his best-selling album of the decade, *Waylon and Willie*.

Waylon Jennings's country roots first led him toward rock in 1958, when he joined Buddy Holly on bass. (It was Jennings who gave up his seat to the Big Bopper on the flight that killed the Big Bopper, Holly, and Ritchie Valens.) Throughout the 1960s, Jennings fought hard for artistic freedom; his influences ran as far afield as Dylan and the Beatles. He even had a minor hit with "MacArthur Park" with the Kimberleys in 1969. Like the rest of the outlaws, Jennings resisted easy categorization and musical limitations, but he was always respectful of his roots. "The ultimate irony of the Outlaws," Bill Malone has said, "may be that, while drawing upon a diverse array of musical sources and reaching out to new audiences, they did more to preserve a distinct identity for country music than most of their contemporaries who wore the 'country' label."[66]

Malone's comment was directed at artists like Kenny Rogers and Dolly Parton, who achieved incredible mainstream success with material that hugged the middle of the pop/country road. Emmylou Harris took a different route. Harris was a truly eclectic performer who managed to stay grounded in tradition even as she explored rock-based material with her versatile Hot Band. While the group was adept at playing traditional acoustic country, their electric numbers were bold enough to be linked with a more extreme development in country-identified rock, which came to be known as redneck rock or, more politely, southern boogie.

Little distinguishes southern boogie bands—the Allman Brothers, the Marshall Tucker Band, Lynyrd Skynyrd, the Charlie Daniels Band, Molly Hatchett, and ZZ Top—from hard-rock bands other than their truculent identification with the South. Like other hard-rock bands, these groups were based in blues and country; their music was loud and sometimes crude; and they exhibited the same macho posturing, albeit with a bit of "good ole boy" flair. At a time when much of rock had become a pale imitation of its former self, however, these bands, even with their reactionary tendencies, sounded refreshing. If Dylan had recovered country for the mainstream rock scene, southern boogie returned rock 'n' roll to the soil.

> *I*f Dylan had recovered country for the mainstream rock scene, southern boogie returned rock 'n' roll to the soil.

The prototypical southern boogie band was the Allman Brothers, which featured brothers Duane and Greg Allman on guitar and keyboards, Dickie Betts on guitar, Berry Oakley on bass, and Jai Johanny "Jaimo" Johanson and Butch Trucks on drums. Duane had been a session player at Fame Studios in Muscle Shoals, backing artists like Aretha Franklin and Wilson Pickett. He was also the second lilting lead guitar on Eric Clapton's *Layla*. At their best, the Allmans were a tight, disciplined unit with intricate instrumental harmonies over a strong percussive base. They first came to the attention of the national audience with *Idlewild South* (1970). *Eat a Peach* (1972), the band's first Top Ten album, contains Duane's last recordings. (Duane was killed in a motorcycle accident before the album was completed; a year later, Berry Oakley died in a similar accident.) The band continued after Duane's death, recording their best-selling album, *Brothers and Sisters,* which hit number one on the album charts and yielded the number two hit single "Ramblin' Man" in 1973. That same year, along with two other acts— the Band and the Grateful Dead—the group headlined a single show at Watkins Glen, New York, that attracted some 600,000 fans, dwarfing even Woodstock in audience size. Although commercial success continued unabated throughout the decade, greatness, that very elusive quality, remained out of reach after the loss of Duane.

The Allman Brothers were the prototypical southern boogie band. Except for its identification with the South, there was little that separated southern boogie from hard rock in general. The Allmans' signature sound included rhythm and blues influences and intricate instrumental harmonies.

The Marshall Tucker Band, named for the owner of the band's rehearsal space, was softer and more laid back than the other southern boogie bands, but still in the mold of country rock. Like the Allmans, the group was signed to Phil Walden's Capricorn label. They toured with the Allmans and, along with other Capricorn acts, did benefits for Jimmy Carter. The Tucker Band was respectable enough to be rewarded with gigs at the White House after Carter's victory, but other southern rockers lived life closer to the edge.

Lynyrd Skynyrd, a variant spelling of the name of the high school gym teacher who suspended the group for wearing long hair, were fiercely proud to be southern. The band's first two albums—arguably their best—were produced by Al Kooper. The first contained "Freebird," a ten-minute tribute to Duane Allman that became something of a signature song for the group. The second had the group's best-selling single, "Sweet Home Alabama," an explicit defense of the southern way of life in response to Neil Young's "Southern Man." If southern rock had an ideological component, this was it. (It would pop up again in Charlie Daniels's "The South's Gonna Do It Again.") With four gold and four platinum albums by 1980, Lynyrd Skynyrd found a ready audience, if not critical praise, for their music, which was as wild and rowdy as their personal lives. The beginning of the end for the group came in 1977 when a plane crash claimed the lives of lead singer Ronnie Van Zant and band members Steve and Cassie Gaines.

The band's natural successor was Molly Hatchett, a group that first entered the Top Twenty in 1979 with the platinum-selling *Flirtin' with Disaster.* But the group soon entered a period of decline and effectively disbanded following a number of personnel and genre changes in the 1980s.

ZZ Top was a Texas-based trio that took southern rock into the 1980s. Their influences ranged from acid rock to the down-home blues of John Lee Hooker and Elmore James. Album titles like *Tres Hombres, Fandango!, Tejas, Deguello,* and *El Loco* suggested a Tex-Mex cultural influence. They had flirted with heavy metal as early as 1975, when they included the metal classic

"Tush" on *Fandango!*. In the 1980s, after the trio adopted their anonymous bearded look, they attempted a more conscious, blues-based metal/pop fusion.

When all was said and done, the southern rockers could be distinguished from their hard-rock contemporaries only by geography and, in some cases, personal appearance.

Mad with Power: Heavy Metal

Depending on one's perspective, the softer rock and soul styles of the 1970s represented either a withdrawal from the political engagement of the 1960s, a reevaluation of its efficacy, a fore-grounding of music as entertainment, or a new strategy for making the world a better place. In contrast, heavy metal represented an absolute rejection of the peace and love ethos. The music was too intense to be regarded as entertainment, and it was too self-absorbed to worry about making the world a better place. It was the critics' worst nightmare: hard rock taken to the extreme, with no socially redeeming features. Or so it seemed.

Heavy metal represented an absolute rejection of the peace and love ethos. It was the critics' worst nightmare: hard rock taken to the extreme, with no socially redeeming features. Or so it seemed.

The origins of the genre's name can be traced to a number of sources. It is used in chemistry to describe the heavier elements in the periodic table. In literature, the term has been ascribed incorrectly to the William Burroughs novel *Naked Lunch* and correctly to his later novel *Nova Express*. Most agree that its first appearance in popular music occurred in the line "heavy metal thunder" from Steppenwolf's "Born to Be Wild" (1968), a Top Ten single that became a biker anthem after it was featured in the film *Easy Rider*. In rock journalism, the term is usually credited to the incomparable Lester Bangs, one of the few critics who would touch the music with a less-than-ten-foot pole.

By the time heavy metal coalesced into a genre in the early 1970s, it had developed several distinctive elements. Chief among these was sound quality: "The essential sonic element in heavy metal is power, expressed as sheer volume," Deena Weinstein has claimed.[67] "If there is one feature that underpins the coherence of heavy metal as a genre," Robert Walser has noted, "it is the power chord" (a chord that is strummed at deafening volume and held to maximum sustain).[68] The power of heavy metal was intended to overwhelm its listeners, to flood them in a kind of sonic tidal wave. Heavy metal was not a violent break from hard rock; rather, it was a logical extension of hard rock with sufficient variation to defy its detractors' simplistic characterization of it as a wall of noise.

According to Weinstein, the origins of heavy metal lie in blues-based rock and psychedelic music.[69] Walser concurs with Weinstein's analysis but adds classical music to the list of sources.[70] Thus, heavy metal bears the influences of Muddy Waters, Howlin' Wolf, B. B. King, and Chuck Berry at one extreme, and Bach, Beethoven, Mozart, and Vivaldi at the other. As always, the genre's boundaries were a matter of subjective judgment. Black Oak Arkansas occupied the territory between metal and southern boogie. The J. Geils Band played hard blues-based rock, but their Boston contemporaries, Aerosmith, moved closer to heavy metal. Bachman-Turner Overdrive, from Canada, formed after guitarist Randy Bachman left Guess Who ("These Eyes," "American Woman"), pushed boogie to the limit on "Takin' Care of

Business" and unleashed Who-like power chords on "You Ain't Seen Nothin' Yet," but fell just short of metal in the eyes of most observers. According to Walser, "[t]he sound that would become known as heavy metal was definitively codified in 1970 with the release of *Led Zeppelin II,* Black Sabbath's *Paranoid,* and *Deep Purple in Rock.*"[71] The ascension of these three pivotal bands illustrates the diversity of sources that produced the genre.

Heavy metal's immediate acid and blues rock antecedents were what one might expect. Eric Clapton, Jeff Beck, and Jimmy Page, the lead guitarists who fronted the Yardbirds, marked the path. Clapton and Beck had always been blues aficionados. As a founding member of Cream, Clapton overlaid the blues with the psychedelic experience. Cuts like "Sunshine of Your Love" began to pull together the elements that define heavy metal: pounding bass and drums, blaring guitar, and screeching vocals. Jimi Hendrix was a parallel acid/blues influence who added incredible virtuosity to deafening sonic distortion. A number of U.S. groups, including Blue Cheer ("Summertime Blues," 1968) and Steppenwolf also pushed the boundaries of volume and distortion. In heavy metal, these elements were fueled by power chords, already evident in the music of the Kinks and the Who. These influences guided Jimmy Page when he sought to extend the work of the Yardbirds in a new configuration: Led Zeppelin.

For U.S. audiences in particular, Led Zeppelin—Jimmy Page (guitar), Robert Plant (vocals), John Paul Jones (bass), and John Bonham (drums)—became the archetypal heavy metal group. Initially billed as the New Yardbirds, Led Zeppelin (reportedly, the Who's immodest drummer, Keith Moon, quipped that the group's music would go over like a "lead zeppelin") filled the void for fans looking for a new intensity in rock. From the release of the group's first self-titled album in 1969, Zeppelin was a hit. Each of their eight subsequent albums released before the end of the 1970s rose to number one or two on the pop charts. Aided by the business acumen of manager Peter Grant, the group set concert attendance records all over the United States. They were ignored, however, by the rock press.

Black Sabbath followed a similar heavy metal road and enjoyed an equally poor relationship with the press. The group

For many Americans, Led Zeppelin defined heavy metal. Despite a broad range of influences, however, they were not accepted in art rock circles. Instead, they were trashed from the left for their sexism and condemned by the right for their fascination with the occult.

started as Earth, a working-class, hippie blues rock band from Birmingham, England. They changed their name to Black Sabbath, taken from an old Boris Karloff horror movie. The name change coincided with a move to a louder, more aggressive style and something of a break with the group's hippie past. In their new incarnation, the group paralleled Zeppelin's success, with five platinum albums in a row in less than four years, peaking with *Master of Reality* in 1971. For this feat, they were charged with a "complete lack of subtlety, intelligence, and originality."[72] Continued *Los Angeles Times* critic John Mendelsohn, "Black Sabbath's . . . new songs are as indistinguishable from its old songs as its old songs are from one another."[73]

This type of blanket dismissal was reminiscent of the things parents and critics said about rock 'n' roll when it first emerged in the 1950s. Complaints that heavy metal was too loud, that you couldn't hear the words, that it all sounded the same overlooked considerable variation in the music. Led Zeppelin, for instance, was influenced by everything from U.S. soul music to Celtic mysticism; their first album ran the gamut from sluggish blues to ethereal ballads. *Led Zeppelin III* (1970) balanced the hard rock riffing on cuts like "Immigrant Song" with a whole side of largely acoustic music. A folkish influence continued on the group's fourth album, *Led Zeppelin IV* (1971), with Page on mandolin in "The Battle of Evermore." The album included the group's seminal "Stairway to Heaven," which builds from an acoustic intro to a blistering climax, with Plant's piercing tenor soaring over Page's deafening salvo of raw guitar licks.

Complaints that heavy metal was too loud, that you couldn't hear the words, that it all sounded the same overlooked considerable variation in the music. Led Zeppelin was influenced by everything from U.S. soul music to Celtic mysticism; their first album ran the gamut from sluggish blues to ethereal ballads.

Deep Purple had an even broader range of influences, as well as a strong psychedelic bent and the beginnings of that conscious incorporation of classical virtuosity that would become increasingly important to the genre. The group first hit the Top Ten with "Hush" in 1968. The use of an organ gave the group a fuller sound than most of their contemporaries and landed them at first in the company of groups like Vanilla Fudge, who described their music as "psychedelic symphonic rock," and Iron Butterfly. Vanilla Fudge interpreted songs like the Supremes' "You Keep Me Hanging On" and the Beatles' "Eleanor Rigby" as if they were being played at a speed slower than most turntables could go, thereby creating in listeners the feeling of a drug-induced effect. Working in a similar way, Iron Butterfly parlayed the droning, seventeen-minute "In-A-Gadda-Da-Vida" from their debut album of the same name into Atlantic's best-selling record.

Deep Purple evidenced a comparable psychedelic connection on *The Book of Taliesyn*. Music from this album was used in the science-fiction movie *2001: A Space Odyssey,* the ultimate filmic acid trip. Classical influences also became evident in Deep Purple's music early on; both guitarist Ritchie Blackmore and organist John Lord had studied classical music. The critical and financial success of Lord's *Concerto for Group and Orchestra* (1970) suggested that the group would follow the trajectory of an art rock ensemble, but Blackmore balked, feeling "that the whole orchestra thing was a bit tame. I mean, you're playing in the Royal Albert Hall, and the audience sits there with folded arms, and you're standing there playing next to a violinist who holds his ears every time you take a solo. It doesn't make you feel particularly inspired."[74] Blackmore wanted to make use of classical resources, but in the context of heavy metal. He described the chord pattern for his solo on "Highway Star" from Deep Purple's best-selling album, *Machine Head* (1972), as "a Bach progression." His guitar playing became the hallmark

"Smoke on the Water"

Artist: *Deep Purple*

Music/Lyrics by Ritchie Blackmore, Ian Gillan, Roger Glover, Jon Lord, and Ian Paice

Label: *Warner Bros (1972),*

from the LP *Machine Head*

If you were between the ages of 13 and 20 in 1972, and you had an electric guitar, you learned the opening riff of "Smoke on the Water." This compelling, repetitive, distortion-soaked guitar riff is one of the hallmarks of hard rock and heavy metal, and aspiring young electric guitar players in the 1970s honed their craft by learning it. Thanks to the success of this song, Deep Purple is included in most discussions of "proto-metal," but this classification doesn't really give us the big picture of their complex stylistic background.

At the end of the 1960s and the beginning of the 1970s, the lines between "heavy metal" and "hard rock" were not clearly defined. To add confusion to the issue, many proto–heavy metal bands shared certain elements with "art" or "progressive" rock bands: complicated musical structures, orchestral electronic effects, and an obsession with technical virtuosity. Deep Purple navigated several of these channels. After experimenting with blues and art rock, the band regrouped in the early 1970s with a new bassist and vocalist, and the new band (Ritchie Blackmore, guitar; Jon Lord, keyboards; Ian Paice, drums; Roger Glover, bass; and Ian Gillan, vocals) had a somewhat "harder" rock sound, even though they never completely let go of their classical leanings.

Musical Style Notes

The famous opening guitar riff of "Smoke on the Water" has all the hallmarks of a blues lick: the movement from the keynote to the lowered third note of the scale, the flatted fifth note of the scale sliding back down to the fourth, and the use of rhythmic syncopation (see, for example, the second bar where the first note appears on the "and" between the first and second beats).

Beat:	1 + 2 + 3 + 4 +	1 + 2 + 3 + 4 +	1 + 2 + 3 + 4 +	1 + 2 + 3 + 4 +
Scale Degree	1 ♭3 4 1	♭3 ♭5 4	1 ♭3 4 ♭3	1 1
Actual Note	G B♭ C G	B♭ D♭ C	G B♭ C B♭	G G

Note: "♭3" indicates the flattened third step of the scale.

When the rhythm section enters, however, we know it's rock and roll just from the driving rhythmic pattern. Listen for the bass player's relentless repeated tonic note (tonic being "do," the first note in a major or minor scale).

Ian Gillan's vocal sound is strongly associated with hard rock and heavy metal—a high tenor sound with a certain amount of raspiness—and is a perfect compliment to the distorted guitar tone, accomplished by raising the volume to a level in excess of what the amplifier can handle (overdriving the amp), resulting in a gritty sound.

"Smoke on the Water" is also a good example of instrumentation built up in layers, a technique used by a number of art rock and heavy metal bands. (Led Zeppelin's "Stairway to Heaven" is another very famous example.)

Musical "Road Map"

TIMINGS	COMMENTS	LYRICS
0:00–0:18	Begins with the famous distorted guitar riff, henceforth referred to as the "SOTW" riff.	
0:18–0:27	Another guitar track is layered in, with high-hat cymbal.	
0:27–0:35	Drum adds backbeat to texture (drum strike on second and fourth beats of each bar).	
0:35–0:52	Bass layered in, playing steady "eighth notes" (one-and-two-and-three-and-four-and)	
0:52–1:26	Verse 1	*Montreux . . .*
1:26–1:55	Refrain, "Smooooke on the waaaa-ter," followed by "SOTW" riff, two times	*Smoke on the water . . .*
1:55–2:29	Verse 2	*They burned down . . .*
2:29–2:58	Refrain, "Smooooke on the waaaa-ter," followed by "SOTW" riff, two times	*Smoke on the water . . .*
2:58–3:39 3:39–3:56	Ritchie Blackmore guitar solo over the structural form of the verse Solo ends over the "SOTW" riff.	
3:56–4:29	Verse 3	*We ended up . . .*
4:29–5:39	Refrain, "Smooooke on the waaaa-ter," followed by "SOTW" riff, four times; music fades as guitar begins to solo.	*Smoke on the water . . .*

of precision and virtuosity that defined the next generation of metal guitarists. It shows up clearly on *Machine Head,* which includes the group's best-known single, "Smoke on the Water."

By the mid-1970s, a whole generation rockers moved proudly toward heavy metal, taking paths that their predecessors had followed. Some came from psychedelia. For example, Rush, a Canadian group, had begun by playing Cream and Iron Butterfly covers in 1974, using a classic power trio lineup. With the 1976 release of *2112,* loosely based on right-wing novelist Ayn Rand's *Anthem,* Rush merged progressive rock with the heavier sound that became their signature sound and commercial breakthrough. When Judas Priest released *Rocka Rolla* in 1974, they were a hard acid-rock band. By *Sad Wings of Destiny,* released one year later, however, they were squarely in the heavy metal camp. Uriah Heep took a similar road. Ted Nugent made a more gradual break from his psychedelic past (as leader of the Amboy Dukes) to a solo career that reached a heavy metal peak with the release of *Cat Scratch Fever* in 1977. Some came from blues-based rock. When Aerosmith was first signed to Columbia in 1972, the group was considered Boston's answer to the Rolling Stones. Lead singer Steven Tyler even looked (and pranced) a bit like Mick Jagger. By the time *Toys in the Attic* made the Top Forty in 1975, the group had begun edging toward the lighter side of heavy metal, a niche they occupied successfully throughout the 1980s. Bad Company, a group under the tutelage of Zeppelin's manager, Peter Grant, played predictable heavy blues-based rock. Although they could emulate Zeppelin's stance on cuts like "Can't Get Enough" and "Ready for Love," they could not match Zeppelin's talent or success. Humble Pie, a blues-based rock ensemble aimed at younger fans, was beginning to move toward metal when guitarist Peter Frampton left to become a solo superstar. The James Gang from Cleveland had been aiming at metal with more eclectic influences when guitarist Joe Walsh left for a stint with the Eagles and his own solo career.

In the classical realm, one guitarist in particular followed in Blackmore's footsteps and rewrote the book on virtuosity and sophistication, thus helping to usher in the new wave of heavy metal guitarists that dominated the 1980s: Eddie Van Halen. Van Halen and his drummer brother, Alex, were born in the Netherlands but raised in California, where they trained to become classical musicians until the lure of rock won out. With Michael Anthony on bass and David Lee Roth on vocals, Van Halen was a high-energy act right from the beginning. Signed by Warner in the late 1970s, the group's debut LP, *Van Halen* (1978), made the Top Twenty. Every subsequent album charted higher than the one before it until the group hit number one in 1985. While Van Halen owed its early success partially to Roth's athletic, overtly sexual (some would say sexist) performances, the group's defining and sustaining force was Eddie Van Halen's pathbreaking guitar style. Like many of his contemporaries, Van Halen was drawn to hard rock through the blues. The combination of blues emotionality, hard rock aggressiveness, Van Halen's classical discipline, and his sophisticated knowledge of music theory enabled him to propel metal guitar playing to new heights. According to Walser, Van Halen's solo on the appropriately titled "Eruption" from the group's debut album heralded the arrival of the new virtuosity in heavy metal. Walser describes the solo as "one minute and twenty-seven seconds of exuberant and playful virtuosity, a violinist's precise and showy technique inflected by the vocal rhetoric of the blues and rock and roll irreverence."[75] *Guitar Player* magazine chose Van Halen as the best rock guitarist for five years in a row.

Just as it is important to recognize the range of influences that comprised heavy metal, it is equally important to recognize that these influences were used in the service of the blustering, sexist, hard-rock scene that provided its context. Perhaps the best example is Zeppelin's "Whole Lotta Love," a rip-off of Willie Dixon's "You Need Love," which appeared on *Led Zeppelin II*. While the thundering rhythm underpinning Plant's insistent shrieking vocals and Page's chugging guitar and buzzsaw fills laid out the parameters of classic metal, the song itself illustrates why most critics were so antagonistic to the music. "I have felt over the past year and a half a steadily increasing disaffection with rock's male chauvinism," wrote Robert Christgau shortly after the song's release. "I am acutely uncomfortable with songs of cock-pride (Led Zeppelin's "Whole Lotta Love," for instance)."[76] For a number of groups (and critics), Plant's macho posturing and Page's phallic guitar thrusts defined heavy metal.

Only one U.S. band could rival Led Zeppelin in its unique combination of macho swagger, commercial success, and critical disdain: Grand Funk Railroad, a group that began in Flint, Michigan. Grand Funk played raw, basic rock that was not terribly distinctive and, as often as not, out of tune; they added little to the corpus of this music other than a few tunes by guitarist Mark Farner. That the group achieved any success at all is surprising; that they became one of the top five rock bands in the world is astounding. Grand Funk tallied eleven gold albums in a row—eight of them Top Ten—peaking with *We're an American Band* and a number one single of the same name in 1973. It is all the more incredible that the band achieved this status with almost no radio play and an almost total lack of press coverage. The only possible explanation is that near-unanimous condemnation conferred on the group the ultimate in outsider status. It was hyped to the fullest by the group's manager, Terry Knight.

The lack of critical recognition for the genre meant that most acts had to support their albums with grueling tours. These live shows tended to be ear-splitting spectacles of testosterone-drenched rock that aroused aggression more than sexuality. As a result, the audiences for metal concerts were predominantly young, white, working-class men, engaging in rites of male bonding with abandon. It was in the milieu of live performance that metal earned its nickname—cock rock. In the context of a burgeoning women's movement, it was a damning indictment, although in certain metal circles it was probably taken as a compliment. Heavy metal was a bastion of male dominance and privilege. In the 1970s, there were no women in heavy metal. The only women who even came close to the genre were the Wilson sisters, Ann and Nancy, who rose to prominence as key members of Heart. Even though Heart's debut release, *Dreamboat Annie* (1976), pictured Ann and Nancy bare-shouldered on either side of a red heart, their combination of ballads and near-heavy metal rock propelled them past novelty status all the way to number seven on the pop charts. Subsequent hits like "Barracuda" confirmed the group's ability to rock with the best of them. In time, the group achieved a superstar status that carried them through the 1980s. In the 1970s, however, Heart was an anomaly.

If heavy metal was condemned—or, more likely, avoided—in progressive circles for its sexism, it was assaulted from the right for its fascination with the occult. Fundamentalist

Just as it is important to recognize the range of influences that comprised heavy metal, it is equally important to recognize that these influences were used in the service of the blustering, sexist, hard-rock scene that provided its context.

groups accused Led Zeppelin of including satanic messages on "Stairway to Heaven" through backmasking, the process of recording passages backward. Groups like Black Sabbath and Judas Priest (formed in 1974) attracted attention simply by virtue of their names. Album titles such as *Sabbath Bloody Sabbath* and *Sin After Sin* only added fuel to the hell fire. Police agencies argued that Australia's AC/DC (also founded in 1974) stood for Anti-Christ/Devil's Children; given metal's preoccupation with power, the more obvious reference to electric currents should have been considered an equally likely acronym. In 1990, Zeppelin's Robert Plant chastised Americans for their inability to understand the British sense of irony and sarcasm. "There was . . . a lot of humor in the music," he explained in a retrospective interview. "Not all this glowering satanic crap. . . . [I]t's very American. Nowhere else in the world has anybody ever considered it or been concerned or bothered at all about that."[77] Still, Black Sabbath's Ozzy Osbourne marketed the connection with satanism most effectively, particularly in his solo career in the 1980s, when it became an even more volatile issue.

Faced with a widespread lack of industry support, if not outright hostility, metal came to wear its outsider status like a badge of honor; after all, part of its mission was to fly in the face of respectability. Blue Öyster Cult, a New York metal group in the Black Sabbath mold, used occult-style lyrics written by critic Richard Meltzer, who was also a vocalist for the group, and added Nazi paraphernalia to their metal regalia. Even with such trappings, their biggest hit "(Don't Fear) The Reaper" tended toward a pop sound, with sweet harmonies and just a hint of metal in the instrumental break. Blue Öyster Cult and Motörhead also added gratuitous umlauts to their names to conjure up a more generic gothic horror, a practice continuing into the 1980s with Mötley Crüe and others.

It was not just that the shows got harder and heavier or that strange animal rituals and awesome pyrotechnics were added; it was that heavy metal began to challenge the traditional concept of masculinity from within its exclusionary male environment. This was the last place one would have expected to find cracks in the facade of male sexuality.

Other heavy metal artists pushed the limits of decorum through performance and personal appearance. It was not just that the shows got harder and heavier or that strange animal rituals and awesome pyrotechnics were added; it was that heavy metal began to challenge the traditional concept of masculinity from within its exclusionary male environment. This was the last place one would have expected to find cracks in the facade of male sexuality. By the early 1970s, women and gays had become sufficiently vocal that gender roles and sexual preferences were no longer beyond questioning. Mick Jagger had long played with androgyny, but to find the beginnings of gender-bending in that area of heavy metal that blossomed into glitter or glam rock was most unexpected. Among the weirdest acts was a group of white, middle-class suburban athletes from Phoenix, Arizona, who named themselves after their leader, a minister's son who called himself Alice Cooper. Alice Cooper represented a clear break with the counterculture. "Even hippies hated us," Alice has said, "and it's hard to get a hippie to hate anything."[78] They made no pretense to authenticity or blues roots. Television was their main influence. Musically, the group was as subtle as a train wreck; they simply plastered their fans against the wall with noise. The group's big break came the night they cleared the posh club Cheetah after only three songs. Frank Zappa was sufficiently impressed that he signed them to his label, which brought them to the attention of its parent, Warner.

Kiss played metal as heavy as anyone and were eminently successful at it. Their equally heavy use of makeup suggested a connection to the ascending glam rock movement that challenged traditional gender roles as never before.

By 1976, the group had brought out eight gold or platinum albums, including the number one *Billion Dollar Babies* (1973) and a few memorable hit singles like "Eighteen" (1971) and "School's Out" (1972). Still, Alice Cooper's importance to rock history has much more to do with their outrageous stage antics than their music. These antics, which included cutting the heads off baby dolls, were invariably embellished by the press. The boa constrictor that Alice performed with became the biggest snake in the world; when a chicken was trampled by the audience, it became Alice biting the heads off live chickens and drinking their blood. The group's members performed in spandex, high-heeled boots, and makeup. Forget that they looked about as feminine as Frank Sinatra; these guys wore makeup at a time when "real men"—especially heterosexual ex-athletes from Phoenix—did not wear makeup. They represented a perverse challenge to the security of fixed gender roles.

Kiss, a group that played metal as heavy as anyone with a posture that was just as macho, made makeup their trademark. As with Alice Cooper, the fact that Kiss racked up eight gold or platinum albums in the 1970s and were still going strong at the end of the following decade is less important to rock history than the image they presented. Members of Kiss did not just apply cosmetics; they donned whole personas. Bassist Gene Simmons became a ghoulish monster; drummer Peter Criss, a cat; guitarists Paul Stanley and Ace Frehley, a clown and a spaceman. The group's gimmick of never being photographed without their makeup—a gimmick to which they held fast until 1983—added measurably to their mystique.

All That Glitters Does Not Sell Gold

The success of Alice Cooper and Kiss proved that the limits of decorum and personal appearance could be pushed and, during the early 1970s, there was a short-lived movement in rock that pushed them over the edge. Glam, or glitter rock, challenged traditional notions of masculinity and femininity as no other music had. As Iain Chambers has written, "'Glam' or 'glitter' rock's inroads into the public figure of male sexuality, in which the chameleon figure of David Bowie was seminal, seemed to crack an image brittle with repression."[79] In the United States, the focal point for the developing glitter scene was New York's Mercer Art Center, where groups like the Forty-Second Street Harlots, the Miamis, Teenage Lust, and the transvestite Wayne County held forth. It was here that the New York Dolls became local favorites. The New York Dolls played a brand of rock that would have placed the group somewhere near the Rolling Stones on the popular music continuum, but the music was tinged with the kind of informed cynicism that could be bred only in New York. Mostly burned-out, working-class dropouts, they performed in full drag—high heels, tights, miniskirts, and bright red lipstick. Why they were surprised when people related to them as a "bunch of transsexual junkies or something"[80] is baffling. Even with albums produced by Todd Rundgren (*New York Dolls*, 1973) and girl group veteran Shadow Morton (*Too Much Too Soon*, 1974), the Dolls never really got beyond cult status. Lead singer David Johansen did achieve some measure of pop success in the 1980s as Buster Poindexter.

The glitter scene in England was more developed, extending the music's reach to the rarefied atmosphere of art rock in one direction and teenybopper pop in another. When the tantalizing Marc Bolan shortened the name of his group from Tyrannosaurus Rex to T. Rex, he signaled a move to an electric hard rock style ("Bang a Gong [Get It On]," 1972) and brought the world of sequins and platform boots to teen fans. By the time of Bolan's death in 1977, many of his fans had switched their allegiance to the Sweet ("Little Willy," "Ballroom Blitz," "Fox on the Run," "Love Is Like Oxygen").

The glam rocker who invested the music with its most lasting artistry and memorable theatrics was David Bowie. As Iain Chambers stated:

> His "feminine" pose and extravagant attire speak an indeterminate language, an androgynous code. But the narcissistic atmosphere this image invokes is in turn richly ambiguous. . . . Such a public display in self-fascination gestures towards the possibility of loosening the sexed male subject from previous, more predictable, moorings.[81]

When Bowie's early hard-rock style failed to capture a substantial following, he created new personas for himself, mindful that such brazen artificiality represented a break with the rock authenticity he had once embraced.

Born David Jones, Bowie took his surname from the Bowie knife to avoid being confused with the Monkees' lead singer, Davy Jones. When Bowie's early hard-rock style failed to capture a substantial following, he created new personas for himself, mindful that such brazen artificiality represented a break with the rock authenticity he had once embraced. Drawing on influences as diverse as mime, the Beat poets, Dylan, Oscar Wilde, and Andy Warhol, Bowie pointed the way to the future.

"Changes"

Artist: David Bowie
Music/Lyrics by David Bowie
Label: RCA (1971), from the
LP *Hunky Dory*

Considered by many to be the greatest of the glam-rock artists of the early 1970s, David Bowie's music actually reveals a wide range of influences, from r&b to art rock, from disco to punk. "Changes" demonstrates his considerable ability to integrate seemingly disparate stylistic elements, which is one of his great strengths as an artist. The song was not a chart-topper at the time of its release, which is ironic considering that it ultimately became one of his best-known songs.

The lyrics of "Changes" seem to celebrate Bowie's mercurial approach to both his public persona and his musical style. He is famous for having re-created himself a number of times: r&b saxophonist; ex-mod-art-rocker; androgynous Ziggy Stardust glam-rock queen; the Thin White Duke of his self-described Plastic Soul period (which postdated "Changes"). Bowie's lyrics are sophisticated, often personal (at least in reference to the character he's currently inhabiting), and sometimes narrative. In "Changes," he appears to be looking back at his own personal history, trying to come to grips with some thread of continuity running through the impermanence of our notions of self.

Musical Style Notes

Each section of "Changes" appropriately seems to morph from one musical style to another. The almost jazzy synthesizer introduction glides into a rhythm track with a New Orleans–style piano riff that recurs at various points in the song. The idiosyncratic, asymmetrical phrasing of the verse occurs over jazz-influenced chord changes, flowing seamlessly into a classic 1960s Kinks-style chorus (compare "Waterloo Sunset"), with its steady 1-2-3-4-1-2-3-4 beat and harmonized vocals, plus a call-and-response effect between the line "Turn and face the strange . . . " and the word "Changes." The catchy "Ch-ch-ch-ch" that begins the word "Changes" recalls the Who's "My Ge-ge-ge-generation"; in both songs, the stuttering may be a subtle reference to "prellies," the mods' drug of choice, which often caused a kind of stuttering side effect. After a second jazz-influenced verse and "Ch-ch-ch-ch-Changes" chorus, the Kinks' influence returns in the bridge, which is followed by another chorus. The song ends with a mellow, jazz-style sax solo over piano and bass. (Bowie began his musical career as a sax player.)

The other performers on "Changes" are guitarist Mick Ronson, bassist Trevor Bolder, drummer Mick Woodmansey, and keyboardist Rick Wakeman.

Musical "Road Map"

TIMINGS	COMMENTS	LYRICS
0:00	Introduction: keyboard, synthesizer.	
0:09	Entrance of rhythm track with New Orleans–style piano riff.	
0:20	Verse 1	*I still don't know. . .*
	Vocals: jazz-influenced melody over synthesizer, piano, bass.	
0:53	Chorus	*Ch-ch-ch-ch-Changes. . .*
1:12	Ending passage of chorus: Note how the voice and the instruments are all articulating in unison.	*Time may change . . .*
1:20	Transitional passage; New Orleans–style piano riff heard again.	
1:29	Verse 2	*I watch . . .*
2:01	Chorus	*Ch-ch-ch-ch-Changes . . .*
2:20	Return of unison passage that ends chorus.	*Time may change . . .*
2:27	Bridge section	*Strange fascination,*
2:42	Chorus	*Ch-ch-ch-ch-Changes . . .*
3:00	Return of unison passage that ends chorus; repeats.	*Time may change . . .*
3:12–3:31	Jazz sax coda (ending section) over synthesizer, piano, bass.	

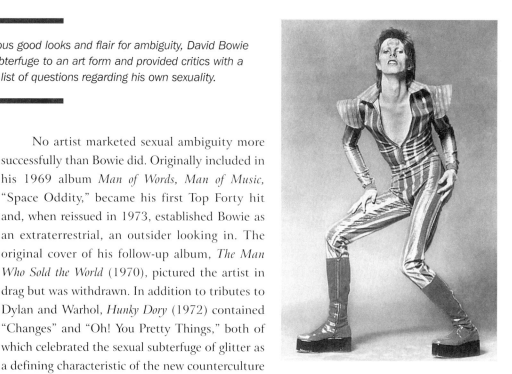

No artist marketed sexual ambiguity more successfully than Bowie did. Originally included in his 1969 album *Man of Words, Man of Music,* "Space Oddity," became his first Top Forty hit and, when reissued in 1973, established Bowie as an extraterrestrial, an outsider looking in. The original cover of his follow-up album, *The Man Who Sold the World* (1970), pictured the artist in drag but was withdrawn. In addition to tributes to Dylan and Warhol, *Hunky Dory* (1972) contained "Changes" and "Oh! You Pretty Things," both of which celebrated the sexual subterfuge of glitter as a defining characteristic of the new counterculture and provided great copy for questions about Bowie's own preferences. His chiseled good looks offset by orange hair and platform boots presented a most androgynous package. By 1972, Bowie was more than ready to inhabit his alien alter ego, Ziggy Stardust. The tour supporting the release of *The Rise and Fall of Ziggy Stardust and the Spiders from Mars* was a lavish glam rock extravaganza. During this period, Bowie announced his bisexuality. He continued projecting sexual ambiguity through other personae on *Aladdin Sane* (1973) and *Diamond Dogs* (1974).

Credit for Bowie's marketing triumph was due, at least in part, to his manager, Tony De Fries, who also managed Lou Reed, Iggy Pop and the Stooges, and Mott the Hoople. This network placed Bowie in a line that led directly to punk and drew those other artists into the orbit of glam. *Aladdin Sane* included "Jean Genie," a tribute that linked Iggy Pop with Jean Genet. In 1972, Bowie produced Iggy Pop's *Raw Power* as well as Lou Reed's *Transformer,* which included Reed's only hit single, "Walk on the Wild Side," a darkly focused paean to sexual adventurism. That same year, Bowie produced Mott the Hoople's *All the Young Dudes,* which gave the group a new lease on life. The association with Bowie and the juxtaposition of the album's title cut with songs like "One of the Boys" and Lou Reed's "Sweet Jane" (about a New York transvestite) located the straight (in all senses) rock group in the middle of the trendy gayness of glam.

If Bowie drew U.S. artists from the world of Warhol into the orbit of glam, other British acts used pop art principles to develop the style further. Bryan Ferry of Roxy Music used "throwaway clichés and amusing phrases that you found in magazines" in his early lyrics.[82] The group's first single, "Virginia Plain" (1972), took its title from a brand of cigarettes. The cover of *For Your Pleasure* (1973) featured seductive, black satin–like surfaces. Roxy Music's early sound resulted from the tension (musical and otherwise) between Ferry and Brian Eno, who joined the group in 1971 as a "technical expert," with no musical training. Eno's input moved the music in a direction that held sound and style to a higher value than musicianship per se. After leaving Roxy Music, Eno joined Bowie on a retreat to Berlin, where the two collaborated on three albums of avant-garde synth-pop.

Between his Ziggy Stardust period and his retreat to Berlin, Bowie went through a number of changes. In embracing the artificial, he had led the way from hippie idealism toward the eruption of punk. In 1975, he took another unexpected turn, swapping "the sci-fi future" of his glam period "for the uniform of white soul boy."[83] After *Diamond Dogs,* he moved to Sigma Sound Studios in Philadelphia, the spiritual center of soft soul. There he recorded *Young Americans,* an album that Peter York would later describe as "avant-garde disco."[84] The title cut became a hit, and "Fame" provided Bowie with his first number one U.S. single. Lou Reed had anticipated the move in *Sally Can't Dance* in 1974, but his outing was sandwiched between other experiments in heavy metal and white noise and no one noticed. It was Bowie who became the first white performer of note to straddle both punk and disco.

By the early 1970s, the established music industry, with its expanded infrastructure, had consolidated its hold over the rock and soul styles that grew out of the 1960s. Corresponding with the disintegration of the social movements that had defined the era, the music fragmented into a number of substyles. While the mellow sounds of singer/songwriters and Philadelphia soft soul tended to dominate the pop mainstream, there was another trajectory that led from hard rock to heavy metal to glam. In the fragmentation of popular music that ensued, audiences that might have overlapped in an earlier time were treated as discrete entities. This trend reached its zenith in the late 1970s in the emergence of punk and disco, whose audiences were viewed as mutually exclusive. Punk and disco were thus positioned as the two poles of pop that would define the extremes of a decade in which rock began to lose its status as outsider art.

LEARN MORE

Chapter Questions on MyMusicKit

Punk and Disco: The Poles of Pop

When the U.S. music business passed the $2 billion mark in the early 1970s, many assumed that sales would continue to climb indefinitely. When the industry doubled in size between 1973 and 1978, surpassing $4 billion in annual sales in 1978, the assumption appeared to be correct. An era of mergers had consolidated the industry into a rationalized music machine. Industry marketing suggested that, with a generous expenditure of promotional dollars, sufficient radio exposure, and a tour supporting a new release, any proven artist could almost guarantee millions of dollars in return.

As the country's leadership shifted from the lackluster and conservative Gerald Ford to the pleasant but largely ineffectual Jimmy Carter, the rock 'n' roll rebellion that had begun in the 1950s seemed, to many, on the verge of being tamed. Popular music was becoming centrist, corporate, safe.

As the country's leadership shifted from the lackluster and conservative Gerald Ford to the pleasant but largely ineffectual Jimmy Carter, the rock 'n' roll rebellion that had begun in the 1950s seemed, to many, on the verge of being tamed. Popular music was becoming centrist, corporate, safe.

If popular music could be drawn as a bell curve, the center section would house a number of middle-of-the-road artists who borrowed soft rock styles for pop-sounding lounge acts. Beginning with "(They Long to Be) Close to You" in 1970, the Carpenters, for example, parlayed a combination of rock covers and originals into twenty Top Forty hits in just over a decade. Barry Manilow, formerly the piano accompanist in the gay bathhouse where Bette Midler got her start, produced twenty-five Top Forty singles and became one of the industry's biggest stars. At the height of his career, three of his albums in a row—*This One's for You* (1976), *Barry Manilow Live* (1977), *Even Now* (1978)—sold over 3 million copies each. Neil Diamond topped both of them. Between 1970 and 1986, he scored thirty-six Top Forty singles and twenty gold and platinum albums. It is a telling commentary on the state of popular music in the 1970s that the most popular singles for the years 1974, 1975, and 1976, respectively, were "The Way We Were" by Barbra Streisand, "Love Will Keep Us Together" by the Captain and Tennille, and "Silly Little Love Songs" by Paul McCartney and Wings.

The pop rockers of the time were only slightly more adventurous. The album that dominated the charts in 1976 was Peter Frampton's *Frampton Comes Alive!* As a member of Humble Pie, Frampton had flirted with heavy metal; as a solo artist, he became a teen idol, more interested in melodic sweetness than volume. His first Top Thirty album, *Frampton* (1975), showcased the songs that would become his major hits ("Show Me the Way," "Baby, I Love Your Way," "Do You Feel Like We Do") as melodic rockers with an acoustic feel. *Frampton Comes Alive!,* which charted for nearly two years and sold over 10 million copies, made a nod toward his origins by including the same songs at hard rock volume.

Fleetwood Mac was a more mature version of these same rock tendencies. With their roots in John Mayall's Bluesbreakers, Fleetwood Mac really gelled when Britons Mick Fleetwood and John and Christine McVie added the acoustic/electric guitar stylings and sweet harmonies of Americans Lindsay Buckingham and Stevie Nicks to the group. Their self-titled 1975 album hit number one, but it was *Rumours* (1977) that earned them a mythic place in rock lore. *Rumours* was a straight-ahead, upbeat pop rock album that hit number one and generated four hit singles, including the number one "Dreams." The album sold 10 million copies in the United States and 25 million worldwide. When the group's follow-up album, *Tusk,* sold 4 million copies, it was pretty ho-hum.

In the mid-1970s, the music industry was basking in sales figures like the ones outlined here. In 1976, the Eagles' *Hotel California* sold 11 million copies. Also released that year, Stevie Wonder's *Songs in the Key of Life*, Linda Ronstadt's *Hasten Down the Wind*, Boz Scaggs's *Silk Degrees*, and Boston's *Boston* each sold more than 3 million copies. The platinum releases that year by Bob Dylan, Chicago, the Doobie Brothers, the Rolling Stones, Kansas, Ted Nugent, Rush, Foghat, Rod Stewart, and Elton John seemed almost routine.

As a gay man, Elton John added a bit of spice to the mainstream. With his Presleyesque glitter tendencies and wild array of custom-made eyeglasses, John was like the Liberace of rock, inserting a bit of glam's flair and showmanship during one of rock's most colorless periods. Well before *Blue Moves*, his first platinum album, he was a bona fide rock star with seven number one albums, five of them in a row. With his long-time collaborator, Bernie Taupin, he was also a prolific writer who captured the spirit of vintage rock 'n' roll with a sense of humor. Early standout hits like "Rocket Man," "Crocodile Rock," "Goodbye Yellow Brick Road," and "Bennie and the Jets" celebrated the entertainment value of a well-crafted song without succumbing to the self-importance of art rock. Throughout the late 1970s, John produced hit singles and platinum albums, always remaining a cut above the formula mentality of the time.

A few other artists also offered something in the way of rock artistry during this period. Billy Joel, a piano man like Elton John, was an intensely personal songwriter who was able to muster a bit of John's flamboyance in concert. Like Bruce Springsteen, Joel added a rock edge to the craft of the singer/songwriter but projected a more conventional image. On *The Stranger* (1977) and *52nd Street* (1978), which rose to numbers two and one, respectively, he explored cultural themes and created portraits of everyday life with drive and sophistication, laying the groundwork for a career that would carry him past the next decade. Borrowing from jazz, r&b, and rock, Steely Dan introduced a rare level of instrumental sophistication. Named after the dildo in William Burroughs's *Naked Lunch,* Steely Dan was essentially a studio band founded by quirky writer/instrumentalists Walter Becker and Donald Fagan, who assembled different side musicians for various album projects. Although the group rarely toured, their fluid rhythms, cryptic lyrics, and exacting production generated sales. *Pretzel Logic* (1974), *Aja* (1977), and *Gaucho* (1980) all went Top Ten.

Aside from the creative energy of a few such artists, the center of rock had begun to take itself and its audience for granted. From the mid-1970s to well into the 1980s, groups like Bob Seger and the Silver Bullet Band, Foghat, Styx, and Supertramp, followed by Foreigner, Journey, Air Supply, and REO Speedwagon, provided competent but not terribly inspired music. It appeared that the mainstream music industry had become such a well-oiled machine that, with little innovation or passion, any second-rate rock group could be assured of radio play, full stadiums, and platinum record sales. However, other styles of music still in their formative stages were positioned at the periphery of this cultural continuum; initially, few suitable venues existed for them and they were well beyond the pale of radio play. At one extreme stood punk; at the other, disco. In different ways and for different reasons, they would shake rock out of its complacency, at least for a time.

It appeared that the mainstream music industry had become such a well-oiled machine that, with little innovation or passion, any second-rate rock group could be assured of radio play, full stadiums, and platinum record sales.

Punk Versus Disco

Obvious distinctions separate disco and punk. Disco was smooth, sleek, and sensual; punk was dense, discordant, and defiant. Disco depended on technological sophistication and studio production; punk's three chords could be hammered out by any garage band. Disco dancers aspired to the controlled energy of the gymnast or the precision of group choreography; punks in the "mosh pit" approximated the antics of a tag-team wrestling match. "[P]ogo dancing—jumping up and down and flailing one's arms," observed Charles M. Young, "is as far as one can get from the Hustle."[1] Disco proudly took its place among other black dance music styles. *Rolling Stone*'s Mikal Gilmore suggested that those "rock purists" who dismissed it as "a frivolous form of expression might do well to remember that rock & roll and rhythm & blues were dance styles, too, before they became art forms."[2] Punk's aim was to deconstruct rock 'n' roll, bleeding it of its black rhythmic influences until only noise and texture remained. Robert Christgau noted that punk "differentiates itself from its (fundamentally black and rural) sources by taking on the crude, ugly, perhaps brutal facts of the (white and urban) prevailing culture, rather than hiding behind its bland facade."[3] These differences were mirrored in fashion statements that pitted polyester leisure suits against black leather bondage gear and ripped T-shirts held together by safety pins.

Such blatant differences between disco and punk tended to obscure their similarities. Both were initially shunned by radio (albeit for different reasons) and forced to develop their own countercultural networks. Both were condemned as contributing to the destruction of Western civilization—punk with its nihilism, disco with its decadence. Both encouraged active—indeed, fanatical—participation among their audiences. Finally, both arose in reaction to the complacency of the music that preceded them. Compare, for example, Andrew Kopkind on disco with Simon Frith on punk. "Disco in the '70s is in revolt against rock in the '60s," Kopkind explained. "Disco is 'unreal,' artificial, and exaggerated. It affirms the fantasies, gossip, frivolity, and fun of an evasive era."[4] Frith, describing the impetus for punk, wrote that "the reason why teenage music must be *remade* is because all the original rock 'n' rollers have become boring old farts, imprisoned by the routines of show biz. . . ."[5] The motivation and effect of both genres were the same—to intensify the feeling of the moment in an otherwise uncertain world.

Yet most critics decried disco as escapist and embraced punk as politically progressive. According to Frith, "The return to rock 'n 'roll roots is, in itself, a radical rejection of record company habits and punk's musical simplicity is a political statement. The ideology of the garage band is an attack on the star system."[6] Although disco spawned its own multibillion-dollar subindustry and punk barely registered a blip in sales, disco made no overt anti-establishment statement, while punk's political possibilities, real or imagined, captured the attention of rock critics who had cut their teeth on the political movements of the 1960s. As a result there has been considerable distortion in the way in which the histories of punk and disco have been recounted. As Andrew Kopkind complained in 1979, "John Rockwell was still writing Hegelian analyses of the Sex Pistols in the Sunday *Times* when two-thirds of the city was listening to Donna Summer and couldn't tell Mr. Rotten from Mr. Respighi."[7]

Although disco was seldom intentionally political, it may well have had a larger political impact than punk. The conflict between punk's progressive urges and its flirtation with Nazi imagery often confounded its potential to pull people together. Disco brought people together across lines of race, class, and sexual preference, especially in the United States. In such a context, antidisco slogans like "Disco sucks" can be seen more as racial (and sexual) epithets than as statements of musical preference, and the systematic avoidance of disco by the rock critical establishment can be construed as racist. As Mikal Gilmore suggested in 1977:

> **A**ntidisco slogans like "Disco sucks" can be seen more as racial (and sexual) epithets than as statements of musical preference, and the systematic avoidance of disco by the rock critical establishment can be construed as racist.

> [W]henever a phenomenon is given blanket dismissal, you can be sure something deeper is at work. And what's going on here is that rock fans, like the proverbial cake, have been left out in the rain. . . . [C]oincident with Saturday Night Fever, disco achieved anthem-like status with urban, working-class youth. . . . [R]ock pride was wounded. Somehow, an entire grassroots movement had passed us by: No wonder Clash fans cry, "Disco sucks!"[8]

By the time the decade ended, disco had swamped the music business and punk had imploded. While disco would collapse shortly thereafter, punk would be born again as new wave, incorporating such a wide range of influences that it even included disco.

Punk: Rock as (White) Noise

The tendency to focus on punk's political impact has corresponded with the tendency to emphasize its British origins. This is because punk's arrival in Britain coincided with right-wing advances and decaying social conditions, which gave the music a more critical political edge.

In the United States, where the Carter presidency offered a brief respite from the preceding eight years of conservative government, punk was less disruptive and more easily incorporated into the star-making machinery of the music industry.

In putting punk's most political foot forward, many observers look first to the Sex Pistols, a British group that caused a political furor in their country even before releasing their first single in 1976. While political impact is one valid measure of the importance of a cultural form, it is not the best way to trace its origins. The emergence of U.S. punk, in fact, predates its British eruption by nearly two years. While the Sex Pistols may have set the standard in England, their debut album, *Never Mind the Bullocks,* never registered on the Top Forty album or singles charts in the United States. Indeed, it was rare in the United States for any punk group to transcend cult status, much less to have a hit record. This fact underscores one of the most salient features of the punk movement: Its myth was always more powerful than its reality.

Central to the myth of the Sex Pistols was Malcolm McLaren, the group's manager. McLaren fancied himself a Machiavellian manipulator with a master plan to use the power of the music industry against itself in the service of radical social change. In fact, he was never a committed activist. He was fascinated, however, by the 1968 student revolts in Paris and influenced by the tactics of the French situationists, who created media-savvy situations as a way of transforming everyday life. He and his partner, Vivienne Westwood, owned a clothing store, catering first to impeccably attired teddy boys and then leather-clad rockers, as each became fashionable. Despite McLaren's claim to have created the Sex Pistols, the group's guitarist, Steve Jones, and its drummer, Paul Cook, had already started a group called the Strand (named after the Roxy Music song) before they met McLaren. Jones and Cook afterward sought out McLaren to be their manager (bassist Glen Matlock joined later). Complicating the picture was the addition of lead singer John Lydon (Johnny Rotten), who would vie with McLaren for control of the group until the end. Lydon couldn't sing and had no sense of rhythm, but according to *Rolling Stone*'s Charles M. Young, he had three qualities to recommend him: "1) his face had the pallor of death; 2) he went around spitting on poseurs he passed on the street; and 3) he

At that point, McLaren saw the Sex Pistols more as a vehicle for selling T-shirts and trousers than as point men in an anarchist revolt.

was the first to understand the democratic implications of punk."[9] At the time Lydon joined the group, McLaren and Westwood had reopened their store as a shop called Sex—hence the group's name. At that point, McLaren saw the Sex Pistols more as a vehicle for selling T-shirts and trousers than as point men in an anarchist revolt.

McLaren claimed that, before the Sex Pistols, he had managed the New York Dolls. In fact, he met the Dolls in 1973, when they were already the toast of the underground, and became obsessed with the group, joining them on their European tour later that year. By the fall of 1974, the group was in trouble. The Mercer Art Center had physically collapsed, leaving the Dolls without their major venue; their second album had stalled at number 167; drummer Billy Murcia had died of a drug overdose; guitarist Johnny Thunders and drummer Jerry Nolan had serious heroin habits; and bassist Arthur Kane was struggling with incipient alcoholism. Finally, Marty Thau, the group's manager, dropped them. At this point McLaren entered the picture. As a friend, he did right by the group, finding hospitals and drug treatment programs. As a manager, a relationship that was never formalized, he simply orchestrated the Doll's last gasp. He dressed the group in red patent leather with hammer-and-sickle flags for a

Malcolm McLaren did more than anyone to promote the myth of punk and himself. As manager of the Sex Pistols, he transformed passing events into the stuff of legends.

backdrop and sent the press a manifesto rather than an invitation to their upcoming shows. "Out went Glam, in came Communism," said historian Jon Savage.[10] By most accounts, the band was tight, but with no substance to their posture, their newest attempt at outrage had no beneficial effect. "You get beat up for being a fag," observed photographer Bob Gruen, "but you get killed for being a Commie."[11] Metaphorically speaking, this is exactly what happened to the Dolls, as their three-year run at celebrity abruptly came to a halt.

Born in the U.S.A.

During the descent of the Dolls, New York trash rock had gotten considerably more stripped down. As 1973 turned into 1974, club owner Hilly Kristal was reopening his Bowery hangout for bikers and winos as a country music bar called Country Blue Grass and Blues (CBGB). Tom Verlaine and Richard Lloyd from the band Television convinced Kristal to book underground rock acts instead. Within months, CBGB had become the heart of the New York rock underground. Its only competition was Max's Kansas City. By the time McLaren returned to New York to preside over the Doll's demise, Hilly Kristal was hosting the scene that would yield Patti Smith, Blondie, the Ramones, and the Talking Heads.

The first wave of punk rockers on both sides of the ocean recognized the important legacy of the Velvet Underground and Iggy Pop and the Stooges from the 1960s. At the poles of the Velvet Underground's creative axis were Lou Reed and John Cale. The Brooklyn-born Reed appeared to be your average college student; he liked a range of music from doo wop and rhythm and blues to jazz. After college, he became an assembly-line songwriter at Pickwick Records. Cale had a degree in classical music; his tastes ran to the avant-garde sounds of Stockhausen, John Cage, and La Monte Young. The buzzsaw sound of Cale's modified electric viola became part of the early Velvet trademark sound and an inspiration to a generation of punks. Their sound was rounded out by guitarist Sterling Morrison and drummer Maureen Tucker.

The Velvet Underground's repertoire, instrumentation, and avant-garde excursions into feedback and white noise were in place before their fabled association with Andy Warhol began. Warhol gave the group a slot at the Factory (his umbrella for diverse multimedia projects), which was undoubtedly the best offer a band with material like "Heroin" and "Black

Angel's Death Song" could get in 1966. His only direct intervention was to install the striking Hungarian-born blonde singer Nico in the band as a more visually appealing focal point than the deadpan Reed. The group's debut album, *The Velvet Underground and Nico,* was released in 1967. During this period, the group joined Warhol's touring multimedia show, the Exploding Plastic Inevitable.

Iggy Pop (born James Osterberg) was an uncultivated working-class kid from Ypsilanti, Michigan, who had spent his high school years playing in bands. He was first exposed to the New York underground at a performance of the Exploding Plastic Inevitable in 1966, leading to his introduction to Warhol, affair with Nico, and subsequent induction into the art rock scene. In 1968, Pop founded the Psychedelic Stooges (later, the Stooges) with the "unremittingly inept" Asheton brothers (Ron on guitar, Scott on drums). By this time, he had developed a style that, according to MC5 manager John Sinclair, "had gone beyond performance—to the point where it was really some kind of psychodrama."[12] The Stooges' material was unstructured ramblings with such titles as "Asthma Attack," "Goodbye Bozos," and "Search and Destroy." Six months after the band formed, they were signed to Elektra. Iggy's choice of John Cale to produce their first album created a direct link between the Stooges and the Velvet Underground. Shortly thereafter, Iggy was engaging in onstage acts of self-mutilation (like cutting his chest with drumsticks) that would earn him the title Godfather of Punk.

By the end of the 1960s, the Velvet Underground had released two more albums—*White Light/White Heat,* which included their classic seventeen-minute tale of horror, "Sister Ray," and *The Velvet Underground*—and Elektra had issued the Stooges' self-titled debut album. So few venues would book either act, however, that it was almost impossible to promote their releases. By the early 1970s, the Stooges had disbanded and, of the original Velvet Underground, only Sterling Morrison remained. Two years later, David Bowie convinced the Stooges to reunite, but they could never keep it together for very long. By the time CBGB took off in 1974, the Stooges and the Velvet Underground had more value as historical referents than as current practitioners.

Punk's maxim was: Whatever is popular, do the opposite. If hippies wore bell-bottoms, punks would wear straight legs. If hippies ate health food, punks would embrace junk food. If 1960s rock was inspired by psychedelic drugs (marijuana, LSD), punk would embrace amphetamines (speed) on the way up and heroin coming down. Punk politics was, if anything, the politics of refusal: the refusal to conform; the refusal to act with decorum; and, in some cases, the refusal to learn how to play music. Aside from this fragile unity, the most distinctive thing about the early New York punk groups was just how different they were from each other. Consider, for example, Patti Smith's spoken-word rock poetry and mannish attire versus Blondie's breathy pop and lead-singer Deborah Harry's peroxide persona; the Ramones' bikers-on-speed sound and image versus the preppiness of the Talking Heads. The group that paved the way for these opposites was Television.

Television, the first noteworthy CBGB group, was a ramshackle outfit that helped pioneer the punk practice of learning on the gig. Although the group's guitarist Tom Verlaine cited the Rolling Stones, John Coltrane, and the free jazz of Albert Ayler among his influences, a mid-1970s review proclaimed that the group had "no musical or socially redeeming

Punk politics was, if anything, the politics of refusal: the refusal to conform; the refusal to act with decorum; and, in some cases, the refusal to learn how to play music.

characteristics, and they know it"[13]—which was likely taken as a compliment. Key to these endearing attributes was bass player and former poet Richard Hell. Anticipating punk's antiglam, antihippie fashion, Hell supplied Television's look—torn-up T-shirts and close-cropped hair. He also contributed the punk classic "Blank Generation"—an answer song of sorts to the Who's "My Generation." The song was taken as an early indicator of punk nihilism, but Hell insisted that its message was misunderstood: "To me, 'blank' is a line where you can fill in anything. It's positive."[14] By the time Television released its first independent single, "Little Johnny Jewel" (1975), tension between Verlaine and Hell had forced the latter out of the group. In 1977, a reconstituted Television recorded the album *Marquee Moon*, one of the more interesting artifacts of the era. That same year, Hell committed "Blank Generation" to an eponymous album with his new group, The Voidoids. By then, punk was being called new wave.

Patti Smith was the first artist associated with CBGB to become famous. Smith attended Pratt Institute, an art school in Brooklyn, in the late 1960s, where she met photographer Robert Mapplethorpe, her first mentor. She and Mapplethorpe took up residence at the Chelsea Hotel, then frequented by Warhol and William Burroughs, among others. Smith—who fell in love with playwright Sam Shepherd, with whom she co-authored *Cowboy Mouth* (1971)—was becoming known as a poet and a rock journalist, writing primarily for *Creem* and *Rolling Stone*. She had also begun performing her work, accompanied on electric guitar by Lenny Kaye, a well-known rock journalist. A later boyfriend (Allen Lanier, keyboardist for Blue Öyster Cult) and a sabbatical in Paris took her further in her journey toward the fusion of poetry and rock 'n' roll. Upon her return, she opened for the New York Dolls during the final days of the Mercer Art Center. After its collapse, she and Kaye began appearing regularly as a duo. However, it was not until they added pianist Richard Sohl that they began to approximate the amalgam of free verse and improvisatory rock with which Smith would become identified.

The trio recorded their first single, "Piss Factory" backed with "Hey Joe" (1974), with Tom Verlaine on lead guitar. "Piss Factory" was an autobiographical account of the horrors of factory work; the meaning of "Hey Joe" was transformed by an introductory poem about Patty Hearst's exploits with the Symbionese Liberation Army. The single's release coincided with Smith and Television sharing a memorable residency at Max's

Patti Smith recorded the first punk album of note. Her androgynous attire, bohemian lifestyle, and successful fusion of rock and poetry suggested the possibility of new directions for music and new roles for women.

Kansas City. In the spring of 1975, the same double bill confirmed CBGB as New York's premiere rock club and, around that time, the Patti Smith Group was signed to Arista. By the time *Horses* was released in 1976, the group had added Ivan Kral on bass and Jay Dee Daugherty on drums, with John Cale as producer. *Horses* was not only the first punk album of note, it was one of the few to enter the Top Fifty. Smith, whose trademark of a man's white shirt and tie suggested new roles for women, was well on the way to stardom when she fell off a ten-foot stage and broke her neck. *Easter* (1978), the album that marked her return, included the decidedly unpunk hit single "Because the Night," supplied by Bruce Springsteen.

In 1974, while Television and Patti Smith were in residence at Max's, the Ramones and Blondie made their debuts at CBGB. The Ramones were formed by middle-class kids from Forest Hills, Queens. Jeff Hyman (Joey), John Cummings (Johnny), Doug Colvin (Dee Dee), and Tom Erdelyi (Tommy) each adopted "Ramone" (Paul McCartney's first pseudonym) as his surnom de punk. Unlike other punk groups, the Ramones played only original material. "We couldn't figure out how to play anybody else's songs," explained Johnny.[15] Stylistically, they stripped rock 'n' roll naked with unadorned, rapid-fire guitar bursts, pneumatic drumming, and abrupt, minimalist lyrics rarely longer than eight lines. The Ramones filled in the

((• **HEAR MORE**
The Ramones on
My MusicKit

The Ramones played faster songs with shorter lyrics than anyone connected to the New York punk scene. Their rapid-fire delivery pointed the way for British punk.

"I Don't Wanna Be Learned, I Don't Wanna Be Tamed"

Artist: The Ramones
Music/Lyrics by The Ramones
Label: Rhino, 2001 rerelease of
The Ramones (1976)

Higher, faster, louder, briefer—it's the Ramones!

The Ramones were, at the same time, the simplest and, one might say, the most abstract of punk bands. Recognizing their own musical limitations, they set out to recover the brevity, simplicity, and hammer-headed directness of earlier "punks" like Jerry Lee and Elvis. Though some thought they came across as complete knuckleheads, their musical style and ethos make great sense as a sly-yet-ferocious assault on the bloated, late 1970s art rock. Where art rock was deemed pretentious, the Ramones were defiantly modest. Where art rock sought symphonic breadth and staged extravaganzas, the Ramones kept everything short (their sets at New York's famed CBGB's club rarely exceeded a half-hour). Where art rock was ruled by banks of pedals and stacks of electronic keyboards, the Ramones kept it to the guitars, the chords, and the (deafeningly loud) amps. The uncomplicated yet defiant lyrics are vaguely political, yet not nearly as direct an affront as those sung by groups like the Sex Pistols or as consciously intellectual as punk poets like Patti Smith. Not by accident, the Ramones also borrowed the straightforward forms, repetitive melodies, and pounding four-on-the-floor rhythms of surf music.

"I Don't Wanna Be Learned, I Don't Wanna Be Tamed" was originally recorded as a demo. It was included as a bonus track on Rhino's rerelease of the 1976 LP *The Ramones*.

Musical Style Notes

The structure of "I Don't Wanna Be Learned, I Don't Wanna Be Tamed" couldn't be more straightforward: three 12-bar sections, the second and third of which contain lyrics sung over the first 8 bars, followed by the first 4 bars played instrumentally. The abrupt ending sounds sudden because the harmonic resolution to this point has been coming at the end of the 12-bar form, and they never get there (but then, that's the whole point). The entire song lasts only one minute.

The sound characteristics—driving drum hits on every beat, loud and extremely distorted guitars, and unpolished vocals—are all typical of early punk rock, New York style. The ersatz British accents, on the other hand, were a Ramones' specialty.

Musical "Road Map"

TIMINGS	COMMENTS	LYRICS
0:00–0:01	Countdown	"One, two,—"
0:01–0:18	Introduction, instrumental, 12 bars	
0:18–0:34	Verse Same form as introduction. Lyrics last 8 bars, 4-bar instrumental transition into next "verse."	"And I don't wanna—"
0:34–0:51	Verse Exactly the same as 0:18–0:34	"And I don't wanna—"
0:51–1:00	Instrumental, consisting of the 8-bar verse, but with no lyrics sung— song ends abruptly where the sung verse would have ended.	

blank of Richard Hell's generation with a repertoire of refusal, including "I Don't Care," "I Don't Wanna Be Learned, I Don't Wanna Be Tamed," and "I Don't Wanna Go Down to the Basement." "We didn't write a positive song until 'Now I Wanna Sniff Some Glue,'" Dee Dee later quipped.[16] The band usually ran through a set with dizzying speed, with few songs longer than two minutes.

Critical praise—in the *SoHo Weekly, Rock Scene, Hit Parader,* and the *Village Voice*—was not long in coming. When London's *New Musical Express* did its first spread on the New York punk scene in 1975, the Ramones were the featured artists. Sire Records signed the group—the second punk act after Patti Smith to secure a record contract. Seymour Stein of Sire played a pivotal role in developing punk, eventually also signing the Talking Heads, the Dead Boys, Richard Hell and the Voidoids, and the Pretenders.

The Ramones' eponymous debut album (1976) delivered all the manic energy of the group's live performances. The album bombed in the United States but was the talk of London, at least in part because there was no similar domestic product. Their second album, *Leave Home* (1977), did even more poorly in the United States than their first, but it cracked the Top Fifty in Great Britain and yielded a hit single there, "Sheena Is a Punk Rocker." Although the Ramones pointed the way for British bands, it was not until Rocket to Russia (1978) that the group finally broke into the U.S. Top 100 LPs. By this time, British punk/new wave was in full swing, and London had overtaken New York as the cutting edge of the new trend.

Although the Ramones pointed the way for British bands, it was not until Rocket to Russia (1978) that the group finally broke into the U.S. Top 100 LPs. By this time, British punk/new wave was in full swing, and London had overtaken New York as the cutting edge of the new trend.

Blondie also found London to be the best launching pad for success in the United States. The group (named after the comic strip character) was formed by lead singer Deborah Harry and guitarist Chris Stein from the remains of their former group, the Stilettos. Blondie's success was slowed by some early personnel changes. Between their CBGB debut and their first LP, bassist Fred Smith left to join Television, Ivan Kral was stolen by Patti Smith, and drummer Billy O'Connor quit to go to law school. Thus, the five-piece lineup on their self-titled debut album (on the Private Stock label) included only Harry and Stein from the original group. The addition of Jimmy Destri on Farfisa organ gave the group a distinctive camp feel that harkened back to the pop sounds of the 1960s. Although the album did not generate a ripple in U.S. sales, it brought the group to the attention of Chrysalis, which purchased their contract for $500,000. Their second album, *Plastic Letters,* also flopped, though the cut "Denis" (a remake of Randy and the Rainbow's "Denise") went to number two on British charts. Blondie hired Mike Chapman, formerly of the sure-bet British bubblegum producer/songwriter team of Chinn and Chapman, to produce *Parallel Lines* (1978), which marked the group's breakthrough in the United States. It peaked at number six and included the disco-influenced number one single, "Heart of Glass."

Although the Talking Heads, like other first-generation groups, were formed in 1974, and although they achieved mass market success in the United States before either Blondie or the Ramones, they are sometimes considered apart from the first wave of CBGB groups. As of their 1975 debut, they already knew how to play; their sets had structure, even rigidity; and they embraced rhythm and blues as a strong element in their otherwise pop rock sound. Still, their

Combining breathy pop vocals with a Marilyn Monroe persona, Blondie's Deborah Harry added disco and rap influences to punk.

presentation was sufficiently minimalist and self-conscious to earn them a place on the art rock side of punk.

The Talking Heads had begun to take shape at the Rhode Island School of Design in 1973, when guitarist/vocalist David Byrne and drummer Chris Frantz formed the Artistics. The following year, they—along with Tina Weymouth, Frantz's girlfriend—headed for New York, where the CBGB scene reignited their desire to play music. With Weymouth on bass, they were an instant hit. Hilly Kristal loved them; the press loved them; other groups were jealous of them. Within two months of their debut, they were headlining with the Ramones; the following year, they signed with the Ramones' label, Sire. Before recording their first single, "Love Goes to Building on Fire" (1976), they added Jerry Harrison, a keyboardist from the proto-punk band the Modern Lovers. *Talking Heads '77,* the group's first album, made it into the Top 100. Although primarily a pop-sounding LP, singles like "Psycho Killer" showed an ironic punk edge. Their next three albums were produced by Brian Eno, who would see them through the punk era into the next decade. *More Songs About Buildings and Food* (1978) included a Top Thirty cover of Al Green's "Take Me to the River" that showcased the Talking Heads' affinity for African American music, a cornerstone of their sound in the 1980s.

By the time the Talking Heads played their first CBGB gig, it was apparent that New York was not the only punk mecca in the United States. When the New York well ran dry for the Velvet Underground in the late 1960s, a Boston club called the Boston Tea Party became their second home. In fact, Boston's Modern Lovers, led by Jonathan Richman, were the first band to embrace the Velvet Underground fully. Cleveland was also a burgeoning punk scene in the early 1970s. The Mirrors, the Electric Eels, and Rocket from the Tombs all began there. While the Mirrors and the Eels faded, the Rockets split into two groups that earned places in

Even though the Talking Heads fashioned a minimalist arty sound, they never lost their affinity for African American music. This combination of influences served them well in the 1980s.

punk history: Pere Ubu ("Thirty Seconds over Tokyo," "Life Stinks," "Final Solution") and the Dead Boys ("Sonic Reducer").

Devo (from *deevolution*) was formed in Akron, Ohio, by art students from Kent State University in 1972. With inverted flowerpot hats and jerky robotic movements defining their image, Devo was signed to Virgin in 1978, and Brian Eno was recruited to produce their first album, *Are We Not Men? We Are Devo!* One of Devo's first singles, "Jocko Homo," and their punk send-up of the Rolling Stones' "Satisfaction" were hits in Britain, but the group remained a cult item in the United States until the next decade.

"Anarchy in the U.K."

CBGB showcased over thirty new groups at its 1975 Festival of Unsigned Bands months before Britain's Sex Pistols played their first gig. But while punk developed earlier in the United States, the social conditions that engendered it were more profoundly disturbing in Britain. Unemployment had reached record highs, and the country was in its deepest recession since World War II. Although labor attempted to respond to these onslaughts, the fascist National Front was growing stronger and the conservative Margaret Thatcher had become prime minister. The optimism of the postwar years was giving way to cynicism, and the consensus of values that had regulated social and political life was coming unraveled.

> **C**BGB *showcased over thirty new groups at its 1975 Festival of Unsigned Bands months before Britain's Sex Pistols played their first gig. But while punk developed earlier in the United States, the social conditions that engendered it were more profoundly disturbing in Britain.*

In such a climate, even the name Sex Pistols, with its obvious connections to youth, violence, and sex, caused a stir. Thus, finding suitable venues was a problem from the moment they started performing in 1975. The pub rock scene was dominated by Dr. Feelgood, the Stranglers, and Eddie and the Hot Rods—groups who played loud, fast, aggressive rock but who never quite made it into the inner circle of punk. The Pistols' initial tour of Britain was staged mostly in college venues, and attendance seldom reached triple figures. Still, by the summer of 1976, they had built a small following and were ready for slightly larger events. Then, in Manchester, the Sex Pistols unleashed "Anarchy in the U.K."—the call to arms that would establish them as the vanguard group in a nationwide movement. Manchester led to an appearance on Granada TV's *So It Goes,* where they again performed "Anarchy in the U.K.," this time on national television.

This performance inspired Joe Strummer, a guitarist for a group called the 101ers, who had taken their name from the number of the torture room in George Orwell's *1984.* With the guidance of manager Bernie Rhodes, a colleague of McLaren's, Strummer teamed up with Mick Jones and Paul Simonon from another group (London SS) to form the Clash. The group took its name from the word used most often in tabloid headlines about class and race relations in Britain. If, as Jon Savage has suggested, "[p]unk's breakthrough was to unite people who saw pop in terms of social realism and those who viewed it as artistic expression," the Clash, more

((•)) **HEAR MORE**
Malcolm McLaren
on MyMusicKit

Johnnie Rotten's painful engagement with his music captures the aesthetic of the Sex Pistols. The "destroy" T-shirt with the swastika juxtaposed against the Union Jack speaks to their contradictory politics.

"Anarchy in the U.K."

Artist: The Sex Pistols
Music/Lyrics by Paul Cook, Steve Jones,
Glen Matlock, and Johnnie Rotten
Label: EMI (1976)

John Lydon/Rotten understood, better than anyone in rock 'n' roll since John Lennon, the way that one generation's scandal could be the next generation's opportunity. Just as Lennon had told a Command Performance audience to "rattle your jewelry" in lieu of applause, Rotten had put a safety pin through a Xerox of Queen Elizabeth's portrait. Both were purely symbolic acts—working-class anger masquerading as mere impudence—but both carried a powerful symbolic message. Neither of these "angry young men" was prepared to accept the previous generation's sense of propriety, and each built a career out of calculated (and brilliantly musical) outrage. Both Lennon and Lydon saw rock 'n' roll as a way out—and a chance for a few swipes at the ruling class along the way.

The players in this 1976 incarnation of the Sex Pistols were Johnnie Rotten (a.k.a. John Lydon), vocals; Steve Jones, guitar; Glen Matlock, bass; and Paul Cook, drums. "Anarchy in the U.K." was released as a single in 1976 and was also included on the LP *Never Mind the Bollocks, Here's the Sex Pistols.*

Musical Style Notes

The driving, drum-hit-on-every-beat and the high-volume guitar distortion of the Sex Pistols place them squarely in the sonic category of punk rock, but claims that the Sex Pistols were unable to play their instruments are highly exaggerated. The musical structure of "Anarchy" is not simplistic, but it contains a typical verse-chorus pop-song construction with two contrasting guitar solo sections. While it may rely on the three primary chords in a major key—what musicians call I, IV, and V—it's no less harmonically sophisticated than many blues songs or British invasion–style songs from the previous decade. The most frequent chord progression here (the one you hear while Johnny's singing "I am an antichrist") is a frantic, sped-up version of the same chord progression that repeats endlessly in Muddy Waters' "I'm a Man," although the distortion and the different rhythm may render it unrecognizable. The first guitar solo is played over a completely different set of chords (for musicians, the II and III chord in the key). The second guitar solo modulates (changes key) a whole step and is an almost complete replica, whether intentionally or not, of the guitar part from the Searchers' 1964 hit "Needles and Pins" (which, interestingly enough, was also covered by the Ramones in 1978). Rotten's lyric style may be confrontational and coarse, but his delivery is impeccable and "in sync" with the rhythm and the harmonic changes of the music, right down to the last snarl.

Musical "Road Map"

TIMINGS	COMMENTS	LYRICS
0:00–0:06	Instrumental introduction	
0:06–0:14	Instrumental introduction	[spoken] Right . . . now! . . .
0:14–0:28	Verse 1	*I am an antichrist . . .*
0:28–0:43	Chorus	*I . . . wanna be . . .*
0:43–1:00	Verse 2	*Anarchy for the U.K. . . .*
1:00–1:12	Chorus	*I . . . wanna be . . .*
1:12–1:31	Guitar solo 1	
1:31–1:45	Verse 3	*How many ways . . . ?*
1:45–2:00	Chorus	*I . . . wanna be*
2:00–2:14	Guitar solo 2 ("Needles and Pins" quote)	
2:14–2:29	Verse 4	*Is this the M.P.L.A. . . .*
2:29–2:43	(Chorus, with new words)	*just . . .*
2:43–3:11	Chorus (four times)	*I . . . wanna be . . .* *I . . . wanna be . . .*

than any other group, took social(ist) realism to its artistic and political limits.[17] At the time, Frith wrote that punk's message "comes most powerfully and most ambiguously from the Sex Pistols, but it comes most clearly from the Clash."[18] The group was the Sex Pistols' major competition and, in fact, outlasted them by years.

The Clash seemed more grounded in the real world than other punk groups and far more likely to take up the cry of the British working class. While the Sex Pistols explored nihilism with songs like "Pretty Vacant," "Seventeen," "Problems," and "Submission," the Clash were more socially engaged, with material such as "London's Burning"; "I'm So Bored with the U.S.A.," a searing commentary on popular culture; and "White Riot," stirred by clashes between young blacks and police at the Notting Hill Carnival. In the spirit of punk, the Clash's "1977" proclaimed an end to Elvis, the Beatles, and the Rolling Stones, but the group also took on the issues of racism ("Police and Thieves"), unemployment ("Career Opportunities"), and class ("What's My Name").

Perhaps oddly for radical punks, both the Sex Pistols and the Clash aspired to major label status. Meanwhile, Stiff Records, a British independent founded in 1976 by two pub rock entrepreneurs, Dave Robinson and Andrew Jakeman (a.k.a. Jake Riviera), provided an early home to other punk groups. Robinson had managed Brinsley Schwarz, a pub rock group, and Graham Parker, whose intense r&b sound (*Howlin' Wind,* 1976) straddled the fence between pub rock and punk. Brinsley vocalist Nick Lowe became Stiff's house producer and an artist in his own right. He eventually supervised all of Elvis Costello's early work, with Riviera doubling as Costello's manager. Stiff signed the Damned, an apolitical group whose members liked speed and noise. They were the first unmistakably punk group to land a record contract in Britain and the first to

The Clash had their sights set on nothing short of a socialist revolution through music. Not surprisingly, they were accompanied by heavy security whenever they arrived in the United States.

hit the Top Thirty with "New Rose," about an amphetamine rush. The Vibrators, another Stiff group that was equally lacking in moral authority, recorded the slightly off-color "We Vibrate."

In his effort to secure a major label contract for the Sex Pistols, McLaren organized the Punk Rock Festival, which was staged at London's 100 Club in September 1976. It featured, among others, the Sex Pistols, the Clash, the Buzzcocks, the Damned, the Vibrators, and Siouxsie and the Banshees, a group assembled at the last minute from Sex Pistols hangers-on. The group originally included Sid Vicious, who later joined the Pistols, and Marco Pirroni, who joined Adam Ant. Vocalist Siouxsie Sioux was the group's focal point. They saw no point in trying to learn any songs at such a late date, so they debuted without a repertoire. Their set was a mess, but a memorable one.

The Punk Rock Festival was plagued by technical difficulties, professional rivalries, political differences, violence, and several arrests. In short, it was a roaring success, especially for the Sex Pistols. In October, the group signed with EMI; in November, "Anarchy in the U.K." was released as a single. A tour with the Clash, the Damned, and Johnny Thunders' Heartbreakers was

> **T**he Punk Rock Festival was plagued by technical difficulties, professional rivalries, political differences, violence, and several arrests. In short, it was a roaring success.

planned to promote the record. In December, however, the Sex Pistols were interviewed on Thames TV's *Today* show by Bill Grundy, who goaded Steve Jones into calling him a "dirty fucker" and a "fucking rotter" on the air. In the ensuing scandal, deejays across Great Britain (with the notable exception of John Peel) refused to play the song. Of the twenty-one dates booked for the Anarchy tour, the Sex Pistols were banned from all but three. Even so, with sales of more than 50,000, "Anarchy in the U.K." entered the Top Twenty before Christmas.

In January 1977, amid fallout from the Grundy appearance, EMI dropped the Sex Pistols. A&M picked them up in March for £50,000 and dropped them a week later for an additional £25,000 buyout. Not bad for a group with only one single. In Manchester, the Buzzcocks issued an EP called "Spiral Scratch" on their own New Hormones label; they sold 15,000 copies. Stiff signed a distribution deal with Island Records just in time to push the Damned's first album, *Damned Damned Damned*, into the U.K. Top Forty. United Artists had already signed the Stranglers, and Polydor had picked up the Jam. The biggest news, however, was that, in March 1977, the Clash had signed with CBS for a £100,000 advance. The Grundy interview had put punk over the top and the music industry was finally taking notice.

The Clash's self-titled debut album (1977) clearly stamped punk with the imprint of social realism and was, in the words of Jon Savage, "the first major Punk statement."[19] Unfortunately, it was not released in the United States. It wasn't until the beginning of the 1980s that the Clash did well in the U.S. market. *London Calling* (1980) and *Sandinista!* (1981) charted Top Thirty and *Combat Rock* (1982) went Top Ten, yielding the group's only U.S. Top Ten single, "Rock the Casbah."

In the punk tradition, Siouxsie Sioux performed with the Banshees before the band had a repertoire. A testament to their staying power, Siouxsie and the Banshees went on to play the first Lollapalooza Festival in 1991.

While CBS was promoting the Clash, McLaren was scrambling for a new contract for the Sex Pistols, eventually going with Virgin. By this time, Sid Vicious had replaced Glen Matlock on bass. In 1977, Queen Elizabeth II's silver jubilee provided the perfect opportunity for the Sex Pistols to reassert their primacy. They planned to release "God Save the Queen" (recorded immediately after the Virgin signing), which baldly accused the monarchy of being a "fascist regime." But the single proved difficult to get out: The pressing plant held up production; platemakers refused to make the liner notes plates; radio and TV stations rejected ads; retail outlets refused to place orders; and the single was banned from the airwaves. Needless to say, all of this provided incredible publicity. The record was finally released in late May (still a few weeks before the planned celebrations) and was selected as the Single of the Week by all four British music weeklies. By the end of Jubilee Week, it had sold 200,000 copies. But for some official tampering—resulting in a blacked-out song title and group name being listed in the number one slot for the week of 18 June 1977—it would have topped the British charts. The song thrust the Sex Pistols' rhetoric up against real-world politics. Verbal attacks became physical, and the group, which had not yet recorded an album, could only tour in secret. The Sex Pistols had definitely made rock 'n' roll "dangerous" again, and the movement they helped to set in motion had barely hit its stride.

Flirtation with Fascism: The Underbelly of Punk

In their rush to shock, punks often seized on any image that could be counted on to produce a strong reaction. No image filled that bill as well as the swastika. If 1960s rock had been marked by its associations with the political left, punk gravitated equally toward symbols at the other end of the political spectrum. For most punks, though not all, flaunting the twisted cross was an exercise in confrontational art rather than a political endorsement of fascism. However, that fine distinction, which is rife in punk's recapitulations of itself, overlooked the importance of historical meaning.

For most punks, flaunting the twisted cross was an exercise in confrontational art rather than a political endorsement of fascism. However, that fine distinction, which is rife in punk's recapitulations of itself, overlooked the importance of historical meaning.

Ron Asheton of the Stooges pioneered the use of Nazi swastikas, iron crosses, and jackboots, soon mirrored by other groups. (He went on to form a band in Los Angeles called New Order, a reference to Hitler's plans for the future.) One of the high points of the Cleveland scene in 1974 was Special Extermination Night, which featured Rocket from the Tombs, the Mirrors, and the Eels. Swastikas adorned the poster advertising the event. The Eels, whose members wore ripped T-shirts with white-power logos and swastikas, were easily the most offensive group. The lyrics to their "Spin Age Blasters" were taken from the slogan "Pull the Triggers on the Niggers" displayed at the American Nazi Party headquarters in Cleveland. Pere Ubu released a 1976 single called "Final Solution" (the name of Hitler's plan to exterminate the Jews). The Dead Boys showed up at CBGB's 1976 Festival of Unsigned Bands wearing Nazi uniforms.

The Dictators, from upstate New York, played a brand of rapid-fire rock that occupied a cultural space between the New York Dolls and the Ramones. In 1977, they released their first album on Asylum, entitled *Manifest Destiny*—a reference to the belief that white settlers were predestined to dominate the land that is now the United States. Early Ramones song titles, such as "Blitzkrieg Bop" and "Today Your Love, Tomorrow the World," contained explicit references to Nazism.

These references were widespread in the punk world. Per their situationist leanings, Malcolm McLaren and Vivienne Westwood had already noted that swastikas could be harnessed to effectively disrupt the flow of everyday life. When the New York Dolls had toured Europe in 1973, with McLaren in tow, they had added the occasional swastika to their trash drag queen attire. In Germany, a blathering Johnny Thunders had told the press that the Dolls wanted to play a benefit at Bergen-Belsen, the site of a former concentration camp, "for all the Nazis who gotta hang out in trees in fuckin' South America."[20] Sid Vicious wore T-shirts with swastikas; Siouxsie Sioux wore a swastika armband. The Clash had objected strenuously to the Banshees' use of the swastika at the 100 Club festival, and Adam Ant was criticized early on for Nazi references in his lyrics, but these tendencies continued. In 1977, the Sex Pistols started performing a song called "Belsen Was a Gas," written earlier by Sid Vicious. The next generation of British groups included Joy Division, whose name was taken from concentration camp brothels; they evolved into a U.K. group called New Order.

The swastika was only one of many disruptive symbols used by punks. For instance, when the Sex Pistols first performed the song that would become "Anarchy in the U.K.," McLaren and Westwood had designed the "Anarchy" shirt to complement it. The outfit was an ideological mishmash, combining small portraits of Karl Marx and flying swastikas with slogans like "Only Anarchists Are Pretty," and set off by an armband reading "Chaos." "The intention was the group should not be politically explicit, but instead should be an explosion of contradictory, highly charged signs."[21] In this politics of confusion, punk irony became problematical.

As Robert Christgau has pointed out, in a statement widely applicable beyond the Ramones:

> *Unless you think the Ramones identify with Charlie Manson, the Texas chain-saw killer, CIA men, SLAers, geeks, glue-sniffers, and electroshock patients—an absurd misreading as far as I'm concerned—then you must conclude that their intention is satiric, and the same applies when they turn to fascist characters.*[22]

"The problem," Christgau noted, "is that irony is wasted on pinheads."[23] Lester Bangs made a cogent argument against the use of the outrageous: "Another reason for getting rid of all those little barbs is that no matter how you intend them, you can't say them without risking misinterpretation by some other bigoted asshole; your irony just might be his cup of hate."[24] Bangs recounted the story of Miriam Linna (of the Cramps), quoted in the punk fanzine *New Order*: "I love the Ramones [because] this is the celebration of everything American—everything teenaged and wonderful and white."[25] Pictured in leather and shades, she was brandishing a pistol in front of the Florida headquarters of the United White People's Party. Nico, too, was unmistakably clear when, after performing "Deutschland Uber Alles" at CBGB, she told an interviewer that she "didn't like negroes." In such a context, the intended irony of Patti Smith's "Rock & Roll Nigger" might well have been lost on many punk fans.

The political climate of the 1970s further confused any punk attempts at irony. In the United States, the curious concept of reverse discrimination had arisen. The logic of the Civil

Rights Act of 1964 was turned on its head when the Supreme Court ruled in 1978 that Alan Bakke's civil rights as a white person had been violated by the University of California's affirmative action policy. The landmark decision signaled the growing strength of a concerted attack on affirmative action and a tremendous resurgence of white supremacist organizations. In this climate, any punk attempts to deconstruct racially loaded terms and symbols could only have unintended consequences. Not even the Clash were above misinterpretation. "White Riot" had been intended as a statement that the white working class should stand up for its rights as blacks had done at Notting Hill. In the atmosphere of racially charged conservatism, however, it was sometimes taken as a racist rallying call for whites to oppose black insurrection. Taken literally, the lyrics to "God Save the Queen" could be (mis)heard as a call to save the "fascist regime." This is exactly what happened at an early Clash/Sex Pistols concert when the Student Union at Lanchester Polytechnic in Coventry refused to pay the groups, calling them "these fascists."

With the rise of the National Front in Britain, it did not take much to fan the flames of racial hatred. But the most inflammatory statements by musicians came not from the punks but from the ranks of the British rock aristocracy.

With the rise of the National Front in Britain, it did not take much to fan the flames of racial hatred. But the most inflammatory statements by musicians came not from the punks but from the ranks of the British rock aristocracy. In 1976, David Bowie was quoted as saying, "I think I might have been a bloody good Hitler."[26] He then staged his return from Berlin to London with what appeared to be a Nazi salute. While Bowie later apologized, Eric Clapton did not. Clapton interrupted a concert in Birmingham, England, in August 1976 with a drunken speech urging support for Enoch Powell, then the most rabid antiblack member of Parliament. In response, a letter of protest signed "Rock Against Racism" was fired off to all the popular music weeklies, precipitating well over 100 enthusiastic replies in the first week alone.

Rock Against Racism: Progressive Punk

Rock Against Racism (RAR) was a broadly based mass movement in the United Kingdom, and its sole purpose was opposition to the National Front. According to RAR historian David Widgery, the organization had a multilevel strategy.

> On one level Rock Against Racism was an orthodox anti-racist campaign simply using pop music to kick political slogans into the vernacular. But on another level, it was a jail break. We aimed to rescue the energy of Russian revolutionary art, surrealism and rock and roll from the galleries, the advertising agencies and the record companies and use them again to change reality, as had always been intended. And have a party in the process.[27]

RAR's energy and creativity came from graphic and fashion designers, photographers, actors, and punk and reggae musicians. Political direction was supplied primarily by the Socialist Workers Party, which later formed the Anti-Nazi League, which then merged with RAR.

In late 1976, around the time "Anarchy in the U.K." came out, RAR began staging concerts. By the following year, it was attracting hundreds of thousands of fans to major events. RAR's antiracist strategy of showcasing multicultural Britain in a positive light required packaging black and white acts together. In doing so, a tilt toward reggae predominated. As Jon Savage has explained, "Any fascist ambiguity in Punk was fueled by the way that the style had bled Rock dry of all black influences; one way to overcome any taint of white supremacy was to affirm visible links with Reggae."[28] Thus, major RAR events paired reggae groups with punk bands: Aswad with the Adverts, the Cimarrons with Generation X, Steel Pulse with the Clash. Reggae was prevalent, of course, in Britain's West Indian enclaves; but it had also been popular since the late 1960s with disaffected British white youths attracted to its hypnotic rhythms and unflinching "rude boy" stance. Its trajectory among white youth, however, had not always been progressive.

In the late 1960s, skinheads adopted reggae as the marshall music to accompany racist attacks. By the mid-1970s, they had become adherents of punk. Some were racist Nazi sympathizers; others liked the music and opposed its fascist leanings. Thus, part of RAR's mission was to claim punk—and reggae—for the left, driving a wedge between racist skinheads and those with more progressive tendencies. Sham 69 was a sizzling punk band that had performed for RAR, but it had a sizable skinhead following who chanted "Sieg Heil" at their concerts and plastered Nazi emblems everywhere. Rock Against Racism was able to turn the tables by pairing Sham with a Southall reggae outfit called Misty, thus forcing skinheads to attend a biracial benefit to see their favorite group. This punk/reggae convergence projected a unique symbolic power that contributed significantly to the powerful feeling of racial unity at many RAR events. At one show in 1977, one member of Generation X and one of the Cimarrons joined hands aloft while the entire audience chanted "Black and white. Black and white." Billy Idol remembered the experience as "one of the greatest nights of my life."[29] The Cimarrons responded by recording a single called "Rock Against Racism."

Bob Marley's influence was key to the widespread appeal of reggae. Following in his wake, Jamaican reggae artists—from the polemical Burning Spear and the anthemic Peter Tosh to the more pop-oriented Jimmy Cliff and Third World—contributed to a virtual subindustry of reggae influences that affected not only the music of black Britons but also that of white punks. In the United States, where conditions favored the influence of rhythm and blues, reggae never had a terribly profound impact in the pop market. Prior to the release of the 1973 cult classic reggae film *The Harder They Come* (starring Jimmy Cliff) and its soundtrack album, the only Jamaican releases to crack the U.S. market had been Millie Small's "My Boy Lollipop" (1964), produced by Chris Blackwell, and Desmond Dekker's "The Israelites" (1969). In the late 1960s, Johnny Nash, a middle-of-the-road r&b singer from Austin, Texas, recorded Bob Marley's "Guava Jelly," then covered Marley's "Stir It Up" in 1973, which hit number twelve on the U.S. charts. His own reggae-inflected "I Can See Clearly Now" (1972) went to number one. When white U.S. artists gravitated toward reggae, it was usually for a touch of exotica, as in Paul Simon's "Mother and Child Reunion" (1971). In 1980, Blondie embraced the style on "The Tide Is High," which became a number one hit.

Throughout the 1970s, white British artists were often more successful with reggae than were its Jamaican originators. It was a discouraging testament to the prevailing distribution of cultural resources that Eric Clapton's number one cover of Marley's "I Shot the Sheriff" (1974) outsold the Wailers' original not only in England and the United States, but also in Jamaica. Clapton never repaid this debt by supporting RAR, preferring instead a safer charitable path that stretched from George Harrison's Concert for Bangladesh to his memorable appearance at Live Aid. Marley, on the other hand, released "Punky Reggae Party" in solidarity with RAR's reggae/punk alliance.

As the RAR push to unite black and white met the reggae explosion, a number of integrated bands were formed that delved into ska, the lighter, faster form of Jamaican dance music preceding reggae. From Coventry came Selecter and the Specials; from London, Madness; and from Birmingham, the English Beat. The groups recorded for a label called 2-Tone, a bow to the interracial character of the bands and their music. UB40, another ska-influenced band, came shortly thereafter, taking its name from the British unemployment form.

In attempting to build as broad a base as possible, RAR also reached across lines of sexual orientation and gender. Gay activist Tom Robinson unfurled the first "Rock Against Sexism" banner while performing at an RAR concert. Robinson played it safe with his first single, "2-4-6-8 Motorway," which made the U.K. Top Ten, but "Up Against the Wall," from his first album, captured the politics of punk as well as any song. At RAR concerts, he moved even straight audiences to tears with his heart-wrenching performances of "Glad to Be Gay." RAR's endorsement of progressive sexual politics dovetailed nicely with a potential that had been inherent in punk from the beginning: the creation of new cultural spaces for women. In New York, women appeared in groups like DNA and Mars wearing black jeans, boots, T-shirts, and leather jackets—the same defiant image used by the men—and put out the same angry, dissonant sound as the men. The sound was christened "no wave" in opposition to new wave. "It was liberating," exclaimed Adele Bertei, organist for the Contortions, "we were just like the boys, finally, we could do what the fuck we wanted to, without any sexist bullshit."[30] A poet named Exene Cervenka and her husband, John Doe, led X, a Los Angeles group. Dissecting Los Angeles with a caustic wit and a rapid-fire beat, the group was able to make the jump to a major label, Elektra, and producer Ray Manzarek.

In London, there was Siouxsie Sioux and the Banshees, and the Slits, an all-female band that translated a maelstrom of noise into a message of female power. Members of the Slits joined early RAR benefits. Poly Styrene, a portly, biracial woman with braces and an acid wit, formed X-Ray Specs by placing an ad in *Melody Maker*. After only three performances, they released their first record, "Oh Bondage! Up Yours!" In 1978, the group joined the Clash, Steel Pulse, the Tom Robinson Band, and others as headliners of RAR's biggest event at Victoria Park. By then, even Siouxsie and the Banshees had publicly distanced themselves from fascist icons. RAR had had its intended effect.

The Rock Against Racism movement provided a context that nurtured the more progressive impulses in punk. In return, punk and reggae musicians supplied the left with the cultural politics needed to reach youth. It was one of the most successful marriages of music and politics ever to occur.

In the British general election of 1979, the National Front was soundly defeated. To be sure, Margaret Thatcher's exploitation of white Britain's racial fears played a major role in rallying the conservative vote for the Tories, but the effect of RAR cannot be discounted. The Rock Against Racism movement provided a context that nurtured the more progressive impulses in punk. In return, punk and reggae musicians supplied the left with the cultural politics needed to reach youth. It was one of the most successful marriages of music and politics ever to occur.

Riding the New Wave

For the most part, the RAR movement coincided with the heyday of punk's first generation of performers. By the second generation, punk had been born again as new wave. While punk's wit, irony, flair for the outrageous, and politics of the absurd were never completely abandoned, the new artists were somewhat less oriented toward shock for its own sake, a bit more adept musically, and infinitely more successful commercially. In the United States, Blondie and the Talking Heads easily assumed the new wave label. The Clash made the transition while touring the United States so extensively they lost contact with their home base. In Britain, the label was assumed by Elvis Costello, the Police, and the Pretenders, all of whom were connected in their own ways to some form of progressive political activism.

If any single performer bridged the gap between punk and new wave and embodied all the contradictions contained therein, it was Declan Patrick McManus, a.k.a. Elvis Costello. When Costello started recording for Stiff, he was married, had a son, and had not given up his day jobs, one of which was a computer operator for Elizabeth Arden, a company he skewered as a "vanity factory" on "I'm Not Angry." Costello combined the words of a poet with the temper of a madman. He told the press "revenge and guilt" were his primary motivations for his songs.

Costello left Stiff in late 1977. His debut album, *My Aim Is True,* was issued on Columbia, as were all of his subsequent U.S. releases. Costello had genuinely catholic tastes in popular music. He released more than a dozen original homages to American r&b on *Get Happy!!* (1980), and he packaged his favorite country songs on *Almost Blue* (1981). Only Joe Jackson rivaled his eclecticism. Jackson explored reggae on *Beat Crazy* (1980); paid homage to Cab Calloway and Louis Jordan on *Jumpin' Jive* (1981); and delved into r&b, salsa, jazz, and funk on *Night & Day* (1982), which also yielded his biggest U.S. hit, "Steppin' Out." Costello generated hit after hit in Britain but managed only one U.S. Top Forty single, "Every Day I Write the Book" (1983). His albums, however, usually garnered respectable chart positions, unlike most of the British new wave pack.

HEAR MORE
Elvis Costello on MyMusicKit

No topic was outside the reach of Costello's acerbic wit or immune to his hostility. He bit the hand that fed his success on "Radio, Radio" and vented his misogyny on "Green Shirt." No less contradictory than the punks who had preceded him, he was a staunch supporter of RAR. Inspired by RAR's punk/reggae fusion, his first big hit in Britain, "Watching the Detectives" (1977), was a lively reggae track backed by the Rumour. He contributed a number of antifascist songs to the RAR movement—"Less Than Zero" from *My Aim Is True* (1978), "Goon Squad" from *Armed Forces* (1979), among others—and shared the stage with Aswad at RAR's Brixton Carnival Two in 1978. None of this, however, kept him from getting into trouble in the United States the following year when Bonnie Bramlett belted him for muttering racial slurs about Ray Charles. Although his anger often got the best of him, he remained a darling of the critics throughout his career. At the end of the 1980s, he was still charting decently in the lower reaches of the U.S. Top Forty.

Like Costello, the Police—Sting (bass and vocals), Andy Summers (guitar), and Stewart Copeland (drums)—rose from the British punk scene; but unlike Costello, the group had little support in the punk community, which viewed them as too commercial because they appeared in TV ads. Copeland's brother Miles managed the group. The Police were thrown into the new wave category primarily because of their nod toward reggae, which can be heard in early hits such as "Can't Stand Losing You" and "Roxanne." *Reggatta de Blanc* (1979), the title of the group's second album, is patois for "white reggae."

Like Costello, the Police broke into the U.S. market by touring small clubs. But they were not parlaying an already solid British base into U.S. success; they entered both markets simultaneously, and when they hit, their success was immediately mainstream. Sting's rugged good looks were broadly appealing, and the group's white reggae style was sufficiently rock to be appreciated by the critics. The material they wrote was good. "Message in a Bottle" and "Walking on the Moon" from *Reggatta de Blanc*, and "Every Little Thing She Does Is Magic" and "Spirits in the Material World" from *Ghosts in the Machine* (1981), rank among the more engaging songs of the era.

In the early 1980s, the band's members embarked on solo projects—Sting as an actor; Summers as a photographer; Copeland as his musical alter ego, Klerk Kant. They reunited for *Synchronicity* in 1983. The LP included their biggest hit, "Every Breath You Take," and remained in the number one slot for seventeen weeks; it also turned them into one of the biggest rock acts in the world. Members have since gone their separate ways, with Sting drawing most of the attention. In the late 1980s, he became active in Amnesty International.

If the Police used the new cultural possibilities offered by the punk/reggae fusion to become successful, Chrissie Hynde walked through the door that punk had opened for women. Born in Akron, Ohio, Hynde attended Kent State for three years without being aware of the punk scene developing in her own backyard. In 1973, she moved to London, where she wrote for *New Musical Express,* clerked for

If the Police used the new cultural possibilities offered by the punk/reggae fusion to become successful, Chrissie Hynde walked through the door that punk had opened for women.

While the Police had little sympathy in the punk community, they achieved more commercial success than most groups in the punk/new wave category. After they peaked, they tended to go their separate ways, with Sting remaining in the limelight as a solo artist.

McLaren and Westwood, and eventually formed the Pretenders. The group started with a cover of the Kinks' "Stop Your Sobbing," and two moderate tempo singles, "Kid" and "Brass in Pocket," the last of which promptly went to number ten in Great Britain. In the United States, the group's 1980 eponymous debut album charted respectably, with material ranging from aggressive, no-holds-barred rock ("Tattooed Love Boys," "Precious") to reggae ("Private Life") and ballads ("Lovers of Today"). *Pretenders II* (1981) also did well and was followed by their biggest single, "Back on the Chain Gang" (1983), later included on *Learning to Crawl*.

As the Pretenders' front woman, Hynde projected a tough-chick-in-leather image with uncommon grace and dignity. In 1983, she had her first child, who then accompanied her on tour. While her lifestyle owed a lot to the women's movement, Hynde's views on marriage and the family were quite conventional. As she later said, "It's not sexist to say that a woman's place is in the home looking after children."[31] In 1985, she married Jim Kerr of Simple Minds and took time off to have another baby. Though feminism was not among her strongest motivations, Hynde did pursue vegetarianism and animal rights vigorously toward the end of the decade.

As new wave journeyed toward mainstream success, several artists sought to retain the edge and anticommercialism of early punk. Black Flag, X, the Minutemen, Fear, the Germs, and the Circle Jerks sought to increase punk tempos to the limits of human endurance while they railed against the conditions of everyday life. This was hard core; the dance that accompanied it was called slamming. To the uninitiated, slamming could easily be mistaken for fighting, and indeed, many hard-core bands seemed more interested in concert brawls than in making records. In addition to Los Angeles, post-punk stalwarts held forth from other locales, notably Minneapolis, where Hüsker Dü came from; San Francisco, home of the Dead Kennedys; and Washington, D.C., which spawned Fugazi.

Key to the development of hard core was SST, an independent label started by Black Flag in 1981. Black Flag went through several personnel changes before arriving at the lineup that featured Henry Rollins as lead singer. A bodybuilder and poet, Rollins unleashed a fury in his vocals that was well suited to the hard-core beat. On Black Flag's debut LP, *Damaged,* Rollins seemed to delight in celebrating depression and inflicting pain (mostly on himself). Before the group released its second album, *Slip It In,* Rollins left to form his own group.

SST was also the musical home of the Minutemen and Hüsker Dü. Given the speed of their music, the Minutemen were aptly named. "On their first few recordings," Robert Palmer noted, "the Minutemen got through every song in under two minutes, many in under one, and still had time to sing each song through once, insert a manic guitar break and sing the song again."[32] Early Hüsker Dü was often compared to the Minutemen. On *Land Speed Record* (1982), one of their first releases, they more than lived up to the comparison.

The Washington, D.C., variant of hard core was called *straightedge* because its adherents were encouraged to avoid drugs, alcohol, and promiscuous sex. The straightedge philosophy was perhaps best captured in "Out of Step" by Minor Threat. After their founder, Ian MacKaye, disbanded the original group, he formed Fugazi, which took hard core in a more political direction, railing against racism, sexism, and environmental destruction.

The most politically oriented band in the hard-core scene was the Dead Kennedys, founded in 1978 by Jello Biafra, the group's lead singer and a dedicated left-wing activist. On their first album, *Fresh Fruit for Rotting Vegetables* (1980), Biafra's biting satire was applied to issues ranging from poverty ("Kill the Poor") to U.S. involvement in Southeast Asia ("Holiday in Cambodia"). "California Über Alles" skewered then-governor Jerry Brown and other "zen fascist" devotees of the California lifestyle. For the group's second outing, *In God We Trust, Inc.* (1981), they rewrote "Über Alles" as "We've Got a Bigger Problem Now," applying the same caustic wit to Ronald Reagan.

While hard-core was pushing punk to the limit, new wave was incorporating other influences that pointed the music back to its roots. Early punk had strayed as far from black influences as one could get; the connection was rebuilt primarily through reggae in Britain and rhythm and blues in the United States.

While hard-core was pushing punk to the limit, new wave was incorporating other influences that pointed the music back to its roots. Early punk had strayed as far from black influences as one could get; the connection was rebuilt primarily through reggae in Britain and rhythm and blues in the United States. The Talking Heads, for example, had always maintained a strong connection to rhythm and blues. It was a logical extension of the group's sound to use African drummers on *Fear of Music* (1979). Their unique synthesis of black and white reached its zenith on *Remain in Light* (1980), which featured Nona Hendryx (formerly of LaBelle) guesting on vocals and Bernard Worrell (formerly of Parliament) on keyboards. Some new wavers even began to make alliances with the dance craze that was threatening to swallow the music industry whole—disco. Blondie had always been based on a send-up of 1960s pop; their breakthrough single in the United States, "Heart of Glass" (1979), had begun as a parody of disco. In the hands of pop producer Mike Chapman, however, it became a genuine dance-floor hit and a number one single. That same year, Third World released a full-fledged disco hit called "Now That We Found Love." One year later, Devo scored their only U.S. hit single with "Whip It," another dance-floor favorite. Disco was what was happening and, at the beginning at least, the site of enormous creativity. "I'm cynical about rock music," said canny new waver David Byrne. "The innovations in popular music seem to be more often in disco and funk in the last ten years."[33]

Disco: The Rhythm Without the Blues

"After 1970, when psychedelia gave way to a vogue for downers," Stephen Holden has written, "public dancing hit a low point. About the only people who didn't stop dancing were blacks and gays."[34] Add Latinos to Holden's list as well. The clubs frequented by the dancers were called discos, from the French word *discothèque*—or record library. Discos had been around in the United States since the early 1960s. Some of these clubs, like New York's Peppermint Lounge, referred to by *Rolling Stone* as "rock & roll discos,"[35] booked live acts like Joey Dee and the Starlighters, whose forty-five minute versions of songs such as "Shout" and "Peppermint Twist" propelled patrons into a sweat-drenched dance frenzy. By the early 1970s, discos used light shows, most featured DJs; and the dancers had added their own pharmacological embellishments. Unlike the hallucinogens favored by 1960s rockers, the downers preferred by heavy metal fans, or the speed that fueled punk, disco drugs of choice were cocaine and poppers (amyl and butyl nitrate). "It was about communal dance ecstasy," Tom Smucker has written. "A new brew of 1970s self-absorption and 1960s collectivity, mixing aerobics, the pick-up singles bar, drug highs and light shows . . . made the dance floor, rather than the concert hall, the locus of orgasmic revelation."[36]

Long before it became a genre unto itself, disco was whatever was played in dance clubs. "At the start, it was an amalgam of pirated songs," Barbara Graustark reported in *Newsweek* in 1979. "In black, Latino and gay all-night clubs on Fire Island, in New York City, and San Francisco, club deejays would create non-stop sequences of dance music by weaving together twenty minute medleys of tunes by Diana Ross, Barry White, The Temptations and Marvin Gaye."[37] Isaac Hayes and MFSB were also early favorites. At this point, disco was simply called "party music." As the sound began to evolve, its inspiration came from far and wide: "From Latin music, it takes its percolating percussion, its sensuous, throbbing rhythms; from the '60s 'funk' music of James Brown and Sly Stone, it borrows a kicky bass-guitar line; from Afro-Cuban music, it repeats simple lyric lines like voodoo chants; and like early rock 'n' roll, it exploits the honking saxophones of black rhythm and blues," Graustark noted.[38] Often, nuances of musical taste indicated sexual preference. In the words of club deejay Danae:

> *Straight disco is heavy-duty funk, the driving sound, that has all the power without much of the emotion. Gays like to hear black women singers; they identify with the pain, the irony, the self-consciousness. We pick up on the emotional content, not just the physical power. The MFSB sound was gay, Barry White was a gay sound, so is Donna Summer, Gloria Gaynor.*[39]

Latin music was primarily an outside influence. Salsa was just coming into its own, a separate subindustry with its own record labels (notably, Fania), distribution networks, and performance venues. Although Fania All Stars compilations like *Spanish Fever* and *Crossover* contained disco material, and Fania often supplied disco deejays with records, there was little direct crossover to pop. Aside from Disco Tex and His Sex-O-Lettes ("Get Dancin'," 1974) and Foxy ("Get Off," 1978), both of which hit the Top Ten, disco produced few Latino stars, probably because of the difficulties—well documented in Rubén Blades's poignant film *Crossover Dreams*—of interacting with the mainstream culture.

Proto-Disco: The Funk Connection

Funk's impact on disco was direct but limited. By the early 1970s, soul, like the rest of popular music, had splintered. In the center, Stevie Wonder had a firm hold on the pop soul audience, just as the Jackson 5 appealed to their younger brothers and sisters. At one end of the soul spectrum was the lavish, sweet sound of Philadelphia. At the other end was funk, the more caustic, percussive sound, descended from James Brown, whose choppy, jagged rhythms interrupted the smooth forward motion of its Philadelphia cousin. Early on, it seemed as if self-contained funk bands such as Kool and the Gang; the Ohio Players; and Earth, Wind & Fire would make a major contribution to disco. Even a white funk band from Scotland, Average White Band ("Pick Up the Pieces," "Cut the Cake"), and a mixed unit from Oakland, California, Tower of Power ("What Is Hip"), appeared to be cutting a good bit of funk mustard. However, as the dance-floor mania became a more and more upscale trend, the cruder sensuality of post-Sly, James Brown–inspired funk was eclipsed by the more polished sound associated with Philadelphia and the controlled, high-tech energy and propulsive

As the dance-floor mania became a more and more upscale trend, the cruder sensuality of post-Sly, James Brown–inspired funk was eclipsed by the more polished sound associated with Philadelphia and the controlled, high-tech energy and propulsive (some would say relentless) 4/4 beat of what came to be known as Eurodisco.

(some would say relentless) 4/4 beat of what came to be known as Eurodisco. In many ways, dance music was at its most creative when it combined elements of all these styles: the sweet soul tenor vocal over Earth, Wind & Fire's funky instrumental on "Shining Star" or Donna Summer's soulful delivery over producer Georgio Moroder's clean, clear, driving synthesizer tracks on "Hot Stuff," which won a rock Grammy at the height of disco.

The funk sound had developed over a long period and was absorbed all too soon. Like a number of their Philadelphia soul mates, the Ohio Players had formed in the 1950s and labored for years before hitting the Top Forty in 1973 with "Funky Worm." Although they recorded five gold albums and a handful of hit singles—"Skin Tight," a dance-floor favorite, and "Fire" and "Love Rollercoaster," which hit number one—they disappeared from the Top Forty in 1976, even before disco peaked. Wild Cherry, another funk band from Ohio, picked up where they left off, with "Play That Funky Music" in 1976. Kool and the Gang formed in the mid-1960s and first hit the Top Forty in 1973 with "Funky Stuff." After two follow-up Top Ten singles ("Jungle Boogie" and "Hollywood Swinging"), they had no more big hits until the inclusion of "Open Sesame" on the 1978 *Saturday Night Fever* soundtrack gave them a new lease on life. They came back with three Top Ten singles in a row—"Ladies Night," "Too Hot," and the classic "Celebration"—that took them successfully into the 1980s.

Earth, Wind & Fire formed later than either the Ohio Players or Kool and the Gang, and did better. Throughout the disco era, they turned out nothing but platinum-selling Top Ten albums. Founded in 1969 by Maurice White, they did not have a stable lineup until Philip Bailey was added as co-lead vocalist in 1973. A session drummer at Chess Records, by the 1970s, White had absorbed a catalogue of styles from American jazz and soul to African folk drumming. *That's the Way of the World* (1975), the soundtrack of a documentary film about the band, was the group's first number one album. It contained all the musical elements that would wrestle for prominence in disco—funk guitar and horn licks punctuating African American and Latin rhythms, all providing a bottom for lavish strings and sweet harmonies with a James Brown tightness that could be rivaled only by the studio precision of Eurodisco. *That's the Way of the World* included the group's only number one single, "Shining Star." Under White's leadership, Earth, Wind & Fire transformed their spiritual interests in Egyptology into a media-savvy image. While they had a keen eye for commercial opportunities, they never lost sight of their funk roots. Their rendition of the Beatles' "Got to Get You into My Life" from Robert Stigwood's film version of *Sgt. Pepper* was one of the few bright spots in an otherwise abysmal movie. The group was also one of the first African American acts to tour with theater sets and special effects. Even at their most grandiose, however, Earth, Wind & Fire seemed to be well within the bounds of soul orthodoxy when compared with George Clinton.

George Clinton was to funk what glam was to rock. His first group, the Parliaments (formed in 1955), had the straight soul hit "(I Wanna) Testify" in 1967 on Berry Gordy's Revilot label. Following a contract dispute, Clinton found his way to white hippies, LSD, and the music of Jimi Hendrix. Attired in sequined jumpsuits and a blonde wig, the new George Clinton (a.k.a. Dr. Funkenstein, Maggot Overlord, Uncle Jam) could be viewed as either a black Frank Zappa or a psychedelic James Brown. In many ways, Clinton was the

missing link between the 1960s focus on mind expansion and the 1970s preoccupation with the body.

Clinton presided over the extensive and hopelessly complicated Parliament/Funkadelic empire. For these overlapping and interconnected groups, he used a core of side musicians—Eddie Hazel, Gary Shider, and Mike Hampton on guitar, Bernard Worrell (later with the Talking Heads) and Junie Morrison on keyboard, and James Brown alumni Bootsy Collins on bass, and Fred Wesley and Maceo Parker on horns. Funkadelic recorded Clinton's wild, psychedelicized funk excursions for Warner. Parliament recorded shorter, if not simpler, material for Casablanca. Spin-off projects, which Clinton encouraged, were signed by any number of other labels. The Horny Horns, led by Wesley and Parker, were signed to Atlantic, as were the Brides of Funkenstein. Worrell also issued a solo LP on Arista before joining the Talking Heads. Hazel recorded as a solo artist for Warner, who also signed Bootsy's Rubber Band. The P-Funk vocal chorus comprised Parlet, a group who recorded three albums on Casablanca.

Parliament/Funkadelic had a prodigious output with reasonably impressive sales figures. At the height of the disco craze, six of Parliament's albums placed in the Top Thirty, as did two of Funkadelic's. But disco was primarily a singles medium. As album-oriented groups, Parliament/Funkadelic's music was not readily available to those who lived only for the dance floor. Parliament/Funkadelic had only three Top Thirty singles—"Tear the Roof off the Sucker

George Clinton is either a black Frank Zappa or James Brown on acid, depending on how you look at it. The mission of his P-Funk empire was to "rescue dance music from the blahs."

(Give Up the Funk)," "Flash Light," and "One Nation Under a Groove." By the late 1970s, their brisk album sales in the pop market represented an alternative to disco more than one of its formative influences.

Up from the Disco Underground

When disco began to emerge as a genre, most of its releases were by black artists. In this sense, early disco was part of the continuing development of black dance music. Among the records that made the rare crossover from clubs to radio was "Soul Makossa" (1973), an obscure French import by a Cameroonian artist named Manu Dibango. Dibango thus became the first African musician to have an international hit. The next year, "Rock the Boat" by the Hues Corporation and "Rock Your Baby" by George McRae both hit number one. B. T. Express scored in 1975 with "Do It ('Til You're Satisfied)," as did Tavares with "It Only Takes a Minute." By 1975, when Van McCoy and the Soul City Orchestra established the hustle as the most important new dance craze since the twist, disco was showing signs of respectability, but the music industry had not yet taken notice.

Gloria Gaynor's "Never Can Say Good-Bye" (1975)—reportedly one of the first records especially mixed for club play—was the first disco hit to chart as disco. She was unable to follow up with another hit until 1979, when her aptly titled "I Will Survive" went to number one. Gaynor's mistake had been to record a dynamite disco hit as the music industry was just beginning to recognize disco as a trend. It was Donna Summer who ultimately became disco's queen. But even as her "Love to Love You Baby" rose to number two early in 1976, the established recording industry continued to ignore disco. According to Andrew Kopkind of the *Village Voice*:

> *The record companies seemed bewildered by what they had, and promo people continued their quirky disregard of the disco category in their portfolios. Instead, they inflated passing fancies into seismic cultural events: Peter Frampton, reggae, and punk, for example. Not that some of those sounds or stars lacked merit; certainly Springsteen, Bob Marley, and the best of the New Wave deserve seats high in rock and roll heaven. But disco would soon swamp them all, and nobody was watching.*[40]

Without promotion from the major record companies, disco was rarely heard on the airwaves. (The one exception was New York's top black station, WBLS, where deejay Frankie Crocker played many of the early disco club hits.) Forced to remain underground, disco continued to receive its primary exposure in clubs, popularized only by the creative genius of the disco deejays who "became taste-making alchemists-engineers with cults that followed them from club to club."[41] Like the music they played, these deejays were initially shunned by record companies. To get records, they were expected to make the rounds to each label individually. Eventually, they organized themselves into "record pools," or central distribution points, where new releases could be discussed and new tastes created. As late as 1979, about fifty functioning pools could be found in major markets scattered across the country. This network of record pools and nightclubs became an alternative to the airplay marketing structure of the music business. Deejays were able to break hits from the dance floor capable of selling upward of 100,000 copies in New York City alone with almost no radio play—no mean achievement in an industry that had committed billions of dollars to the airplay system of marketing.

Deejays were able to break hits from the dance floor capable of selling upward of 100,000 copies in New York City alone with almost no radio play—no mean achievement in an industry that had committed billions of dollars to the airplay system of marketing.

HEAR MORE
Audio links to Selected Year-End Disco Hits on MyMuiscKit

Disco's following was not just a fleeting, if dedicated, underground party culture; it was a significant record-buying public. As early as 1976, the year-end pop charts were bursting with disco acts whose records were among *Billboard*'s forty most popular that year. Over the next couple of years, disco continued to swell its ranks on the pop charts.

Although as many acts were signed by major labels as by independents, the majors neither promoted the music nor supplied its key innovations. When disco hit, the majors simply contracted with independents for distribution or rode the disco wave with their own artists. By and large, disco's creative energy came from independent producers and upstart independent labels. Consider Richard Finch and Harry Wayne Casey, who made TK Records one of the premiere disco labels. Casey was a songwriter in Miami, Florida, and knew the club scene; Finch, a bassist, worked as an engineer at TK Records in Hialeah. Together they wrote and produced George McRae's "Rock Your Baby" for TK, which gave the small independent its first entree to disco. Finch and Casey then formed KC and the Sunshine Band, a black, white, and Latino ten-piece unit that established TK's position in disco. In 1975, the band released three singles that, like "Rock Your Baby," hit number one on both the pop charts and the r&b charts: "Get Down Tonight," "That's the Way (I Like It)," and "Shake Your Booty." Finch and Casey turned out two more number ones—"I'm Your Boogie Man" and "Please Don't Go"—and a number of lesser hits. Their strong r&b feel, which came to be known as the Miami Sound, contributed significantly to the funk side of disco.

The SalSoul label tried to fill a niche in the disco market that combined salsa and soul. Its founders, three Syrian Jewish brothers—Ken, Joe, and Stanley Cayre—with an interest in Latin music, had relocated from Miami to New York. Afro-Filipino Joe Bataan provided the Cayre brothers with their salsa-soul-disco link in 1973, when he recorded a full-length album for them entitled *SalSoul*. This album included the single "Latin Strut," an early dance floor hit during the ascent of disco. The album gave the Cayres a name for their new label and "Latin Strut" provided the funding to capitalize it when Columbia Records, sensing crossover possibilities, bought the rights to the song for $100,000.[42] The Cayres' concept for SalSoul was to produce disco that had "an R&B rhythm and Latin percussion with a pretty melody on top."[43] For this sound, they turned toward Philadelphia, where they contracted with Vince Montana, an Italian American Latin music aficionado, to assemble the SalSoul Orchestra, an ensemble that numbered as many as 50 players, including some of the best conductors and arrangers and hottest percussionists in the business, not to mention more than a dozen strings. Their first release, "The SalSoul Hustle" (1975), became a number one disco single; "Tangerine," a cover of a Jimmy Dorsey tune, crossed over to pop. Ultimately, however, the lush string arrangements and pretty melodies sounded too saccharine and SalSoul too often found itself on the novelty side of disco.

Casablanca was an independent label that backed into disco through its association with Donna Summer. Summer, a high school dropout from Boston, was in Munich, in the German production of *Hair*, when she fell into an alliance with Eurodisco producer Georgio Moroder. Summer could belt out a song, but for what would become her first U.S. hit single, Moroder created a symphonic mix of drum machine rhythms and synthesized sounds and then cleared the studio so that Summer could repeat the song's one-line lyric over and over in a breathy whisper while simulating the sound of orgasm twenty-two times. To introduce the song to the U.S. audience, Moroder took a three-minute demo of "Love to Love You Baby" to Neil Bogart of Casablanca Records. Bogart, known in the previous decade as the Bubblegum King, had produced groups like Ohio Express and the 1910 Fruitgum Company for Buddah. He had recently founded Casablanca, whose roster included the heavy metal group Kiss and George Clinton's Parliament. The addition of Summer would point Casablanca in yet another direction. It was perhaps Bogart's inclination to take chances that attracted Moroder to his label.

((•)) **HEAR MORE**
Donna Summer
on MyMusicKit

Donna Summer clutches one of her four Grammy awards. While she had the talent to rise above her disco queen image, the pressures of fame and fortune ultimately caused her to turn her back on disco altogether.

"Last Dance"

Artist: Donna Summer
Music/Lyrics by Paul Jabara
Label: Casablanca (1978), from the LP *On the Radio* and the soundtrack to the film *Thank God It's Friday*

In the slick, sophisticated sound-world of disco, the producer took on a role of primary importance. In "Last Dance," we hear the winning combination of Eurodisco producers Giorgio Moroder and Pete Bellotte and the gospel-tinged vocals of Donna Summer. Summer, born in Boston, was already enjoying considerable career success in Europe when her sensuous 1976 disco hit "Love to Love You Baby" became a huge hit in the United States. "Last Dance" was part of the soundtrack to the film *Thank God It's Friday* (in which Summer also played the role of aspiring singer Nicole Sims). The song won both a Grammy and the 1978 Academy Award for Best Original Song.

Musical Style Notes

The slow-dance beginning of "Last Dance," with its shimmery, bell-like synth-percussion effects and tremolo strings, gives way after the first verse to the classic sound of disco: synthesized bass and drums, multiple keyboards, string-heavy orchestral textures, and a driving rhythm track with a steady, pounding emphasis on each beat. Summer's strong, vibrant voice carries over this thick texture beautifully, demonstrating disco's gospel and soul roots with her vocal improvisations and vocal melismas (multiple notes sung over one syllable).

In the second repetition of the fast-tempo chorus to "Last Dance," we can also hear an example of a musical technique called modulation, which is another term for "changing key." The "key" of a piece refers to a specific set of notes (scale) and chords used to create the melody and harmony of a musical piece. This set of notes, or scale, has a particular keynote. If you were to sing the well-known do-re-mi-fa-so-la-ti-do scale, the "do" would be the keynote. In the second chorus to "Last Dance," the scale, keynote, and harmonies are all shifted up in pitch a half-tone. This technique is common in pop music, where it is used to create a sudden change to a "brighter" sound, which in turn gives the aural illusion of a spike in the energy and brilliance of a piece.

Musical "Road Map"

TIMINGS	COMMENTS	LYRICS
0:00–0:15	Introduction; instrumental with melismatic vocal (*Melisma*: many notes sung over one syllable—in this case "hooo.") Sonic "colors" added with bells and other synthesized percussion.	
0:15–1:15	Verse 1—slow ballad version of verse	*Last dance . . .*
1:15–1:19	Pause on sustained chord	
1:19–1:35	Chorus New faster dance tempo begins.	*So let's dance . . .*
1:35–2:05	Verse repeats in new faster dance tempo.	*Last dance- . . .*
2:05–2:12	Chorus	*So let's dance*
2:12–2:24	Chorus modulates to a new, higher key. (See Musical Style Notes above.) Chorus ends with long-held vocal note.	*So let's dance*
2:24–3:15	This section features the instrumental musical content of the first half of the verse, with vocalization on syllable *hoo* sung over instrumental section, with vocal melisma added.	
	Second half of verse with lyrics repeats in the new key.	*I need you*
2:55–3:15	This section features the instrumental musical content of the chorus, with vocal improvisations: "Come on, baby. Dance that dance," etc.	*Come on,*
3:15	Final chord	

Summer became a mainstay of Casablanca's financial health. At her peak, she delivered three number one albums and eight Top Ten singles in a row, including "MacArthur Park," "Hot Stuff," and "Bad Girls," all of which reached number one. "Last Dance," from the film *Thank God It's Friday*, earned her the first of four Grammies in 1978. Summer had trouble rising above her sultry disco seductress persona, but she had enough talent to seek more. In 1979, she sang with Barbra Streisand on "No More Tears (Enough Is Enough)." Her ambition was also evident, if not fully realized, on her autobiographical disco miniopera, *Once Upon a Time*. Under the pressures of fame and fortune (and a lawsuit against Casablanca), she became a born-again Christian in the early 1980s and turned her back on disco.

Bogart added the Village People to his roster in 1978. A gay-oriented novelty act whose members dressed as a cowboy, an Indian, a hard hat, a soldier, a cop, and a leather freak, the Village People were assembled by Jacques Morali, a French producer. Morali's upbeat, anthemic melodies and the group's animated, karate-chop delivery were presented as camp disco to the general public. For those in the know, however, the irony of hits such as "Macho Man," "Y.M.C.A.," and "In the Navy" was not particularly subtle. With worldwide sales of 10 million albums, the Village People added measurably to Casablanca's fortunes. In 1978 alone, the fledgling company grossed $100 million.

Independent producers were as important to disco's creativity as independent labels were to its production. This was especially so in Europe, where producers like Cerrone and Alec Costandinos made quasi-symphonic disco concept LPs such as *Love in C Minor* and *Love and Kisses*, respectively. Costandinos turned to literary sources for *Romeo and Juliet* and *The Hunchback of Notre Dame*. Eurodisco and its U.S. counterpart had significant differences. While Eurodisco albums were often conceived as a conceptual whole, U.S. disco was oriented toward individual songs and was more r&b-based. Freddie Perren in the United States, for example, produced albums that were aggregations of singles, which varied in function, tempo, and mood, with no segues between songs. As an independent producer (originally with Motown), his first successes included the Sylvers' Jackson 5–ish "Boogie Fever" and Tavares's pop-oriented "Heaven Must Be Missing an Angel" and "Who Dunit." In the late 1970s, he produced Gaynor's "I Will Survive" and Peaches and Herb's disco hit "Shake Your Groove Thing"—but neither of their albums were all disco. In contrast, Georgio Moroder thought of himself as a composer. For Donna Summer's *Live and More* LP, Moroder wrote "Heaven Knows" to complement the rhythm and feeling of "MacArthur Park," the song it follows, thereby maintaining the same tempo and emotional edge for the entire album side.

In some ways, Eurodisco album-length compositions attempted to do the work of club deejays. In the United States, where the success of disco depended, at least at first, on deejay creativity, the music developed as a singles medium. In fact, a whole new subindustry of twelve-inch, 45 rpm singles (the so-called disco mix) opened to accommodate the specific needs of club deejays for extended play and heavy bass. This innovation would provide the foundation for rap records in the next decade.

Eurodisco album-length compositions attempted to do the work of club deejays. In the United States, where the success of disco depended, at least at first, on deejay creativity, the music developed as a singles medium.

Mainstream Disco: The Bee Gees Boogie Down

In keeping with the popular music tradition of black innovation and white popularization, it was not until a white supergroup—the Bee Gees—came to dominate the scene that disco finally took on the mantle of respectability. According to Andrew Kopkind, 1978 saw

> several disco stars achieve the necessary "crossover" effect, bringing the music out of the subcultural ghettoes into mainstream life. The Bee Gees were crucial to that passage; they made disco safe for white, straight, male, young, and middle-class America. What Elvis Presley did for black rhythm and blues, … the Brothers Gibb have done for disco.[44]

By the time that Barry, Maurice, and Robin Gibb struck disco gold, they had already been through at least three musical incarnations. They began their hit-making career as a Beatles sound-alike act with "New York Mining Disaster 1941/Have You Seen My Wife Mr. Jones" in 1967. After a few more hits, they embarked on undistinguished solo careers. Their reunion in the early 1970s again produced hits ("How Can You Mend a Broken Heart" at number one), but no distinctive voice until Atlantic producer Arif Mardin helped them create their disco-era persona. On *Main Course,* he encouraged the r&b feel evident on cuts like "Jive Talkin'," a number one hit in 1975. On "Nights on Broadway," Barry unveiled the falsetto that would become the group's disco trademark, perfecting the sound on "You Should Be Dancing,"

The Brothers Gibb had been through a number of incarnations before achieving superstardom as top-selling disco artists. Their music crossed the dance fever over to the mainstream with a level of saturation that almost guaranteed a backlash.

which rose to number one in 1976. When Robert Stigwood commissioned them to write the soundtrack for the feature film *Saturday Night Fever,* they captured the disco crown.

The Bee Gees had always been associated with Stigwood. In 1967, they were signed to a five-year management contract with Brian Epstein's NEMS company when Stigwood was its director. Reportedly, Stigwood paid $2,500 for a 51 percent interest in their publishing.[45] Beginning with *Main Course,* all Bee Gees recordings had been released on his RSO label. Stigwood was a master at "crossover media," in which a product in one medium sells a product in another. *Newsweek*'s David Ansen described the process as "album sells theater ticket, play sells movie rights, soundtrack album sells movie, movie sells soundtrack album."[46] Stigwood bought the performance rights to the *Jesus Christ Superstar* album in 1970; he was also involved with the production of the film version of *Tommy,* the Who's rock opera, in 1975 and with *Grease, Evita,* and *Sgt. Pepper's Lonely Hearts Club Band* in 1978, months after he produced *Saturday Night Fever,* whose music he already owned.

Stigwood's crossover media plan was orchestrated to perfection with *Saturday Night Fever.* "How Deep Is Your Love," from the soundtrack album, rose to number one about two months before the film's release. By the time the film broke in 504 theaters, "Stayin' Alive," which opens the movie, was number one. "Every time the deejay announced 'Stayin' Alive'," crowed RSO Records president Al Coury, "he said, 'That's from the movie *Saturday Night Fever* starring John Travolta.' It was millions and millions of dollars of free publicity."[47] Two months later, "Night Fever," from which the film took its name, occupied the number one slot, which, of course, kept the film in circulation that much longer. This kind of marketing would become the rule in the 1980s, a decade dominated by video clips and movie tie-ins.

The success of *Saturday Night Fever* was unprecedented. The film grossed $130 million in its first U.S. run; the soundtrack album sold 15 million copies in the United States and 30 million worldwide, becoming the best-selling record in history at the time. In addition to the Bee Gees' three number one hits, the LP generated hits for Tavares ("More Than a Woman"), the Trammps ("Disco Inferno"), and a number one single for Yvonne Elliman ("If I Can't Have You"), all within the film's initial run. The film even showcased the Latin side of disco with David Shire's "Salsation," Midway through the year, RSO estimated that its 1978 revenues would be somewhere between $300 million and $500 million. The biggest winner of all, however, was Polygram, the Netherlands-based conglomerate that distributed both RSO and Casablanca.

After *Saturday Night Fever*, it became impossible to ignore disco. Artists of all persuasions jumped on the disco bandwagon. Cher's "Take Me Home" reached number eight; Dolly Parton contributed "Baby I'm Burnin'"; jazz flautist Herbie Mann had a disco hit with "Superman." Even the Rolling Stones and Rod Stewart became disco converts. The Stones' "Miss You" sold 2 million copies, and Stewart scored the best-selling single of his career, "Da Ya Think I'm Sexy?" With such guaranteed hit-making artists on board, radio and television soon followed suit.

The commercial potential of disco came to full bloom when WKTU, an obscure soft rock station in New York, converted to an all-disco format. Within months, WKTU went from a dreary

The commercial potential of disco came to full bloom when WKTU, an obscure soft rock station in New York, converted to an all-disco format. Within months, WKTU went from a dreary 0.9 share of the market to an unbelievable 11.3 share, making it the most listened-to station in the country.

0.9 share of the market to an unbelievable 11.3 share, making it the most listened-to station in the country. This was in December 1978. By March 1979, some 200 disco stations were broadcasting in major markets, from Miami to Los Angeles, and syndicated television programs such as *Disco Magic* and *Dance Fever* had brought the dancing craze to the heartland. That year, disco records captured eight out of fourteen pop Grammy awards. Over 36 million adults thrilled to the musical mixes of 8,000 professional deejays who worked just a portion of the estimated 20,000 disco clubs. According to varying estimates, disco accounted for 20 to 40 percent of *Billboard*'s chart action. All in all, the disco phenomenon spawned an industry with annual revenues ranging between $4 and $8 billion.

The entire disco apparatus now became harnessed to the service of industry profits. The music business soon replicated the 120-beat-per-minute formula ad nauseam. Record pools now served as marketing tools, supplying the record companies with crucial demographic data. Everything from Glenn Miller's "Chattanooga Choo-Choo" to the theme from "Star Wars," to Stravinsky's "Firebird Suite," fell prey to the relentless disco beat; Beethoven's "Fifth Symphony" was an early victim. Percy Faith even recorded a disco version of "Hava Nagila." In the hands of the industry, disco seemed to gobble up everything in its wake.

By this time, disco had come to symbolize the mindless overindulgence its critics had complained about in the first place. Even disco sympathizers acknowledged "its empty excesses, its superficiality, its desperate trendiness."[48] The disco underground, once a haven for the disenfranchised, had surfaced as affluent-chic. Disco "is the height of effete snobbery," snapped one observer, "the ultimate in mindless narcissism. Disco is Margaret Trudeau, Truman Capote, Cher, and all their vacuous Studio 54–*People* magazine cronies."[49] Many black artists began to complain that they had to submit to the demand for disco. "We're in a period of the McDonald's of music, where it's mass-marketed like junk food," lamented Melba Moore, whose "You Stepped into My Life" was a disco hit. "I don't know what *good* is any more."[50] In any given week, as many as forty of *Billboard*'s Hot 100 were disco releases. With the market saturated to this degree, a backlash was inevitable, and given disco's particular history, it was bound to have racial overtones.

The Hard Rock Reaction

The most visceral antidisco reactions came from the hard rock/heavy metal axis of popular music. As John Travolta won the urban white youth market for disco, and scores of radio stations across the country converted to a disco format almost overnight, FM rock radio responded to its loss of audience share by initiating various antidisco campaigns. Dave Marsh, writing in *Rolling Stone,* explained their motivation:

> *As competition becomes fiercer, each station must settle for a narrower demographic range. Right now the goal is males, ages eighteen to thirty-four . . . [They] are the most likely to see disco as the product of homosexuals, blacks, and Latins, and therefore they're the most likely to respond to appeals to wipe out such threats to their security. It goes almost without saying that such appeals are racist and sexist, but broadcasting has never been an especially civil-libertarian medium.*[51]

Georgia Christgau had pointed out these tendencies in New York six months earlier.

> *Three progressive FM rock stations in New York run anti-disco campaigns. It's not hard to do—radio is already segregated black from white. At a sellout show of Twisted Sister, a local group with a white following, a banner displayed from the balcony read, "We hate disco because it sucks." This isn't opinion, it's willful ignorance, racism feeding on paranoia. . . .* [52]

The height of antidisco mania occurred on 12 July 1979 when Chicago deejay Steve Dahl staged a "Disco Demolition Night" for station WLUP (the Loop) at a White Sox doubleheader. Drawn by the Loop's nonstop hype, 47,795 fans (more rock than baseball) paid their way into Comiskey Park, while about half that number either gate-crashed or swarmed around outside. As soon as Dahl blew up a cache of disco records between games, hordes of rock crazies stormed the field, tearing up turf and chanting "Disco sucks!" at the top of their lungs. When park security was unable to restore order, the Sox were forced to forfeit the second game.[53]

In the frenzy of the antidisco campaigns, hard rock fans generalized their antidisco feelings to include all black music, while rock radio fanned the flames of racism. As Robert Hilburn has written:

> *Rock-oriented radio stations could have educated this young audience on the historical link between rock and black music by programming classic Motown-Stax-Hendrix tracks or the rock-oriented tracks by such contemporary black stars as Stevie Wonder, Prince, Donna Summer, and Rick James. Eager to be culturally in tune with their listenership, however, the stations carelessly picked up on the anti-disco sentiment and fell into racist programming policies: They simply stopped playing all black records.* [54]

Although FM rock radio, called album-oriented rock (AOR) at the time, viewed disco as a serious threat to its well-being, it was in no real financial danger. AOR was programmed on the basis of sophisticated market research that targeted the record-buying habits of the population with the most disposable income. Needless to say, AOR's reliance on such research meant that it often excluded black music. WKTU may have been the most listened-to station in 1979, but with an estimated "annual pretax income of about $6 million on revenues of $9 million," AOR station KMET in Los Angeles was by far the most lucrative.[55] The economic reality for radio was that "disco pulled in an audience that was older, younger, more female or less affluent than desired. And it was easy to see that stations that had stuck to hard rock—KMET in Los Angeles, for instance—were prospering in just the demographic areas radio needed. So rock rose."[56]

As rock radio reasserted its primacy, black-oriented radio stations were forced to adopt a new format—Urban Contemporary. Black radio had often had to attract a white listenership just to maintain respectable ratings; the competitive environment of the 1970s added even more pressure to appeal to a more affluent demographic. According to Pablo Guzman: "To satisfy everyone in the spirit of the lowest common denominator and to appease big-budget advertisers who were still nervous about the 'black' tag, black references were dropped, music that was 'too funky' was abandoned in favor of white 'crossover' and UC was born."[57] Stations retained black artists in the soul, funk, and jazz idioms who were central to their playlists—Stevie Wonder, Donna Summer, Rick James, Third World, Funkadelic, Quincy Jones, and

George Benson—and added white acts that fit the format—David Bowie or Hall and Oates. As the strategy began to show returns, bewildered black listeners wondered why their stations were programming more and more white artists. Though assuring listeners of their commitment to the black audience, stations continued to drift toward the mainstream market.

Urban Contemporary was an interesting concept because it was designed as a multiracial format. It was also quite successful, surpassing even AOR stations in many instances. Still, while Urban Contemporary programmers provided greater access to white musicians on what had been black-oriented stations, black performers did not gain greater access to rock radio. Urban Contemporary may well have been a net loss for black artists.

> **W**hile Urban Contemporary programmers provided greater access to white musicians on what had been black-oriented stations, black performers did not gain greater access to rock radio. Urban Contemporary may well have been a net loss for black artists.

By the end of the 1970s, punk—born again as new wave—had assimilated such diverse musical influences (from Jamaican ska to electronic music, to disco itself) that it had expanded beyond categorization. Dance-oriented cuts like Blondie's "Heart of Glass," the Clash's "Magnificent Seven," and Spandau Ballet's "Freeze" found their way into disco clubs, further blurring the line between genres. Disco, as a distinct musical style, became so bloated that it began to collapse under its own weight, and black artists began to move in different musical directions. Traditional soul artists such as Smokey Robinson and Stevie Wonder reappeared on the year-end pop charts. At the same time, a new style of black music known as rap was born. Artists like the Sugar Hill Gang, Kurtis Blow, and Grand Master Flash and the Furious Five transformed the street poetry of Harlem and the South Bronx into black popular culture. Other black artists—notably Prince—moved in a rock-oriented direction. Indeed, the artist who dominated in the 1980s was Michael Jackson, the best-selling pop star in history. Jackson's ascent to superstardom was initially hampered by technological advances that allowed the transfer of radio's restrictive programming policies to the new medium of music television. As economic imperatives propelled the music industry toward a strategy of globalization, however, the 1980s witnessed a significant reshuffling of the musical deck. Even as the industry moved toward greater concentration, African American artists achieved superstar status in unprecedented numbers, and popular music became more politically engaged than in any period since the 1960s.

LEARN MORE
Chapter Questions on MyMusicKit

Are We the World? Music Videos, Superstars, and Mega-Events

The murder of John Lennon on 8 December 1980 put the big chill to any vestiges of the 1960s idealism that had survived the me decade, just as the election of Ronald Reagan one month earlier made it clear that the country was moving in a new political direction. The Keynesian economic strategies of pump priming and deficit spending that had defined the Democratic Party's fiscal policy since the 1930s no longer held sway among the electorate. Reagan's laissez-faire new federalism, which some labeled voodoo economics, promised that deregulation of big business and tax cuts for the rich would yield a balanced budget and benefits that trickled down to everyone. Instead, the federal government experienced its worst deficit in history to date, and the gap between rich and poor steadily widened.

The murder of John Lennon on 8 December 1980 put the big chill to eliminated any vestiges of the 1960s idealism that had survived the me decade, just as the election of Ronald Reagan one month earlier made it clear that the country was moving in a new political direction.

When Reagan was elected in 1980, the music industry, like society as a whole, was in a state of flux. Disco had fallen victim to its own predictability and the racist backlash of hard rock fans. At the same time, punk had evolved into new wave, an umbrella category so diverse that it was nearly meaningless. As a result, the music industry's marketing categories were temporarily thrown into disarray. For a time, the term *new music* was used to describe everybody from Blondie to Michael Jackson.

In 1979, the U.S. music industry suffered its first major recession in thirty years. Its phenomenal growth in the mid-1970s had led many to believe that it was nearly recession-proof.

Between 1978 and 1979, however, revenues from the sale of recorded music in the United States declined by 11 percent—from an all-time high of $4.1 billion, to $3.7 billion.[1] Over the next few years, U.S. sales fluctuated, bottoming out at $3.6 billion in 1982. International sales followed a similar trajectory, falling 18 percent in three years, from $11.4 billion in 1980 to $9.4 billion in 1983.[2]

LEARN MORE
Learning objectives on MyMusicKit

Hardly the stock market crash of 1929, the decline in revenues was significant for an enterprise that had more than doubled in size in the preceding five years. Within the first five months of decline, 700 record-company employees lost their jobs.[3] Between 1980 and 1986, CBS alone eliminated over 7,000 positions worldwide.[4] Production became more restrictive, making it harder for new acts to break into the business. One estimate suggests that record companies signed about 50 percent fewer artists during the recession than they had previously.[5] Accordingly, the number of new U.S. releases was cut nearly in half over the six-year period from 1978 (4,170) to 1984 (2,170).[6]

Any number of reasons were proffered for the slump. The industry itself favored home taping and piracy as the best explanations. Home taping of music (considered illegal by the industry) was, by far, the weaker explanation because market research showed that the people buying blank tapes were precisely the people buying music. (The introduction of portable cassette players in Walkmans, boom boxes, and car stereos had opened up new opportunities for listening to music. By 1983, the year the U.S. music business recovered from the recession, prerecorded cassettes surpassed record albums in unit sales.) The figures on piracy were more convincing. In 1979, when the U.S. industry was plagued with overstock returns, Al Coury, president of RSO, estimated that 20 to 40 percent of the returns to his company were illegal duplicates.[7] In 1982, the International Federation of the Phonographic Industry (IFPI) estimated piracy at 11 percent of the total market in the United States and Canada, 21 percent in Latin America, 30 percent in Africa, and 66 percent in Asia.[8]

The industry's explanations tended to omit the possibilities of a less-than-exciting period in music, a saturated market, and the failure of its own promotional apparatus. They also failed to note the diversion of their own capital into other ventures, including the burgeoning home video market for films and games. In 1982, for example, Warner's Atari division (maker of Pac Man) accounted for two-thirds of total corporate profits, while its recording interests posted losses of over $100 million.[9] A year later, however, the situation was reversed, as Atari faced losses in the hundreds of millions of dollars and a pared-down record division was once again on its way to financial health. The introduction of the video cassette recorder (VCR) in the late 1970s had created a home market for films on video. By 1980, *Billboard* had started its Video Sales chart, followed in 1982 by its Video Rentals chart. Many record companies, from independents such as RSO, Casablanca, and Island to major conglomerates such as Warner Communications and CBS, had developed film divisions and were betting on strong connections among film, video, and music in the near future. VCR penetration among consumers grew modestly at first but approached 75 percent by the end of the decade.

The technological advances of the late 1970s and early 1980s were about to transform the way in which music was produced and consumed. By the early 1980s, advances in satellite transmission had made possible instantaneous national exposure for recording artists as well as

*B*y the early 1980s, advances in satellite transmission had made possible instantaneous national exposure for recording artists as well as worldwide simultaneous broadcast of performances. At the same time, the global penetration of portable cassette technology provided for individualized reception anywhere in the world.

worldwide simultaneous broadcast of performances. At the same time, the global penetration of portable cassette technology provided for individualized reception anywhere in the world. In the United States, the impact of these new transmission capabilities became apparent in 1981 with the creation of the most powerful music outlet ever—MTV.

Early Music Television: They Want Their MTV

👁 SEE MORE
MTV documentary on MyMusicKit

The presentation of music in a visual context, be it dancing or a live concert, has long been seen as an indispensable part of its promotion. A pop performance is as intrinsically a visual experience as an auditory one. One asks, "Have you ever *seen* Springsteen live?" not "Have you ever *heard* Springsteen live?" The visual impact of a performance enables music to deliver its full measure of pleasure. Many of the first sound films were musicals. For a brief time in the 1960s, video jukeboxes (the Scopitone in France and the Color Sonics machine in the United States) showed groups performing the selected record. In the late 1970s, it was only logical that the visual context for music should become television.

Of course, television had been used to promote popular music for quite some time. In the 1950s and 1960s, recording artists had appeared regularly on family variety shows, and *American Bandstand* had provided national exposure for rock 'n' roll stars. In the 1960s and 1970s, shows like *Shindig, Hullabaloo, The Monkees, The Archies,* and *The Partridge Family,* were organized around rock. The Beatles' promotional film clips for "Penny Lane" and "Strawberry Fields" were produced for television and anticipated some of the videographic techniques used in the 1980s. Indeed, the 1975 film clip for Queen's "Bohemian Rhapsody" is often remembered as the first music video. Music television in the 1980s, however, ushered in a new and innovative era, as video became the standard method for marketing popular music.

The deregulation of television at the start of the 1980s encouraged a massive expansion of cable services throughout the United States and a dramatic increase in the number of available channels, all of which required new forms of programming. At the same time, technological developments enabled the hitherto unconnected media of television, film, and computer games to converge under the rubric of "home video." Soon home stereo was added to the mix, as Robert Pittman, MTV's founding father, recognized in 1981: "We're now seeing the TV become a component of the stereo system. . . . MTV is the first attempt to make TV a new form, other than video games and data channels."[10]

The U.S. music industry was fairly slow to warm up to music videos—a high-budget item with an unknown market. Indeed, music videos have never become consumer commodities in quite the same way as records, tapes, and compact discs. Even in 1989, sales of music videos were a paltry $115 million in the United States, compared to sales of sound recordings at $6.5 billion.

Still, Pittman and his colleagues recognized that music videos could promote the music itself and deliver potential consumers to advertisers.

Thus, with an initial investment of $20 million, MTV, the first twenty-four-hour music video cable channel, was launched on 1 August 1981 by Warner Communications and the American Express Company. The channel, described by Marshall Cohen, then–vice president of marketing, as "the most researched channel in history," was devoted to the science of demographics or, to use Pittman's term, *psychographics*. With 85 percent of its mostly white suburban viewers falling between the ages of twelve and thirty-four, MTV promised to deliver the perfect consumers for a tight economy.[11] In its first year, 125 sponsors bet on that promise and the gamble paid off handsomely. With only 40 percent of the country wired for cable at the time, MTV expanded in two years from an initial 2.5 million subscribers to 17 million in 1983, becoming the fastest growing cable channel in history. It was unquestionably the most effective way for a record to get national exposure.

In his book *Dancing in the Distraction Factory,* Andrew Goodwin identified three periods in MTV's development.[12] The first, 1981 to 1983, was characterized by a twenty-four-hour continuous flow of music with little in the way of discrete programs. During this period, MTV was, in essence, a visual radio station with an album-oriented rock (AOR) format, no news, and continuous music punctuated only by advertisements and the bland patter of the on-camera veejays (video jockeys).

The second period, 1983 to 1985, marked a second launch, as the channel became available in the New York and Los Angeles markets for the first time. During this period, a number of new music video outlets were created to fill in the gaps left by MTV's rock-oriented programming. Black Entertainment Television (BET) devoted about six hours per week to its *Video Soul* program, the primary outlet for video exposure of black artists. USA Cable Network's *Night Flight* showcased the work of some black and Latino acts. *The Nashville Network,* which began in 1983, offered about eighteen hours of country music daily. WTBS inaugurated *Night Tracks,* a program that used a kind of Top Forty format. The networks also moved into music videos with NBC's *Friday Night Videos* and ABC's *Hot Tracks.* MTV bested its U.S. competition at this time by negotiating exclusivity arrangements with a number of major record companies, giving it exclusive broadcast rights to certain videos for one month in return for annual payments of hundreds of thousands of dollars. This period marked the beginning of a major commitment to heavy metal and the ascendancy of the performance clip, a live performance video in which the interaction between the band and their fans served as an indicator of metal authenticity.

The third period saw a broadening of musical scope and a deeper commitment to youth culture. Videos aimed at viewers twenty-five to fifty-four were transferred to the adult-oriented VH-1, a second MTV Networks music video channel. This period also witnessed the departure of Robert Pittman as MTV's auteur and the abandonment of the continuous flow of music in favor of discrete programming, which would eventually rival the cluttered schedules of the networks.

Goodwin has astutely pointed out that most studies of MTV have a postmodernist bent because they focus disproportionately on the first period and Pittman's tenure. During the first period, according to Goodwin, the continuous flow of music "blurred the categories of art-rock and pop, thus contributing toward a conflation of popular and high-cultural discourses."[13] In that period, the U.S. music industry was reluctant to enter the video market, forcing MTV to rely on British music videos, which "tended toward the abandonment of narrative" as groups "eschewed the bland realism of performance videos."[14]

Music videos had developed earlier in Britain because the paucity of radio stations in Britain and throughout Europe had caused British record companies to seek exposure for their artists on television programs such as Britain's *Top of the Pops.* MTV, through these videos (or promo clips), offered bands entry to the U.S. market that was less expensive, cumbersome, and chancy than transatlantic national tours. The videos were conceived as promotional; they were made by producers and directors from the ranks of advertising and they used marketing aesthetics—fast cuts, ever-changing camera angles, eye-catching visuals, and a panoply of special effects. This aesthetic is at the heart of the perception that postmodernism had arrived.

Britain was swept up in the new romantic movement, which, in its reaction to punk, combined black-influenced dance music, synthesizer pop, and a sense of disco glitz in a strikingly visual and unabashedly commercial package that was well suited to televisual presentation.

Adding to this perception was the fact that Britain, at the time, was swept up in the new romantic movement, which, in its reaction to punk, combined black-influenced dance music, synthesizer pop, and a sense of disco glitz in a strikingly visual and unabashedly commercial package that was well suited to televisual presentation. Drawing on the repetitive electronic sounds of Can and Kraftwerk from Germany, British acts like Gary Numan and Ultravox made dance-oriented synth-pop safe for Spandau Ballet ("To Cut a Long Story Short"), Depêche Mode ("Just Can't Get Enough"), Soft Cell ("Tainted Love"), and other new romantics. While the movement itself was short-lived, MTV exposure contributed heavily to the success of these groups.

Throughout Pittman's tenure, MTV devoted a significant portion of its airtime to introducing white rock acts from other English-speaking countries. The channel's first video, "Video Killed the Radio Star," was by Buggles, a British group, and Australia's Men at Work owed their U.S. success completely to MTV. Beginning in 1982, the channel showcased so many English groups (Adam Ant, Billy Idol, Flock of Seagulls, New Order, After the Fire, Thomas Dolby, and ABC, among many others) that it contributed significantly to what can only be described as a second British Invasion. In doing so, MTV propelled Human League's "Don't You Want Me?" to number one on the charts and prolonged the musical lives of the Kinks and the Hollies. It also rejuvenated the career of the supremely telegenic David Bowie when it placed his video of "Let's Dance" in heavy rotation (about half a dozen plays per day) in 1983, giving him his first Top Ten hit in seven years. Other British groups who were proponents of what was called the new pop (Eurythmics, Culture Club, and Duran Duran, among others) also made their U.S. debuts in 1983 on MTV and parlayed their exposure into international superstardom. Annie Lennox of Eurythmics played with androgyny on "Sweet Dreams" while Boy George of Culture Club performed gentle, soulful dance cuts like "Do You Really Want to Hurt Me," "I'll Tumble 4 Ya," and "Karma Chameleon," decked out in heavy makeup and flowing female frocks. In both instances, the music was as satisfying as the visual images were striking. It was Duran Duran, however, that used the visual medium to greater advantage than any other act at the time.

As *Eurythmics*, Annie Lennox and Dave Stewart offered considerable talent and a fresh sound, while Lennox called attention to gender roles as she played with androgyny.

The physical attractiveness of the group (which formed in 1978) was an early indicator of one of the prime requirements for video success. Shortly after the recruitment of the alluring, almost pretty, Simon Le Bon as lead vocalist in 1980, Duran Duran had become the favorite of the teeny bopper set in Britain. Their first video, "Girls on Film," directed by former musicians Kevin Godley and Lol Creme, was so steamy/erotic/sexist (depending on one's perspective) that it was limited in its ability to get public exposure, which naturally identified Duran Duran as a group to watch, so to speak. The videos for "Rio" and "Hungry Like the Wolf," released in the United States in 1983, established them as international superstars. Though group members tried to defend their aesthetic choices as parody, in the eyes of the critics, Duran Duran was clearly eschewing punk's oppositional politics in favor of jet-set images in exotic locations. The video "Wild Boys," directed by Russell Mulcahy, was a surrealistic, science-fiction montage that epitomized the advertising technique of juxtaposing disparate images.

Thanks in large measure to MTV, the second British Invasion, according to *Billboard*, "became a certifiable matter of public record on 16 July 1983, upon which date no fewer than eighteen singles of British origin charted in the American Top Forty, topping the previous high of fourteen, set on July 18, 1965."[15] While many British videos were, in fact, visually more interesting than their U.S. counterparts, MTV's selection process favored British groups at the expense of U.S. artists—especially African American ones. Britain's Thompson Twins ("In the Name of Love") was one of the few integrated groups to appear on the channel. A tally of *Billboard*'s MTV listings showed that, of nearly 100 videos aired the week of 16 July 1983, none by African American artists were in heavy rotation or medium rotation and no new ones had been added to the playlist. No concerts or specials by African American artists had been shown in the history of the channel. Of the U.S. videos shown, the only African American one was Donna Summer's "She Works Hard for the Money," which was in light rotation. Overall, only three black acts (all from other countries) were in medium or heavy rotation.[16] The channel was roundly trashed in the popular press for its racism, which *People* magazine summed up in one line: "On MTV's current roster of some 800 acts, 16 are black."[17] MTV executives claimed that few black artists recorded the kind of rock 'n' roll that their format required. The argument was circular: If the channel's format targeted a largely white suburban audience, then the format itself was racially biased—it could not be used to explain away the racial bias. Furthermore, how could MTV justify programming Phil Collins's note-for-note cover of the Supremes' "You Can't Hurry Love" when Motown acts were getting no airplay? On what basis was Hall and Oates's rhythm and blues (r&b) crossover music considered rock 'n' roll if r&b crossovers by African American artists were not? The channel's racism was exposed on the air when David Bowie caught veejay Mark Goodman off guard with a question about the lack of black artists on the channel. Replied Goodman: "Of course, also we have to try and do what we think not only New York and Los Angeles will appreciate, but also Poughkeepsie or the Midwest. Pick some town in the Midwest which would be scared to death by Prince, which we're playing, or a string of other black faces, or black music."[18]

Perhaps the most blatant act of racial exclusion was MTV's rejection of five Rick James videos at a time when his album *Street Songs* had sold almost 4 million copies. An MTV spokesperson gave the standard reply: "We play rock and roll. We don't play Rick James because he's funk."[19] The response was particularly unconvincing because MTV was playing Prince heavily at the time. While the case could certainly be made that James had a "blacker" sound than Prince, trying to set a rigid outer limit on rock 'n' roll somewhere between Prince's "Little Red Corvette" and James's "Superfreak" could only be considered an exercise in hair splitting. Of course, one possible explanation was the fact that Prince was signed to Warner, an MTV parent company, while Rick James recorded for Motown. In any case, at the time, MTV steadfastly continued its refusal of Rick James videos.

Michael Jackson and the incredible success of *Thriller* finally blew MTV's format argument out of the water. Jackson had already demonstrated his crossover appeal as a member of the Jackson 5 on Motown and as a solo artist on Epic. His first Epic album, *Off the Wall* (1979), produced by Quincy Jones, sold multiplatinum and yielded four Top Ten singles. Still, the album was only a warm-up for *Thriller*, which was number one for thirty-seven weeks in 1983 and generated an unprecedented seven Top Ten singles. It also accounted for a record twelve Grammy Awards in 1983. In fact, *Thriller* set so many records that a consideration of its artistic merit can easily get buried under its impressive statistics. The fact is that *Thriller* was a musical tour de force. Its songs and arrangements were well crafted, its production was crisp and

Because of criticism over reported physical alterations, charges of alleged child abuse, and unfavorable coverage of his failed marriage to Lisa Marie Presley, it is easy to lose sight of the fact that Michael Jackson once broke down racial barriers, set unimaginable sales records, and provided the inspiration and leadership for charity rock in the United States.

uncluttered, its dance grooves were positively infectious, and Jackson's vocals were flawless. On *Thriller*, Michael Jackson demonstrated the versatility that should have earned him the title King of Pop, but given the racial politics of fame, he could only capture that crown by coronating himself a decade later.

On Thriller, **Michael Jackson demonstrated the versatility that should have earned him the title King of Pop, but given the racial politics of fame, he could only capture that crown by coronating himself a decade later.**

The album had something for just about everyone. Its first hit was "The Girl Is Mine," an upbeat pop duet with Paul McCartney that was guaranteed to pull in a middle-of-the-road, adult rock audience. It was followed by "Billie Jean," an exquisitely pulsing rocker with obvious dance floor appeal that was number one for seven weeks. The song that displaced it was "Beat It," an overture to hard rockers that used Eddie Van Halen on guitar. As "Beat It" began its descent from the number one slot, Jackson appeared on *Motown 25,* a TV special celebrating Motown's twenty-fifth anniversary. The show, aired 16 May 1983, reunited first- and second-generation Motown acts such as Stevie Wonder, Marvin Gaye, the Supremes, the Temptations, the Four Tops, and the Jacksons, all of whom, except Stevie Wonder, had long since departed the label. Michael had agreed to appear on the condition that he be allowed to perform "Billie Jean," the only non-Motown song of the evening. As the song's throbbing rhythms came up from the band and a black fedora appeared from nowhere, Jackson teased his audience to shrieks of delight. He then launched into a dance routine that married the fluidity of Fred Astaire to the acrobatics of break dancing, unleashing his now fabled moonwalk on millions of awestruck viewers for the first time. With a single performance, Michael Jackson boosted the sales of *Thriller* beyond all known records.

Even so, MTV at first refused to air the "Billie Jean" or "Beat It" videos. On "Billie Jean," advertising veteran Steve Barron portrayed Jackson as a shadowy figure who leads a private detective through a surreal street scene and vanishes into thin air just as he is about to be captured. Bob Giraldi, also from the world of advertising, shot "Beat It" as a straight ensemble dance number that reportedly used real Los Angeles gang members as well as professional dancers. Both videos made as good use of the medium as any British video and their appeal should have been self-evident, but still MTV resisted. Whether because of the overwhelming popularity of "Billie Jean" or, as widely rumored, because CBS Records threatened to pull all its videos from MTV unless the channel aired Jackson's videos, MTV finally relented.

HEAR MORE
Thriller on
MyMusicKit

"Beat It"

Artist: Michael Jackson
Music/Lyrics by Michael Jackson
(with Quincy Jones)
Label: Epic (1983), from the LP *Thriller*

Funk, disco, and metal meet with visceral force in "Beat It," one of the many huge hits from Michael Jackson's 1983 LP *Thriller*. The precision disco beat and catchy "hook," laid down by L.A.'s finest studio musicians, was further enhanced by a pyrotechnic metal guitar solo by Eddie Van Halen (who, honored and excited by being asked to participate on a Michael Jackson song, reportedly refused to take any money for the session).

Often considered the high point of Jackson's career, *Thriller* and its spin-off videos wedded the masterful production and arrangement skills of producer Quincy Jones with the James Brown–influenced dance and vocal virtuosity that was evident in Jackson even as a 10-year-old Motown star. Both the LP and the videos were lavish, expensive productions, and the associated musical mini-movies raised the bar for music videos in general. *Thriller* catapulted Jackson through the race barrier of white-dominated AOR radio and 1980s MTV, and broke the field of music video wide open for the next wave of funk-influenced African American artists such as Prince.

Musical Style Notes

The backbone of the song "Beat It" is provided by a disco-style electronic drum track, synthesizers, and drum set (played by Steve and Jeff Porcaro of the band Toto), over which a repetitive and compelling melodic vamp is played by bassist Steve Lukather (also of Toto) and guitarist Paul Jackson. Adding to the texture are multiple keyboards, played by Bill Wolfer and Greg Phillinganes (of Stevie Wonder's Wonderlove Band). Layered over this are Michael Jackson's multi-tracked vocals and Eddie Van Halen's guitar solo.

The musical structure is straightforward and typical of song forms found in both rock and disco—verse-verse-chorus—with an improvisatory section (the guitar solo) followed by the repetition of several choruses (see below).

Fun fact: At 2:45 you can hear something that sounds like knocking on a door and then a door closing. Legend has it that this was an engineer who didn't realize Van Halen was about to begin recording his solo.

Musical "Road Map"

TIMINGS	COMMENTS	LYRICS
0:00–0:11	Introduction—synthesized gong sound followed by sharp rhythmic synth hits.	
0:11	Synthesized disco style. Drum track enters.	
0:25–0:39	Repeating guitar/bass vamp begins.	
0:39–0:53	Verse 1	*They told him . . .*
0:53–1:06	Verse 2	*You better run . . .*
1:06–1:27	Chorus (All parts sung by Jackson)	*Beat it . . .*
1:27–1:41	Verse 3	*They're out . . .*
1:41–1:55	Verse 4	*You have to . . .*
1:55–2:29	Chorus	*Beat it . . .*
2:29–2:49	Instrumental interlude providing a transition to the guitar solo. (Listen for the knocking at 2:45.)	
2:49–3:18	Eddie Van Halen's guitar solo.	
3:18–4:17	"Beat it" chorus begins again and repeats until the end of the track.	*Beat it . . .*

Both proceeded to become two of the most popular videos ever—"Billie Jean" widely remembered as the video that broke the color line on MTV.

Having spent $150,000 on the production of "Beat It"—when most videos cost $35,000 to $45,000—Jackson went on to push production costs to the limit by hiring film director John Landis to shoot a $300,000, fifteen-minute version of "Thriller." Jackson recovered his investment when a documentary called *The Making of Michael Jackson's* Thriller, which included the video of the song, sold nearly one-half million copies in 1984.

While charges of racism provided MTV with its first controversy, the treatment of women and the portrayal of gender roles in music videos overall have engendered the longest running debates. The vast majority of MTV videos, particularly in the early years, were by white men aiming for a white male audience; women in these videos were used to hook young male viewers. Early examples include the J. Geils Band's "Centerfold," ZZ Top's "Legs," Van Halen's "Hot for Teacher," and Robert Palmer's "Addicted to Love." Given videos' promotional nature and the fact that many directors came from advertising—where it is axiomatic that sex sells—the sexism in these efforts cannot be attributed to innocent experimentation with a new art form. As Kevin Godley, codirector of Duran Duran's "Girls on Film," has noted, "People are always accusing that video of sexism, and of course they're right. . . . We were very explicitly told by Duran Duran's management to make a very sensational, erotic piece that would be for clubs, where it could get shown uncensored, just to make people take notice and talk about it."[20]

> **W**hile charges of racism provided MTV with its first controversy, the treatment of women and the portrayal of gender roles in music videos overall have engendered the longest running debates.

However, the objectification of women in music videos was not uniform, monolithic, or fixed. As one example, Madonna was routinely taken to task for objectifying herself in her early videos ("Like a Virgin," "Material Girl"). She defended the practice on the basis that she was in control of her image, and critics and her audience have since claimed her as a progressive rock star. "Material Girl," in particular, has been subjected to more scholarly (and mostly feminist) rereadings than any other video.[21] Male stars did not always exploit female images. Lionel Richie's "Hello" and Phil Collins's "One More Night," for example, displayed respect for women. Early music videos sometimes challenged the traditional images of men and women. Annie Lennox and Boy George played with androgyny, as mentioned earlier, and girl-next-door Olivia Newton-John released one of the most popular, if overexposed, videos of the decade, "Physical," which ended somewhat ironically with gay male couples leaving a gym arm-in-arm.

Cyndi Lauper, Donna Summer, and Pat Benatar tried different ways of giving a voice to women. The title of Lauper's debut album, *She's So Unusual* (1984), aptly described the singer with the extreme New York accent, rainbow-colored hair, and thrift-shop fashions. Lauper's three-octave range gave her four Top Ten hits in a row and propelled her to instant, if short-lived, superstardom. On the video of her first hit, "Girls Just Wanna Have Fun," shot in her own home with her real mother, Lauper resisted the confines of traditional feminine roles and used imaginative computer graphics to make the point. Donna Summer's "She Works Hard for the Money" depicted a single, working mother oppressed on the job and faced with the drudgery of housework and ungrateful kids. The bleakness of her life is eased at the end of the video as women from all walks of life gather together to dance in the streets. Pat Benatar's "Love Is a Battlefield" took a similar line. In the video, Benatar portrays a young woman thrown out of her suburban home by unbending parents and forced to work in an urban brothel. She finds strength when she intervenes on behalf of a friend threatened by a surly patron. The video ends with the women dancing defiantly into the street, expressing both female solidarity and the pleasure of dancing together.

MTV debuted at exactly the right time for a music industry battling a recession. By late 1982, record companies could count on a 10 to 15 percent increase in sales for acts that debuted on MTV. Stray Cats sold about 2 million copies of *Built for Speed* (1982) on the strength of the videos for "Rock This Town" and "Stray Cat Strut." The engaging video for the Greg Kihn Band's "Jeopardy" shot the single to number two in 1982. By the week of 10 October 1983, seventeen of *Billboard*'s Top Twenty albums had videos on MTV. Artists took the power of the new medium so seriously that Stevie Nicks scuttled an $85,000 Civil War drama shot for "Stand Back" because she thought she looked overweight in the video.

Given its impact, MTV could have had a major effect on the music industry's star system, particularly because it differed from radio in one significant way. "We play 80 percent new music, 20 percent old," boasted Robert Pittman. "Radio is just the opposite."[22] Radio recognized MTV's power and often added new artists on the basis of video success. This trend indicated that breaking new artists could have been the music industry's way out of the recession, but the major record companies adopted a different and far less democratic strategy.

Superstars: The Road to Economic Recovery

By 1983, the combination of the recession, the U.S. music industry's slowness in embracing music videos, and MTV's reliance on white British acts and its unwillingness to air African American artists had resulted in U.S. pop charts that listed little U.S. music. *Boston Globe* critic Steve Morse noted, "The American pop charts these days have a shocking lack of true American music—especially country rock, blues, soul, rockabilly, folk and rhythm and blues. Or for that matter, black funk and rap music—two more recent styles that have been unable to transcend cult status."[23]

At the same time, as a result of the multiracial programming of Urban Contemporary stations and MTV's preponderance of new music, AOR radio—now the most conservative and segregated format in radio—experienced a significant decline.[24] Responding to these pressures, Lee Abrams, AOR's founder, unveiled a new format called Superstars 83. By year's end, Superstars 83 had been radically revised—ironically, following MTV's reluctant and belated lead—to include black crossover acts like Lionel Richie, Donna Summer, Eddy Grant, Prince, and, of course, Michael Jackson. The appearance of black artists on AOR stations suggested some new developments in the music industry.

In 1978, five transnational music corporations—RCA, CBS, Warner, EMI, and Polygram—controlled, through ownership, licensing, and/or distribution, more than 70 percent of an international music market worth over $10 billion.[25] Both CBS and RCA had reported in 1977 that more than half of their sales came from their international divisions; at the time, however, a marked division still existed between artists aimed at the domestic market and those marketed primarily outside the United States. The surprisingly high international sales figures of the late 1970s were the result of international artists outselling domestic artists. (Spanish balladeer Julio Iglesias, for example, barely made a dent in the U.S. market in the 1970s, even though he lived in the United States and was the best-selling artist in the world at the time.) Despite good international sales in the 1970s, the domestic market was still the main focus of U.S. record companies.

The systematic exploitation of the world market as a condition of further growth did not become dominant until the 1980s. Key to this development was the recognition that the industry's recovery that began in 1983 "was due more to the runaway success of a handful of smash hits than to an across-the-board pickup in album sales."[26] Of course, nothing embodied this reality better than *Thriller*. By 1984, when domestic sales of $4.4 billion indicated that the U.S. music industry had at least returned to its 1978 level of prosperity, *Thriller* was on its way to becoming the best-selling album of all time, eventually reaching sales of some 40 million units worldwide. Its success triggered an era of blockbuster LPs featuring a limited number of superstar artists as the solution to the industry's economic woes. *Thriller* thus underscored the two most salient aspects of the industry's recovery: concentration of product and expansion into international markets.

Of course, globalization affected the treatment of artists at home. "Increasingly, the big record companies are concentrating their resources behind fewer acts," reported the *Wall Street Journal*, "believing that it is easier to succeed with a handful of blockbuster hits than with a slew of moderate sellers."[27] Accordingly, in 1984, Warner Records dropped over thirty artists from its roster, including Arlo Guthrie, Van Morrison, and Bonnie Raitt, who were not quite up to par in terms of sales. (Some, like Raitt, went on to achieve their greatest successes at other labels.) The major labels could have begun scouring the world for new, exciting, and diverse talent, but instead that became a task for independent labels. In the cost-cutting fever generated by the recession, major companies looked to reap greater rewards from fewer artists.

The major labels could have begun scouring the world for new, exciting, and diverse talent, but instead that became a task for independent labels. In the cost-cutting fever generated by the recession, major companies looked to reap greater rewards from fewer artists.

If 1983 belonged to Michael Jackson, 1984 was the year of Prince. Just as Jackson would become the King of Pop, Prince was the heir-apparent to Little Richard, Jimi Hendrix, and Sly Stone, synthesizing funk and rock as masterfully as Sly and the Family Stone had before him. As singer, guitarist, and producer, Prince was able to do all by himself what Michael Jackson needed Quincy Jones and Eddie Van Halen to do for him. Born of an interracial union in middle-class, middle-American Minneapolis, Prince Rogers Nelson, known at the time as Prince, was signed to Warner in 1978 and granted an unprecedented degree of artistic autonomy for a teenager who used music as a vehicle for some very strange notions about sexuality and religion. His first albums were entirely self-written, self-played, and self–produced, and he sang all his own songs. "Soft and Wet" from *For You* (1978), an album dedicated to "God," gave an early taste of themes later included on *Dirty Mind* (1980), which contained odes to incest ("Sister") and oral sex ("Head") as well as other ditties that radio would not touch. Prince seemed quite at home appearing in concerts in black lace underpants, backed by the provocative

Despite the fact that Prince projected a mysterious and seductive R-rated persona in the early 1980s, his music still took the mainstream by storm.

female trio Vanity. For the double LP *1999* (1982), Prince moved closer to the rock mainstream, producing three major hits, including "Little Red Corvette," which became one of the first videos by an African American artist to air on MTV. However, it was not until *Purple Rain* (1984) that Prince was finally crowned.

For *Purple Rain*, Prince assembled the Revolution, a new band that was integrated racially and sexually. Released as both an album and a film of the same name, *Purple Rain* was the kind of triumph of cross-media marketing that Robert Stigwood would have envied. Before the movie opened, "When Doves Cry," the album's first single, had already reached number one; "Let's Go Crazy" hit number one shortly thereafter. The title song was then released and rose to number two. All in all, the soundtrack album, which sold 14 million copies, yielded five hit singles for Prince and two more for the Time, while the movie video sold half a million units within six months of its release. The album's artistry was impressive. The stark rhythms of "When Doves Cry" and the frenzied pace of "Let's Go Crazy" seemed to play fast and loose with the rules of pop, yet both reached number one. On video, Prince unleashed some dance moves that approached Jackson's finesse, and guitar playing that rivaled the best of the heavy metal virtuosos. It was Prince's finest hour.

Purple Rain's occupation of the number one position for twenty-four weeks delayed Bruce Springsteen's entrance into the top slot. *Born in the U.S.A.*, released about the same time as *Purple Rain*, ascended to number one and tied *Thriller*'s record of generating seven Top Ten singles. The album remained in the Top Forty for nearly two years, eventually selling some 15 million copies in the United States and making Springsteen the hottest artist of 1985.

Unlike many other superstars, Springsteen always felt more comfortable on stage than on video. An early clip for "Atlantic City," from his acoustic *Nebraska* album, was a black-and-white collage of mundane images of the Atlantic City boardwalk, parking lots, and casino scenes; Springsteen himself never appeared. Springsteen combined the image of a hard-driving, blue-collar rock 'n' roller with that of a socially conscious 1960s romantic so effectively that he could project the persona of a working-class hero without pretense, even as he carried home tens of millions of dollars from the sale of *Born in the U.S.A.* On that album, Springsteen brought together the unbridled energy of *Born to Run* and the sober portraits of everyday life that comprised *Nebraska*. In "Glory Days" he sang with passion about the troubles of a former high-school baseball star and a divorced prom queen. "My Hometown" was a thoughtful, searching ballad about the deindustrialization of small-town America. "Born in the U.S.A." was a wail about the racism and senselessness of the Vietnam War and the cruel fate that befell its veterans. The song's hook line was so powerful (and so ambiguous) that both the Republican and Democratic presidential candidates in 1984 tried to appropriate the song. Springsteen avoided endorsing

"Born in the U.S.A." was a wail about the racism and senselessness of the Vietnam War and the cruel fate that befell its veterans. The song's hook line was so powerful (and so ambiguous) that both the Republican and Democratic presidential candidates in 1984 tried to appropriate the song.

either of them, concentrating instead on playing benefit concerts to raise money for food banks, soup kitchens, striking miners, and unemployed steelworkers.

Whitney Houston outsold Springsteen, but she never reached his heights as a political icon or culture hero. The daughter of soul singer Cissy Houston and a cousin of Dionne Warwick, Houston, an actress and a model before coming to the attention of Clive Davis at Arista Records, was made for music television. Because few black acts, particularly black female acts, were aired, however, her promotional clips were few and far between. Even so, the playful video for "How Will I Know" helped to maintain her 1985 self-titled debut album in the Top Forty for seventy-eight weeks after it had entered the charts at number one. By the time she released "Where Do Broken Hearts Go" from her second album, *Whitney,* she had tallied seven number one hit singles in a row, a feat unheard of since the Beatles.

Whitney Houston came from a family of rhythm and gospel giants. Although she has tended to play it safe musically, she is capable of combining Aretha Franklin's range and power with her cousin Dionne Warwick's ability to transform pop fluff into a thing of soulful beauty.

Houston had Aretha Franklin's range and power but tended to play it safe as an artist, thus emerging more as pop entertainer than soul diva. "Saving All My Love for You" and "Didn't We Almost Have It All" were fairly standard pop ballads, as was her surefire remake of George Benson's "Greatest Love of All." "How Will I Know" and "I Wanna Dance with Somebody" were middle-of-the-road, if somewhat spirited, dance numbers. What made these songs work as well as they did was Houston's infectious delivery. In this, she was a lot like her cousin Dionne Warwick, who could transform the most vacuous pop material into something soulful. Had she been more adventurous in her material, she might have approached Aretha Franklin's stature as an artist, rather than just topping her sales figures.

Lionel Ritchie was another superstar of this period. As a founding member of the Commodores—playing saxophone and then becoming lead vocalist and main songwriter—he was a versatile performer whose goal had always been maximum crossover. The Commodores' songs routinely registered in the upper reaches of the pop and r&b charts in the 1970s. "Three Times a Lady," a Grammy-nominated number one hit, even earned Richie a country songwriter award from ASCAP in 1978. He went solo in 1981 under the tutelage of Kenny Rogers's manager, Ken Kragen. In 1983, Richie released *Can't Slow Down,* which went to number one in the middle of Michael Jackson mania and remained in the Top Forty for seventy-eight weeks. The album sold 10 million copies and generated five Top Ten singles, including "All Night Long (All Night)" and "Hello," which reached number one, aided by MTV videos. Had it not been overshadowed by *Thriller,* the album would have been the talk of the industry. Richie repeated his success with *Dancing on the Ceiling* (1986), which also went to number one, and issued a documentary on the making of the title song's video, as Jackson had with "Thriller." After "All Night Long (All Night)," Richie's hits tended to be well within the bounds of pop convention, including those with movie tie-ins and high-tech videos.

Madonna combined good promotion, danceable material, engaging choreography, and visual appeal into just the kind of superstar package that the industry wanted. Between 1984

"Born in the U.S.A."

Artist: Bruce Springsteen
Music/Lyrics by Bruce Springsteen
Label: Columbia (1984)

What makes a rock 'n' roll anthem? The term *anthem* originally referred to a sacred vocal piece, usually sung by a church choir. Over the years, *anthem* has come to refer to songs that have symbolic, cultural, or spiritual meaning (for example, national anthems like the "Star-Spangled Banner"). There are particular songs in the history of rock 'n' roll that have generated a strong experience of cultural identity or community. (It also helps if the song has a particularly compelling or hypnotic refrain.) By this definition, Bruce Springsteen's "Born in the U.S.A." is one of the major rock anthems of the early 1980s.

"Born in the U.S.A." is written from the point of view of a Vietnam vet in the late 1970s and early 1980s, having come home to rejection, hardship, and discrimination in the workplace. The song also underscores the fact that it was largely working-class and minority Americans who fought in Vietnam. However, the irony of this song's history is the frequency with which it has been misinterpreted. In 1984, conservative columnist George Will held it up as a shining example of conservative American values; shortly thereafter, President Reagan made a famous reference to the song in a reelection speech. The song is still sometimes misread as a militant "pro-America, right-or-wrong" song, usually by people who know only the words of the refrain and have filled in the blanks themselves.

Musical Style Notes

"Born in the U.S.A." has an interesting asymmetrical structure. While it's basically an example of a verse and refrain form, there are instances in which the refrain ("Born in the U.S.A.") is played but not sung, and in one case, a verse that is extended by a couple of lines, which draws the ear of the listener to that particular verse ("I had a brother at Khe Sahn . . . "). The band also changes the musical texture at certain points, adding and dropping instruments, which lends expressive color to different parts of the text.

The powerful beginning consists of the refrain tune, played by Roy Bittan on keyboard synthesizer and Max Weinberg on drums. (This huge, reverberant drum sound was very popular in the early 1980s and can be heard in the recordings of many other artists, notably Phil Collins.) The other members of the "Born in the U.S.A." version of the E Street Band are Clarence Clemons, saxophone; Danny Federici, keyboards; Bruce Springsteen, guitar and lead vocals; Garry Tallent, bass; and Steven Van Zandt, guitar and vocals.

Musical "Road Map"

TIMINGS	COMMENTS	LYRICS
0:00–0:17	Introduction Keyboard synthesizer and drums, playing the tune of the "Born in the U.S.A." refrain.	
0:17–0:33	Verse 1 (Bruce Springsteen, vocals)	*Born down . . .*
0:33–0:49	Refrain	*Born in the U.S.A. . . .*
0:49–1:04	Verse 2 Entrance of entire band; sound texture thickens.	*Got in . . .*
1:04–1:20	Refrain	*Born in the U.S.A. . . .*
1:20–1:36	Verse 3	*Come back . . .*
1:36–1:53	Refrain music, without words	
1:52–2:22	Verse 4 Note the slightly longer verse—there is no expected line of text after "He's all gone." The next two lines correspond in length to the second half of the other verses.	*I had a brother . . .* *He had a woman . . .*
2:22–2:39	Verse 5 Band drops out; drums synth	*Down in the shadow . . .*
2:39–2:55	Refrain	*Born in the U.S.A. . . .*
2:55–3:11	Refrain Whole band reenters here.	*Born in the U.S.A. . . .*
3:11–3:57	Instrumental refrain, three times Whole band	(Springsteen punctuates this with spontaneous vocalizations—"No, no, no," etc.)
3:42	(Springsteen yelling in background.)	
3:57–4:12	Synthesizer and bass continue refrain. Music; guitar (free form). Drum solos under synth and bass.	
4:12–4:37	Whole band reenters, still playing refrain. Sound gradually fades.	

and 1987, she had twelve Top Ten hits in a row. Nine of them came from two albums, *Like a Virgin* (1984) and *True Blue* (1986). Both albums hit number one and remained in the Top Forty for a year. Madonna began her career as a disco diva with dance-floor hits such as "Holiday," "Borderline," and "Lucky Star" and then used music videos to make the transition to rock star with "Like a Virgin" and "Material Girl." In her videos and live performances, she displayed an adult sexuality that inspired lust in teenage boys, emulation in young girls, and outrage in their parents. Her penchant for Christian iconography sometimes recalled Prince's uneasy marriage of sex and religion. Over the years, she has continued to push sexual expression to the limit of public acceptability and sometimes beyond. Ambitious to the core and one of the most astute businesspeople in the industry, Madonna has always managed to use controversy to generate sales. All of her albums have been certified platinum.

> **M**adonna began her career as a disco diva and then used music videos to make the transition to rock star. In her videos and live performances, she displayed an adult sexuality that inspired lust in teenage boys, emulation in young girls, and outrage in their parents.

A handful of other artists had extraordinary chart runs that generated similar megasales, rounding out the profile of about two dozen or so superstars who could carry the entire music industry. Their multiplatinum figures represented a dramatic statement of how concentrated the industry had become. Interestingly, for many of these artists—the Pointer Sisters certainly come to mind—this period represented some of their best work. In some respects, the industry had come full circle and returned to the days before rock became art, when albums were aggregates of singles. In those early days, however, LPs were crammed with filler in order to sell the artist's current hit at a higher price. In the 1980s, albums were carefully constructed repositories of quality material—designed not as conceptual wholes like *Sgt. Pepper* but as time-release capsules, with individual cuts marketed to the public at precise moments. The goal was not to sell the single—singles had become largely promotional—but to keep the album in circulation and on the pop charts for months on end. As we have seen, music television and cross-media marketing, particularly movie tie-ins, were crucial to this development. (See tables below for additional information.)

Throughout her career, Madonna has tested the limits of acceptable sexual expression. A talented dance/pop diva as well as a consummate businesswoman, she has always managed to turn controversy into record sales.

"Like a Virgin"

Artist: Madonna
Music/Lyrics by Billy
Steinberg and Tom Kelly
Label: Sire, from the LP
Like a Virgin (1984)

From her disco beginnings to her most recent work, Madonna's music has always been about dance. Her intense personal style and charisma, ultrasexual image, pioneering fashion sense, controversial use of religious iconography, and chameleon-like changes in personae are all part of her unique mystique. Musically, however, this Italian American's roots are in African American musical genres. The beat is straight out of disco, and the song structures are straight out of soul and even out of Motown, punctuated with the melismatic "wooo-hooos" of a gospel singer.

"Like a Virgin" was Madonna's first number one single (and remained at number one on the *Billboard* charts for six weeks in 1984). The "Like a Virgin" video was also extremely successful, despite controversy about its sexual content, and it helped catapult her to worldwide fame. One of the most successful artists of the last three decades, Madonna has sold over 300 million records internationally.

Musical Style Notes

The introduction to "Like a Virgin," with its compelling bass-synth pattern, establishes its dance beat immediately. The prevailing sonic texture of disco is also evident in the instrumentation, heavy on synthesizer and keyboards. The verses of "Like a Virgin" have a two-part structure. We hear 8 bars (measures) of music and lyrics, followed by another 8 bars that feature the same music but with different lyrics, continuing into a chorus, which is also 8 bars long. This musical structure, while found frequently in disco, is also found in a lot of Motown songs; in fact, the structure, harmony, and rhythm of "Like a Virgin" are reminiscent of a number of Motown hits (listen again to the beginning introduction, and compare it with the beginning of the Four Tops' 1965 hit "Sugar Pie Honey Bunch"). "Like a Virgin" is a particularly good illustration of the way in which elements of different African American genres—r&b, soul, Motown, and disco—combined to create the building blocks of 1980s dance music.

The players on "Like a Virgin" are bassist Bernard Edwards, guitarist Nile Rodgers, drummer Tony Thompson, synth/keyboardist Rob Sabino, and singer Madonna Louise Ciccone.

Musical "Road Map"

TIMINGS	COMMENTS	LYRICS
0:00–0:07	Synthesized bass and keyboard introduction	
0:07–0:43	Verse 1	*I made it . . .*
0:43–1:00	Chorus	*Like a virgin . . .*
1:00–1:35	Verse 2	*Gonna give you . . .*
1:35–1:52	Chorus	*Like a virgin . . .*
1:52–2:08	Instrumental bridge, layered over with melismatic vocal part on the syllables *woo hoo*	
2:08–2:28	Verse 3 (half as long as previous verses)	*You're so fine, . . .*
2:28–2:44	Chorus	*Like a virgin . . .*
2:44–3:00	The instrumental musical material of the chorus continues, with vocal improvisations, using the words of the chorus.	*Like a virgin . . .*
3:00–3:35	Further vocal improvisations over music of the chorus, now using vocal syllables as well as slightly changed lyrics (Track fades to ending.)	*oh-ho . . .* *Can't you hear . . .*

Selected Albums with One-Year Top Forty Chart Runs, 1983–1986

ARTIST	ALBUM (YEAR)	TOP FORTY CHART RUN
Michael Jackson	*Thriller* (1983)	Ninety-one weeks
Huey Lewis and the News	*Sports* (1983)	Seventy-one weeks
Lionel Richie	*Can't Slow Down* (1983)	Seventy-eight weeks
Madonna	*Like a Virgin* (1984)	Fifty-two weeks
	True Blue (1986)	Fifty-two weeks
Billy Ocean	*Suddenly* (1984)	Fifty-seven weeks
Pointer Sisters	*Breakout* (1984)	Sixty-five weeks
Bruce Springsteen	*Born in the U.S.A.* (1984)	Ninety-six weeks
Tina Turner	*Private Dancer* (1984)	Seventy-one weeks
Wham!	*Make It Big* (1984)	Fifty-six weeks
Phil Collins	*No Jacket Required* (1985)	Seventy weeks
Whitney Houston	*Whitney Houston* (1985)	Seventy-eight weeks
Anita Baker	*Rapture* (1986)	Seventy-two weeks
Janet Jackson	*Control* (1986)	Seventy-seven weeks
Steve Winwood	*Back in the High Life* (1986)	Sixty weeks

((•● **HEAR MORE**
Audio links for long-running Top Forty Albums on MyMusicKit

Chris Blackwell explained in 1986, "If you're in the entertainment business on the music side, you really need to be in films as well because I think they're really joining into one business."[28] In this way, too, the industry had come full circle. Just as Tin Pan Alley had solidified its dominance through its relationship with Hollywood films in the 1930s and 1940s, record companies now did so in the 1980s. Indeed, music had become so integral to films that it affected how they were made. In the 1970s, *Saturday Night Fever* (the film) had made it difficult to hear the Bee Gees' "Stayin' Alive" without imagining John Travolta strutting down the streets of Brooklyn. *Flashdance* and *Footloose* created similar associations in the 1980s; the 1987 sleeper hit *Dirty Dancing* completed the fusion of music and film. *Dirty Dancing*'s soundtrack music became the focal point of the film. Bob Buziak, the RCA president who authorized both film and soundtrack, noted at the time:

> The movie *Back to the Future* grossed $150 million and had a No. 1 single with Huey Lewis; the soundtrack album only sold 600,000. That's because the music was "wallpapered" into the movie, and the songs were not an essential part of the emotional experience. For a soundtrack to be really successful—like *Top Gun* or *The Big Chill*—you have to hear what you see.[29]

By harnessing all the technology and marketing tools at its disposal, the music industry created a small, internationally popular roster of superstars who could generate unheard-of profits. Revenues increased steadily after 1983, even though total unit sales declined from 680 million in

Selected Top Ten Hits with Movie Tie-Ins, 1984–1986

ARTIST	SONG (YEAR)	MOVIE
Phil Collins	"Against All Odds (Take a Look at Me Now)" (1984)	Against All Odds
Kenny Loggins	"Footloose" (1984)	Footloose
Pointer Sisters	"Neutron Dance" (1984)	Beverly Hills Cop
Huey Lewis and the News	"The Power of Love" (1985)	Back to the Future
Billy Ocean	"When the Going Gets Tough, the Tough Get Going" (1985)	Jewel of the Nile
Lionel Richie	"Say You, Say Me" (1985)	White Nights
Tina Turner	"We Don't Need Another Hero (Thunderdome)" (1985)	Mad Max: Beyond Thunderdome
Berlin	"Take My Breath Away" (1986)	Top Gun
Kenny Loggins	"Danger Zone" (1986)	Top Gun
Madonna	"Live to Tell" (1986)	At Close Range

HEAR MORE
Audio links for Top Ten Hits with Movie Tie-Ins on MyMusicKit

1984 to 618 million in 1986. In other words, the U.S. music business was making more money selling fewer recordings. This development was aided by another technological advance: the compact disc (CD), introduced simultaneously by Sony and Phillips in the late 1970s. As a digital configuration, the CD promised better sound quality and ease of use than either records or tapes. Although CDs cost no more to produce than records or tapes, demand allowed companies to charge more for them. In 1986, "[t]he sale of 53 million CDs generated almost as much income ($930 million) as the 125 million LPs sold ($983 million)."[30]

Perhaps the most striking fact about the new star system was that a significant number of the superstars—Michael Jackson, Prince, Lionel Richie, Tina Turner, Whitney Houston, Billy Ocean, the Pointer Sisters, Janet Jackson, Anita Baker, Stevie Wonder, Kool & the Gang, Luther Vandross, and Diana Ross—were African American. This may have been the first indication that the greater cosmopolitanism of a world market could change the complexion of popular music at home. International acceptance, it appeared, provided clout that could lead to superstardom at home. Nineteen of the Top Fifty albums of 1985 were by black artists. Eight of the twelve most popular hits of 1986 were by African American artists, four of whom were women. As *Billboard*'s Paul Grein noted in 1986:

> *Perhaps the most striking fact about the new star system was that a significant number of the superstars were African American. This may have been the first indication that the greater cosmopolitanism of a world market could change the complexion of popular music at home.*

> *Black music has been setting the pace in pop for the past four years, with Michael Jackson, Lionel Richie, and Prince & the Revolution leading the way. . . . [I]n 1986 . . . female artists came to the forefront. . . . The popularity of black female singers was dramatized in June, when "Whitney Houston," Patti LaBelle's "Winner in You" and Janet Jackson's "Control" held down the top three spots on the Top Pop Albums chart. It was the first time that black artists—or female artists, for that matter—had ever achieved that monopoly.[31]*

During this time, African American producers such as Quincy Jones, Nile Rogers, Narada Michael Walden, Jimmy Jam, and Terry Lewis also came to the fore and paved the way for L. A. Reid and Babyface Edmunds toward the end of the decade.

Most of the white artists who achieved superstardom during this period were heavily influenced by black music. Madonna started as a disco artist and kept abreast of the urban dance music scene throughout her career. Phil Collins had enjoyed a fruitful relationship with the Earth, Wind & Fire horn section since his earliest solo hits. George Michael—formerly of Wham! (which evidenced a Motown influence)—regularly crossed over to the black music market; in 1989, he won the American Music Award for Best Black Male Vocal. Bruce Springsteen's music had r&b roots. Indeed, according to *Billboard,* the rest of the white rock scene was "in something of a sorry state. Urban/dance-oriented rock sounds seemed to garner the lion's share of chart success in 1986, with major names such as Robert Palmer, Peter Gabriel, and Steve Winwood all leaning more toward r&b than rock on their platinum releases."[32]

In the 1980s, record companies came to realize that their products' longevity was the key to their financial well-being. If black artists could demonstrate staying power, then black artists would become superstars. Second in importance to longevity was breadth of audience. The strategy of appealing to as wide an audience as possible led to the release of a number of well-calculated cross-racial/cross-ethnic duets in the 1980s.

When Paul McCartney teamed up with Stevie Wonder in 1982 to record "Ebony and Ivory," the recording was seen as a breakthrough for racial harmony. McCartney then sang with Michael Jackson on "The Girl Is Mine" in 1982 and "Say, Say, Say" in 1983. This latter recording was supported by one of the few interracial videos on MTV, although one had to wade past the trappings of minstrelsy in its staging, costuming, and blackface makeup to appreciate its significance. These projects can be viewed optimistically as attempts to break down the segregation of the music industry or cynically as two commercial giants cashing in on each other's superstardom. Julio Iglesias was introduced to the U.S. mainstream through two 1984 duets, one with Willie Nelson ("To All the Girls I've Loved Before") to see if he might spark the country end of the market and one with Diana Ross ("All of You") to test his appeal among black listeners. Other cross-racial pairings ranged from pop-oriented commercial gambits to socially conscious anthems.

These cross-racial successes encouraged record companies to spread even single acts to multiple marketing categories. In 1985, Kool & the Gang released *Emergency,* which, on the strength of three Top Ten singles, remained in the Top Forty for nearly a year. The group finished the year in the number one position on the black music charts and among the top twenty acts on the pop, adult contemporary, and dance charts. Madonna registered on the same four charts that same year, topping both the pop and dance categories. Stevie Wonder also found acceptance in these marketing categories when "Part-Time Lover" (1985) reached number one on all four charts during 1985. As a whole, in their attempts to consolidate cross-racial markets, these efforts brought a new dimension to the very term *crossover.* A few crossover projects seemed to have a higher purpose. "Sisters Are Doin' It for Themselves" (1985), by Eurythmics and Aretha Franklin, included a video portraying women in a broad range of leadership roles. Proceeds from the sale of the number one single "That's What Friends Are For" by Dionne

Warwick and Friends (Elton John, Gladys Knight, and Stevie Wonder) went to finance AIDS research. But these efforts had the benefit of hindsight, as they ventured down a trail that had been blazed some eight months earlier by the ultimate crossover recording—"We Are the World."

Charity Rock and Mega-Events: Who is the World?

International superstars and technological wonders like satellite transmission and the portability of cassettes had, by the mid-1980s, made popular music truly global. Perhaps nothing better illustrates this phenomenon than the string of socially conscious mass concerts and all-star performances, known as mega-events, that began in 1985 with Band Aid, Live Aid, and "We Are the World." Because these projects, somewhat cynically dubbed charity rock, also aided transnational record companies in finding new markets, they have sometimes been written off as politically irrelevant. More often than not, however, this judgment is too facile.

While a handful of major corporations have always exercised tight economic control over the international music market, acquiring the lion's share of the market is not synonymous with determining the form, content, style, and impact of popular music. If anything, in their relentless pursuit of higher profits, record companies have tended to relinquish artistic control and to move further and further away from the creative process. By the beginning of the 1980s, music, to the transnational corporate giants, had become a "bundle of rights" for things like television, movies, and advertising. Focused on these new sources of income, the industry cared little to intervene in musical content except when forced to do so (see Chapter 10).

In their relentless pursuit of higher profits, record companies have tended to relinquish artistic control and to move further and further away from the creative process.

Thus, in the mid-1980s, popular music tended to develop according to two opposing principles that corresponded roughly to the extremes of the commercialism/authenticity continuum. On the commercial end, record companies discovered that their back catalogues were gold to filmmakers and advertisers. Ben E. King's "Stand by Me" was featured in an eponymous film, and Levi used it to sell jeans in Britain; as a result, the 1961 r&b classic reentered the British charts and generated brisk sales in the United States as well. Cream's "I Feel Free" was used to sell cars; the Doors' "Riders on the Storm," to sell tires. The Beatles' "Revolution" turned up as the soundtrack for a Nike commercial. In the 1990s, even Dylan's "The Times They Are A-Changin'" was used to promote an accounting firm. "What's new about the rock/ad agency tie-in," said Simon Frith, "is not the exploitation of stars' selling power as such . . . but the use of anticommercial icons to guarantee the 'authenticity' of the product they're being used to sell."[33] If commercialism compromised authenticity, it was recovered somewhat by the more humanitarian impulse of charity rock. This humanitarian bent was colored, according to John Rockwell of the *New York Times,* by "rock's leftist bias," which "arose from its origins as music by outsiders" and "was solidified by the 1960's, with its plethora of causes and concerns . . . Rock music was the anthem of that change—racial with the civil-rights movement, and also social, sexual, and political."[34]

Christmas in Ethiopia: The Advent of Charity Rock

The story of charity rock begins with the energy and imagination of Bob Geldof, leader of the Boomtown Rats, an Irish punk group. Inspired to action by a BBC documentary on Ethiopian famine, Geldof, with Midge Ure of Ultravox, wrote "Do They Know It's Christmas." He then organized the biggest names in British popular music to record the song as Band Aid, with all proceeds donated to famine victims. "Do They Know It's Christmas" became the biggest selling U.K. single ever, totaling 7 million copies worldwide. Geldof tried to organize a similar project in the United States but was stonewalled by some artists. "Look, they viewed me as a minor pop singer from England," he told *Rolling Stone.* "From their point of view, it's like Joe Blow calling up. . . . But if Ken Kragen calls up, they know it's kosher. They know that Lionel [Richie] and Quincy [Jones] will be there and that you're gonna have a good show."[35] This is, of course, exactly what happened.

In the United States, charity rock was organized by Harry Belafonte and Ken Kragen, who, as manager for both Lionel Richie and Kenny Rogers, covered a broad range of pop terrain with the credibility that Geldof lacked. Artistic leadership was provided by African Americans, with Michael Jackson way out front. "We Are the World," co-written by Jackson and Richie, was produced by Quincy Jones, with Jackson as music director. It was released by an all-star ensemble called U.S.A. (United Support of Artists) for Africa—also the name of the organization administering the record's profits. Kragen served as president of U.S.A. for Africa.

"We Are the World" brought together a range of artists who might not otherwise have appeared on the same stage. In so doing, the project opened the door to bolder undertakings like "Sun City."

"We Are the World" was an upbeat pop ditty structured around cameo appearances by the biggest names in U.S. popular music—Michael Jackson, Lionel Richie, Bruce Springsteen, Kenny Rogers, Billy Joel, Madonna, Cyndi Lauper, Diana Ross, Huey Lewis, Bob Dylan, Stevie Wonder, Ray Charles, and more. Because it fit promoter Bill Graham's description of 1980s rock as "the voice of corporate America," it proved to be an easy target for the critics. "With *We Are the World*, I know what they *meant*," said Jackson Browne. "But on the other hand, that's the problem with North America. We think we *are* the world!"[36] When it was released, Greil Marcus argued that the song

> *sounds like a Pepsi jingle—and the constant repetition of "There's a choice we're making" conflates with Pepsi's trademarked "The choice of a new generation" . . . and the true result will likely be less that certain Ethiopian individuals will live . . . than that Pepsi will get the catch phrase of its advertising campaign sung for free by Ray Charles, Stevie Wonder, Bruce Springsteen, and all the rest.*[37]

There was also a distasteful element of self-indulgence in the "saving our own lives" line because the performers were proclaiming their own salvation for singing about an issue they would never experience on behalf of a people most of them would never encounter. Even so, "We Are the World" became for charity rock what "We Shall Overcome" was to the civil rights movement and helped to clear the way for Live Aid, the largest single event in human history.

Live Aid made Marshall McLuhan's global village something of a reality for at least sixteen hours. It was organized as an act of will by Geldof, who conned, cajoled, even resorted to what he called "moral blackmail" to convince more than sixty artists (not to mention promoters, ticket sales agencies, merchandising concerns, sponsors, satellite operators, and radio and television stations) to donate their time and/or money to the cause. The event was organized as a Band Aid project. U.S.A. for Africa did not participate as an organization and neither Jackson nor Richie appeared, though the concert closed with an ensemble rendition of "We Are the World." The concert was staged simultaneously at Wembley Stadium in London and JFK Stadium in Philadelphia on 13 July 1985, and it was broadcast either live via fourteen satellites or pretaped to more than 1.6 billion people in 160 countries.

Although the widely rumored Beatle reunion with Julian Lennon sitting in for John never happened, Live Aid had its share of classic rock 'n' roll moments. Keith Richards and Ron Wood of the Rolling Stones joined Bob Dylan for an all-star performance of "Blowin' in the Wind." Mick Jagger teamed up with Tina Turner for what one newsweekly called a "delightfully lascivious" version of "State of Shock." The Who played together for the first time in three years, and Led Zeppelin and Crosby, Stills, Nash & Young reunions occurred, although time and various indulgences had taken their toll. Daryl Hall and John Oates joined former Temptations David Ruffin and Eddie Kendricks for some show-stopping choreography. Phil Collins managed to perform at both Wembley and JFK by zooming across the Atlantic on the supersonic Concorde. Geldof's own magic moment occurred when he was hoisted onto the shoulders of Paul McCartney and Pete Townshend on stage for all the world to see.

"We Are the World" became for charity rock what "We Shall Overcome" was to the civil rights movement and helped to clear the way for Live Aid, the largest single event in human history.

HEAR MORE
Bob Geldof on
MyMusicKit

Shared by 1.6 billion people in 160 countries, Live Aid was the largest single event in human history. The live concert was staged simultaneously at Wembley Stadium in London and JFK Stadium in Philadelphia.

In both the popular and trade presses, the concert was celebrated and criticized—celebrated for "weld[ing] together popular art and humane politics, for using the power, energy and invention of rock & roll to accomplish something of practical social value"[38] and criticized for its paucity of black and Latino artists and its trivialization of the issues. MTV, which carried the full sixteen-hour telecast, was the primary target for criticism in the United States because its veejays showed more interest in displaying themselves than in the issues at hand or the value of rock history. As the reunited Led Zeppelin launched into their seminal "Stairway to Heaven," the cameras cut to Martha Quinn looking enraptured. The performance of rap group Run-D.M.C., one of the few youth-oriented black groups booked for the event, was short-shrifted so that MTV could cover Sting's backstage arrival. Although the veejays could not be blamed for directorial decisions, their interview questions seldom went deeper than "What does Live Aid mean to you?" Hype, glitter, and industry gossip routinely took precedence over education, analysis, and a call to action.

Comparisons with other rock events abounded, the most obvious being to Woodstock. Indeed, Joan Baez opened the Philadelphia show with, "Good morning, you children of the 1980s. This is your Woodstock and it's long overdue." In point of fact, however, Baez's comments reflected wishful political thinking. Woodstock was the product of a bygone era; it was experienced as participatory, communitarian, and anticommercial. Live Aid was an unabashed celebration of technological possibilities in a period of yuppie conservatism, with corporate sponsors—AT&T, Eastman Kodak, Chevrolet, and Pepsi—that would have been anathema to the Woodstock generation. "The politics of Woodstock were antiauthoritarian, antiestablishment, antiwar," said commentator Pete Hamill. "The American Live Aid audience was part of a new American generation that thinks Ronald Reagan is a wonderful president, Rambo a wonderful role model, and Grenada a wonderful war."[39]

Still, as Will Straw pointed out, "The most underrated contribution rock musicians can make to politics is their money, or ways in which that money might be raised."[40] The actual take from Live Aid was $67 million, a staggering amount of money by any fund-raising standard. Even so, Geldof, who was nominated for the Nobel Peace Prize for his efforts, recognized its limitations: "I'm aware that a million dollars is a lot of money, but when 130 million people are affected by this problem, even $67 million is nothing."[41] The question remained as to what extent Live Aid had served the cause at hand versus to what extent it had served capital. At the 1986 ceremony of the British Phonographic Industry's (BPI) awards, Norman Tebbitt of the Thatcher administration "extolled Live Aid as a triumph of international marketing."[42] On this side of the Atlantic, John Costello, vice president of Pepsi, said: "Live Aid demonstrates that you can quickly develop marketing events that are good for companies, artists, and the cause."[43]

Mega-Events: The Politics of Mass Culture

To many, charity rock was a contradictory phenomenon. It provided activist musicians with a platform for political expression on a previously unthinkable scale while enabling the music industry to exploit a gold mine of untapped markets. Such competing tendencies encouraged a new view of mass culture. Far from being considered a cultural wasteland of mindless consumption, many activists now came to see mass culture as "contested terrain"—an ideological cauldron in which new values could be forged.

To many, charity rock was a contradictory phenomenon. It provided activist musicians with a platform for political expression on a previously unthinkable scale while enabling the music industry to exploit a gold mine of untapped markets.

Band Aid, Live Aid, and U.S.A. for Africa created a climate in which musicians worldwide felt compelled to develop African famine relief projects. For a partial list: as Northern Lights, Canada's top pop stars recorded "Tears Are Not Enough"; West Germany's all-star Band fur Ethiopia released "Nackt im Wind"; as Chanteurs Sans Frontieres, thirty-six French singers offered "Ethiopie"; Belgium contributed "Leven Zonder Honger"; the Netherlands, "Samen"; Australia, "E.A.T." (East African Tragedy); and fifty African artists, including Youssou N'Dour, Hugh Masakela, Manu Dibangu, and King Sunny Ade, recorded "Tam Tam Pour L'Ethiopie."[44] These efforts created the cultural space for progressively bolder projects, including some that targeted issues closer to home. An offhand comment by Bob Dylan about the plight of the family farm, made from the stage at Live Aid, prompted Willie Nelson, John Cougar Mellencamp, and Neil Young to organize Farm Aid two months later. Nelson cajoled country artists from Kenny Rogers and Glen Campbell, to Alabama and the Charlie Daniels Band, to Merle Haggard and Loretta Lynn to perform. Young and Mellencamp pulled in rockers ranging from Billy Joel and Don Henley, to Eddie Van Halen and Sammy Hager, to X and the Blasters. The concert brought together a unique coalition of rock and country artists who were uncommonly respectful of one another, raised $10 million, and became an annual event that has extended into the new millennium.

Other, more politicized ventures followed, including Sun City, two Amnesty International tours, and two tributes to (South) African National Congress leader Nelson Mandela. Using "We Are the World" as a model, guitarist Little Steven, from Springsteen's E Street Band, assembled more than fifty rock, rap, r&b, jazz, and salsa artists to create the recording "Sun City," a politically charged anthem supporting the UN-sponsored cultural boycott of South Africa, which was then under white minority rule. "Sun City" urged musicians not to perform at the lavish Las Vegas–like entertainment complex of the same name that was located in one of the so-called South African homelands. Symbolically, it upped the political stakes of all-star recordings significantly.

In some ways, "We Are the World" was the logical extension of the crossover strategy developed in the mid-1980s. It was a pop-oriented tune that primarily used rock, country, and r&b artists who had achieved mainstream acceptance. Live Aid had broadened the politicization of mass culture a bit more by including heavy metal acts like Judas Priest and Ozzy Osbourne, new wave groups like Simple Minds and the Boomtown Rats, r&b artists like Patti LaBelle and Ashford and Simpson, and rappers like Run-D.M.C. "Sun City" pushed this process even further with a powerful composition and an explicitly anti-apartheid message. It had a broad range of artists—jazz great Miles Davis; salsa stars Ray Baretto and Rubén Blades; rappers Afrika Bambaataa and Run-D.M.C.; and two South African groups, the Malopoets and Via Afrika, who risked personal reprisals for participating—as well as politically outspoken artists such as Jackson Browne, Bonnie Raitt, Peter Garrett from Midnight Oil, and Bono from U2. Its video masterfully intercut scenes of the horrors of apartheid with cameo appearances of the performing artists. It climaxed with the ensemble cast singing the anthemic chorus at a New York divestment rally at CitiBank, then segued seamlessly to a demonstration in South Africa with black South Africans singing "Nkosi Sikelel' iAfrica," the (unofficial) black South African national anthem. The creators of "Sun City" also encouraged their audience to become informed and active on the issue. The album jacket, for example, was filled with information about apartheid, and a teacher's guide showed how to use the record and the video in the classroom.

In 1986, U2, then an up-and-coming Irish rock band from Dublin, headlined the Conspiracy of Hope, a U.S. tour for Amnesty International. As a group of politically progressive, devout Christians, U2 represented an organization that advocated for prisoners of conscience around the world. Formed in 1977, U2 first cracked the U.S. Top Forty in 1983 with *War,* which included "Sunday Bloody Sunday," the group's most poignant political commentary. With the release of *The Unforgettable Fire* (1984), which included the hit single "Pride (In the Name of Love)," they began their ascent to superstardom. By 1987, they were the hottest rock act in the world. *The Joshua Tree,* released that year, went to number one and charted in the Top Forty for more than a year, winning the 1987 Grammy Award for album of the year.

Jack Healy, then executive director of Amnesty International USA, organized the Conspiracy of Hope Tour and engineered the connection between rock and the human rights movement. One of the tour's goals was to recruit new "freedom writers" to participate in

Amnesty's letter-writing campaigns on behalf of prisoners of conscience. Thus, as part of the event, the tour targeted six political prisoners, three of whom were freed within two years as a result. In addition, Amnesty/USA added some 200,000 volunteers to the organization. "Previous to 1986, we were an organization post forty," said Healy. "Music allowed us to change the very nature of our membership."[45] In 1988, Healy organized a world tour, the Human Rights Now! Tour, featuring Springsteen, Sting, Peter Gabriel, Tracy Chapman, and Youssou N'Dour as headliners supported by acts from host countries. Sting, who had left the Police in the mid-1980s, was riding high from the successes of *The Dream of the Blue Turtles* (1985) and . . . *Nothing Like the Sun* (1987). Gabriel's *So* (1986), the best-selling album of his solo career, had catapulted him to international superstardom, and he was already well respected as the prime mover of WOMAD, the international World of Music, Arts, and Dance Festival. Chapman's self-titled debut album hit number one in 1988, enabling Healy to add some diversity (musical and otherwise) to the bill. N'Dour was Senegal's most popular artist and a master of the African funk, rock, and jazz fusions becoming popular internationally. Springsteen was Amnesty's best-selling artist, but the tour had as big an effect on him as he had on it. As Healy recalled:

> *I remember Bruce Springsteen saying that he'd played to his first black audiences on the Human Rights Now! Tour in Zimbabwe and the Ivory Coast. We played to Shintos in Japan, Hindus in India, uptight Orthodox Christians in Greece, a mix of religions in Zimbabwe and a lot of Muslims in the Ivory Coast. And Bruce was loved by all of them; he rocked the stadiums everywhere.*[46]

After the tour, Amnesty boasted 420,000 members worldwide, with an average age of twenty.

Two massive international concerts were staged at Wembley Stadium on behalf of Nelson Mandela: the first on 11 June 1988 to celebrate his seventieth birthday—while he was still imprisoned in South Africa; and the second on 16 April 1990 to celebrate his release two months earlier. The eleven-hour birthday tribute featured a remarkably diverse roster of first-rate talent[47] and was broadcast to an estimated 600 million people in more than sixty countries.

In calling for the release of Mandela, the leader of the African National Congress (ANC)—an organization considered illegal by most countries broadcasting the concert—the tribute raised the political stakes for mega-events once again. The stage was adorned by a thirty-foot scrim of Mandela's image perched tastefully atop the slogans "Isolate apartheid" and "The struggle is my life." The massive speaker columns were flanked by exact replicas of the late Keith Haring's "Free South Africa" poster. Just as "Sun City" pushed the limits of politicized pop, urging artists and fans to move from charity to action, the Mandela shows also broadened the political scope of tours, asking audiences to help bring structural change to South Africa.

Just as "Sun City" pushed the limits of politicized pop, urging artists and fans to move from charity to action, the Mandela shows also broadened the political scope of tours, asking audiences to help bring structural change to South Africa.

The first Mandela tribute had to balance the need to recruit stars who could ensure the event's financial success with the need to present artists committed to the cause at hand. In the push to book name acts, artists like Billy Bragg and South Africa's Johnny Clegg were passed over for Whitney Houston and others—for which the event's organizers were roundly criticized. However, Houston was one of the first artists to commit to the festival and delivered the most animated performance of the day. Her overwhelming popularity helped make the event attractive to broadcasters all over the world, and she was a favorite of the imprisoned ANC leaders. Ahmed Kathrada, an ANC rebel serving a life sentence with Mandela, sent a message that was distributed by the local Anti-Apartheid Movement and quoted in *Rolling Stone*: "You lucky guys. What I wouldn't give just to listen to Whitney Houston! I must have told you that she has long been mine and Walter's [Sisulu] top favorite. . . . In our love and admiration for Whitney we are prepared to be second to none!"[48]

Organizers of the second concert, An International Tribute for a Free South Africa, had only fifty-four days to produce the event. Still, they assembled an impressive lineup of artists, with stars like Peter Gabriel, Tracy Chapman, Bonnie Raitt, Anita Baker, Neil Young, Natalie Cole, and Lou Reed, among many others. The 72,000 tickets sold out faster than any other event in the history of Wembley Stadium. Of course, the real headliner was Nelson Mandela. His presence made the concert irresistible to broadcasters from some sixty-three countries worldwide. Even South Africa proposed to carry the show, a proposal eventually rejected by the ANC in support of the cultural boycott of that country. Thus, it was all the more shocking that not one U.S. broadcaster would air the event. The only North American broadcaster was MuchMusic, Canada's equivalent of MTV.

Mandela, with his dignified but forceful demeanor and steadfast refusal to compromise his principles, drove home his anti-apartheid message to hundreds of millions of people throughout the world. He indicated his understanding of the power of mega-events when, backstage, he thanked the performing artists for their efforts:

> *Over the years in prison I have tried to follow the developments in progressive music. . . . Your contribution has given us tremendous inspiration. . . . Your message can reach quarters not necessarily interested in politics, so that the message can go further than we politicians can push it. . . . We admire you. We respect you, and above all, we love you.*[49]

Environmental concerns were also on the international political agenda in the late 1980s. Early in 1989, Geffen Records and cable music channel VH-1 promoted a project for

Greenpeace, an international environmental group. As its contribution, VH-1 produced over two dozen minute-long spots with celebrities discussing environmental issues. Artists from U2 and the Talking Heads to John Cougar Mellencamp and Belinda Carlisle donated twenty-seven hit songs to an album, *Rainbow Warriors,* released as *Breakthrough* in the former Soviet Union. It became the top-selling record in that country, with all proceeds split between Greenpeace and the Soviet Foundation for Survival and Development of Humanity. Our Common Future, another environmental extravaganza, was staged at Lincoln Center in 1989; participants included Bob Geldof, Sting, Midnight Oil, Herbie Hancock, and actor Richard Gere, as well as scientists and world leaders, who used that platform to voice their concerns over global environmental decline. It was a little unnerving for some, however, to see Margaret Thatcher delivering a taped message about Britain's fears for the environment. Clearly, the show's politics were compromised by sponsorship of the event by multinational corporations, including Sony, Panasonic, and Honda.

Dave Marsh has been particularly critical of corporate involvement in mega-events, claiming that it robs "charity-rock of one of its most important selling points: the selflessness of its motivation."[50] Given the scale of mega-events, however, most would be impossible without some kind of corporate sponsorship. Amnesty's Human Rights Now! Tour would have gone bankrupt had not Reebok bailed it out. The mega-events of the 1980s developed a momentum that obliged corporations and world leaders to accommodate initiatives that were essentially humanitarian or progressive.

Indeed, this momentum affected the culture of popular music in general. As Simon Frith and John Street have noted: "The paradox of Live Aid was that while in the name of 'humanity' it seemed to depoliticise famine, in the same terms, in the name of 'humanity' it politicised mass music."[51] Mellencamp's "Rain on the Scarecrow," about the despair of modern rural life, was connected to his involvement in Farm Aid. Jackson Browne's interest in Central America led to "Lives in the Balance," a moving criticism of U.S. intervention in Central America. Likewise, there was a resonance between Sting's participation with Amnesty International and his "They Dance Alone," about the widows of "disappeared" political activists in Chile. With "Luka" (1987), singer/songwriter Suzanne Vega highlighted the issue of child abuse. A number of rap groups, including Public Enemy, Boogie Down Productions, and Stetsasonic, participated in "Self-Destruction," the anthem of the Stop the Violence movement, which protests black-on-black crime. For Spike Lee's film *Do the Right Thing,* Public Enemy contributed "Fight the Power," the soundtrack for the most powerful statement about racism in the 1980s. By the end of the 1980s, there was scarcely a social issue that was not associated in a highly visible way with popular music and musicians.

The 1980s mega-events also had an unintended but progressive side effect on the music industry itself. Because these performances included a broad range of artists, the outlets that carried the performances contributed significantly to undermining the apartheid of the industry's traditional formats, which were fragmented by class, race, age, and ethnicity. "Whoever buys ['Sun City']," remarked coproducer Arthur Baker, "is going to be turned on to a new form of music, just as whoever sees the video is going to be turned on to an artist they've never seen before."[52] For a brief time in the 1980s, the internationalization of the music industry became a two-way process, albeit a limited one. While Anglo-American music was disproportionately broadcast to a worldwide audience, artists like Youssou N'Dour and Sly and Robbie did gain greater access to the world market. It was more than a coincidence that the emergence of world music (also known as world beat) in developed countries paralleled the development of charity rock. A greater awareness of world cultures, in turn, influenced the character of mainstream popular music at home. Jackson Browne incorporated Central American sounds on *Lives in the Balance* (1986); David Byrne of the Talking Heads explored Afro-Brazilian music on *Rei Momo* (1989). Perhaps the best-known—and most controversial—fusion of mainstream popular music and international music styles was Paul Simon's *Graceland,* in many ways a pivotal album of the 1980s.

Released in 1986, *Graceland* was based primarily on South African musical styles and incorporated an incredible diversity of cultural influences, ranging, in the words of ethnomusicologist Steven Feld, from

> *Quirky 1960's Long Island/Brill Building Simon lyrics, pedal steel guitar riffs from a Nigerian Jùjú band player via Nashville recordings, vocals from Senegalese Youssou N'Dour on break from recording projects with British pop star Peter Gabriel, and everything else from Synclavier samplers and drum machines to the Everly Brothers and Linda Ronstadt . . . with exemplars of zydeco . . . and East Los Angeles Chicano rock and roll. . . .*[53]

Historically, the album has taken its place as a defining contribution to that amorphous category of world music or world beat. As such, it has been at the heart of highly politicized discussions concerning musical appropriation and ownership on the one hand, and cultural imperialism on the other. On the album, Simon demonstrated his talent as a musician with a fine ear for exotic sounds. He offered three times union scale for sessions and gave appropriate co-writer credits on collaborative songs. He was respectful of South African music and worked with notable black South African artists like Ladysmith Black Mambazo and other first-rate studio musicians. The album also featured performances by Los Lobos and zydeco legend Rockin' Dopsie. The result was a hauntingly beautiful compilation that effectively linked South African rhythms with a range of regional ethnic U.S. influences.

Applying his ability as a singer/songwriter and fine ear for multicultural sounds, Paul Simon created one of the most celebrated and criticized albums of the 1980s. He is pictured with the late Joseph Shabalala, leader of Ladysmith Black Mambazo, who were among the featured South African artists to appear on Graceland.

Still, as critics noted, most of the album was recorded in South Africa in violation of the UN cultural boycott. (This may explain why Simon appeared on "We Are the World" but refused to participate in the more radical Sun City project, which directly supported the cultural boycott.) In using Linda Ronstadt, who had performed at Sun City, as a backup vocalist, Simon simply added to the insult of his own violation of the cultural ban. If his purpose was to showcase black South African music, one had to wonder why he named the album after the estate of Elvis Presley, a white American who had captured the rock 'n' roll crown by employing (some would say imitating) African American musical styles. Simon was also criticized for registering the producer's credit and all the copyrights in his own name, which ensured him any music awards as well as the lion's share of subsequent royalties. He was likewise vulnerable to the charge that his songs avoided political content. Under considerable international pressure, he added explicitly anti-apartheid performers such as Miriam Makeba and Hugh Masakela to his 1987 Graceland Tour.

Because Simon considered himself anti-apartheid (he recorded in South Africa but did not perform there), he and many others tended to dismiss the criticisms. He felt vindicated after receiving both the 1986 Grammy Award for Album of the Year and the 1987 producer's Grammy for Record of the Year. Accordingly, *Graceland* was celebrated, according to Feld, as "a melding of mainstream 'world' pop and African 'folk' musics; the major anti-apartheid consciousness-raising and publicity event of 1987; and a major international market breakthrough for the South African musicians."[54] Five years later, however, on the eve of Simon's 1992 South African tour—the first by a major U.S. artist after cultural sanctions were lifted—the offices of the promoter and sound company were bombed by the Azanian National Liberation Army. While the tour was supported not only by the white minority government but also by two of South Africa's main black organizations (the ANC and the Inkatha Freedom Party), many in South Africa felt that lifting sanctions was premature and that Simon was an appropriate target because of the *Graceland* controversy. In the international community, *Graceland* produced passionate responses on both sides of the political divide, reinforcing the notion of mass culture as contested terrain.

Mega-events themselves faded from view in the early 1990s, coinciding with the disintegration of the Soviet Union and the establishment of global capitalism as a single worldwide economic system. They did not reappear until opposition to this new economic order had reached mass-movement proportions. But by then, the contradictions involved in negotiating music's dual role as cultural force and commercial product had become all but unmanageable. In 2005, the twentieth anniversary of Live Aid, Bob Geldof organized Live 8, an eleven-concert global extravaganza, designed to "make poverty history" by pressuring the world's richest countries, known as the G8, to pledge increased aid and greater debt relief for Africa.[55] Two years later, Al Gore spearheaded Live Earth to spread his "inconvenient truths" about the environment to a global audience through 24 hours of concerts on seven continents. Just as Live Earth issued a "call to action," Live 8 promoted itself as a movement-building exercise, announcing on its website: "We don't want your money. We want you." But rather than adopt the oppositional politics of the antiglobalization movement, Live 8 organizers chose to negotiate with

But rather than adopt the oppositional politics of the antiglobalization movement, Live 8 organizers chose to negotiate with the G8, leaving a trail of broken promises and reducing the audience to consumers of the event rather than developing their potential as political activists.

the G8, leaving a trail of broken promises and reducing the audience to consumers of the event rather than developing their potential as political activists. As of this writing, neither campaign had significant concrete accomplishments to point to, although such events do provide an opportunity keep critical issues in the public eye.

LEARN MORE
Chapter Questions
on MyMusicKit

By the mid-1980s, the music industry had bounced back from the doldrums of worldwide recession and had resumed its pattern of more or less steady growth now tied to international sales. If Michael Jackson's Thriller *represented the revitalization of the music industry as an international cultural force, Paul Simon's* Graceland *embodied all the contradictions involved in trying to manage the unequal distribution of cultural power. Technological advances had brought the cultures of the world closer together, and while these developments created possibilities for musical expression that were new and exciting, they also allowed the music industry to centralize its operations. In attempting to use the power of popular music to foster greater understanding and empathy among different cultures, mega-events politicized popular music while providing the music industry with access to new international markets. In both instances, they generated considerable controversy. During this period in the United States, new developments in rap and heavy metal became the focus for controversy. By the late 1980s, rap and metal had become the defining elements of a new disaffected youth culture and precipitated the most concerted attempt to regulate popular music since rock 'n' roll's payola hearings.*

Rap and Metal: The Voices of Youth Culture

10

In the mid-1980s, a powerful convergence of forces took place in popular music. Aided significantly by technological advances, mega-events politicized popular music to a greater extent than at any time since the 1960s. At the same time, MTV—itself a product of new technology—renewed its focus on youth culture. As in the 1960s, a connection emerged among youth, music, and politics that soon became most apparent in the phenomenal expansion of rap and heavy metal. At this cultural moment, the Parents Music Resource Center (PMRC), a Washington-based pressure group, launched its campaign against explicit lyrics in popular music. The music industry found itself embroiled in a battle over the values and principles that would guide the country into the next decade and perhaps the next century. The PMRC initially targeted heavy metal; as rap gained in prominence, however, it became the focal point of conservative wrath.

> **A**s in the 1960s, a connection emerged among youth, music, and politics that soon became most apparent in the phenomenal expansion of rap and heavy metal.

Technology, of course, has been a central factor in forging links among youth, their music, and politics. Just about all successful popular recording artists make use of technological advances, but rap and metal artists, more than others, have incorporated these advances into the very essence of their music. Both styles have also sought to upend the underlying logic of the improvements. While the history of sound recording can be read as a quest to eliminate noise, both rap and metal have used "cleaner" technology precisely to achieve a "dirtier" sound. Metal has used it in the service of volume and distortion; rap, in the organization of its disparate sonic elements.

Given metal's preoccupation with power, it has always relied greatly on technology. The heavily distorted guitar sound—the most obvious sign of heavy metal power—occurs when an amplifier is overdriven (driven beyond its capacity to deliver a clean sound). In the 1960s, Jimi

Hendrix achieved this effect through the creative use of feedback, using the operating noise of the amplifier to overwhelm the signal of the guitar. In the 1980s, Eddie Van Halen used a voltage regulator to increase power to his amp. Heavy metal vocalists often use vocal distortion boxes to create a menacing growl.

In the case of rap, dual turntable rigs were transformed into full-fledged musical instruments, and boom boxes became localized radio stations, often to the dismay of nearby listeners. In the mid-1980s, rap artists began to use samplers (digital devices capable of recording, storing, and reproducing any sound in nature perfectly) and drum machines to construct the basic building blocks of a rap composition: the rumbling bass tones that can destroy car radio speakers, familiar beats looped into endless repetition, found sounds and prerecorded tracks reshuffled into an original sound collage.

One aspect of rap that is analogous to power in heavy metal is the concept of noise. As rap has strayed further and further from middle-class conventions, it has come to be defined less by melody and harmony and more by the notion of organized sound or noise. In titling her seminal analysis of rap *Black Noise,* Tricia Rose used the noun to explicate not only rap's relationship to technology but also a new development in the history of black orality and a cultural device for political resistance.[1] Public Enemy's "Bring the Noise," for example, assaults the listener with a dense mix of samples and synthesized noise. Borrowing from the gospel call-and-response style, Chuck D's vocal exhortation "Turn it up!" is answered by DJ Terminator X with furious record scratching (back cueing a record with the sound system turned on). As a whole, then, "Bring the Noise" mounts a defiant challenge to mainstream listeners through its intentionally aggravating use of noise.

> **B**oth rap and heavy metal have used the power of noise to assault traditional musical conventions and to trace the boundaries of youth culture. In doing so, they have provided highly visible targets for the self-proclaimed custodians of good taste.

Both rap and heavy metal have used the power of noise to assault traditional musical conventions and to trace the boundaries of youth culture. In doing so, they have provided highly visible targets for the self-proclaimed custodians of good taste. At the same time, both genres have their defenders. Reflexive dismissals of metal's racism and misogyny—common during its first wave—have tended to give way to more complex rereadings of the music in some people's efforts to understand the youth culture of the 1980s and 1990s. Similarly, issues of violence and misogyny in rap have become part of a dialogue about class, age, and gender differences within the black community and the relationship of black youth to the mainstream culture. As a result, both genres have become arenas for what can be viewed as a battle for American values.

The Continuing History of Heavy Metal

After its initial surge in the early 1970s, heavy metal seemed destined to be a short-lived phenomenon. First-generation fans began to move on to new styles and the succeeding generation of (white) youth gravitated toward punk. Still, metal never disappeared completely. Artists like Ted Nugent, Aerosmith, and Kiss had consistent runs of gold and platinum releases throughout the late 1970s. As the statement of a more or less coherent subculture, however, the music was in decline. Feminist criticism of metal's misogyny had caused many thinking fans to reevaluate the music, and punk had supplanted metal's "empty virtuosity" with a more defiant political statement. Beginning at the turn of the decade, however, a resurgence of the music transformed it into the dominant expression of youth culture in the 1980s.

Heavy Metal: The New Wave

Key to the metal revival were the groups that *Sounds* magazine dubbed and promoted as "the new wave of British heavy metal." These groups—Iron Maiden, Def Leppard, Motörhead, Saxon, Venom, Angelwitch, Diamond Head, and so on—filled the void after first-wave British metal groups like Deep Purple and Led Zeppelin ceased touring or went into tax exile. Judas Priest, still in its ascent, had temporarily abandoned the British audience following their successful U.S. tour as the opening act for Zeppelin in 1977. (They redeemed themselves partially with the release of *Stained Class* in 1978.) Two of the new groups—Iron Maiden and Def Leppard, both founded in the midst of punk—achieved worldwide success. AC/DC, created in Australia in 1974 around a core of British ex-patriots, rode the new wave in the United States. The nucleus of AC/DC was brothers Angus and Malcolm Young on guitars and Bon Scott on lead vocals. Having achieved Australian and British chart success with early releases such as *Let There Be Rock* and outrageous stage shows, AC/DC broke into the U.S. Top Forty with the more occult-oriented *Highway to Hell* (1979) just before Scott died from the effects of alcoholism. With Brian Johnson as his replacement, AC/DC's momentum continued with three Top Ten long-playing records (LPs) in a row, climaxing with *For Those About to Rock We Salute You* in 1981, which went to number one. Def Leppard shared AC/DC's management. Their debut album, *On Through the Night* (1980), established them as part of Britain's new wave. Aided by MTV, Def Leppard's *High 'n' Dry* (1981) broke into the U.S. Top Forty. Iron Maiden opened for Judas Priest, which helped push their debut album to number four in Great Britain, but they did not hit the U.S. Top Forty until 1982, with Bruce Dickinson as lead singer on *The Number of the Beast,* another album that appealed to fascination with the occult.

No particular brand of metal dominated the British new wave. Motörhead attracted a punk following with pounding cuts played at breakneck speed—for example, "Overkill" and "Bomber"—thus aligning the band with the speed metal style that grew out of L.A. hard core. They continued in this vein throughout the 1980s, peaking early with *Ace of Spades* and the live album *No Sleep Till Hammersmith.* Iron Maiden, fairly eclectic in its references and musical moods, leaned toward traditional heavy metal; pegged by *The Number of the Beast* as a Satanist group, they used Satanism as one of several sources to explore morality, power, and chaos. "Run for the Hills" addressed the plight of Native Americans; "Stranger in a Strange Land" and "Sea of Madness" spoke to the alienation of youth. Guitarist/composer Steve Clark brought his classical training to Def Leppard's style. On *High 'n' Dry*, the group's producer, Mutt Lange, played up the music's melodic elements, propelling them toward a more pop sound—described somewhat disparagingly by Philip Bashe as "metal pop" and by Deena Weinstein as "lite metal."[2]

HEAR MORE
Heavy Metal on MyMusicKit

Even with such variation, certain elements united these new wave groups under the heavy metal banner. "What all the new bands did share," Weinstein has written, "was a general heavy metal sensibility, along with youthfulness and a strong emphasis on visual elements."[3] According to Robert Walser, "[T]he new wave of metal featured shorter, catchier songs, more sophisticated production techniques, and higher technical standards."[4] In the United States, Van Halen was the embodiment of these characteristics. Throughout the 1980s, the group turned out nothing but Top Ten platinum albums; *1984,* on the charts for over a year, yielded the number one single "Jump." Until he was replaced in the mid-1980s, lead singer David Lee Roth provided a striking visual focus with his macho aerobic performances, and lead guitarist Eddie Van Halen had been setting the standard for technical virtuosity for years.

Randy Rhoads was another standout guitar virtuoso of heavy metal. Like Van Halen, Rhoads was classically trained and claimed influences that ranged from Alice Cooper to Vivaldi. He made a name for himself as a member of Quiet Riot, a hard-rocking metal act from Los Angeles, then became Ozzy Osbourne's lead guitarist, linking the new virtuosity with traditional British heavy metal. Rhoads's classical influence can be heard on two 1981 recordings, "Goodbye to Romance" and "Mr. Crowley," and a live recording of "Suicide Solution," released on *Tribute* in 1987, five years after Rhoads's death in a plane crash. Following his death, the torch of virtuosic brilliance was picked up by Sweden's Yngwie Malmsteen. Although his debut release in 1984 led *Guitar Player* to name him Best Rock Guitarist in 1985, Malmsteen did not break into the U.S. Top Forty until three years later, with *Odyssey*. More of a musician's musician than a commercial success, Malmsteen "adapted classical music with more thoroughness and intensity than had any previous guitarist, and he expanded the melodic and harmonic language of metal while setting even higher standards of virtuosic precision."[5]

Of course, virtuosity in heavy metal—indeed, in the context of Western music generally—as Walser has astutely pointed out, "has always been concerned with demonstrating and enacting a particular kind of power and freedom that might be called 'potency.' Both words carry gendered meanings, of course; heavy metal shares with most other Western music a patriarchal context wherein power itself is construed as essentially male."[6] Thus, unsurprisingly, throughout its first generation, heavy metal was the exclusive province of (young, white) males. No female musicians to speak of played heavy metal, unless one extends the genre's boundaries to include the Wilson sisters from Heart. Indeed, precious few women attended metal concerts; those who did were accepted as subcultural equals only when they conformed to the masculine codes of dress (jeans and black T-shirts) and evidenced the proper knowledge and love of the music. Women in "feminine" garb were usually regarded as groupies, on hand to service the band sexually. It wasn't until 1980 that an all-female metal band released an album in the United States—*Demolition* by Girlschool, part of the British new wave. They achieved some respect and chart position in Britain after touring with Motörhead; U.S. success, however, never came their way.

Around 1983, the next wave of metal began to arrive from Los Angeles. Groups like Mötley Crüe and Ratt tended toward a glam rock appearance, harkening back to the New York Dolls, and a *lite* metal sound. Mötley Crüe opened for Kiss in 1983, which helped to push the

P*recious few women attended metal concerts; those who did were accepted as subcultural equals only when they conformed to the masculine codes of dress (jeans and black T-shirts) and evidenced the proper knowledge and love of the music.*

group's *Shout at the Devil* album into the Top Twenty. Ratt first hit the Top Ten with *Out of the Cellar* in 1984. Other L.A. groups included Quiet Riot, Dokken, and W.A.S.P. Quiet Riot scored two hit singles—"Cum on Feel the Noize" (1983) and "Bang Your Head (Metal Health)" (1984) from their *Metal Health* album—rare for a metal band at the time. Dokken's *Tooth and Nail* (1984) failed to crack the Top Forty but found a spot on *Hit Parader*'s Top 100 Metal Albums, as did their Top Twenty *Back for the Attack* (1987). The latter promoted a consistent image of male victimization at the hands of the femme fatale, an oft-used misogynist device in metal. Though they had a hard-core following, W.A.S.P. never had a major hit in the United States. The group's importance was blown out of all proportion when right-wing critics of heavy metal discovered "Animal (F**k like a Beast)," a song disturbing to many in its celebration of the sheer physicality of sex.

The Los Angeles metal scene was given a boost by the U.S. '83 Festival, organized by Steve Wosniak, co-founder of Apple Computer. Taking heed of the audience fragmentation that had occurred since the 1960s, Wosniak organized the event around different genres on different days. The heavy metal day—with Ozzy Osbourne and Judas Priest from Britain; Scorpions from Germany; Triumph from Canada; and Van Halen, Quiet Riot, and Mötley Crüe from Los Angeles—drew the largest crowd. The festival and the fact that the major U.S. groups were from L.A. prompted other metal acts, including Poison and Guns 'N' Roses, to relocate. Poison, in particular, was well suited to the glam look and the lighter sound that characterized much of the L.A. scene. The group's carefully tended, artfully moussed, blow-dried hair led it, along with Ratt and the lesser known White Lion, to be dubbed "hair" bands. Female artists like Lita Ford and Vixen emerged from that scene, too, and achieved a measure of metal fame in the late 1980s.

Crucial to the growth of metal, particularly the L.A. variety, was its MTV exposure. The genre had been largely excluded from radio since its beginnings. While some album-oriented rock (AOR) stations programmed metal in the late 1970s, they cut back on it significantly in the early 1980s during ratings wars with other formats. Even fledgling MTV was reluctant to air heavy metal. During its second period, however, MTV "programmed heavy metal with a vengeance."[7] Among its more prominent metal groups were Mötley Crüe, Quiet Riot, Dokken, Twisted Sister, and Scorpions. According to Andrew Goodwin,

> *as MTV expanded from the main urban centers of the United States on the coasts into midwestern cities and towns, it needed to reach out with music that appealed to the rockist tastes of its new demographics. Furthermore, the network was no longer dependent on a relatively small number of clips originating in Europe. These factors colluded to generate MTV's embrace of heavy metal music.*[8]

Heavy metal's MTV success led to its increased programming on radio. The real payoff, of course, was in sales. *Billboard* reported that the music's market share jumped after a year of heavy play on MTV from about 8 percent in 1983 to 20 percent in 1984.[9]

Metal's advance was slowed temporarily in 1985 when right-wing Christian fundamentalist groups and various conservative civic, professional, and watchdog organizations pressured MTV into cutting back on its metal programming. MTV tried to justify its acquiescence by claiming that it had cut back to focus on more cutting-edge product, but according to Linda Martin and Kerry Segrave, "[A]s most of the industry saw it . . . MTV was bowing to the pressure of various conservative watchdog groups who had been complaining."[10] This campaign had immediate results: Metal's market share dropped to 15 percent in the first quarter of 1985.[11] By this time, however, metal had developed an irrepressible momentum. By the end of 1986, the demand for it had become so great that MTV created a weekly all-metal program, *Headbangers' Ball*, that gave the music its due and placed some of its more objectionable videos in an after-hours slot. *Headbangers' Ball* had 1.3 million viewers each week, becoming MTV's most popular show.

For a music defined, in part, by transgression, increased acceptance into the mainstream of U.S. popular culture was a mixed blessing. In many ways, the bonds of the heavy metal subculture had been forged in the cauldron of exclusion and outsider status. Before mass acceptance, songs could be longer, instrumentals could be privileged over vocals, and live performance could be accorded a higher cultural value than studio production. And hit singles were unnecessary. But mainstream recognition brought pressure for a more polished (commercial) sound. Thus, metal's expansion beyond its original subcultural following paralleled its fragmentation.

Metal Fragments

By the late 1980s, the heavy metal press had become rife with distinctions among categories. *Traditional* or *classic heavy metal* was used to describe the original sound of wildly distorted guitar, heavy bass and drums, and raw, unadorned vocals. *Lite* or *pop metal* emphasized sweeter vocals, even harmony. *Glam metal* was defined by a particular look. *Thrash* and *speed metal* featured faster tempos derived from punk. *Death metal,* a subcategory of speed/thrash, focused on the issue of death. *Black metal* focused on Satanic themes, with *white metal* its Christian counterpart. For all these distinctions, however, there were really only two camps. At one end of the spectrum was lite metal and at the other were the groups lumped together as speed/thrash metal.

Lite metal groups like Def Leppard, Quiet Riot, Van Halen, Mötley Crüe, and Bon Jovi were favored by MTV, gained greater access to radio, and expanded into stadium-size venues. Lite metal initially transformed the metal audience from subculture to mass culture and altered its gender balance.[12] A number of lite metal albums signaled the transition. Def Leppard's *Pyromania* (1983) reached number two and remained on the charts for over a year. The album's three hit singles generated album sales of 7 million units, a sure sign that metal was moving beyond subculture status. Quiet Riot's *Metal Health* and Van Halen's *1984* made similarly impressive showings, peaking at numbers one and two, respectively.

These albums also marked the period when the MTV performance clips came into frequent use. This was, according to Goodwin, "a direct result of the need for heavy metal acts to establish an 'authentic' (i.e., documentary rather than fictional) set of images and to display musical competence."[13] According to E. Ann Kaplan, these clips were typical of the "nihilist heavy metal video," in which

> the male body is deliberately set up as object of desire: zoom shots pick up male crotches and bare chests in an erotic manner and instruments are presented as unabashed phallic props. . . . [T]hese videos . . . adopt a challenging, aggressive stance toward the fans and spectators. . . .[14]

While Kaplan aptly describes metal's preoccupation with reinforcing an unstable and insecure masculinity, she acknowledges that "a more complicated set of discourses" was involved. David Lee Roth, who was let go as Van Halen's lead singer shortly after "Jump" became the group's most popular single, argued that "a lot of what I do can be construed as feminine. My face, or the way I dance, or the way I dress myself for stage."[15] The lure of androgyny as a transgressive social practice was strong in metal, particularly among glam metal groups. It complicated metal's masculinist codes and, in conferring prestige on traditionally female signs, may have accounted for some of metal's positive appeal among young women.

The lure of androgyny as a transgressive social practice was strong in metal, particularly among glam metal groups. It complicated metal's masculinist codes and, in conferring prestige on traditionally female signs, may have accounted for some of metal's positive appeal among young women.

Romance was adopted as a metal topic in the mid-1980s, also clearly extending metal's appeal to women. Before this, themes of romantic love had been conspicuously absent from the genre, which helped to maintain metal as a bastion of male bonding. Offering a broader analysis, Walser notes: "Until the mid 1980s one of these three strategies—misogyny, exscription, androgyny—tended to dominate each heavy metal band's 'aesthetic.' A fourth approach, increasingly important in recent years, 'softens' metal with songs about romance; this kind of music has drawn legions of female fans to metal."[16] The pivotal album in this regard was Bon Jovi's *Slippery When Wet* (1986).

Bon Jovi was formed in New Jersey in the early 1980s. In its first incarnation, the group sported many characteristics of the standard heavy metal band—doom and gloom lyrics, macho performances, a leather/mascara look, and the powerhouse sound of distorted guitar. In keeping with metal's preoccupation with power and phallocentric imagery, the group's first Top Forty album was named *7800° Fahrenheit,* the temperature of an erupting volcano. For *Slippery When Wet,* however, Bon Jovi traded in their leathers and makeup for the more casual bluejean look of rock authenticity. Lead singer Jon Bon Jovi projected a vulnerability rare among heavy metal artists, which allowed the group to draw effectively on pop's tradition of love songs. Put together, these new elements had enormous appeal for female fans; *Slippery When Wet* became one of the decade's best-selling albums. It rose to number one on the charts and stayed in the Top Forty for well over a year, generating two number

Jon Bon Jovi, leader of the group that bears his surname, started out as a leather-clad rocker who then drew legions of female fans to heavy metal with themes of romance and his vulnerable good looks.

"Jump"

Artist: Van Halen
Music/Lyrics by Van Halen
Label: Warner Brothers,
from the LP *1984* (1984)

One of the most famous synthesizer intros in the history of rock 'n' roll begins this classic 1984 hit by Van Halen. While Van Halen was known as a heavy metal band, this song is a quintessential pop hit in terms of its structure, its unforgettable hook, the power of the rhythm section, the rocking guitar solo, and the joyous and infectious refrain. Synthesizers, invented in the 1950s but only widely employed in rock beginning in the 1970s, had become associated with some of the most pretentious excesses of art rockers, as well as the often sterile and sometimes antiseptic dance beats of 1980s new wave and disco. Eddie Van Halen was the first musician since Pete Townsend (who had practically reinvented the rock synthesizer with his definitive parts on *Who's Next?*) to understand that synths could *rock*, that (plugged into a Marshall amp and turned up to 10) they could deliver just as much visceral power as a Les Paul guitar.

Musical Style Notes

Eddie Van Halen's signature virtuoso guitar style featured a technique known as two-handed tapping, exploiting the heavily amplified electric guitar's sensitivity and response. Guitarists for decades had employed the techniques called hammer-ons and pull-offs, in which the fretting-hand's fingers would tap down on the strings, or pull them sideways, thus providing two or more notes for each pick stroke. Eddie Van Halen was the first metal guitarist to exploit the possibility of *both* hands tapping down on the fingerboard. This in turn allowed Eddie—a trained pianist who had grown up playing Bach and Mozart—to play very fast, two-part, widely spaced, cascading, classical-style solos at screeching volume. In his speed, imagination, ability to construct totally memorable guitar riffs, fantastic command of guitar tones, and telepathic communication with drummer/brother Alex, Eddie was unquestionably the most influential hard-rock guitarist of the late 1970s and early 1980s.

Like so many great pop hits, "Jump" opens with a first iteration of the fantastic hook, a simple, synth-driven chord progression that recurs as a refrain throughout the tune. Though the band was widely criticized for having "gone soft" because the A section features synth instead of heavy guitar, the simple, repetitive, major-key straightforward synth chords provide a wonderful contrast to the B section and to the minor-key guitar solo.

In the B section, you can also hear the bass playing a syncopated rhythm. A syncopation happens when one plays between the main beats or when two instruments play in different rhythmic units against each other. Here, for example, the bass temporarily counts in 6, and the rest of the group counts in 4. The bass then transitions at the end of the line to get back "in sync" with everyone else. Here is that relationship written out in a chart:

count in 4	1	+	2	+	3	+	4	+	1	+	2	+	3	+	4	+	1
Can't you	see	me	stand-	ing	here	I	got	my	back	a	gainst	the	rec-	ord	ma-	chine	
bass notes:	/			/			/			/		/		/		/	/
count in 6	1	2	3	4	5	6	1	2	3	4	5	6	(1	2	3	4)	1

The players in this version of Van Halen were Eddie Van Halen, guitar, keyboards, Oberheim OB-XA synthesizer, and background vocals; Alex Van Halen, drums; Michael Anthony, bass and background vocals; and David Lee Roth, lead vocal.

Musical "Road Map"

TIMINGS	COMMENTS	LYRICS
0:00–0:14	Introduction: fat-sounding synth bass note, over which we hear the repeated chord progression that constitutes the famous "Jump" riff. This is punctuated with drum kicks and a scream by singer David Lee Roth.	
0:14–0:28	Rhythm track is layered over synthesizer riff.	
0:28–0:59	Verse 1, section A Two sections, 8 bars each	*I get up . . .* *And I know . . .*
0:59–1:15	B section; new melody and lyrics. Listen to syncopation in bass at beginning (see Musical Style Notes above).	*Can't you see . . .*
1:15–1:30	Chorus	*Might as well . . .*
1:30–	Verse 2 (only 8 bars—half as long as Verse 1)	*Ah, oh! . . .*
1:45	B section returns.	*Can't you see me . . .*
2:01	Chorus	*Ah, might as well . . .*
	Roth yells "JUMP!"—which cues guitar solo.	
2:17	Eddie Van Halen's guitar solo	
2:31	Solo focus switches to synthesizer (also played by Eddie Van Halen).	
3:05	Reprise of synth introduction riff	
3:19	Chorus (repeats until fade)	*Might as well . . .*
3:35	Chorus repeats, fade to end.	

one hit singles, including "Livin' on a Prayer," a classic love-conquers-all composition. In part because the group included keyboards, Bon Jovi's inclusion in the heavy metal category is controversial in certain circles. However, Walser has convincingly argued that their music falls within the genre: "Features of heavy metal are evident in the timbres and phrasing of both instruments and vocals. . . . The sustained and intense sounds of heavy metal are channeled behind the romantic sincerity of pop, while smooth, sometimes poignant synthesizer sounds mediate the raw crunch of distorted guitar."[17]

If lite metal was the expansionist wing of metal, speed/thrash metal was preservationist, seeking to fortify the boundaries of an exclusionary male subculture.

Against this backdrop of upbeat, forward-looking pop crossover, speed/thrash metal, which emerged in reaction to the perceived compromises of lite metal, turned inward to forestall the further dilution of the genre. If lite metal was the expansionist wing of metal, speed/thrash metal was preservationist, seeking to fortify the boundaries of an exclusionary male subculture. In the words of Deena Weinstein:

> *Speed/thrash can be understood as an attempt to reclaim metal for youth and especially for males by creating a style that is completely unacceptable to the hegemonic culture. Speed metal represents a fundamentalist return to the standards of the heavy metal subculture.*[18]

Speed/thrash metal began as a West Coast phenomenon (primarily in Los Angeles and San Francisco) with groups like Metallica, Slayer, Testament, Megadeth, Exodus, and Possessed, who eschewed the glamour and popularity of lite metal in favor of an underground club scene where the subculture could be maintained more easily. They were later joined by other groups, including Anthrax, Nuclear Assault, Suicidal Tendencies, Annihilator, and Sepultura. Speed/thrash's creators were influenced as much by hard-core punk as by earlier forms of heavy metal. From punk came faster tempos, more hostile postures, and menacing vocals; from heavy metal came sheer volume and ensemble virtuosic precision. Lyric content, according to Weinstein, "specializes in chaos. Sex is rarely mentioned, alcohol and drugs are judged to be bad rather than pleasurable. . . . Themes of lust and romance are ceded to lite metal."[19] The resultant fusion, according to the *Boston Globe,* was "ugly, nasty, angry."[20] Still, while speed/thrash metal tended to focus on the darker side of life, as evidenced in the growth of death metal, it was not, as many of its detractors have claimed, simply empty nihilism. Societal themes ran through the music. Metallica's *. . . And Justice for All* expressed a concern for justice, while Nuclear Assault's "Inherited Hell," Testament's "Greenhouse Effect," and Metallica's "Blackened" all raised environmental issues.

Metallica became the best-known and best-selling speed metal group. Formed in Los Angeles in the early 1980s and influenced by L.A. hard core, they began by playing covers of British new wave metal bands at breakneck speed. Their *Masters of Puppets* (1986) became the first platinum-selling speed/thrash album, suggesting significant crossover success. Even so, most fans and critics felt that Metallica remained loyal to the subculture. "Remaining true to a tough identity incompatible with MTV, AOR, or even college radio," wrote one critic, "Metallica are the first in years to build a big career in American rock disregarding the dictates of all three. They've called their own shots, kept their integrity, and rallied their support on the strength of their music and non-image."[21] *. . . And Justice for All* (1988) achieved Top Ten status and platinum sales with almost no radio play.

Like most heavy metal groups, Metallica enjoys an intimate relationship with power and technology. What is rare is that they have been able to achieve official artistic recognition and overwhelming commercial success without losing subcultural credibility.

By this time, metal's popularity had exceeded all expectations. After Bon Jovi's *Slippery When Wet* became the most popular record of 1987, *Billboard* reported, "[f]ive more metal bands cracked the top five: Cinderella, Poison, Whitesnake, Mötley Crüe, and Def Leppard. At one point in June, five of the top six albums were by metal-leaning acts."[22] These were the Osbourne/Rhoads *Tribute* LP; Mötley Crüe's *Girls, Girls, Girls*; Poison's *Look What the Cat Dragged In*; Bon Jovi's *Slippery When Wet*; and Whitesnake's self-titled LP. In 1988, metal accounted for eleven of the fifty best-selling albums of the year, and in 1989 ten of the top forty most popular albums were metal. At this level of success, the genre was impossible to ignore. Accordingly, in 1988, the National Academy of Recording Arts and Sciences (NARAS) established a Grammy Award for Best Hard Rock/Metal Performance. Metallica delivered a sizzling performance of "One" at the awards telecast and was widely expected to win the Grammy. By including hard rock in the category, however, NARAS was able to appease its conservative elements and award the prize to the largely irrelevant Jethro Tull. Metal was not given its full due until the following year, when NARAS separated hard rock from heavy metal and Metallica finally walked off with a Grammy.

Among the ten most popular albums of 1989 were two LPs by Guns 'N' Roses, a new L.A. group. *Appetite for Destruction,* their Top Forty debut, rose to number one and charted for seventy-eight weeks, generating three Top Ten singles. Guns 'N' Roses quickly became the new bad boys of heavy metal. Rising from the L.A. street scene, they wrote and played with raw emotion that resonated with many alienated young whites—and others. As *Rolling Stone* put it, "You didn't have to be a runaway to relate to the feelings of dislocation, terror and excitement that mingled in the likes of 'Paradise City' or 'Welcome to the Jungle.'"[23] At the same time, on "One in a Million" the group fueled (and exploited) some fans' racial/sexual fears, insecurities, and hostilities when lead singer Axl Rose spoke of African Americans and homosexuals as

"... And Justice for All"

Artist: Metallica
Music/Lyrics by James Hetfield,
Lars Ulrich, and Kirk Hammett
Label: Elektra, from the LP ...
And Justice for All (1988)

Musical Style Notes

Music Terminology Demystified: What Is a Riff?

A riff is a repetitive musical phrase characterized by a memorable melody and a compelling rhythmic pattern. It can be used as an introduction or as a steady pattern that repeats throughout a piece. Three classic but quite different examples can be found in the Beatles' song "Birthday" from the *White Album*; the 2-bar riff that permeates Run-D.M.C.'s tune "Rock Box," and the memorable guitar riff Duane Allman wrote for Derek and the Dominoes' song "Layla." In the case of heavy metal, a song's signature riff often features a driving rhythm and considerable speed and energy, like the signature riff in Metallica's "... And Justice for All."

Writer Richard Gehr has described Metallica's music as "mini-epics of ear-shattering volume and mind-boggling speed." These "epics" are actually created by assembling sections of music based on instrumental riffs. James Hetfield has stated that the members of Metallica regularly create musical riffs, which they often write down or record for future use, partnering song lyrics with instrumental riffs that seem to fit the mood, and adding additional riffs and patterns that correspond with the changing content or mood of the different lyric sections. This creative method works well to produce these musical mini-epics, with their multiple contrasting sections, just as classical composers crafted melodic themes that would then be manipulated and reiterated in different sections of large-scale musical compositions.

Musical "Road Map"

TIMINGS	COMMENTS	LYRICS
0:00–0:22	Introduction: electric guitar	
0:22–0:28	Second guitar added.	
0:28–0:34	Drums and bass enter.	
0:34–0:39	Drums out—guitars continue.	
0:39–0:45	Drums and bass reenter.	
0:45–0:56	Introduction form repeated with all instruments.	
0:56–1:01	Transition section, characterized by percussive texture and full stops.	
1:07–1:21	Introduction ends—the actual song form begins here, with the steady speed metal percussion style, marked by occasional syncopations (accents placed between the beats).	
1:21–1:41	The song's signature riff begins here.	
	(Note the use of syncopations and sophisticated and complex rhythms.)	
1:41–2:11	Another guitar is layered into the sound texture.	

TIMINGS	COMMENTS	LYRICS
2:11–2:31	Verse 1, A section of melody	*Halls of Justice . . .*
2:31–2:55	Verse 1, B section of melody	*The ultimate . . .*
2:55–3:16	Chorus	*Nothing can save . . .*
3:16–3:37	Signature riff returns.	
3:37–3:58	Verse 2, A section	*Apathy . . .*
3:58–4:21	Verse 2, B section	*The ultimate . . .*
4:21–4:53	Chorus	*Nothing can . . .*
4:53–5:05	Return of percussive transition section heard at 0:56.	
5:05–5:29	Guitar solo, part 1	
5:29–5:55	Guitar solo, part 2	
5:55–6:22	Tempo begins to slow down.	
6:22–7:27	Beginning of new instrumental section, with slower tempo, repeating melody, and descending chord pattern (the bass notes of the chords move progressively lower in pitch).	
7:27–7:47	Signature riff returns.	
7:47–8:09	Verse 3, A section	*Lady Justice has been raped . . .*
8:09–8:33	Verse 3, B section (same lyrics in each verse)	*The ultimate in vanity . . .*
8:33–8:54	Chorus	*Nothing can save us . . .*
8:54–9:07	Riff continues, with additional guitar sound layered in.	
9:07–9:41	Final section—repeat of the last section of the chorus, followed by the repetition of the signature riff leading to the end off the song.	*Seeking no truth . . .*
9:41–9:43	Ending tag—guitar plays alone, followed by three percussive chords.	

"niggers" and "faggots." The group incurred the wrath of the more progressive elements of the rock critical establishment, but their popularity continued unabated into the next decade. *Use Your Illusion I* and *Use Your Illusion II* both finished among the twenty most popular albums of 1992.

By the end of the 1980s, metal had become so expansive that there was even space for a handful of African American and female artists. Most prominent among the former was Living Colour, led musically and spiritually by guitar virtuoso Vernon Reid. Reid was a founder of New York's Black Rock Coalition, whose express purpose was to reclaim rock 'n' roll's black roots. Living Colour was the perfect articulation of the organization's position. Reid and his group drew on every major movement in black music—from blues and jazz to hip hop, from Jimi Hendrix and Sly Stone to James Brown and George Clinton—to fashion their brand of metal. Living Colour first hit the Top Ten with *Vivid* in 1989; they finished 1989 just a bit below Guns 'N' Roses on the year-end pop charts and received the Hard Rock Grammy for "Cult of Personality."

Living Colour's success made the absence of other African Americans more conspicuous, especially because most heavy metal musicians had found their way into the genre through the blues and Hendrix.

Living Colour's success made the absence of other African Americans more conspicuous, especially because most heavy metal musicians had found their way into the genre through the blues and Hendrix. From Thin Lizzy in the 1970s to King's X in the 1980s, even racially mixed groups could be counted on one hand. Historians of the genre have tried to explain this absence in various ways. Walser has pointed to metal's history as a British working-class style, while Weinstein has pointed to black "cultural self-segregation."[24] Weinstein's argument contradicts the founding principle of Living Colour and does not account for why the group had so much difficulty getting signed to a label or marketed. In the end, the band was put into a new marketing category, *funk metal,* as were other black metal artists, who, according to Weinstein, "brought the contribution of their separate musical culture to metal, grafting themselves onto it."[25]

In assessing the significance of racism in heavy metal, one must wonder how much the antidisco campaigns of hard rock radio stations in the late 1970s served to widen the already existing racial divide. Racial tensions flared between Living Colour and Guns 'N' Roses when the groups opened for the Rolling Stones in Los Angeles in 1988. Both traded harsh, racially charged barbs on and off stage, which, given the pattern of racial exclusion in metal, created the impression that metal was foreign territory for black artists. Still, it is important to note that, except for isolated examples such as Guns 'N' Roses' "One in a Million," explicitly racist themes seldom showed up in the music's content.[26]

For female artists, the road to metal success, even at the height of metal mania, was almost impassable. While the explosion of lite metal helped create more gender-balanced audiences, they opened few doors for female performers. Heart had a run of LPs that reached numbers one, two, and three, respectively, and scored with a number of singles, beginning with "What About Love" (1985), that approached the sound of a power ballad. Joan Jett and the Blackhearts also hit the Top Twenty in 1988 with *Up Your Alley,* but the inclusion of either act in heavy metal would be hotly contested among most fans. Only two female acts who achieved national recognition were incontrovertibly metal—Lita Ford and Vixen. Ford had performed

Lita Ford was one of the only women artists to achieve any measure of success or respect within heavy metal. To get to that point she paid her dues for more than a decade.

with Joan Jett as a member of the Runaways in the mid-1970s. After years as a solo artist, she released her first album, *Out for Blood* (1983, Polygram), but did not garner national attention until she changed labels and managers. She felt the switch to RCA and Sharon Osbourne, manager of husband Ozzy Osbourne, allowed her to be herself. *Lita* (1988) brought her into the Top Thirty, and its hit single, "Close My Eyes Forever," co-written with Ozzy Osbourne, entered the Top Ten. When Ford said in a *Metal* interview, "I wear my balls on my chest," she spoke volumes about the contradictory demands placed on a female performer in a masculinist subculture.[27] Vixen worked as an unsigned performing ensemble for years before landing a contract with EMI. The group's eponymous debut album, released in 1987, was among the most popular albums of 1989, eventually selling over 1 million copies. By 1990, metal bands had glutted the market, and metal sales slumped. Black pop now dominated the pop charts, and rap had begun to push metal aside as the cutting-edge statement of youth culture.

Hip Hop, Don't Stop

Rap music must be understood historically as one cultural element within a larger social movement known as hip hop, which also includes break dancing and, to some extent, graffiti art. The movement was nothing short of a new way of life. As Tim Carr has noted:

> *Hip Hop is to funk what bebop was to jazz . . . a new strain of an old form, stripped down and revved up, rejuvenated. The Young Turks challenging the old masters. Just as bebop replaced stiff collared swing orchestras with Zoot-suited combos . . . so has hip hop emerged as a musical style with a brand new way of walking, talking, dancing, and seeing the world.[28]*

Hip hop, with roots in the gang cultures and ghetto communities of the South Bronx and Harlem, originated at the same time as disco but developed for more than five years in almost complete isolation. According to David Toop, "[s]ince nobody in New York City, America, or the rest of the world wanted to know about the black so-called ghettos—the unmentionable areas of extreme urban deprivation—the style was allowed to flourish as a genuine street movement."[29]

Old School Rap

The early culture heroes of hip hop, like those of disco, were the DJs. Following the norms of gang culture, certain DJs dominated particular geographical territories. As early as 1973, pioneer Bronx-style DJs such as Kool Herc, soon followed by Afrika Bambaataa and Grandmaster Flash, had already begun to distinguish themselves from their disco counterparts by including hard-core funk such as Jimmy Castor's "It's Just Begun," the Incredible Bongo Band's "Apache," and James Brown's "Get on the Good Foot," and developing new ways of handling records. Kool Herc, for example, played only a record's hottest, most percussive portion, known as the break. These sustained peaks of dance beats created a musical collage that came to be called break-beat music, and the young b-boys and b-girls who danced to it came to be known as break dancers. Meanwhile, on the West Coast, the Original Lockers, a dance troupe, introduced the robotic movements known as popping and locking that would rejuvenate hip hop dancing in the 1980s.

These sustained peaks of dance beats created a musical collage that came to be called break-beat music, and the young b-boys and b-girls who danced to it came to be known as break dancers.

HEAR MORE
Hip Hop on
MyMusicKit

Hip hop DJs tried to outdo each other by spinning outrageous combinations of records. One of Afrika Bambaataa's sets, for example, might include the theme from the *Pink Panther*, the Beatles, the Rolling Stones, Grand Funk Railroad, Kraftwerk, and the Monkees in addition to James Brown, Sly and the Family Stone, and the Jackson Five. "Hip hop," noted David Toop, "was the new music by virtue of its finding a way to absorb all other music."[30] By 1976, DJs had transformed records and turntables from mere sound carriers into full-fledged rhythm instruments through the introduction of technical innovations such as scratching.

As their popularity increased, the best Bronx-style DJs outgrew small house parties and moved into clubs, community centers, and finally into auditoriums, some of which could accommodate up to 3,000 people. In these larger venues, DJs began to use crew members as emcees (MCs) to provide vocal entertainment as a means of crowd control. Like break dancing, MCing, as it was first known, started as a solo art. MCs soon developed their unique styles, eventually known as rapping. Among the first solo MCs were Eddie Cheeba, DJ Hollywood, and later Kurtis Blow. Grandmaster Flash expanded the idea to include whole groups of MCs. Soon rap groups were popping up all over the Bronx and Harlem, using names like Double Trouble, the Treacherous Three, the Funky Four Plus One, and the Furious Five (started by Flash). Afrika Bambaataa worked with several rap groups, including the Jazzy Five, the Cosmic Force, and the Soulsonic Force. By around 1978, MCs had begun to surpass DJs in cultural importance.

Out of his love of music and his experiences as a South Bronx gang member and a follower of the Black Panthers, Afrika Bambaataa, a pioneer hip hop DJ and leader of the Soulsonic Force, fashioned the Zulu Nation as an inclusive hip hop posse.

Although the style of early rap groups evolved spontaneously, rap's roots can be traced through Caribbean island traditions back to West African griots. In the United States, rap's ancestors include field hollers, work and prison songs, competitive urban word games like signifying and the dozens, scat singing, the rhymes of Muhammed Ali, the politically potent verse of the Watts Prophets and the Last Poets, and finally the lyrics of artists such as James Brown and Gil Scott-Heron. The hip hop movement followed an African American progression, but a strong Latino presence also existed. African American DJs incorporated Latin music into their mixes, just as Puerto Rican DJ Charlie Chase (of the Cold Crush Brothers) played funk. Other notable Puerto Rican DJs and MCs included Whipper Whip and Rubie Dee (Fantastic Five), and O.C. and Devastating Tito (Fearless Four). The most famous of the break-dance crews, the Rock Steady Crew, was predominantly Puerto Rican.[31]

Bronx-style rapping, around since 1976, was not recorded commercially until 1979. Before that, rapping existed only in live performance or on homemade cassettes. It is surprising, therefore, that the first two rap records did not come from that neighborhood. "King Tim III (Personality Jock)" was recorded by the Fatback Band from Brooklyn, and "Rapper's Delight" was made by the Sugar Hill Gang based in New Jersey. "Rapper's Delight" used classic hip hop rhymes recorded over "Good Times" by Chic; it made the lower reaches of the pop Top Forty, eventually selling some 2 million copies.

Given its lineage, it was inevitable that rap would include topical themes. The first recorded rap to deliver a serious message was "How We Gonna Make the Black Nation Rise" (1980) by Brother D and Collective Effort. The style and political priorities of message rap had been anticipated by two earlier albums, *Hustler's Convention* and *Rappin' Black in a White World*. *Hustler's Convention* was recorded in New York by Lightnin' Rod, a.k.a. Jalal Nuridin, who had been the leader of the Last Poets. His powerful prison poetry over tracks by members of Kool and the Gang inspired many early MCs. *Rappin' Black in a White World* was recorded by the Watts Prophets. By the late 1960s, both the Poets and the Prophets had become targets of the FBI's infamous COINTELPRO operation and neither received their artistic or commercial due at the time. Two decades later, samples of their work could be found on albums by hip hop artists such as Def Jeff, Too Short, Tim Dogg, and A Tribe Called Quest.

The phenomenal success of "Rapper's Delight" first alerted the mainstream media to the existence of hip hop—which was now "discovered" by the music business, the print media, and the film industry in turn—and Bronx DJs entered the downtown New York club scene. Afrika Bambaataa proceeded to spin at the Mudd Club, the Ritz, the Peppermint Lounge, Negril, Danceteria, and the Roxy, where he hosted crowds of up to 4,000 people. Films like *Wild Style*, *Flashdance*, *Breakin'*, and *Beat Street* soon followed, bringing hip hop to a mass audience. Unfortunately, the mass media often rip cultural phenomena from their historical contexts. Watching *Flashdance*, one might think Jennifer Beals had invented break dancing. The only hints of historical accuracy in the film portrayed the Rock Steady Crew dancing to Jimmy Castor's "It's Just Begun." Similar disjunctures were evident on vinyl. The first so-called rap record to reach pop number one was Blondie's "Rapture" (1981). That same year, Chris Frantz and Tina Weymouth of Talking Heads formed Tom Tom Club and recorded "Wordy Rappinghood," followed by the hip hop–influenced "Genius of Love." While respectful of hip hop culture, these were still outsiders reaping the rewards of early rap.

Some of the most enduring Bronx-based rap records were also produced during this time. "Planet Rock" (Afrika Bambaataa and the Soulsonic Force) and "The Message" (Grandmaster Flash and the Furious Five) were released in 1982 and showcased all the innovations of hip hop culture. Borrowing freely from Kraftwerk's "Trans Europe Express," "Planet Rock" used a

Roland TR 808 drum machine and rhymes that were, according to Steven Hager, "a dreamy, utopian throwback to the 1960s" to create a formidable dance floor and retail hit.[32] "The Message" heralded greater lyric sophistication and a tilt toward topical themes, as soon seen in "Problems of the World" by the Fearless Four and "White Lines (Don't Do It)" by Grand Master Melle Mel and the Furious Five.

> *In the early 1980s, the never-ending debate on whether rap would continue began. In the final analysis, these debates were irrelevant. Hip hop had already influenced cultural forms from ballet and modern dance to fashion design and studio art, not to mention pop, rock, funk, soul, and jazz.*

In the early 1980s, the never-ending debate on whether rap would continue began. In the final analysis, these debates were irrelevant. Hip hop had already influenced cultural forms from ballet and modern dance to fashion design and studio art, not to mention pop, rock, funk, soul, and jazz. The evidence could be found in Herbie Hancock's use of DJ Grandmaster D.ST on the Grammy-winning "Rockit," and Grandmaster Melle Mel's rapid-fire rap introduction to Chaka Khan's "I Feel for You," which hit the Top Ten in 1984.

Hip Hop: The Next Generation

By the mid-1980s, a second generation of New York rap artists had sprung up, including Whodini, The Force MDs, The Fat Boys, and Run-D.M.C, and a fledgling hip hop scene was developing in Los Angeles. A mobile L.A. DJ crew called Uncle Jam's Army (after the Funkadelic album *Uncle Jam Wants You*) played music at L.A. street parties, while clubs served the downtown crowd. Prominent among the local DJs were Dr. Dre and Yella from the World Class Wrecking Cru, which eventually metamorphosed into N.W.A. (Niggas With Attitude). Also on the West Coast scene were Ice-T and Kid Frost. Ice-T—a New York transplant and star of the documentary *Breaking and Entering*—rapped harder than most of his contemporaries. Kid Frost was hip hop's first Chicano nationalist. Both Ice and Frost at first played to predominantly Chicano audiences. In 1984, station KDAY made a significant commitment to hip hop when, through the efforts of its program director, Greg Mack, all the popular New York groups performed in Los Angeles.

The growth of New York hip hop moved rap from the twelve-inch single (the

Run-D.M.C. represented the beginnings of a second generation of rappers. Their hard, boastful rhymes combined with rock influences helped bring rap to the attention of the mainstream audience.

industry standard for dance music since disco) to the album. Key to this transition was the success of *Run-D.M.C.* (1984), the first gold rap album. The group that gave its name to the album represented a departure from first-generation rappers in a number of ways. Joseph Simmons (Run), Darryl McDaniels (DMC), and Jason Mizell (Jam Master Jay), all college educated, came from the lower-middle-class neighborhood of Hollis, in Queens. Run-D.M.C. had their sights set on conquering both the rock and rap markets. On their second album, *King of Rock*, they proclaimed their conquest and backed it up with hard, boastful rapping complemented by the Hendrix-like live guitar of Eddie Martinez on tracks like "Rock Box" and "King of Rock." While hip hop DJs had always used rock tracks in their mixes, Run-D.M.C.'s use of live guitar was novel. Martinez was a bridge to rock and a reminder of the Latino presence in hip hop—a presence further emphasized in the LP's use of mixes by Tony Torrez and the Latin Rascals.

In 1986, Run-D.M.C. released *Raising Hell*, which went to number three on the charts and sold 3.5 million copies. For the album, producer Rick Rubin suggested remaking Aerosmith's "Walk This Way" (1977), one of Jam Master Jay's favorite rock selections, as a duet between Run-D.M.C. and Aerosmith's Steven Tyler and Joe Perry, who were just returning to music from an extended bout with drugs and alcohol. The song's video is a metaphor for the contradictions inherent in crossing over. It opens with the two groups performing on opposite sides of a wall. Initially annoyed with each other's sound, they eventually break through the wall and Run-D.M.C. ends up performing with Aerosmith to an all-white audience, leaving their own audience behind.

The only album to rival *Raising Hell*'s sales was *Licensed to Ill* by the Beastie Boys, white bohemians from Manhattan. They were branded as rap's first major affront to decency because of their on- and off-stage antics and their first hit single, "You've Got to Fight for Your Right to Party." Signed to black-owned Def Jam, the Beasties were the first significant white performers in rap. Over the next few years, considerable inroads continued to be made into the album and cassette markets by East Coast rap releases such as UTFO's *Lethal*, L. L. Cool J's *Bigger and Deffer*, Whodini's *Open Sesame*, Heavy D. & the Boyz's *Living Large*, Eric B. & Rakim's *Paid in Full*, Salt-N-Pepa's *Hot, Cool & Vicious*, and the Fat Boys' *Crushin'*.

Eight of *Billboard*'s Top Thirty black albums for the week of 28 November 1987 were rap albums.

By this time, the Los Angeles rap scene, which featured harder rhymes set to the slower pace of L.A. cruising, was coming into its own. In 1986, Ice-T recorded "Six in the Morning," which spoke of early morning police raids and threw in a bit of gratuitous misogyny. The recording led to Ice-T's six-year

As one of the original gangsta rappers, Ice-T was controversial from the start. Still, he was able to fashion a credible film career and make a bridge to heavy metal with Body Count. *While some of his political decisions were open to debate, his business sense was unerring.*

"Rock Box"

Artist: Run-D.M.C.

Music/Lyrics by Larry Smith,
Joseph ("Run") Simmons, Darryl
("DMC") McDaniels

Label: Def Jam (1984), from
the LP *Run-D.M.C.*

Founded in the early 1980s by Joseph "Run" Simmons, Darryl "DMC" McDaniels, and Jason "Jam Master Jay" Mizell, Run-D.M.C. is often credited with breaking down the barrier between hip hop and mainstream rock and roll, introducing hip hop to a huge listening audience that had previously either been unaware of it or viewed it as an exclusively urban, African American street phenomenon. Run-D.M.C.'s cover of Aerosmith's "Walk This Way" was a huge crossover hit. This was the first rap video played on MTV. However, a strong rock element was present from the very beginning in their music, and you can hear on "Rock Box," which is from their first LP.

Musical Style Notes

"Rock Box" contains many stylistic elements of hip hop:

- A sampled drum rhythm track (although the actual beat is a hard rock style).
- Rap-style vocals, with dialogue between Run and DMC, voice doublings and echo effects used to highlight certain words, and rhythmic lyric repetitions.
- Turntable cuts from Jam Master Jay.

In addition to this, however, a definitive rock element is present. The prevailing drum rhythm is a trap-set style, hard rock backbeat—with the emphasis on beats 2 and 4, as opposed to the relentless 1-2-3-4 equal quarter notes heard in some sampled drum tracks. The opening riff, doubled on guitar and bass (first occurring at 0:12), would sound completely at home on any heavy metal album. Layered over this is the guitar work of Eddie Martinez, whose wailing solos on "Rock Box" were played live in the studio and were reminiscent of a sound more likely to be associated with Hendrix or Stevie Ray Vaughan than with hip hop mixes.

Musical "Road Map"

TIMINGS	COMMENTS	LYRICS
0:00–0:08	Rap intro—RUN Electric guitar and sampled drum rhythm track is established, then stops.	*RUN: Run—Run—D—DM—MC—C*
0:08–0:32 0:12	Rhythm track reestablished. Repeating bass guitar, heavy metal style riff established. Electric guitar solo (Eddie Martinez).	
0:32–1:11	Part 1 RUN begins. Echo effects and DMC's added. Voices are used to highlight and accentuate certain words. The word *fade* is both a verbal conclusion and a musical cue that leads into the instrumental break.	*RUN: For all you sucker . . .*

TIMINGS	COMMENTS	LYRICS
1:11–1:29	Instrumental section: Overdubbed electric guitar solo Sampled rhythm track Synthesizer	
1:30–1:54 1:36	Part 2 RUN begins. DMC enters over Run's "Never, never."	*RUN: Because the rhymes . . .* *DMC: Took a test . . .*
1:54–2:03	Run jumps in with "Bust into the party . . ."	*RUN: Bust into . . .*
2:03–2:32	DMC begins; Run joins occasionally to punctuate a word or phrase. Echo effects used again to highlight certain words.	*DMC: So listen . . .*
2:32–3:15	RUN–DMC dialogue Turntable cuts from Jam Master Jay.	*RUN–DMC: Our DJ's better*
3:15–3:34	Dialogue between Run and DMC	
3:34–3:58	Improvised rap, with lots of rhythmic repetition of words and syllables.	*Jay Jay Jay . . .* *We don't . . .*
3:58–4:27	Guitar solo can be heard under rap lyrics	*My, my man . . .*
4:27–5:27 5:11	Synth chord pops and cues next section of rap; guitar continues at intervals throughout. Lyrics and music begin to fade.	*Re, remember . . .*

Public Enemy was among the most socially conscious and politically controversial groups in rap. Their early albums elevated production values and political commentary to a new level.

association with Warner that produced *Rhyme Pays* (1987), *Power* (1988), *Iceberg* (1989), and *OG* (1990). Also in 1986, a sixteen-year-old Ice Cube wrote "Boyz N the Hood," with Eazy E providing the vocals over a grinding, bass-heavy rhythm track created by Dre and Yella. This relationship led to the formation of N.W.A. and the music now called gangsta rap. Although Los Angeles is usually considered home to gangsta rap, the style can be traced to earlier artists, including Philadelphia rapper Schoolly-D's "PSK," which projected a chilling image of gang membership and directly influenced Ice-T; and to New York duo KRS-One and Scott La Rock of Boogie Down Productions, whose *Criminal Minded* included cuts like "South Bronx" and "9mm" that used gangsta vocabulary.

As the Los Angeles rap scene began to bloom, Public Enemy (PE)—who wrote rap's most politically advanced lyrics—formed in New York. They hailed from Long Island and were an extended posse (or crew): leader Chuck D; MC Flavor Flav; DJ Terminator X; a production team ("the Bomb Squad") of Bill Stephney, Hank Shocklee, and Eric "Vietnam" Sadler; Professor Griff as minister of information; and a paramilitary troop of bodyguards known as Security of the First World (S1W). PE sought to advance black nationalism and Afrocentricity with tracks as compelling and technically advanced as they were controversial. After cutting their teeth on *Yo! Bum Rush the Show,* the group hit their stride with *It Takes a Nation of Millions to Hold Us Back* (1988) and *Fear of a Black Planet* (1990). On *Nation of Millions,* PE positioned themselves among a host of black leaders, including Marcus Garvey, Rosa Parks, Steven Biko, Martin Luther King, Malcolm X, and Nelson and Winnie Mandela. "This literal act of insertion by Public Enemy into the tradition of black resistance," Brian Cross has written, "collapses the boundary between popular culture and politics."[33]

As 1988 continued, message rap raised the consciousness of its fans and the blood pressure of its enemies in equal measure.

As 1988 continued, message rap raised the consciousness of its fans and the blood pressure of its enemies in equal measure. The *Nation of Millions* cover had a logo with a bereted silhouette caught in the crosshairs of a rifle sight. That same year, KRS-One, after the shooting death of his partner Scott La Rock, released *By Any Means Necessary.* Invoking the famous Malcolm X photograph, the album cover showed KRS-One looking out of the window with a gun. Clearly, hip hop culture had already become highly politicized by the time N.W.A. released *Straight Outta Compton* (1988). N.W.A. added to the controversy by portraying Los Angeles gang life without any distance or moral judgment. Brian Turner, president of Priority, the label that distributed N.W.A., defended the group:

> *What impressed me about N.W.A. and Eazy-E was that these guys lived the things they talk about. All I was hearing on the news was the perspective of the police and outsiders—you never get the perspective of the actual guy they're talking about. When I saw what these guys wrote, it really hit me that their side of the story is important to tell.*[34]

Not everyone agreed with Turner. Something of a generation gap had developed in black music; nowhere was this more apparent than on black radio. At the time, *Billboard* charts distinguished between sales and airplay for the Top Forty black singles. Of the twenty-eight rap songs that reached its Top Forty sales chart in the first forty-six weeks of 1988, only sixteen registered on its airplay chart.[35] Clearly, rap was not receiving airplay commensurate with its sales. Tony Gray, program director at WRKS in New York, tried to explain:

> *Those records appeal to a specific demographic, primarily 12- to 18-year-olds, or perhaps 12- to 24-year-olds. The battle that [black] radio stations have is that they do need to play popular music, but for marketing reasons they have to be concerned with the 25-plus listeners as well. You don't want to alienate those listeners because that's where the bulk of your revenue comes from.*[36]

To some, the split between rap and other black popular music represented more than a generation gap—it indicated class divisions within the black community. Bill Adler, publicist for Run-D.M.C., L. L. Cool J, and Public Enemy, among others, put it starkly: "Black radio is run by 'buppies' [black urban professionals]. They've made a cultural commitment to a lifestyle that has nothing to do with music on the street. . . . This music very rudely pulls them back on the street corner, and they don't want to go."[37] Artists themselves often identified "bourgeois blacks" as the main source of resistance to rap.

Of course, rap's detractors had no lack of issues to point to. From different quarters, rap was roundly chastised for bigotry, sexism, and/or violence. The cries of anti-Semitism directed at Public Enemy's Professor Griff reached a peak when he claimed in a *Washington Times* interview that Jews were responsible for "the majority of wickedness that goes on in the world."[38] (Griff was subsequently fired and then rehired as liaison to the black community.) In the *New York Times*, critic Jon Pareles berated Professor Griff but also stated that PE's "overall message is one of self-determination for blacks."[39] As to rap's sexist tendencies, Harry Allen noted:

> *When Ice-T releases a record called "Girls, Let's Get Buck Naked and Fuck" . . . when 2 Live Crew on a cut called "S & M" calls to women to bring their "d_ _k-sucking friends," when Ultramagnetic M.C.'s Kool Keith . . . talks about smacking up his bitch in the manner of a pimp, sisters understandably scream.*[40]

"Hip-hop is sexist," Allen concluded, but he added, "it is also frank."[41] One wonders if rap would have been so upsetting if it had not been so frank. Still, while sexism has never been a stranger to any genre of popular music or any aspect of U.S. life, rap's sexism—for example, its widespread and demeaning references to women as "bitches" and "hoes"—should not be excused.

Evidence of a change in hip hop's sexual politics became visible in 1985 when Roxanne Shanté's "Roxanne's Revenge," the answer track to "Roxanne Roxanne," UTFO's insult song, beat the original at its own game. However, it was the overwhelming commercial success of Salt-N-Pepa's double platinum debut LP, *Hot, Cool & Vicious* (1988), that finally convinced some rap labels to promote female rappers, many of whom had been part of the hip hop underground for years.

> *After six years of releasing records, Def Jam finally recorded Nikki D's "Daddy's Little Girl," their first track by a female rapper, and Public Enemy recruited Sister Souljah to the ranks. In Los Angeles, Ice Cube put his support behind Yo Yo, co-producing her scorching* Make Way for the Motherlode. . . . *Yo Yo . . . founded the Intelligent Black Woman's Coalition, hoping to reverse the low status and self-esteem that women were clearly suffering in the face of such a concerted shut-out by men.*[42]

By the end of the decade, women had added a new voice to hip hop. Pointing to releases like "Paper Thin" (MC Lyte), "Independent Woman" (Roxanne Shanté), and "Ladies First" (Queen Latifah), critics tended to portray women rappers as female correctives to adolescent male sexual ranting. However, the reality is more complex.[43] Not all male raps were sexist. (Consider, for example, "Date Rape" by A Tribe Called Quest.) But trying to shoehorn groups like Hoes with Attitude or Bitches with Problems into a feminist mold was obviously problematic. In fact, even the most progressive female rappers resisted the feminist tag, seeing it as a label for a white middle-class movement that existed in tension with their commitment to racial solidarity. Perhaps this commitment, more than a tacit approval of male sexism, was what made most female rappers reluctant to speak out publicly against their male counterparts.

Even the most progressive female rappers resisted the feminist tag, seeing it as a label for a white middle-class movement that existed in tension with their commitment to racial solidarity.

The woman who best managed this conflict between racial solidarity and feminism was Queen Latifah. Projecting a powerful and dignified image, Latifah developed "a forthright rapping approach that sidestepped the dissing clichés."[44] Through cuts like "Dance for Me" and "Come into My House," she established herself as a rapper as talented as her male counterparts. She released her first album, *All Hail the Queen,* on Tommy Boy in 1989. On the video for its most popular cut, "Ladies First"—performed as a duet with her "European sister" Monie Love—Latifah positioned herself as a military strategist alongside black women activists such as Sojourner Truth, Angela Davis, and Winnie Mandela, thus offering a pro-female version of the predominantly male lineage portrayed in other political rap videos.

Queen Latifah was one of the most intelligent and articulate women in rap. Her forceful rhymes added measurably to the chorus of female voices that began to emerge in the late 1980s. In the 1990s she starred in the television sitcom Living Single, then made the leap to films.

Still, rap's objectification and exploitation of women continued. It was expressed most straightforwardly by the Miami-based 2 Live Crew on *Move Something* (1988) and *As Nasty as They Wanna Be* (1989).

Violence was the third issue that rap's critics frequently decried. The confrontational stance and uncompromising lyrics of Public Enemy ("Fight the Power") and N.W.A. ("_ _ _ _ tha Police") and the skirmishes at rap concerts fueled the notion that rap promoted violence. Violence had occurred at some shows, but that did not distinguish rap concerts from rock concerts or, for that matter, any number of sporting events. Rappers themselves addressed this problem head-on. Following the leadership of critic Nelson George, in 1989, a number of rap groups—Stetsasonic, Boogie Down Productions, and PE, among others—initiated a campaign called Stop the Violence, aimed at black-on-black crime. Among other projects, these groups helped create "Self-Destruction," the all-star rap recording that became the movement's anthem. The following year, West Coast rappers followed suit with "We're All in the Same Gang."

Ironically, the West Coast effort occurred amid bitter splits among members of the N.W.A. posse. Following the success of *Straight Outta Compton,* Ice Cube left the group over disputes about creative control and money. Looking to the Public Enemy orbit for support and inspiration, he "sought to bring the gangsta style of rhyming from the west to the apocalyptic beats of the Bomb Squad."[45] The result was the Top Twenty *Amerikkka's Most Wanted,* one of 1990's best-selling albums. It launched Ice-Cube on a highly successful solo career in rap and led to his best-selling LPs *Death Certificate* (1991), *Predator* (1992), and *Lethal Injection* (1993). N.W.A. responded with *Efil4zaggin* in 1991, after which Dr. Dre also left the group. He returned as a solo act the following year with *The Chronic* (the term for a particularly strong strain of marijuana).

While the press criticized gangsta violence and hip hop misogyny, a good deal of rap spoke positively about real issues. "Any examination of rap's lyrical content," wrote David Nathan, "reveals a very high percentage of anti-violent, anti-drug messages, many aimed at improving self-esteem, encouraging the youth of the 80s to continue their education and approach adulthood with a positive approach."[46] This side of rap, which stood in sharp contrast to the lyric vacuity of most black pop at the time, tended to get lost in the controversy. "Self-Destruction" sold nearly 500,000 units and never even registered in the black airplay Top Forty.

Despite the turmoil surrounding rap, major record companies were quick to recognize the sound's financial potential. While few major labels signed rap acts directly, buy-ins and distribution deals with successful rap indies became commonplace.[47] Majors generally left creative functions at the street level and simply provided independents with superior distribution, which increased rap's access to mainstream outlets. As a result, rap tended to get more support on pop radio than on black radio. Even MTV initiated a rap show. Buried at first in a late-night weekend slot, *Yo! MTV Raps* soon moved to a daily afternoon slot and became one of the channel's most popular shows. In 1988, NARAS added a rap category to the Grammy Awards. However, it refused to include the rap award in its live telecast, which led four of the five nominees, including winners D.J. Jazzy Jeff & the Fresh Prince, to boycott the show. Shortly thereafter, *Billboard* quietly added a rap chart to its pages.

Rap tended to get more support on pop radio than on black radio. Even MTV initiated a rap show. Buried at first in a late-night weekend slot, Yo! MTV Raps soon moved to a daily afternoon slot and became one of the channel's most popular shows.

Entrance into the mainstream led to exposure in other media. After winning the rap Grammy, Will Smith (the Fresh Prince) landed a starring role in a prime-time sitcom, *The Fresh Prince of Bel Air.* Rappers showed up on other African American sitcoms, including *A Different World* and *Cosby.* The poignant comedy/variety show *In Living Color,* grounded in a hip hop aesthetic, featured artists like Monie Love and Queen Latifah, who later had her own sitcom,

"Ladies First"

Artist: Queen Latifah

Music/Lyrics by Dr. Shane Faber, Mark James (DJ Mark the 45 King), Simone Johnson, Dana Owens (Queen Latifah), Anthony Peaks

Label: Tommy Boy, from the CD *All Hail the Queen* (1989)

Queen Latifah's music is an example of the immediacy and the community basis in which hip hoppers develop their rhymes. A talented, disciplined, and hardworking musician, she came under the influence of Kris Parker, otherwise known as KRS-One, who, as a producer and rapper with Boogie Down Productions, had developed an explicitly Afrocentric, antiviolent, and "conscious" hip hop approach. As part of this group, Latifah, whose stage name means "delicate and sensitive" in Arabic, fashioned a proud, empowered female response to the misogyny and gangsta violence of much hip hop. In "Ladies First," Queen Latifah and guest artist Monie Love use the medium of hip hop, a genre that in many cases objectifies women, to deliver a message about the strength and autonomy of women, thus creating a powerful, courageous new identity for women in hip hop and leaving no question about whether female rappers can compete with the guys.

Musical Style Notes

The instrumental tracks of "Ladies First" feature the trademark hip hop techniques of synth programming and sampling, in which digital samples of extant sound files are used as building blocks for a new composition, and often repeat, or loop, the samples. These samples can be anything from turntable scratching to preexisting recordings (see Puff Daddy's "I'll Be Watching You"), to the funky horns and the sampled alto sax squeal heard on "Ladies First." Vocally, we hear another hallmark of hip hop, which is a dialogue between two rappers, each reinforcing the other's point of view and adding to the argument.

Musical "Road Map"

TIMINGS	COMMENTS	LYRICS
0:00–0:18	Introduction Synthesized, funk-style horn and drum samples.	
0:18–0:29	Verse 1	Queen Latifah: *The ladies*
0:29–0:53	Verse 1 (response)	Monie Love: *A-yo, . . .* Male voice: *Yeah, . . .*
0:53–1:12	Verse 2	*Believe me . . .*
1:12–1:30	Verse 2 (response)	*I break*
1:30–2:04	Instrumental interlude—same material as Introduction.	
2:04–2:14	Verse 3	*Who said . . .*
2:14–2:24	Verse continues, with dialogue between Queen Latifah and Monie Love.	Monie Love: *My sister, . . .* Queen Latifah: *Sure, . . .*
2:24–2:59	Verse 4 (response)	*Yo, praise me . . .*
2:59–3:13 3:13–3:17	Verse 4 (response)	Queen Latifah: *Contact . . .*
3:17–3:56	Horn samples continue. Break at 3:35; sound reduced to only drum and alto sax samples. Music fades; ends 3:56.	

Living Single. Quincy Jones, producer of *Fresh Prince,* also attempted to build bridge generations and cross musical boundaries in the production of his award-winning 1989 LP, *Back on the Block,* which brought together diverse musical talents such as Sarah Vaughn, Ella Fitzgerald, Siedah Garrett, Al Jarreau, Bobby McFerrin, Take 6, Ray Charles, Chaka Khan, Al B. Sure, James Ingram, and Barry White with rappers like Ice-T, Melle Mel, Big Daddy Kane, and Kool Moe Dee.

It was in film, however, that rap made some of its most powerful statements. When Kid N Play parlayed their LP *Funhouse* into the film *House Party* (plus a sequel and a Saturday-morning cartoon show), they only hinted at the connections between rap and topical film. Spike Lee's *Do the Right Thing,* powered by the hip hop force of Public Enemy's "Fight the Power," tied rap and topical film tightly together. Following the success of Lee's devastating treatment of race relations, a rash of black-directed films appeared about life in the 'hood, including *Straight Outta Brooklyn, Juice, New Jack City,* and *Boyz N the Hood.* The last two starred Ice-T and Ice Cube, respectively, and featured their music. These films were far more realistic in their portrayal of urban life and far more demanding in their political analysis than the break-dance movies of the mid-1980s or the so-called blaxploitation films of the early 1970s.

In 1990, rapper/dancer Hammer (then M. C. Hammer) scored another first for rap with *Please Hammer Don't Hurt 'Em,* which logged twenty-one weeks at number one on the pop charts and became the best-selling rap album ever. With sales of over 10 million copies, it outdistanced its nearest competitor by a factor of two. Ambitious to the core, Hammer set his sights on nothing short of toppling Michael Jackson. Roundly dissed by the hip hop nation for playing to mainstream sensibilities, Hammer enlisted James Brown to bolster his credibility. In the long-form prologue to the "2 Legit to Quit" video, Brown anoints Hammer as his godson and directs him to "bring back the glove"—an obvious reference to Michael Jackson and therefore to the pop crown.

Ironically, Hammer's pop tendencies may have created cultural space for his main competition, Vanilla Ice. After Ice toured as Hammer's opening act, his LP *To the Extreme* skyrocketed to number one on the pop charts and multiplatinum certification, temporarily displacing Hammer himself. Ice ran into credibility problems when it was discovered that part

of his biography had been falsified to make him look more "street." This drive "to be more 'authentic,'" according to Kristal Brent Zook, "demonstrates that an increasing sense of African-American solidarity seems to inspire an increasingly blatant demand for inclusion among (some) white people who now sense themselves uncomfortably shifting from center

In 1990, Hammer (formerly known as M.C. Hammer) recorded the best-selling album in rap and promptly earned the wrath of the hip hop community for selling out. While his raps were not the strongest, there may also have been a certain amount of jealousy in the reaction.

to margin."[48] Another group of white rappers, Young Black Teenagers, included a song called "Proud to Be Black" in their debut album, pushing identification with black culture to the limit. Other white rap groups, such as Third Base, gained acceptance by other rappers based on a certain repudiation of white skin privilege in their own lifestyles.

The success of Los Angeles gangsta rap led both Hammer and Vanilla Ice to follow up their earlier successes with harder images—Hammer looking like a gangsta, Ice wearing dreadlocks and publicly embracing marijuana. However, Los Angeles was home to an incredible diversity of rappers. In 1989, Chicano Kid Frost recorded the bilingual *Hispanic Causing Panic.* He was joined in short order by Cubanos Melloman Ace and Skatemaster Tate. Named after the discharge of a shotgun, the Boo Yaa Tribe—Samoans from southeast Los Angeles—were a formidable-looking group of ex–gang members. Toop notes their "raps are written in hardcore prison slang, with joy, pleasure, identity and emergence expressed in metaphors of death, violence, intimidation, fear and imprisonment."[49] Against this background, the group's members have talked openly about their respect for women in their culture. The most diverse posse in the Los Angeles hip hop scene were the groups associated with the Soul Assassins. At the center of that posse was Cypress Hill (with Grandmixer Muggs, an Italian; B-Real, a Chicano; and Sen Dogg, a Cuban). Known for their "old school" hook lines and harmonic approach and B-Real's characteristic nasal whine, Cypress Hill's 1991 debut single, "How I Could Just Kill a Man," propelled the group to national recognition. Songs dealing with hot-button issues such as drugs ("I Wanna Get High") and violence ("Cock the Hammer") brought further recognition. Their second album, *Black Sunday* (1993), debuted at number one on the pop charts. Muggs soon set up the Soul Assassins as a production company that included FunkDoobiest and House of Pain. Among FunkDoobiest's members were Puerto Rican and Sioux MCs and a Mexican DJ. House of Pain was Irish with a Latvian DJ. With the 1992 single "Jump Around" and the LP *Fine Malt Lyrics,* House of Pain achieved national fame, bringing something of the Irish experience to hip hop.

By the early 1990s, then, hip hop had become, as Brian Cross wrote, "a voice for many different subjectivities—women, Chicano, Cubano, Asian, Irish, gay, and all the variants covered by black, Jamaican, Dominican, etc."[50] According to Cross, far from detracting from the African American cultural priorities that determined the trajectory of rap, hip hop's expansion "brings the struggle of African-Americans to many new ears, thereby providing a new perspective on one's own problems."[51] From an isolated street culture, hip hop had grown in less than twenty years into a global phenomenon. Perhaps because of this success, it became the focus of such a ferocious backlash.

Regulating Popular Music: The Politics of Censorship

Popular music has never been a stranger to controversy or opposition. Herman Gray has noted three periods of particularly strong opposition: the response to jazz in the early part of the twentieth century, the reaction against rock 'n' roll in the 1950s and 1960s, and the 1980s wave of controversy associated with heavy metal and rap.[52] No matter what the genre, certain themes run through all three periods. Some people fear that sensual rhythms can overcome rationality or that lyrics can undermine moral values. Because of these fears, people have attempted at times to link these genres to drug abuse, lawless behavior, and general moral decline. In turn, all of these problems have been projected to some degree onto race.

In Lawrence Grossberg's view, the most recent round of attacks on popular music from the mid-1980s onward can be ascribed to the new conservatism espoused by Christian fundamentalists, conservative elitists, and organizations like the PMRC.[53] His analysis is shared by Nan Levinson, a Tufts University professor and correspondent for *Index on Censorship*. "Though usually played as revolts of the fed up," Levinson has said, "these skirmishes are likely to be nurtured or orchestrated by organizations of the extreme moralist right."[54] Both Grossberg and Levinson believe these groups are linked by common tenets, such as a narrow interpretation of the "Christian way of life," and certain sound-bite concepts, such as "family values," that are media codes for conservatism.

Aligning with the new conservatism, the popular press began to cast music as a social irritant and its detractors as defenders of decent society.

Aligning with the new conservatism, the popular press began to cast music as a social irritant and its detractors as defenders of decent society. The nation's shift toward the political right during the Reagan–Bush years (1981–1992) made essentially conservative arguments more appealing to many erstwhile liberals. The assumption—often made tacitly—was that popular music communicated messages through its lyrics, visual images, hypnotic rhythms, subliminal suggestions, and sheer volume to an impressionable young audience, thus producing direct and uniform effects on their behavior. Of course, musical communication is far more complicated than this. As Susan McClary and Robert Walser have pointed out:

> *Music relies on events and inflections occurring on many interdependent levels (melody, rhythm, harmony, timbre, texture, etc.) simultaneously. Each of these has something of a syntactical dimension—a grammar of expectations, normal continuity, etc.—and also a wide-open semiotic dimension. . . . When all these levels are operating at the same time, . . . we are dealing with a tangle that pages and pages of words can only begin to unpack.[55]*

Add to this the visual dimension of music video, which frequently eschews narrative organization altogether, and the complexity of communication increases significantly. Music is polysemic: It communicates on many levels at once. Its meaning may be different for different people in different places, and that meaning may change over time. This is not to suggest that popular music has no effects; it was certainly related in some way, for example, to the social transformations of the 1960s. Today, however, that same music is used to sell beer, cars, and running shoes. During the mega-events of the 1980s, popular music mobilized masses of people toward particular political ends. At the same time, it opened new markets for and delivered new consumers to transnational corporations.

The proposition that lyrics and images glorifying violence or the degradation of women contribute to those same proclivities in society must be taken seriously. However, music must be considered in proportion with many variables that bear on these problems—including class, age, race, gender, ethnicity, sexual orientation, employment status, housing, education, religion, drug laws, obscenity standards, health status, nutrition, the availability of social services, the economy, and the political climate. In the 1980s and 1990s, however, as in the jazz era and the heyday of rock 'n' roll, the reaction to popular music seemed to lack such a sense of proportion. Indeed, many critics seemed to hold popular music solely responsible for (and even more harmful than) the social problems it referenced, as in the government investigation initiated by the PMRC in 1985.

The Parents Music Resource Center

The Parents Music Resource Center (PMRC) was founded in early 1985 by a group of prominent women in Washington, D.C. Founding members included Tipper Gore, wife of then-senator Al Gore; Sally Nevius, whose husband had chaired the D.C. city council; Pam Howar; and Susan Baker, whose husband, James Baker, was then secretary of the treasury. Of the twenty original members—dubbed the Washington wives—seventeen were married to influential Washington politicians.[56] Concerned, as they said, "about the growing trend in music toward lyrics that are sexually explicit, excessively violent, or glorify the use of drugs and alcohol"—as evidenced in Prince's "Nikki Darling" and Madonna's "Like a Virgin"—they decided to exploit their personal connections to "educate and inform parents about this alarming trend as well as to ask the industry to exercise self-restraint."[57] The PMRC consistently maintained that it was in favor of voluntary measures, not censorship, and that it was not opposed to all forms of popular music.

(((• **HEAR MORE** Tipper Gore on MyMusicKit

With a contribution from Mike Love of the Beach Boys and office space donated by Coors Beer (known for its anti-unionism and its donations to extremely conservative organizations), the group set up shop and formed an alliance with the national Parent/Teacher Association (PTA), gaining access to 5.6 million PTA members. The PMRC wanted the music industry to publish the lyrics to all new releases and institute a rating system ("X" for explicit lyrics, "V" for violence, "O" for occult, and so on). In August 1985, Stan Gortikov, then president of the Recording Industry Association of America (RIAA), offered a compromise generic warning: "PARENTAL ADVISORY/EXPLICIT LYRICS." Acknowledging the legitimacy of the PMRC's concerns, he cited only legal and logistical problems as the reason for the compromise.

Such problems did exist. "Unlike the motion picture industry, which rates about 325 films a year," Gortikov noted, "the recording industry releases 25,000 songs annually, which would require a process for rating 100 tunes a day."[58] He also pointed out that

As the leader of the Mothers of Invention, Frank Zappa was as creative and idiosyncratic as he was uncompromising and disciplined. In 1985, he played a prominent role at the PMRC hearings as an outspoken defender of First Amendment rights.

publication of lyrics without the publisher's permission would violate copyright laws. There were even greater difficulties of interpretation. As Simon Frith asserted long ago, different consumers attach competing meanings to their experiences of music.[59] Recording practices like echo, distortion, and backward masking (recording passages backward), which have led to charges of subliminal messages, further complicate any discussion of meaning. The mind boggles at the thought of a committee trying to make definitive cultural sense out of all of this, especially given the confusion over meaning that the music industry itself reported during the hearings. Frank Zappa recalled one record company executive who forced his group to excise the phrase *And I still remember mama with her apron and her pad/ Feeding all the boys at Ed's Cafe* because he thought that the word *pad* referred to a sanitary napkin.[60]

If Gortikov's willingness to compromise suggested that the music industry had surrendered to minimal pressure, it began to make more sense when the PMRC rejected his suggestion and unleashed its full powers or, more accurately, that of its members' mates. In September, the Senate Committee on Commerce, Science, and Transportation held public hearings on the PMRC's charges. Among others on the committee were John Danforth (chair), and Fritz Hollings and Al Gore, whose wives were PMRC members. Gortikov knew that the industry faced both legislation and regulation if it did not cooperate. Adding further pressure on the industry to cooperate was the home-taping bill (H.R. 2911), championed by record companies, which would have levied a tax on blank tape, enabling record companies to recover millions of dollars in revenues presumably lost because of home taping. Representative Thomas Downey was a sponsor of the bill and a past recipient of the RIAA's culture award; his wife was a PMRC member. When hearings on the House bill stalled, the industry looked to the Senate for help; the co-sponsor of the Senate bill (S. 1739) was Al Gore.

> **T**he 1985 PMRC hearings were reminiscent of the 1959 payola hearings. Once again, morally high-toned critics advocated protecting innocent children from the evils of popular music. Testimony from the young people allegedly affected was notably absent.

The 1985 PMRC hearings were reminiscent of the 1959 payola hearings. Once again, morally high-toned critics advocated protecting innocent children from the evils of popular music. Testimony from the young people allegedly affected was notably absent. Unlike the payola hearings, however, the players did not fall into neatly defined interest groups. Important labels, including MCA, A&M, and Geffen, initially broke ranks with the RIAA and joined a group of smaller labels to form an anticensorship group, the Musical Majority. While Smokey Robinson and Mike Love spoke out against so-called porn rock, artists ranging from Frank Zappa and Dee Snider of Twisted Sister to John Denver and Donny Osmond denounced the rating system.

Denver testified about the dangers of being overly literal in interpreting lyrics, recounting how some radio stations had refused to broadcast his "Rocky Mountain High" because they thought it was about drugs. PMRC co-founder Susan Baker had attempted to anticipate such warnings by pointing out earlier that Cole Porter's "The Birds Do It, The Bees Do It" could hardly be compared to W.A.S.P.'s "F-U-C-K Like a Beast."[61] However, Baker neglected to mention that the W.A.S.P. song had never been released in the United States or that the Porter classic *could* be compared to the Captain and Tennille's "Do That to Me One More Time," which, according to Zappa, had appeared on the PMRC's original hit list.[62] Omissions like these left many openly suspicious of the proceedings. "Beneath the 'save the children' rhetoric," editorialized *Rolling Stone*, "is an attempt by a politically powerful minority to impose its morality on the rest of us."[63]

In November 1985, shortly after the hearings, a compromise was reached between the RIAA and the PMRC. Essentially, the PMRC ended up agreeing to Gortikov's original proposal. With a voluntary rating system now in place, questions remained about what was considered offensive and how serious it was. These were the arenas in which the PMRC scored its greatest victories in terms of framing the issues and capturing public attention.

The Issues: Sex, Drugs, and Rock 'n' Roll Revisited

In 1988, the PMRC produced a video, *Rising to the Challenge,* outlining "five major themes" of concern to them in popular music:

1. Abuse of drugs and alcohol
2. Suicide
3. Graphic violence
4. Fascination with the occult
5. A sexuality that is graphic and explicit[64]

The PMRC claimed that these themes "occurred consistently in some rock music and especially in heavy metal."[65] At the time, they maintained that heavy metal was "the most disturbing element in contemporary music," claiming that "much of it dwells on themes that glorify rape, sado-masochism, violence, and suicide."[66] The fact is that, beginning with Chaucer's *Canterbury Tales,* Shakespeare's *Romeo and Juliet,* and Dante's *Inferno,* sex, drugs, violence, suicide, and the devil have always been compelling themes in Western art and often in the lives of its practitioners. "[Berlioz's] program for the *Symphonie Fantastique,*" Walser has noted, "explicitly connects opium use with the rhetorical splendor of his music. Abuse of alcohol is well documented for composers such as Schumann, Schubert, and Mussorgsky."[67] Wagner's music has long been associated with imperialism and violence. It is no coincidence that director Francis Ford Coppola selected Wagner's "Ride of the Valkyries" to accompany the bombing of a Vietnamese village in *Apocalypse Now. People* magazine reported that "Cole Porter's 'Love for Sale' was considered so 'blue' that it could be broadcast only in instrumental form. . . . Duke Ellington's 'The Mooche' was considered so provocative that some blamed it for a national rise in incidents of rape."[68]

In their video, the PMRC tried to make its point by drawing attention to Mötley Crüe vocalist Vince Neil's conviction in a drunk driving accident that took the life of another musician. Neil's irresponsibility notwithstanding, such behavior was hardly limited to heavy metal artists, and the vast majority of incidents involving heavy metal artists were far less serious. The PMRC argued that times had worsened since Elvis, but Elvis could match drug habits and violent outbursts with anyone. As to the music itself, Walser has noted that an "examination of eighty-eight [heavy metal] song lyrics reprinted by *Hit Parader* reveals relatively little concern with violence, drug use, or suicide."[69]

In targeting heavy metal—and then rap—the PMRC and their allies were drawing a line between themselves and youth. In so doing, they made it clear that other forms of music—even other forms of popular music—would not be subjected to the same scrutiny. Country music, for example, remained largely untouched by the PMRC, even though it has often dealt with themes of sex, violence, and alcohol. Critic Dave Marsh noted this double standard when he wrote, "Imagine how the rapper Ice Cube would be denounced for a song about drunkenly disrupting an old girlfriend's wedding and threatening the groom, then setting out on a bender with his crew. That is exactly the story line of Garth Brooks's 'I've Got Friends in Low Places.'"[70]

In some ways, the country music industry relished the attacks on rap and heavy metal. "Every morning when they play that stuff," said Jimmy Bowen, head of Nashville's Liberty Records, "people come running to us."[71] Frank Zappa even suggested that the rating system would "have the effect of protectionist legislation for the country music industry."[72] This is not to suggest that country's increased appeal was due only to the campaign against rap and metal. In a conservative political period, one would expect a music that has always been coded conservative to thrive. Occasionally, explicit political connections were drawn between country music and the new conservatism—as with Randy Travis's 1990 hit "Point of Light," written expressly for the first President Bush—but the real payoff for country music was in expansion and sales. Albums by country artists like Randy Travis, George Strait, Clint Black, and Garth Brooks began to appear regularly among the best-selling pop albums of the year, historically a rare occurrence for country music. In 1992, Garth Brooks alone had five albums among the year's most popular, including *Ropin' the Wind* at number one—the first country album ever cited as top pop album of the year.

The selective application of their research to rap and metal raised serious questions about whether the PMRC campaign was really about truth in advertising, as they claimed. In his testimony at the PMRC hearings, Stan Gortikov hinted at a more troubling agenda when he expressed the "fear that the only acceptable translation of the wishes of the PMRC will somehow constitute a de facto first stage form of censorship."[73] Since the rating system was created in 1985, many retail record outlets have, in fact, refused to carry stickered products, fearing organized consumer protests over them. These stores included department stores like Sears and J. C. Penney as well as music chains like Record World, Disc Jockey, and Camelot Music, the second largest chain in the country. The hugely influential Wal-Mart chain took the practice one step further, refusing to carry a growing list of nonstickered records, too.[74] (Wal-Mart had distinguished itself prior to this by refusing to stock thirty rock magazines, including *Rolling Stone, Creem,* and *Tiger Beat,* on the basis that they were "pornographic."[75] This policy was implemented while the giant warehouse chain was still selling guns.) By 1990, nineteen states had considered legislation requiring lyric labeling; some proposed laws would subject stores to criminal liability if they carried stickered product.[76] (At the same time, a spate of proposed legislation aimed to regulate live concerts and volume levels on boom boxes.) In 1992, the police chief of Guilderland, New York, sent a letter to local music stores warning about the legality of selling stickered records, even though selling stickered records was not illegal.[77] That same year,

four record outlets in Omaha, Nebraska, were charged with violating the state's harmful-to-minors law when they sold stickered LPs to teenagers.[78] If the warning label was simply to alert parents to controversial material, as the PMRC contended, why was it being used as a basis for criminalization? The fact is that the 1985 PMRC hearings marked the beginning of an intensified effort to put popular music on trial.

Shortly after the hearings, Ozzy Osbourne was sued by a couple who alleged that his song "Suicide Solution" had caused their nineteen-year-old son, John McCullom, to shoot himself. The case became a cause célèbre for the PMRC; the song and McCullom's death were highlighted in *Rising to the Challenge* a few years later. Because the lyrics referred to suicide as "the only way out," Osbourne's claim that the song was antisuicide was less than convincing, although the court dismissed the lawsuit. The arguments over the lyrics' meanings simply underscored the complexity of how music communicates. As Walser has pointed out, "Music does not simply inflict its meanings upon helpless fans . . . indeed, the evidence suggests that only a tiny minority of fans found 'Suicide Solution' depressing rather than sobering and thought-provoking."[79]

A late-1980s ABC *20/20* broadcast corroborated Walser's view. The show addressed a suicide case involving two Chicago teenagers, Nancy Grannan and Karen Logan, who were found dead clutching a note with the lyrics to Metallica's "Fade to Black." The PMRC blamed the song for encouraging suicide. The *20/20* segment included interviews with high school students and journalist Charles M. Young. Said Young, "Heavy metal speaks to the anger and despair of teenagers today the same way the blues used to speak to the despair and anger of black people in the South. Without heavy metal, there would probably be more suicides because metal and certain other forms of rock give teenagers something to believe in that they get no place else."[80] While Metallica acknowledged the tragedy in an interview in *Parade* magazine, bassist Jason Newsted also said, "I wish you could hear all the kids that come up to us and say, 'If it weren't for "Fade to Black" . . . I'd be dead now.' Or, 'You guys helped me through those times, to want to continue my life.' And there's hundreds of those."[81]

The most celebrated suicide case was the 1992 lawsuit alleging that subliminal messages on Judas Priest's *Stained Class* caused Ray Belknap and Jay Vance of Reno, Nevada, to kill themselves. Because lyrics about suicide had already been ruled protected speech in the

Osbourne trial, the plaintiffs built their case around alleged subliminal commands in the LP to "do it" and backward messages exhorting "try suicide," "suicide is in," and "sing my evil spirit." When it was revealed that Vance and Belknap came from severely troubled backgrounds that could easily have accounted for their suicides, Judas Priest was cleared of all charges. The judge found that subliminal messages, if any, on the album were neither intentional nor necessary to explain the suicide pact. He did leave the door open, however, to future lawsuits in ruling that "subliminal messages and 'backmasking' . . . are not protected speech under the First Amendment."[82]

Subliminal messages and backmasking also figured heavily in charges of Satanism, an issue revealing the affinity between the PMRC and the religious right. Prominent among Christian fundamentalists attempting to link popular music and Satanism were James Dobson, leader of Focus on the Family; Dan and Steve Peters, ministers in St. Paul; and the Reverend Donald Wildmon, head of the Mississippi-based American Family Association. In the late 1980s and early 1990s, with the PMRC's Susan Baker on its board of directors, Focus on the Family campaigned vigorously to remove "objectionable" records from stores. The Peters brothers, who lectured widely on the evils of popular music, were endorsed by PMRC co-founder Sally Nevius, who said, "It was guys like them who got the rock & roll wrecking ball rolling in the right direction."[83] While no organizational connection existed between Wildmon's group and the PMRC, a 1990 *Time* magazine article, titled "No Sympathy for the Devil," suggested an ideological one, describing the campaigns of both groups in similar terms.[84]

In 1985, the Back in Control center— a counseling program that advocated "deprogramming" youth who had fallen under the spell of heavy metal— estimated that over 1 million Americans were in covens.

Wildly divergent estimates are given as to how widespread and how dangerous Satanism is. In 1985, Darlyne Pettinicchio, a consultant on gangs for police agencies and a staffer at the Back in Control center—a counseling program that advocated, among other things, "deprogramming" youth who had fallen under the spell of heavy metal—estimated that over 1 million Americans were in covens.[85] In contrast, David Alexander wrote in the *Humanist* that the number was under a thousand. He also pointed out that Satanism was a protected religion under the First Amendment and that no Satanists had been charged in any ritual crimes.[86] Law enforcement agencies, in particular, have tended to view Satanism as dangerous. Writing in *The National Sheriff*, Robert J. Barry maintained that "Satanism is on the rise in America. Hardly a day passes without reports of violent acts conducted by Satanists. Across the country law enforcement organizations are receiving reports of homicide, mayhem, assault, suicide, child abuse and animal mutilations that are linked with the satanic occult."[87] Barry went on to claim, "One of the major contemporary movements exploiting Satanism is the music industry and its punk rock and 'heavy metal' productions."[88] Despite little evidence to validate Barry's claim—other than the sensational arrest of Richard Ramirez, the alleged Night Stalker, described by the press as "an AC/DC fan who had apparently been obsessed by Satanism"[89]— the issue of Satanism in popular music persisted. It reached fever pitch in 1990 when New York's cardinal John J. O'Connor warned his flock that "diabolically instigated violence is on the rise"[90] and noted that "some kinds of rock music" were the devil's tool, singling out Ozzy Osbourne's "Suicide Solution" as an example.[91] This was three weeks *after* J. Gordon Melton, head of the Institute for the Study of American Religion, reported that "press reports of satanic activities showed no increase and that upon investigation many of the most dramatic reports turned out to be without basis."[92]

If the crusaders who attacked heavy metal were serious about making the connection between popular music and violent crime, why didn't they challenge Tom Metzger, a former Ku Klux Klansman and leader of the White Aryan Resistance (WAR), and his son John when they organized an Aryan Woodstock for their followers in 1989? Where were they when *New York Times* critic Jon Pareles took Public Enemy to task for their anti-Semitism and criticized Guns 'N' Roses for their use of *nigger* and *faggot*?[93] Because neither racism nor bigotry had been on their agenda, these concerns went largely unmentioned until Pareles reframed the issues.

The way a problem is framed can shape responses to it. Nowhere was this more apparent than in the PMRC's concern over "a sexuality that is graphic and explicit," a phrasing that made sexuality itself the problem. Thus, no distinctions were permitted between sexuality that is violent and degrading to women and sexuality that is mutual and sensuous. In this phrasing, it mattered not whether a woman was a passive victim or actively in control of her sexual choices. The only thing that mattered was that sex was talked about. The PMRC's inability to make finer distinctions led only to the conclusion that "sex is bad," a disorienting and repressive message for teenagers at a crucial stage in their sexual development.

Madonna was the main target of the PMRC's concerns about sexuality. Susan Baker said that "Like a Virgin" moved her to become a founding member of the PMRC. Pam Howar expressed the concern that Madonna was teaching young girls "how to be porn queens in heat."[94] Madonna had expressed her sexuality consistently and boldly and was forthright in her promotion of safe sex, speaking out publicly on the issue, performing at AIDS benefits, including informational materials in her albums, and distributing condoms at her concerts. In so doing, she had become a major source of irritation for the PMRC and the religious right. Transforming the role of undergarments and taking liberties with Christian iconography only added to their ire.

Her "Justify My Love" was, for some, the final straw. The video contained not-quite-explicit sex, made more complicated by insinuations of homosexuality and group sex. Its sexuality was soft and gentle, and it forced her fans to grapple with the complexities of sex that her critics would sooner have avoided by preaching abstinence. There was certainly room for discussion concerning her choice of images, but for the PMRC, the issue was closed. "Justify My Love" earned the distinction of being the first video officially banned by MTV, a status that quickly turned it into the best-selling music video in history.

Battles over sex in popular music have tended to pit First Amendment defenses against fundamentalist dismissals of all sexually provocative material as obscene. In December 1985, shortly after the PMRC's hearings, a young girl from Los Angeles purchased the Dead Kennedys' *Frankenchrist* album, which included the poster *Penis Landscape* by the award-winning Swiss artist H. R. Giger. Her parents were so horrified at the graphic portrayal of ten male appendages that they called the California attorney general's office to complain. In April 1986, Jello Biafra, the band's leader, was arrested for distributing harmful material to a minor. Criminal charges were also leveled at his record company, his distributor, the L.A. wholesaler, and even the sixty-seven-year-old owner of the pressing plant that manufactured the record. The store that sold the record was not charged because, according to the police, "[t]hey were cooperative and took the record off the shelves."[95]

The Dead Kennedys' bust had all the markings of a test case. Apparently, the district attorney thought that the label, Alternative Tentacles, would be an easy target because it was a small company that could ill afford an expensive legal battle.[96] Biafra, however, decided to fight. Defending his artistic choices as political speech, he argued that the Giger poster resonated with themes that ran through the *Frankenchrist* album. Whatever the courts may have thought of the wacky, activist history of the Dead Kennedys, Jello Biafra was a worthy opponent and a serious political figure. In 1979, he had run for mayor of San Francisco and placed fourth in a field of ten candidates. The case ended with all defendants cleared, but the protracted legal battle bankrupted Alternative Tentacles and ended the career of the Dead Kennedys.

This obscenity case was followed by several others that received nationwide coverage. In June 1988, Tommy Hammond, the owner of a small record store in Alabama, was arrested on obscenity charges for selling 2 Live Crew's *Move Something* to an adult undercover agent. At the time of his arrest, the album had not been judged obscene by any court. In fact, Hammond kept the albums behind the counter and refused to sell them to minors because they carried a warning sticker. Nevertheless, four months after his arrest, Hammond was fined $500 by a municipal court judge, who declared the album obscene. Hammond appealed and was eventually acquitted, but neither 2 Live Crew nor sellers of their albums were done with obscenity charges.

In 1990, 2 Live Crew's LP *As Nasty As They Wanna Be* became the first recording to be declared obscene by a federal district court. After the ruling, the group was arrested for performing some of the album's material at an adults-only nightclub. Charles Freeman, an African American record-store owner from Fort Lauderdale, Florida, was also arrested for selling the LP. Like the Dead Kennedys, 2 Live Crew was thought to be an easy target. Cuts that detailed sex in every imaginable position were bound to be considered offensive by many, and the record was produced by a small, independent label that had no money for an extended legal battle.

The 2 Live Crew case is important not only because it tested the strength of the First Amendment, but also because it confronted the racism associated with the application of the obscenity laws.

The 2 Live Crew case is important not only because it tested the strength of the First Amendment, but also because it confronted the racism associated with the application of the obscenity laws. Presently, a three-pronged legal test determines obscenity. A work must (1) lack serious literary, artistic, political, or scientific value; (2) when taken as a whole, appeal to prurient interest; and (3) be patently offensive, as judged by community standards.[97] Given this third prong, what the Supreme Court has called the "dim and uncertain" line separating obscenity from constitutionally protected speech can change from one locale to another. A work judged obscene in Florida may be perfectly legal in New York; which was, in fact, the case with the 2 Live Crew recording. The complexity of determining community standards was the basis of 2 Live Crew's defense. Appearing as an expert witness, eminent African American scholar Henry Louis Gates, Jr., testified that 2 Live Crew's risqué rhymes were part of the venerable tradition of competitive African American word games such as signifying and playing the dozens, and that judging the legal status of 2 Live Crew's work, therefore, required a familiarity with "black codes," which had been absent in the original determination of obscenity.[98] The defense prevailed and 2 Live crew was acquitted. That didn't help Charles Freeman, who was convicted and fined $1,000 for selling the record in a separate trial. The obscenity ruling itself was overturned on appeal in May 1992 and finally laid to rest when the U.S. Supreme Court refused to challenge the appellate decision.[99]

Charges of obscenity in rap have been second only to charges of violence. Such charges became particularly loud in the 1992 election year, primarily because of the political fallout from the uprising in Los Angeles following the Rodney King verdict. (In that case, L.A. police were found not guilty in the brutal beating—captured on video—of King, an African American.) Cultural and political differences resulted in considerable distortions of what was actually being said. When President Clinton characterized rapper/activist Sister Souljah's comments as "full of hatred," David Mills, the *Washington Post* reporter who had interviewed her, noted in an article for *Essence,* "Clinton really *did* take her comment out of context. Souljah was describing the attitude of the L.A. rioters, not prescribing future action."[100]

In the same time period, the rap/metal song "Cop Killer" from Ice-T's *Body Count,* which he had been performing for over a year, sparked further national debate over rap's seeming encouragement of violence. For some, the song captured their outrage over the King verdict. At the same time, its violent imagery prompted others, including dozens of police organizations, to call for a boycott of Time Warner, then the parent company of Ice-T's record label. In the ensuing controversy, both conservative and liberal public figures denounced the record. Some tried (unsuccessfully) to ban it under federal sedition laws. "Maybe I underestimate my juice," said a bewildered Ice-T, "but there's people out there with nuclear bombs, people with armies, and the president has time to sit up and get into it with me?"[101]

While the furor over "Cop Killer" was similar to the furor over N.W.A.'s "_ _ _ _ tha Police" a few years earlier, the environment was quite different. Most of the world had seen the video of Rodney King's beating and knew the police had been absolved. These events recontextualized the messages of both songs. While it is easy to understand why some police officers found the song upsetting, it is interesting that the National Black Police Association denounced the Warner boycott, noting that "Cop Killer" "did not happen in a vacuum. People have always expressed their feelings and opinions through songs, and they are talking about how African-American people have been victimized by police brutality. And that is very real. Where were those organizations when Rodney King was beat up and when that verdict came in?"[102] The association was disappointed when Ice-T agreed to pull the song from future pressings of the album. Like many others, it feared that the action would send "a negative message to other artists."[103]

Shortly afterward, three rappers made headlines for allegedly crossing the line into violence in real life. In August 1993, Snoop Doggy Dogg, as he was then called, was charged in connection with the fatal shooting of Philip Woldemarian in Los Angeles. In the incident, his bodyguard, not Snoop, shot Woldemarian. The rapper pleaded not guilty and was eventually acquitted. In October, Tupac Shakur was arrested for aggravated assault in the shooting of two off-duty Atlanta police officers. Three weeks later, he was arrested again with two friends on charges of sexual assault (for which he eventually did time). Public Enemy frontman Flavor Flav was arrested for attempted murder and criminal possession of a firearm. He had confronted his girlfriend's alleged lover with a gun and fired one shot into the ground. Fortunately, he had enough presence of mind to check himself into the Betty Ford Clinic for crack abuse. Still, his irresponsible behavior compromised Public Enemy's message of positive self-determination for African Americans.

Although Snoop Dogg was only indirectly involved in violence, his case received more publicity than the others because he had just made music history. On 11 December 1993,

Tupac Shakur grappled with the contradictions of the gangsta lifestyle in his art and in his life.

DoggyStyle became the first debut album ever to enter the *Billboard* pop charts at number one; it sold more than 800,000 units in its first week. Snoop, a protégé of rapper/producer Dr. Dre, was distinguished from other rappers by his style, described in the *New York Times* as "gentle." "[W]here many rappers scream," said *Times* reporter Touré, "he speaks softly." Touré then added, "While Snoop delivers rhymes delicately, the content is anything but."[104]

For Tupac Shakur, both incidents initially seemed out of character. Described as quiet and shy, Shakur was a formally trained actor who had received an NAACP Image Award nomination for his role in the film *Poetic Justice.* His hit single "Keep Ya Head Up," according to Havelock Nelson, "speaks urgently and respectfully about the struggles of black women."[105] Thus, many observers of the hip hop scene found Shakur's behavior troubling. Havelock Nelson argued, "Shakur . . . is endangering more than just his own career. He and other rappers who can't get a grip are also helping set the stage for hip hop's last blast. With their buck-wild actions, these artists are unwittingly playing into the hands of forces fed up with heightened levels of black achievement."[106]

Rap had been roundly criticized when its art simply imitated life. The media blitz following these incidents seemed to suggest the more disturbing possibility that there was no difference between the two.

Rap had been roundly criticized when its art simply imitated life. The media blitz following these incidents seemed to suggest the more disturbing possibility that there was no difference between the two. According to this logic, rap could be held responsible for all social disintegration. As David Toop pointed out, however, "[c]hildren carry automatic weapons like Uzis and sell crack in the streets. Babies are born with AIDS and teenagers are shot dead for their shoes. Music may be powerful and influential but no music is strong enough to create this kind of social decay."[107] When James Brown ran afoul of the law, no one said funk was to blame. The fact that Tupac Shakur served time for some of his actions should be no different. Such instances cannot be used legitimately to indict a whole genre of music.

Following these incidents, media outlets began falling over themselves to outdo each other's antiviolence policies. Black radio station WBLS in New York banned violence and profanity from its broadcasts. The rap magazine *Rap Sheet* stopped carrying advertisements that pictured guns. Black Entertainment Television (BET) instituted a no-guns policy in the videos they aired. These moves coincided with an escalation of protests against gangsta rap from within the black community. In late December 1993, the National Political Congress of Black Women (NPCBW), which boasted a membership of 2,500, staged demonstrations in Washington, D.C., against two record retail outlets, Nobody Beats the Wiz and Sam Goody. The organization was joined in civil disobedience by activist Dick Gregory and endorsed by the National Council of Negro Women, the NAACP, and Jesse Jackson's National Rainbow Coalition, among others. Beginning in February 1994, both the House and Senate scheduled hearings on gangsta rap. Senator Carol Moseley Braun, an African American who chaired the Senate committee, proposed a rating system—the same idea abandoned in 1985 as too unwieldy—"to prevent records from getting into the hands of children."[108] No rappers were invited to testify at the first round of hearings. But one aspect of these inquiries differed significantly from the PMRC investigation. While the participants who criticized rap—most of whom were African Americans—did not condone violent or misogynist lyrics, nearly all recognized the legitimacy of black rage and placed their comments in the context of societal disintegration. "The issue is not whether to spurn, regulate, restrict, segregate, or otherwise curb the distribution of hip hop music," said David W. Harleston of Rush Associated Labels. "Rather, the issue is whether we, as a community and nation, are prepared to address the very issues that have given rise to the lyrics that some find so troubling."[109] The question that followed logically was not Why are some rappers so offensive? but rather, Why do so many fans find offensive rappers appealing? This question suggests a consideration of popular music as one variable among the myriad of social forces that affect the quality of life.

After 1994, rap hearings began to subside, only to pick up again two years later with the shooting deaths of Tupac Shakur and Biggie Smalls. At the time of Shakur's death in 1996, his fourth album, *All Eyez on Me*, which debuted at number one, had sold 3 million copies, placing him squarely in the company of top-selling artists. Shakur had built his career steadily, with the release of three previous albums (*2pacalypse Now* [1991], *Strictly 4 My N.I.G.G.A.Z.* [1993], *Me Against the World* [1995]) and well-received appearances in a number of films (*Juice* [1992], *Poetic Justice* [1993], *Above the Rim* [1994]), and with two more films in the can (*Gridlock* and *Gang Related*). Two years before his death, Shakur had been shot five times during a robbery in New York. He implied that Biggie Smalls and Sean "Puffy" Combs, the head of Smalls's label, Bad Boy Records, were involved or knew the shooter's identity, a charge that Smalls and Combs denied. The accusation placed the shooting within the age-old East Coast/West Coast rap rivalry; Shakur recorded for L.A.-based Death Row Records, run at that time by Marion "Suge" Knight, who was widely suspected of having ties to organized crime. Knight had publicly insulted Combs and Bad Boy at the 1995 *Source Awards* show in New York. For his part, Shakur had baited Smalls viciously on "Hit 'Em Up," on which he claimed to have had sex with Smalls's estranged wife, Faith Evans. Shakur was shot in Las Vegas while riding in Knight's car. He died one week later, on 13 September 1996.

Biggie Smalls, who recorded as The Notorious B.I.G., grew up big and tough on the streets of Brooklyn, but had a gift for constructing rhymes. If Shakur displayed a siege mentality on *Me Against the World,* B.I.G. fortold his own death on his debut album, *Ready to Die* (1994). After Shakur's death, Combs tried to end the hostility between Bad Boy and Death Row, as he and Smalls prepared for the release of Smalls's second album, *Life After Death.* Both felt that Smalls was on the verge of a major breakthrough. Trying to put Shakur's death behind them, Smalls and Combs ventured to Los Angeles (with extra security) in March 1997 to present an award to Toni Braxton at the *Soul Train Awards*. The following night, after leaving a party, Smalls was shot dead in his car. As of this writing, the murders of Tupac and Biggie remain cold cases. Combs paid tribute to his friend and protégé on a chart-topping duet with Faith Evans titled "I'll Be Missing You." It was a single from his own debut as rapper Puff Daddy. Fittingly, he titled the album *No Way Out*.

LEARN MORE
Chapter Questions
on MyMusicKit

Against the odds, metal had risen from the embers of a dying 1970s subculture. Rap emerged from one of the most dispossessed communities in the country. By the late 1980s, they had become the primary musical expressions of youth culture. Working from the bottom up, these styles seemed to thrive on the indifference, even hostility, of the music industry. They engendered fanatical devotion among their fans and a ferocious backlash among their detractors. In this sense, these styles were decidedly political, whether they intended to make an overt political statement or not. The intensity of feelings generated by rap and metal resonated with the profound rethinking of American values that characterized the period. As such, these types of music were frequently the targets for government investigations and the wrath of conservative social organizations. In the 1990s, a new sound that was labeled alternative began competing for national attention among youths. For many, alternative was the fulfillment of the political promise of punk a decade later. Alternative emerged as an intensely personal music with a discordant sound, and its artists initially adopted a doggedly anticommercial posture. Paradoxically, the music became wildly successful.

Packaging Pop Trends: The Search for the Next Big Thing

The success of rap and metal at the dawn of the 1990s reminded many of precisely that aspect of rock 'n' roll that had so distressed the moral guardians of the 1950s: that the music of the most disenfranchised—angry blacks and irreverent working-class whites— could be the most compelling culturally, politically, and economically.

Accordingly, *Rolling Stone*'s Mikal Gilmore remembered 1990 as "the year in which rock & roll was reborn."[1] Something of a postmodern twist to this rebirth became apparent as the major-market breakthrough of what had been called alternative music brought about a further disintegration of the barriers between cult and mass, margin and mainstream, underground and commercial, and (ultimately) serious art and popular culture. As boundaries collapsed, the music business faced a crisis of categories and began packaging musical trends in the latter half of the decade according to tried-and-true marketing categories based on age, gender, ethnicity, and, of course, race.

> *The success of rap and metal at the dawn of the 1990s reminded many of precisely that aspect of rock 'n' roll that had so distressed the moral guardians of the 1950s: that the music of the most disenfranchised—angry blacks and irreverent working-class whites—could be the most compelling culturally, politically, and economically.*

At first, rap and metal developed separately along racial lines. Except for their shared commitments to technology and transgression, these genres evolved in fairly distinct ways— rap, based on sophisticated electronic beats and def(t) linguistic juxtapositions; metal, based on guitar virtuosic precision and sheer loudness. Beneath these two main youth cultural trends, however, lay an underground of post-punk alternative sounds in which genre boundaries were not always so clear or well defended.

Cross-genre influences were becoming more conspicuous as the 1990s dawned. According to Gilmore, Living Colour's second long-playing record (LP), *Time's Up*, "fused punk rhythms and speed metal leads with a complex harmonic architecture derived from the

367

LEARN MORE

Learning objectives
on MyMusicKit

avant-garde sensibility of legendary jazz saxophonist Ornette Coleman."[2] Living Colour's mission was to reclaim rock 'n' roll as black music. Cuts like "History Lesson" and "Pride" drove the point home. At the same time, Faith No More, an all-white post-punk band, released *The Real Thing,* which "took a personalized, raplike delivery and intercut it with hard-edge metallic textures."[3] Faith No More had been knocking around the San Francisco underground for eight years and had two previous albums—*We Care a Lot* (1985) and *Introduce Yourself* (1987). Bolstered by MTV support for the single "Epic," *The Real Thing* went gold. "Between these two bands," Gilmore said, "the face of modern rock was virtually overhauled this last year."[4]

Both Living Colour and Faith No More were among 1990's best-selling pop artists and enjoyed substantial mainstream market sales. Notably, the label *alternative* was applied to both groups. That year, Sinéad O'Connor, another mainstay of alternative music, released her second album, *I Do Not Want What I Haven't Got.* Propelled by her heart-wrenching video of Prince's "Nothing Compares 2 U," the album was number one on *Billboard*'s pop charts for six weeks, achieving double platinum certification. Combining Irish pathos with punk rage, O'Connor's 1987 debut album, *The Lion and the Cobra,* had won her a devoted following in the alternative category. With even more challenging material, *Do Not Want* sold millions of copies. This level of success raises the question: Alternative to what?

The most popular music of the 1960s signified an alternative to mainstream values even as it dominated sales. In this sense, the term *alternative* connotes opposition or resistance to established norms. While the mainstream music industry can control the marketplace economically, it cannot determine the meaning of the music. For all the saccharine teen pop that clogged the airwaves, it was still possible for the targeted polemics of Rage Against the Machine to sell platinum. An established rocker like Bruce Springsteen could still shake up the status quo with "American Skin (41 Shots)," about the murder of Haitian immigrant Amadou Diallo. Content to focus on developing new revenue streams, the major record companies had long since distanced themselves from the creative process. As a result, popular musicians enjoyed more autonomy than most other popular artists. The failure to understand this fact is at the heart of our inability to grasp the contradictions inherent in the notion of alternative music.

Sinéad O'Connor displays the Video of the Year, Best Female, and Post-Modern video awards she won for "Nothing Compares 2 U" in 1990. It was that kind of recognition that began to collapse alternative into the mainstream.

The idea that music can retain its integrity only *before* it reaches a mass public leads to the tendency to lionize artists when they are least successful and to dismiss them precisely at the moment of their greatest impact.

The idea that music can retain its integrity only before it reaches a mass public leads to the tendency to lionize artists when they are least successful and to dismiss them precisely at the moment of their greatest impact.

A culture war of sorts has been going on since rock 'n' roll appeared, and most often the battles have been fought in the arena of popular music. The music industry has responded differently at different times. In the 1950s, the majors generally aligned themselves with the more conservative elements of society in resisting rock 'n' roll. The writers, performers, deejays, and independent record companies that produced and disseminated the music challenged the industry's established powers and emerged victorious. From the mid-1960s on, the majors realized that independent labels were key to the industry's future success and began to rely on them for research and development. Most independent labels ferreted out niches of unsated consumer demand and/or test-marketed new musical forms; the majors then bought them outright, distributed their products, or signed their most successful artists. This was the pattern with punk and disco (1970s) and with rap and metal (1980s). The only things that changed in the 1990s were the speed and efficiency with which the mainstream music industry was able to incorporate new trends.

Alternative as Mainstream

In the 1980s, the music usually labeled *alternative* had its roots in the punk movements of the 1970s and their 1980s post-punk (as opposed to new wave) variants. However, the label was applied in one way for African American artists and in another for white artists. The fact that African American artists as diverse as the metallic Living Colour, the folk-oriented Tracy Chapman, blues musician Robert Cray, and soul singer Terrence Trent D'Arby were labeled *alternative* speaks more to race-based marketing strategies than to a shared aesthetic. Chapman outgrew the confines of the label when her self-titled debut LP went to number one on the pop charts, but as a black female acoustic folk singer, she was still in a class by herself. Her search for a musical home led her to headliner status on the Amnesty International tours and eventually to Farm Aid V, where she shared the stage with Living Colour's Vernon Reid. She collaborated with Reid and Bobby Womack on her third album, *Matters of the Heart,* in 1992. In 1991, Reid and his group, still falling through the cracks of conventional marketing categories, joined the first Lollapalooza tour, adding breadth to the alternative music festival. When Living Colour previewed their 1992 lineup, with Doug Wimbish on bass, they chose the legendary New York punk club, CBGB, to do so.

White alternative groups, though also sounding different from one another, derived from a more coherent lineage that included the Dead Kennedys from San Francisco, Fugazi from Washington, D.C., and R.E.M. from Athens, Georgia, and the groups associated with the hardcore SST label (Black Flag and the Minutemen from Los Angeles, Sonic Youth from New York, Dinosaur, Jr., from Massachusetts, and Hüsker Dü from Minnesota). Athens and Minneapolis had established the viability of regional alternative scenes, but it was Seattle that put the music over the top.

Seattle: From Sub Pop to Superstars

Seattle had earlier spawned the fathers of guitar-based instrumental rock 'n' roll, the Ventures, and the greatest psychedelic guitarist of them all, Jimi Hendrix. In fact, Seattle had had a thriving alternative scene for years. At its center was the Sub Pop label, founded by Bruce Pavitt and Jon Poneman. Among the groups that recorded for Sub Pop were Soundgarden, Nirvana, Pearl Jam, Alice in Chains, Smashing Pumpkins, Mud Honey, L7, the Afghan Whigs (from Cincinnati), and Screaming Trees. Seattle's radio stations KCMU and KJET supported these groups early on, as did a developed alternative press that included the now-defunct *Backlash* and the *Seattle Rocket*. Prior to the 1990s, all the groups lived around Seattle and played to local audiences. In 1991, however, Nirvana released their major label debut album on David Geffen's DGC imprint. *Nevermind* went national with a vengeance. Aided significantly by MTV's decision to push the video of its haunting single "Smells Like Teen Spirit" to anthem-of-a-generation status, *Nevermind* managed to displace Michael Jackson's *Dangerous* from the number one slot on the pop charts, if only for a week. *Nevermind* sold 3 million copies in four months and continued to sell 100,000 copies a week. Nirvana embodied all the contradictions of alternative music and fell victim to its pressures early on. The beginning of the end started with the group's ascent to rock superstardom once Seattle was discovered.

Although Nirvana most readily comes to mind when considering the incorporation of alternative into the mainstream, the Seattle gold rush actually began with the signing of Soundgarden to A&M in 1988.

Although Nirvana most readily comes to mind when considering the incorporation of alternative into the mainstream, the Seattle gold rush actually began with the signing of Soundgarden to A&M in 1988. Soundgarden had contributed three tracks to a 1986 compilation album called *Deep Six*, which marked the rise of the Seattle scene. Earlier, Soundgarden had recorded two extended play discs (EPs) for Sub Pop and a Grammy-nominated LP for SST entitled *Ultramega OK*. Kim Neely described *Ultramega OK* as "a pastiche of psychedelia, blistering hardcore and wrecking-ball blooze wrapped up with odd tunings and time signatures [that] was a sonic fuck-you to the candy-ass poodlehead bands that were clogging the charts at the time."[5] In the late 1980s, Soundgarden's promise prompted major label a&r personnel to descend on Seattle in search of the next big thing. Columbia signed Alice in Chains, Pearl Jam went to Epic, and Nirvana signed with DGC.

((•)) **HEAR MORE**
Kurt Cobain on
MyMusicKit

As rock 'n' roll hard luck tales go, the story of Nirvana and the late Kurt Cobain, the group's leader and spiritual center, was not atypical. The group originally hailed from Aberdeen, Washington, a dying lumber town that passed on to its inhabitants depression, disillusionment, and dysfunction. Cobain was a product of all three. Playing around Olympia, Tacoma, and Seattle, Nirvana came to the attention of Sub Pop, which issued a test single in 1988, "Love Buzz" backed with "Big Cheese." That year, the group contributed "Spank Thru" to a sampler called *Sub Pop 200,* an early anthology of the dark, brooding guitar-based sludge that came to be known as grunge. The following year, Sub Pop released Nirvana's first full-length LP, *Bleach,* which had respectable regional sales, showcased Cobain's songwriting, and resulted in the DGC signing. By this time, Cobain and bassist Krist Novoselic had settled on Dave Grohl as the band's permanent drummer. *Nevermind* and its hit single captured "a defining moment in rock history," argued Anthony DeCurtis. "Nirvana transformed the '80s into the '90s."[6]

With the release of Nevermind, *Nirvana introduced alternative to the mainstream with a vengeance. Here, the late Kurt Cobain shrinks at the prospect of fame while Krist Novoselic sports a T-shirt advertising Sonic Youth, their labelmates at DGC.*

The impact of *Nevermind* was a huge burden to Cobain. How could he be the spokesperson for a generation when he could barely keep his own life together? Ultimately, what he called "medicating" himself (with heroin) and being photographed with the barrel of an M-16 in his mouth said more about his pain than wearing a T-shirt that read "Corporate Magazines Still Suck" for Nirvana's *Rolling Stone* cover said about his integrity.

Following the runaway success of *Nevermind,* alternative bands began entering the mainstream as never before. Pearl Jam's debut album, *Ten,* went straight to number two and, with sales of 7 million copies, could still be found among the top 100 albums three years later. The group's follow-up album, *Vs.* (1993), entered the charts at number one. Alice in Chains enjoyed similar success: In October 1992, with their 1990 debut, *Facelift,* still on the charts, the group's second album, *Dirt,* entered the *Billboard* 200 at number six. That same week, Pearl Jam's *Ten* held the number seven slot, and the multi-artist compilation soundtrack to Cameron Crowe's *Singles,* the film that put Seattle on the big screen, was at number ten.

With the 1993 release of *In Utero,* Nirvana's long-awaited studio follow-up to *Nevermind,* Cobain told *Rolling Stone,* "I've never been happier," appearing on the cover in a suit and tie. This was Cobain's other side: the brilliant singer/songwriter who tried to exorcise his demons through his art; the genuine misfit who longed for the normalcy of love and family, which he tried to find in his marriage to Courtney Love (leader of the female-dominated punk band Hole) and the co-parenting of their child, Frances Bean. Ultimately, however, the portrait he painted for *Rolling Stone* was the forgery of a man in serious denial. His relationship with Love was a tumultuous foray into co-dependency, complete with guns, drugs, domestic

"Smells Like Teen Spirit"

Artist: Nirvana

Music/Lyrics by Kurt Cobain,
Dave Grohl, Krist Noveselic

Label: DGC, from the CD
Nevermind (1991)

The debut album of the power trio Nirvana, led by the intelligent, talented, and unhappy 24-year-old Kurt Cobain, established grunge as a popular style. Nirvana's 1991 disc *Nevermind*, chock-full of dark, angry, powerful, and hook-ridden rock anthems, garnered extensive critical acclaim. The album's hit single "Smells Like Teen Spirit" reached the Top Ten, and in some cases the number one position, internationally.

In contrast to some of the poseurs who throughout rock's history had made a profession of portraying the anguished artist, Cobain was both truly brilliant and truly tormented, and the wave of angst, rage, and despair unleashed in his lyrics gained him a reputation as spokesperson for Generation X, a title he regarded with ambivalence. Chronically depressed and a heroin addict, Cobain ended his life in 1994.

Musical Style Notes

Nirvana's instrumentation falls into the category of power trio—guitar (Kurt Cobain), bass (Krist Noveselic), and drums (Dave Grohl)—a combination that has a long history in the world of rock 'n' roll, although it was used in different ways. For power trios like the Jimi Hendrix Experience, it was all about the virtuoso lead guitarist; for others, the guitar was primarily employed as a rhythm instrument, while the bass laid down structurally simple but prominent lines, and the drums were the "star" attraction that filled the extensive available sonic space. Like the Who's Keith Moon or Led Zeppelin's John Bonham, Dave Grohl's drums are the instrumental power engine driving Nirvana's guitar riff–based songs.

"Smells Like Teen Spirit," though perceived at the time as a new alternative musical phenomenon, is in many ways a classic pop single, with a fantastic guitar hook, simple repeated chord progression, and cathartic shout-along chorus. The song's signature succession of chords is in a dark, minor key, and functions somewhat outside the normal harmonic expectations of rock 'n' roll (for those who have studied music theory, the chord progression is I, IV, III, VI).

Structurally, the song has a verse-chorus form, but the verse has two parts: an A section that features new lyrics each time and a B section with the same hypnotic, repetitious "hello" lyric each time. The chorus continues the technique of repetition but moves from hypnotic to a litany of rage and despair. This combination of introspective, atmospheric, soft verse and hard, screaming chorus is a strong stylistic marker of grunge rock.

Musical "Road Map"

TIMINGS	COMMENTS	LYRICS
0:00–0:25	Introduction: electric guitar begins with the song's signature chord progression. Drums enter at 0:07. Other instruments join at 0:09, including guitar, now playing with distortion.	
0:25–0:34	Introduction ends with reduced volume, transition to verse.	
0:34–0:50	Verse 1	*Load up . . .*
0:50–1:06	B section, which provides transition from the verse to the chorus.	*Hello, hello,*
1:06–1:31	Chorus Note the change in energy and sonic texture—harder rock sound, screaming vocals.	*With the . . .* *Entertain us . . .*
1:31–1:47	Instrumental transition to Verse 2	
1:47–2:04	Verse 2	*I'm worst . . .*
2:04–2:20	B section	*Hello, hello, . . .*
2:20–2:45	Chorus	*With the . . .*
2:45–2:53	Instrumental transition	
2:53–3:33	Guitar solo over musical content of verse	
3:25–3:33	Ends with instrumental transition to Verse 3	
3:33–3:50	Verse 3 (Note feedback in background.)	*And I forget . . .*
3:50–4:05	B section	*Hello, hello, . . .*
4:05–4:58	Chorus Last line repeats nine times Sound fades on last chord, with guitar feedback.	*With the . . .* *A denial . . .*

violence, overdoses, detoxes, and police interventions. Neither were things much rosier on the artistic front. The release of *In Utero* had been fraught with last-minute title and track changes. Cobain had wanted to title the album *I Hate Myself and Want to Die* after a song he had written for the LP, but he pulled the song just prior to release because he feared no one would get the joke. (It subsequently appeared as the lead track on the otherwise lackluster *The Beavis and Butt-Head Experience.*) After the album's release, he authorized Geffen to remove the collage of fetuses from the album's back cover and to change the title of "Rape Me," the album's most controversial song, to "Waif Me." Because Cobain equated compromise with selling out, these changes must have eaten away at his artistic soul.

Cobain's suicide surprised no one (although press reports greatly exaggerated the damage). Still, people were unprepared for what they discovered on 8 April 1994. In the greenhouse above his garage, Cobain had pressed the barrel of a 20-gauge shotgun to his head and pulled the trigger. Commentators spoke of Cobain's death with a profound sense of loss, though they did not excuse the suicide. Aware that troubled teens might emulate his actions, Courtney Love repeatedly called her late husband an "asshole" as she read his suicide note aloud. Donna Gaines, author of *Teenage Wasteland,* a superb book on teen suicide, wrote in *Rolling Stone*: "His suicide was a betrayal; it negated an unspoken contract among members of a generation who depended on one another to reverse the parental generation's legacy of neglect, confusion and frustration. Cobain broke that promise. He just walked."[7] Thus, Nirvana's contribution to the music that bore their imprint was cut short.

Following Cobain's death, a number of more established bands from outside Seattle—notably R.E.M. and Sonic Youth—continued to propel alternative toward the mainstream.

R.E.M.'s career was a model that Cobain might have liked for Nirvana—mainstream success at a pace that could be handled without abandoning artistic or personal integrity.

R.E.M.'s career was a model that Cobain might have liked for Nirvana—mainstream success at a pace that could be handled without abandoning artistic or personal integrity. When Cobain died in 1994, R.E.M.'s 1992 outing, *Automatic for the People,* had already logged seventy weeks on the pop charts, after peaking at number two. Formed in Athens, Georgia, in 1980 as a jangly, inaccessible folk rock unit, R.E.M. was as beholden to 1960s-era Byrds as to any punk influences. *Rolling Stone* selected their first full-length album, *Murmur* (1983), as album of the year over Michael Jackson's *Thriller* and the *Village Voice* lavished similar best-of praise on it at a time when the album had sold only 150,000 copies. From *Murmur* on, most of R.E.M.'s albums sold slightly better than the one before. In 1987, *Document* became their first million seller; *Green,* their 1988 major label debut, occasioned their first arena-level tour; *Out of Time* (1991), their first number one album, joined *Nevermind,* as one of the releases that forced major labels to take alternative acts more seriously. In 1991, R.E.M. tallied seven Grammy nominations, further erasing the distinction between alternative and mainstream. *Out of Time* actually bested *Nevermind* for the Best Alternative Music Grammy. R.E.M. also walked away with additional trophies for Best Pop Performance and Best Short-Form Video for "Losing My Religion," *Out of Time*'s hit single.

Throughout their career, the members of R.E.M. have kept their personal lives private and have tried to be musically and politically progressive. Michael Stipe, the group's leader, has

R.E.M. has enjoyed success at a pace they could handle without compromising their artistic or personal integrity. If Kurt Cobain could have done likewise, it might have changed the course of his life.

championed environmental causes, animal rights, and antinuclear campaigns. His nonprofit film company, C-00, has produced public service announcements about AIDS, homelessness, and racism. Several R.E.M. songs have explicitly political themes. For example, "Fall on Me" (from *Life's Rich Pageant,* 1986) deals with acid rain, "Welcome to the Occupation" (*Document*) protests U.S. intervention in Central America, and "Ignoreland" (*Automatic for the* People) is an anti-Republican anthem. Other songs—such as "The One I Love," "Losing My Religion," and "I Took Your Name"—raise the politics of the personal. It was a testament to the strength of the group's fan loyalty and artistic staying power that, some fifteen years later, R.E.M. was still being reviewed as a model of musical integrity.

At the time of Cobain's death, Sonic Youth had just released *Experimental Jet Set, Trash and No Star,* the group's third DGC album. Formed in the early 1980s, two of its members, guitarists Thurston Moore and Lee Ranaldo, had played with avant-garde musician Glenn Branca's group. There they learned the approach that became their trademark: using unconventional tunings to bend standard pop songs completely out of shape. Sonic Youth was to 1990s alternative what the Velvet Underground had been to 1970s punk—a formative influence with avant-garde tendencies and a distinctly New York posture. Their style and the dark side of their musical vision resonated in Seattle. Splitting their vocals between Moore and bassist Kim Gordon, they recorded several albums for independents before signing with DGC. On cuts like "JC" and "Swimsuit Issue" from *Dirty* (1992), their second DGC album, Gordon combined overt sexuality with uncompromisingly feminist lyrics. In her creative mix of femininity and feminism, Gordon served as a role model for post-punk female bands, such as Babes in Toyland, L7, and Hole, and an inspiration for groups like Bikini Kill, Bratmobile, and Sleater-Kinney from the underground feminist punk movement known as riot grrrl. Just as it had for 1970s punk, the rules-don't-apply attitude of the alternative scene encouraged women to experiment with new roles and sounds.

Lollapalooza: Mainstreaming the Counterculture

Alternative took its place, along with rap and metal, as one of the predominant voices of youth culture. Rap, metal, and alternative fans were perceived as distinct audiences in part because the music industry marketing apparatus—like society at large—was divided along lines of race and culture. Still, they had a fair amount in common, including their age and alienation from the establishment, and they were united in their commitment to transgression—of musical conventions, of societal values, of behavioral norms. If these genres were already individually threatening and controversial, what could be more upsetting than putting them all together? No doubt this thought crossed the mind of Perry Farrell, the leader of Jane's Addiction, when he organized the first Lollapalooza festival in 1991.

Farrell and his partners joined forces to stage a multi-act touring music festival like the ones held annually in England. Jane's Addiction, who had recently broken into the Top Twenty with their album *Ritual de lo Habitual,* headlined the tour. Other acts included Living Colour, Nine Inch Nails, Ice-T and Body Count, the Henry Rollins Band, the Butthole Surfers, and Siouxsie and the Banshees. In a summer when mainstream acts flopped or lost money, the seven-act, twenty-one-city Lollapalooza tour—assault, really—played to a total of 430,000 people and grossed $10 million. "Lollapalooza became," as *Boston Globe* critic Jim Sullivan wrote, "the surprise smash summer tour of 1991, an artistic success and a substantial moneymaker in a recession-plagued season."[8]

Capturing the tour's unifying element, the *New York Times* titled Jon Pareles's review "Howls of Rage." Henry Rollins delivered the vein-popping punk fury that had characterized his stage demeanor since fronting Black Flag in the early 1980s. The Butthole Surfers bashed away at acid-induced, punk-influenced three-chord garage rock. Over a mechanized industrial beat, Trent Reznor continued the nihilistic rants that had pushed Nine Inch Nails' *Pretty Hate Machine* to platinum sales. Siouxsie and the Banshees, the only female-fronted act, carried forward the punk spirit of an earlier generation. Living Colour delivered messages about everything from racism to the environment with music as scorching as ever. Jane's Addiction drifted, in Pareles's words, "from heavy metal stomps to scrabbling funk to finger-picking folk rock. . . . Mr. Perkins added a touch of Latin Timbales to rock rhythms, while Morgan Fichter on violin brought hints of country and Arabic music to some songs."[9] It was Ice-T, however, who put the show over the top, both musically and politically. After rapping for half his set, he brought out his new thrash metal band, Body Count. It was at Lollapalooza that he first performed "Cop Killer," the song that got him in so much political hot water one year later, at Lollapalooza. Like the Butthole Surfers, he openly brandished firearms on stage, vowing to avenge police brutality, and teamed up with Farrell for a provocative version of Sly Stone's "Don't Call Me Nigger, Whitey."

Perhaps more than its music, what made Lollapalooza "alternative" was the continual projection of political messages, concerning everything from censorship to the first Gulf War, and the presence of many left-leaning activist organizations.

Perhaps more than its music, what made Lollapalooza "alternative" was the continual projection of political messages, concerning everything from censorship to the first Gulf War, and the presence of many left-leaning activist organizations, including the National Abortion Rights Action League; Refuse and Resist; the Hyacinth Foundation, an AIDS group; and Handgun Control, Inc. Organizers for the 1992 Lollapalooza—an election year—were clear in their intent: "We got a lot of people registered [to vote] last year and this year signing people up is even more important."[10] The political booths for Lollapalooza '92 included Rock the Vote and College Democrats as well as the more radical gay activist organization ACT-UP, the militant environmental organization Greenpeace, the controversial animal rights group People for the Ethical Treatment of Animals (PETA), the Cannabis Action Network, and the Coalition for the Homeless.

Lollapalooza '92 planners expanded the tour from twenty-one cities to thirty-six cities. Unable to get headliners such as Neil Young and R.E.M., organizers had to settle for a lineup that included the Red Hot Chili Peppers, Pearl Jam, Soundgarden, Ice Cube, Ministry, The Jesus and Mary Chain, and Lush (with a second stage for lesser-known acts like Cypress Hill, the Boo Yaa Tribe, and Sharkbait). In the five months it took to put the show together, however, Pearl Jam's *Ten* and the Chili Peppers' *Blood Sugar Sex Magik* both made the Top Ten, peaking at numbers two and three, respectively. Soundgarden's *Badmotorfinger* had gone Top Forty, and Ice Cube's *Death Certificate,* which had peaked at number two, was still riding the charts. The festival nearly doubled its audience (to 800,000) and its take (to $19 million).

The Red Hot Chili Peppers provided some of the most interesting music, its sound sometimes recalling early hip hop sources like Jimmy Castor and Parliament-Funkadelic grafted onto heavy metal. Formed in the early 1980s, the group had worked the Los Angeles underground for years. "Loved and scorned in equal measure as tattooed punk-funk loons obsessed with the horizontal rumba," David Fricke has said, "the Chili Peppers are skateboard-culture heroes, recognized even by their detractors as early pioneers of the mosh-pit marriage of funk, rap, and thrash that Living Colour and Faith No More took to the bank."[11] Following their self-titled 1984 debut LP, they recorded *Freaky Styley* and *The Uplift Mofo Party Plan* before hitting pay dirt with *Mother's Milk* in 1989. During this period, the band struggled through lead singer Anthony Kiedis's heroin addiction and the heroin-overdose death of guitarist Hillel Slovak. *Blood Sugar Sex Magik* marked the group's Warner debut in 1991. "Under the Bridge," the unlikely hit single that kicked them into the Top Ten, detailed Kiedis's ordeal with drugs.

In terms of musical range, Lollapalooza '92 was similar to its predecessor, but a kind of formula mentality was setting in. Kiedis insisted that the 1992 lineup was "way too male" and,

By the time Lollapalooza '92 hit the road, Pearl Jam was so well known that the alternative festival was well on its way to becoming a mainstay of the summer concert circuit. Lead singer Eddie Vedder is held aloft by the crowd as he explores the darker side of life.

especially on the main stage, "way too guitar-oriented."[12] By 1993, the festival had become an institution. Headline positions on the main stage became slots to be filled. Alice in Chains replaced Soundgarden; Dinosaur Jr. took Pearl Jam's slot. Arrested Development, with their multiplatinum 1992 debut album, *3 Years 5 months & 2 days in the Life of . . .*, still on the charts, represented rap. Fishbone, from Los Angeles, was the West Coast ska to gospel to heavy metal answer to New York's Living Colour. Front 242 took over the industrial niche vacated by Ministry and Nine Inch Nails. Primus closed the show with snappy, quirky, quasi-funk. Again, only one female act took the stage—Babes in Toyland. Nirvana spurned the event. With Perry Farrell playing a lesser creative role, Lollapalooza '93 became, in the words of critic Steve Pond, "the year Lollapalooza doesn't like to talk about."[13]

By 1993, other artists had developed alternatives to the alternative festival, the most notable of which was Alternative Nation, featuring the Spin Doctors, Soul Asylum, and Screaming Trees. By tour time, the Spin Doctors' 1991 debut, *A Pocket Full of Kryptonite*, had reached platinum status. Soul Asylum's *Grave Dancer's Union* had already gone platinum. (The group's video for the single "Runaway Train" featured listings of missing children and led to a gig at the White House as President Clinton signed the youth service bill.) Screaming Trees' *Sweet Oblivion* album and "Nearly Lost You" single from the *Singles* soundtrack announced the group's arrival after eight years and six albums. Like Lollapalooza, Alternative Nation was a summer-long tour that played to hundreds of thousands in sold-out shows across the country. It was dubbed by *Rolling Stone* "the Little Lollapalooza That Could."

In 1994, with Farrell again playing an active role, Lollapalooza regained its artistic footing. The festival featured Smashing Pumpkins, the Beastie Boys, George Clinton and the P-Funk All Stars, the Breeders, A Tribe Called Quest, L7, Green Day, and others. (This time, Nirvana had agreed to appear but cancelled after Cobain's suicide.) Because Smashing Pumpkins' *Siamese Dream* was already double platinum and the Beastie Boys' *Ill Communication* entered the charts at number one before the tour, the festival was vulnerable to the criticism of being too mainstream. However, all the Lollapalooza tours crossed lines of class, race, and gender in ways that most tours avoided like the plague. Lollapalooza faded from view in the late 1990s, survived by other ensemble tours like H.O.R.D.E. and Lilith Fair that were aimed at more specialized audiences. While it lasted, however, Lollapalooza presented a reasonably representative cross section of what was going on musically in youth culture, and did so with far more heart, spontaneity, and political awareness than the festival held on the twenty-fifth anniversary of Woodstock. Because Woodstock '94 performances were broadcast only on pay-per-view, MTV was temporarily reduced to the rock equivalent of the Home Shopping Network with its incessant merchandising schemes to make up for the lack of performances. It was so not alternative.

What About Country Music?

All the column inches devoted to alternative tended to obscure the biggest commercial breakthrough of the 1990s—country music. If the early 1990s belonged to any one artist, it was Garth Brooks. *Billboard* listed Brooks as Top Pop Album Artist and Top Country Album Artist for the years 1991, 1992, and 1993. In 1992, NBC aired a Garth Brooks special opposite a

CBS Michael Jackson special. Jackson placed sixty-sixth in the ratings, while Brooks finished among the ten highest-rated shows. All six of his albums—*Garth Brooks, No Fences, Ropin' the Wind, In Pieces, Beyond the Season,* and *The Chase*—could be found among the 100 most popular albums of 1993. (*No Fences* and *Ropin' the Wind* had sold about 10 million copies each by year's end.) *Ropin' the Wind* caused the pop side of the industry to stand up and take notice. Released in September 1991, the album went straight to number one and remained there for eight weeks. After fending off challenges from Hammer, Guns 'n' Roses, U2, Michael Jackson, and Nirvana, *Ropin' the Wind* regained the number one position in January 1992 for another ten weeks.

Brooks was neither your average superstar nor your average country singer. A paunchy, slightly balding singer from Yukon, Oklahoma, he made it big with no major tale of woe to hang his considerable hat on. While exposed early on to country greats like Merle Haggard and George Jones, he also praised Kiss, Kansas, Electric Light Orchestra (ELO), and Styx. His music was unlike that of "new traditionalists" such as Ricky Skaggs and Emmylou Harris (both of whom achieved a certain amount of crossover appeal in the early 1980s by updating honky-tonk heroes like Hank Williams and Lefty Frizzell) and unlike the pop country that followed the success of the film *Urban Cowboy*. Brooks came from a generation of country artists whose blend of folk, country, and rock 'n' roll ran the gamut from the songs of James Taylor to the mellow country rock of the Eagles, to the raucous southern boogie of Lynyrd Skynyrd. His performance style was steeped in the arena rock aesthetic, including theater smoke, pyrotechnics, and sophisticated lighting effects.

Needless to say, Brooks's fame caused a shakeup in Nashville and highlighted a generation gap in country music. Not only was Brooks a best-selling country artist under the age of forty (indeed, the ten best-selling country artists of 1992 were all under forty), but also his material challenged some of country music's most sacred cows. In 1991, the Nashville Network (TNN) refused to air the video of "The Thunder Rolls," in which a woman shoots her abusive husband.

Brooks was neither your average superstar nor your average country singer. A paunchy, slightly balding singer from Yukon, Oklahoma, he made it big with no major tale of woe to hang his considerable hat on.

"We Shall Be Free," a response to the Rodney King beating, includes lines supportive of gay rights. Brooks played two benefits that raised $1 million for South Central Los Angeles. He also defended his music. "No one could doubt that we did country music,"

Garth Brooks, more than any other artist, dominated the early 1990s and turned country music into the biggest commercial breakthrough of the decade. With his roots in the country tradition, he packed his live performances with all the glitz of an arena rock show.

he told one interviewer in 1993. "One thing was who I surrounded myself with: two guys from Kansas, three from Oklahoma. Out in front you've got steel guitar, fiddle, you got hats, we're all wearing Wranglers and Ropers." While he acknowledged his shows' arena rock mentality, his bottom line was that he and his band were "just a bunch of country bumpkins who got lucky. And *know* that they got lucky."[14]

Brooks's crossover triumph and overwhelming popularity opened up unprecedented space on the pop charts for other country artists. Between 1991 and 1996, Clint Black, Reba McIntyre, Travis Tritt, Vince Gil, Trisha Yearwood, Dwight Yoakam, George Strait, Billy Ray Cyrus, Mary Chapin Carpenter, Tim McGraw, and Faith Hill were among the best-selling pop artists of a given year. In 1992, country radio had an 11.6 percent market share, second only to adult contemporary's 18.1 percent. TNN's 1.6 percent cable channel market share may not have set any records, but it was higher than MTV's 0.6 percent. At least two Garth Brooks albums could be found among the year's best-selling albums for every year of the decade except 1997. The year Brooks was absent, a teenaged LeAnn Rimes placed three albums among the 50 best-selling albums, including *Blue* at 5.7 million copies and counting. Bracketing Rimes's success, Shania Twain's *The Woman in Me* and *Come on Over* were among the ten best-selling albums of 1996 and 1998, respectively. Two years later, *Come on Over* was still among the twenty best-selling albums of the year.

Like Brooks, Ellen "Shania" Twain (her nickname taken from the Ojibway Indian word for "I'm on my way") was not your average country artist. She was born in Windsor, Ontario, and turned to music in her early twenties to help support her family after her parents were killed in a car crash. Her self-titled debut album won little critical praise, but her sexy video for "What Made You Say That" caught the attention of Mutt Lange, whose producer credits included AC/DC, Def Leppard, and the Cars. Lange became Twain's producer (and husband), propelling her next two albums to multiplatinum success. At twelve times platinum without touring, *The Woman in Me* made Twain a superstar before most of her fans had seen her live. In 1998, she started a two-year world tour in support of *Come on Over,* which had two versions: a country version for the U.S. audience and a pop-oriented international version. By the end of the decade, *Come on Over* had sold 34 million copies worldwide, the most ever by a female artist. Twain and Lange then retreated to their new home in Switzerland to concentrate on raising a family.

The female partner of another couple—Faith Hill and Tim McGraw, both top country performers and touring partners—also scored in the late 1990s. Following a string of country crossover successes in the mid-1990s, Hill unveiled a new, sexier image and more pop-oriented material for *Breathe* (1999), whose title song became the best-selling single of 2000. Like alternative, country was now fully pop.

Black Music at the Base

In the feeding frenzy for alternative and the ascent of country, it was easy to lose sight of the fact that in most instances, African American musical styles had powered the pop machine. But the industry had long treated rap as the elephant in the room.

In the feeding frenzy for alternative and the ascent of country, it was easy to lose sight of the fact that in most instances, African American musical styles had powered the pop machine. But the industry had long treated rap as the elephant in the room, even as it benefited enormously from rap's sales figures. By the opening years of the new millennium, hip hop–related artists—especially rappers—had become the predominant trend on the year-end pop charts. This phenomenon had begun with the explosion of gangsta rap in the early 1990s and the marriage of rap and traditional rhythm and blues (r&b) that the music industry eventually dubbed r&b/hip hop.

Hip Hop with Soul: The New R&B

Prominent among the diverse array of musical tastes that surfaced in the early 1990s were r&b vocal styles that combined the smooth balladry of r&b veterans like Barry White and Luther Vandross with the hip hop–inflected harmonies of acts like Boyz II Men, En Vogue, TLC, Color Me Badd, Jodeci, Mary J. Blige, and Silk. This smooth r&b sound—initially referred to as *hip hop doo wop* or *hip hop soul*—often bore the signatures of African American writer/producers: Teddy Riley, credited with inventing new jack swing with his group Guy ("Groove Me" and "Teddy's Jam," 1987); Sean "Puffy" Combs, who established the signature sound of Mary J. Blige (*What's the 411?*, 1991) before he became a mogul; and Antonio "L.A." Reid and Kenneth "Babyface" Edmunds, who founded LaFace Records in 1989, home to TLC and Toni Braxton. Braxton's self-titled 1993 debut eventually sold eight times platinum, generating five hit singles. She hit her stride on her sophomore outing, *Secrets* (1996), featuring the erotic "You're Makin' Me High" backed with the Diane Warren–penned blockbuster "Un-break My Heart," both number one hits and both Grammy winners.

TLC was discovered by Reid's writer/producer wife, Pebbles, and signed to LaFace in 1991. They were launched as a sexy novelty act with *Ooooooohhh . . . On the TLC Tip,* whose pop/rap/hip hop singles "Ain't 2 Proud 2 Beg," "Baby, Baby, Baby," and "What About Your Friends" propelled the album to multiplatinum status. *CrazySexyCool* (1994) revealed a more seasoned group with a polished r&b sound. Generating four Top Ten singles—"Creep" and "Waterfalls" at number one—the album sold about 11 million copies. Following *CrazySexyCool*, personal and financial troubles kept TLC out of circulation until their spectacular comeback with *Fan Mail* in 1999.

The top-selling smooth r&b group of the decade was Boyz II Men. With Michael Bivins (of New Edition and Bell Biv Devoe fame) as their manager, they went from Philadelphia's Creative and Performing Arts High School to Motown Records, where they quickly became the label's best-selling act. "Motownphilly," the first single from their debut album, *Cooleyhighharmony,* showcased their musical roots. For the soundtrack of Eddie Murphy's film *Boomerang,* they cut a smooth Babyface ballad called "End of the Road," which spent a then-record-breaking thirteen weeks at number one on the pop charts. *Boyz II Men II* (1994) established them as the premier r&b harmony group of the new era, selling 17 million copies—Motown's best-selling album ever. Its two number one singles—"I'll Make Love to You" and "On Bended Knee"—were collaborations with producers Babyface, and Jimmy Jam and Terry Lewis, respectively. The former song spent fourteen weeks at number one, breaking their previous record, and a duet with Mariah Carey, "One Sweet Day" (1995), logged sixteen weeks at number one. The Boyz themselves produced *Evolution* (1997), but Jam and Lewis wrote its number one single. Sean "Puffy" Combs co-wrote and co-produced three of its other singles. Although *Evolution* debuted at number one, sales stalled at about 2 million copies, beginning a downward trend in their popularity, which continued with *Nathan Michael Shawn Wanya*, released in 2000.

Destiny's Child emerged in Houston in 1990 and paid seven years of dues before getting signed to Columbia in 1997, while still in their teens. Their eponymous debut album sold well, but it was their second outing, *The Writing's on the Wall* (1999), and one of its hit singles, "Say My Name," that established them as pop superstars. Unfortunately, at this point the original group self-destructed. After a series of high-profile lawsuits and verbal exchanges in the press, their new lineup included Beyoncé Knowles, who had long since become the group's focal point, her cousin Kelly Rowland, and newcomer Michelle Wallace. Their third album, *Survivor* (2001), sold four times platinum, with "Bootylicious" at number one. After that, group members embarked on solo projects, with Beyoncé ascending to superstardom in the new millennium.

If there was any one artist who left the biggest imprint on this new sound, it was writer, producer, performer, and professional basketball player R. Kelly. Raised in South Side Chicago, Kelly saw music and sports as avenues out of poverty. Through the efforts of his high school music teacher, music gained the edge (although Kelly did sign a contract with the Atlantic City Seagulls). Kelly has written and/or produced music for artists such as Toni Braxton, Mary J. Blige, Whitney Houston, Boyz II Men, and Michael Jackson, and by 1991 had released his own platinum solo debut, *Born into the 90s*. Controversy greeted his five times platinum second album, *12 Play* (1993), whose sexually explicit singles "Sex Me (Parts I and II)," "Bump N' Grind," and "Your Body's Callin'," coupled with his equally suggestive stage show, both delighted and enraged fans across the country. It didn't help that the following year, he produced fifteen-year-old Aaliyah's debut, *Age Ain't Nothing but a Number,* amidst rumors (later proved to be true) that he had married the underage star.

In 1994, Kelly formed a bond with gospel singer Kirk Franklin. His eponymous third album, while still sexually charged, reflected Franklin's influence and certainly did no harm to his career. *R. Kelly* (1995) was his first album to hit pop number one. It sold four times platinum and generated three platinum singles— "You Remind Me of Something," "Down Low (Nobody Has to Know)," and "I Can't Sleep Baby (If I)." In 1997, Kelly appeared at one of Franklin's concerts, proclaiming: "Every day I seem to be falling in love with the Lord. . . . I used to be flying in sin—now I'm flying in Jesus."[15] By then he had written the G-rated

High drama and personnel changes did not keep Destiny's Child from becoming superstars.

"I Believe I Can Fly" for the *Space Jam* sound-track (reportedly at the behest of Michael Jordan), which he performed at the Franklin concert to wild applause. At the end of the decade, he was still riding high with the two-disc *R.* (1998), which sold seven times platinum. It was propelled by a duet with Celine Dion, "I'm Your Angel," which had a six-week run at number one. *TP-2.com* (2000) also went to number one on the album charts, extending Kelly's popularity into the new millennium.

The multitalented R. Kelly could have achieved upward mobility through sports, but he chose music instead.

A collaboration with Jay-Z on a remix of "Fiesta" from *TP-2.com* led to the idea of creating an album together. "The best of R&B. The best of rap. Let's put it together and see what happens," said Kelly.[16] *The Best of Both Worlds* was expected to be the crowning achievement of the music that *Billboard* had officially dubbed r&b/hip hop in 1999, renaming the r&b charts to reflect the music's evolution. On the eve of its release, *Vibe* magazine called the album "the ulti-mate union of hip hop and r&b."[17] Kelly was at the top of his game as he belted out "The World's Greatest," his hit single from the *Ali* soundtrack, at the opening ceremony of the Winter Olympics in Salt Lake City. But that very morning the *Chicago Sun-Times* had broken a story about a videotape of Kelly allegedly having sex with a fourteen-year-old girl. As the tape's lurid details became public, along with other tapes and civil suits, plans for *The Best of Both Worlds* stalled. The song "Come to Daddy" was jettisoned, although other tracks like "Naked" and "P***y" made the cut. In addition to mushrooming legal problems, such as the twenty-one-count indictment relating to the original tape, many critics felt that the album didn't measure up artistically. For whatever reason—or for all of them—*The Best of Both Worlds* flopped. R&b/hip hop continued to develop in the able hands of artists like Mary J. Blige, whose *No More Drama* (2001) revealed a mature r&b diva with a hip hop edge. But Kelly's career was seriously destabilized; his 2002 single—"Heaven, I Need a Hug"—said it all.

Rap: The Elephant in the Room

By the 1990s, hip hop geography had expanded beyond the East Coast/West Coast poles that had figured into the deaths of Tupac Shakur and Biggie Smalls, and was now creating new vocabularies of place and space. Rap was not simply a buck-wild street culture; it was a major corporate enterprise, with the most successful artists often playing the multiple roles of performing artist, writer, producer, and label head and taking on appellations like *mogul* and *impresario.* As Keith Negus astutely pointed out, "[R]appers who have often been identified solely with 'the street' are also executives."[18]

Rap was not simply a buck-wild street culture; it was a major corporate enterprise, with the most successful artists often playing the multiple roles of performing artist, writer, producer, and label head and taking on appellations like mogul and impresario.

The artist who best exemplified the move from the street to the executive suite was Sean "Puffy" Combs, a.k.a. Puff Daddy (later P. Diddy, then Diddy). "I strive to be known as a mogul entrepreneur," he told *Rolling Stone* in 1997, but even then he was plagued by the notion that "I've gotten my fame through tragedies. My successes have been overlooked."[19] For Puffy, the tragedies began in earnest in 1991 when an oversold New York celebrity basketball event that he promoted resulted in a stampede that left nine people dead. In 1997, Puffy's relationship to Biggie Small's assassination drew frenzied press. Two years later, he was accused of breaking the arm and jaw of Interscope executive Steven Stoute over a dispute about a video. He was arrested in 2000 (along with his then-girlfriend Jennifer Lopez and rapper Shyne) for a shootout at Club New York in which three people were injured. But if trouble seemed to follow Puffy wherever he went, so did success.

((• **HEAR MORE**
Puff Daddy on
MyMusicKit

By 1997, Combs's Bad Boy Entertainment empire grossed $200 million and employed 300 people. That year, Combs—who, as producer, had already launched the careers of Mary J. Blige, Mase, Lil' Kim, Foxy Brown, Jodeci, and, of course, Notorious B.I.G. (Biggie Smalls)—recorded his first album, *No Way Out*, as rapper Puff Daddy. Credited to Puff Daddy and the Family (which included other Bad Boy artists such as Mase, Lil' Kim, the Lox, 112, Black Rob, Faith Evans, and Notorious B.I.G.), *No Way Out* was certified seven times platinum. Its first single, "I'll Be Missing You," a duet with Faith Evans (the late Smalls's estranged wife), was Puffy's eulogy to his friend and protégé that was based on a sample of the Police's "Every Breath You Take." On "Pain" he recalled several tragedies in his life, including Smalls's murder. "Is This the End" marked his decision to carry on as B.I.G.'s heir. Another single, "It's All About the Benjamins" ($100 bills—which exhibit Benjamin Franklin's picture), became an anthemic metaphor for the unabashed materialism at the center of the new hip hop culture. Puffy was considered a lightweight rapper and a sample-heavy producer, having borrowed from David Bowie's "Let's Dance" (for "Been Around the World") and Love Unlimited Orchestra's "I Did It for Love" (for "The Benjamins"); he even teamed up with Jimmy Page to use the melody from Led Zeppelin's "Kashmir" (for "Come with Me"). Defending the practice on *Forever* (1999)—on which he sampled Earth, Wind & Fire's "Fantasy" (for "Angels with Dirty Faces") and Christopher Cross's "Sailing" (for "My Best Friend")—Puff Daddy asked reporters: If what he does is so easy, why haven't others followed suit?

Combs reinvented himself as P. Diddy in 2001, releasing a gospel album (*Thank You*) and a rap album (*The Saga Continues*). The latter was a production extravaganza with over a score of rappers and singers and yielded the rock-inflected "Bad Boy for Life," Diddy's biggest single in a long time. Intended to announce that Bad Boy was still in the house, it also showed that the label had lost some of its most talented rappers.

With significant tragedies along the way, Sean "Puffy" Combs parlayed his knowledge of street life and studio production into a successful hip hop empire.

"I'll Be Missing You"
Artist: Puff Daddy & 112
Music/Lyrics by Sean Combs (with samples from Sting's "Every Breath You Take")
Label: Bad Boy (1997)

"I'll Be Missing You" is a tribute to slain hip hop star Notorious B.I.G. (a.k.a. Biggie) written by his friend and mentor Puff Daddy (now known as Diddy), one of the richest and most successful men in the American music industry. Built on a sample from Sting's hit "Every Breath You Take," it features Diddy, Biggie's widow Faith Evans, and the Atlanta-based hip hop group 112. "I'll Be Missing You" is a prime example of a hit song that references a specific event, which in turn opens up a world of cultural associations and thus forms an integral part of the informed listener's experience of the song.

Musical Style Notes

Sampling, in which a digitized segment of a preexisting song is used as the basis for a new composition, is a well-known hip hop technique and one particularly associated with Puff Daddy/Diddy. The practice is not without controversy; while some look at it as a way of remaking or covering a successful pop song, others see it as a kind of culturally sanctioned plagiarism. But borrowing has a time-honored history in Western music, and both sampling and borrowing create multiple semiotic layers that affect the listener's reception of the piece.

The layers and associations found in "I'll Be Missing You" include the following:

- The introductory sample of Samuel Barber's Adagio for Strings, used for countless movie tearjerkers.
- The omnipresent sample of Sting's "Every Breath You Take," with its compelling, repetitious bass line and its original, somewhat obsessive love lyric.
- The reference to gospel's tradition of powerful death-and-redemption songs in the quote from "I'll Fly Away," sung at 4:51.

Musical "Road Map"

TIMINGS	COMMENTS	LYRICS
0:00–2:14	A sample of a choral rendition of composer Samuel Barber's *Adagio for Strings,* over which Puff Daddy narrates a memorial speech.	*Every day . . .*
0:10	Vocal narration starts.	*. . . face again.*
2:14–3:04	The sample of "Every Breath You Take" begins, the narration wraps up, and Puff Daddy begins the rap.	*Seems like . . .*
3:04–3:41	The beginning of the chorus overlaps with the last line of the rap. Chorus is singing, "Every breath you take." The words have been changed, including the final line of the original, which is here changed to *"I'll be missing you."*	*Every breath . . .*
3:41–4:15	Sample continues; Puff Daddy raps.	*It's kind . . .*
4:15	Chorus returns with "Every breath" melody, again overlapping with the last line of the rap. Over the chorus, Faith Evans (?) is singing an obbligato (additional) line: I miss you . . . yeah yeah	*Every breath . . .*
4:41	Chorus has been singing in unison; here they break into harmony at *"What a life to take."*	*What a life . . .*
4:47	Here the "Every breath" sample continues, but the sung melody breaks away with *"Somebody tell me why."*	
4:51	Singers begin singing a line from the gospel song "I'll Fly Away."	
5:07	Chorus begins the short, repetitive melodic phrase that also ends the original Sting song but with different words. As with the original, they are harmonizing at the interval of a "third" (two voices singing a distance of three notes from one another).	*Every night . . .*
5:17	Puff Daddy begins speaking again, while the chorus continues. Track fades while Puff Daddy is speaking.	*Every day . . .*

Diddy's empire suffered another setback in 2002 when Arista dropped Bad Boy. Although Diddy soon scored another distribution deal with Universal, he had already been dislodged from his position of dominance.

In 1998, Combs was edged aside for mogul entrepreneur of the year by one Percy Miller, a.k.a. Master P. That year P, as he called himself, recorded his fourth album, the multiplatinum *MP Da Last Don,* which he claimed would be his last. Not because he was finished with hip hop—in fact, he kept recording—but because he wanted to build "the profile of a businessman, not a gangsta."[20] By then, P had built his No Limit record store into a label and a multimedia empire, earning $56 million that year (compared to Puffy's $53.3 million). The No Limit Army, as its stable of artists was called, included the production team Beats by the Pound and P's younger brothers, Silkk The Shocker and C-Murder, as well as Mo B. Dick and Mia X, who also recorded collectively as TRU (The Real Untouchables). Master P had grown up in the Calliope projects in New Orleans, a tough neighborhood in one of the country's most violent cities; tales of crime and violence were commonplace in his music. No Limit's first release, *The Ghetto Is Trying to Kill Me*—a straight-ahead gangsta rap album with hard beats, deep bass, and NC-17 lyrics—became a substantial underground hit. Gangsta was now No Limit's signature sound, and in 1998, Master P bought Snoop Dogg out of his Death Row contract and signed him to No Limit. Snoop returned the favor with "Still a G Thang" from *Da Game Is to Be Sold, Not to Be Told,* which debuted at number one.

As to his own career, *Only God Can Judge Me* (1999), P's follow-up to *MP Da Last Don,* peaked at number two on the album charts; his chart position began to slip with *Ghetto Postage* (2000) and *Game Face* (2002). During this period, P had become an actor-writer-producer-director (co-starring in his own Miramax film, *I Got the Hook-Up!*), an author, and a sports agent (representing Derek Anderson of the Cleveland Cavaliers and Ron Mercer of the Boston Celtics). A serious athlete himself, P played basketball in a UCLA summer league in 1988 and joined the Charlotte Hornets in 1999 (but was dropped four days before the season opened). In addition to No Limit Records, No Limit Films, and No Limit Sports Enterprises, a No Limit clothing line (Soldier Gear) and a multimillion-dollar deal with Converse, Inc. completed the picture. These ancillary commercial enterprises seemed to substantiate what Keith Negus emphasized as the "need to be wary of the increasingly routine rhetoric and romanticization of rap musicians as oppositional rebels 'outside' the corporate system, or as iconoclasts in revolt against 'the mainstream'—a discourse that has often been imposed upon rap and not necessarily come from participants within hip hop culture itself."[21]

No Limit's location in New Orleans highlighted another aspect of this new hip hop era: Production was no longer confined to New York and Los Angeles.

No Limit's location in New Orleans highlighted another aspect of this new hip hop era: Production was no longer confined to New York and Los Angeles. In 1992, Nelson George had written that "rap's gone national and is in the process of going regional,"[22] noting that a national audience had been getting some rap from regional sources: Miami (2 Live Crew), Houston (Geto Boys), Seattle (Sir Mix-A-Lot), and San Francisco (Too Short). By the mid-1990s, the geography of hip hop also included the Midwest and what Tony Green referred to as the "Dirty South."[23] New Orleans boasted not only Master P's No Limit Army, but also Mystikal on Jive Records; the Cash Money label with Juvenile, B.G., Turk, and Lil' Wayne (who recorded solo and collectively as the Hot Boys), and Big

Tymers. The LaFace label (OutKast, Goodie Mob) and So So Def (Jermaine Dupri, Lil' Bow Wow, Da Brat) were headquartered in Atlanta, where Def Jam opened a subsidiary in 2000 with Scarface as president and Ludacris as flagship artist. Timbaland and Magoo represented Virginia Beach, as Bone Thugs-N-Harmony did with Cleveland, and (later) as Eminem did with Detroit. A next generation of labels had sprouted in rap's historical strongholds: Dr. Dre had launched Aftermath in Los Angeles; New York boasted Roc-A-Fella (Jay-Z) and Ruff Ryders (DMX). Observed Murray Forman:

> Today the emphasis is on place, and groups explicitly advertise their home environments . . . or else they structure their home territory into titles and lyrics, constructing a new internally meaningful hip hop cartography. . . . [P]roducers have also demonstrated a growing tendency to incorporate themselves as localised businesses (often buying or starting companies unrelated to the music industry in their local neighborhoods . . .). Extending Nelson George's observation, it now seems possible to say that rap, having gone regional, is in the process of going local.[24]

Puffy opened Justin's Restaurant and hired Sister Souljah to run his $2 million Daddy's House social programs. Master P started a basketball foundation for underprivileged youth and donated $500,000 to keep open some schools and churches in his neighborhood.

To some extent, the decentralization of rap could be recognized in regional production styles. The New York sound of the 1980s, as exemplified by the frenetic, layered sounds that the Bomb Squad produced for Public Enemy, represented the pace and density of New York life. The more laid-back, bass-heavy productions of N.W.A. in Los Angeles reflected a car culture that encouraged cruising and the use of powerful sound systems with deeper bass. By the release of Dr. Dre's *The Chronic* (1992), the sound had been codified into the G-funk production style that emphasized slow beats underpinning lengthy samples of traditional late-1970s funk. Florida, also a car-centered society, favored deep, subwoofer bass sounds (referred to there as *booty bass* or *booty boom*). After Biggie Smalls's death, Bad Boy's production style became softer, even more sample heavy, and more pop-oriented. The gangsta style reasserted its primacy after Dr. Dre turned Eminem, the white rapper from Detroit, into the country's most successful hip hop artist at the end of the decade.

Into the new millennium, the style that most defined the Dirty South was called bounce, as in Mystikal's 2002 hit "Bouncin' Back (Bumpin' Me Against the Wall)." Commentators could agree that bounce was about dance beats, but they traced the style to different sources, including Luther Campbell's booty bass in Miami. Campbell noted that "Miami is not really a Southern city; it's a Caribbean city—Jamaicans, Cubans, Haitians, Puerto Ricans, Bahamians. So what I did was add all those elements together."[25] British critic and bounce producer Nik Cohn took bounce back to 1980s New Orleans, also in many ways a Caribbean city. Said Cohn: "Before Master P or Cash Money, there was bounce. It started in the late 1980s, a wild mix of rap and Mardi Gras Indian chants and second line brass-band bass patterns and polyrhythmic drumming and gospel call-and-response."[26]

The major labels were only too happy to distribute these overwhelmingly successful new rap indies. Still, the majors preferred to keep rap at arm's length. Aside from the constant political pressure

The majors preferred to keep rap at arm's length. Aside from the constant political pressure from watchdog organizations and elected officials concerned about lyrics, rap's propensity to sample other copyrighted records presented a real headache for major companies.

from watchdog organizations and elected officials concerned about lyrics, rap's propensity to sample other copyrighted records presented a real headache for major companies. Hip hop artists often operated as extended social groups—posses, crews, collectives of all types. At Bad Boy, it was called the Family; Master P built the No Limit Army; Snoop Dogg had Tha Dogg Pound; and Wu-Tang was a Clan. This was confusing to an industry structured around carefully parsed contracts and tracking of artists to determine chart position, market share, royalties, and so on. These loose alliances manifested themselves in the continual appearance of artists on each other's recordings, sometimes across labels. To take just one example, "It's All About the Benjamins" credited not only Puff Daddy and the Family, but also The Notorius B.I.G., Lil' Kim, The Lox, Dave Grohl, Perfect, FuzzBubble, and Rob Zombie.

Perhaps the most collective operation in rap was Wu-Tang Clan. Wu-Tang was consciously assembled as a loose confederation of MCs—RZA, Genius (GZA), Ol' Dirty Bastard (ODB), Method Man, Raekwan the Chef, Ghostfaced Killah, U-God, Inspectah Deck, and Masta Killa—who performed collectively as Wu-Tang Clan and also recorded as solo artists. Started by Genius (GZA) and Ol' Dirty Bastard, it was the musical genius of producer RZA (pronounced Rizza)—whose signature sound of menacing beats, sparse samples, and surrealistic soundscapes underpinned the group's violent martial arts humor—that enabled Wu-Tang to realize its vision. Following their success with *Enter the Wu-Tang: 36 Chambers* (1993), released on their own Loud label, they landed the perfect deal with RCA, allowing individual members to record solo with anyone and any label.

After many solo projects and the release of their second group effort, *Wu-Tang Clan Forever* (1997), the group had achieved major crossover success, coupled with business ventures

Wu-Tang Clan combined group efforts, solo projects, and incredible merchandizing into a loose-knit hip hop operation that almost defied description.

that included a clothing line (Wu Wear), a video game for Playstation (*Wu-Tang: Shaolin Style*), and a comic book (*The Nine Rings of Wu-Tang*). Other solo projects followed. Their prodigious output occurred amid continual legal skirmishes, usually involving Ol' Dirty Bastard on weapons or assault charges. By the end of 2000, the Clan was hard at work on a new group project, *The W*, with all the original members except ODB, then a fugitive from a court-ordered drug rehabilitation program. (He still appeared on the album, via previously recorded rhymes.) The full Clan—minus ODB, who was now in jail—assembled again in 2001 to record their fourth group album, *Iron Flag*. It wasn't until 2007 that Wu Tang Clan recorded another full studio album. By then ODB had died of a heart attack.

Beginning in the late 1990s, rap artists launched several successful ensemble tours. Bad Boy's No Way Out tour, for instance, featured Puffy and the entire Bad Boy Family—plus artists like Jay-Z, Foxy Brown, Busta Rhymes, and Usher—and played to sold-out houses everywhere. But the 1999 Hard Knock Life tour set the standard. Headlined by Jay-Z, whose third album, *Vol. 2 . . . Hard Knock Life*, had gone quadruple platinum, the fifty-four-date tour also featured DMX as co-headliner, the duo of Method Man and Redman, and DJ Clue. The tour stood out among rap tours because it earned an impressive $18 million and suffered no cancellations, artist drop-offs, or violence. It gained further respectability by donating money to the families of the Columbine victims. The Hard Knock Life tour was the model for later tours, like the Ruff Ryders/Cash Money tour of 2000, which featured Ruff Ryders' DMX and Cash Money's Juvenile as co-headliners, with both labels' other artists as support. (By this time, Juvenile's *400 Degreez* had been certified triple platinum.) While the tour had fewer scheduled dates than Hard Knock Life, it was booked into larger, mostly coliseum-level venues with greater ticket sales potential. But the tour was marred by a violent backstage brawl in Boston, which left six people stabbed, two of them critically.

One of the most successful (and controversial) tours of the period was Up in Smoke (2000), featuring Snoop Dogg; Ice Cube; MC Ren; Dr. Dre; and Dre's protégé, Eminem. Eminem (born Marshall Mathers, III) grew up mostly around Detroit in what he described as a dysfunc-

HEAR MORE
Eminem on
MyMusicKit

tional family. He quit school in the ninth grade, fathered a child, and lived with Haile and her mother, Kim, in a crack-ridden Detroit neighborhood. In short, Mathers had street cred. He came to Dre's attention when the latter heard the *Slim Shady* EP that Eminem had released independently in 1997. In 1999, the duo worked together on the full-length *Slim Shady LP*, which entered the charts at number two and was certified three times platinum before the year was out. Slim Shady was the alter ego that allowed Eminem to take revenge on the world, killing his mother, killing the mother of his child,

The fact that Eminem achieved both commercial success and critical acclaim with violent, misogynistic rhymes outraged many.

getting even with the high school bully who beat him up, ripping Pamela Anderson's breasts off, and taking every drug imaginable at the same time. For his second outing, Eminem came out from behind his Slim Shady persona to assume his real identity on *The Marshall Mathers LP* (2000). With material as venomous as his first album, *Marshall Mathers* sold 7 million copies in its first year.

The overwhelming commercial successes of *Slim Shady* and *Marshall Mathers* outraged most observers of the cultural scene. The fact that both received critical raves—Dre, for his skilled production; Eminem, for his verbal dexterity—was like pouring gasoline on a fire. "When Ice-T sang about murdering a cop, he got dropped from his record label," wrote Renée Graham. "When Eminem raps about butchering his wife and brutalizing homosexuals, he gets a Grammy nod for album of the year."[27] The fact that Eminem was white was even more troubling for different people for different reasons. For some, it meant that a double standard was being applied—one for black artists and another for white. For others, it meant that the Up in Smoke tour would reach an unprecedented crossover audience. Everyone's fears were realized. Up in Smoke played to predominantly white audiences—and the more provocative the material, the louder the cheers. At the same time, the shows were well produced and the audiences well behaved. The white rapper from Detroit had turned himself into a superstar and, in the process, brought hard-edged rap to a new generation of middle-class white teens. He then starred in *8 Mile*, a movie based loosely on his rap persona.

> **U**p in Smoke played to predominantly white audiences—and the more provocative the material, the louder the cheers. At the same time, the shows were well produced and the audiences well behaved.

New York was still the center for hard-core rap, but New York rap, too, had become significantly more decentralized. In its rundown of the fifty most influential hip hop players, *Rolling Stone* identified the particular borough or 'hood that each New York artist "represented"—Beastie Boys (Manhattan), Busta Rhymes (Brooklyn), KRS-One (the Bronx), Mase (Harlem), Wu-Tang Clan (Staten Island), etc.[28] Puff Daddy and his Bad Boy empire had gotten most of the notoriety, but Russell Simmons had parlayed Def Jam (LL Cool J, Method Man, Redman, Foxy Brown) into a multimedia empire that included film (*The Nutty Professor*), television (*Def Comedy Jam*), a clothing line (Phat Farm), and distribution deals with Roc-A-Fella and Ruff Ryders, home to Jay-Z (Brooklyn) and DMX (Yonkers), respectively. Nas (Queens) had scored a major label deal with Columbia/Sony.

With literate rhymes and tough beats, Nas evoked the harsh reality of street life in the Queensbridge projects on his major label debut, *Illmatic*. Jay-Z, from Brooklyn's Marcy projects, was a promising student who found himself immersed in the seamier side of street life until rap showed him a way out. His debut album, *Reasonable Doubt* (1996), a classic of the genre, is often compared to Nas's *Illmatic*. The two sparred repeatedly for New York's rap throne in the aftermath of Biggie Smalls's death. Jay-Z also entered the East Coast/West Coast fray with "Brooklyn's Finest," a vicious response to Tupac's "Hit 'Em Up." At the same time, he ventured across turf lines to collaborate with the hottest rappers in the business: Notorious B.I.G., Ja Rule, and DMX on the East Coast; Ludacris and Missy Elliott in the South; and Snoop Dogg and Too Short on the West Coast. Nas enjoyed a steady stream of hits by some of the best producers in the business—"If I Ruled the World" (the Trackmasters), "Hate Me Now" (Puff Daddy), "Nas Is Like" (DJ Premier), and "You Owe Me" (Timbaland)—before his career

started to go into decline. Sensing weakness, Jay-Z called Nas out on "Takeover," to which Nas responded on "Ether" (from *Stillmatic*, 2001), which then prompted Jay-Z's "Super Ugly." Though the release of *Stillmatic* represented something of a come-back, Nas never quite regained his undisputed prominence in New York rap. Jay-Z, on the other hand, became so successful that his Roc-A-Fella label (founded with Damon Dash) became a corporate empire with its own talent roster (Beanie Sigel, Cam'ron, M.O.P.), a stable of in-house producers (Just Blaze, Kanye West), a clothing line (Roca Wear), and a film division (*Paid in Full*, *State Property*). Even with all this commercial success, Jay-Z never lost his focus on the music.

Jay-Z had hit his stride on *Vol. 2 . . . Hard Knock Life*, part of a trilogy bracketed by *In My Life, Vol. 1* (1997) and *Vol. 3 . . . Life and Times of S. Carter* (1999). For *Vol. 2*, he featured numerous fellow rappers, including DMX and Ja Rule, while collaborating with some of the best-known producers in the business such as Puffy and Teddy Riley, whose memorable, radio-friendly hooks generated a string of hit singles such as "Hard Knock Life (Ghetto Anthem)." He scaled back somewhat for 2000's *The Dynasty: Roc la Familia*, which primarily featured Roc-A-Fella's in-house rappers. The album hit number one and went platinum. For *The Blueprint* (2001), there was only one guest shot—Eminem on "Renegade." Propelled by demand for "Izzo (H.O.V.A.)," one of the hottest singles of the year, *The Blueprint* went to number one and multiplatinum certification. When Jay-Z first laid claim to the New York rap throne on 1997's "The City Is Mine," many wondered if he was serious. By 2001, there was no longer any doubt that he was. His ill-fated collaboration with R. Kelly on *Best of Both Worlds* seemed like a mere bump on the road to an ever-brighter future that included a committed relationship with Beyoncé Knowles of Destiny's Child and ascension to the presidency of Def Jam. After record-ing *The Black Album* (2003), Jay-Z announced his intention to retire. It didn't last. By 2005, he was recording again and attending to all aspects of his new executive position.

DMX, from Yonkers, spent part of his childhood in several group homes and by his early teens was no stranger to the criminal justice system. Touré described him as "tough at a glance . . . sonic testosterone . . . a direct descendent of Tupac." Continued Touré: "He raps in the roughest and grimiest voice in hip hop, the sound of gravel hitting the grave. His records speak of death constantly, crime casually, moral consequences occasionally."[29] After a few unre-warding years at Ruffhouse, DMX switched to Def Jam. There his first two albums, *It's Dark and Hell Is Hot* (1998) and *Flesh of My Flesh*, both debuted at number one on the *Billboard 200* in the same year—a first for any artist, hip hop or otherwise. DMX was also a devoted husband and father who shunned publicity and overly high drama in his personal life, despite clashes with the law. His 2000 entry, *. . . And Then There Was X,* entered the charts at number one, eventually selling 5 million copies. By then, he had had major supporting roles in the Jet Li action film *Romeo Must Die* and Steven Segal's *Exit Wounds. The Great Depression* (2001) was his fourth straight album to debut at number one.

DMX's success marked the entry of producer Irv Gotti, formerly Jay-Z's DJ. Gotti started out as Irv Lorenzo, a small-time drug dealer from Hollis, Queens, the neighborhood that spawned Def Jam founder Russell Simmons and Run-D.M.C. Because he acted like a boss, Jay-Z had called him Gotti, after the New York crime boss, and the name stuck. It was Gotti who brought DMX and Ja Rule to Def Jam and helped restore the label's glory. It was also Gotti who launched Ashanti's career. Gotti produced what he called "chick records . . . records that niggas ain't mad at and women love."[30] Examples include "What's Luv" (Fat Joe and Ashanti), "Foolish" (Ashanti), "Baby" (Ashanti), "Ain't It Funny" (Jennifer Lopez and Ja Rule), and "Down for You" (Ja Rule, Charli Baltimore, Vita, and Ashanti).

In 1997, Gotti formed a joint venture with Def Jam, which he called, fittingly, Murder, Inc. and signed Ja Rule as its flagship artist. In Gotti's hands, Ja Rule scored an early success with *Venni Vetti Vecci* (1999), modeled after DMX's hard-core style. For his second outing, *Rule 3:36* (2000), Gotti took Ja in a more pop direction, adding female background singers. He perfected this formula on Ja's third album, *Pain Is Love* (2001), which featured collaborations with Jennifer Lopez ("I'm Real") and Ashanti ("Always on Time"). The move toward pop added measurably to Ja Rule's crossover appeal but cost him at street level. DMX attacked him relentlessly in the press. Ja retaliated with "Fuck with Us" from his fourth album, *The Last Temptation* (2002). By this time, Ja Rule had become one of the most financially successful rap artists of the early 2000s. But if he was smarting all the way to the bank, he was also watching his back.

The new generation of hard-core New York rappers returned the most publicized rap back to its gangsta roots. Unlike the rappers who had dominated New York, from Run-D.M.C. to Public Enemy—all college graduates from middle-class backgrounds—the new rap stars had gone to the school of hard knocks.

The new generation of hard-core New York rappers returned the most publicized rap back to its gangsta roots. Unlike the rappers who had dominated New York, from Run-D.M.C. to Public Enemy—all college graduates from middle-class backgrounds (even Puff Daddy attended Howard University)—the new rap stars had gone to the school of hard knocks. Their frustrations were often directed toward each other in verbal jousts like the ones between Jay-Z and Nas and DMX and Ja Rule, but the attacks on Ja Rule escalated in the hands of Eminem and his New York protégé, 50 Cent. The latter punched Ja Rule in Atlanta, called him out on "Wanksta" (from the *8 Mile* soundtrack), and began a concert set with snippets from Ja Rule's music videos, commenting on each: "I know that's not hip hop, you know that's not hip hop."

50 Cent began life as Curtis Jackson, also in Hollis, Queens. According to street lore, he became a second-generation crack dealer at age twelve, earning up to $5,000 a day. At twenty-four he was shot nine times at point-blank range; one of the bullets pierced his jaw, producing his signature slur on record. With street cred like that, it's no wonder that the bidding for his contract reached a reported $1 million when Eminem and Dr. Dre signed him to the Shady/Aftermath label. At that point, the war with Ja Rule and Murder, Inc. really heated up.

50 Cent's first album on his new label, *Get Rich or Die Tryin'*, went double platinum in three weeks, largely on the strength of the Dr. Dre–produced party anthem, "In Da Club." The album also included "Back Down," part of the continuing salvo of insult songs directed at Ja Rule. Ja responded with "Loose Change," on which he took on 50 Cent, Eminem, and Dre. Reportedly, Ja Rule's crew also stabbed 50 Cent at the Hit Factory. Eminem, 50 Cent, and Busta Rhymes then verbally ganged up on Ja Rule, setting new rhymes to the instrumental track of Tupac's "Hail Mary." Ja fired back with "Guess Who Shot Ya."

If all of this had just been verbal sparring, a time-honored tradition in rap, it would not have been especially disturbing. But as 50 Cent himself said: "This ain't no rap war."[31] It got more intense when the press started trying to connect the dots to the 2002 execution-style murder of Jam Master Jay (of Run-D.M.C.) in his Hollis, Queens, studio. 50 Cent had met Jay in 1996 when 50 was making mix tapes such as "How to Rob" (now an underground classic), which details ripping off hip hop and r&b stars, from Mariah Carey to Jay-Z. Jam Master Jay was apparently instrumental in brokering a deal for 50 Cent with Columbia Records, for which Jay got the lion's share of the advance. 50 Cent had earlier admitted to having a long-standing feud with drug distributor Kenneth "Supreme" McGriff, who was being investigated for bankrolling Murder, Inc. at the time of Jay's murder. The press wanted to know whether 50 Cent's gripe with Murder, Inc. and Ja Rule was somehow linked to Jay's murder. Whatever the truth, 50 Cent (and his six-year-old son) spent the early 2000s wearing bullet-proof vests wherever they went. Rap was capitalizing more than ever on its connections to the street, even as it became more fully integrated into the social and corporate fabric of American life.

Though the most publicized rap of the era was drenched in testosterone, other tendencies existed as well. In OutKast's *All Music Guide* entry, for example, John Bush credited the group with taking "Southern hip hop in bold, innovative new directions: less reliance on aggression, more positivity and melody, thicker arrangements, and intricate lyrics."[32] By *Stankonia* (2000), OutKast had already enjoyed a run of hit singles and platinum sales. Also from Atlanta, Ludacris had emphasized the "dirty" in Dirty South with his first hit single, "What's Your Fantasy" (2000), and more so with its remix. Other hit singles followed, such as the Neptunes-produced "Southern Hospitality." For his third album, *Word of Mouf* (2001), Ludacris modulated his gangsta style (if not his sexism) with more subtlety and humor as in "Area Codes." Featuring a broad range of styles, *Word of Mouf* aspired to pop rap mass appeal. Meanwhile, in New Orleans, Mystikal's *Let's Get Ready* (2000) incorporated Southern soul in the album's James Brown–influenced lead single, "Shake Ya Ass," continuing in this vein on "Bouncin' Back (Bumpin' Me Against the Wall)" from *Tarantula* (2001). Both singles were produced by the Neptunes. These artists may have retained their edge as they became mainstream, but the most popular rap artists of 2001 and 2002—Shaggy and Nelly, respectively—were unabashedly pop.

Shaggy's album *Hot Shot* was the second most popular album of 2001, behind the Beatles' *1*. By the end of the year, *Hot Shot* had been certified six times platinum. Born in Jamaica but raised in Brooklyn, Shaggy was the antithesis of the New York gangsta: He was polite, well mannered, and completely nonthreatening. His breakthrough single, "Oh Carolina" (1993)—a remake of Prince Buster's original, with Latin percussion over a sample of the *Peter Gunn*

theme—was recorded while he was in the U.S. military and released after he had served in the first Gulf War. Shaggy continued recording in what he called his dog-amuffin style throughout the 1990s, but he did not achieve pop stardom until *Hot Shot.*

Nelly picked up where Shaggy left off. In 2001, he was two notches below Shaggy as the fourth most popular pop artist in *Billboard's* tally; in 2002, he was number one. Nelly was born in St. Louis but moved to suburbia before street life could take its toll. With his laid-back Southern drawl, tongue-twister rhymes, and infectious pop hooks, he burst onto the rap scene in 2000 with the blockbuster album *Country Grammar* and its lead single of the same name. By the time Universal signed him a year later, the album had been certified eight times platinum. His first Universal outing, *Nellyville* (2002), went straight to number one on the pop charts and stayed there for seven weeks, propelled by the Neptunes-produced single, "Hot in Herre," Indeed, the week *Nellyville* was released, Nelly was number one on ten different *Billboard* charts. Even with some (minimal) gangsta posturing, he did nothing that would risk losing any portion of his vast pop audience; his duet with Justin Timberlake ("Work It") served only to consolidate his teen base.

Many women rappers rose to fame during this period. Foxy Brown, Lil' Kim, and Charli Baltimore—the latter two of whom were lovers and protégés of Biggie Smalls—hailed from New York. Missy "Misdemeanor" Elliot presided over her own record-company empire in Virginia. Eve, a former stripper from Philadelphia, became the lone woman in the Ruff Ryders crew. Da Brat, from Chicago, signed with Jermaine Dupri's So So Def in Atlanta. Solé came from Kansas City, and Mia-X was discovered by Master P in New Orleans. Most of these rappers paid homage to their elder sisters like Queen Latifah but started out taking a much more over-the-top sexualized approach. Referred to early on as hard-edged harlots and the reigning divas of raunch, these women rappers have been celebrated and criticized not only for their street-tough raps and NC-17 lyrics, but also their stage outfits and demeanor that leave little to the imagination.

After a few false starts, Eve won a rap competition to join the Ruff Ryders. She scored double platinum on *Let There Be Eve . . . Ruff Ryders First Lady* (1999), which entered the pop charts at number one, the first rap album by a woman to do so. But it was her duet with No

Doubt's Gwen Stefani on "Let Me Blow Ya Mind" (from *Scorpion,* 2001) that really broke Eve to the mainstream audience and earned her a Grammy, too. She continued her successful rap career on *Eve-Olution* (2002), broke into film (*XXX, Barbershop*), and contracted with the UPN network to produce and star in a sitcom bearing her name.

Before breaking away from the pack as an artist, Missy Elliott had established herself as a notable writer and producer, owning her own company, The Gold Mine, and working along-side producer and friend Timbaland to create hits for other artists (such as "One in a Million" for Aaliyah). As a rapper, she hit platinum on her first outing, *Supa Dupa' Fly* (1997), and more than held her own with *Da Real World* (1999), which attempted to reclaim the word *bitch* as a positive term. "Elliott doesn't sling the b-word around in the misogynistic way of her male hip hop cohorts," said Vanessa Jones. "Instead, Elliott reclaims it, making it the description of choice for strong women."[33] From there, the hits just kept coming (in part thanks to Timbaland's appealing dance grooves): "She's a Bitch" and "Hot Boyz" from *Da Real World*; "Get Ur Freak On" and "One Minute Man" from *Miss E . . . So Addictive* (2001); and "Work It" from *Under Construction* (2002). If she could be criticized for retreating into a formula mentality on *This Is Not a Test* (2003), she returned the focus to her skills as a rapper and songwriter on *The Cookbook* (2005). Elliott's vocal talents—she is a consummate rapper and an able soul singer—have made her one of the few artists to span the worlds of rap, r&b/hip hop, and electronic dance music. Her artistry creates a rap that is hard, sexy, playful, and danceable, unencumbered by the encroachments of the thug life.

> ***E****lliott's vocal talents have made her one of the few artists to span the worlds of rap, r&b/hip hop, and electronic dance music. Her artistry creates a rap that is hard, sexy, playful, and danceable, unencumbered by the encroachments of the thug life.*

Despite the media's single-minded focus on rap's violent side, clearly a range of styles reflected other tendencies, too. Hip hop also ventured into political territory, most notably with the Hip Hop Summit Action Network. Begun in 2001 with Def Jam founder Russell Simmons in charge, the Action Network mobilized rappers, hip hop executives, and black political leaders, from Ben Chavis, then of the NAACP, to Louis Farrakhan of the Nation of Islam. The network took on issues such as freedom of speech and social injustice as well as political campaigns like voter registration and reforming punitive drug laws. Such efforts showcased the positive activities of hip hop nation but were seldom reported with the same gusto as the sensationalized acts of violence.

Missy Elliott established herself as a rapper, producer, and woman to be reckoned with.

Other Contenders for the Next Big Thing

Historically, the music industry has been organized around stars—superstars, really. Its major operations—the formidable marketing apparatus, radio promotion, music videos, and live performance touring circuits—have required eventual superstardom to function most effectively. As a result, major labels have risked millions of dollars searching for that one act that would make it all worthwhile. This strategy leads to the culturally unappealing logic that a single artist who can sell 40 million units—as Michael Jackson did with *Thriller*—is worth more than forty acts who can sell 1 million units apiece. Such an artist saves the costs of mounting forty different marketing campaigns. It is by design, then, that major record companies promote as few artists as possible. As Anthony DeCurtis observed in 1992, "[i]nstead of investing in and nurturing a wide range of new talents, record companies are betting wildly like drunks at the roulette table, hoping that one big score—whether by an old favorite or a new lucky number—will cover all past debts."[34]

((• **HEAR MORE**
Mariah Carey on
MyMusicKit

In the 1990s, the artist that the music industry promoted to the greatest economic advantage was Mariah Carey, who combined incredible talent with the best business plan on the planet. With her multi-octave range and good pop/dance/r&b material, Carey was paired with top-notch professionals and approached by Columbia as a major investment from day one. "We don't look at Mariah Carey as a dance-pop artist," said Columbia executive Don Ienner. "We look at her as a franchise."[35] (Columbia must have regarded her subsequent marriage to label head Tommy Mottola as a corporate merger.) Her 1990 eponymous debut album rolled out four number one singles in a row. Two of them, "Vision of Love" and "Love Takes Time," hit number one in three markets—pop, adult contemporary, and r&b. Indeed, every Carey album of the decade was launched with a single that went to number one.

Choosing to debut "Vision of Love" on *The Arsenio Hall Show*—then the late-night last word in black New York hipness—suggested that Carey (and Columbia) felt secure enough about her pop appeal to play to her black audience. During this period, Carey's racial makeup—her mother is a white New York opera singer and her father is a black Venezuelan—received as much press as her music. Her second album, *Emotions,* also featured r&b and ballads with cross-market appeal. From very early on, one got the impression of an enormous talent following a calculated program of career development—from her *MTV Unplugged* appearance, which yielded a number one cover of the Jackson 5's "I'll Be There," to her "All I Want for Christmas Is You," which hit the pop charts for the 1994, 1995, and 1996 holiday seasons. *Daydream* (1995) straddled the r&b and adult contemporary audiences with hit singles like "Fantasy," which sampled the Tom Tom Club's "Genius of Love," and "One Sweet Day," a duet with Boyz II Men. Carey came out with *Butterfly* in 1997, with the unreleased

Mariah Carey was considered a hot property at Columbia from the moment she was signed. She lived up to expectations when her multi-platinum self-titled debut album brought her the Best New Artist and Best Pop Vocal Performance, Female, Grammys in 1990.

"Love Takes Time"

Artist: Mariah Carey
Music/Lyrics by Mariah Carey and Ben Margulies
Label: Columbia, from the CD
Mariah Carey (1990)

As with many Urban Contemporary vocal artists in the 1980s and 1990s, Mariah Carey's appeal combined vocal pyrotechnics, impeccably polished and sophisticated musical settings, and an equally polished and sophisticated public persona. An attractive person of mixed ethnicity, with a five-octave range and astonishing technical facility, Carey was typically enlisted to provide vocal fireworks on ballad or dance tracks crafted by top-dollar producers. She appeared repeatedly on the *Billboard* Top 100, her hit singles always accompanied by carefully produced and staged music videos that emphasized the glamour of her lifestyle, wardrobe, and beauty.

Musical Style Notes

Mariah Carey's melismatic vocal style comes from the tradition of virtuosic soul singers such as Aretha Franklin and the late Minnie Riperton, whose influence is easily heard in Carey's music. Carey also shares with Riperton the ability to amaze audiences by singing in the ultra-high flute, or whistle, register.

The sophistication and technical perfection of the instrumental settings found in songs such as "Love Takes Time" provide an entire background on which Mariah Carey's vocal technique can be displayed, just as the setting of a diamond is crafted to show off the jewel. The message is not necessarily that of the text, which is the typical sad love song, but rather that of the plush, meticulous, and expensive musical and visual framing—and in that sense, the style is the diametric opposite of text-centric genres like hip hop. The musical structure itself is a very standard pop-song formula: verse-chorus-verse-chorus-bridge-chorus.

Musical "Road Map"

TIMINGS	COMMENTS	LYRICS
0:00–0:15	Introduction: melismatic, textless vocals; synth keyboards and strings; minimal percussion. Note descending bass line (traveling downward in pitch), a common chord progression often used for pop ballads.	
0:15–0:46	Verse 1 Same sound texture as introduction.	*I had it all . . .*
0:46–1:24	Chorus Addition of multitracked vocals; slightly thicker sound texture. Vocal increase in energy and power as the chorus progresses.	*Love takes time . . .*
1:24–1:54	Verse 2 Drum track enters, creating a thicker, stronger rhythmic backdrop.	*Losing my mind . . .*
1:54–2:28	Chorus Additional drum backbeat added, which further strengthens the rhythmic pulse.	*Love takes time . . .*
2:28–2:59	Bridge Note the rhythmic syncopation at 2:51, which matches the voice. Very high-range background vocals enter at the transition into the next chorus.	*You might . . .*
2:59–3:30	Chorus	*Love takes time . . .*
3:30–3:46	Final section: Sonic texture brought down to the much simpler, quieter Sound of the introduction. Drum roll leads to final chord.	*I don't wanna . . .* *. . . alone.*

single of the same name hitting the Top Twenty. *Butterfly,* along with its video, added more hip hop, r&b, and cheesecake to Carey's usual mix. Shortly afterward, she and Mottola split up; her next album, *Rainbow* (1999), featured the number one single "Heartbreaker." Without losing one iota of her pop appeal, Carey continued her move toward hip hop and r&b on *Rainbow,* which featured guest shots by Jay-Z, Snoop Dogg, Da Brat, and Missy Elliott.

As the new millennium began, Mariah Carey had recorded more number one singles than any other female artist in any genre—including at least one in every year of her debut decade—and she had sold an incredible 105 million units in under ten years.

As the new millennium began, Mariah Carey had recorded more number one singles than any other female artist in any genre—including at least one in every year of her debut decade—and she had sold an incredible 105 million units in under ten years. Given this kind of success, it is perhaps not all that surprising that the major labels stuck to their superstar marketing strategies, ponying up millions for contracts in the 1990s that were surely unprecedented, and perhaps unrecoverable.

Janet Jackson initiated the 1990s round of high-stakes contracts when she switched from A&M to Virgin in 1991. With only two albums (both number one's) and one tour to her credit, she scored a reported $50 million deal that Richard Branson, chairman of Virgin Records, compared to buying a Rembrandt.[36] In the same year, Aerosmith returned to Columbia with a new deal worth upward of $30 million. In 1991, Mötley Crüe re-signed with Elektra for $25 million to be paid over four albums. ZZ Top scored $30 million at RCA. The Rolling Stones landed a $40 million three-album deal with Virgin. Even these contracts paled in comparison with those offered to Madonna, Michael Jackson, and Prince, reportedly each worth over $60 million. The frenzied bidding peaked in August 1996 when R.E.M., of all groups, scored an $80 million five-album deal with Warner—the largest contract in record-company history.

These artists and their handlers were cashing in on the outlandish sums of money that had changed hands in recent mergers, such as Matsushita's 1990 purchase of MCA and its affiliated labels for $6.6 billion. "When you hear that your record company has been sold for 20 or 30 times its earnings," said Tim Collins, Aerosmith's manager, "you think, 'I want a piece of that.'"[37] The incredible amounts of money involved in these deals led artists to become more aware of their key role in companies' overall profitability, and a new understanding of the value of catalogue sales simply added to the performers' growing realization of their own worth. Back catalogue had always been valuable because an artist's hit records generally boost sales of his or her earlier recordings. With the advent of the compact disc, back catalogue became even more important because consumers began buying CDs of recordings they already owned. In the early 1990s, back catalogue sales were estimated to be as much as 40 percent of all album sales. Thus, for many artists, their back catalogue was their most valuable asset.

For both artists and companies, a second and perhaps more attractive aspect of back catalogue related to the practice of linking groups and songs with films and/or products. Advertising proved to be very lucrative with the Beatles selling sneakers, Elton John crooning for Sassoon, and Madonna shilling for Pepsi. By the mid-1990s, record companies thought of themselves more as exploiters of rights than as producers of records. Their new mission was to develop as many revenue streams as possible. For a while, they were on a roll. Then the bottom fell out—well, sort of.

In his 1996 front-page, year-end wrap-up for the *New York Times*, Neil Strauss noted that "[g]rowth in the $12 billion [U.S.] record industry, which for more than a decade has ranged from 12 to 20 percent annually, has slowed to a virtual standstill."[38] Strauss and others offered various explanations for the phenomenon: record companies' pursuit of singles rather than development of long-term careers; the industry's focus on new technologies instead of on the music; a natural decline in catalogue sales as baby boomers completed the replacement of their LPs; the industry's failure to recognize the potential of urban music; and the industry's typical reliance on a handful of superstars.

Some of the biggest superstars no longer sold like superstars. In the early 1990s, new releases by Madonna and Prince (now called "the artist formerly known as Prince" or simply "the Artist") rose and fell on the charts as never before. Prince sustained himself with three greatest-hits packages; Madonna, with a $50 "art" book—*Sex*—of suggestive photographs of herself. Pearl Jam outsold Michael Jackson. By 1996, the industry's superstar strategy appeared flawed because many multiplatinum artists turned out products that fell far short of record-company expectations. To take just one instance: Following *Monster*'s success at 2.7 million units sold, R.E.M. kicked off their $80 million contract with *New Adventures in Hi-Fi* selling under 1 million units—way below expectations. Note the irony in this brand of industry thinking: It is only in the context of sales of 5 to 10 million units that sales of 1 million can be considered "disappointing." Nevertheless, with an overall pattern of flat sales, the industry was clearly in trouble. In an eighteen-month period, the Wherehouse, Peaches, and Camelot outlets, three of the largest record retail chains in the country, filed for bankruptcy. Four of the six major labels underwent significant staff cuts.

Those who remained continued searching for the next big thing. As 1996 drew to a close, all indicators seemed to point toward urban dance music. WKTU, New York's Top 40/Dance station, became the number one station in the market, with the largest listening audience in the country (which also happened when it converted to an all-disco format some twenty years earlier). For a good part of 1997, the music industry tried to promote what they called electronica, a catch-all phrase that included everything from hip hop, dance pop remixes, and r&b-flavored dance music to the sounds of acid house, techno, and their multiple variants that had been seeping into the United States from England and the continent for years.[39] When that failed, the music industry tried to exploit trends based not so much on genre but rather on gender, age, and ethnicity—The Year of the Woman, The Year of Teen Pop, and The Year of Latin(o) Music.

Sounds Without Stars: Electronic Dance Music

The story of house and techno, the major styles that comprised electronica, is a convoluted tale of trans-Atlantic cross-fertilization and ever-evolving substyles and scenes that is complicated further by multiple, and at times conflicting, interpretations of musical categories, cross-racial codes, sexual etiquette, the significance of drug use, and the meaning of subcultural style.[40] European styles and scenes have dominated both the academic discourse and public

The story of house and techno is a convoluted tale of trans-Atlantic cross-fertilization and ever-evolving substyles and scenes that is complicated further by multiple, and at times conflicting, interpretations of musical categories, cross-racial codes, sexual etiquette, the significance of drug use, and the meaning of subcultural style.

understanding of these musics, at times obscuring their origins, which date back to the late 1970s and early 1980s in Chicago, Detroit, and New York. Long before pivotal British figures such as Paul Oakenfeld, Danny and Jenni Rampling, and Nicky Holloway returned from Ibiza to revitalize the stagnant British club scene, the music that had captured their bodies and spirits issued from seminal DJs/producers like Frankie Knuckles in Chicago, Larry Levan in New York, and Juan Atkins, Derrick May, and Kevin Saunderson (the Belleville Three) just outside of Detroit.

From 1977 until 1983, Frankie Knuckles spun at the Warehouse, a Chicago dance club where audiences favored up-tempo disco mixes drawn from Philadelphia soft soul, New York dance music, and Eurodisco, played at around 124 beats per minute. The Warehouse gave its name to the sound—house music. Knuckles assembled his remixes on reel-to-reel tape, adding his own machine-made four-to-the-floor kick drum (a defining sound of house), beefed-up bass, and other special effects, like his signature locomotive steam engine sound. Two labels—Trax and DJ International—handled most of Chicago house. Jesse Saunders's and Vince Lawrence's remix of First Choice's "On and On" (Trax, 1983) is generally acknowledged to be the first commercially available house recording, and "Love Can't Turn Around" by Farley "Jackmaster" Funk and Jesse Saunders (on DJ International) became house's first international hit, breaking into the U.K. Top Ten in 1986. The predominant dance style at the Warehouse was called jacking, referring to a type of frenzied, sexualized body movement. As house became popular in Britain, a number of jack tracks made the British charts, including "Jack the Groove" by Raze and Steve Silk Hurley's "Jack Your Body." Chicago made it clear that disco hadn't died; it had gone underground. And the term *underground* meant it had returned to its roots in mostly black and Latino gay club culture. "House didn't just resurrect disco," asserts Simon Reynolds, "it intensified the very aspects that most offended the disco-phobes: the mechanistic repetition, the synthetic and electronic textures, the rootlessness, the 'depraved' hypersexuality and 'decadent' drugginess."[41]

Meanwhile, in New York, Larry Levan was spinning for a more upscale, gay crowd at the Paradise Garage, home to the slower, more soulful variant of the music, which became known as garage. There he transformed his remixes of Loose Joints' "Is It All Over My Face" (1980), Taana Gardner's "Heartbeat" (1980), ESG's "Moody" (1981), and N.Y.C. Peech Boys' "Don't Make Me Wait" (1982) into dance floor magic. When Knuckles sent him a copy of Jamie Principle's "Baby Wants to Ride" (Trax, 1984), Levan "flipped over it and started playing it at the Garage," thereby exposing house to a broader audience.[42]

Frankie Knuckles developed the sound of house music at the Warehouse in Chicago.

In the Detroit area, Atkins, May, and Saunderson, three middle-class blacks from the suburb of Belleville who launched techno, had cut their musical teeth on the sounds of WGRP deejay Charles "the Electrifyin' Mojo" Johnson, whose heady, eclectic mixes melded everything from Prince and Parliament/Funkadelic to Kraftwerk and electropop. Recording (with partner Rick Davis) as Cybotron, Atkins began transforming Mojo's eclectic tastes into funky, rhythmically complicated tracks, featuring Atkins's deep, resonant vocals and a background of murky psychedelic sounds. Cybotron's "Alleys of Your Mind" (1981) shares the spotlight with the lesser known "Sharevari" by A Number of Names as the first techno recording.[43] Derrick May hit his stride performing as Rhythim Is Rhythim in 1987. Using the rich bank of bass guitar sounds in the Yahama DX-100 keyboard to produce complex staccato bass lines, overlaid with other electronic sounds, May's 1987 releases, "Nude Photo" and "Strings of Life," became defining moments in the evolution of techno. While Atkins became the spiritual leader of techno and May its chief alchemist, Kevin Saunderson achieved the greatest commercial success. Forming the group Inner City, Saunderson released *Big Fun* in 1989 on his own KMS label. It spawned four singles that went to number one on the dance charts—"Big Fun," "Good Life," "Ain't Nobody Better," and "Do You Love What You Feel"—with "Good Life" crossing over to pop as well.

House and techno, then, were the sounds that took British club culture by storm in the late 1980s. Techno originally entered Britain as a subset of house imports; it was codified as black dance music, but it was not specifically labeled techno until Virgin Records released the compilation *Techno: The Dance Sound of Detroit* in 1988. Aided significantly by the warm, feel-good, physio-psychedelic rush provided by the drug Ecstasy (abbreviated simply as E), the music then became known as acid house. The particular mix of cultural elements also produced remarkable gender-bending effects. According to Simon Reynolds, "Gay behavioural codes and modes of expression were entering the body-consciousness of straight working-class boys, via Ecstasy."[44] This new sensibility was evident in "Acid Trax" by Chicago's Phuture and was reflected in popular British dance club singles such as Jolly Roger's "Acid Man" and D-Mob's "We Call It Acieed," which went to number three on the British charts.

After U.S. imports melded with British homegrown product and morphed into acid house, the scene outgrew the clubs and expanded to all-night events—raves—with crowds of up to 20,000 "turning on, tuning in, and freaking out" in aircraft hangers, abandoned warehouses, and open fields along London's M25 highway. A moral panic ensued over the drug excesses of the burgeoning rave culture. In this context, the term *acid house* was dropped and replaced by *techno,* now used as an umbrella term that included electronic dance styles coming out of Europe—a new definition far removed from the music's Detroit origins. As Sarah Thornton put it, "[T]he shift from the first to the second kind of techno, from a 'black' to a 'white' sound, is accompanied by a shift in the discourses about their places of origin. Later techno was said to be a musical Esperanto. It was not considered to be the sound of any particular city or any definite group but rather as a celebration of rootlessness."[45] Thus, when this later techno was fed back into the

A *moral panic ensued over the drug excesses of the burgeoning rave culture. In this context, the term* acid house *was dropped and replaced by* techno, *now used as an umbrella term that included electronic dance styles coming out of Europe—a new definition far removed from the music's Detroit origins.*

United States, it was bundled with an aura of white Europeanness. "In Detroit," asserts Simon Reynolds, "everybody assumed Cybotron were white guys from Europe," a perception no doubt increased by Cybotron's liberal appropriation of Kraftwerk and other sounds from the European avant garde.[46]

As British rave culture fragmented into progressively narrower scenes, the house/techno sound underwent further transformations into various substyles, including deep house, hard core, ambient, hip house, jungle (a.k.a. drum and base), and trip hop, among others. A second generation of young, energetic ravers pushed house toward the more up-tempo and anthemic hard core, rocking the body to new extremes with tracks such as Unique 3's "The Theme," Shut Up and Dance's "Raving I'm Raving," and the Prodigy's "Charly" and "Everybody in the Place." Meanwhile, there was a resurgence of interest in chill-out ambient music to replenish the spirit. Examples include the KLF's *Chill Out*; 808 State's "Pacific State"; S'Express's "Mantra for a State of Mind"; and the Orb's "Fluffy Little Clouds," "Backside of the Moon," and "A Huge Evergrowing Pulsating Brain That Rules from the Centre of the Ultraworld." The more sedentary enjoyed Warp's self-described "electronic listening music" compilation, *Artificial Intelligence* (1992).

These scenic changes also signaled social and aesthetic divisions along the fault lines of class, sexual orientation, and, in particular, race. As the working-class rave culture expanded, clueless, and presumably lower-class, newcomers were disparaged as "acid teds"—a play on the teddy boys of the 1960s. In gender terms, Sarah Thornton points out that "in America, house and acid house were perceived first and foremost as gay and could be heard only in gay clubs until they were re-exported back to the United States as 'English acid house.'"[47] As to race, adjectives like *progressive* or *intelligent*—as in progressive house or intelligent techno— were often used to indicate music that had been drained of its African American influences and also marked a retreat from dance culture itself, such as with Warp's *Artificial Intelligence* compilation.

As the hypersyncopated break-beats of hard core attracted more black Britons to the rave scene, more black influences appeared in the music. Jungle was such a phenomenon. Lacking the metronomic kick drum that underpinned much of house and disco, jungle combined reggae samples with deep hip hop baselines and dense layers of percussion. Credit for the first use of the term probably goes to black promoter Paul Chambers, who released the uncredited single "Jungle Techno" around 1992. According to Matthew Collin, jungle was immediately understood as "black youth reasserting control over what was originally the black music of Chicago, New York and Detroit," even though it was widely known that half the contributing DJs and producers were white.[48] Among junglists, the drugs of choice switched from Ecstasy and speed to marijuana and champagne. If the stereotype of the hard-core raver had been "a sweaty, shirtless white teenager," the stereotypical junglist was "a head-nodding, stylishly dressed black twenty-something with hooded eyes, a joint in one hand, and a bottle of champagne in the other."[49] The term *jungle* was controversial, conjuring up images of primitivism, urban violence, and miscegenation. Shut Up and Dance, a highly politicized rave duo ("White White World," "Autobiography of a Crackhead"), denounced the term as racist. For many, the term *drum and bass* was more acceptable because that was primarily what the music was about anyway.

The first to experiment with the jungle style of distilling break-beats into complex percussive webs were DJs like Fabio and Grooverider, who drew on influences from house, hard core, reggae, hip hop, soul, jazz, ambient, and techno. But Goldie put the sound over the top. A veteran of the hip hop break-dancing and graffiti art scene, Goldie released tracks as part of Rufige Cru and under his own alias, Metalheadz. Goldie made his mark with "Terminator," on which he perfected the junglist technique of time stretching—using pitch control to create the illusion of changing tempos. His masterpiece, "Timeless," the title track of the 1995 album of the same name, appeared shortly after two other concept jungle albums—4 Hero's *Parallel Universe* and *Black Secret Technology* by A Guy Called Gerald. *Timeless* stands, in the words of Simon Reynolds, as jungle's *Sgt. Pepper*—"half genre-bending brilliance, half ill-advised attempts to prove Goldie's versatility."[50] Because jungle tended to explore the underside of rave culture, it was labeled dark and invariably linked—as were black youth more generally—to violence and the use of harder drugs. At this point, the scene split along racial lines, with white ravers gravitating toward happy hard core to regain the feel-good vibe of the Ecstasy culture.

Trip hop was likewise criticized—by its practitioners as a media invention and by its detractors, who saw nothing new in the music. Trip hop was an ethereal, down-tempo form of hip hop, designed mostly for listening. Contrary to the "keepin' it real" imperatives of U.S. hip hop, trip hop's goal was to keep it as unreal as possible. Its best-known practitioners included Massive Attack, Tricky, Portishead, and LA-based DJ Shadow. The style was defined with Massive Attack's *Blue Lines* (1991), which included raps by Tricky and instrumental programming by Portishead's Goeff Barrow. While *Blue Lines* retained the essence of hip hop—break-beat rhythms and looped samples—it also included atmospheric guitar riffs and trancelike melodies, proceeding at a tranquil 90 bpm or less. *Protection* (1994), their follow-up, was less well received; its sequel, *No Protection* (1995), fared considerably better. Portishead's *Dummy* (1994) used Beth Gibbons's bluesy vocals and elements of house and film soundtrack music, winning fans beyond the rave culture. *Dummy* received the prestigious Mercury Music Prize and sold 150,000 copies in the United States after "Sour Times" went into regular rotation on MTV. DJ Shadow, a white b-boy from southern California, gained attention abroad as a master sampler on the strength of singles like "Entropy," "In Flux," "Lost and Found," and "What Does Your Soul Look Like?" His debut album, *Endtroducing* (1996), was greeted with critical acclaim, although Shadow remained practically unknown in the U.S. hip hop scene.

Tricky was easily the most colorful figure in the trip hop scene. Appearing at times in a wedding dress and mascara, Tricky played with gender as much as with genre. Following the success of his first single, "Aftermath" (with vocalist Martina), his debut album, *Maxinquaye* (1995), entered the British charts at number two. In it, he combined a sense of social consciousness with ponderous rhythms, orchestral arrangements, and ominous background sounds. It was quite a package. In the words of Simon Reynolds: "Racially, stylistically, sexually, Tricky is one slippery fellow. *Maxinquaye* is an unclassifiable hybrid of club and bedroom music, black and white, rap and melody, song and atmospherics, sampladelic textures and real-time instrumentation. It sucks you into the polysexual, transgeneric, mongrelized mind-space inside Tricky's skull."[51] Following his second album, *Nearly God,* a collection of tracks featuring Bjork,

Trip hop was an ethereal, down-tempo form of hip hop, designed mostly for listening. Contrary to the "keepin' it real" imperatives of U.S. hip hop, trip hop's goal was to keep it as unreal as possible.

Neneh Cherry, Cath Coffey, Alison Moyet, and others, Tricky was signed by Polygram for *Pre-Millennium Tension* (1996).

These were the rough contours of the house/techno scene abroad as the U.S. music industry began to take notice and tried to bundle everything into one category: electronica. As 1997 dawned, the groups to watch were the Prodigy, the Chemical Brothers, Underworld, and the most recognizable DJ/producer of them all—Moby. The prodigy behind the Prodigy, Liam Howlett—a classically trained pianist turned hip hop b-boy—burst onto the rave/hard core scene with "Charly" (1991), which hit number one on the British dance charts and crossed over to pop number three. Harnessing rave energy to pop appeal, titles like "Hyperspeed," "Full Throttle," and "G-Force" captured the youthful exuberance of their music. Their debut album, *The Prodigy Experience* (1992), picked up by Elektra in the United States, added polished pop hooks to the break-beat foundation. Considered hopelessly commercial by the ultra-hip—the Prodigy was playing at rock festivals by this time—Howlett continued to release underground singles that passed muster on the dance floor. The group's 1994 double album, *Music for the Gilted Generation,* launched an all-out assault against the British crackdown on illegal raves. Following the success of their nonalbum single "Firestarter" (U.K. number one, U.S. number five), a bidding war broke out for their contract, with Madonna's Maverick label ultimately winning. The Prodigy's third album, *The Fat of the Land* (1997), went straight to number one in the United States—and just about everywhere else.

The Chemical Brothers rose to popularity on the wings of a rave-meets-rock 'n' roll hybrid called big beat, with artists like Fatboy Slim and Bently Rhythm Ace. Beginning musical life as the Dust Brothers, Chemical Brothers Ed Simmons and Tom Rowlands debuted with *Exit Planet Dust* (1995), a compilation of bombastic, guitar-laden, siren-screeching (but still dance floor friendly) techno for headbangers. They extended their rock credentials on the follow-up single, "Setting Sun," with Oasis's Noel Gallagher supplying the vocals. *Dig Your Own Hole* (1997)—which entered the British charts at number one, U.S. at number fourteen—was an even more eclectic, hard-rocking album, underpinned with layered rhythms and sophisticated electronics. Underworld started as a funk rock group and evolved toward a more techno (but still rock-oriented) sound with the addition of DJ Darren Emerson. Following the success of *Dubnobasswithmyheadman* (1994), Underworld scored a U.S. deal with TVT. *Second Toughest in the Infants* (1996) was released to critical acclaim, with the

Laying polished pop hooks over a breakbeat foundation, the Prodigy scored a number one album in the United States.

nonalbum single "Born Slippy"—featured in the soundtrack to *Trainspotting*—boosting sales of the album. While these groups were built on a firm foundation of electronic dance music, they succeeded in the U.S. pop market in part because of their more rock-like presentation as bands. Their limited success was strong enough to convince rockers such as U2 to flirt with the style, as they did on *Pop* (1997). Madonna, of course, had always kept one foot in the dance market.

New York-based Moby took a somewhat different tack. Born Richard Melville Hall, Moby became a radical Christian and a vegan activist. Based on "Go," his successful remix of the *Twin Peaks* theme, and his 1992 high-energy eponymous debut techno album, Moby was signed to Elektra Records, for whom he recorded *Everything Is Wrong* (1994). It won critical raves but no corresponding commercial success. In 1996, he abandoned techno for political activism and progressive rock on *Animal Rights*. He returned to techno for *I Like to Score* (1997), but didn't hit his stride until *Play* (1999), a master stroke of musical production and a marketing triumph. All eighteen tracks were licensed for use in films, television programs, and advertisements before the album peaked on the charts (it eventually won multiplatinum certification). According to *Wired*, "The dozen and a half songs on *Play* . . . have been sold hundreds of times for commercials, movies, and TV shows—a licensing venture so staggeringly lucrative that the album was a financial success months before it reached its multiplatinum sales total."[52] Moby consolidated his skills on *18* in 2002. By this time he had become important enough to be verbally attacked by Eminem on "Without Me."

But Moby was a rarity. Electronica as an enterprise never became the next big thing. It remained largely the province of the underground, in the able hands of DJ crews like San Francisco's Invisibl Skratch Piklz and New York's X-ecutioners. The cuts that dominated the U.S. dance charts in the late 1990s were club remixes of artists from other genres: Bjork ("Big Time Sensuality"), k.d. lang ("Lifted by Love," "Sexuality"), Celine Dion ("Misled"), Reba McEntyre ("You Keep Me Hanging On"), Gloria Estefan ("You'll Be Mine [Party Time]," "Tres Desos [Three Wishes]," "Reach"), and Toni Braxton ("You're Making Me High," "Unbreak My Heart," "I Don't Want To"). Summing up 1997, *Billboard*'s Marilyn Gillen wrote: "The planned phenomenon of 'electronica' was still being assessed as the year closed out, though its impact on cash registers seemed less than electric."[53] Ultimately, electronic dance music was the product of master turntablists and remixers—propellerheads working with samplers, drum machines, and computers—rather than the charismatic front-men and -women who fit the industry's conception of superstars.

> **U**ltimately, electronic dance music was the product of master turntablists and remixers—propellerheads working with samplers, drum machines, and computers—rather than the charismatic front-men and -women who fit the industry's conception of superstars.

The Year(s) of the Woman and the Rage Rock Backlash

Although women comprise over 50 percent of the population, they are underrepresented in the upper reaches of most fields of endeavor, including popular music. Consequently, when women break through, it is considered a trend. The *Boston Globe's* Steve Morse identified this trend twice in the 1990s—once, when he declared: "Time to call 1996 what it was: pop music's Year of the Woman"[54]; then again in 1999, as women swept the Grammy Awards. Women also did very well in the intervening years. Initially, Morse noted not only the superstar entries of

Alanis Morisette's *Jagged Little Pill,* 1996's best-selling album, and Celine Dion's multiplatinum *Falling into You* but also the impact of lesser-known artists like Joan Osborne, Natalie Merchant, Ani DiFranco, Tori Amos, Suzanne Vega, and Shawn Colvin, as well as women fronting mixed-gender groups such as Delores O'Riordan (Cranberries), Gwen Stefani (No Doubt), and Lauryn Hill (Fugees). In fact, the six best-selling albums of 1996 were by women or woman-fronted groups: Morisette, Dion, Mariah Carey's *Daydream,* the Fugees' *The Score,* Shania Twain's *The Woman in Me,* and the all-female soundtrack to *Waiting to Exhale.* Women also took five of the six top spots the following year. Newcomers included the Spice Girls (*Spice*), No Doubt (*Tragic Kingdom*), Jewel (*Pieces of You*), and LeAnn Rimes (*Blue*).

A number of things were striking about this trend. One was the number of genres represented, including pop/dance (Mariah Carey, Spice Girls), alternative/pop rock (Alanis Morisette), folk rock (Jewel), country (Shania Twain, LeAnn Rimes), and hip hop (Lauryn Hill). Equally interesting was that three of the year's six biggest sellers hailed from Canada—Alanis Morisette, Celine Dion, and Shania Twain. Dion carried the Canadian torch into 1998, dominating the top two slots with a central presence on the *Titanic* soundtrack, followed by her own *Let's Talk About Love.* Twain was close on her heels at number five with *Come on Over,* which set an all-time album sales record for a female artist. They were joined by compatriot singer-songwriter Sarah McLachlan, whose *Surfacing,* which began its ascent in 1997, announced her entrance into the elite of pop superstars.

McLachlan had developed a solid career as a singer-songwriter beginning with her debut album, *Touch,* in 1989. After working on a documentary in Southeast Asia about poverty and child sexual abuse, she returned to the studio, hitting her stride on *Fumbling Towards Ecstasy* (1994). In 1996, she founded Lilith Fair, a self-described "celebration of women in music," which featured only female-led acts (although at times male backup musicians outnumbered the women on stage). Lilith Fair was the most successful concert tour of 1997. Between 1997 and 1999, its final year, it grew into a multicity, multidate event featuring dozens of artists on multiple stages. Lilith Fair was for women what Lollapalooza was for alternative: a spectacular showcase that demonstrated it could succeed against all odds. And as with Lollapalooza, the organizers injected social consciousness into the event. With one dollar from every ticket sold being donated to a charitable organization, Lilith Fair was able to distribute some $700,000 in 1997 alone to a variety of progressive women's organizations. Throughout its run, McLachlan maintained a hands-on relationship with the festival and was the only headliner to perform every date. She was selflessly devoted to the festival's goals and causes; at the same time, her strong presence at the 1997 festival helped propel *Surfacing,* just released, to four times platinum sales, generating three hit singles in the process. By the time she called it quits in 1999, her *Mirrorball* album was in the Top Ten.

Lilith Fair was criticized for gravitating toward the softer end of the female performance spectrum, focusing primarily on singer-songwriters like Fiona Apple ("Criminal"), Paula Cole ("Where

((•● **HEAR MORE**
Sarah McLachlan
on MyMusicKit

Sarah McLachlan rose to prominence in the Year(s) of the Woman and founded Lilith Fair, the most important women's tour of the 1990s.

Have All the Cowboys Gone"), Shawn Colvin ("Summer Came Home"), Joan Osborne ("One of Us"), and Suzanne Vega ("Luka"). "The cartoon image of Lilith," wrote James Sullivan retrospectively in the *San Francisco Chronicle,* "has been one of anguished young maidens with wispy songs to sing."[55] As the festival grew in popularity, however, it also grew in diversity. In 1998 and 1999, artists included Erykah Badu ("On and On"), Missy "Misdemeanor" Elliott ("Hot Boyz"), Lauryn Hill ("Doo Wop [That Thing]"), Queen Latifah ("Ladies First"), Me'Shell Ndegéocello ("Wild Night," with John Mellencamp), and the Dixie Chicks ("There's Your Trouble"), as well as Bonnie Raitt, Sinéad O'Connor, and the Pretenders. Even teen sensation Christina Aguilera came on board briefly in 1999. Asked where all this variation was in 1997, McLachlan responded: "We asked them all last year and they said no."[56] By 1999, Lilith Fair had concluded with a powerful female sound.

Women also dominated the 1999 Grammy Awards in a sweep that the *Boston Globe*'s Morse dubbed, once again, the Year of the Woman. Top honors went to Sheryl Crow, Alanis Morisette, Shania Twain, the Dixie Chicks, Madonna, Celine Dion, and Lauryn Hill (who took five trophies, a record for a female artist). Crow took Best Rock Album for *The Globe Sessions* and Morisette walked away with Best Rock Song and Best Female Rock Vocal Performance for "Uninvited." The Dixie Chicks upset Shania Twain for Best Country Album, but Shania shared the writing credits for Best Country Song and walked off with Best Female Country Vocal for "You're Still the One." Madonna picked up Best Pop Album and Best Dance Recording for *Ray of Light.* Brandy and Monica ("The Boy Is Mine") and Patti Labelle ("Live! One Night Only") won awards in the r&b category, Deniece Williams and Cissy Houston in gospel, and Patti Page in Best Traditional Pop Vocal Performance.

The youngest of fourteen children, Celine Dion had been a veteran of the Francophone Quebec music scene since performing in her parents' club at age five. She made her bid for international stardom on the strength of her first all-English album, *Unison.* When it crossed national and linguistic boundaries, she scrambled to appease her French-speaking base by very publicly refusing to accept the Canadian Felix Award for Anglophone Artist of the Year. Still, her career choices bowed at least partially to the dictates of U.S. tastemakers. On her second all-English album, *Celine Dion* (1992), she was paired with notable songwriters such as Diane Warren and Prince, who supplied "With This Tear." The album includes "Beauty and the Beast," the animated film's title song. She was confirmed as an international superstar with *Falling into You* (1996), best-selling album in 1997, and winner of both the Album of the Year and Best Pop Album Grammys. *Let's Talk About Love* (1999) was released on the same day as the soundtrack of the film *Titanic.* Dion's "My Heart Will Go On," from that soundtrack, was featured on both albums and pushed both to international sales of 27 million units.

Lauryn Hill had more options than most people. Still in high school, she landed a recurring role on the soap opera *As the World Turns* and played a role in the Whoopi Goldberg film *Sister Act 2.* She wrote poetry, played high school basketball, ran track, and was a cheerleader and homecoming queen. She went to Columbia University and continued to work with childhood friends Wyclef Jean and Prakazrel ("Pras") Michel as a member of the Fugees, whose *The Score* (1996)—at 17 million units—was the best-selling hip hop album ever. Propelled by Hill's infectious vocal on the cover of "Killing Me Softly," *The Score* was the socially conscious hip hop album of the year with its combination of deep beats and insightful commentary juxtaposed against an incredible musicality. Throughout, Hill continued to work with the Refugee Project, which she started in 1996 to assist underprivileged and at-risk youth. Before launching her solo career, however, she took time off when her son, Zion—whose father is Bob Marley's son Rohan—was born.

The Miseducation of Lauryn Hill (1998) was Hill's solo debut—a big band jazz–meets–hip hop extravaganza incorporating soul, rap, reggae, and hip hop. In 1999, it earned her the Album of the Year and the Best New Artist, R&B Song, R&B Album, and R&B Vocal Performance Grammys. Critical praise was unequivocal. Hill's largely autobiographical work touched on issues from racism and sexism to spirituality and self-confession, eliciting comparisons to touchstone works such as Marvin Gaye's *What's Goin' On* and Joni Mitchell's *Blue*. In addition to the warmth and sensitivity of her vocals, Hill also brought considerable savvy to the album as producer and grace to the Grammy Awards. Still, she had no illusions about the music industry. "This is a very sexist industry," she exclaimed. "They'll never throw the genius title to a sister. They'll just call her 'diva' and think it's a compliment. It's like our flair and vanity are put before our musical and intellectual contributions."[57]

Perhaps it was the overwhelming success of Lilith Fair or the continued dominance of women in the pop arena, but 1999 marked the beginning of a backlash against the preponderance of women in high places.

Perhaps it was the overwhelming success of Lilith Fair or the continued dominance of women in the pop arena, but 1999 marked the beginning of a backlash against the preponderance of women in high places. While even some of the female singer-songwriters like Alanis Morisette had been described as "angry"—in her case, because of the uncensored lyrics of "You Oughta Know"—their anger did not compare to the fury that issued from the rock bands labeled rage rockers by the press. The acts most often mentioned included Korn, Limp Bizkit, and Kid Rock. All came from white working-class and mostly southern backgrounds, all combined elements of rock and rap in their music, and all had achieved platinum sales. They came together at an event deemed the antithesis of Lilith Fair—Woodstock '99. "If Lilith catapulted women front and center in the popular culture," opined the *Boston Globe*'s Joan Anderman, "Woodstock '99 flung them not merely back into the wings but to a far darker place, where men rule with iron—and if it suits them, violent—fists."[58]

Woodstock '99 was staged at Griffis Air Force Base in Rome, New York. Essentially a slab of concrete surrounded

Limp Bizkit became one of the focal points for male rage in the late 1990s. With an aggressive stage show and titles like "Nookie," no one was surprised.

by barbed wire, with nary a shade tree in sight, the promoters could not have selected a more inhospitable site. While nudity abounded in 1967, the nakedness vibe in 1999 was different. Here the scene was like an amphitheater strip club, with shirtless goons demanding that women "show us your tits"—forcibly if necessary, or in exchange for cigarettes, beer, drugs, or water. In the sets by Korn and Limp Bizkit, the mosh pit seemed more violent than usual; women were routinely groped and dozens of fans were injured. "Don't let anybody get hurt," said Limp Bizkit's seemingly concerned Fred Durst, who then added, "but I don't think you should mellow out. That's what Alanis Morisette had you motherfuckers do," referring to her earlier, admittedly sluggish performance.[59] Limp Bizkit then broke into their hit single "Nookie" and the mosh pit exploded—a rape allegedly occurring in the pit during Limp Bizkit's set.

The Red Hot Chili Peppers closed the show. In another context, the Chili Peppers bursting on stage buck naked could have been celebrated as an act of sexual freedom. Juxtaposed against scenes of forced sexuality (four rapes were reported), their exuberance became part of a different reality. Closing with a rendition of Jimi Hendrix's "Fire" might also have taken on a more benign meaning were it not linked to a growing number of bonfires that prompted the health services to abandon the site. The festival degenerated into a finale of arson and rioting by fans, who were justifiably outraged at the poor sanitary conditions, lack of shade, and exorbitant prices for food and water.

Another kind of rage was also expressed at Woodstock '99 and elsewhere during this period—that of rock-rap ensemble Rage Against the Machine. As self-defined socialists, Rage had taken up the causes of the Native American activist Leonard Peltier; the Zapatista rebels in Chiapas, Mexico; and imprisoned black journalist Mumia Abu-Jamal. Like the other rage rockers, Rage incorporated rap into their music, but with a political edge, as in "Vietnow" from *Evil Empire* (1996). Led by Mexican American vocalist Zac de la Rocha and biracial guitarist Tom Morello, Rage criticized the macho posturing of gangsta rappers like Tupac and Notorious B.I.G., as well as the misogynistic lyrics of several artists. Following the success of *The Battle of Los Angeles* (1999), and just after de la Rocha left the band, Rage released *Renegades*, an album of covers of, among others, the Rolling Stones' "Street Fighting Man," Afrika Bambaataa's "Renegades of Funk," and Cypress Hill's classic "How I Could Just Kill a Man," all recorded with the group's signature political edge.

Teen Pop: Boy Bands and Teen Queens

Rage rockers were also the antithesis of another phenomenon—teen pop, represented by artists such as the Backstreet Boys, 'N Sync, Britney Spears, and Christina Aguilera. But there is more to such stark dichotomies than meets the eye. With rage rock described by the press as everything that is aggressive, hateful, and misogynistic and teen pop as wholesome and family-oriented, one might imagine that the former's audience would be limited to angry white men, with young girls gravitating toward teen pop. The reality is far more complex. "Contrary to popular opinion," says Joan Anderman, "not every adolescent heart is aflutter for the Backstreet Boys and 'N Sync. Girls from the suburbs and girls from the city, girls who live in tiny hamlets overseas and in Midwestern trailer parks, are dedicated followers of the new crop of coarse, venomous rockers."[60] In this context, the 1999 *Rolling Stone* Readers Poll—which bestowed top honors on Korn, Limp Bizkit, Kid Rock, and Eminem as well as on the Backstreet Boys and Christina Aguilera—cannot be read as a simple gender division.[61] It is quite likely that young women as well as young men voted for all of them.

> **T**he striking combination of innocence and sexuality of the new teen sensations was, in some ways, a throwback to early-1960s pent-up sexuality—a preoccupation with titillation, as in the beach party movies.

The striking combination of innocence and sexuality of the new teen sensations was, in some ways, a throwback to early-1960s pent-up sexuality—a preoccupation with titillation, as in the beach party movies. The rage rockers manifested a rougher sexuality (some would call it sexism)—Marlon Brando's and James Dean's alienated hoodlums combined with the Stones' "Street Fighting Man" and taken to the extreme—but it clearly had its appeal. Some young women always see the attraction of the dangerous, adventurous, outlaw bad boy, which is an archetype that appears in popular culture and in everyday life. Christina Aguilera talked openly about wanting to date a "roughneck." She was linked in the press to Fred Durst (of Limp Bizkit) and Eminem, who skewered her sexual reputation on "The Real Slim Shady."[62]

There was a certain incestuousness about the new teen pop infrastructure and a shared ethic among the most successful artists about their role as teen idols. Britney Spears and Christina Aguilera, as well as 'N Sync's Justin Timberlake and JC Chasez, were members of the *Mickey Mouse Club* class of 1993. Both the Backstreet Boys (BSB) and 'N Sync shared management with Lou Pearlman's Continental Management Company. BSB became disillusioned when Pearlman created 'N Sync without telling them, then sued for back royalties. 'N Sync also left over money issues; they joined Johnny Wright's Wright Stuff management company, which started with the New Kids on the Block and moved on to Britney Spears. 'N Sync then left RCA for Jive Records, home to both Britney Spears and the Backstreet Boys; and all three acts have worked with the crack writer-producer team headed by the late Denniz Pop and his protégé Max Martin at Sweden's Cheiron Studios. Auditions for *Star Search* and a Southern Baptist upbringing were themes that run through many of these artists' backgrounds. An intense work ethic and rigorous sense of discipline characterized all the successful careers; the result was a curious combination of youthful energy and seasoned professionalism, accompanied by an acute sense of their responsibilities as role models to a generation.

Dating back to Sonny and Cher, the Partridge Family, the Jackson 5, and the New Kids on the Block, there was nothing particularly new about the teen pop phenomenon. From the mall tours of Tiffany and the more self-assured, r&b-flavored pop of Debbie Gibson to the "girl power" feminism of the Spice Girls and No Doubt, there has been a market for this music. The difference at the end of the twentieth century was just how systematic and all-pervasive it seemed to be. In addition to those boy bands and teen queens already mentioned, one found the funkier 98 Degrees, LFO, Mandy (Moore), Jessica Simpson, and the well-respected Hanson. Monica and Brandy, and Destiny's Child were among the few African American acts who could be considered part of the phenomenon. Teen pop peaked in 1999. That year, three of the four best-selling albums of the year were *Millennium* (Backstreet Boys) at number one, . . . *Baby One More Time* (Britney Spears) at number two, and *'N Sync* in the number four slot, with Christina Aguilera edging into the Top Forty with her self-titled debut. The year 2000 showed a slight shift, with 'N Sync taking over the top slot and Spears's *Oops! . . . I Did It Again* and Aguilera's debut in the Top Ten. By this time, the Backstreet Boys had slipped due to contractual problems.

The Backstreet Boys, the oldest of the new boy bands, had been around since 1993. Signed by Jive in 1994, they became major hitmakers in Europe, though it wasn't until 1997 that they made it in the United States. That year, a self-titled compilation of their European hits plus some new material—including "Quit Playing Games (with My Heart)," "As Long As You Love Me," "Everybody (Backstreet's Back)"—took the United States by storm, eventually selling 13 million copies. Their follow-up album, *Millennium* (1999), broke Garth Brooks's first-week sales record, toting up 1.1 million units. The tour supporting the album sold out all 53 dates (765,000 tickets) in one day. Together, *Backstreet Boys* and *Millennium* racked up some 60 million copies in worldwide sales. BSB eventually left Pearlman, but stayed with Jive, reportedly signing a $60 million five-album deal.

From the start, BSB felt threatened by 'N Sync. They were angry with Pearlman for developing the group and were particularly upset when 'N Sync's sophomore effort, *No Strings Attached* (on Jive), sold 2.4 million copies, more than doubling BSB's first-week sales record. With so many similarities to the Backstreet Boys—five clean-cut twenty-somethings from Orlando recording very highly produced pop singles and schooled by the same handlers—'N Sync distinguished themselves as somewhat edgier and more savvy. They hit pay dirt with their very first (self-titled) album, which sold more than eleven times platinum and remained on the charts over two years, generating the hit singles "Tearin' up My Heart," "Here We Go," and "I Want You Back." They also recorded a hit version of "God Must Have Spent a Little More Time on You" as a duet with Alabama and "Music of My Heart" as a duet with Gloria Estefan, and

The oldest of the new boy bands, the Backstreet Boys became a major teen sensation but kept looking over their shoulders as 'N Sync gained on them.

performed a duet with Puerto Rico's Son By Four at the first-ever Latin Grammy Awards show—thereby disseminating their music to new audiences. *Rolling Stone*'s Anthony Bozza wrote, "'N Sync seem no different from Backstreet . . . but they are. . . . 'N Sync tap into some of the same teen angst and psychosexual anxiety at the heart of much darker stuff, like teen horror movies and grunge."[63]

'N Sync's third outing, *Celebrity,* was more mature and musically diverse. Still tethered to Cheiron's pop base, the group ventured much farther afield, using the Neptunes to produce "Girlfriend" and techno producer BT to produce "Pop" over "Max Headroom-style frackle-stutter edits" of Timberlake beatboxing.[64] *Celebrity* marked something of a break for them; it has been compared to Michael Jackson's *Dangerous,* due in no small part to the tonality and phrasing of Timberlake's vocals. "Justin could've been raised in the black church," quipped the Neptunes' Pharrell Williams.[65] At the end of 2001, the album had been certified five times platinum and was still on the charts. 'N Sync and the Backstreet Boys peaked when they placed second and third among the top-grossing live acts worldwide, taking in $90.2 million and $89.8 million, respectively, for their 2001 tours.

Britney Spears burst onto the charts in late 1998 and took the music to new heights over the next two years. As 2000 came to a close, her first album, *. . . Baby One More Time,* had been certified thirteen times platinum and was still riding the charts, and her second, *Oops! . . . I Did It Again,* was at number five and climbing, eventually selling 9 million units. The title songs from both albums, like her stage act, were loaded with sexual innuendo. The fact that the first album's hook line was prefaced with "hit me" raised concerns about female masochism, a charge that Spears shrugged off. "It doesn't mean physically hit me," she told Steven Daly. "It means just give me a sign."[66] Spears made her stage debut at age five. Later signed to Jive records, every aspect of her career was mapped out and Spears was a full collaborator, calling many of the shots. As her co-manager Larry Rudolph explained, "She knows exactly what her audience wants. She is her audience."[67]

Spears sought to project a more grown-up image for her third album and brought in the Neptunes to produce the single "I'm a Slave 4 U." Released in late 2001, *Britney* became her third album in a row to debut at number one. By this time, she was dating Justin Timberlake, and the media attention lavished on their (short-lived) romance added to the celebrity status of both. During this period, she also landed a lucrative Pepsi endorsement. But *Britney* sold below expectations (around 4 million copies) and none of its

Britney Spears combined sexual innuendo, disciplined professionalism, and a strong business plan into one of the most successful careers in teen pop, then spiraled out of control.

singles broke into the Top Ten, even with the steamy video for "I'm a Slave 4 U." Spears decided to take a much-needed sabbatical after an onstage meltdown on the final day of her 2002 world tour.

Obvious similarities, Christina Aguilera had often been compared to Britney Spears her fellow former Mouseketeer. But given her vocal range and power—which earned her the chance to record "Reflection" for the soundtrack to Disney's *Mulan* before her first album was released—comparisons with artists like Whitney Houston and Mariah Carey would not have been out of line. She beat both Britney Spears and Macy Gray for the Best New Artist Grammy in 2000—an upset victory all the more incredible because RCA had

Because of obvious similarities, Christina Aguilera had often been compared to Britney Spears her fellow former Mouseketeer. But given her vocal range and power, comparisons with artists like Whitney Houston and Mariah Carey would not have been out of line.

reined her in, keeping the album well within teen pop conventions. Her 1999 eponymous debut entered the charts at number one and sold better than 8 million copies before it peaked. Its first single, "Genie in a Bottle," whose infectious hook line propelled it straight to number one, became the most popular single of the year. It was the perfect metaphor for the state of her career and the bottled-up teenage sexuality that typified so much of the music. Still riding the charts in 2000, *Christina Aguilera* generated two more number one singles—"What a Girl Wants" and "Come on Over Baby (All I Want Is You)." Born of a white mother and an Ecuadorian father, Aguilera is part Latina, a side of her identity she decided to explore in more depth. As 2000 came to an end, she had three albums in the Billboard 200: *Christina Aguilera* at number twenty-six and climbing fast; *My Kind of Christmas*, her holiday entry; and *Mi Reflejo* (My Reflection), the Spanish version of her debut album. And she hadn't yet recorded what the press was calling her sophomore album.

Aguilera took two years to complete her second studio album, *Stripped*. During this period, she came of age in a most extroverted fashion, bragging to one interviewer that her genital piercings had "gotten a lot of compliments," to which she quickly added: "From my gynecologist."[68] Aguilera was certainly entitled to celebrate her newfound adult sexuality, but on *Stripped*, as in real life, she seemed overwhelmed by it, compelled to flaunt it, unable to place it in any kind of perspective. Despite her protestations that the title referred to her "stripped of all the hype, the gloss, the controversy, the rumors,"[69] her nude photos on the album cover (as well as on the *Rolling Stone* cover) suggested otherwise, as did "Dirrty," the first single. Her Linda Perry collaboration, "Beautiful," broke into the Top Ten, and although *Stripped* quickly rose to number two on the charts, it failed to generate sales even approaching those of her first album. Tracks like "I'm OK," about her father's abuse of her mother, revealed the pain of a young woman working through serious childhood issues. Gone was the pretty, perky Christina of nineteen; replacing her was the alter ego she called Xtina (tattooed on the back of her neck), who represented her "dark, mysterious, kind of edgier side."[70] In the time it took to record her second album, the teen pop space in popular culture was already being taken over by a generation of somewhat more serious, less overtly sexual female artists ranging from Norah Jones and Vanessa Carlton to Avril Lavigne and Pink. However, while Christina and Xtina struggled to come to an accommodation, Aguilera could still rely on one of the best vocal instruments in the business, and she still had all that Latin music to explore.

"... Baby One More Time"

Artist: Britney Spears
Music / Lyrics by Max Martin
Label: Jive, from the CD ... *Baby One More Time* (1998)

Britney Spears's appeal is not only aural but strongly visual as well—presented, like Britney's role model, Madonna, in the company of impeccable choreographies and virtuosic dance montage. Britney's early song hits were simple, repetitive, written by others, and essentially conceived as vehicles for carefully staged theater. Whether innocent or salacious, soulful or funky, Britney's hits reflected the industry's emphasis on marketing elements over artistic individuality. Some may question the artistic credibility of this approach; however, Britney's powerful, sultry, and amazingly flexible voice still shines through any amount of glitz and hype.

Musical Style Notes

While 1960s producer Phil Spector had to fill the studio with live performing bodies to get his famous "wall of sound," today's producers (in this case, Max Martin and Rami) can get an incredibly thick instrumental and vocal texture with a few live musicians, a recording studio, and a computer. Other than the acoustic and electric guitar and bass, all the other instrumental sounds on the CD ... *Baby One More Time* (drums, multiple keyboards) are created by synth programming. There is also a lot of electronic processing done on the vocals, in terms of both doubling parts and manipulating the actual vocal sound, with compression, reverb, and other effects. Armed with this technology and an artist with Spears's strong and remarkably fluid natural voice, the sky's the limit in creating vocal effects.

Structurally, "... Baby One More Time" has a verse-chorus form; the verse has two distinctly different melodic sections (indicated in the Musical "Road Map" as the A and B sections of the verse). The chorus is memorable—one of those refrains that runs through your mind for the rest of the day—culminating with the memorable "Hit me baby one more time" hook.

An interesting variation happens at 2:05 in the piece, where new musical material is introduced into the verse. Then at 3:07, the new material is interwoven with the chorus, creating the effect of a call and response between groups of vocalists (some of them overdubbed).

Musical "Road Map"

TIMINGS	COMMENTS	LYRICS
0:00	Introduction, prominent piano sound, steady drumbeat, guitar with wah wah effect also heard in background.	*Oh baby baby . . .*
0:12	Verse 1 (A section of verse) Note	*how was I . . .*
0:32	(B section of verse) Background vocals added.	*Show me . . .* *'cause I need—*
0:43	Chorus Multiple vocals	*My loneliness . . .*
1:04	Verse 2 (A section of verse) Solo voice with background vocals added as verse progresses.	*Oh baby baby . . .*
1:24	(B section of verse)	*Show me . . .*
1:35	Chorus Multiple vocals	*My loneliness . . .*
1:55	Reprise of introduction material	
2:05	New Verse 1, altered and expanded with musical material from the chorus. This verse begins like the others, but the second line is missing. At the fourth line ("I must confess"), a new melody is heard, with more background vocals, bringing an entirely new musical element into the song. The end of the variation picks up the last 4 bars of the chorus, with the last line "hit me baby one more time."	*Oh baby baby . . .* *. . . hit me baby . . .*
2:47	Chorus Multiple vocals	*My loneliness . . .*
3:07	Chorus repeats. Here the musical material of the chorus (overdubbed, multitracked vocals, including Britney's) is interwoven with the musical material from the altered verse/chorus heard at 2:05 (Britney and multitracked background vocals). Last line: Instrumental track drops out; "Hit me baby one more time" is sung a cappella, and then the final chord is struck.	*My loneliness . . .* *And give me . . .* *Hit me baby . . .!*

The Latin Boom and Beyond: A Decade of Latin(o/a) Music(ians)

In a season of "Years of . . . ," 1999 could also be called the Year of the Latin Pop Explosion, and not without some justification. It was the year that Ricky Martin shook his bon bon into the hearts of millions. And it was the year that Carlos Santana recorded *Supernatural*, which earned him a record-tying eight Grammys. Among the Latino/a artists who had Top Ten pop hits that year were Christina Aguilera ("Genie in a Bottle," "What a Girl Wants"), Marc Anthony ("I Need to Know"), Gloria Estefan ("Music of My Heart" with 'N Sync), Enrique Iglesias ("Bailamous"), Jennifer Lopez ("If You Had My Love," "Waiting for Tonight"), and, of course, Martin ("Livin' La Vida Loca," "She's All I Ever Had," "Shake Your Bon Bon"), and Santana ("Smooth" featuring Rob Thomas). These pop successes were the surface manifestations of broader and deeper changes taking place in the Latino community, which came to fruition over the course of the next decade.

Between 1990 and 2005, according to census data, the number of immigrants in the United States (documented and undocumented) rose from 19.8 million to 35.7 million, "a number larger than the population of California."[71] More of these immigrants—about 11 million—came from Mexico than from any other country. As of 2004, the U.S. Census Bureau listed over 40 million residents of the United States as being of "Hispanic Origin,"[72] surpassing African Americans as the country's largest ethnic group. New arrivals no longer limited themselves to the historical points of entry like California, New York, Texas, and Florida. Dramatic increases occurred in Indiana, South Dakota, Delaware, Missouri, Colorado, and New Hampshire,[73] resulting in a nationally dispersed Latino population. Just as internal migration during World War II created national markets for regional musics, international immigration in the age of globalization would profoundly alter the U.S. cultural landscape once again.

In 1997, the National Academy of Recording Arts and Sciences (NARAS) gave its blessing to the formation of a Latin Grammy organization, the Latin Academy of Recording Arts and Sciences (LARAS), and also established a new Best Latin Rock/Alternative Grammy of its own, essentially recognizing that the *rock en español* of groups like Mana, Los Fabulosos Cadillacs, Café Tacuba, and Molotov had gained a foothold in the United States. During this period, other events also raised the profile of Latin music in the mainstream. *Selena*, a feature-length Hollywood biopic about the Queen of *Tejano* Music—following her untimely death in 1995—catapulted Jennifer Lopez (in the title role) to pop stardom. Ry Cooder's accidental blockbuster album, *The Buena Vista Social Club*, whose stylistic assortment of *son, descarga, danzón, mambo, cha-cha-cha, guajiro,* and *bolero* elevated a forgotten group of aging traditional Cuban musicians like Ibrahim Ferrer and Compay Segundo to international star status. Finally, Paul Simon's well-promoted, but ultimately flawed Broadway production of *The Capeman* provided a crossover platform for artists like Marc Anthony, Ednita Nazario, and Rubén Blades with its mixture of everything from doo wop and gospel to modern *salsa* and *merengue*. Meanwhile, Gloria Estefan continued to turn out her signature *salsa*-fied dance music, and even New York Puerto Rican rapper the late Big Pun(isher) hit the Top Thirty with "Still Not a Player." By the time LARAS staged its own separate prime-time Latin Grammys telecast in 2000, Martin and Santana were positioned to take home multiple trophies.

Ricky Martin was the Puerto Rican version of the teen pop superstars. At age twelve, he was a (replaceable) member of the international teen sensation *Menudo*. Following some

With a well-timed shake of his bon bon, Ricky Martin ushered in a Latin pop explosion just before the turn of the century.

successful soap opera work (*General Hospital*), a stint on Broadway (*Les Miserables*), and a string of four successful solo albums (totaling sales of 15 million units), Martin jump-started the late-1990s Latin pop explosion with his electrifying performance of "Cup of Life" at the Grammys. In May 1999, Columbia released Martin's first English-language album, *Ricky Martin,* which shot to number one, and he began "Livin' La Vida Loca" in earnest. It was so *loca*, in fact, that 2001 found him sharing the stage with Wayne Newton and Destiny's Child at the presidential inaugural, where he "persuaded [President George W.] Bush to come onstage and give his pelvis a twitch or two (albeit small, tastefully presidential ones)."[74]

At the time of Martin's ascent, Santana appeared to be a 1960s superstar past his prime. He had not had a Top Forty album or single since 1982. Some seventeen years later, an angel named Metatron, whom Santana says visits him frequently, told him, "You will be inside the radio frequency for the purpose of connecting the molecules with the light," which Santana immediately understood to be a new album, on the radio, connecting people with their spiritual selves.[75] Santana delivered Metatron's message verbatim to Arista president Clive Davis, who, being a veteran of the sixties himself, also understood. If Santana was the spiritual force behind *Supernatural,* Davis was its architect, planning the album as half vintage Santana and half collaborations—with Rob Thomas from Matchbox Twenty, Dave Matthews, Everlast, Lauryn Hill, Cee-Lo, Mana, Eagle Eye Cherry, and Eric Clapton. Arista released the album in June 1999, with "Smooth" (featuring Rob Thomas) as its first single. Both album and single went to number one, taking *Supernatural*'s sales past 10 million. If Martin was the brash young Latino crossover heartthrob of the moment (despite the buzz of his being gay), Santana comported himself more like an elder statesman of music. Both men stressed the importance of family and spirituality in their lives.

If Martin was the brash young Latino crossover heartthrob of the moment (despite the buzz of his being gay), Santana comported himself more like an elder statesman of music. Both men stressed the importance of family and spirituality in their lives.

The success of Martin and Santana created space for other Latin artists on the pop charts—most notably Jennifer Lopez and later Shakira. In 1999, when Lopez recorded *On the 6* (after her childhood New York subway line), she had already established herself as one of the highest paid actresses in Hollywood, commanding up to $9 million per movie. With major label backing from Epic and with producers of the caliber of Emilio Estefan and Sean "Puffy" Combs (with whom she had a high-profile, tortured affair), *On the 6* reached sales of 6 million and Lopez scored a number one single with "If You Had My Love." For her second outing, *J.Lo,*

"Livin' La Vida Loca"

Artist: Ricky Martin
Music / Lyrics by Desmond Child
and Robi Draco Rosa
Label: Sony, from the CD
Martin (1999)

Musical Style Notes

"Livin' La Vida Loca" instantly establishes its Latin musical influence with its percussion style, dance rhythms, and brass-heavy instrumentation. Layered over this are Martin's vocals, Rusty Anderson's treble-heavy, surf-style guitar solos, and, near the end of the track, a dazzlingly high trumpet part played by Tony Concepción. Structurally, it is a verse-chorus form; the verse has two sections of contrasting melodic content, and the chorus features an extremely catchy hook in the "Livin' La Vida Loca" line at the end—the kind of musical phrase that gets stuck in your brain for the rest of the day. With the hook, the dance rhythms, the surf licks, and Martin's charismatic vocal style, the different elements of "Livin' La Vida Loca" comprised a sure-fire formula for a hit single.

The musicians on "Livin' La Vida Loca" are Ricky Martin, lead vocal; Rusty Anderson, guitar; Randy Cantor, keyboards; Robi Draco Rosa, background vocals; Rafael Solano, percussion; and Tony Concepción, trumpet.

Musical "Road Map"

TIMINGS	COMMENTS	LYRICS
0:00–0:13	Instrumental introduction: full band, including horn section, Latin percussion.	
0:13–0:29	Verse 1, A section of the melody (short guitar interlude before verse 2).	*She's into superstitions . . .*
0:29–0:40	Verse 2, A section of the melody.	*She's into new sensations . . .*
0:40–0:53	Verse 2, B section of the melody vocal harmony.	*She'll make you . . .*
0:53–1:20	Chorus	*Livin' la vida loca . . .*
1:20–1:31	Same music as Introduction	
1:31–1:41	Verse 3, A section of the melody texture change at beginning.	*Woke up . . .*
1:41–1:55	Verse 3, B section of the melody.	*She never drinks . . .*
1:55–2:22	Chorus	*Livin' la vida loca . . .*
2:22–2:32	Guitar instrumental solo. (Note surf style.)	
2:32–2:46	New verse, B section only.	*She'll make you . . .*
2:46–3:08	Chorus	*Livin' la vida loca . . .*
3:08–3:35	Chorus repeats	
3:35–4:01	Guitar instrumental solo (overlaid with super-high trumpet solo; listen at 3:46); takes the track to the end at 4:01.	

she continued in the dance/pop vein with singles such as "Love Don't Cost a Thing," although expectations were higher than the album delivered. A compilation of remixes followed, with J.Lo entering politically sensitive territory by using the word *nigger* on the Murder, Inc. remix of "I'm Real" (featuring Ja Rule). With her street cred in question, the first single from her third full-length studio album, *This Is Me . . . Then* (2002), was "Jenny from the Block," on which Lopez tried to convince her listeners that she was still just plain folks from the 'hood. Following her tabloid romance with Ben Affleck and marriage to Marc Anthony, she released *Rebirth* (2005). By 2007, she had embraced her Latino roots, releasing the all Spanish *Como Ama una Mujer*, but hedged her bets with a tour supporting the more pop-oriented *Brave*.

Shakira Isabel Mebarak Ripoll was born in Barranquilla, Colombia; her father, born in New York, is of Lebanese descent. At thirteen, she auditioned for a Sony executive in Barranquilla, who signed her to a three-record deal. She was already a pop superstar throughout Latin America—performing her own rock-oriented compositions—before coming to the attention of her U.S. fans. Influenced by rockers such as Aerosmith, Nirvana, and Tom Petty, Shakira's third album, *Pies Descalzos* (*Bare Feet*), released in 1995, went to number one in eight different countries and kept generating hit singles until it reached sales of nearly 4 million units. In 1998, she hired Miami Latin music mogul Emilio Estefan as her manager/producer to record *Dónde Están Los Ladrones?* (*Where Are the Thieves?*). A bigger worldwide hit than her previous album, it also spent eleven weeks at number one on the U.S. Latin album chart. Poised for crossover success in the United States, Shakira allied herself with impresario Freddy DeMann, who had nurtured the careers of Madonna and Michael Jackson. Her *MTV Unplugged* special was the channel's first-ever Spanish-language cablecast. Released as an album in 2000, *MTV Unplugged* was her third platinum album in a row and earned her a Grammy for Best Latin Pop Album.

Determined to remove any remaining obstacles to mainstream pop superstardom, Shakira dyed her hair blonde and taught herself English well enough to sing and write in it. Then she recorded *Laundry Service* (2001), her first (mostly) English album, for which she wrote or co-wrote every song. Within a year of its release, *Laundry Service* achieved triple platinum sales, propelled by the infectious Latin/dance/rock groove of "Whenever, Wherever." Shakira had earned a reputation as a serious *rockera* and a writer of poetic lyrics, described by one critic as "emphatically self-expressive and somewhat surreal."[76] Following an ambitious tour to support *Laundry Service*, Shakira took an extended break, during which she wrote about sixty songs in English and Spanish. A selected number were released six months apart in 2005 in two albums divided by language: *Fijacion Oral, Vol. 1* and *Oral Fixation, Vol. 2*. Both albums hit the Top Five on the pop album charts and earned Shakira a massive crossover audience. *Vol. 2* was rereleased in 2006 to include her runaway hit single "Hips Don't Lie" (featuring Wyclef Jean); its video portrayed Shakira at her sensual best, combining erotic but tasteful dance moves from her Middle Eastern heritage with a hot Latin dance groove. By 2006, Shakira had become a truly global pop star, incorporating influences ranging from pop, rock, and disco to *cumbia*, *tejano*, and reggaeton into a coherent bilingual musical project.

The disparate events and variations of style that created the late-1990s Latin boom not only showcased the diversity of artists and musics that constituted the Latin music category, they also begged the question: What is Latin music? Shakira is a case in point. Clearly a rocker, albeit no stranger to Latin sensibilities, Shakira's entry in the *All Music Guide* lists her only in the Latin genre, primarily because of her ethnicity. Rock is not mentioned as one of her styles, even though it is the driving force of her current music. In what sense, then, is music like Shakira's "Latin"? LARAS sidestepped the question, describing the inadequacy of the term in the opening line of one of its website pages: "'Latin Music' has never been more than a short-hand for a universe of rhythms and styles as diverse as the people who created them. For a while it was a useful convention. Not any more."[77] Operationally, Latin music has been defined as music made by Latinos for Latinos—which begs another question: Who is Latino?

In the United States, *Latino* is used as an umbrella term referring to people of Latin American descent who live permanently in the United States. It is a social construct that purports to describe a number of very different cultures and ethnic groups, each of which has a different historical relationship to the United States and to each other. According to ethnomusicologist Deborah Pacini Hernandez, the major social function of the term is to distinguish people of Latin American descent from others in the United States.[78] But as Pacini Hernandez points out, Cubans, Puerto Ricans, Mexicans, Colombians, Salvadorans, Dominicans, and so forth, cannot be reduced to a single ethnic category any more than Western Europeans can. The experiences of Chicanos, who have been a major presence in the Southwestern United States since the Spanish-American War, are different from those of newcomers from the Spanish Caribbean, whose major waves of immigration didn't start until after World War II. The term *Latino* is often used synonymously with the more prevalent (and more controversial) term *Hispanic*, which extends the umbrella to include Spain. There is also debate about whether Latino includes immigrants from Portuguese-speaking Brazil, whose musical styles are well represented in the Latin Grammy categories.

The term *Latino* has historically been associated with the Spanish language, which is of particular importance in the United States, where pop hits are English-only. The eruption of *salsa* in the 1970s, therefore, was not simply the start of a hot new dance music; as a Spanish-only music, it was also a referendum on political allegiances and cultural authenticity. (The Rubén Blades film *Crossover Dreams* [1985] offers a powerful explication of these complexities.) Over time, however, the relationship among language, musical form, and identity changes. Many Latino/a musicians, such as Jennifer Lopez, were either born in or raised in the United States and grew up speaking little Spanish. The most popular late-1990s youth-oriented Latino magazines such as *Hispanic, Urban,* and particularly *Frontera* attempted to incorporate styles like rock and rap into positive Latino identities without the taint of inauthenticity. In these magazines, the guest vocal of Celia Cruz, the Queen of Salsa, on Wyclef Jean's hip hop version of "Guantanamera" was viewed as positively as was Sen Dogg, the Afro-Cuban member of Cypress Hill, starting the hard-core punk outfit SX10. In the final analysis, the formation of ethnic identities is a historically fluid process forged in the cauldron of changing social relations and ideological imperatives, rather than something tied to the immutable characteristics of a particular musical tradition or song form. Nowhere was this cultural hybridity more evident than in the formation and dispersion of reggaeton.

Reggaeton is a quintessentially hybrid music that combines elements of hip hop and Jamaican dancehall filtered through Spanish Caribbean sensibilities. The simple response to the origins of reggaeton is that it was born in Panama and raised in Puerto Rico. The more complete answer involves the interweaving of disparate sonic elements across national boundaries, linguistic barriers, and separate (and unequal) marketing structures. In the end, reggaeton became the first genre with Spanish vocals ever to find mainstream acceptance in the United States.

Prior to the birth of reggaeton, Jamaican reggae had traveled not only to London and New York, but also to Puerto Rico and Panama, where descendants of Jamaican workers had begun performing what was called reggae en español. During the same period, New York–based Puerto Ricans transported rap to Puerto Rico, where it was soon indigenized as *rap en español* by artists like Vico C. By the late 1980s, Panamanian artist El General ("Tu Pum Pum," 1988), considered by many to be the father of reggaeton, had adapted the insistent bounce of dancehall reggae for Latin American audiences. Significantly, El General was living in New York, when he recorded many of his hits. With lyrics in Spanish, this music had enormous appeal in Puerto Rico, where Jamaican dancehall had already achieved widespread popularity. Indeed, as Puerto Rican DJs like Playero and DJ Nelson developed the sound further, they were so drawn to Jamaican artist Shabba Ranks's "Dem Bow," with its minimalist dancehall beat punctuated by snare drum accents, that this "riddim," initially created by producer Bobby Digital, became a defining characteristic of the music. Around the mid-1990s, these elements began to coalesce into what is now known as reggaeton. But it wasn't until New York–based N.O.R.E.'s "Oye Mi Canto" (2004)—a driving appeal to inclusiveness and pan-Latino identity—opened the door to reggaeton in the United States and Daddy Yankee's *Barrio Fino,* with its ubiquitous hit single "Gasolina," flooded the market that reggaeton became a mainstream phenomenon.

From 2004 to 2005, *Billboard* reported that Latin music was the only category of music that had registered growth.[79] The magazine attributed the expansion to Shakira and reggaeton. Shakira herself incorporated a reggaeton sound on "La Tortura," a duet with Alejandro Sanz, from *Fijacion Oral, Vol. 1.* The song's video was reportedly the first in Spanish to go into regular rotation on MTV. Indeed, on 30 July 2005, every Top Ten song on the Latin Tropical Airplay chart had some connection to reggaeton. Also at this time, Daddy Yankee's *Barrio Fino* was the best-selling Latin album in the country and the first reggaeton album to debut at number one on the Latin charts.

Daddy Yankee had been an important figure in the Puerto Rican underground since the early nineties and had started building a higher reggaeton profile later in the decade. With Universal's promotional clout behind *Barrio Fino* in 2004, he was first out of the gate for the crossover crown of mainstream U.S. acceptance. Although "Gasolina"—a bouncy dance track that was a playful metaphor for sex—was the single that caught on in the United States, the album also contained several other well-produced songs that received significant exposure on Latin radio, including "Lo Que Paso, Paso" and "No Me Dejes Solo" (featuring Wisin & Yandel) and "Like You," which crossed over to pop. Daddy Yankee entered into a joint venture with Interscope for *Barrio Fino: En Directo* (2005), which also hit number one on the Latin charts and sent its lead single "Rompe" to number 24 on the Hot 100, confirming Daddy Yankee as the most important reggaeton artist to date.

HEAR MORE
Reggaeton on MyMusicKit

Daddy Yankee had been a pivotal artist in the Puerto Rican underground for more than a decade before his ubiquitous single "Gasolina" conquered the mainland mainstream.

Other reggaeton artists who were vying for mainstream U.S. exposure included Tego Calderón, Don Omar, and Wisin & Yandel. If Daddy Yankee was the party animal in the house, Calderón (*El Abayarde,* 2002) was the thinking person's reggaeton artist. On cuts like "Loiza," he challenged his fans to address the issue of racism in the Spanish Caribbean. His 2004 follow-up, *El Enemy de los Guasíbiri,* showed a deeper commitment to reggaeton just as the music was catching on in the United States. Wisin & Yandel's staccato single "Rakata" had peaked at number two on the Latin charts, but it wasn't until *Pa'l Mundo* hit number one in 2005 that they solidified their position in the mainstream reggaeton boom. Don Omar's *The Last Don* (2003) was considered classic reggaeton as soon as it was released. His "Reggaeton Latino" (2005) was a number one Latin hit and a lively statement of pan-Latino solidarity.

If there was some competition for king of reggaeton, there was no question who was queen. One of the few women in a male-dominated and often misogynistic environment who could compete as an equal, Ivy Queen had been around the Puerto Rican underground dance scene since before reggaeton. Her debut album, *En Mi Imperio* (*In My Empire*), appeared in 1996. Four albums, a slew of hit singles, and a Shakira-like makeover later, she joined the 2005 reggaeton explosion with *Flashback,* a collection of old and new music that included "Cuéntale" at number one on the Latin singles charts.

As reggaeton made more inroads into the U.S. mainstream, many listeners reported a certain sameness to "all, not some" reggaeton tunes, as the *Village Voice* put it.[80] One reason for that perception could have been that a single production team, Luny Tunes, had dominated the music. Luny (Francisco Saldana) and Tunes (Víctor Cabrera) were born in the Dominican Republic and raised in Peabody, Massachusetts. Moving to Puerto Rico at the invitation of DJ Nelson, they quickly eclipsed all other reggaeton producers in their uncanny ability to generate hits, including Daddy Yankee's "Gasolina," Don Omar's "Dale Don Dale," and Wisin & Yandel's "Rakata." Among their many accomplishments was the incorporation of Dominican elements of *bachata* and *merengue* into reggaeton. As one well-known DJ in Puerto Rico noted, "Luny Tunes contributed something very positive, because they . . . made it what it is, a tropical music, in that way it distinguished it from hip hop."[81] Their compilation albums, *Mas Flow* (2003), *La Trayectoria* (2004), and *Mas Flow, Vol. 2* (2005), became some of reggaeton's best-selling albums.

One of the few women who could hold her own in the Puerto Rican underground, Ivy Queen projected a strong female image as she performed at the 2006 Latin Grammys at Madison Square Garden.

First and foremost a type of club music, reggaeton's gut-level appeal was most apparent on the dance floor, where the prevailing dance style, *perreo* (doggystyle), invited sexualized movements that went well beyond suggestive. Reggaeton had always been criticized—for violence, for misogyny, for being inferior music. But it was criticized most severely for its overt sexuality. Such criticism, of course, only served to confirm its outlaw status, which helped make the music and the scene so attractive in the first place.

The ability of reggaeton to generate hits from the dance floor, as with disco before it, forced radio to take it more seriously. Stations formatted for hip hop and r&b began adding a few reggaeton cuts like "Oye Mi Canto" and "Gasolina." Then some Spanish-language stations began moving toward a reggaeton-centric format eventually dubbed *Hurban* ("Hispanic urban"). History was made when KXOL-FM in Los Angeles switched from easy listening to reggaeton in the summer of 2005 and went from eighteenth to second in market share—and to first among listeners twelve to twenty-four years old.[82] Immediately following, Univision flipped eight major market stations to a reggaeton-centered format they called *La Kalle* ("the street"), Clear Channel converted four stations, and others followed suit. "We've found that the appeal of reggaeton is universal," said Clear Channel senior vice president for programming, Tom Poleman. "It's not just about Latin listeners; white suburban kids have a lot of passion for it."[83]

In 2006, four of the five most popular Latin albums of the year were reggaeton albums, with Don Omar's *King of Kings* crossing over to number seven on the pop album charts. Tego Calderón had signed with Atlantic and had begun to venture beyond reggaeton on *The Underdog/El Subestimado*. By this time, everyone from Jay-Z, Alicia Keys, and R. Kelly to Sean Paul, Ricky Martin, and Ja Rule had come calling on Luny Tunes for remixes. In 2007, the momentum continued. Daddy Yankee's long-awaited *El Cartel: The Big Boss*, a dance floor delight featuring duets with high-profile pop-rappers like will.i.am, Fergie, and Akon, hit number nine on the pop album charts. Wisin & Yandel's *Wisin vs. Yandel: Los Extraterrestres* hit pop number fourteen. Ivy Queen contributed *Sentimiento*, at number four on the Latin charts. Meanwhile, Calle 13 emerged as the hottest new act in Latin popular music. They seemed to appear from nowhere to garner three Latin Grammys for their self-titled debut album in 2006 and two more for *Residente o Visitante* (the duo's nicknames) in 2007. College educated, professionally trained, politically astute, and sensitive to the gender issues that often dog reggaeton, Calle 13 expanded the reggaeton pallette to include influences from throughout the Americas. Whether or not reggaeton had already had its moment in the sun, it could certainly be seen as a case study of how global cultural flows would affect the character of popular culture in the future.

LEARN MORE

Chapter Question on MyMusicKit

The music industry began the 1990s with the pleasant surprise that a local music scene from Seattle could spread to a national market and would define a generation. The fact that the major players were unable to follow up this success with another such mass phenomenon coincided with a downturn in industry fortunes at mid-decade that was reflected in flat sales. To regain its lost footing, the industry tried packaging a number of trends based on age (teen pop), gender (women), ethnicity (Latino/a), and so on, but to no avail. Of course, the staples in the industry marketing bag, from country to rap, continued to sell, but such musics had long since established identities that would not permit promoting them as next big things. Country still had a regional aura that smacked of Nashville commercialism even as it dominated the national pop charts. Rap had always been kept at arm's length by the major labels for a variety of reasons, ranging from the uncomfortable gaze of conservative watchdog organizations to the impossible collectivity of its business and artistic practices; rappers routinely collaborated with one another across contractual lines. The failure of the music industry to completely pigeonhole consumers spoke to a truth that the major labels have never fully grasped: that most consumers' tastes are far more diverse than music industry marketing strategies permit. The question was whether this fact would prove to be the industry's undoing as it confronted the devastating effects of 9/11 and the challenge of digital downloading in the new millennium.

Taking Care of Business: Popular Music in the New Millennium

12

By 1999, according to the International Federation of the Phonographic Industry (IFPI), the international music business was worth $38.5 billion annually in worldwide sales. The mergers that accompanied the industry's good fortune made the acquisitions of a decade earlier seem downright small-time and introduced changes in the structure of the transnational music business that pointed to a decline in U.S. dominance. In 1990, when Matsushita bought MCA (which included Geffen and Motown) for $6.6 billion, it seemed extravagant compared to Sony's earlier purchase of CBS Records (renamed Sony Music) for only $2 billion.[1] Then, in 1998, Canada's Seagram Company combined the holdings of MCA (acquired from Matsushita in 1995) and Polygram (purchased for $10.4 billion) into a single corporate entity called, modestly enough, the Universal Music Group. Operating in forty-eight countries, the new megafirm boasted a 23 percent market share of worldwide sales. This was followed in short order by the unprecedented and ill-fated $165 billion takeover of Time-Warner by America Online. At this point, five transnational corporations controlled close to 80 percent of the worldwide sale of recorded music.

These mergers led to a significant downsizing of staff (as these new gigantic companies moved to capitalize on economies of scale) and significant cutbacks in artist rosters (as they set about constructing a global marketing apparatus that demanded superstardom for success). In the merger that created Universal, for example, the artist roster at affiliated label A&M was cut from ninety artists to eight.

Technological developments suggested a reevaluation of the industry's core business model, but the major labels did not heed the call. By the early 2000s, it was clear that the future of music would be tied to free-floating digital sound files traveling across the Internet. The music industry had always treated the Internet with caution and suspicion,

LEARN MORE
Learning objectives
on MyMusicKit

425

and had remained largely unaware of the research on file compression that had been going on for years at Germany's Fraunhofer Institute. The institute's audio compression standard MP3, which shrinks an audio CD file to one-tenth its original size without appreciable loss of quality, had been approved in 1992. But it wasn't until computer clock speeds and network capacity increased enough to permit efficient transfers of MP3 files at the turn of the new millennium that MP3 threatened to become the Trojan horse that could topple the music business.

It wasn't until computer clock speeds and network capacity increased enough to permit efficient transfers of MP3 files at the turn of the new millennium that MP3 threatened to become the Trojan horse that could topple the music business.

The terrorist attacks of 11 September 2001, which pushed the country into costly and questionable wars in Afghanistan and Iraq, had a devastating effect on the economy, which had already begun to decline, and introduced a new role for music. Patriotism became *de rigueur*, and protest and dissent were muffled in the name of individual sensitivity and/or national security.

By the early 2000s, the music business had experienced a profound reversal of fortunes, posting a 25 percent decline from 2000–2003; this led to yet another round of mergers and cutbacks. What had been the "Big Five" at the turn of the new millennium became the "Big Four" in 2004, when Sony Music and BMG merged. That same year, Edgar Bronfman, Jr., the heir to the Seagram fortune, having sold Universal to Vivendi in France, bought the Warner Music Group for $2.6 billion after Time-Warner cut its music division loose from the disastrous AOL-Time Warner merger. The Sony-BMG merger resulted in the loss of 2,000 staff positions, and the restructuring plan for the new Warner Music Group called for the elimination of another 1,000 jobs.[2] By this time, not a single major transnational record company remained in U.S. hands. These were the contours of the international music industry in the early years of the new millennium.

They Want Their MP3

Before online etailer MP3.com was forced into bankruptcy by the major record labels, it had posted thousands of MP3 files on its website for easy download. But it was peer-to-peer (P2P) technologies like Napster, Gnutella, and Freenet that realized MP3's full potential. Developed by Shawn Fanning, a Northeastern University student at the time, Napster was a combination search engine, communication portal, and file-sharing software that facilitated sharing MP3 files; to logged-in users, it granted access to all other Napster users and the MP3 files they chose to share. As early as 2000, the worldwide Napster community was estimated to be as large as 40 million users. Newer technologies took the process one step further. Gnutella and Freenet allowed direct user-to-user contact, making it much more difficult to track users or files. Freenet enabled such direct transactions with any file type—audio, video, text, databases, etc.— and added file encryption and user anonymity.

((•● **HEAR MORE**
Napster on MyMusicKit

These developments were of great concern to the music industry, which had become significantly more concentrated at a time when technological advances demanded a model of decentralization. The Internet and MP3 linked consumers directly with the artists and music of their

choice, thus bypassing the record companies completely. As an unprotected format, MP3 left the industry with no way to regulate its use. MP3 usage quickly gained momentum. According to a 1999 article, "[a]bout 846 million new CDs were sold last year. But at least 17 million MP3 files are downloaded from the Net *each day*. That adds up to almost 3 billion in the first six months of 1999."[3] And that was before Napster was fully unleashed. A later study estimated that Napster users downloaded 1.3 billion songs in September 2000 alone, and that at any given moment, 640,000 Napster users were online together.[4]

Rather than embracing the Internet's potential and taking the lead in developing affordable, user-friendly methods of downloading music, the music industry retreated into a protectionist mode, seeking to prop up its dated business model of manufacturing and selling CDs. Fearful of a decline in sales, the industry adopted a two-pronged strategy of legislation and litigation: advocating for expanded copyright laws and suing alleged infringers. New, restrictive legislation strengthened corporate copyright protection and narrowed the terrain of fair use. A flurry of legal actions ensued, primarily targeting MP3.com and Napster, and demonizing their users as pirates and thieves.

Legislation and Litigation

To grasp the severity of these actions, it is important to understand that copyright law has never simply mandated an exclusive contract to exploit the fruits of one's creativity. Rather, it has been a balancing act, weighing the legal protection of intellectual property and providing an incentive for creative work against the public rights of access to information and freedom of expression. The U.S. Constitution states: "The Congress shall have power . . . to promote the progress of science and useful arts, by securing for limited times to authors and inventors the exclusive right to their respective writings and discoveries."[5] Harvard's William Fisher has asserted that most legal scholars have

Copyright law has never simply mandated an exclusive contract to exploit the fruits of one's creativity. Rather, it has been a balancing act, weighing the legal protection of intellectual property and providing an incentive for creative work against the public rights of access to information and freedom of expression.

interpreted the founding fathers' primary concern as the promotion of learning; protecting authors was a means to that end.[6] This perspective has been reaffirmed over the years in provisions regarding the public domain, personal use, fair use, and rights of access. It was reiterated in the late 1980s House Report on the Berne Convention Implementation Act of 1988: "'The constitutional purpose of copyright is to facilitate the flow of ideas in the interest of learning' . . .

[T]he primary objective of our copyright laws is not to reward the author, but rather to secure for the public the benefits from the creations of authors."[7]

The legislation of the late 1990s inverted these priorities by serving the interests of corporate capital over those of the general public. The No Electronic Theft Act of 1997 prosecuted people who accessed copyrighted materials electronically without authorization, whether or not they realized any "commercial advantage or private financial gain,"[8] and thus criminalized a range of practices once considered fair use. The Digital Millennium Copyright Act of 1998 made it illegal to circumvent any technological measures protecting sound recordings and other copyrighted material. The Sonny Bono Copyright Term Extension Act (1998) extends U.S. copyrights owned by corporations to ninety-five years and individually held copyrights to the life of the author plus seventy years, effectively eliminating the public domain for anything written during the lifetime of any current listener.

The music industry launched its first legal salvo against online music in October 1998, targeting Diamond Multimedia's Rio, a portable MP3 player. Fearing piracy on a grand scale, the Recording Industry Association of America (RIAA) sought to enjoin Diamond under the Digital Audio Home Recording Act of 1992, which levied a tax on digital audio recorders and blank media. The courts ruled in favor of Diamond for the very narrow reason that the legislation targeted only recording devices and the Rio was considered a storage device.

Undaunted, the RIAA sued MP3.com, then the best-known source of online MP3 files. In late 1999, MP3.com constructed an online database of some 60,000 commercially available CDs and gave free access to users who inserted a matching CD into a computer and "beamed" its contents to My.MP3.com. The RIAA alleged infringement of the copyrights of all the major label recordings in the database. Because MP3.com had not negotiated licensing arrangements, it had little chance to win the suit. Still, its argument—that once someone buys a recording, the music industry should no longer have control over its use—remains a point of debate.

Artists themselves were divided on the question. Paul McCartney sued MP3.com, and P. Diddy and others spoke out against file sharing, while Prince praised Napster as "an exciting new development in the history of music."[9] Unsigned artists turned overwhelmingly to the Internet for self-promotion. Roger McGuinn, founder of the Byrds and veteran of twenty-five albums on four different labels, testified at the 2000 U.S. Senate hearings on digital music: "In most cases a modest advance against royalties was all the money I received for my participation in these recording projects."[10] In contrast, he stated that MP3.com

offered an unheard of, non-exclusive recording contract with a royalty rate of 50% of the gross sales. . . . MP3.com not only allowed me to place these songs on their server, but also offered to make CDs of these songs for sale. They absorbed all the packaging and distribution costs. So far I have made thousands of dollars from the sale of these folk recordings on MP3.com, and I feel privileged to be able to use MP3s and the Internet as a vehicle for my artistic expression. MP3.com has offered me more artistic freedom than any of my previous relationships with mainstream recording companies. I think this avenue of digital music delivery is of great value to young artists, because it's so difficult for bands to acquire a recording contract. When young bands ask me how to get their music heard, I always recommend MP3.com.[11]

By the end of 2000, MP3.com had settled with all the major labels for an estimated $170 million and had revived My.MP3.com as a subscription service. Competing etailers such as myplay and Musicbank were negotiating similar licensing arrangements. But these services failed because they could not compete with the power and potential of peer-to-peer file-sharing networks like Napster. It was Napster that crystallized all the music industry's fears about piracy and theft.

The RIAA filed suit against Napster on behalf of eighteen powerful record companies in December 1999, alleging "contributory and vicarious" copyright infringement. Another suit, brought by the heavy metal group Metallica (joined by Dr. Dre), further polarized the music world. Their monitoring showed that 330,000-plus Napster users had downloaded 1.4 million Metallica songs during a three-day period.[12] Metallica demanded that Napster remove the violators from their service in a lawsuit that also named three universities. Napster, according to its own antipiracy policy, complied and removed all the named users. As required by law, however, Napster also issued a statement that anyone who felt that they had been falsely identified could petition the company for reinstatement. After the first 17,000 users had petitioned Napster, Metallica's lawyer decried: "What Napster has done is create 17,000 liars."[13] Such statements alienated the most dedicated segment of the record-buying public. Wrote P. J. Huffstutter in the *LA Times*: "The industry's crusade to block technological innovation has been taken as a declaration of war against young music fans, traditionally its most fervent customers. Fighting back, computer-savvy kids have united and are turning a business dispute into a holy war."[14]

In March 2001, the court enjoined Napster to take all "reasonable" steps to block any copyrighted songs from its network upon receiving notice from the record companies. The RIAA gave Napster a list of some 675,000 protected works with 8 million file names that it wanted blocked; Napster was unable to comply with such demands. By summer 2001, the wildly popular file-sharing network had been effectively shut down.

Piracy and Theft

Using loaded terms like *piracy* and *theft*, the music industry argued that file swapping and digital downloading were tantamount to stealing. Had they been able to get past their fears of lost revenue and understand these practices in more value-neutral terms, the major labels might have been able to see Napster's worth as a promotional vehicle. In a University of Southern California study conducted in 2000, 73 percent of students who downloaded MP3s reported that they still bought the same number of, or more, CDs,[15] which was also reported by 87 percent of downloaders in a different study.[16] Indeed, according to the industry's own mid-year 2000 figures—a period of heavy Napster activity—an RIAA press release stated: "The number of full-length CDs . . . is at an all-time high, growing 6.0% from this time last year, . . . which suggests once again, that consumer demand for music in the form of a CD remains the mainstay."[17] The importance of this pattern cannot be emphasized enough: During Napster's heyday, CD album sales were still on the rise. Who, then, were the pirates and thieves?

The music industry argued that file swapping and digital downloading were tantamount to stealing. Had they been able to get past their fears of lost revenue and understand these practices in more value-neutral terms, the major labels might have been able to see Napster's worth as a promotional vehicle.

The music industry's projection of such terms onto consumers and MP3 services deflected attention from its own less-than-ethical practices. Though the industry has generally cast its policing actions as "protection for creative musicians," the evidence suggests that its goal has always been to protect corporate profits. One-sided contracts have always dominated the industry—with low royalty rates, unfair publishing arrangements, multiyear renewals that keep an artist tied to a particular label, and advances against royalties that keep artists perpetually in debt. Indeed, artists' major sources of revenue have generally been concerts and merchandising, with royalties usually accruing to record companies as repayment of advances. In 1999, at the behest of the RIAA, Mitch Glazier, then majority counsel to the House Judiciary Subcommittee on Intellectual Property—and later the RIAA's chief lobbyist—slipped a three-line amendment into an omnibus appropriations bill that made all recordings "works for hire"—in effect, reducing artists to hired hands of the record companies. Master recordings, which previously had reverted to artists after thirty-five years, became the property of the record companies forever. President Clinton signed the bill into law without debate. After intense pressure from artists like Don Henley and Sheryl Crow, who organized the Recording Artists Coalition, the law was reversed the following year.

In May 2000, the Federal Trade Commission (FTC) settled a suit against all the major labels involving a price-fixing scheme—minimum advertising price programs (MAPS)—whereby these companies paid stores to advertise particular CDs in return for specifying minimum retail prices in the ads. Calling them "coercive agreements," FTC chairman Robert Pitofsky stated: "There was no plausible business justification for this other than to get prices up."[18] According to the suit, consumers were overcharged $500 million for CDs in a two-year period. The settlement obligated the major labels to refrain from MAPS-like programs for seven years, resulting in potential savings for consumers of an estimated $17 million per month.

Such behavior makes it evident that terms like *piracy* and *theft* are relative. These terms also put a narrow, negative spin on considerably more complicated issues. If one replaces them with phrases such as *file sharing* and *community building*, for example, a far more positive picture of the Napster community emerges.

Regardless of lawsuits and verbal attacks, it was clear from the beginning that the industry had to incorporate certain Napster features if it were to survive. First, Napster set the standard for user friendliness. More important, Napster and similar services offered a music library that cut across artists, songs, and labels, enabling users to compile CDs of exactly the music they wanted. Individual labels—divided by imprint, genre, race, language, and so on—couldn't duplicate this kind of resource. Finally, Napster users did not simply trade music files; they communicated with each other. They shared ideas and feelings, argued passionately about music, and turned each other on to new sounds. In short, they self-selected into communities of taste, which constituted a better promotional vehicle than anything the music industry had ever had at its disposal.

Throughout the Napster controversy, many observers felt that the major labels were using the courts to buy time until they could figure out how to enter the online record business on their own terms. Key to this prospect was the industry's search for a secure digital format to use for commercial music downloading. The Secure Digital Music Initiative (SDMI) was envisioned as a standard that would encode a sound file with a digital watermark identifying its owner and origin, thus discouraging piracy on the Internet. After nearly two years of experimentation with four types of watermarks, Princeton computer scientist Edward Felten and a team of students defeated all four.[19] The initiative never came to fruition.

The Music Industry in a Post-Napster World

By 2001, the major labels had inaugurated two online music services. Pressplay, a joint venture of Sony and Vivendi Universal, included deals with Yahoo, Roxio, the Microsoft Network (MSN), and—interestingly—MP3.com. MusicNet, a competing project of AOL Time-Warner, BMG, and EMI, partnered with RealNetworks and reportedly agreed to allow Napster to license its catalogue. At launch, both services were restricted to the catalogues of the participating labels and offered only limited access to digital music, for a monthly fee. The two services aligned themselves with bitter Internet rivals Microsoft and RealNetworks, which only hampered collaboration and cross-label licensing. Pressplay was based on Microsoft's Windows Media Player; MusicNet used RealNetworks' RealOne Player. Meanwhile, the U.S. Department of Justice launched an antitrust investigation of MusicNet and pressplay to determine if the major labels had colluded to set rates and terms.

Not surprisingly, next-generation Napster clones such as Grokster, Morpheus, and KaZaA jumped in to fill the void left by the major labels. For the first week of 2002, for instance, the RealOne Player was downloaded 18,000 times, compared with 1.5 million downloads for Morpheus and 1 million for KaZaA.[20] As of the year ending September 2002, the free KaZaA software had been downloaded 120 million times.

Facing competition of this magnitude, the RIAA continued prosecuting alleged offenders, even as the major labels were strengthening their online presence. Beginning in October 2001, the RIAA joined forces with the Motion Picture Association of America (MPAA), following essentially the same strategy used against Napster. But the RIAA received stunning setbacks in its suits against Grokster, Morpheus, and KaZaA. First, an appeals court in The Netherlands ruled that distributing the KaZaA software there did not violate copyright law, stipulating: "Insofar as there are acts that are relevant to copyright, such acts are performed by those who use the computer program and not by KaZaA."[21] Then, in April 2003, in what amounted to a complete reversal of the Napster decision, Los Angeles federal judge Stephen Wilson ruled that Grokster and Morpheus were not liable for the infringing practices of their users. Basing his decision on the famous 1984 Sony Betamax case, which recognized that these technologies are capable of "substantial non-infringing uses," the judge noted that Napster opened itself to liability by playing an active role in connecting its users, whereas Grokster and Morpheus had no control over the actions of their users once they downloaded the software.[22] Denied the legal basis for eliminating peer-to-peer services, the music business began suing thousands of individual consumers.

While the initial threat of prosecution precipitated a drop in music downloading over the summer of 2003, file sharing had already grown to proportions that even the Napster community couldn't have imagined. The RIAA estimated that 2.6 billion copyrighted song files were being traded over P2P networks every

Napster opened itself to liability by playing an active role in connecting its users, whereas Grokster and Morpheus had no control over the actions of their users once they downloaded the software.

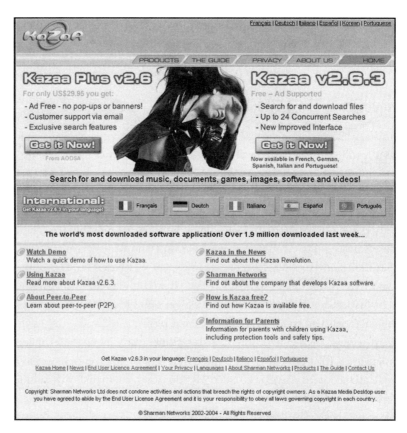

Second generation file-swapping services like KaZaA dwarfed even the Napster community in numbers of users.

month; KaZaA was leading the pack, with over 230 million users, up from 100 million one year earlier.[23] Market research data showed a steady increase in the number of P2P users online at any given time, from 3.8 million in August 2003 to 6.7 million in October 2004.[24]

Industry figures on the decline in CD sales ranged from 26 percent to 31 percent between 2000 and 2003, and file sharing was always cited as a major source of the problem. According to Forrester Research, however, the decline since 2000 had been 15 percent, with only 35 percent of that due to unauthorized downloading.[25] A more definitive study by economists at the Harvard Business School and the University of North Carolina concluded: "Downloads have an effect on sales which is statistically indistinguishable from zero."[26] Indeed, for the most popular albums—"the top 25 percent that had more than 600,000 sales"—the study found a *positive* correlation between downloading and sales. "For every 150 songs downloaded . . . sales jumped by one CD."[27] This study was compelling because it relied not on interviews, but on a comparison of data from 1.75 million downloads during a seventeen-week period with Nielsen SoundScan sales data during the same period. Whatever the actual figures, it had to be admitted that, while punitive lawsuits might make file swappers fearful of downloading for a time, they certainly were not designed to stimulate CD sales.

The San Jose *Mercury News* put it best when it editorialized: "Suing your customers, as a long-term strategy, is dumb."[28] But sue they did.

Beginning in April 2003 the RIAA surprised hundreds of thousands of file swappers with an email message that read:

> *It appears that you are offering copyrighted music to others from your computer. . . . When you break the law, you risk legal penalties. There is a simple way to avoid that risk: DON'T STEAL MUSIC, either by offering it to others to copy or downloading it on a "file-sharing" system like this. When you offer music on these systems, you are not anonymous and you can easily be identified.*[29]

In fact, the RIAA had already sued four college students for allegedly uploading 27,000 to 1 million songs each. The lawsuits asked for damages of $150,000 per song (the maximum under the Digital Millennium Copyright Act), effectively suing the students for billions of dollars. The RIAA located the students by intercepting their Internet addresses on the P2P networks, then sending subpoenas to their Internet service providers (ISPs) for their real names and addresses.

Verizon—an ISP subpoenaed for subscribers' information—fought the case vigorously because the controversial fast-track subpoena process in the Digital Millennium Copyright Act allowed copyright holders to obtain subpoenas from court clerks, without having to go before a judge or first file a lawsuit. Civil liberties groups joined the case, concerned about privacy and due process. Verizon and other commercial ISPs were also alarmed that the burden of copyright enforcement would fall on them. Eventually, over 100 commercial ISPs and universities were subpoenaed. Some universities readily turned over the contact information of the alleged student violators. Others, like Massachusetts Institute of Technology (MIT) and Boston College, opposed the subpoenas, arguing that they violated provisions of the Family Education Rights and Privacy Act.

The music industry also experimented with other measures during this time. Some major labels piloted copy-proof CDs—essentially, corrupted audio CD files that not only couldn't be copied but also wouldn't even play in some CD-ROM drives. Some industry defenders began posting corrupted files on P2P networks. Senator Orrin Hatch, chair of the Senate Judiciary Committee, who earned $18,000 in songwriting royalties in 2003, actually endorsed developing technological ways of destroying the computers of downloaders.[30]

In June 2003, Verizon lost on appeal, which opened the floodgates to over a thousand new subpoenas. These translated into 261 individual lawsuits, which included a twelve-year-old honor student from a New York public housing project and a seventy-one-year-old grandfather. Preteen Brianna Lahara, whose mother settled out of court for $2,000, became the poster child for the heavy-handed tactics of the music industry. Grokster president Wayne Rosso offered to pay the bill, denouncing the RIAA as "the show-business version of the Taliban."[31] By this time, the RIAA altered its demand letter to urge downloaders to settle out of court. It also promoted an amnesty program called Clean Slate, which reportedly protected users against prosecution if they signed a statement saying they had illegally downloaded files and would refrain from doing so again. The Electronic Frontier Foundation (among others) correctly pointed out that the RIAA could not prohibit lawsuits by its member labels or other rights holders; thus, signing the affidavit would be tantamount to giving them a signed confession with no guarantees against prosecution.

Undeterred by the lack of access to mass subpoenas and a constant stream of bad press, the RIAA continued targeting individuals for the next few years. As of October 2005, most of the 3,300 alleged file traders who had settled out of court had forked over $3,000 to $11,000 apiece, creating a handsome new revenue stream for the music business.[32] By May 2006, more than 18,000 people had been sued in the United States alone, with another 5,500 in eighteen other countries.[33] As of June 2006, none of these cases had been adjudicated in court—in other words, not a single person had been convicted of any wrongdoing. Indeed, the first case to go to trial targeted Patricia Santangelo, a single mother of five, whom the judge described as "an Internet-illiterate parent, who does not know Kazaa from kazoo, and who can barely retrieve her e-mail."[34] Santangelo surprised industry lawyers by insisting on going to trial, rather than settling out of court, and fought the RIAA to a standstill, becoming a P2P folk hero in the process. In April 2007, her case was dismissed with prejudice, which meant that the RIAA could not sue her again. But in 2009, after the RIAA went after two of her children, the family agreed to settle for $7,000.

Santangelo's case emboldened others like Tanya Anderson, who not only beat the RIAA and recovered her legal fees, but also countersued and petitioned the court for class action status for her case. Still, of the 40,000 people the RIAA claims to have targeted, fewer than 100 have decided to go to court.[35] In December 2008, the RIAA announced that it was discontinuing its strategy of suing individuals, but decided not to drop cases already in progress, two of which turned out to be landmark victories for the music industry. Jamie Thomas-Rassett had been fined $220,000 by the courts for downloading 24 songs in 2007, but was granted a new trial in 2009 because the judge found the penalty excessive. Incredibly, the verdict in the second trial raised the penalty to $80,000 per song, or $1.92 million. Concurrently, the industry pursued graduate student Joel Tennenbaum; he retained Harvard lawyer Charles Nessen, who petitioned the court to stream the trial on the Internet (but the RIAA balked) and built his case around a fair use defense (which Judge Nancy Gertner disallowed). In the end, Tennenbaum was fined $675,000. As of this writing, it was unclear how these cases would fair upon appeal. Meanwhile, "The $675,000 Mixtape" of the 30 songs Tennenbaum was accused of sharing became available for free download on The Pirate Bay.

Throughout its campaign of suing individuals, the music industry never lost sight of the central role of the P2P networks. In 2004, the Australian music industry decided to go after KaZaA.

> **T**he first question, was where KaZaA called home. While its domain name was registered to an Australian company called LEF Interactive, its software was licensed to a company in Estonia, its servers were in Denmark, and its Web interface was owned by Sharman Networks, officially located on the island of Vanatu.

The first question, however, was where KaZaA called home. While its domain name was registered to an Australian company called LEF Interactive—which took its name from the French slogan *liberté, égalité, fraternité*—its software was licensed to a company in Estonia, its servers were in Denmark, and its Web interface was owned by Sharman Networks, officially located on the island of Vanatu. The major labels got court permission to raid the offices of Sharman Networks and the homes of its executives to search for evidence of copyright infringement. In September 2005, the court ruled that Sharman had encouraged copyright infringement on KaZaA and that it was liable for 90 percent of the industry's legal fees (millions of dollars). The major labels were also expected to petition for several billion dollars in damages. Seeing the writing on the wall, KaZaA prohibited Australians from downloading its software and agreed to settle with the music industry.

By this time, Grokster and its co-defendant, StreamCast Networks (owner of Morpheus), had met a similar defeat. In June 2005, the U.S. Supreme Court unanimously ruled that companies that actively encourage or induce users to engage in illegal file trading are liable for their users' actions. Wrote Justice David Souter, "[w]e hold that one who distributes a device with the object of promoting its use to infringe copyright, as shown by clear expression or other affirmative steps taken to foster infringement, is liable for the resulting acts of infringement by third parties."[36] Though the Court did not rule that Grokster and Morpheus were liable, instead referring the case back to the lower court, Souter's opinion stated clearly that both companies "took active steps to encourage infringement."[37] StreamCast pledged to continue fighting the case. Grokster settled for $50 million in damages and stopped distributing its software. The Grokster website (www.grokster.com) went dark, except for the following statement:

> The United States Supreme Court unanimously confirmed that using this service to trade copyrighted material is illegal. Copying copyrighted motion picture and music files using unauthorized peer-to-peer services is illegal and is prosecuted by copyright owners. There are legal services for downloading music and movies. This service is not one of them.

Until *Grokster*, the primary limitation on suits against a service provider for "contributory and vicarious infringement" had been the 1984 *Sony Betamax* standard of "substantial non-infringing uses." Congress tried to bypass this standard in the so-called INDUCE Act, under which companies could be held liable for encouraging their users to engage in illegal activity. Even though the legislation failed, Souter's opinion, which "premises liability on purposeful, culpable expression and conduct," clearly established a new standard, which narrowed the "substantial non-infringing uses" standard applied by the appeals court in *Grokster* a year earlier.[38]

In the end, it was not clear what effect the *Grokster* decision would have on P2P and technological innovation generally. By the time the decision was handed down, a third generation of more sophisticated and further decentralized P2P networks like BitTorrent and eDonkey had arisen. A new chapter was added to this saga in 2009 when the four founders of The Pirate Bay—reportedly the biggest host of BitTorrent trackers in the world—were found guilty of assisting in copyright infringement in a Swedish court and sentenced to one year in prison and fined a total of $3.5 million. Again, the practical value of the decision was unclear because the company's servers had long since been moved to Thailand.

Throughout this period, there was only one legal downloading service that showed any real promise—Apple's iTunes (Music) Store. Launching its new venture in spring 2003 over the slogan "Downloads done right," Apple began with a catalogue of some 200,000 songs from five major companies and offered users simplicity, affordability, convenience, and flexibility. The iTunes interface was as user-friendly as any file-sharing service: Songs sold for $.99 per single ($9.99 for most albums), and the user was permitted easy transferability to Apple's iPod portable music player and unlimited CD burning. With that simple formula, the iTunes Store shocked and delighted record-company executives when it sold 1 million songs in each of its first two weeks of operation—at a time when iTunes was available to less than 1 percent of the record-buying public. Shortly afterward, Apple then introduced a Windows-compatible version of the

In capturing the imaginations of digital downloaders, the iPod became the gold standard for digital media players and a cultural icon for portable music (and video).

iTunes software and invited 150 representatives from independent labels to participate in the venture on an equal footing with the majors.

Apple's accomplishment also had some limitations. The sound files available for download were copy-protected AAC files, a version of the newer MP4 format. On the upside, unlike MP3, MP4 is public domain software; it boasts better compression and better sound quality than MP3—but its files will not play on traditional MP3 players. AAC also includes the capability of digital rights management (DRM), which allowed Apple to "authorize" loading the files onto a limited number of computers at a time. While such limitations were minimal and easily managed, it was easy to see how additional restrictions could propel users back toward unrestricted peer-to-peer networks.

Apple's success with such a small market share encouraged other companies to try to compete with the company in the more lucrative PC market. The most interesting venture was proposed by Roxio, who acquired the rights to the Napster brand at fire sale prices. Then, in May 2003, Roxio bought pressplay and launched an online music store using the pressplay technology and the Napster brand name.[39] In 2006, Microsoft went toe-to-toe with Apple with their own MP3 player—the Zune. Amazon entered the business in 2008, posting only unrestricted MP3 files with a variable pricing scheme.

Despite such efforts by other companies, Apple continually vanquished all competitors, maintaining a market share in the 70 percent range, with all other online services dividing the remains with single-digit market shares. Since its debut in 2001, Apple's iPod had established itself as the icon of digital music (and then photo and video) players. Other services found it difficult to beat Apple's combination of style, ease of use, and seamless hardware/software integration. By 2005, the online store was outselling bricks-and-mortar outlets like Tower Records and Sam Goody. In February 2006, the iTunes Music Store sold its 1 billionth song.[40] By 2009, that figure had mushroomed to 6 billion. Perhaps even more impressive, by September 2009, Apple had sold 220 million iPods.

Apple's success might have pointed the way to the future for the music industry. But instead of taking a serious look at its core business model, the industry flailed about, squandering consumer trust on unenforceable laws and punitive lawsuits and jockeying for position amidst changing label configurations and economic and political upheaval.

Apple's success might have pointed the way to the future for the music industry. But instead of taking a serious look at its core business model, the industry flailed about, squandering consumer trust on unenforceable laws and punitive lawsuits.

Popular Music Post-9/11

The 11 September 2001 terrorist attacks on the United States shook the country out of its complacency regarding national security, prompted an outpouring of sympathy from around the world, and sent the economy into a serious decline. These events also ushered in something of a new role for contemporary popular music. Historically, the rock and rap axis of U.S. popular music had most often been associated with rebellion, defiance, resistance, and opposition. Post-9/11, this same music was also conscripted into the service of mourning, healing, nation-building, and patriotism.

Music outlets monitored listener call-ins closely as indicators of their audience's frame of mind after the attacks. While classic rock stations fielded requests for old chestnuts like John Lennon's "Imagine" and Simon and Garfunkel's "Bridge over Troubled Water," heavy metal outlets pushed the sonic envelope with Jimi Hendrix's "Star Spangled Banner" and Metallica's "Don't Tread on Me." Songs in demand at country stations leaned toward patriotic anthems like Johnny Cash's "Ragged Old Flag," Brooks and Dunn's "Only in America," and Lee Greenwood's "God Bless the USA." MTV sought to establish a nonviolent tone with "Imagine," Bob Marley's "One Love," Prince's "When Doves Cry," and Pearl Jam's "Alive."

Artists' involvement ranged from individual financial contributions to huge mega-events. Dr. Dre donated $1 million to a victim's relief fund; artists playing New York at the time, like the Black Crowes and Incubus, donated their proceeds. Before the attacks, Bono had teamed up with hip hop producer Jermaine Dupri to remake Marvin Gaye's classic "What's Goin' On" for Artists Against AIDS Worldwide; after 9/11, they added the United Way's September 11 Fund to the list of recipients. Arista rereleased Whitney Houston's stirring 1991 Super Bowl performance of the "Star Spangled Banner," with proceeds earmarked for New York firefighters. Sony refused to release Michael Jackson's "What More Can I Give," recorded with Destiny's Child, Backstreet Boys, Tom Petty, and Seal, among others, because its producer had ties to gay pornography. Still, the October 22 *United We Stand* benefit in Washington, D.C., at which it was performed, raised $3 million. Paul McCartney headlined the *Concert for New York City* in Madison Square Garden, which raised $30 million for the New York Fire Department. The Beastie Boys organized New Yorkers Against Violence—the only event explicitly committed to nonviolent solutions to terrorism—as a two-night fundraiser with guests Moby, Michael Stipe, Bono, Mos Def, and the Strokes.

Perhaps the most impressive happening was *America: A Tribute to Heroes,* a telethon staged on September 21, ten days after the attacks. It featured twenty-two artists, with fifty actors staffing the telephones, and was transmitted over the four major commercial networks as well as thirty cable channels without credits or commercial interruptions. Artists included Bruce

Springsteen, Celine Dion, Mariah Carey, U2, Sting, Stevie Wonder, Neil Young, Paul Simon, Tom Petty, Billy Joel, Jon Bon Jovi, Richie Sambora, Sheryl Crow, Dave Matthews, Eddie Vedder, Limp Bizkit, Enrique Iglesias, Alicia Keys, Wyclef Jean, Faith Hill, the Dixie Chicks, and Willie Nelson. The telethon generated an estimated $160 million from its East Coast broadcast alone, making it the largest single fundraising event in history even before the compilation CD was released.

A Tribute to Heroes was an understated, reverential event that encapsulated the new role for music. Punk, rap, and metal, as performance styles, were excluded because the dominant aesthetic of the tribute was MTV Unplugged. There were no heavy sounds, aggressive rhymes, or sonic distortions that might have signified discord or disunity; overt expressions of patriotism were downplayed, but understood. Stage sets were unadorned, bathed in soft backlight in the red/orange and blue/green ranges of the spectrum and illuminated by the white light of candles, creating a hint of the colors of the American flag. For security reasons, the program was broadcast from undisclosed locations in New York, Los Angeles, and London. There was no live audience, no stage risers, and no artist introductions or credits; celebrity was consciously obscured in order to engender a sense of what Tom Hanks called "our larger American family."

There were some poignant moments, such as Will Smith's introducing Mohammad Ali as a Muslim or the footage of Muslim children in America expressing fears of retaliation. Stevie Wonder chastised those who "hate in the name of God or Allah" in his introduction to "Love's in Need of Love Today." Tom Petty's mildly aggressive rendition of "I Won't Back Down" was offset by Neil Young's stirring performance of Lennon's "Imagine," which conjured up visions of a world with neither religions nor countries and "nothing to fight or die for." A number of songs, such as Enrique Iglesias's "Hero" and Billy Joel's "New York State of Mind," were irrevocably resignified by the event. Significantly, the all-cast version of "America the Beautiful" that closed the show included the second verse, which calls on America to "Confirm thy soul in self-control/Thy liberty in law."

The finale of America: A Tribute to Heroes *both celebrated and challenged the country in a time of crisis.*

In contrast to the somber tone of the *America Tribute*, the *Concert for New York City* was a brash, commercialized, public extravaganza staged at Madison Square Garden on behalf of the city's police, fire, and health workers, which signified the change in mood, emotional tone, and political will taking place as the United States invaded Afghanistan. With minimal diversity provided by Jay-Z and Destiny's Child, the bill was dominated by British and American rockers, including Billy Joel, Bon Jovi, John Mellencamp, David Bowie, Eric Clapton, the Who, Mick Jagger and Keith Richard, Elton John, and Paul McCartney. Musically, the concert was a tribute to brash, white, male, mostly guitar-based rock in both its lineup and performance styles. As headliner, McCartney was seen as the primary link between the first British Invasion and the present political alliance between Britain and the United States. He showcased "Freedom," a new song that included the cautionary line "Anyone who tries to take it away, they'll have to answer." The theme of revenge had been previewed in Bon Jovi's "Wanted Dead or Alive," echoing President Bush's statements about Osama bin Laden. But the Who drove the message home. Opening their set with classic Pete Townshend power chords on "Who Are You?"—now a query to the terrorists—the group performed their high-energy single in front of a Union Jack background and closed with "Won't Get Fooled Again," the Union Jack now flanked by two U.S. flags.

Given the imperative for emotional healing following the 9/11 tragedy, the historical anti-establishment role of rock might have appeared inappropriate to the crisis. Still, as artists rushed to show their support for a grieving nation, many seemed to retreat from long-held principles. U2's defining image of Bono parading with a white flag as he ranted against war on "Sunday Bloody Sunday," was rather different than the U2 at the Super Bowl halftime show in 2002, where Bono displayed the American flag lining of his jacket and the band unfurled a larger-than-life scrim of the names of all the 9/11 victims. At that same halftime show, Paul McCartney, who had seriously criticized the British occupation of Northern Ireland when he wrote and recorded "Give Ireland Back to the Irish" in 1972, related differently to the prospect of another long-term occupation on his new song "Freedom." As talk of helping and healing gave way to the rhetoric of revenge and retribution, those who chose to dissent found that a new reality had taken hold.

As talk of helping and healing gave way to the rhetoric of revenge and retribution, those who chose to dissent found that a new reality had taken hold.

Corporate Radio and the New Patriotism

Measured responses to 9/11were soon eclipsed by a more fervent patriotism in popular culture and in government rhetoric and actions. In the music field, corporate radio played a major role in narrowing the range of cultural expression. Right after the attacks, for example, Clear Channel, the largest radio chain in the United States, issued a list of nearly 200 songs to its member stations that executives felt were inappropriate to play. The list included some obvious choices (Metallica's "Seek and Destroy," AC/DC's "Shot Down in Flames") and some not so obvious ones (Carole King's "I Feel the Earth Move," the Bangles' "Walk Like an Egyptian"). Its inclusion of *all* Rage Against the Machine songs raised the specter of censorship. Defended by Clear Channel as an act of sensitivity toward the victims' families and denounced by its critics as an act of suppression, the list was part of a running battle between those concerned with civil liberties and freedom of expression and those prioritizing the need for national unity and internal security.

What made the Clear Channel list so important—and the touchstone for the debate on civil liberties—was the network's power, which derived from the terms of the 1996 Telecommunications Act. The 1996 law, twelve years in the making, was the first major overhaul of telecom policy since the Communications Act of 1934; it covered everything from radio, television, and telephone to cable TV and the Internet. The controversial Communications Decency Act attached to the legislation (and declared unconstitutional by the Supreme Court one year later), drew attention away from one of the law's central provisions—the relaxation of cross-ownership rules for media corporations. Clear Channel was a clear beneficiary. In 1995, before passage of the bill, Clear Channel owned 43 radio stations. By the early 2000s, it owned over 1,200 stations in the United States, which took in 20 percent of the industry revenues in 2001; it owned over 700,000 billboards; it controlled 65 percent of the U.S. concert business; and it posted total revenues exceeding $8 billion.[41]

In the early 2000s, according to one major news outlet, four companies controlled 90 percent of radio ad revenue.[42] This level of concentration has serious implications for programming. "In one recent week," reported *Rolling Stone* in August 2001, "the forty top modern-rock stations added a total of sixteen new songs, and the biggest forty-five Top Forty stations added a total of twenty."[43] By this time, even major record companies decried the difficulty of breaking new artists on the centrally programmed chain, and artists complained that if they chose not to perform at a Clear Channel concert venue, they would pay the price in radio play.

As the nation went to war against Iraq, Clear Channel adopted an activist posture that marked a new role for corporate radio. During this period, demonstrations erupted both against and for the war. At first the pro-administration "Rally for America" demonstrations appeared to be organized from the ground up as spontaneous local events and were reported as such. It was then revealed that the rallies were being organized and sponsored by Clear Channel. "While labor unions and special interest groups have organized and hosted rallies for decades," wrote Tim Jones in the *Chicago Tribune*, "the involvement of a big publicly regulated broadcasting company breaks new ground in public demonstrations."[44] Added former Federal Communications Commission (FCC) commissioner Glen Robinson, "I can't say that this violates any of a broadcaster's obligations, but it sounds like borderline manufacturing of the news."[45]

Clear Channel's support for administration policy might have been motivated by its upcoming business before the FCC—business that would have allowed it to expand considerably, particularly into television. Paul Krugman, writing in the *New York Times*, traced a direct connection from President Bush to Clear Channel:

> *The vice chairman of Clear Channel is Tom Hicks. . . . When Mr. Bush was governor of Texas, Mr. Hicks was chairman of the University of Texas Investment Management Company, called Utimco, and Clear Channel's chairman, Lowry Mays, was on its board. Under Mr. Hicks, Utimco placed much of the university's endowment under the management of companies with strong Republican Party or Bush family ties. In 1998 Mr. Hicks purchased the Texas Rangers in a deal that made Mr. Bush a multimillionaire.*[46]

It is always threatening to free expression when a public media company enjoys this degree of intimacy with any government agency, let alone the White House. The question is how this relationship affected popular music and culture in the post-9/11 context.

Country Music Goes to War

From the buildup of the U.S. war in Afghanistan in 2001 to the U.S. invasion of Iraq in March 2003, the nation's attention was captured by a number of country songs that followed a rough trajectory from thoughtful reflection to strident fight songs. In October 2001, Alan Jackson penned "Where Were You (When the World Stopped Turning)," which went straight to number one on the country singles hart and crossed over to the Top Thirty on the pop charts. "Where Were You" was a thoughtful rumination on the kinds of things people might have been doing when the World Trade Center towers were struck. Aaron Tippin weighed in with "Where the Stars and Stripes and the Eagle Fly," which became the ninth most popular song of 2001. Lee Greenwood's "God Bless the USA"—which appeared on four different compilations by the end of 2001—came in at number six for that year and number eleven for 2002. Both talked of pride in America and the willingness to pay a price to defend freedom. It is remarkable that these songs found their way into the year-end Top Ten with only a couple of months of sales.

From the buildup of the U.S. war in Afghanistan in 2001 to the U.S. invasion of Iraq in March 2003, the nation's attention was captured by a number of country songs that followed a rough trajectory from thoughtful reflection to strident fight songs.

During the buildup of the first Gulf War, Greenwood's anthem, written in 1984, became the title song on his 1990 album of the same name. At that time, Greenwood had turned to patriotism to bolster a flagging career, but his career foundered again by the mid-1990s.[47] The 9/11 attacks propelled his song back into the upper reaches of the pop charts. Similarly, Tippin released "You've Got to Stand for Something" in 1991, from his debut album of the same name, in the wake of the first Gulf War. The song became a Top Ten hit. A decade later "Where the Stars and Stripes and the Eagle Fly" was a crossover hit that reached the pop Top Twenty. Other artists also had patriotic entries dating back to the buildup of the first Gulf War. In 1990, Hank Williams, Jr. released "Don't Give Us a Reason," which told "old Saddam" that "you figured wrong." Billy Ray Cyrus contributed "Some Gave All" from the 1992 album of the same name. Indeed, the patriotic fervor of the first Gulf War propelled Whitney Houston's "Star Spangled Banner" into the Top Twenty the first time it was released.

The events of 9/11 had produced a somewhat reflective patriotism in pop country, but the rhetoric surrounding the war in Afghanistan and the increasing demonization of Iraq set a different tone. Toby Keith's "Courtesy of the Red, White and Blue (The Angry American)" from *Unleashed* (2002) captured the new, vengeful attitude more than any other song. With a number of platinum releases to his name, Keith was no stranger to stardom, but it was "Courtesy"—warning "We'll put a boot in your ass/It's the American Way"—that made him a household name. On the strength of the hit single, *Unleashed* hit number one in 2002 and had been certified double platinum by year's end. In the countdown to the war in Iraq, Darryl Worley's "Have You Forgotten," went to the top of the country chart in five weeks, reminding listeners "about bin Laden/Have you forgotten?"

Alan Jackson attempted a thoughtful reflection on the tragedy of 9/11.

"Courtesy of the Red, White, and Blue (The Angry American)"

Artist: Toby Keith

Music/Lyrics by Toby Keith Coval

Label: Dreamworks Nashville, from the CD *Unleashed* (2002)

Musical Style Notes

Music has been used to rally the troops since ancient times, from the thundering drums of ancient armies to the bagpipes of Scottish regiments. In "Courtesy of the Red, White, and Blue," Toby Keith also uses layers of sound to "rally" his listeners. The song's structural simplicity (multiple verses and a repeating chorus) helps in this regard because it does not distract from the sonic texture and the associations they evoke in the listener. Keith varies the instrumentation to fit the lyrics, using the most transparent texture (one solo instrument) to highlight and emphasize certain lyrics, and then adds layers of sound to build emotion as he works up to the defiant chorus, where the drums enter. In the last chorus, the keyboards also use a synthesized effect that results in the sound of the melody being played by large bells that are doubled by electric guitar, illustrating the lyric "when you hear mother freedom start a 'ringin' her bell."

Musical "Road Map"

TIMINGS	COMMENTS	LYRICS
0:00–0:24	Guitar chord, followed by Verse 1, accompanied by one acoustic guitar.	*American girls . . .*
0:24–0:43	Verse 2 Bass, acoustic and electric guitar added.	*My daddy . . .*
0:43–1:03	Verse 3 Sound texture thickens.	*Now this nation . . .*
1:03–1:34	Chorus Drums enter; background vocals enter.	*Hey, Uncle Sam . . .*
1:34–1:52	Guitar solo	
1:52–2:17	Return to Verse 1 texture: vocals and sparse acoustic guitar. Keyboards layered in the background, at a low volume. Note dramatic pause before the "boot" line at 2:11.	*Justice . . .*
2:17–3:14	Chorus The song's thickest musical texture happens here. Note bells—these are synthesized and played by a keyboard, and they are doubled by the electric guitar. Song ends with a loud, sustained chord, punctuated by a final stroke of the same chord.	*Hey, Uncle Sam . . .*

Pat Garrett continued in this vein with "Saddam Stomp," which made a second mistaken connection between Saddam Hussein, the Iraqi leader, and bin Laden. These were followed by Clint Black's "I Raq and Roll," which warned America's enemies to "be careful where you tread," and Lynyrd Skynyrd's "Red, White, and Blue," summed up by singer Johnny Van Zant as "love it or leave it," providing the group with its first hit in years.

The fact that many of these songs became year-end best sellers suggests that they hit a nerve among the U.S. populace, whose support for U.S. foreign policy was still strong during the buildup to Iraq. The momentum they created encouraged artists from other genres to get on board. R. Kelly contributed "A Soldier's Heart"; Ray Stevens scored with a novelty track "Osama—Yo' Mama," criticizing bin Laden's mother for not raising him correctly; Neil Young released "Let's Roll," in honor of the passengers on Flight 93. This song presented his more liberal rock fans with something of a dilemma. As critic John Metzger put it:

> While ["Let's Roll"] pays tribute to those on ill-fated Flight 93 . . . it's also impossible not to take it as supportive of the current Administration and their poorly planned war-run-amuck. To be fair, at the time of the song's writing, America was in shock and was more willing to concede to its leaders' whims. But with lines like, "We're goin' after Satan/On the wings of a Dove," the song now stands as an odd statement from someone like Young who long has rallied against war and unjust government policy.[48]

The problem with the more conservative country artists wasn't that they were resolute in their defense of U.S. policy or that their hits were prowar—popular culture had been able to accommodate different points of view since Barry McGuire's "Eve of Destruction" went head-to-head with Barry Sadler's "Ballad of the Green Berets" in 1965. The problem was that they left no room for any other point of view. Steve Earle is a case in point. As much a rocker as a country artist, Earle's songwriting is sharp and edgy, tending toward outlaw country, and his progressive politics have seldom won him friends in Nashville. As concerned as anyone about 9/11, Earle attempted a complex consideration of the issues at a time when country music was moving toward a more strident patriotism. On "John Walker's Blues"—about John Walker Lindh, the "American Taliban"—from *Jerusalem* (2002), he attempted to get inside Walker Lindh's head to explore why an American youth searching for truth in Islam would take up arms with the Taliban. While *Jerusalem* was a Top Ten country album that crossed over to pop, Earle was routinely denounced as a traitor by conservative commentators.

The boycott of the Dixie Chicks was even more dramatic. The Dixie Chicks rose to superstardom on the strength of their 1998 multiplatinum debut major label release, *Wide Open Spaces,* which delivered solid material, great musicianship, and a female trio having a genuinely good time; it offered little that was controversial. Their follow-up, *Fly* (1999), went to number one, continuing in the same vein except for the single "Goodbye Earl," about the murder of an abusive husband, which caused a stir at several country stations. For their September 2002 release, *Home,* the Chicks went deeper into their country roots with traditional instrumentation and few concessions to pop sensibilities. Nevertheless, *Home* debuted at number one on the *Billboard 200* and garnered not only Country Music Awards, but also American Music Awards, People's Choice Awards, and four Grammys. The Chicks were selected to sing the national anthem at the 2003 Super Bowl. In the spring of 2003, however, while on tour in London, lead singer Natalie Maines told her

The problem with the more conservative country artists wasn't that they were resolute in their defense of U.S. policy or that their hits were prowar. The problem was that they left no room for any other point of view.

HEAR MORE
The Dixie Chicks
on MyMusicKit

audience: "We're ashamed the president of the United States is from Texas," an obvious reference to George W. Bush's decision to invade Iraq. Although she apologized to President Bush within days, calling her remarks "disrespectful," the Dixie Chicks were banned on seventy-four country radio stations. The message was clear: It was not an option to criticize the president in wartime.

However, the boycott emboldened the Chicks. At the first show of the U.S. leg of their tour, they performed "Truth #2," about standing up for one's beliefs, during which they showed video footage of civil rights, gay rights, and prochoice demonstrations, while slogans like "freedom" and "truth" were projected on the screen. Maines told her audience, "If you're here to boo, we welcome that, because we welcome freedom of speech."[49] Despite the country radio boycott, their sixty-two-date U.S. tour nearly sold out. Maines traded barbs with Toby Keith, whose "Courtesy of the Red White and Blue" she had called "ignorant." The jousting reached its climax when Maines appeared on the Country Music Awards telecast wearing an F.U.T.K. T-shirt.

The Toby Keith–Dixie Chicks rivalry could be seen as a referendum on the extremes in country music over the next few years. Keith's *Shock'n Y'All*—possibly a play on "Operation Shock and Awe, " the opening campaign in the Iraq War—debuted at number one on the *Billboard 200* in 2003 and placed him at the top of five year-end country charts in 2004. Having won a massive conservative country audience with *Unleashed,* Keith played to these same fans on *Shock'n Y'All,* minus the didactic rants and strident patriotism. On *Honkytonk University* (2005), Keith included a shout-out to his "boys in Afghanistan and Baghdad City," but remained essentially focused on the hard-core country themes of hard drinking and failed relationships, a trend he continued with even more versatility on *White Trash with Money* (2006).

The Dixie Chicks underwent a folk-rock makeover for *Taking the Long Way* (2006), an album rooted in country but reflective of their new sophistication as international superstars. It debuted at number one on both the pop and country charts, demonstrating a substantial country music fan base. Although their tour suffered in some conservative regions, the album's provocative first single, "Not Ready to Make Nice," made it clear that the Chicks were not ready to back off their views. "I'd rather have a smaller following of really cool people," said Martie Maguire, "than people who have us in their five-disc changer with Reba McEntire and Toby Keith."[50]

Before criticizing President Bush, the Dixie Chicks were the darlings of the country music scene.

"Not Ready to Make Nice"

Artist: The Dixie Chicks
Music/Lyrics by the Dixie Chicks
Label: Sony, from the CD
Taking the Long Way (2006)

The Dixie Chick's hit song "Not Ready to Make Nice" is Natalie Maines's defiant refusal to back down after receiving death threats for a comment she made to an English audience in 2003, just as the United States was about to invade Iraq. While the group suffered bans on radio airplay and their concert attendance declined, their May 2006 CD *Taking the Long Way* sold a half-million copies in the United States in the first week of its release.

Musical Style Notes

"Not Ready to Make Nice" features the Dixie Chicks' signature multiple vocals and country-rock instrumentation (acoustic and electric guitars, bass, drums, fiddle, keyboards). Its structure is straightforward but not simple: The verse-verse-chorus form used frequently in a country ballad is made more complex by the addition of a lyrically crucial bridge (this is where the death threats are referred to in very specific terms) and an instrumental section that functions as a transition from the bridge back to the chorus, with no intervening verse. The ending is a reprise of Verse 1, but it ends abruptly halfway through, driving home the message of the lyric and leaving harmony unresolved. In other words, the song does not return at the end to the musical tonic, or keynote, and this results in the absence of an aural perception of finality.

Musical "Road Map"

TIMINGS	COMMENTS	LYRICS
0:00–0:11	Instrumental introduction; prominent acoustic guitar, keyboards.	
0:11–0:36	Verse 1 Acoustic guitar still prominent.	*Forgive—sounds good . . .*
0:36–0:58	Verse 2 Drums enter.	*I'm through . . .*
0:58–1:24	Chorus Multiple vocals enter.	*I'm not ready . . .*
1:24–1:48	Verse 3	*I know you . . .*
1:48–2:14	Bridge section (this is the section that tells the actual story of the death threats made to Maines).	*I made my . . .*
2:14–2:24	Instrumental transition. Orchestral texture layered in.	
2:24–2:48	Chorus Orchestral texture continues; multiple vocals.	*I'm not ready . . .*
2:48–3:13	Chorus, repeated, with vocal *obligato* (additional sustained vocal part) added.	
3:13–3:27	Transitional passage—same as introduction.	*What it is . . .*
3:27–3:53	Verse 1	*Forgive—sounds good . . .*
3:53	Song ends abruptly at the last line of the verse.	*. . . but I'm still waiting.*

Dissent Unplugged

While prowar anthems emerged as year-end best sellers, almost no protest music was heard on the radio. This absence was especially notable by the time of the war in Iraq. Although the U.S. peace movement had initially greeted the war in Afghanistan with ambivalence, it echoed worldwide opinion in opposing any invasion of Iraq. Many peace activists began to wonder if protest music had died. Writing for the University of Peace, Joseph Schumacher opined:

While prowar anthems emerged as year-end best sellers, almost no protest music was heard on the radio. Many peace activists began to wonder if protest music had died.

> *The sorry state of musical political protest is surprising given that the American, Australian and British Governments joint invasion of Iraq galvanized global anti war sentiment unlike any other single action since the Vietnam War. The millions of people who marched against the war in the weeks preceding and during the Iraq invasion sent a powerful message for peace across the world. What has been conspicuously missing is a soundtrack to the phenomenon.*[51]

In fact, plenty of protest music was being produced; it simply wasn't being aired. Noting that popular music and songs had "played a crucial role in the national debate over the Vietnam War," Brent Staples argued in the *New York Times* that "[a] comparable song about George W. Bush's rush to war in Iraq would have no chance at all today. There are plenty of angry people, many with prime music-buying demographics. But independent radio stations that once would have played edgy, political music have been gobbled up by corporations that control hundreds of stations and have no wish to rock the boat."[52]

Other observers felt that a climate of intolerance for opposing viewpoints had caused many artists to censor themselves. "We've seen dozens of acts quietly bury their edgier songs," complained Jeff Chang in 2002. "The Strokes pulled a song called 'New York Cops' from their album and Dave Matthews decided not to release 'When the World Ends' as a single."[53] In 2003, Madonna reportedly withdrew a completed video for her "American Life" single because it portrayed her wearing Army fatigues, tossing a grenade at a President Bush–like figure. When artists performed controversial protest material, they often paid a price, even if in small ways. Bruce Springsteen performed "American Skin (41 Shots)," about the police killing of Hatian immigrant Amadou Diallo, at one of his New York dates; it cost him his customary after-concert police escort to the airport. Jethro Tull was banned from classic rocker WCHR-FM in New Jersey for complaining that drivers who hung American flags from their cars were confusing nationalism with patriotism. "As far as we're concerned," said program director and on-air personality Phil LoCascio, "this ban is forever."[54]

Still, a number of stalwarts continued to release antiwar material. Pearl Jam disparaged the president on "Bushleaguer" (2002), claiming "He's not a leader/He's a Texas leaguer." Public Enemy reinforced this notion on "Son of a Bush" (2003). On "Combat Rock" (2002), Sleater-Kinney's Carrie Brownstein shouted, "Where is the protest song . . . ? Dissent's not treason." Given the dearth of protest material, the album that garnered all the mainstream press was Springsteen's *The Rising* (2002). The return of the E Street Band would have been cause for celebration in itself, but Springsteen's thoughtful politics strengthened the album further. On songs like "Into the Fire," "You're Missing," and "Lonesome Day," Springsteen did what he does best—give voice to the unheard and build bridges among a diversity of groups. In the end, however, *The Rising* was a retrospective engagement with the intense emotions of 9/11 more than a forward-looking critique of U.S. foreign policy. In the absence of radio play for protest songs, many artists posted songs for free download. (The accompanying table has a sampling of those posted between spring 2002 and spring 2003; please note that many links have probably expired.) Nevertheless, in an unfriendly radio climate, the Internet offered only limited possibilities for disseminating protest music.

For the three-year period from 9/11 until the 2004 presidential election, the most provocative anti-administration songs came from the progressive sectors of punk and rap. Before the invasion of Afghanistan, Anti-Flag released "911 for Peace" (on *Mobilize,* 2002), on whose chorus Justin Sane repeatedly shouted, "I don't wanna die, I don't wanna kill." Anti-Flag was founded in 1993 as an old-school, in-your-face punk band with explicitly left-wing politics. On *The Terror State* (2003), which opens with a direct assault on the president's veracity, the group took on issues ranging from the war to the economy. That same year, NoFX weighed in with "The Idiot Son of an Asshole," taunting both Bush presidents with an endless repetition of the song's title. Green Day delivered a certified antiwar blockbuster with *American Idiot* in 2004, with "Holiday" breaking ground by getting adult contemporary radio play.

Despite its penchant for violence, misogyny, and unabashed materialism, rap dispensed the fullest and most radical critiques of U.S. foreign policy. One of the first substantive responses to 9/11 was "Makeshift Patriot," released by slam poet/rapper Sage Francis in October 2001. It opens with a live audio track recorded by Francis at Ground Zero five days after the attacks. Its extended rap over a churchlike organ captures the horror and contradictions of that fateful September day. Francis is clear, however, about the outcome. "Freedom will be defended," he acknowledges, but quickly adds, "at the cost of civil liberties."

Some rap responses were more circumspect, reflecting the ambivalence of the rap community itself. Outkast's "The Whole World" (2001) presented an impressionistic, gut-level response to the initial attacks set to an up-tempo beat. Talib Kweli expressed contradictory feelings toward police and other officials on "The Proud" (2002), accusing them of killing "my people everyday" and admiring them for their selflessness at Ground Zero. On Wu Tang Clan's "Rules" (2001), Ghostface Killah, angry and bewildered over the bombings, shows respect toward Osama bin Laden when he says, "No disrespect, that's where I rest my head. I understand you gotta rest yours too nigga." But when he realizes that his people are dying as a result, he takes matters into his own hands: "Mr. Bush sit down, I'm in charge of this war."

As the war in Afghanistan began to segue into talk of invading Iraq, some rappers took a more radical stance. Mr. Lif opened "Home of the Brave" (2002) with a speech

> **D**espite its penchant for violence, misogyny, and unabashed materialism, rap dispensed the fullest and most radical critiques of U.S. foreign policy.

Protest Music on the Internet (Spring 2002–Spring 2003)

Beastie Boys "In a World Gone Mad" (www.beastieboys.com)

Luka Bloom "I Am Not at War with Anyone" (www.lukabloom.com)

Billy Bragg "The Price of Oil" (www.billybragg.co.uk)

Chuck D "A Twisted Sense of God" (www.slamjamz.com)

Zack de la Rocha (with DJ Shadow) "March of Death" (www.marchofdeath.com)

Nanci Griffith "Big Blue Ball of War" (www.nancigriffith.com)

Mick Jones "Why Do Men Fight" (www.poptones.co.uk)

Lenny Kravitz "We Want Peace" (www.rockthevote.org)

John McCutcheon "We Know War" (www.folkmusic.com)

John Mellencamp "To Washington" (www.mellencamp.com)

Meshell Ndegeocello "Forgiveness & Love" (www.meshell.com)

Leslie Nuchow "An Eye for an Eye (Will Leave the Whole World Blind)" (www.slammusic.com)

R.E.M. "The Final Straw" (www.remhq.com)

Spearhead "Bomb the World" (www.spearheadvibrations.com)

Cat Stevens "Peace Train" (www.yusufislam.org)

System of a Down "Boom!" (www.systemofadown.com)

((• **HEAR MORE** Audio links on MyMusicKit

by John F. Kennedy that considered thoughtful protest as "the basis of all human morality." Lif accused Bush of stealing the presidency, asserted the complicity of the media, and suggested that war in the Middle East could only divert people's attention from other pressing issues, such as a recession at home. Paris had addressed the 1991 Gulf War with "Bush Killa." On "What Would You Do?" from *Sonic Jihad* (2003), whose cover depicts a 747 about to crash into the White House, he named Bush as having the most to gain from a war and accused the administration of creating an enemy to justify its actions. Paris sputters, "It's plain to see / the oldest trick in the book is make an enemy / of phony evil now the government can do its dirt." On "Why?" (2004), Jadakiss asked pointedly, "Why did Bush knock down the towers?"

Even some higher-profile rap artists expressed dissatisfaction. On "Rule" from *Stillmatic* (2002), Nas asked Bush to "call a truce, world peace, stop acting like savages." The Black Eyed Peas scored a major Top Forty radio hit in 2003 with "Where Is the Love?" (an uncredited collaboration with Justin Timberlake), which proclaimed, "A war is goin' on but the reason's undercover." Eminem included some critical verse in cuts like "Business" and "My Dad's Gone Crazy" on *The Eminem Show* (2002). In "Square Dance," he cautioned young people about joining the war effort. For *Encore* (2004), Eminem (and Dr. Dre) produced a Spartan album with straightforward lyrics, unleashing a barrage of criticism on "Mosh" as Eminem intoned, "Fuck Bush, until they bring our troops home." Many of these songs were released within the chart life of the country singles that dominated the national airwaves. They could have contributed to a national debate but instead received only limited exposure.

Some musicians joined Musicians United to Win Without War (MUWWW), a group that aligned itself with the broad-based Win Without War coalition, which tried to prevent the invasion of Iraq. MUWWW described itself as "a loose coalition of contemporary musicians who feel that in the rush to war by the Bush administration the voices of reason and debate have been trampled and ignored."[55] The group included the usual suspects, ranging from David Byrne and Sheryl Crow to Ani DiFranco and Fugazi, as well as newcomers as diverse as Missy Elliot, Dave Matthews, and Bubba Sparxxx. At MUWWW's founding press conference, Russell Simmons and Ben Chavis of the Hip Hop Summit Action Network joined in the name of the hip hop community. Rockers and rappers launched an energetic voter registration campaign, quickly signing up nearly 100,000 new voters. Punks took a more aggressive and partisan stance. Under the leadership of Fat Mike from NOFX, they formed Punkvoter (www.punkvoter.com), dedicated to building a "united front in opposition to the dangerous, deadly, and destructive policies of George Bush, Jr." As Fat Mike told *The Nation*, "It's time to get mad."[56]

Although the invasion of Iraq proceeded apace, all this activity revealed considerable antiwar sentiment and enabled progressive musicians to rediscover their historical voice of protest. Significantly, the Win Without War coalition included organizations and individuals who had also protested concentration in the mass media, the erosion of artists' and consumers' rights, and the restrictive globalization policies of the World Trade Organization (WTO). Attempting to pull these disparate strands of activism into a united movement, in November 2003, Billy Bragg launched the "Tell Us the Truth" tour—which also featured Tom Morello (formerly of Rage Against the Machine) performing as the Nightwatchman, Steve Earle, Lester

Chambers of the Chambers Brothers, and rapper Boots Reilly of the Coup. The tour was sponsored by the AFL-CIO, Common Cause, the Future of Music Coalition, Free Press, and the Axis of Justice. Around this time, some music industry liberals from Nashville formed Music Row Democrats to make clear that conservatives did not speak for everyone in the country music business. Although these developments represented a significant cross section of center-left U.S. political thought, they were neither loud enough to drown out the chorus of nationalist anthems nor sufficiently compelling to recapture the White House for the Democrats in 2004.

As the war in Iraq dragged on, public opinion began to shift against it in the run-up to the 2006 midterm elections. Before 2005 was out, the Rolling Stones had chastised President Bush on "Sweet Neo-Con," and System of a Down continued their successful activist progressive rock career with the multiplatinum double album (released in two parts), *Mesmerize/Hypnotize,* both halves of which entered the charts at number one. On "B.Y.O.B." from *Mesmerize,* frontman Serj Tankian asked pointedly, "Why don't presidents fight the wars?" In 2005, Anti-Flag made the previously unthinkable leap to a major label with their politics intact and in 2006, they released *For Blood and Empire,* an album brimming with anti-Bush sentiment and criticism of the Iraq War. That year, Neil Young released *Living with War*, a full 180 degrees from his pro-administration stance following 9/11. At the time, Young described it on his website as "a metal version of Phil Ochs and Bob Dylan . . . metal folk protest?" Its most controversial cut, "Let's Impeach the President," was a straight-ahead rocker that called the White House to task over "why we have to send our men to war." Around this time, the floodgates seemed open for antiwar material; artists included Pink ("Dear Mr. President"), Pearl Jam ("World Wide Suicide"), the Pet Shop Boys ("I'm with Stupid"), the Flaming Lips' ("Haven't Got a Clue"), and the Roots ("False Media"). Music Row Democrats released a country compilation album, the *MRD Song Pack,* featuring many songs directly critical of the president and the war in Iraq, such as Billy Braddock's "Thou Shalt Not Kill" and Nanci Griffith's "Big Blue Ball of War." P. F. Sloan even recorded a new version of the classic antiwar song he had written in 1965, "Eve of Destruction."

Bruce Springsteen's *We Shall Overcome: The Seeger Sessions* entered the pop charts at number three and was certified gold within weeks. The album, with over a dozen musicians, showcased a broad range of Pete Seeger material. Springsteen opened the tour supporting the album in hurricane-ravaged New Orleans, performing the album's tunes as well as an updated version of Blind Alfred Reed's "How Can a Poor Man Stand Such Times and Live?" that included a pointed reference to "President Bystander." Interviewed about the federal

Throughout the post-9/11 period, Billy Bragg continued to promote the voice of protest in popular music.

response to Hurricane Katrina, Springsteen had words that echoed Neil Young's provocative single: "Obviously, get rid of the president," said Springsteen. "When you see the devastation [in New Orleans] and realize the kind of support the city will need to get back on its feet, there's no way to make sense of someone pushing for more tax cuts for the 1 percent of the 1 percent of the population. It's insanity and a subversion of everything America is supposed to be about."[57] Springsteen added a Seeger song to the tour in an updated version that summed up his feelings about the Iraq War—"(If You Love Your Uncle Sam) Bring 'Em Home." Despite the reappearance of protest music, the Iraq War survived not only the 2006 midterm elections, but also the ascension to the presidency in 2008 of Barak Obama, the first African American president of the United States and the only mainstream candidate to have opposed the war from the start.

Back to Business as Usual

In the post-9/11 period, getting back to business as usual took on a perverse urgency in the music industry, as elsewhere. But with the technological advances of peer-to-peer technology and the devastation of the economy wrought by the terrorist attacks, it was no longer quite clear what "usual" was. Immediately following the attacks, the ability simply to go shopping became the measure of a nation unbowed by terrorism. For many in the music industry, business as usual meant not only recovering lost revenues but restoring the dominance of rock, as if the familiar sounds of loud rock bands offered some reassurance of normalcy. But this vision overlooked the gains made by country music and undervalued yet again the degree to which rap and hip hop had become the foundation of U.S. popular culture.

For many in the music industry, business as usual meant not only recovering lost revenues but restoring the dominance of rock, as if the familiar sounds of loud rock bands offered some reassurance of normalcy.

The Return of Rock

By early 2002, some guitar-based bands, who had been successful before 9/11, had seemingly reasserted the primacy of rock. "With Creed, Linkin Park, and Nickelback all at the top of the charts," reported *Rolling Stone* in February 2002, "record companies are getting back to the business of rock."[58]

These multiplatinum mainstream rockers were the most visible segment of an even broader range of guitar-based rock sounds developing at the club level. The label *post-grunge* was variously applied to all these groups, more because they had formed after the peak of the Seattle scene than because of their sound. For example, Linkin Park routinely incorporated not just classic rock, but old school rap and electronic influences, too, in their debut album, *Hybrid Theory* (2000), which sold eight times platinum by 2002, and in their multiplatinum *Meteora* in 2004. Indeed, the post-grunge appellation was attached to guitar-based bands, from Blink 182 (*Take Off Your Pants and Jackets,* 2001) and Sum 41 (*All Killer No Filler,* 2001) to Staind (*Break the Cycle,* 2001) and Lifehouse (*No Name Face,* 2001). Lifehouse's "Hanging by a Moment" (2001) marked the first time since 1988 that a male rock group had the number one song of the year; in 2002, this distinction went to Nickelback's "How You Remind Me," marking the apex of the trend identified by *Rolling Stone.*

The year 2001 also marked the first time in four years that Creed did not finish the year as the top mainstream rock band. Florida-based Creed was formed in 1995 as a Seattle-influenced grunge metal outfit by singer/lyricist Scott Stapp and guitarist/composer Mark Tremonti. Stapp grew up in a Christian fundamentalist home, which definitely influenced his writing. As to the first album, Stapp says: "I was still dealing with guilt issues about all the Ten Commandments and all the other things the Bible says that I wasn't living in my life."[59] As a result, the group has often been deemed an alternative Christian band, a label they have only halfheartedly denied. Their debut album, *My Own Prison* (1997), generated four number one singles on *Billboard*'s mainstream rock radio charts—"My Own Prison," "Torn," "What's This Life For," "One"—and sold 5 million copies over the next two years. Their follow-up, *Human Clay* (1999), entered the pop charts at number one and sold 10 million copies. Their next three singles, "Higher," "What If," and "With Arms Wide Open," topped the charts, too, providing the group with seven number one radio singles in a row. *Weathered,* released in November 2001, also entered the charts at number one and sold 5 million copies in its first two months. Throughout their career, they have received nothing but critical disdain as a hopelessly derivative and formulaic group. Fortunately for them, this has always been a surefire formula for massive sales among hard rock groups.

After Creed disbanded following a 2002 car accident in which Stapp sustained a back injury that lead to various drug dependencies, other guitar-based bands came to the fore. Matchbox Twenty, a stereotypic post-grunge rock band, had a steady stream of Top Ten albums, including *More Than You Are* in 2002. That year, Lifehouse continued their post-grunge angst on *Stanley Climbfall.* Linkin Park reprised its marriage of buzzsaw guitar riffs and hip hop

Like many hard rockers before them, Creed parlayed critical disdain into massive sales.

elements on its second number one multiplatinum album, *Meteora* (2003). Staind also scored a second multiplatinum number one pop entry, *14 Shades of Grey* (2003), and followed it with *Chapter V* (2005), its third number one album in a row. Hoobastank's 2003 post-grunge entry, *The Reason,* went to number three on the album charts; 3 Doors Down parlayed their first Top Ten single, "Kryptonite," into a run of Top Ten albums, peaking with *17 Days,* which hit number one in 2005. Nickelback crafted the most stable career for themselves, following up 2001's "How You Remind Me" with "Someday" from *The Long Road* (2003) and "Photograph" from *All the Right Reasons* (2005), becoming, in effect, the archetypal post-grunge Top Forty band.

These coliseum-level acts were joined by a resurgence of guitar-based garage rock bands at the club level, too. Throughout 2002, groups like the Strokes (*Is This It?*) from New York, the White Stripes (*White Blood Cells*) from Detroit, the Hives (*Veni, Vidi, Vicious*) from Sweden, and the Vines (*Highly Evolved*) from Australia generated a significant buzz in international music centers such as New York and London.

But why this sound? Why at this time? One commentator interviewed by *Rolling Stone* in early 2002 pointed out that "you can't ignore what's happened in this country since September 11th. There's been a change of tenor in the music scene."[60] Another noted that pop sales had declined substantially and opined, "Rock has started to fill that void."[61] By the end of the year, *Billboard*'s Larry Flick reported, "One growing form of expression has been simple guitar-based rock, which has swept aside the squeaky-clean pop that dominated the U.S. market in recent years."[62] The above comments positioned rock only in opposition to teen pop, ignoring the gains of country music and its relevance to the post-9/11 period. But perhaps it is not too far-fetched to propose that, in the disorientation following 9/11, many mainstream fans, who would not have related to country anthems, found comfort in the familiar sounds of

Beginning in 2002, Detroit's White Stripes generated significant international buzz.

guitar-based rock and that, in the buildup for the war in Afghanistan, the more aggressive sounds of hard rock might have been the preferred sounds for this group.

This is not to suggest an easy homology between rock and war—indeed, in the sixties rock was perceived, if anything, as antiwar—nor that these groups were particularly identified with the war effort. Rather, this speculation is simply to wonder out loud why certain production styles become popular when they do and to reflect on the social functions of music in a given social context. To complicate the analysis, guitar-based rock was not the only trend that threatened to displace saccharine teen pop; other trends rivaled, even eclipsed, these post-grunge sounds in popularity and sales.

Singer/Songwriters Emote

Balancing the male-dominated, angst-ridden post-grunge sounds of the period, a new generation of female singer/songwriters eclipsed teen pop with a more soulful brand of introspection. These women were not creations of Disney nor products of the recording studio; all were serious artists, gifted songwriters, and talented performers. Some, like Michelle Branch, Avril Lavigne, and Pink, signed recording contracts before they were out of their teens. Others were musical prodigies with an impressive pedigree of artistic training. Alicia Keys had graduated as valedictorian from the High School for the Performing Arts in Manhattan before entering Columbia University at age sixteen. Norah Jones studied at the High School for Performing and Visual Arts in Dallas. Vanessa Carlton attended the School of American Ballet before embarking on a career in music.

Balancing the male-dominated, angst-ridden post-grunge sounds of the period, a new generation of female singer/songwriters eclipsed teen pop with a more soulful brand of introspection.

By the time Carleton released her platinum debut, *Be Not Nobody,* and its best-selling single, "A Thousand Miles," in 2002, this music was recognized as something of a trend. Its beginnings could be seen in Michelle Branch's *The Spirit Room* (2001) or even in Nelly Furtado's *Whoa, Nelly!* (2000), but it was defined by the tastefully stunning debut of Alicia Keys's *Songs in A Minor,* released in 2001. Powered by the ubiquitous, gospel-inflected single "Fallin'," the album hit number one and sold four times platinum before the year was out. Born of an interracial couple and raised by her white mother, Keys identified herself as black and displayed a maturity and self-confidence well beyond her years. Influenced by everyone from Marvin Gaye to Prince, to Biggie Smalls, to Chopin ("Chopin is my dawg"), Keys was also blessed with a manager who was loyal to a fault and a record company that learned to let a sixteen-year-old write and produce her own tracks. She conquered the *Tonight Show* and the *Oprah Winfrey Show* and generated significant buzz on MTV with the video for "Fallin'" before the album was released. At the 9/11 benefit *America: A Tribute to Heroes,* Keys performed a soulful version of Donny Hathaway's classic "Someday We'll All Be Free," but hers was not a knee-jerk patriotism. Describing her ambivalence, she told one reporter: "All day I been seein' everyone rockin' flags in they hats and on the street and I'm torn. . . . I see lies in that flag. I can't suddenly be all patriotic. But this is about human life beyond any country or flag."[63]

Alicia Keys clearly took her place among other soul divas like Jill Scott and India.Arie, but she also helped carve out the cultural space occupied by singer/songwriters like Norah Jones and Vanessa Carlton. Her long-awaited second album, *The Diary of Alicia Keys,* completed in 2003,

Alicia Keys' tasteful debut CD defined the new sound of female singer/songwriters.

didn't so much break new ground as confirm the staying power of the youthful Keys. With tracks ranging from the waltz-time "If I Ain't Got You" to the reggae-inflected "You Don't Know My Name," Keys demonstrated the same sophisticated musicality and soulful delivery that made her first album the defining moment of a new trend. *Diary* went to number one and multiplatinum certification, and it finished 2004 as the year's fourth most popular album. In the time between Keys's two blockbuster releases, Jones and Carlton, as well as Lavigne and Pink, had all enjoyed platinum releases.

Norah Jones—who, like Keys, listed Chopin as an influence—took the music forward into the terrain of pop jazz and what she described somewhat jokingly as "soft cock rock." Jones never traded on the fact that her father is Ravi Shankar, the world-famous sitar master. After a period of waitressing and playing low-paying club dates, she scored a contract with Blue Note. Her mellow, sultry delivery on *Come Away with Me* propelled her debut album to eight times platinum certification and netted her an impressive five Grammy Awards, including Album of the Year, Record of the Year ("Don't Know Why"), and Best New Artist, and stayed on the album charts for three years. "Don't Know Why," never a blockbuster hit single, nevertheless became an instant classic. Jones's sophomore album, *Feels Like Home* (2004), was not a major departure from her signature sound, described by her guitarist Adam Levy as "this cocktail of Ray Charles and Etta James, and Bill Evans on piano, and these simple country vocals, the way Loretta Lynn sings, so direct you can't ignore it."[64] The album sold 1 million copies in its first week and finishing 2004 as the fifth most popular album of the year, one notch down from Keys's *Diary*.

Avril Lavigne, a small-town Canadian teen signed to Arista at 16, was positioned as the Britney slayer—a guitar-carrying teen icon who did not appear manufactured and whose music (there are conflicting stories about how much of it she wrote) ranged from teen pop to hard rock. *Let's Go* (2002), her debut album, was produced by Antonio L. A. Reid and was propelled by three Top Ten singles—"Complicated," "Sk8er Boi," and "I'm with You"—written in collaboration with the Matrix

HEAR MORE
Norah Jones on
MyMusicKit

Norah Jones' sultry delivery produced incredible sales for someone signed to a jazz label.

"Don't Know Why"

Artist: Norah Jones
Music/Lyrics by Jesse Harris
Label: Blue Note, from the CD
Come Away with Me (2002)

The media makes much of the fact that Norah Jones is the daughter of Indian sitar master Ravi Shankar, but Jones paved her own musical path, and her style is firmly rooted in American popular music genres. Her music contains elements of jazz, soul, and even country music, and her mellow, sensuous vocal style recalls a number of great female jazz and soul singers (she has cited Billie Holiday as an important early influence). In 2004, *Time* magazine listed her as one of the year's most influential artists, because of her straightforward vocal delivery and avoidance of technological gimmickry.

Musical Style Notes

Music Terminology Demystified: What Is a Bridge?

A bridge is a section of a song that usually occurs after at least two repetitions of the main verse melody. Its tune differs from that of the verse, providing a contrasting section that then connects again to the main verse melody, which usually features either a new lyric verse or a repeat of Verse 1.

Structurally, "Don't Know Why" is classic pop ballad: verse/verse/bridge/verse/bridge/verse, with the final line of each verse serving as a lyric refrain. Stylistically, it features a folk- and jazz-influenced acoustic flavor. Songwriter Jesse Harris played guitar on the track; the other players are bassist Lee Alexander, violinist Jenny Scheinman, organist Sam Yahel, and Norah Jones on acoustic and electric piano and vocals.

Musical "Road Map"

TIMINGS	COMMENTS	LYRICS
0:00–0:11	Introduction—instrumental guitar, piano, bass, drums.	
0:11–0:38	Verse 1	*I waited . . .*
0:38–1:00	Verse 2	*When I saw . . .*
1:00–1:22	Bridge	*My heart . . .*
1:22–1:44	Verse 3	*Out across . . .*
1:44–2:06	Bridge 2	*My heart . . .*
2:06–2:27	Instrumental over bridge—piano, guitar, bass, drums.	
2:27–3:06	Verse 4 with extra last line *"don't know why . . . "*	*Something . . .*

songwriting team. *Let's Go* achieved sales of 4 million in six months. It lent credence to her ability to topple teen pop, clearly demonstrated her potential for future growth, and established her as a major player in the new singer/songwriter trend. *Under My Skin* (2004), released while she was still in her teens, debuted at pop number one and revealed a somewhat more mature Lavigne. Not the blockbuster of her first release, *Under My Skin* remained on the charts for over a year; it sold over 2 million copies and yielded her biggest single in the United States, "My Happy Ending." Lavigne then took a break from music, branching out into film and modeling, and marrying Sum 41 frontman Deryck Whibley in July 2006. She returned to the limelight with *The Best Damn Thing* (2007), whose pop-punk hit single "Girlfriend" topped her U.S. sales of "Happy Ending."

Label-mate Pink started her career before Lavigne; her first outing was a well-crafted but undistinguished dance pop album that sold double platinum. Having toured as the opening act for 'N Sync, however, she was in danger of becoming just another teen pop act. But Pink was fiercely independent and deeply distrustful of all authority figures, including recording executives. For her second album, *M!ssundaztood* (2001), she fought her label for artistic control, teamed up with Linda Perry (of 4 Non Blondes) to write most of the material, and delivered an unlikely product that offered everything from dance/pop ("Get the Party Started") and mainstream rock ("18 Wheeler") to deeply personal confessionals ("Family Portrait," "Dear Diary," "My Vietnam"). By the end of 2002, *M!ssundaztood* had been certified four times platinum and had established Pink as her own person. She worked with Rancid's Tim Armstrong to produce *Try This* (2003), a rock-based, eclectic mix of everything from ska to electronica. She returned in 2006 with *I'm Not Dead,* cranking up the dance rhythms and taking shots at Paris Hilton ("Stupid Girls"), George W. Bush ("Dear Mr. President"), and others. Neither album duplicated the sales of *M!ssundaztood,* but both hit the Top Ten and confirmed Pink as a talented risk taker. Her fifth studio album, *Funhouse* (2008), was propelled to five times platinum sales by her first number one solo single, "So What."

Nelly Furtado's career bracketed the trend of female singer-songwriters in the early 2000s and has run the gamut of popular music styles from the eclectic *Whoa,*

Pink's independence and distrust of authority propelled her to multi-platinum sales.

Nelly! (2000) to the all-Spanish *Mi Plan* (2009). A single mom from Toronto, Furtado is conscious of her working-class background and Portuguese roots; speaks four languages; and loves Toronto for its multicultural character, support for gay marriage, and commitment to grassroots political activism.[65] Her musical tastes are even broader than Pink's, running from rhythm and blues (r&b)/hip hop and alternative to Portuguese *fado*, Brazilian *bossa nova*, and Indian *raga*. On *Whoa, Nelly!* Furtado received critical acclaim for her adventurous genre blending; the album generated two Top Ten singles, "Turn Off the Light" and "I'm Like a Bird," which earned her a Grammy for Best Female Pop Vocal Performance. Following the disappointment of *Folklore* (2003), Furtado took time off, returning in 2006 with *Loose*, a (mostly) Timbaland-produced album that hit number one and further showcased her ability to incorporate global cultural influences into a pop sound. While the hip hop–influenced "Promiscuous" (featuring Timbaland) provided her with a number one single in the United States, other songs ranged from the pop-oriented "Maneater" to the Latin-tinged "Te Busqué" (featuring Juanes), to the reggaeton-influenced "No Hay Igual," recorded with members of Calle 13. In 2009, she released an entire album in Spanish. While oriented toward a Latino audience, *Mi Plan* was hardly a side project of a pop superstar. All the songs were written by Furtado in collaboration with various Latino artists. And having gone to school with Timbaland on *Loose*, Furtado recorded *Mi Plan* with a strong rhythmic base designed to have plenty of appeal in the pop market.

Pink and Furtado took the role of singer/songwriter in fresh new directions, while a new generation of male singer/songwriters returned the craft to its roots in the early 1970s. These included John Mayer (*Heavier Things*), Jack Johnson (*On and On*), Jason Mraz (*Waiting for My Rocket to Come*), David Gray (*A New Day at Midnight*), Pete Yorn (*Day I Forgot*), and Howie Day (*Stop All the World Now*). All enjoyed chart successes in 2003. Jon Pareles commented on the significance of their music for the period: "All it takes is turning on a pop radio station or MTV to get the strange feeling that the mid-1970's have returned: the days of post-Vietnam and post-Watergate letdown, oil crisis, unemployment and soothing soft rock to provide consolation for it all."[66] As if to consecrate the link to the 1970s, not only did period icon James Taylor release a new album, but his and Carly Simon's son Ben Taylor debuted with *Famous Among the Barns*.

Initially, no one stood out from the new crowd of singer/songwriters as much as Dave Matthews, described by Pareles as "a brooding songwriter strumming an acoustic guitar."[67] The fact that he was born in apartheid South Africa made it all the more interesting that he achieved international superstardom with his band of three black (Boyd Tinsley, Carter Beauford, LeRoi Moore) and two white (Stefan Lessard, Matthews) musicians. Signed to RCA in the mid-1990s, the Dave Matthews Band released three platinum (or better) studio albums before replacing longtime producer Steve Lillywhite with the more mainstream Glen Ballard for the double platinum *Everyday* (2001), a move that upset many fans. *Busted Stuff* (2002) remixed much of the unused material from previous Lillywhite sessions. Both albums were among the year-end best sellers for 2002. Besides being an extremely successful touring act, the band continued to produce platinum live albums

> **P**ink and Furtado took the role of singer/songwriter in fresh new directions, while a new generation of male singer/songwriters returned the craft to its roots in the early 1970s.

As introspective as any singer/songwriter, Dave Matthews assembled an integrated rocking band and become politically engaged.

and some moved on to solo projects, too. Matthews further distinguished himself from his ouvre by his activist bent and progressive political stands. He has served on the Board of Farm Aid since 2000; in 2004, he joined Bruce Springsteen on the Vote for Change Tour; and he has since played benefits for Tibet and the victims of Hurricane Katrina and the Virginia Tech shootings.

While none of the new crop of singer-songwriters adopted Matthews's activist politics, John Mayer and Jack Johnson achieved the most commercial success. Johnson was an accomplished surfer before moving into songwriting and filmmaking while attending the University of California–Santa Barbara. His *On and On* hit number three in 2003, catapulting him to the upper reaches of touring acts. By then, even his debut release, *Brushfire Fairytales* (2001), had gone platinum, confirming his star power. Johnson's sunny disposition and feel-good sound defined his work even when he addressed topical issues such as materialism ("Gone") and war ("Traffic in the Sky"). Delivering more of the same, *In Between Dreams* (2005) fared best of all, peaking at number two on the album charts. It wasn't until *Sing-A-Longs and Lullabies for the Film Curious George* (2006) that he achieved his first number one album. For *Sleep through the Static* (2008), he returned to his laid-back, hushed vocal delivery even on the topical title song.

Following a stint at the Berklee College of Music in Boston, Mayer enjoyed indie success with *Inside Wants Out* (1999) before signing with Columbia. On the strength of his major label debut, *Room for Squares* (2002), Mayer walked off with the 2003 Grammy for Best Male Pop Vocalist. His second major label effort, *Heavier Things* (2003), went to number one and platinum certification. All three albums could be found among *Billboard*'s most popular albums of 2003.

John Mayer's music provided comfort to a generation in pain.

Mayer considered *Continuum* (2006) as the third of a trilogy recorded with a pared-down trio of guitar, bass, and drums. He continued in the same vein for *Battle Studies* (2009), which he described in promotional interviews as a "heartbreak handbook."

It is fair to say that the music of these artists is sensitive, direct, and heartfelt. Still, descriptions of it in places like the *All Music Guide* offer less than flattering insights into its social functions. In reviewing *On and On,* one critic wrote, "Fans will enjoy Johnson's soothing ballads and boy-next-door charms, never looking beyond the surface of the songs themselves."[68] Mayer's *Heavier Things* was described as "music that floats through the speakers nicely and never leaves much of a lasting impression."[69] This is music that was designed to soothe while shielding the listener from the problems of the world. In the words of Jon Pareles: "Mr. Mayer and his fellow songwriters often play the same comforting role as their forebears. Turning away from the bad news of the outside world, they focus on personal affairs: mostly romance, but also the endless processes of self-invention and finding a place in the world."[70] As if to challenge Pareles, Mayer claimed on his website that, for *Continuum,* he was ready to tackle "big themes." Nevertheless, on "Waiting for the World to Change," his Grammy-winning topical single from the album, the singer abdicates all personal agency and waits for the world to magically change, in effect confirming Pareles's view.

Idol Worship

Another post-9/11 popular culture phenomenon offered similar diversions from world problems, ironically in the name of "reality"—that is, "reality TV," with its signature music program, *American Idol*. The model for *American Idol* was *Popstars*, a late-1990s New Zealand television show that inspired a British variant called *Pop Idol* in 2001. In the hands of media Svengali Simon Fuller and his colleagues Simon Cowell and Simon Jones, the *Pop Idol* format became an international franchise. In the United States, Fremantle North America, owned by the German conglomerate Bertelsmann, produced the show. After being turned down by all U.S. networks, *American Idol* was picked up by Fox, which is owned by media mogul Rupert Murdoch's conservative News Corporation, headquartered in Australia. Acting on a tip from his daughter in England, Murdoch reportedly told his executives, "Don't look at it. Buy it! Right now!"[71] *American Idol* quickly became the number one Nielsen-rated television show in the country, averaging 31.6 million viewers a week in 2006.[72] By then, it was being aired in over 100 countries.

The contest begins with public, nationwide auditions for thousands of singers age sixteen to twenty-eight. These early sessions have produced endless fodder for celebrity gossip columnists, *Saturday Night Live* skits, and culture vultures across the blogosphere, keeping the show constantly in the public eye. When the contestants get whittled down to thirteen finalists, audience voting becomes the mechanism for progressing toward victory. In addition to the $1 million first prize, the winners (and sometimes other finalists) are typically offered record contracts with one of Sony-BMG's affiliated labels. They are also signed to management contracts with 19 Entertainment, Fuller's massive international artist development company headquartered in Britain, which oversees the idols' record and movie deals, live shows, merchandising, and endorsements.

> **W**ithin only a few years, naysayers had to admit that American Idol had produced a group of democratically elected superstars who had proven themselves in the marketplace.

Within only a few years, naysayers had to admit that *American Idol* had produced a group of democratically elected superstars who had proven themselves in the marketplace. Beginning with the first season in 2002, *American Idol* veterans steadily built their presence in the popular market. First-season winner Kelly Clarkson scored the best-selling single of that year with "A Moment Like This," later included on her debut album, *Thankful* (2003). Clarkson was at home in front of the camera and able to handle everything from Aretha Franklin covers to middle-of-the-road pop; her first-season victory made it more difficult to dismiss the show out of hand. While *Thankful* didn't bowl anybody over, it showcased Clarkson's versatility to advantage and eventually rose to number one on the pop charts. On her second effort, *Breakaway* (2004), Clarkson established herself as an artist with staying power. On the strength of hit singles ranging from pop balladry ("Because of You") to arena rockers ("Since U Been Gone"), the album sold over 5 million copies and netted Clarkson two Grammys in 2006. *My December* (2007), revealed Clarkson as a writer and rocker with an edge; it was released over the loud and very public objection of label head Clive Davis, who disapproved of the star's new direction. Clarkson returned to the pop fold and the top of the charts in 2009 with "My Life Would Suck Without You" from *All I Ever Wanted*.

(((• HEAR MORE
American Idol on
MyMusicKit

In 2003, second-season runner-up Clay Aiken and winner Ruben Studdard entered the Hot 100 Single Sales chart at numbers one and two, with "This Is the Night" and "Flying Without Wings," respectively, and held the top two positions for *Billboard*'s year-end tally. By this time, Clarkson's *Thankful* and Aiken's *Measure of a Man* had hit number one on the album charts, selling millions of copies each, and Studdard's *Soulful* debuted in the number one slot at the end of the year. *Soulful* had a cohesive r&b/hip hop feel to it, and its distinctive sound served to separate Studdard from the pop sound that had defined the Clarkson and Aiken releases. Studdard had narrowly edged Aiken aside for the second season crown by only 134,000 votes out of 24 million cast. But Aiken beat Studdard to marketplace and to the cover of *Rolling Stone,* becoming, in effect, the season's champion. One couldn't help but wonder whether the fact that Aiken is white and Studdard is black had something to do with it.

In 2004, *Idol* contestants recorded the three best-selling singles of the year and four of the top six, including third-season winner Fantasia (Barrino) at number one with "I Believe"—the first time a new artist had debuted at number one on the *Billboard Hot 100* with her first single.

Fantasia, as she is billed, is a soul/gospel powerhouse with a booming Broadway voice. Her debut album, *Free Yourself*, reached the Top Ten and sold 2 million copies.

By 2005, the idols had made chart inroads across the board. Fourth-season winner Carrie Underwood, the first "country" idol, had the best-selling pop single and best-selling country single of the year with "Inside Your Heaven." Her runner-up, Bo Brice, scored the second best-selling single with his version of the same song. Clarkson placed two singles in the year-end Hot 100 Songs—"Since You Been Gone" and "Behind These Hazel Eyes"—and scored the number one adult contemporary hit with "Breakaway." Fantasia emerged as the number one adult r&b artist and new r&b/hip hop artist. Studdard had the number one gospel album of the year with his second entry, *I Need an Angel*, and Aiken finished the year with the number one Christian album, *Merry Christmas with Love*. *American Idol* winners or runners-up had walked off with seventeen number one honors on *Billboard*'s year-end tallies, with Clarkson racking up nine of them.

Underwood's *Some Hearts* (2005) charted for the whole of 2006, ending up as the number one pop album of the year, something no Idol debut had ever done. As an *Idol* winner with a debut album that was eventually certified six times platinum, Underwood faced an interesting dilemma: How does a singer maintain credibility as a country singer when she or he is already a pop superstar? For her sophomore album, *Carnival Ride* (2007), she went deeper into her country roots, contributing a number of her own songs, and managed to retain her small-town-girl persona, despite her incredible success. In addition to winning numerous music awards, at 26, she became the youngest member of the Grand Ole Opry. She was also twice voted "world's sexiest vegetarian" by People for the Ethical Treatment of Animals (PETA).

Over the next couple of seasons, with a few notable exceptions—Jordin Sparks's self-titled platinum debut album (2007); David Cook's eleven chart singles in 2008—Idol offered little that was distinctive (despite Sanjaya Malakar's folk-hero celebrity). Many finalists turned in "less than expected" sales, with several being dropped from their labels. Even respectable gold album sales for his eponymous debut album were not enough to keep 2006 title holder Taylor Hicks from getting the ax. During this period, *Idol's* biggest successes came from those who had been voted off the show—Chris Daughtry's multiplatinum debut with his new rock band, DAUGHTRY; Jennifer Hudson winning an Oscar for her role in *Dreamgirls*. It wasn't until the contentious final round of season eight (2009), pitting Adam Lambert against Kris Allen, that *Idol* hysteria once again hit the stratosphere.

In the run-up to the season eight finale, it seemed clear that the flamboyant, openly gay, over-the-top Adam Lambert, with his stunning vocal range and confident power-pop delivery, would be the 2009 *American Idol*. From "Born to Be Wild" to Aerosmith's "Cryin'," to the Sam Cooke classic "A Change Is Gonna Come," there was no song that Lambert couldn't deliver with passion. There was also some sense that *Idol* needed a showstopper like Lambert to prove it wasn't just another TV talent show, especially considering Allen's clean-cut image and laid-back delivery on time-honored chestnuts such as Marvin Gaye's "What's Goin' On" and Bill Withers's "Ain't No Sunshine." The judges gushed over Lambert: "You are a rock god!" screamed Kara DioGuardi; "Dawg, you're one of the best we've ever had on this stage," said Randy Jackson; "You dare to dance in the path of greatness," opined Paula Abdul; Simon Cowell offered his highest compliment, a quiet standing ovation.[73]

Then, inexplicably, Kris Allen won. One couldn't help but wonder whether the goth fashion statement with black nail polish or the widely circulated photographs of Lambert kissing other young men had anything to do with this. Former runner-up Clay Aiken, who had recently come out as gay himself, added fuel to the fire in criticizing Lambert's performance of Johnny Cash's "Ring of Fire" as "contrived," "awful," and "slightly frightening." Voting irregularities

Adam Lambert's on- and off-stage demeanor may have jolted onlookers out of their comfort zone, but his musical talents could not be denied.

were reported, like ATT providing free phones and power-texting workshops at house parties in Allen's home state of Arkansas, but these were dismissed as unconfirmed or indecisive. The show announced that a slim majority (not reported) of the 88 million or so *Idol* voters confirmed that they were not ready to embrace Adam Lambert as their idol. In the end, *American Idol* may have demonstrated that it was another middle-of-the-road TV show, but it was still the one that more people watched than any other.

Black Artists, Hip Hop Aesthetics, and Pop Success

The return of guitar-based rock may have provided some sense of familiarity following a period of profound social dislocation, while a new generation of singer-songwriters and television idols protected their audiences from thinking about the difficult social issues that swirled about them. But in some ways, these trends papered over another pattern that was revealed on 11 October 2003: *Billboard* reported that, for the first time in the magazine's history, all ten of the Top Ten pop hits in the country were by black artists, nine of them rappers, with Beyoncé at number one with "Baby Boy." Once again, most observers had failed to notice the elephant in the room until it sat down on the sofa. Critic Nelson George was quick to claim the ultimate victory. "The battle's been won," said George. "Hip-hop is the new American music."[74] That statement may have been a bit over the top, but it echoed David Toop's statement of some twenty years earlier: "Hip hop was the new music by virtue of its finding a way to absorb all other music."[75]

HEAR MORE
Audio links for *Billboard* Top Ten Singles, 11 October 2003, on MyMusicKit

What happened was that hip hop singles had made the transition from urban radio to Top Forty radio, which reflected the broadest demographic and formed the basis for the *Billboard Hot 100* chart. But the *Hot 100* is more heavily weighted to radio play than to sales; it is the *Billboard 200*, the mainstream album chart, that reflects the bulk of sales. Had black artists captured the Top Ten album positions, George's statement would have been unassailable. Still, he was correct that even the hardest rappers had become more oriented toward the crossover market and that hip hop aesthetics had exerted a defining influence on other styles, from teen pop to r&b. Artists like Bubba Sparxxx and Nappy Roots even offered country rap. In that sense, hip hop had become "the new American music" or, at the very least, a new paradigm that may have surpassed rock in cultural importance.

> *Even the hardest rappers had become more oriented toward the crossover market and hip hop aesthetics had exerted a defining influence on other styles, from teen pop to r&b. In that sense, hip hop had become "the new American music" or, at the very least, a new paradigm that may have surpassed rock in cultural importance.*

The Top Ten sweep by black artists marked a pattern that many in the music industry found troubling. Their concerns were blunted for a time because black rappers were still sharing top honors with whites from other genres at year's end. Still, it would not have been a stretch even in 2003 to say that black hip hop artists were first among equals—certainly in mainstream influence, but also in popularity and sales. Indeed, *Billboard*'s first three Top Pop Artists of the Year were black, and six of the ten most popular songs of 2003 were by black artists. More important, this was a baseline from which their presence only expanded.

If the year was owned by any single artist, it was 50 Cent. *Rolling Stone*'s April 3 cover pictured him as buff and as mean as he could be. By this time he had become the most controversial figure in rap, if not in popular culture generally. His exploits had already generated so much buzz that when his much-anticipated debut, *Get Rich or Die Tryin'*, was finally released, it sold a record-breaking 872,000 units in five days, powered by the ubiquitous feel-good single "In Da Club." He had the number one single of 2003 from the number one album of the year, making him *Billboard*'s Top Pop Artist of the Year, with two other black artists—R. Kelly (*Chocolate Factory*) and Sean Paul (*Dutty Rock*)—in positions two and three, respectively. The same year, 50 Cent's G-Unit posse released the platinum-selling *Beg for Mercy*. Although he was nominated for an impressive five Grammys, he was shut out of the winner's circle. Particularly angered at not being named Best New Artist of the Year, he tried to block Evanescence (whose *Fallen* had remained on the album charts for two years) from receiving the award.

Three other rap or r&b/hip hop acts—Jay-Z, OutKast, and Beyoncé—bested all artists with six nominations each in 2003. Beyoncé opened the Grammy Awards telecast with a stunning medley of Prince tunes and her hit single "Crazy in Love," accompanied by Prince. At the end of the night, Beyoncé went home with her boyfriend, Jay-Z, who won two Grammys for his guest appearance on "Crazy in Love," and with five of the six awards for which she was nominated. She lost, however, to Coldplay's *Clocks* for Record of the Year. The year 2003 was something of a breakout year for Beyoncé, who left Destiny's Child to become a solo artist, releasing *Dangerously in Love* in June. By year's end, it had sold 2 million copies and eventually generated five Top Ten pop singles, including two at number one—"Crazy in Love" with Jay-Z and "Baby Boy," enhanced by the staccato dancehall verse of Sean Paul. The Jamaican rapper

With his fabled penchant for violence and strong rhyming and production skills, 50 Cent emerged as the most popular artist of 2003, a feat he repeated in 2005.

"In Da Club"

Artist: 50 Cent

Music/Lyrics by Curtis James Jackson III (50 Cent), with Mike Elizondo and Andre Young (Dr. Dre)

Label: Shady/Aftermath/Intersc ope, from the CD *Get Rich or Die Tryin'* (2002)

In the wake of the archetypal Brooklyn hip hop of Run DMC and the Afrocentric rapping of Queen Latifah, hip hop made a breakthrough into white radio with so-called gangsta rap. Often focusing, like "In Da Club," on both bicoastal (New York versus Los Angeles) and interpersonal rivalries, gangsta rappers have crafted a much harder, even more minimalist, outlaw approach. As with many gangsta rap songs, "In Da Club" was released in both an "explicit" version and a "clean" version. The explicit version is much more direct in its references to drug use and specific feuds and more liberal in its use of language that some might find offensive.

Musical Style Notes

"In Da Club" is in classic hip hop style: Layers of interlocking rhythms create a compelling, repetitive groove over which the rap is foregrounded. Altogether, the rhythm features a steady sixteenth note pattern (each large beat is subdivided into 4 smaller beats); a syncopated drum track; a syncopated chord progression that repeats throughout the piece; and a synthesized hand-clap track that accentuates the backbeat, forming an interlocking pattern.

Large beat			1	2	3	4	1	2	3	4
Syncopated beat(chords)	1 2 3 4	1 2 3 4	1 2 3 4	1 2 3 4	1 2 3 4	1 2 3 4	1 2 3 4	1 2 3 4	1 2 3 4	1 2 3 4
Hand-claps			X		X		X		X	
Large beat subdivided into 4 beats	1 2 3 4	1 2 3 4	1 2 3 4	1 2 3 4	1 2 3 4	1 2 3 4	1 2 3 4	1 2 3 4	1 2 3 4	1 2 3 4

The vocals alternate between spoken voice—a combination of chanted speech on one note, which may alternate slightly by one tone—and passages that are sung.

Musical "Road Map"

TIMINGS	COMMENTS	LYRICS
0:00–0:15	Verse 1 (spoken). Keyboards and prominent bass. (See Musical Style Notes above for interlocking rhythm pattern.)	*Go, . . .* *It's your birthday . . .*
0:15–0:26	Chorus (chanted on a single note, with occasional variation by one or two tones). Note additional layer of sampled "orchestral" sound.	*You can . . .* *Bottle full . . .*
0:26–0:36	Chorus repeats.	
0:36–1:19	Verse 2 (chanted, speech; changes to a focus on speech as the verse continues; the last lines are sung). "Orchestral" sound drops out and returns at 0:59.	*When I pull up . . .*
1:19–1:30	Chorus (chanted on a single note, with occasional variation by one or two tones).	*You can find . . .*
1:30–1:42	Chorus repeats.	
1:42–1:52	Bridge (sung). (Whistle heard way in the background.)	*My flow, . . .*
1:52–2:23	Verse 3 (chanted speech).	*You should . . .*
2:23–2:34	Chorus (chanted on a single note, with occasional variation by one or two tones).	*You can . . .*
2:34–2:45	Chorus repeats. "Orchestral sample" is mixed up a little more prominently here.	
2:45–3:12	Ending verse—spoken. Chord progression continues; music fades out; ends at 3:12.	*Ha ha . . .* (Laughter)

himself scored the third most popular single of the year, "Get Busy." Beyoncé reunited with Destiny's Child the following year to record their farewell album, *Destiny Fulfilled*.

OutKast had followed up their triple platinum *Stankonia* (2000) with *Speakerboxxx/The Love Below* (2003), for which they won three Grammys. They also became the first rappers to win the Album of the Year award. The double album was also one of the few hip hop albums to be certified diamond (10 million units sold or, as in this case, 5 million for each CD). *Speakerboxxx/The Love Below* was essentially two albums: the first, a Big Boi compilation that continued OutKast's adventurous Dirty South hip hop; the second, an eccentric André 3000 (a.k.a. Dré) foray into funk and soul. Each CD generated a number one hit single—Big Boi's "The Way You Move" and André's "Hey Ya!" which became one of the standout singles of the year.

Black dominance in popular music continued in 2004: Seven of the first ten Top Pop Artists of the Year and eleven of the thirteen most popular singles were by rap or r&b/hip hop artists.

Black dominance in popular music continued in 2004: Seven of the first ten Top Pop Artists of the Year and eleven of the thirteen most popular singles were by rap or r&b/hip hop artists. In addition to artists already mentioned, there were newcomers like Twista (*Kamikazi*) and Kanye West (*The College Dropout*). Usher ruled 2004 in much the same way that 50 Cent had the previous year, only more strongly. Usher recorded the most popular album of the year (*Confessions*) as well as the top two singles ("Yeah!" and "Burn"). *Confessions* sold an incredible 1.1 million units in its first week. The album's first single, "Yeah!" (featuring L'il Jon and Ludacris), which married Dirty South crunk beats to an r&b sound, occupied the number one position on the *Billboard Hot 100* for a record-tying twelve weeks. It was replaced by "Burn," an r&b/hip hop song built around Usher's gentle falsetto, which held the top spot for another seven weeks, giving Usher an unprecedented nineteen-week run at pop number one. The album also generated two other number one singles—"Confessions Pt. 2" and "My Boo," a duet with Alicia Keys—placing Usher at the top of Hot 100 for twenty-eight weeks of the year. Signed to La Face Records by L. A. Reid when he was just fourteen, Usher released his first album while he was still in high school and the platinum-selling *My Way* (1997) shortly after graduating. *Confessions* (2004) was his fourth studio album; it was certified eight times platinum before the year was out.

This was also the year that producer Kanye West stepped out from behind the mixing board and became rapper Kanye West. West was not your average MC. Looking like someone from the pages of *GQ* in his pink Polo shirts and Gucci loafers, he graced the cover of *Time* magazine before Rolling Stone pictured him as Christ with a crown of thorns. West invited controversy wherever he went and he went everywhere. He threw a fit at the *American Music Awards* after country singer Gretchen Wilson bested him for the Best New Artist award. His most-publicized controversy occurred at a benefit for Hurricane Katrina victims, where he launched into an antigovernment rant that climaxed with the pronouncement that "George Bush doesn't care about black people." He also spoke out against homophobia in rap in an MTV interview.

West was raised mostly in the middle-class South Shore suburb of Chicago by his mother, Donda, a college professor, while spending summers with his father, a former Black Panther who became a photographer, marriage counselor, and professor. West dropped out of college after one year to try his hand at music. Creating beats for local Chicago rappers

An unlikely hip hop hero in his upscale, preppy attire, Kanye West proved to be a top-selling rapper and an outspoken political commentator, before he became a "jackass" in the eyes of some.

soon led to gigs at Bad Boy and Roc-A-Fella in New York, where he built a solid reputation as a producer, working with top-tier artists like Keys ("You Don't Know My Name"), Twista ("Slow Jamz"), Ludacris ("Stand Up"), and Jay-Z ("Izzo [H.O.V.A.]," "Takeover," "03 Bonnie & Clyde"). But when he told his colleagues at Roc-A-Fella that he wanted to rap, his request was first met with an awkward standoffishness. "It was obvious we were not from the same place or cut from the same cloth," said Jay-Z. "We all grew up street guys who had to do whatever we had to do to get by. Then there's Kanye, who to my knowledge has never hustled a day in his life. I didn't see how it could work."[76]

Fearing that one of their hottest producers might jump labels, Roc-A-Fella signed West. His first effort, *The College Dropout* (2004), debuted at number two and sold nearly 3 million copies; West received ten Grammy nominations for that album and won three. The album had been delayed by a near-fatal car accident, which West chronicled on his hit "Through the Wire" while his jaw was still wired shut. This plus "Slow Jamz" (with Twista and Jamie Foxx), his hilarious ode to romantic r&b singers, kept West in the public eye while the album was being released. For his second album, *Late Registration* (2005), West used another approach, collaborating with producer Jon Brion, who added horns and strings to the rapper's sample-heavy beats. *Late Registration* went to number one and platinum certification, and won the Grammy for Best Album of the Year. Its singles included "Diamonds from Sierra Leone" and "Gold Digger" (featuring Jaime Foxx in his Ray Charles persona), which went to pop number one.

By 2005, some in the industry took action against black dominance on the pop charts. In February, *Billboard* introduced a new singles chart, the Pop 100. The Hot 100 had *Billboard*'s pop singles chart since 1958; it was the chart that the radio program *American Top 40* had used to create its weekly playlist from 1970 to 1995. It remained *Billboard*'s main chart for tabulating the most popular individual songs. What, then, was the Pop 100? The answer began to emerge after one noticed that every record to reach number one on the *Hot 100* in 2004 was by a black artist (see the table). Simply put, the Pop 100 was created to remedy this situation.

Billboard Number One Hot 100 Singles (2004)

STARTING DATE AT NUMBER ONE	SONG	ARTIST
January 3	"Hey Ya!"	OutKast
February 14	"The Way You Move"	OutKast featuring Sleepy Brown
February 21	"Slow Jamz"	Twista featuring Kanye West and Jamie Foxx
February 28	"Yeah!"	Usher featuring Lil' Jon and Ludacris
May 22	"Burn"	Usher
July 10	"I Believe"	Fantasia
July 17	"Burn"	Usher
July 24	"Confessions Part II"	Usher
August 7	"Slow Motion"	Juvenile featuring Soulja Slim
August 21	"Lean Back"	The Terror Squad
September 11	"Goodies"	Ciara featuring Petey Pablo
October 30	"My Boo"	Usher and Alicia Keys
December 11	"Drop It Like It's Hot"	Snoop Dogg featuring

((• HEAR MORE
Audio links for *Billboard* number one Hot 100 singles for 2004 on MyMusicKit

The Hot 100 was based on sales and airplay data from all radio formats; the Pop 100 limited its data collection to a narrower range of mainstream Top 40 stations, to track what *Billboard* called "mass-appeal mainstream hits"—as if that phrase didn't describe rap.[77] Explained journalist and music librarian Bill Lamb, "By the beginning of the new century, many fans and members of the music industry became concerned that the Hot 100 had become biased in favor of r&b and hip hop music. It was becoming more and more difficult for rock and mainstream pop songs to do well on the Hot 100."[78]

What was really going on was that hard-core rap and r&b/hip hop had captured the taste preferences of white suburban teenagers, and many music executives didn't like that.

> **T**he runaway success of rap and hip hop had allowed many street-toughened black entrepreneurs to become multimillionaires on their own terms, and this challenged narrow mainstream conceptions of the American Dream.

The runaway success of rap and hip hop had allowed many street-toughened black entrepreneurs to become multimillionaires on their own terms, and this challenged narrow mainstream conceptions of the American Dream. Clearly, the Hot 100 was still a more accurate measure of popular taste. The Pop 100 was designed to give white artists in pop, rock, and country a better chance to claim a number one hit song. Ironically, the first song to hit number one on the new

Pop 100 chart was Ciara's "1, 2 Step," a dance-oriented r&b/hip hop single featuring Missy Elliott. Still, the new chart enabled Kelly Clarkson's "Since U Been Gone" to top the year-end recap. Other than that, the two charts were remarkably similar because rap and r&b/hip hop had already made inroads into Top 40 radio territory and because many white artists had adopted hip hop aesthetics and rap styles. Gwen Stefani's "Hollaback Girl"—a jaunty dance pop single with rapped verses—scored number two for the year on both charts.

Even with the new chart, black artists dominated 2005: 50 Cent's *The Massacre* (2005) made the rapper the Top Artist of the Year for the second time in three years. Four singles from the album—"Disco Inferno," "Candy Shop," "Just a Lil Bit," "Outta Control"—hit the Top Ten on both the Hot 100 and the Pop 100. He collaborated with the Game on "How We Do It" and "Hate It or Love It." The Game was a Compton rapper who had joined 50 Cent's G-Unit in 2004, across rap's geographical divide. By the time the singles caught fire, however, the relationship had already gone bad, and 50 Cent dismissed the Game from G-Unit. The rapper finished the year with a video game, *50 Cent: Bulletproof*, and a starring role in a loosely autobiographical film, *Get Rich or Die Tryin'*.

Mariah Carey was the comeback story of 2005. Carey had hit bottom in the early 2000s, complete with suicide notes and erratic behavior—a public and highly publicized breakdown. After signing with Virgin for a reported $80 million, her film musical, *Glitter*, and its accompanying soundtrack album of the same name did so poorly that the movie failed to recover its production costs in its initial U.S. release, and the album barely broke gold sales. Adding insult to injury, Virgin then paid her $28 million to go away. Moving to Island/Def Jam to set up her own label in 2002, her first outing, *Charmbracelet*, failed to lift her career. Three years later, on *The Emancipation of Mimi*, Carey again embraced hip hop and returned to an r&b-based dance pop groove that finally put the early 2000s behind her. The album hit number one and was still riding the charts a year later, having been certified six times platinum. It also generated two number one singles: "Don't Forget About Us" and "We Belong Together," which spent fourteen weeks in the top slot. Carey's next album, $E=MC^2$ (2008) included "Touch My Body," which hit number one on the Hot 100 and the Pop 100. (Because this was her eighteenth number one hit, she tied Elvis; only the Beatles, with twenty, had more). Carey's return demonstrated the resilience of the artist and the centrality of dance grooves and hip hop aesthetics to mainstream success.

Over the next few years, black dominance in the pop market continued. While Carrie Underwood and Chris Daughtry boasted the number one albums of the year for 2006 and 2007, respectively, they were bested for overall pop performance by Chris Brown in 2006 and Akon in 2007. Brown emerged as Billboard's number one pop artist of the year because the combination of his self-titled debut album (released while he was still in high school) and its four hit singles, gave him greater popularity overall. On "Run It!" (the album's first single, which debuted at number one), Brown's youthful innocence was bolstered by hard-edged dance beats and a guest rap by Luther Campbell (of 2 Live Crew fame). In 2007, Akon topped Brown with a hit album, *Konvicted*, and six entries on the year-end Hot 100 (many of them crossover duets). Indeed, in 2007, black artists—Beyoncé, Rihanna, Jay-Z, Akon, will.i.am, T-Pain, Snoop Dogg, and Ludacris—appeared (either solo or as part of a duet) on seven of the ten most popular hits of the year. In 2008, Chris Brown regained the pop crown with *Exclusive* and five hit singles. He was joined on the list by Lil Wayne at number two with *Tha Carter III*, which sold over 1 million copies in its first week; Rihanna at number three with *Good Girl Gone Bad* and five hit singles; and Alicia Keys at number four, with *As I Am*, the most popular album of the year.

All of these artists scored on both the Hot 100 and the Pop 100 (as did Carrie Underwood and Chris Daughtry). In addition, white artists like Fergie, Eminem, and Justin Timberlake, who were routinely referred to as r&b/hip hop acts, charted in similar ways, which made the lack of any clear differentiation between the Hot 100 and the Pop 100 even more striking. In 2006, for example, all of the top ten Hot 100 songs could be found within the top fourteen positions on the Pop 100. The first four positions on both charts in 2007 were inter-changeable and in 2008, the top two songs on both charts were the same and both were by black artists—"Low" by Flo Rida (featuring T-Pain) and "Bleeding Love" by Leona Lewis. Indeed, all of the most popular 2008 entries on the Hot 100 could be found within the upper reaches of the Pop 100. As a result, in June 2009, *Billboard* finally realized the error of its ways and pulled the plug on the Pop 100. It was clear that pop success could no longer be limited by race or genre and that the importance of hip hop aesthetics for artists of all persuasions had simply become a fact of cultural life.

> **I**n June 2009, Billboard *finally realized the error of its ways and pulled the plug on the Pop 100. It was clear that pop success could no longer be limited by race or genre and that the importance of hip hop aesthetics for artists of all persuasions had simply become a fact of cultural life.*

The Future of Music

The opening years of the new millennium were devastating for the major record companies, and it was clear that no amount of suing fans, reconfiguring labels, or cutting artists and staff would be enough to stanch their revenue hemorrhage. By 2009, according to the RIAA, U.S. recorded music sales, adjusted for inflation, had plummeted to less than half of what they were in 1999.[79] Because record companies have occupied the power center of the music business at least since the mid-1950s, the sale of prerecorded music has generally been taken as the major indicator of the health of the industry as a whole. But sales data are really only about the health of record companies. One effect of the downturn in CD sales has been to highlight other sectors of the music business as the search for new business models takes place.

For most artists, CD sales account for relatively little of their income; their main sources of revenue come from live performances and merchandise. For them, the current state of the industry has driven home the importance of touring. Accordingly, in 2006, concert revenues went through the roof. North American receipts alone hit $2.8 billion, a 35 percent increase over the previous year. The dramatic increase in revenue was perhaps not all that surprising given that some of the most lucrative tours in history—Madonna, the Rolling Stones, U2—were on the road. But it wasn't just the industry veterans who benefitted; newer acts like Rascal Flats, RBD, Brad Paisley, Tool, and the Black Eyed Peas also fared well and the major destination fes-tivals like Bonaroo, Coachella, and Austin City Limits attracted huge crowds. What was even more surprising was that, with higher ticket prices, attendance was also up some 14 percent.[80]

The worldwide concert business grossed $3.4 billion in 2006, of which $2 billion went to a single company—Live Nation (the concert arm of Clear Channel that was spun off as an independent entity. Its closest competitors, AEG Live at $543 million and CPI (part-owned by

Live Nation) at $533 million, were a distant second and third, respectively.[81] The concert business had become more concentrated than record companies had, and it was driven primarily by the larger stadium-level acts. The top ten tours took in $1.2 billion themselves; CPI's entire gross came from just three tours—the Stones, Barbra Streisand, and the Who.[82] The question for the future was whether increasing concert revenues would trickle down to the smaller independent promoters. While a number of independents improved their numbers in 2006, the fear was that, because promoters work on such small profit margins, slight shifts in the business could be cataclysmic.

The concert business declined measurably in 2007, but this was partially explained by the relative dearth of megatours that dominated 2006. The North American industry regained its footing in 2008, with an 8 percent rise in revenue, which was offset somewhat by a 2 percent decline in attendance. Many industry veterans noted that the trend of increasing revenues outpacing attendance—higher ticket prices with fewer concertgoers—did not augur well for the future. One booking agent offered this advice: "Pray, be less greedy, superserve the consumer, drop prices, create great tour packages, bundle music with ticket purchases."[83] Some artists seemed to take the advice to heart. U2 named its 2009 360° Tour after its new sound system that enabled them to play stadium shows in the round, thereby expanding the capacity of the stadium and allowing them to achieve higher grosses with lower ticket prices. Coldplay gave a free live album to everyone attending their summer 2009 North American tour. Anecdotal evidence suggested that live concerts were broadly appealing "from teens attending $10 club shows to businessmen filling $100 arena seats."[84]

The one aspect of music sales that everyone was paying attention to was digital sales because it was clear that digital sales would be the currency of the future. Forrester Research projected that digital sales would reach 50 percent of all sales by 2011, but because overall sales had declined so much, it was unlikely that such an increase would make up for the loss of physical CD sales in the forseeable future (which is to say that digital sales would become a larger piece of a smaller pie). And there would likely be some surprises in who benefitted the most from these changes. In 2007, EMI became the only major label to post a larger share of the digital market than the physical one. In contrast, every independent distributor reported a higher percentage of digital sales than physical sales. According to *Billboard*, "[i]ndies are better-positioned to do well in an online era. Their audience tends to be younger and more tech-savvy and the sheer number of indie labels and their vast back catalogs are suited to capture the Long Tail market."[85]

In the past few years, the idea of a long tail market has become one of the most salient features of what the future music business might look like. The idea derived from an article written by *Wired* editor Chris Anderson in 2004, then expanded into a book.[86] In the book, Anderson argued that the conventional music industry logic that only 10 percent of all releases are profitable is based on the scarcity of space for physical products. A bricks-and-mortar retailer like Wal-Mart, for example, has to sell about 100,000 copies of a CD to cover its overhead. Artists who can sell in the 50,000 range never even make it into the store. As a result, these are precisely the artists that the major labels have been pruning from their rosters. In a hit-driven culture, one imagines that demand drops off so sharply for anything less than a hit that there is little reason to expect it to generate any profit.

In a hit-driven culture, one imagines that demand drops off so sharply for anything less than a hit that there is little reason to expect it to generate any profit. But if one imagines a digital world in which there are no manufacturing costs to speak of, no distribution costs, and no requirements for shelf space, a rather different economic picture emerges.

But if one imagines a digital world in which there are no manufacturing costs to speak of, no distribution costs, and no requirements for shelf space, a rather different economic picture emerges.

The subscription service Rhapsody offers hundreds of thousands of tracks to its customers. As with physical retailers, there is high demand for the most popular tracks, which falls off rapidly. But at the point where physical retailers cease stocking any more CDs, demand at Rhapsody keeps going. "Not only is every one of Rhapsody's top 100,000 tracks streamed at least once each month,"says Anderson, "the same is true for its top 200,000, top 300,000, and top 400,000."[87] In the process, people discover that their taste may not be as hit-bound as they thought. This is the long tail. To give some idea of just how profitable the long tail economy can be consider that "Rhapsody streams more songs each month *beyond* its top 10,000 than it does its top 10,000."[88] The picture that emerges is that of a bifurcated industry in which the entities comprising the back end of the long tail could, in the aggregate, rival the major companies for market share. This scenario holds promise for artists at all levels of the business, from obscure blues singers to genre-defying newbies.

Just who are the entities that will manage the long tail? In its 2008 year-end round-up, *Billboard* noted that, in a digital world where touring, merchandising, branding, sponsorships, engaging social networks, and the like, have become as important as album sales, and a label deal is one of a number of options available to artists, management companies have become more central to the task of career development. They have become the hub of activity that once defined record labels. "In short," said *Billboard*, "managers may just be the new labels."[89]

It is certain that, in the near term, the major labels will keep their antennae attuned to potential blockbusters, but there is also mounting evidence that the future of the music business will be as much about niches as about hits, to use Anderson's terms. Moving forward, the major labels might be motivated to experiment with new models for developing and disseminating music. Or they might simply share the marketplace with inventive new companies that cater to independent artists on a more loosely defined, revenue-sharing basis. Whatever the outcome, one thing is sure: It will be a long tail future with more music available than we ever dreamed possible.

<hr>

LEARN MORE
Chapter Questions
on MyMusicKit

As the new millennium dawned, the music industry was hit by a double whammy: Napster and its offspring ushered in an era of unauthorized digital music file swapping, and the events of 9/11 knocked the bottom out of the whole economy. While no one questioned that the future of music would be digital, downloadable, and customized for individual taste, the music industry remained obsessed with copyright protection and centralized control at the expense of user-friendly services. As a result, the major labels tended to lag far behind the third-party services they should have been trying to emulate rather than eliminate. Artists may have been caught in the middle on the copyright question, but record companies were clearly in it for themselves, going after revenues that most often accrued to the labels either as royalties or as artist payback of record-company advances. The majors consolidated their control over a global market, all but eliminated the public domain, and narrowed fair use almost to extinction. Artists themselves continued to derive their income more from touring and merchandising.

The tragedy of 9/11 and subsequent escalation of military engagement brought the more conservative elements of country music to the fore, as the push for a more patriotic popular culture captured the attention of the mainstream audience. The more liberal rock establishment seemed ambivalent in its political responses, which ranged from outright protest to serious self-censorship. With the passage of time, however, the war in Iraq seemed to spiral out of control, transforming public opinion in the process. As the Bush administration sank to its lowest approval ratings ever, protest music resurfaced across genres and the war became the pivotal issue in electing the country's first African American president in 2008.

The drive to return to business as usual in the post-9/11 period prompted a return to the familiar sounds of guitar-based rock and the introspection of earnest singer-songwriters. Amidst all this activity was the continuing momentum of a significant paradigm shift toward hip hop as the foundational template for U.S. popular music. What remained unclear, however, was how all these developments would proceed into the future. The combination of more powerful computers, broadband connectivity, inexpensive storage capacity, and democratic avenues of viral communication held out the possibility that thousands of artists selling a few thousand songs each could, in the aggregate, rival the market for hits. In such a future, the prospects for a vibrant musical culture seem well within reach.

Notes

INTRODUCTION

1. It should be noted that this discussion concerns cultural development as it occurred in European societies. Of course, any number of other societies developed according to different cultural patterns, but the cultural forms and values of the "New World" were informed by those of the European colonial powers; thus, an understanding of cultural development in European societies is relevant to understanding the tensions and complexities of contemporary U.S. culture.

2. This analysis was developed most forcefully by the members of the Frankfurt School, a group of Jewish intellectuals in Germany who were rightly disturbed by Hitler's effective use of the mass media in advancing the cause of fascism in the 1930s and 1940s.

3. Oscar Handlin, "Comments on Mass and Popular Culture," in *Culture for the Millions? Mass Media in Modern Society*, ed. Norman Jacobs (Princeton, N.J.: D. Van Nostrand, 1959), 66.

4. Stuart Hall and Paddy Whannel, *The Popular Arts* (New York: Pantheon Books, 1965), 67–68.

5. Carl Belz, *The Story of Rock*, 2d ed. (New York: Harper Colophon, 1971), 1.

6. Simon Frith, *Sound Effects: Youth, Leisure and the Politics of Rock 'n' Roll* (New York: Pantheon Books, 1981), 54.

7. Charlie Gillett, *The Sound of the City: The Rise of Rock and Roll* (New York: Outerbridge and Dienstfrey, 1970), i.

8. Ibid.

9. Frith, *Sound Effects*, 203.

10. Peter Wicke, *Rock Music: Culture, Aesthetics and Sociology* (Cambridge, Eng.: Cambridge University Press, 1990), 12.

11. Richard Middleton, "Reading Popular Music." Unit 16 of Open University course U203 *Popular Culture*. Milton-Keynes: The Open University, 1981, p. 17.

12. Charles Hamm, *Yesterdays: Popular Song in America* (New York: W. W. Norton, 1983), 358.

13. H. F. Mooney, "Popular Music Since the 1920s: The Significance of Shifting Taste," in *The Age of Rock*, ed. Jonathan Eisen (New York: Vintage Books, 1969), 10, 11.

14. Ibid.

15. Ibid., 10.

16. Christopher Small, *Music of the Common Tongue: Survival and Celebration in Afro-American Music* (New York: Riverrun Press, 1987), 25.

17. Iain Chambers, *Urban Rhythms: Popular Music and Popular Culture* (New York: Macmillan, 1985), 10.

18. Wicke, *Rock Music*, 16–17.

19. The use of the terms *race* and *hillbilly* as marketing categories for music was initiated by producer Ralph Peer. The origin of the terms is explained in detail in the next chapter.

20. David Brackett, "The Politics and Practice of 'Crossover' in American Popular Music, 1963 to 1965." *The Musical Quarterly* (Winter, 1994): 777.

21. Arnold Shaw, *Honkers and Shouters: The Golden Years of Rhythm and Blues* (New York: Collier Books, 1978), 524.

22. "Billboard Adopts 'R&B' As New Name for 2 Charts." *Billboard*, 27 October 1990, 35.

23. Ibid., 6.

24. See Arnold Shaw, *The Rockin' '50s* (New York: Hawthorne Books, 1974), 145.

25. Shaw, *Honkers and Shouters*, 215.

26. Ben Fong-Torres, "The Rolling Stone Interview: Ray Charles," *Rolling Stone*, 18 January 1973, 18.

27. Nick Tosches, *Country: Living Legends and Dying Metaphors in America's Biggest Music* (New York: Charles Scribner's Sons, 1985), 55.

28. Shaw, *Honkers and Shouters*, 497.

29. "To Censor Popular Songs." *Literary Digest* (24 May 1913): 1181.

30. Ibid.

CHAPTER 1

1. Cited in Dale Cockrell, *Demons of Disorder: Early Blackface Minstrels and Their World* (New York: Cambridge University Press, 1997), 45.

2. Ibid., 47.

3. Charles Hamm, *Yesterdays: Popular Song in America* (New York: W. W. Norton, 1983), 131.

4. Eric Lott, "Love and Theft: The Racial Unconscious of Blackface Minstrelsy." *Representations* (Summer 1992): 28.

5. Hamm, *Yesterdays*, 214.

6. Russell Sanjek, *American Popular Music and Its Business: The First Four Hundred Years, Volume II from 1790 to 1909* (New York: Oxford University Press, 1988), 339.

7. Hamm, *Yesterdays*, 288.

8. Sanjek, *American Popular Music, II*, 377. Sanjek further states: "The production of pianos and player pianos reached its all-time high in 1899, when more than 365,000 were manufactured, and it continued to average 300,000 annually until just after World War I" (p. 296).

9. Hamm, *Yesterdays*, 285. Ian Whitcomb puts the figure at 10,000,000 copies over a twenty-year period. See Ian Whitcomb, *After the Ball: Popular Music from Rag to Rock* (Baltimore: Penguin Books, 1974), 4.

10. Sanjek, *American Popular Music, II*, 365.

11. It is interesting to note that at this point, the term *gramophone* was dropped from the language in the United

States (but not in Europe), and *phonograph* became the generic term for all record players.

12. As if to complement the gentility of the series, Johnson then introduced the Victrola, the first console record player, which featured an enclosed turntable, tone arm, and playback horn, and a price tag of $200.

13. Whitcomb, *After the Ball,* 98–99.

14. C. A. Schicke, *Revolution in Sound: A Biography of the Recording Industry* (Boston: Little, Brown and Co., 1974), 67–68.

15. Hamm, *Yesterdays,* 290.

16. Ibid., 325.

17. "The Birth of Our Popular Songs." *Literary Digest* (7 October 1916): 892.

18. *Irving Berlin's America,* PBS documentary produced by Joann G. Young, 1986.

19. Hamm, *Yesterdays,* 340.

20. Gunther Schuller, *Early Jazz: Its Roots and Musical Development* (New York: Oxford University Press, 1968), 24.

21. Whitcomb, *After the Ball,* 26.

22. Joplin never recorded. The recordings attributed to him were actually made from piano rolls he cut. Given the popularity of player pianos at the beginning of the twentieth century, piano rolls became a vehicle for introducing the music of some black artists to mainstream listeners. Because there are no recordings of Joplin himself, however, there remains no definitive statement as to the tempo at which he played his compositions.

23. Gilbert Seldes, *The Seven Lively Arts* (1924; reprint New York: A. S. Barnes, 1957), 71.

24. Hamm, *Yesterdays,* 321.

25. Schuller, *Early Jazz,* 38.

26. Leroi Jones [Amiri Baraka], *Blues People* (New York: William Morrow, 1963), 69.

27. Samuel Charters, *The Country Blues.* (New York: Rinehart and Company, 1959), pp. 34–35.

28. Ibid., 148.

29. William Barlow, "Cashing In," in *Split Image: African Americans in the Mass Media,* 2d ed., ed. Jannette L. Dates and William Barlow (Washington, D.C.: Howard University Press, 1993), 31.

30. Robert Palmer, *Deep Blues* (New York: Viking Press, 1981), 100.

31. Elijah Wald, *Escaping the Delta: Robert Johnson and the Invention of the Blues* (New York: Amistad, 2004), 11–20.

32. A number of black jazz musicians, including New Orleans trumpeter Freddie Keppard, were asked to record by recording companies. They declined because they feared that if recorded, their styles could be studied and stolen. As the innovators of jazz styles, African American artists apparently felt that they had more to lose than to gain by engaging with the new technology.

33. Russell Sanjek, *American Popular Music and Its Business: The First Four Hundred Years, Volume III from 1900 to 1984* (New York: Oxford University Press, 1988), 23.

34. John Storm Roberts, *The Latin Tinge: The Impact of Latin American Music on the United States* (New York: Oxford University Press, 1979).

35. Eileen Southern, *The Music of Black Americans: A History* (New York: W. W. Norton, 1971), 347–348.

36. Ruth Glasser, *My Music Is My Flag: Puerto Rican Musicians and Their New York Communities, 1917–1940* (Los Angeles: University of California Press, 1995), 57

37. Southern, *The Music of Black Americans,* 353.

38. Gleason L. Archer, *History of Radio to 1926* (New York: American Historical Society, 1938), 178.

39. Ibid., 112.

40. Lee de Forest, *Father of Radio* (Chicago: Wilcox and Follett, 1950), 442–443.

41. Sanjek, *American Popular Music, III,* 81.

42. Ibid, 166.

43. Erik Barnouw, *The Golden Web: A History of Broadcasting in the United States, 1933–1953* (New York: Oxford University Press, 1968), 6.

44. Donald Clarke, ed., *The Penguin Encyclopedia of Popular Music* (New York: Viking, 1989), 301.

45. Sanjek, *American Popular Music, III,* 155.

46. Ana M. Lopez, "Are All Latins from Manhattan: Hollywood, Ethnography, and Cultural Colonialism," in *Film and Nationalism*, ed. Alan Williams (Philadelphia: Rutgers University Press, 2002), 198.

47. Gustavo Pérez Firmat, "Latunes: An Introduction." *Latin American Research Review,* December 2008): 180–181.

48. Roberts, *The Latin Tinge,* 50.

49. Firmat, "Latunes," 183.

50. Sanjek, *American Popular Music, III,* 110–111.

CHAPTER 2

1. Charles Hamm, *Yesterdays: Popular Song in America* (New York: W. W. Norton, 1983), 379.

2. Elijah Wald, *How the Beatles Destroyed Rock 'n' Roll: An Alternative History of American Popular Music* (New York: Oxford University Press, 2009), 89.

3. William Barlow, "Cashing In," in *Split Image: African Americans in the Mass Media,* 2d ed., ed. Jannette L. Dates and William Barlow (Washington, D.C.: Howard University Press, 1993), 43.

4. Samuel Charters, *The Country Blues* (New York: Rinehart and Company, 1959), 34.

5. Gunther Schuller, *Early Jazz: Its Roots and Musical Development* (New York: Oxford University Press, 1968), 37.

6. Charters, *The Country Blues,* 27.

7. Schuller, *Early Jazz,* 36.

8. Ingrid Monson, "Jazz Chronological Overview," in African American Music: An Introduction, ed. Mellonee V. Burnim and Portia K. Maultsby (New York: Routlegde, 2006), 147.

9. Wald, *How the Beatles Destroyed Rock 'n' Roll,* 28.

10. Bill C. Malone, *Country Music U.S.A.: Revised Edition* (Austin: University of Texas Press, 1985), 4.

11. Christopher Small, *Music of the Common Tongue: Survival and Celebration in Afro-American Music* (New York: Riverrun Press, 1987), 36.

12. Leroi Jones [Amiri Baraka], *Blues People* (New York: William Morrow, 1963), 70.

13. Malone, *Country Music U.S.A.*, 24.

14. John W. Work, *American Negro Songs* (New York: Crown Publishers, 1960), 34.

15. While Rodgers yodeled on "Sleep, Baby, Sleep" in 1927, he was not the first to do so on record. According to Nick Tosches, that honor probably goes to Riley Puckett, the blind guitarist of the Skillet Lickers, who yodeled three years earlier on the group's Columbia recording "Rock All Our Babies to Sleep." The elusive Emmett Miller may have beat them all to yodeling, but he did not record one until 1925, on "Lovesick Blues." See Nick Tosches, *Country: Living Legends and Dying Metaphors in America's Biggest Music* (New York: Charles Scribner's Sons, 1985), 110–111.

16. Tosches, *Country*, 194.

17. Elijah Wald, *Escaping the Delta: Robert Johnson and the Invention of the Blues* (New York: Amistad, 2004), 28.

18. Jones [Baraka], *Blues People*, 105.

19. Ibid., 100.

20. Many observers, myself included, have written disparagingly about the term *race music*. It is likely, however, that Peer simply took his cue from the African American newspapers in which his company advertised—the *Chicago Defender, the Pittsburgh Courier*—which themselves referred to the African American community as "the race."

21. Jones [Baraka], *Blues People*, 99.

22. Ibid., 89.

23. Charters, *The Country Blues*, 46.

24. Howard W. Odum and Guy B. Johnson, *Negro Workaday Songs* (Chapel Hill: University of North Carolina Press, 1926), 38.

25. Eileen Southern, *The Music of Black Americans: A History* (New York: W. W. Norton, 1971), 398.

26. Charters, *The Country Blues*, 67.

27. Robert Palmer, "Robert Johnson: The Complete Recordings," *Rolling Stone*, 18 October 1990. http://www.rollingstone.com/reviews/album/117645/review/6067403/thecompleterecordings

28. Southern, *The Music of Black Americans*, 386–387.

29. Malone, *Country Music U.S.A.*, 39.

30. Ibid., 40.

31. Ibid., 42.

32. One study conducted by Anne and Norm Cohen concluded that between 1922 and 1924, only 2 percent of country performers' repertoires were of British origin. See Malone, *Country Music U.S.A.*, 44.

33. Ibid., 52.

34. Wald, *Escaping the Delta*, 47–53.

35. Nelson George, *The Death of Rhythm & Blues* (New York: Pantheon Books, 1988), 11.

36. Ibid.

37. Malone, *Country Music U.S.A.*, 152.

38. John Hammond, *On Record* (New York: Penguin Books, 1981), 163.

CHAPTER 3

1. Ian Whitcomb, *After the Ball: Pop Music from Rag to Rock* (Baltimore, MD: Penguin Books, 1974), 199.

2. Russell Sanjek, *American Popular Music and Its Business: The First Four Hundred Years, Volume III from 1900 to 1984* (New York: Oxford University Press, 1988), 176. The dramatic increase of ASCAP's revenues from 1932 to 1937 came about when eleven music publishing houses controlled by Warner Brothers and representing 20 to 40 percent of the music played on the radio returned to ASCAP's fold. Dissatisfied with their share of publishing revenues, they had decided to collect their own royalties independently and had left ASCAP in 1935. They returned August 1936, freeing up some 36,000 songs—including works by George Gershwin and Jerome Kern—that had been out of circulation since January of that year.

3. Nat Shapiro, *Popular Music: An Annotated Index of American Popular Songs: Volume 2, 1940–1949* (New York: Adrian Press, 1965), 6.

4. "ASCAP Defied," *Business Week,* 16 November 1940, 50.

5. Minna Lederman, "Music and Monopoly," *The Nation,* 28 December 1940, 656.

6. Bill C. Malone, *Country Music U.S.A.*, rev. ed. (Austin: University of Texas Press, 1985), 179.

7. Arnold Passman, *The Deejays* (New York: Macmillan, 1971), 64.

8. Sanjek, *American Popular Music, III*, 128.

9. D. Dexter, "1935–1945, Disk Jockey: Origin of the Species," *Billboard*, 27 December 1969, 58.

10. According to the terms of the 1909 Copyright Act, only the underlying composition of a recording could be copyrighted; the recording itself could not. As a result, only writers and publishers received royalties from the broadcast of recorded music.

11. Passman, *The Deejays*, 80. Whiteman and RCA Victor had initiated the suit that led to the lower court decision.

12. Using Ralph Peer's international business connections, the companies had also attempted to record U.S. pop in Latin America, but the attempt failed. In Cuba, the language barrier prevented English-language recordings of broadcast quality. In Mexico, the progressive Mexican musicians' union refused to participate in the strikebreaking strategy.

13. Arnold Shaw, *Honkers and Shouters: The Golden Years of Rhythm and Blues* (New York: Collier Books, 1978), 124.

14. Charlie Gillett, *The Sound of the City: The Rise of Rock and Roll* (New York: Outerbridge and Dienstfrey, 1970), 3.

15. Unlike Sinatra, many Italian American performers anglicized their names. Frankie Lane began life as Frank Paul LoVecchio, Vic Damone as Vito Rocco Farinola, Tony Bennett

as Anthony Dominic Benedetto, and Dean Martin as Dino Crocetti.

16. Whitcomb, *After the Ball,* 200.

17. Gillett, *The Sound of the City,* 9.

18. Leroi Jones [Amiri Baraka], *Blues People* (New York: William Morrow, 1963), 168. Rhythm and blues, of course, developed in the blues tradition of African retentions superimposed on a European melodic and harmonic structure. For a more detailed discussion, see Portia K. Maultsby, "Africanisms in African American Popular Music," in *Africanisms in American Culture,* ed. Joseph E. Holloway (Bloomington: Indiana University Press, 1990); Reebee Garofalo, "Crossing Over, 1939–1992," in *Split Image: African-Americans in the Mass Media,* 2d ed., ed. Jannette L. Dates and William Barlow (Washington, D.C.: Howard University Press, 1993).

19. George Lipsitz, *Class and Culture in Cold War America: "A Rainbow at Midnight"* (South Hadley, MA: J. F. Bergin, 1982), 195–196.

20. Nelson George, *The Death of Rhythm & Blues* (New York: Pantheon Books, 1988), 10.

21. Jones [Baraka], *Blues People,* 160.

22. George, *The Death of Rhythm & Blues,* 9.

23. Jones [Baraka], *Blues People,* 171.

24. Shaw, *Honkers and Shouters,* 278–279.

25. Ibid., 289.

26. Donald Clarke, *The Penguin Encyclopedia of Popular Music* (New York: Penguin Books, 1989), 1217.

27. Edward Zwick, "An Interview with the Father of Hi-Fi: Dr. Peter Goldmark," *Rolling Stone,* 27 September 1973, 44–45.

28. Ibid., 44.

29. Unable to bend like the AM signal, FM waves move in a straight line. Therefore, FM transmission suffers from a line-of-sight problem: irregular topography and the curvature of the Earth prevent transmission over long distances. However, the quality of the signal in terms of frequency response and suppression of interference is far superior to AM transmission.

30. Sanjek, *American Popular Music, III,* 173.

31. *That Rhythm, Those Blues,* PBS documentary produced by George T. Nierenberg, 1988.

32. ABC *20/20,* segment on rap produced by Danny Schechter, 1981.

33. George, *The Death of Rhythm & Blues,* 41.

34. Ibid.

35. Shaw, *Honkers and Shouters,* 509.

36. Among the popular black deejays in the South were "Jockey Jack" Gibson (Atlanta); "Professor Bop" (Shreveport); Larry McKinley and Vernon Winslow (New Orleans); "Sugar Daddy" (Birmingham); "Spider" Burks (St. Louis); Bruce Miller (Winston-Salem); and Nat D. Williams, "Bugs" Scruggs, Larry Dean, and George White (Memphis). Southern white r&b deejays included Zenas "Daddy" Sears (Atlanta). Bob "Wolfman Jack" Smith (Shreveport). Ken Elliott and Clarence "Poppa Stoppa" Hammon (New Orleans). Bill Gordon and Dewey Phillips (Memphis), and Gene Nobles and John Richbourgh (Nashville). A number of southern r&b recording artists—Elmore James, Rufus Thomas, Sonny Boy Williamson, Howlin' Wolf,

Muddy Waters, and B. B. King, among others—had careers as deejays before they became performers. B. B. King acquired his initials from his radio moniker, "the Beale Street Blues Boy."

37. Passman, *The Deejays,* 175.

38. George, *The Death of Rhythm & Blues,* 41.

39. Passman, *The Deejays,* 185.

40. Ibid., 176.

41. Steve Chapple and Reebee Garofalo, *Rock 'n' Roll Is Here to Pay: The History and Politics of the Music Industry* (Chicago: Nelson-Hall, 1977), 56.

CHAPTER 4

1. Charlie Gillett, *The Sound of the City: The Rise of Rock and Roll* (New York: Outerbridge and Dienstfrey, 1970), 1.

2. Nick Tosches, *Country: Living Legends and Dying Metaphors in America's Biggest Music* (New York: Charles Scribner's Sons, 1985), 32.

3. Jim Dawson and Steve Propes, *What Was the First Rock 'n' Roll Record?* (Boston: Faber and Faber, 1992), xvi–xvii.

4. Tosches, *Country,* 28.

5. Robert Palmer, "The Fifties," *Rolling Stone,* 19 April 1990, 48.

6. George Lipsitz, *Class and Culture in Cold War America* (South Hadley, MA: J. F. Bergin, 1982), 214.

7. Steve Perry, "Ain't No Mountain High Enough: The Politics of Crossover," in *Facing the Music,* ed. Simon Frith (New York: Pantheon Books, 1988), 67–68.

8. Greil Marcus, *Mystery Train: Images of America in Rock 'n' Roll* (New York: Dutton, 1975), 166.

9. In *San Antonio Rose: The Life and Music of Bob Wills* (Urbana: University of Illinois Press, 1976), Charles R. Townshend suggests that Walker and his friend Charlie Christian (who was to electric jazz guitar what Walker was to electric blues) were themselves influenced by white western-swing electric guitarists Bob Dunn, who played for Milton Brown and His Musical Brownies, and Leon McAuliffe, a steel guitarist for Bob Wills and His Texas Playboys. In "The Church of the Sonic Guitar," *South Atlantic Quarterly* 90, no. 4 (Fall 1991), Robert Palmer argues that Walker's style is derived from Blind Lemon Jefferson and jazz licks he learned from Christian.

10. Palmer, "The Church of the Sonic Guitar," 652.

11. John Storm Roberts, *The Latin Tinge: The Impact of Latin American Music on the United States* (Tivoli, N.Y.: Original Music, 1985), 136.

12. Gillett, *The Sound of the City,* 42.

13. For a more detailed discussion of the concentration of the music industry during this period, see Richard A. Peterson and David C. Berger, "Cycles in Symbol Production: The Case of Popular Music," *American Sociological Review* (April 1975), 158–173.

14. Erik Barnouw, *The Golden Web: A History of Broadcasting in the United States, 1933–1953* (New York: Oxford University Press, 1968), 221.

15. Arnold Shaw, *The Rockin' '50s* (New York: Hawthorne Books, 1974), 66.

16. Ibid., 235.

17. Richard A. Peterson, "Why 1955? Explaining the Advent of Rock Music," *Popular Music* (January 1990): 113.

18. Langdon Winner, "The Sound of New Orleans," in *The Rolling Stone Illustrated History of Rock 'n' Roll,* ed. Jim Miller (New York: Rolling Stone Press, 1976), 42.

19. John Broven, *Rhythm and Blues in New Orleans* (Gretna, LA: Pelican Publishing Co., 1988), 64.

20. Winner, "The Sound of New Orleans," 46.

21. Arnold Shaw, *Honkers and Shouters: The Golden Years of Rhythm and Blues* (New York: Collier Books, 1978), 190.

22. Shaw, *The Rockin' '50s,* 210.

23. Ibid. Since then, Richard has tried to manage the tension between his ministry and his music career. Invariably, his irrepressible rock 'n' roll spirit shows through.

24. Johnny Otis, as quoted in Steve Chapple and Reebee Garofalo, *Rock 'n' Roll Is Here to Pay: The History and Politics of the Music Industry* (Chicago: Nelson-Hall, 1977), 233.

25. Johnny Ace was the first major rock 'n' roll fatality. He died playing with a loaded gun on tour on Christmas day in 1954, just before "Pledging My Love" hit the pop charts.

26. Preston Love, introduction to *Listen to the Lambs,* by Johnny Otis (New York: W. W. Norton, 1968), xxxv–xxxix.

27. Rubén Guevara, "The View from the Sixth Street Bridge: The History of Chicano Rock," in Dave Marsh, ed., *The First Rock & Roll Confidential Report* (New York: Pantheon, 1985), 116.

28. Michael Lydon, *Rock Folk: Portraits from the Rock 'n' Roll Pantheon* (New York: Dell, 1968), 10.

29. Gillett, *The Sound of the City,* 96–97.

30. Nelson George, *The Death of Rhythm and Blues* (New York: Pantheon Books, 1988), 68.

31. Lydon, *Rock Folk,* 20.

32. John W. Rumble, "Roots of Rock 'n' Roll: Henry Glover at King Records," *Country Music Journal* (Vol. 14, No. 2, 1992): 38.

33. Robey also bought Duke Records from founder James Mattis, who was a deejay for WDIA in Memphis, thus forming the Duke/Peacock complex.

34. Shaw, *Honkers and Shouters,* 479.

35. Peter Guralnick, *Sweet Soul Music: Rhythm and Blues and the Southern Dream of Freedom* (New York: Harper and Row, 1986), 26.

36. Ray Charles and David Ritz, *Brother Ray: Ray Charles' Own Story* (New York: DaCapo Press, 1992), 149.

37. Guralnick, *Sweet Soul Music,* 50.

38. Ibid., 66.

39. Shaw, *Honkers and Shouters,* 444.

40. Wilson suffered a heart attack on stage in 1975 and remained in a coma until he died in 1984.

41. Tony Heilbut, *The Gospel Sound: Good News and Bad Times* (New York: Simon and Schuster, 1971), 76.

42. Among the less memorable answer songs were the Midnighters' "Annie's Aunt Fanny," the El Dorados' "Annie's Answer," Buddy Holly's "Midnight Shift," and the Midnights' (not to be confused with the Midnighters) "Annie Pulled a Humbug."

43. Greil Marcus, "Is This the Woman Who Invented Rock & Roll? The Deborah Chessler Story," *Rolling Stone,* 24 June 1993, 41.

44. Ibid., 43.

45. Doo wop groups with predominantly Italian American membership included the Mello-Kings ("Tonight, Tonight," 1957), the Elegants ("Little Star," 1958), the Mystics ("Hushabye," 1959), and the Capris ("There's a Moon Out Tonight," 1961) and, at the periphery of the style, the Royal Teens ("Short Shorts," 1958) and the Regents ("Barbara Ann," 1961).

46. Buck Ram added Zola Taylor to the Platters largely for show. Both the Skyliners ("Since I Don't Have You," 1959) and the Cleftones ("Heart and Soul," 1961) also performed with female vocalists who had no readily distinguishable roles.

47. Among the groups that could still be associated somewhat with the style were the Duprees ("You Belong to Me," 1962), the Tymes ("So Much in Love" and "Wonderful, Wonderful," 1963), the Vogues ("Five O'Clock World," 1965), and the Fortunes ("You've Got Your Troubles," 1965).

48. Robert Palmer, *Baby That Was Rock and Roll* (New York: Harvest/HBJ, 1978), 19.

49. Steven Loza, *Barrio Rhythms: Mexican American Music in Los Angeles* (Chicago: University of Illinois Press, 1993), 82.

50. Peter Guralnick, *Feel Like Going Home: Portraits in Blues and Rock 'n' Roll* (New York: E. P. Dutton, 1971), 140.

51. Gillett, *The Sound of the City,* 38.

52. Ibid., 30.

53. Shaw, *Honkers and Shouters,* 64.

54. *Blackboard Jungle* was the first Hollywood film to include rock 'n' roll in its soundtrack, which might not have happened without the advocacy of its Tin Pan Alley composers. *Rebel Without a Cause,* starring James Dean and released that same year, and *The Wild One,* released in 1954 with Marlon Brando in the lead role, would have been equally obvious choices for rock 'n' roll soundtracks, but both used big-band soundtracks, which tended to contradict their themes of youth rebellion.

55. Guralnick, *Feel Like Going Home,* 140.

56. Peter Guralnick, *The Listener's Guide to the Blues* (New York: Facts on File, 1982), 80.

57. Guralnick, *Feel Like Going Home,* 149–150.

58. Lydon, *Rock Folk,* 32.

59. Gillett, *The Sound of the City,* 36.

60. Peter Guralnick, "Elvis Presley," in *The Rolling Stone Illustrated History of Rock 'n' Roll,* ed. Jim Miller (New York: Rolling Stone Press, 1976), 35.

61. Guralnick, *Feel Like Going Home,* 142.

62. Guralnick, "Elvis Presley," 35.

63. Ibid., 36.

64. Ibid., 36, 38.

65. Presley died on 16 August 1977, in Memphis, a bloated, drugged-out caricature of his former self.

66. Dawson and Propes, *What Was the First Rock 'n' Roll Record?,* 192.

67. Ibid.

68. Tosches, *Country,* 82.

69. Ibid., 95.

70. Ibid.

71. Ted Fox, *Showtime at the Apollo* (New York: Holt, Rinehart and Winston, 1983), 207.

72. For an excellent discussion of these unsung female rockabillies, see David Sanjek, "Can a Fujiyama Mama Be the Female Elvis? The Wild Wild Women of Rockabilly," in *Sexing the Groove,* ed. Shiela Whitely (New York: Routledge, 1996).

73. *Rock and Roll: The Early Days,* video documentary produced by Patrick Montgomery, 1985.

CHAPTER 5

1. For a more detailed analysis of this, see Steve Chapple and Reebee Garofalo, *Rock 'n' Roll Is Here to Pay: The History and Politics of the Music Industry* (Chicago: Nelson-Hall, 1977), 300–304; and Peter Wicke, *Rock Music: Culture, Aesthetics and Sociology* (New York: Cambridge University Press, 1990), 30–34.

2. Charlie Gillett, *The Sound of the City: The Rise of Rock and Roll* (New York: Outerbridge and Dienstfrey, 1970), 360.

3. Russell Sanjek, "The War on Rock," *Downbeat Music '72 Yearbook* (Chicago: Maher Publications, 1972), 16–19, 62–66.

4. Mitch Miller, "June, Moon, Swoon and Ko Ko Mo," *New York Times,* 24 April 1955, p. 78.

5. This situation was complicated when Frank Sinatra charged Miller with trying to foist BMI material on him while he was still with Columbia in 1956. In response, Miller produced statistics that disproved Sinatra's allegation.

6. Just as Columbia did through its subsidiary OKeh, Victor maintained a presence in the r&b market through its Groove subsidiary, founded in 1953. One memorable Groove recording that hit rock 'n' roll pay dirt was the eerie "Love Is Strange" (1957) by Mickey and Sylvia. Mickey was Mickey "Guitar" Baker, an experienced session guitarist; Sylvia was Sylvia Robinson, who formed Sugar Hill Records, the first rap label of note, in the late 1970s.

7. Gillett, *The Sound of the City,* 74.

8. For an interesting listing of pop/r&b covers, including label and release date, see Philip Ennis, *The Seventh Stream: The Emergence of Rock 'n' Roll in American Popular Music* (Hanover, N.H.: Wesleyan University Press/University Press of New England, 1992), 223–226.

9. Dot achieved the status of a major when it was purchased by ABC-Paramount in 1957.

10. Gillett, *The Sound of the City,* 76.

11. Chapple and Garofalo, *Rock 'n' Roll Is Here to Pay,* 49–52; 246–248.

12. Gillett, *The Sound of the City,* 127.

13. Ed Ward, Geoffrey Stokes, and Ken Tucker, *Rock of Ages: The Rolling Stone History of Rock & Roll* (New York: Rolling Stone Press, 1986), 166.

14. Gillett, *The Sound of the City,* 127.

15. Russell Sanjek, *American Popular Music and Its Business: The First Four Hundred Years, Volume III from 1900 to 1984* (New York: Oxford University Press, 1988), 444.

16. Arnold Shaw, *The Rockin' '50s* (New York: Hawthorne Books, 1974), 176.

17. Henry Schipper, "Dick Clark," *Rolling Stone,* 19 April 1990, p. 70.

18. Ibid.

19. Linda Martin and Kerry Segrave, *Anti-Rock: The Opposition to Rock 'n' Roll* (New York: DeCapo Press, 1993), 24–25.

20. Shaw, *The Rockin' '50s,* 218–219.

21. Shaw, *The Rockin' '50s,* 267.

22. Gillett, *The Sound of the City,* 360.

23. Sanjek, "The War on Rock," 18.

24. Ibid., 19.

25. Ibid., 62.

26. Ibid.

27. Trent Hill, "The Enemy Within: Censorship in Rock Music in the 1950s," *South Atlantic Quarterly* (Fall 1991), 677.

28. Chapple and Garofalo, *Rock 'n' Roll Is Here to Pay,* 52.

29. Greg Shaw, "Instrumental Groups," in *The Rolling Stone Illustrated History of Rock & Roll,* ed. Jim Miller (New York: Rolling Stone Press, 1976), 108.

30. Arnold Shaw, *Black Popular Music in America* (New York: Schirmer Books, 1986), 207.

31. Gillett, *The Sound of the City,* 218.

CHAPTER 6

1. Bernice Johnson Reagon, "Songs That Moved the Movement," *Civil Rights Quarterly* (Summer 1983), 27-35.

2. At the time, mass culture was considered to be a sign of capitalism at its worst. Thus, it was viewed as an irredeemably debased culture, produced only for profit, with no possibility for resistance or opposition, rather than as an arena for cultural struggle. By the end of the decade, politically minded people had begun to rethink this position.

3. Nelson George, *The Death of Rhythm & Blues* (New York: Pantheon Books, 1988), 69.

4. *Hail! Hail! Rock 'n' Roll,* film documentary, directed by Taylor Hackford, 1987.

5. David Hinckley, Liner Notes, *Phil Spector Back to Mono (1958–1969),* Phil Spector Records, 7118-2.

6. Tom Wolfe, "The First Tycoon of Teen," *The Kandy-Kolored Tangerine-Flake Streamline Baby* (New York: Farrar, Straus, and Giroux, 1965), 69.

7. Love has gone on to become an accomplished actress, who is perhaps best known for her role as Danny Glover's wife in the *Lethal Weapon* films.

8. Michael Lydon, "Smokey Robinson," *Rolling Stone,* 28 September 1968, 21.

9. Gerri Hersey, *Nowhere to Run: The Story of Soul Music* (New York: Penguin Books, 1984), 190.

10. Stephen Thomas Erlewine, "Review" (*Bringing It All Back Home*). All Music Guide. http://www.allmusic.com/cg/amg.dll?p=amg&sql=10:hifqxqt5ld0e.

11. George, *The Death of Rhythm & Blues,* 85.

12. Lester Bangs, "The British Invasion," in *The Rolling Stone Illustrated History of Rock 'n' Roll,* ed. Jim Miller (New York: Random House, 1976), 164.

13. Steve Chapple and Reebee Garofalo, *Rock 'n' Roll Is Here to Pay: The History and Politics of the Music Industry* (Chicago: Nelson-Hall, 1977), 70.

14. These two shows, currently available on a single home video as *Born to Rock* (UPA Productions of America, 1982), also included African American artists such as Chuck Berry, Bo Diddley, Ray Charles, James Brown, the Ronettes, and Ike and Tina Turner.

15. Hersey, *Nowhere to Run,* 185.

16. Burdon went on to front the African American ensemble War in the late 1960s, an association that lasted through the release of the painfully titled LP *Black Man's Burdon.* The group then left Burdon, going on to record fifteen hit albums of its own.

17. Anthony Scaduto, *Bob Dylan* (New York: Signet Books, 1973), 203–204.

18. Although it is not hard to imagine that they took this occasion to toke up, it seems quite unlikely that they had not encountered the mind-altering substance in Hamburg, where they flirted with the German art school scene through the influence of Stuart Sutcliffe's girlfriend Astrid Kirchherr.

19. Scaduto, *Bob Dylan,* 204.

20. Ibid.

21. Lillian Roxon, *Lillian Roxon's Rock Encyclopedia* (New York: Grosset and Dunlap, 1971), 78.

22. Ibid., 187.

23. After Vietnam, Sadler worked as a mercenary, hiring himself out in more than half a dozen battles around the world. In September 1988, he took a bullet in the head in Guatemala City.

24. Todd Gitlin, *The Sixties: Years of Hope, Days of Rage* (New York: Bantam Books, 1993).

25. George, *The Death of Rhythm & Blues,* 86.

26. Jim Delahunt, "Whatever Success I Had Was Through the Help of the Good Lord," *Rolling Stone,* 20 January 1968, 13.

27. Peter Guralnick, *Sweet Soul Music: Rhythm and Blues and the Southern Dream of Freedom* (New York: Harper and Row, 1986), 169.

28. Ibid., 332.

29. Hettie Jones, *Big Star, Fallin' Mama* (New York: Viking Press, 1974), 41. The term *Rap* in Jones's quote refers to H. Rap Brown, the militant black leader, whose poetic, fiery speeches may well have been one of rap music's formative influences.

30. Robert Palmer, "James Brown," in *The Rolling Stone Illustrated History of Rock & Roll,* ed. Jim Miller (New York: Rolling Stone Press, 1976), 136.

31. For a more developed discussion of this comparison, see Deborah Pacini Hernandez, *Oye Como Va!: Hybridity and Identity in Latino Popular Music* (Philadelphia: Temple University Press, 2010).

32. Cited in Juan Flores, *From Bomba to Hip-Hop: Puerto Rican Culture and Latino Identity* (New York: Columbia University press, 2000), 82.

33. John Storm Roberts, *The Latin Tinge: The Impact of Latin American Music on the United States* (Tivoli, NY: Original Music, 1979), 167.

34. Flores, *From Bomba to Hip-Hop,* 89.

35. Pacini Hernandez, *Oye Como Va,* 47–48.

36. Ibid., 209.

37. Roxon, *Lillian Roxon's Rock Encyclopedia,* 210.

38. Roxon, *Lillian Roxon's Rock Encyclopedia,* 229.

39. David Crosby, *The Monterey International Pop Festival,* boxed set, Rhino R2 70596.

40. George, *The Death of Rhythm & Blues,* 98.

41. Gitlin, *The Sixties,* 287.

42. *Woodstock,* film directed by Michael Wadleigh, 1970.

43. *Gimme Shelter,* film directed by David Maysles, Albert Maysles, and Charlotte Zwerin, 1970.

CHAPTER 7

1. Michael Lydon, "Rock for Sale," in *The Age of Rock 2: Sights and Sounds of the American Cultural Revolution,* ed. Michael Lydon (New York: Vintage Books, 1970), 53.

2. Steve Pond, "The Seventies," *Rolling Stone,* 20 September 1990, 53.

3. For a detailed discussion of the merger movement, see Steve Chapple and Reebee Garofalo, *Rock 'n' Roll Is Here to Pay: The History and Politics of the Music Industry* (Chicago: Nelson-Hall, 1977), 82–87.

4. Peter Wicke, *Rock Music: Culture, Aesthetics and Sociology* (Cambridge, Eng.: Cambridge University Press, 1990), 121.

5. Ben Fong-Torres, ed., *The Rolling Stone Interviews,* vol. 2 (New York: Warner Books, 1973), 292.

6. Wicke, *Rock Music,* 126.

7. Chapple and Garofalo, *Rock 'n' Roll Is Here to Pay,* 175.

8. Ibid., 109

9. Ibid., 121.

10. Robert Draper, *Rolling Stone Magazine* (New York: Harper and Row, 1990).

11. Jann Wenner, "A Letter from the Editor." *Rolling Stone,* 9 November 1967, 2.

12. Michael Lydon, "The High Cost of Music and Love: Where's the Money from Monterey?" *Rolling Stone,* 9 November 1967, 1.

13. Jann Wenner, "Musicians Reject New Political Exploiters," *Rolling Stone,* 11 May 1968, 1, 22.

14. Draper, *Rolling Stone Magazine,* 157.

15. Jann Wenner, "A Letter from the Editor: On the Occasion of Our Fourth Anniversary Issue," *Rolling Stone,* 11 November 1971, 34.

16. *The Compleat Beatles,* video documentary, produced by Patrick Montgomery, 1982.

17. Ibid.

18. Joe Smith, *Off the Record: An Oral History of Popular Music* (New York: Warner Books, 1988), 242.

19. Simon Frith, *Sound Effects: Youth Leisure and the Politics of Rock 'n' Roll* (New York: Pantheon, 1981), 53.

20. *The Compleat Beatles*, 1982.

21. Ralph Gleason, "Perspectives: Changing with the Money Changers," *Rolling Stone,* 20 January 1968, 9.

22. Ralph Gleason, "Stop This Shuck Mike Bloomfield," *Rolling Stone,* 11 May 1968. 10.

23. John Pidgeon, *Eric Clapton* (London: Panther, 1976), 65.

24. Dave Morse, *Motown* (London: Vista, 1971), 108.

25. Jon Landau, "Soul," *Rolling Stone,* 24 February 1968, 18.

26. Wicke, *Rock Music,* 95.

27. Simon Frith and Howard Horne, *Art into Pop* (New York: Methuen, 1987), 86.

28. Ibid., 109.

29. Ibid., 108.

30. Iain Chambers, *Urban Rhythms: Pop Music and Popular Culture* (New York: Macmillan, 1985), 114–115.

31. Robert Walser, *Running with the Devil: Power, Gender, and Madness in Heavy Metal Music* (Hanover, N.H.: Wesleyan University Press, 1993), 61–62.

32. Irwin Stambler, *Encyclopedia of Pop, Rock & Soul* (New York: St. Martins, 1977), 176.

33. Frith and Horne, *Art into Pop,* 98.

34. *Rolling Stone,* 28 May 1970, 17.

35. Chambers, *Urban Rhythms,* 118.

36. "Wexler Attributes Greater R&B Volume to Black Buyer," *Billboard,* 20 November 1971, 8.

37. Paul Ackerman, "Gortikov Scorches Whitey Trade in NATRA Speech," *Billboard,* 17 July 1969, 1.

38. "New Black Hope," *Billboard,* 17 May 1969, 34.

39. John Lombardi, "Kenny Gamble and Leon Huff and the Resurrection of Jerry Butler and Philly Soul," *Rolling Stone,* 30 April 1970, 39.

40. Nelson George, *The Death of Rhythm & Blues* (New York: Pantheon Books, 1988), 145.

41. Jim Miller, "The Sound of Philadelphia," in *The Rolling Stone Illustrated History of Rock & Roll,* ed. Anthony DeCurtis and James Henke (New York: Random House, 1992), 518.

42. Of course, not all veteran r&b groups were this lucky. The Dells, the model for Robert Townshend's film *The Five Heartbeats,* had been together since 1953. The group's biggest success, "Oh, What a Night" (1969), was a remake of an r&b hit the group had recorded thirteen years earlier. The Dells' last Top Forty hit was in 1973.

43. "Wexler Attributes Greater R&B Volume to Black Buyer," 8.

44. Peter Guralnick, *Sweet Soul Music* (New York: Harper and Row, 1986), 391.

45. Robert Christgau, *Any Old Way You Choose It: Rock and Other Pop Music, 1967–1973* (Baltimore, Md.: Penguin Books, 1973), 217

46. Ibid., 211.

47. Chapple and Garofalo, *Rock 'n' Roll Is Here to Pay,* 80.

48. Katherine Orloff, *Rock 'n Roll Woman* (Los Angeles: Nash Publishing, 1974), 11.

49. Gillian G. Gaar, *She's a Rebel: The History of Women in Rock & Roll* (Seattle, Wash.: Seal Press, 1992), 123.

50. Christgau, *Any Old Way You Choose It,* 212.

51. Stephen Holden, "The Evolution of the Singer-Songwriter," in *The Rolling Stone Illustrated History of Rock & Roll,* ed. Anthony DeCurtis and James Henke (New York: Random House, 1992), 489.

52. Bruce Springsteen can be classified as a singer/songwriter in the same sense that Van Morrison or the solo John Lennon can be; they all composed personal, poetic verse. They also belted it out with incredible intensity; they were hardly soft. Following the breakup of Them, Morrison tasted success on his first solo album, *Blowin' Your Mind* (1967), which had the hit single "Brown Eyed Girl." After a dry spell that included the failure of the critically acclaimed *Astral Weeks,* he regained his footing in 1970 with *Moondance* and *His Band and the Street Choir.* The latter of these yielded the single "Domino," which made the Top Ten. At his most confessional, Lennon transformed months of primal scream therapy into singles like "Cold Turkey" and album cuts like "Mother," from his first solo LP, *John Lennon/Plastic Ono Band* (1970), the album that included "Working Class Hero." Springsteen was that working-class hero.

53. Jon landau, "Growing Young with Rock and Roll," *The Real Paper,* 22 May 1974, 23.

54. Robin Denselow, *When the Music's Over: The Story of Political Pop* (Boston: Faber and Faber, 1989), 180.

55. Ellen Willis, "Beginning to See the Light: Or Rock & Roll, Feminism, and Night Blindness," *Village Voice,* 27 March 1978, 21–22.

56. Christgau, *Any Old Way You Choose It,* 274.

57. Gaar, *She's a Rebel,* 138.

58. Ibid., 136.

59. Cynthia M. Lont, "Women's Music: No Longer a Small Private Party," in *Rockin' the Boat: Mass Music and Mass Movements,* ed. Reebee Garofalo (Boston: South End Press, 1992), 242.

60. Gaar, *She's a Rebel,* 155–156.

61. Bill C. Malone, *Country Music, USA* (Austin: University of Texas Press, 1985), 386.

62. Stambler, *Encyclopedia of Pop, Rock & Soul,* 37.

63. By the time he died from heart failure in the mid-1970s, Parsons was credited with influencing everyone from Emmylou Harris (his protégé) to the Rolling Stones.

64. Christgau, *Any Old Way You Choose It,* 269.

65. Anthony DeCurtis, "The Eagles," *Rolling Stone,* 20 September 1990, 92.

66. Malone, *Country Music, USA,* 404–405.

67. Deena Weinstein, *Heavy Metal: A Cultural Sociology* (New York: Lexington Books, 1991), 23.

68. Walser, *Running with the Devil,* 2.

69. Weinstein, *Heavy Metal,* 16.

70. Walser, *Running with the Devil,* 57–107.

71. Ibid., 10.

72. Stambler, *Encyclopedia of Pop, Rock & Soul,* 57.

73. Ibid.

74. Walser, *Running with the Devil,* 61, citing Mordechai, "Where There's Smoke . . . There's Fire." *Guitar World,* February 1991, 62.

75. Ibid., 68.

76. Christgau, *Any Old Way You Choose It*, 116.

77. J. D. Considine, "Led Zeppelin," *Rolling Stone*, 20 September 1990, 59, 109.

78. Smith, *Off the Record*, 273.

79. Chambers, *Urban Rhythms*, 113.

80. Robert Christgau, *Any Old Way You Choose It*, 303.

81. Chambers, Urban Rhythms, 113.

82. Frith and Horne, *Art into Pop*, 115

83. Chambers, *Urban Rhythms*, 133.

84. Peter York, *Style Wars* (London: Sidgwick and Jackson, 1980). Cited in Chambers, *Urban Rhythms*, 138.

CHAPTER 8

1. Charles M. Young, "Rock Is Sick and Living in London: A Report on the Sex Pistols," *Rolling Stone*, 20 October 1977, 68.

2. Mikal Gilmore, "Disco," *Rolling Stone*, 19 April 1979, 54.

3. Robert Christgau, "A Cult Explodes—and a Movement Is Born," *Village Voice*, 24 October 1977, 57.

4. Andrew Kopkind, "The Dialectic of Disco," *Village Voice*, 12 February 1979, 11.

5. Simon Frith, "Beyond the Dole Queue: The Politics of Punk," *Village Voice*, 24 October 1977, 78.

6. Ibid.

7. Kopkind, "The Dialectic of Disco," 11.

8. Gilmore, "Disco," 54. It should also be noted that a good deal of the antidisco sentiment had to do with the fear of and hostility toward technology replacing live music.

9. Young, "Rock Is Sick and Living in London," 70.

10. Jon Savage, *England's Dreaming: Anarchy, Sex Pistols, Punk Rock, and Beyond* (New York: St Martins Press, 1992), 87.

11. Clinton Heylin, *From the Velvets to the Voidoids: A Pre-Punk History for a Post-Punk World* (New York: Penguin Books, 1993), 87–88.

12. Ibid., 38.

13. Ibid., 120.

14. Ibid., 123.

15. Ibid., 172.

16. Ibid., 174.

17. Savage, *England's Dreaming*, 202.

18. Frith, "Beyond the Dole Queue," 78.

19. Savage, *England's Dreaming*, 330.

20. Ibid., 63.

21. Ibid., 188.

22. Christgau, "A Cult Explodes," 70.

23. Ibid.

24. Lester Bangs, "The White Noise Supremacists," *Village Voice*, 30 April 1979, 45–46.

25. Ibid., 46.

26. Savage, *England's Dreaming*, 242.

27. David Widgery, *Beating Time: Riot 'n' Race 'n' Rock 'n' Roll* (London: Chatto and Windus, 1986), 53.

28. Savage, *England's Dreaming*, 398.

29. Widgery, *Beating Time*, 64.

30. Savage, *England's Dreaming*, 442.

31. Gillian G Garr, *She's a Rebel: The History of Women in Rock & Roll* (Seattle, WA: Seal Press, 1992), 277.

32. Robert Palmer, "New Rock from the Suburbs," *New York Times*, 23 September 1984, 23.

33. Heylin, *From the Velvets to the Voidoids*, 314.

34. Stephen Holden, "The Evolution of a Dance Craze," *Rolling Stone*, 19 April 1979, 29.

35. Tom Smucker, "Disco," in *The Rolling Stone Illustrated History of Rock & Roll*, eds. Anthony DeCurtis and James Henke (New York: Random House, 1992), 562.

36. Ibid.

37. Barbara Graustark, "Disco Takes Over," *Newsweek*, 2 April 1979, 59.

38. Ibid., 58–59.

39. Kopkind, "The Dialectic of Disco," 14.

40. Kopkind, "The Dialectic of Disco," 11.

41. Holden, "The Evolution of a Dance Craze," 30.

42. Deborah Pacini Hernandez, *Oye Como Va! Hybridity and Identity in Latino Popular Music* (Philadelphia, Pa.: Temple University Press, 2010), 58-59.

43. Tim Lawrence, *Love Saves the Day: A History of American Dance Music Culture* (Durham, N.C.: Duke University Press, 2003), 170.

44. Kopkind, "The Dialectic of Disco," 16.

45. Russell Sanjek, *American Popular Music and Its Business: The First Four Hundred Years, Volume III* (New York: Oxford University Press, 1988), 514

46. David Ansen, "Rock Tycoon," *Newsweek*, 31 July 1978, 41.

47. Ibid., 41.

48. Kopkind, "The Dialectic of Disco," 11.

49. Don McLeese, "Anatomy of an Anti-Disco Riot," *In These Times*, 29 August–4 September 1979, 23.

50. Graustark, "Disco Takes Over," 58.

51. Dave Marsh, "The Flip Sides of 1979," *Rolling Stone*, 27 December 1979, 28.

52. Georgia Christgau, "Disco! Disco! Disco! Four Critics Address the Musical Question," *In These Times*, 6–12 June 1979, 21.

53. McLeese, "Anatomy of an Anti-Disco Riot," 23.

54. Robert Hilburn, "Musical Lessons from 1983's First Half," *Cape Cod Times*, 16 July 1983, 12.

55. N. R. Kleinfeld, "FM's Success Is Loud and Clear," *New York Times*, 26 October 1979, Dl.

56. Marsh, "The Flip Sides of 1979," 30.

57. Pablo Guzman, "On the Radio, Part Two," *Rock & Roll Confidential*, January 1984, 2.

CHAPTER 9

1. Recording Industry Association of America (RIAA), *Inside the Recording Industry: A Statistical Overview, Update '86* (New York: Recording Industry Association of America, 1986), 4.

2. Michèle Hung and Esteban Garcia Morencos, *World Record Sales 1969–1990: A Statistical History of the World*

Recording Industry (London: International Federation of the Phonogram Industry, 1990), 85.

3. Paul Grein, "Unemployment Lines: LA Industrial Personnel Face Major Challenges to Rebuild Their Careers," *Billboard,* 19 May 1979, 3.

4. Simon Frith, "Picking Up the Pieces: Video Pop." In *Facing the Music,* ed. Simon Frith (New York: Pantheon Books, 1988), 93.

5. "Record Business Sees Light Ahead—On Video Screen," *Chicago Tribune,* 26 April 1983, 5.

6. RIAA, *Inside the Recording Industry,* 5.

7. Russell Sanjek, *American Popular Music and Its Business: The First Four Hundred Years, Volume III* (New York: Oxford University Press, 1988), 602.

8. Frith, "Picking Up the Pieces," 117.

9. Sanjek, *American Popular Music and Its Business,* 641.

10. Andrew Goodwin, *Dancing in the Distraction Factory: Music Television and Popular Culture* (Minneapolis: University of Minnesota Press, 1992), 133.

11. Eric Gelman, "Rocking Video," *Newsweek,* 18 April 1983, 98.

12. Goodwin, *Dancing in the Distraction Factory,* 132–139.

13. Ibid., 134.

14. Ibid.

15. Parke Peterbaugh, "Anglomania: America Surrenders to the Brits—But Who Really Wins?" *Billboard,* 10 November 1983, 31.

16. *Rock and Roll Confidential,* July 1983, 6.

17. Rebecca Bricker, "Take One," *People,* 4 April 1983, 31.

18. Steven Levy, "Ad Nauseum: How MTV Sells Out Rock & Roll," *Rolling Stone,* 8 December 1983, 37.

19. Bricker, "Take One," 31.

20. Michael Shore, *The Rolling Stone Book of Rock Video* (London: Sidgwick and Jackson, 1985), 86.

21. See, for example, E. Ann Kaplan, *Rocking Around the Clock: Music Television, Postmodernism, and Consumer Culture* (New York: Routledge, 1987); L. Lewis, *Gender Politics and MTV: Voicing the Difference* (Philadelphia, Pa.: Temple University Press, 1990); and Susan McClary, *Feminine Endings: Music, Gender, and Sexuality* (Minneapolis: University of Minnesota Press, 1991).

22. Gelman, "Rocking Video," 97.

23. Steve Morse, "Can American Bands Beat the British Blitz?" *Boston Globe,* 1 January 1984, p. A4.

24. Paul Grein, "AOR Programmers Plan More Variety," *Billboard,* 14 January 1984, 66.

25. Laurence Kenneth Shore, "The Crossroads of Business and Music: A Study of the Music Industry in the United States and Internationally" (Ph.D. Diss., Stanford University, 1983), 248; Hung and Morencos, *World Record Sales, 1969–1990,* 85.

26. Paul Grein, "'83 RIAA Tally: Fewer Biggies," *Billboard,* 14 January 1984, 4.

27. Jeffrey Zaslow, "Music and Money," *Wall Street Journal,* 21 May 1985, 1.

28. Ted Fox, *In the Groove* (New York: St. Martin's Press, 1986), 322.

29. Stephen Holden, "Musical Odyssey," *New York Times,* 9 December 1987, C33.

30. Frith, "Picking Up the Pieces," 102–103.

31. Paul Grein, "Charts '86," *Billboard,* 27 December 1986, Y-4.

32. Steve Gett, "Rock '86," *Billboard,* 27 December 1986, Y-4.

33. Frith, "Picking Up the Pieces," 90.

34. John Rockwell, "Leftist Causes? Rock Seconds Those Emotions," *New York Times,* 11 December 1988, 23.

35. David Breskin, "Bob Geldof: The Rolling Stone Interview," *Rolling Stone,* 5 December 1985, 34.

36. Mark Coleman, "The Revival of Conscience," *Rolling Stone,* 15 November 1990, 71.

37. Griel Marcus, "Rock for Ethiopia" (panel presentation at the Third International Conference on Popular Music Studies, Montreal, Quebec, Canada, July 1985), 17.

38. Pete Hamill, "A Day to Remember," *Rolling Stone,* 29 August 1985, 28.

39. Ibid., 74.

40. Will Straw, "Rock for Ethiopia" (panel presentation at the Third International Conference on Popular Music Studies, Montreal, Quebec, Canada, July 1985), 28.

41. Breskin, "Bob Geldof: The Rolling Stone Interview," 28.

42. Simon Frith, "Crappy Birthday to Punk," *In These Times,* 23–29 April 1986, 20.

43. *Rock & Roll Confidential,* 1985 September, 1.

44. Stan Rijven, "Rock for Ethiopia" (panel presentation at the Third International Conference on Popular Music Studies, Montreal, Quebec, Canada, July 1985), 3–7.

45. Jack Healy, "Mass Concerts/Mass Consciousness: The Politics of Mega-Events" (panel discussion at the New Music Seminar, New York, 17 July 1989).

46. Coleman, "The Revival of Conscience," 80.

47. The bill included Whitney Houston, Sting, Stevie Wonder, Dire Straits, Tracy Chapman, Peter Gabriel, The Fat Boys, Jackson Browne, Natalie Cole, Little Steven, Eurythmics, Freddie Jackson, Phil Collins, UB40, Al Green, Midge Ure, Miriam Makeba, Hugh Masakela, Simple Minds, Sly and Robbie, Aswad, The Bee Gees, Youssou N'Dour, Salt-n-Pepa, and more.

48. Anthony DeCurtis, "Rock & Roll Politics: Did the Nelson Mandela Tribute Make Its Point," *Rolling Stone,* 11 August 1988, 34.

49. Danny Schechter, "Why We Didn't See Wembley," *Africa Report* (July–August 1990), 66.

50. *Rock & Roll Confidential,* September 1985, p. 1.

51. Simon Frith and John Street, "Party Music," *Marxism Today* (June 1986), 29.

52. *The Making of Sun City,* MTV documentary produced by Steve Lawrence and Vinny Longabardo, Karl-Lorimar Home Video, 1985.

53. Steven Feld, "Notes on World Beat," *Public Culture Bulletin* (Fall 1988), 33–34.

54. Ibid., 32.

55. My understanding of Live 8 has been aided by C. Michael Elavsky, "United as ONE: Live 8 and the Politics of the Global Music Media Spectacle," *Journal of Popular Music Studies* (December 2009), 384–410.

CHAPTER 10

1. Tricia Rose, *Black Noise: Rap Music and Black Culture in Contemporary America* (Hanover, N.H.: University Press of New England, 1994).

2. Philip Bashe, *Heavy Metal Thunder: The Music, Its History, Its Heroes* (Garden City, N.Y.: Doubleday, 1985); Deena Weinstein, *Heavy Metal: A Cultural Sociology* (New York: Lexington Books, 1991).

3. Weinstein, *Heavy Metal*, 44.

4. Robert Walser, *Running with the Devil: Power, Gender, and Madness in Heavy Metal Music* (Hanover, N.H.: Wesleyan University Press, 1993), 12.

5. Ibid., 94.

6. Ibid., 76.

7. Andrew Goodwin, *Dancing in the Distraction Factory: Music Television and Popular Culture* (Minneapolis: University of Minnesota Press, 1992), 135.

8. Ibid., 135.

9. Greg Ptacek, "Majors Return to Nuts and Bolts of pre-MTV Metal Marketing Days," *Billboard*, 27 April 1985, HM 15.

10. Linda Martin and Kerry Segrave, *Anti-Rock: The Opposition to Rock 'n' Roll* (New York: DaCapo Press, 1993), 232.

11. Ptacek, "Majors Return to Nuts and Bolts," HM 3.

12. Ibid., HM 15.

13. Goodwin, *Dancing in the Distraction Factory*, 136.

14. E. Ann Kaplan, *Rocking Around the Clock: Music Television, Postmodernism, and Consumer Culture* (New York: Routledge, 1987), 102–103.

15. Roberta Smoodin, "Crazy Like David Lee Roth," *Playgirl*, August 1986, 43, quoted in Walser, *Running with the Devil*, 129.

16. Walser, *Running with the Devil*, 111.

17. Ibid., 121.

18. Weinstein, *Heavy Metal*, 48.

19. Ibid., 50.

20. Jim Miller, "It's Not Only Rock 'N' Roll." *Boston Globe*, 23 August 1991, 94. There were parallel developments in post-punk. Thrash metal was to classic metal what the hard-core sound of Black Flag and SS Decontrol was to new wave. By the time Black Flag leader Henry Rollins left to form his new group, the Rollins Band, its music was defined by yet another fusion category called thrashcore, which included a group called Suicidal Tendencies.

21. Sue Cummings, "Road Warriors," *Spin*, August 1986, quoted in Weinstein, *Heavy Metal*, 160.

22. Paul Grein, "The Year in Charts," *Billboard*, 26 December 1987, Y-4.

23. J. D. Considine, "Metal Mania," *Rolling Stone*, 15 November 1990, 104.

24. See Weinstein, *Heavy Metal*, 66; Walser, *Running with the Devil*, 17.

25. Weinstein, *Heavy Metal*, 67.

26. Walser, *Running with the Devil*, 17.

27. Laurel Fishman, "Lita Ford," *Metal*, May 1988, quoted in Walser, *Running with the Devil*, 132.

28. Tim Carr, "Talk That Talk, Walk That Walk," *Rolling Stone*, 26 May 1983, 22.

29. David Toop, *The Rap Attack 2: African Rap to Global Hip Hop* (London: Serpent's Tail, 1991), 14.

30. Ibid., 154.

31. For an excellent explication of the (primarily) Puerto Rican involvement in early rap as a conjunctive (rather than merely additive) experience, see Juan Flores, *From Bomba to Hip Hop: Puerto Rican Culture and Latino Identity* (New York: Columbia University Press, 2000). See also Raquel Z. Rivera, "Boricuas from the Hip Hop Zone: Notes on Race and Ethnic Relations in New York City," *Centro Journal* (Spring 1996), 202–215.

32. Steven Hager, *Hip Hop: The Illustrated History of Break Dancing, Rap Music, and Graffiti* (New York: St. Martin's Press, 1984), 91.

33. Brian Cross, *It's Not About a Salary: Rap, Race and Resistance in Los Angeles* (New York: Verso, 1993), 50.

34. Alex Henderson, "Active Indies," *Billboard*, 24 December 1988, R-16.

35. Ibid., R-8.

36. Dan Stuart, "Black Radio," *Billboard*, 17 June 1989, B-12.

37. Henderson, "Active Indies," R-21.

38. Jon Pareles, "There's a New Sound in Pop Music: Bigotry," *New York Times*, 10 September 1989, Arts and Leisure, 1.

39. Ibid., 33.

40. Harry Allen, "Hip Hop Madness: From Def Jams to Cold Lampin', Rap Is Our Music," *Essence*, April 1989, 117.

41. Ibid.

42. Toop, *The Rap Attack 2*, 200.

43. For an excellent discussion of this complexity, see Rose, *Black Noise*, 146–182.

44. Toop, *The Rap Attack 2*, 201.

45. Cross, *It's Not About a Salary*, 55.

46. David Nathan, "Rap," *Billboard*, 24 December 1988, R-5.

47. Columbia Records negotiated a custom label deal with Def Jam (L. L. Cool J, Oran 'Juice' Jones, the Beastie Boys, Public Enemy) in 1985. Jive Records (Whodini, Kool Moe Dee, Steady B., D. J. Jazzy Jeff & the Fresh Prince, Boogie Down Productions) entered into distribution arrangements with both RCA and Arista. Cold Chillin' Records (Marly Marl, Roxanne Shanté, Biz Markie, M. C. Shan) signed a distribution deal with Warner in 1987. Warner also bought a piece of Tommy Boy (Stetsasonic, Force MDs, De La Soul, Queen Latifah, Black by Demand, Digital Underground). Delicious Vinyl (Tone Loc, Def Jef, Young M.C.) concluded a national distribution deal with Island. National distribution for Priority (N.W.A., Eazy E, Ice Cube) went to Capitol.

48. Kristal Brent Zook, "Reconstructions of Nationalist Thought in Black Music and Culture," in *Rockin' the Boat: Mass Music and Mass Movements*, ed. Reebee Garofalo (Boston: South End Press, 1992), 262.

49. Toop, *The Rap Attack 2*, 185.

50. Cross, *It's Not About a Salary*, 58.

51. Ibid.

52. Herman Gray, "Popular Music as a Social Problem: A Social History of Claims Against Popular Music," in *Images of Issues*, ed. Joel Best (Hawthorne, N.Y.: De Gruyter, 1989), 143–158.

53. See Lawrence Grossberg, *We Gotta Get Out of This Place: Popular Conservatism and Postmodern Culture* (New York:

Routledge, 1992). For an abbreviated treatment of this discussion, see Lawrence Grossberg, "The Framing of Rock: Rock and the New Conservatism," in *Rock and Popular Music: Politics, Policies, Institutions,* eds. Tony Bennett et al. (New York: Routledge, 1993), 195.

54. Nan Levinson, "Shut Up," *Boston Globe,* 20 February 1994, 79.

55. Susan McClary and Robert Walser, "Start Making Sense: Musicology Wrestles with Rock," in *On Record: Rock, Pop, and the Written Word,* eds. Simon Frith and Andrew Goodwin (New York: Pantheon Books, 1990), 278.

56. Martin and Segrave, *Anti-Rock,* 292.

57. U.S. Congress, Senate Committee on Commerce, Science, and Transportation, *Record Labeling,* 99th Cong., 1st sess., 1985, 11, quoted in Herman Gray, "Rate the Records: Symbolic Conflict, Popular Music, and Social Problems," *Popular Music and Society* (Fall 1989): 6–7.

58. Steven Dougherty, "Parents vs. Rock," *People,* 16 September 1985, 50.

59. Simon Frith, *Sound Effects: Youth, Leisure, and the Politics of Rock 'n' Roll* (New York: Pantheon Books, 1981), 175.

60. Dougherty, "Parents vs. Rock," 50.

61. Gray, "Rate the Records," 9.

62. Frank Zappa, "The Porn Wars," *Penthouse,* May 1989, 78.

63. Editorial, *Rolling Stone,* 7 November 1985, 10.

64. PMRC Video, *Rising to the Challenge,* produced by Teen Vision, Inc., 1989.

65. Ibid.

66. Ibid.

67. Walser, *Running with the Devil,* 140.

68. Dougherty, "Parents vs. Rock," 52.

69. Walser, *Running with the Devil,* 139.

70. Dave Marsh, "What's Being Sold in Country?" *New York Times,* 24 May 1992, 20.

71. Ibid.

72. Robin Denselow, *When the Music's Over: The Story of Political Pop* (Boston, MA: Faber and Faber, 1989), 267.

73. U.S. Congress, Senate Committee on Commerce, Science, and Transportation, *Record Labeling,* 99th Cong., 1st sess., 1985, 11, quoted in Gray, "Rate the Records," 10.

74. David Thigpen, "Up Against the Wall," *Rolling Stone,* 24 February 1994, 16.

75. Jello Biafra, "The Far Right and the Censorship of Music." *Harvard Law Record* (17 April 1987), 11.

76. Marjorie Heins, *Sex, Sin and Blasphemy: A Guide to America's Censorship Wars* (New York: The New Press, 1993), 90.

77. Ibid., 89.

78. Ibid., 92.

79. Walser, *Running with the Devil,* 150.

80. ABC, *20/20,* segment on heavy metal, produced by Danny Schechter, 1987.

81. Lynn Minton, "Is Heavy Metal Dangerous?" *Parade,* 20 September 1992, 12.

82. K. Zimmerman, "Priest Ruling Gives Unclear Message," *Variety,* 3 September 1990, 8, quoted in Steve Jones, "Ban(ned) in the USA: Popular Music and Censorship," *Journal of Communication Inquiry* (Winter, 1991), 77.

83. The editors of *Rock & Roll Confidential, You've Got a Right to Rock* (Los Angeles: Duke and Duchess Ventures, Inc., 1990), 6.

84. Richard N. Ostling, "No Sympathy for the Devil," *Time,* 19 March 1990, 56.

85. Robert J. Barry, "Satanism: The Law Enforcement Response," *The National Sheriff,* February/March 1987, 40.

86. David Alexander, "Giving the Devil More Than His Due." *The Humanist,* March/April 1990, quoted in Walser, *Running with the Devil,* 199–200.

87. Barry, "Satanism," 39.

88. Ibid., 41.

89. Dougherty, "Parents vs. Rock," 46.

90. Ostling, "No Sympathy for the Devil," 56.

91. Reuters, "Of Hard-Rock Demons: A Cardinal Speaks Out," *Boston Globe,* 6 March 1990, 23.

92. Peter Steinfels, "Surge in Satanic Activity Alarms O'Connor," *New York Times,* 6 March 1990, B6.

93. Pareles, "There's a New Sound in Pop Music: Bigotry," 1, 32–33.

94. Dennis Wharton, "D.C. Bluebloods Want X Rating for Porn Rock," *Variety,* 22 May 1985, quoted in Martin and Segrave, *Anti-Rock,* 293.

95. Biafra, "The Far Right and the Censorship of Music," 12.

96. Ibid.

97. Heins, *Sex, Sin, and Blasphemy,* 22–24.

98. Henry Louis Gates, Jr., "2 Live Crew, Decoded." *New York Times,* 9 June 1990, p. A23.

99. Brechner Center for Freedom of Information, *The Brechner Report* (Gainesville: University of Florida, 1992), 2.

100. David Mills, "Rap as Politics: The Sayings of Sister Souljah," *Essence,* September 1992, 20.

101. Alan Light, "Ice," *Rolling Stone,* 20 August 1992, 30.

102. Charlene Orr et al., "Texas Police Pursue 'Cop Killer,'" *Billboard,* 27 June 1992, 79.

103. Greg Sandow, "Fire & Ice," *Entertainment Weekly,* 14 August, 1992, 32.

104. Touré, "Snoop Dogg's Gentle Hip Hop Growl," *New York Times,* 21 November 1993, 32.

105. Havelock Nelson, "Music and Violence: Does Crime Pay?" *Billboard,* 13 November 1993, 109.

106. Havelock Nelson, "The Rap Column," *Billboard,* 4 December 1993, 30.

107. Toop, *The Rap Attack 2,* 170.

108. Bill Holland, "Senate Hearing Examines Gangsta Lyrics," *Billboard,* 5 March 1994, 10.

109. Ibid., 10.

CHAPTER 11

1. Mikal Gilmore, "The Year in Music," *Rolling Stone,* 13–27 December 1990, 13.

2. Ibid., 17.

3. Ibid.

4. Ibid.

5. Kim Neely, "Into the Unknown," *Rolling Stone,* 16 June 1994, 117.

6. Anthony DeCurtis, "Kurt Cobain, 1967–1994," *Rolling Stone,* 2 June 1994, 30.

7. Donna Gaines, "Suicidal Tendencies: Kurt Did Not Die for You," *Rolling Stone,* 2 June 1994, 67.

8. Jim Sullivan, "Lollapalooza: The Sound of Success," *Boston Globe,* 2 August 1992, B25.

9. Jon Pareles, "Howls of Rage, Nine Hours Worth, at Waterloo Village," *New York Times,* 13 August 1991, C13.

10. Peter Watrous, "Good Things Happen to Lollapalooza," *New York Times,* 5 August 1992, C13.

11. David Fricke, "Red Hot Chili Peppers' Naked Truth," *Rolling Stone,* 25 June 1992, 29.

12. Ibid., 29.

13. Steve Pond, "The Trick Is to Be Loved but Not Embraced," *New York Times,* 26 June 1994, sec. 2, 28.

14. Anthony DeCurtis, "Ropin' the Whirl Wind," *Rolling Stone,* 1 April 1993, 35.

15. Greg Kot, "R. Kelly Profile: Legal Woes Don't Stop the Music," *Chicago Tribune,* 9 May 2008. http://www.chicagotribune.com/news/nationworld/chi-r-kelly-0509may09,0,3990976.story.

16. Lola Ogunnaike, "Caught in the Act," *Vibe,* May 2002, 93.

17. Ibid., 92.

18. Keith Negus, *Music Genres and Corporate Cultures* (New York: Routledge, 1999), 85.

19. Mikal Gilmore, "Puff Daddy," *Rolling Stone,* 7 August 1997, 72.

20. Fred Schruers, "Master P," *Rolling Stone,* 29 October 1998, 42.

21. Keith Negus, *Music Genres and Corporate Cultures,* 96.

22. Nelson George, *Buppies, B-Boys, Baps and Bohos: Notes on Post-Soul Black Culture* (New York: HarperCollins, 1992), 80.

23. Tony Green, "The Dirty South," in *The VIBE History of Hip Hop,* Alan Light, ed. (New York: Three Rivers Press, 1999).

24. Murray Forman, "'Represent': Race, Space and Place in Rap Music," *Popular Music,* January 2000, 68–69.

25. David Bry, "The Song of the South," *Vibe,* June 2002, 94.

26. Ibid., 100.

27. Renée Graham, "Is Some Hatred More Acceptable Than Others?" *Boston Globe,* 5 January 2001, C1.

28. "The Hip-Hop 50," *Rolling Stone,* 29 October 1998, 45–57.

29. Touré, "DMX Reigns as the Dark Prince of Hip Hop," *Rolling Stone,* 13 April 2000, 85.

30. Nathaniel Welch, "Hit Man," *Rolling Stone,* 22 August 2002, 54.

31. Touré, "The Life of a Hunted Man," *Rolling Stone,* 3 April 2003, 46.

32. John Bush, "Outkast," *All Music Guide,* 2003. http://www.allmucis.com/cg/amg.dlle.

33. Vanessa E. Jones, "Whose Word Is It Anyway?" *Boston Globe,* 7 July 1999, D1.

34. Anthony DeCurtis, "The Year in Music," *Rolling Stone,* 10–24 December 1992, 26.

35. "1990 Yearbook," *Rolling Stone,* 13–27 December 1990, 72.

36. "Janet Jackson Inks Record $50 Mil. Deal with Virgin Records," *Jet,* 25, March 1991, 60.

37. Fred Goodman, "Big Deals: How Money Fever Is Changing the Music Business," *Musician,* January 1992, 42.

38. Neil Strauss, "For Record Industry, All Signs Are Gloomy," *New York Times,* 4 December 1996, A-1.

39. During this period, this music was the subject of countless news articles and, subsequently, a number of academic books as well. Among the best of these are: Sarah Thornton, *Club Cultures: Music, Media and Subcultural Capital* (Hanover, N.H.: University Press of New England, 1995); Matthew Collin, *Altered States: The Story of Ecstasy Culture and Acid House* (New York: Serpent's Tail, 1997); Hillegonda C. Rietveld, *This Is Our House: House Music, Cultural Spaces and Technologies* (Brookfield, VT: Ashgate, 1998); Simon Reynolds, *Generation Ecstasy: Into the World of Techno and Rave Culture* (New York: Routledge, 1999); Dan Sicko, *Techno Rebels: The Renegades of Electronic Funk* (New York: Billboard Books, 1999); Kai Fikentscher, *You Better Work: Underground Dance Music in New York City* (Hanover, N.H.: University Press of New England, 2000).

40. Because these styles are often presented ahistorically, the listening public has been deluged with a smorgasbord of over 300 sub-subgenres, of which Kembrew McLeod ("Genres, Sub-Genres, Sub-Sub-Genres and More: Musical and Social Differentiation Within Electronic-Dance Music Communities," *Journal of Popular Music Studies,* Spring 2001) has distilled an edited list that includes: "Abstract Beat, Abstract Drum-n-Bass, Acid House, Acid Rave, Acid-Beats, Acid-Funk, Acid-Techno, Alchemic House, Ambient Dance, Ambient Drum-n-Bass, Amyl House, Analogue Electro-Funk, Aquatic Techno-Funk, Aquatic-House, Atomic Breaks, Avant-Techno, Bass, Big Beat, Bleep-n-Bass, Blunted Beats, Breakbeat, Chemical Beats, Chicago Garage, Chicago House, Coldwave, Cosmic Dance, Cyber Hardcore, Cybertech, Dark Ambient, Downtempo Funk, Downtempo Future Jazz, Drill-n-Bass, Dronecore, Drum-n-Bass, Dub, Dub-Funk, Dub-Hop, Dub-n-Bass, Electro, Electro-Acoustic, Electro-Breaks, Electro-Dub, Freestyle, Future Jazz, Futuristic Breakbeat, Futuristic Hardbeats, Futuristic Hardstep, Gabber, Garage, Global House, Global Trance, Goa-Trance, Happy Hardcore, Hardcore Techno, Hard Chill Ambient, Intelligent Drum-n-Bass, Intelligent Jungle, Intelligent Techno, Miami Bass Minimal Techno, Minimal Trance, Morphing, Mutant Techno, Mutated Minimal Techno, Mystic-Step, Neurofunk, Noir-House, Nu-Dark Jungle, Old School, Organic Chill Out, Organic Electro, Organic Electronica, Progressive House, Progressive Low Frequency, Progressive Trance, Ragga, Ragga-Jungle, Rave, Techstep, Techxotica, Trance, Trancecore, Trance-Dub, Tribal, Tribal Beats, Tribal House, Tribal Soul, Trip-Hop, Tripno, Twilight Electronica, Two-Step, UK Acid, UK Breakbeat, Underground, World-Dance."

41. Simon Reynolds, *Generation Ecstasy: Into the World of Techno and Rave Culture* (New York: Routledge, 1999), 24.

42. Hillegonda C. Rietveld, *This Is Our House: House Music, Cultural Spaces and Technologies* (Brookfield, VT: Ashgate, 1998), 23.

43. "Alleys" was released concurrently with Afrika Bambaataa's "Planet Rock," also heavily indebted to Kraftwerk, which typified the New York hip hop sound called electro.

44. Reynolds, *Generation Ecstasy*, 60.

45. Sarah Thornton, *Club Cultures: Music, Media and Subcultural Capital* (Hanover, N.H.: University Press of New England, 1995), 76.

46. Reynolds, *Generation Ecstasy*, 13.

47. Thornton, *Club Cultures*, 73.

48. Matthew Collin, *Altered States: The Story of Ecstasy Culture and Acid House* (New York: Serpent's Tail, 1997), 254.

49. Reynolds, *Generation Ecstacy*, 260.

50. Ibid., 341.

51. Ibid., 330.

52. Ethan Smith, "Organization Moby," *Wired*, May 2002, 91.

53. Marilyn Gillen, "The Year in Business: Ups, Downs, and Rebounds," *Billboard*, 27 December 1997, YE 14.

54. Steve Morse, "In Pop, Women Took New Ground All Over," *Boston Globe*, 29 December 1996, N6.

55. James Sullivan, "Three's the Charm as the Last Lilith All-Women Music Festival Loses Its Sensitive Side," *San Francisco Chronicle*, 15 July 1999, reported on Geocities.com. http://www.sfgate.com/cgi-bin/article.cgi?f=/c/a/1999/07/15/DD90915.DTL.

56. Ibid.

57. Monifa Young, "Interview with Lauryn Hill," *Essence*, June 1998, 74.

58. Joan Anderman, "Shut Up," *Boston Globe*, 3 December 2000, K1.

59. Rob Sheffield, "Rage Against the Latrines," *Rolling Stone*, 2 September 1999, 54.

60. Joan Anderman, "The Female Fans Say They're in It for the Catharsis," *Boston Globe*, 16 July 2000, P1.

61. "Readers Poll," *Rolling Stone*, 20 January 2000, 51.

62. Neil Straus, "The Hit Girl: Christina Aguilera," *Rolling Stone*, 6–20 July 2000, 82, 151.

63. Anthony Bozza, "NSynchronicity," *Rolling Stone*, 30 March 2000, 55.

64. Touré, "True Tales of the Pop Life: 'N Sync," *Rolling Stone*, 16 August 2001, 66.

65. Ibid., 70.

66. Steven Daly, "Britney Spears: Inside the Heart and Mind (and Bedroom) of America's New Teen Queen," *Rolling Stone*, 15 April 1999, 65.

67. Peter Kafka, "The Queen of Teen," *Forbes*, 20 March 2000, 162.

68. Chris Heath, "Has Anyone Seen Christina," *Rolling Stone*, 14 November 2001, 55.

69. Ibid.

70. Ibid.

71. Rick Lyman, "New Data Shows Immigrants' Growth and Reach," *New York Times*, 15 August 2006, 1.

72. US Census Bureau, "Table 11 Population by Sex, Age, Hispanic Origin, and Race: 2004." http://www.census.gov/population/socdemo/hispanic/ASEC2004/2004CPS_tab1.1a.html.

73. Lyman, "New Data Shows Immigrants' Growth and Reach," 1.

74. Joseph P. Kahn, "Musical Chairs Coming Up for the White House," *Boston Globe*, 20 January 2001, C2.

75. Chris Heath, "The Epic Life of Carlos Santana," *Rolling Stone*, 16 March 2000, 41.

76. Mim Udovitch, "Shakira," *Rolling Stone*, 31 October 2002, 102.

77. LARAS, "Universe of Rhythms: The Grammys Guide to Latin Music," 2000. http://www.grammy.com/press/guide_eng.html.

78. Deborah Pacini Hernandez, "Race, Ethnicity and the Production of Latin/o Popular Music," in *Global Repertoires: Popular Music Within and Beyond the Transnational Music Industry*, ed. Andreas Gabesmair and Alfred Smudits (Burlington, VT: Ashgate Publishing Ltd., 2001).

79. Leila Cobo, "Reggaeton Broke Out but Regional Mexican Acts Drove Latin Biz," *Billboard*, Special Section, 24 December 2005, 20.

80. Jon Caramanica, "Grow Dem Bow," *Village Voice*, 12 January 2006. http://www.villagevoice.com/music/0603,caramanica,71722,22.html.

81. Interview with DJ Velcro, Deborah Pacini, and Reebee Garofalo, San Juan, Puerto Rico, 10 May 2006.

82. Agustin Gurza, "The Reggaeton Craze Saw a Quick Burnout with Fans and Radio," *Chicago Tribune*, 19 April 2006, 3

83. Leila Cobo, "Radio Flips for Reggaeton," *Billboard*, 10 September 2005, 47.

CHAPTER 12

1. At the time, the Netherlands-based Phillips Electronics Corporation owned Polygram's affiliated labels (Polydor, Deutsche Grammophon, Mercury, and Decca) and acquired A&M and Island. The German publishing conglomerate, Bertelsmann, purchased RCA Records and its affiliated labels to form BMG. The unexpected demerger of Thorn-EMI left EMI Records (EMI, Capitol, Chrysalis, IRS, and Rhino, among others) on its own.

2. Brian Garrity, "Music Biz Gets a Makeover," *Billboard*, 25 December 2004, YE-53.

3. Vito Peraino, "The Law of Increasing Returns," *Wired*, August 1999, 144.

4. Rachel Konrad, "Napster among Fastest-Growing Net Technologies," CNET News.com, 5 October 2000. http://news.cnet.com/news/0-1005-200-2938703.html.

5. U.S. Constitution: art. 1, § 8, cl. 8.

6. William Fisher, "Theories of Intellectual Property," 2000. http://cyber.law.harvard.edu/people/tfisher/iptheory.pdf.

7. H.R. Rep. No. 609, 100 Congress, 2nd session 23, 1988. Cited in L. Ray Patterson and Stanley W. Lindberg, *The Nature of Copyright: A Law of User's Rights* (Athens, GA: University of Georgia Press, 1991), 49.

8. Kenneth Cohen et al., "No Electronic Theft Act: Policy Development Team Report," Washington, D.C.: U.S. Sentencing Commission, February 1999, 2.

9. Reuters, "Prince Voices Support for Napster," CNET News.com, 9 August 2000. http://news.cnet.com/news/0-1005-200-2482624.html.

10. Statement of Roger McGuinn, Senate Judiciary Committee Hearing on Music on the Internet: Is There an Upside to Downloading? 11 July 2000. http://frwebgate.access.gpo.gov/cgi-bin/getdoc.cgi?dbname=106_senate_hearings&docid=f:74728.pdf.

11. Ibid.

12. See Ron Harris, "Metallica to Napster: Cut Users," *Boston Globe,* 4 May 2000, E4; and Steve Morse, "Napster Strikes Dissonant Chords," *Boston Globe,* 5 May 2000, D18.

13. John Borland, "Napster Says 30,000 Metallica Fans Appeal Ban," CNET, 16 May 2000. http://news.cnet.com/Napster-says-30,000-Metallica-fans-appeal-ban/2100-1023_3-240611.html.

14. P. J. Huffstutter, "Music Makers at Wits' End in Battle with Internet Takers," *Los Angeles Times,* 29 May 2000, A14.

15. Mark Latonero, "Survey of MP3 Usage: Report on a University Consumption Community," The Norman Lear Center, Annenberg School for Communication, University of Southern California, June 2000, 2.

16. "Playboy Poll: Napster Users Buy CD's," MP3 Newswire, 17 August 2000. http://www.mp3newswire.net/stories/2000/playboy.html.

17. RIAA Press Release, "Record Industry Announces 2000 Midyear Shipment Data," Washington, D.C., 25 August 2000. http://www.riaa.com/newsitem.php?news_month_filter=8&news_year_filter=2000&resultpage=&id=3525ABBC-B110-C3F5-8B63-AC4D3802C9C2.

18. Bloomberg News, "FTC Slams Record Labels on CD Sales Practice," 10 May 2000. http://news.cnet.com/2100-1023-240383.html.

19. Hiawatha Bray, "Hackers Go One Up," *Boston Globe,* 26 October 2000, C1.

20. Reuters, "Music Industry Still in First Gear Online," 7 January 2002. http://news.com.com/2100-1023802359.html.

21. Amy Harmon, "Music Industry in Global Fight on Web Copies," *New York Times,* 7 October 2002. http://www.nytimes.com/2002/10/07/technology/07SWAP.html.

22. John Borland, "Judge: File-Swapping Tools Are Legal," CNET News.com, 25 April 2003. http://news.cnet.com/2100-1027-998363.html.

23. Brian Garrity, "Grokster Blasts RIAA Anti-Piracy Tactics," *Billboard.com,* 27 June 2003. Posted on FreeRepublic.com. http://209.157.64.200/focus/f-news/936821/posts.

24. "New P2P File Sharing Stats," *p2pnet.net News,* 22 October 2004. http://p2pnet.net/story/2797.

25. Neil Strauss, "File-Sharing Battle Leaves Musicians Caught in Middle," *New York Times,* 14 September 2003. http://www.nytimes.com/2003/09/14/technology/14MUSI.html.

26. John Schwartz, "A Heretical View of File Sharing," *New York Times,* 5 April 2004. http://www.nytimes.com/2004/04/05/technology/05music.html.

27. Beth Potier, "File Sharing May Boost CD Sales: Study Defies Traditional Beliefs About Internet Use," *Harvard Gazette Archives,* 15 April 2004. http://www.news.harvard.edu/gazette/2004/04.15/09-filesharing.html.

28. Editorial, "The Sound of Lawsuits," *San Jose Mercury News,* 9 September 2003. http://www.bayarea.com/mld/mercurynews/news/opinion/6727444.htm.

29. Sue Zeidler, "Music Industry Sends Warning to Song Swappers," Yahoo News, 29 April 2003. http://msl1.mit.edu/furdlog/docs/2003-04-29_yahoo_reuters_riaa_threat.pdf.

30. "Senator: Trash Illegal Downloaders' PCs," CNN.Com, 18 June 2003. http://www.cnn.com/2003/TECH/internet/06/18/download.music.ap/index.html.

31. Andy Sullivan, "Music Firms, DJ Offer to Pay 12-Year-Old's Fine," Reuters, 11 September 2003. http://www.reuters.com/newsArticle.jhtml;jsessionid=GJHB5ZIZY5BACR-BAEKSFFA?type=topNews&storyID=3431108.

32. *RIAA v. The People: Two Years Later,* Electronic Frontier Foundation, 2005. http://w2.eff.org/IP/P2P/RIAAatTWO_FINAL.pdf.

33. Staff and Agencies, "Music Industry Counts the Cost of Online Piracy," *The Guardian,* 4 April 2006. http://arts.guardian.co.uk/netmusic/story/0,,1746741,00.html.

34. Bruce Gain, "RIAA Takes Shotgun to Traders," *Wired News,* 4 October 2005. http://www.wired.com/entertainment/music/news/2005/10/68951.

35. Heather Green, "Does She Look Like a Music Pirate?" *Business Week,* 5 May 2008. http://www.businessweek.com/magazine/content/08_18/b4082042959954.htm.

36. Justice David Souter, *MGM v. Grokster.* Supreme Court of the United States, No. 04–480, 27 June 2005.

37. Ibid.

38. Ibid.

39. "Roxio Buys Pressplay, to Relaunch Napster," Salon.com, 19 May 2003. http://www.salon.com/tech/wire/2003/05/19/roxio_pressplay/index.html.

40. Matthew Yi, "One Billion Songs Sold on iTunes," *San Francisco Chronicle,* 24 February 2006. http://www.sfgate.com/cgi-bin/article.cgi?f=/c/a/2006/02/24/BUG9THDRI31.DTL.

41. Ray Waddell, "Touring Strong, but Some Numbers Cause Concern," *Billboard,* 28 December 2002, 77.

42. Cynthia Cotts, "Telecom for Dummies, *Village Voice,* 5–11 September 2001. http://www.villagevoice.com/2001-09-04/news/telecom-for-dummies/.

43. Greg Kot, "What's Wrong with Radio," *Rolling Stone,* 16 August 2001, 25.

44. Tim Jones, "Media Giant's Rally Sponsorship Raises Questions," *Chicago Tribune,* 19 March 2003. http://www.chicagotribune.com/news/showcase/chi-0303190157mar19.story.

45. Ibid.

46. Paul Krugman, "Channels of Influence," *New York Times,* 25 March 2003. http://www.nytimes.com/2003/03/25/opinion/25KRUG.html.

47. Tom Roland, "Lee Greenwood," *All Music Guide,* n.d.. http://www.allmusic.com/cg/amg.dll?p=amg&uid=CASS80310101206&sql=B3srz286c054a.

48. John Metzger, "Neil Young Are You Passionate?" *The Music Box,* May 2002, Vol. 9, No. 5. http://www.musicbox-online.com/ny-pass.html.

49. Jenny Eliscu, "Chicks Triumph," *Rolling Stone,* 29 May 2003, 10.

50. Joan Anderman, "Dixie Chicks: A Brief History of an Outspoken Band," *Boston Globe,* 28 July 2006. http://www.boston.com/news/globe/living/articles/2006/07/28/dixie_chicks_a_brief_history_of_an_outspoken_band/.

51. Joseph Schumacher, "Is Protest Music as Dead as Disco?" *Peace and Conflict Monitor,* 12 May 2003. http://www.monitor.upeace.org/innerpg.cfm?id_article=5.

52. Brent Staples, "The Trouble with Corporate Radio: The Day the Protest Music Died," *New York Times,* 20 February 2003. http://www.nytimes.com/2003/02/20/opinion/20THU4.html.

53. Jeff Chang, "Is Protest Music Dead?" CounterPunch. 2 April 2002. http://www.counterpunch.org/changprotestmusic.html.

54. "N.J. Rock Station Won't Play Jethro Tull," Associated Press, 13 November 2003. http://new.music.yahoo.com/jethro-tull/news/n-j-rock-station-wont-play-jethro-tull—12175162;_ylt=AlcZ18t0YGd5y3xXuLx85FgQxCUv.

55. Posted on the MoveOn website: http://www.moveon.org/musiciansunited/.

56. Kristin V. Jones, "Rocking the Hip Hop Vote," *The Nation,* 1 December 2003, 8.

57. Edna Gundersen, "For Springsteen, 'Seeger Sessions' Sends a Message," *USA Today,* 7 June 2006, 3d.

58. Fred Goodman, "Will Rock Trounce Teen Pop," *Rolling Stone,* 28 February 2002, 19.

59. Chris Heath, "Creed's Stairway to Heaven," *Rolling Stone,* 28 February 2002, 40.

60. Goodman, "Will Rock Trounce Teen Pop," 20.

61. Ibid.

62. Larry Flick, "Declining Sales in 2002 Trigger Desire for Less Hype, Better Records, Fresh Blood." *Billboard,* 28 December 2002, 17.

63. Touré, "The Next Queen of Soul," *Rolling Stone,* 8 November 2001, 84.

64. Mark Binelli, "The Accidental Superstar," *Rolling Stone,* 18 March 2004, 54.

65. Austin Scaggs, "Why Is Nelly Furtado's New Album So Loud?" *Rolling Stone,* 19 June 2006. http://www.rollingstone.com/news/story/10603268/why_is_nelly_furtados_new_album_so_loud.

66. John Pareles, "Music; So Sweet, So Sensitive, So Self-Absorbed, So 70's," *New York Times,* 18 May 2003. http://www.nytimes.com/2003/05/18/arts/music-so-sweet-so-sensitive-so-self-absorbed-so-70-s.html.

67. Ibid.

68. MacKenzie Wilson, "On and On," *All Music Guide.* http://www.allmusic.com/cg/amg.dll?p=amg&uid=UIDSUB04031220182845228 1&sql=Allf8zfi3eh2k.

69. Stephen Thomas Erlewine, "Heavier Things," *All Music Guide.* http://www.allmusic.com/cg/amg.dll?p=amg&uid=UIDSUB04031220182.

70. Pareles, "Music; So Sweet, So Sensitive, So Self-Absorbed, So 70's."

71. Bill Carter, "How a Hit Almost Failed Its Own Audition," *New York Times*, 30 April 2006, 1

72. Paul R. La Monica, "No False 'Idol' for Fox," CNN Money.com, 24 May 2006. http://money.cnn.com/2006/05/22/news/companies/idol_fox/index.htm.

73. Jocelyn Noveck, "Whole Lotta Love for 'Idol' Lambert," Boston Globe, 16 May 2009. http://www.boston.com/ae/tv/articles/2009/05/16/whole_lotta_love_for_idol_lambert/.

74. Joan Anderman, "Hip-Hop Setting the Beat," *Boston Globe,* 4 October 2003 http://www.boston.com/news/local/articles/2003/10/04/hip_hop_setting_the_beat/

75. David Toop, *The Rap Attack: African Jive to New York Hip Hop* (New South Wales, Australia: Pluto Press, 1984), 154.

76. Josh Tyrangiel, "You Can't Ignore Kanye," *Time,* 29 August 2005, 54.

77. Silvio Pietroluongo, Minal Patel, and Wade Jessen, "Singles Minded: Hot 100 Adds Digital Sales; Pop 100 Debuts," *Billboard,* 12 February 2005, 64.

78. Bill Lamb, "How to Read the Billboard Charts," Aboutcom, retrieved on 26 August 2006. http://top40.about.com/od/popmusic101/a/billboardcharts.htm.

79. Charles M. Blow, "Swan Songs?" *New York Times*, 1 August 2009. http://www.nytimes.com/2009/08/01/opinion/01blow.html.

80. Ray Waddell, "Burning Up, the Road: Both Dollars and Attendance Prove Touring Is Out of Its Slump." *Billboard*, 23 December 2006, YE-8.

81. Ibid.

82. Ibid.

83. Ray Waddell, "The Rules of the Road: In Uncertain Times, the Live Music Business Posted a Strong 2008." *Billboard*, 20 December 2008, 50.

84. Sarah Rodman, "Music Lovers Pack Halls, Drown the Money Blues," *Boston Globe,* 20 May 2009. http://www.boston.com/news/local/massachusetts/articles/2009/05/20/music_lovers_pack_halls_drown_the_money_blues/.

85. Cortney Harding, "Bigger Bytes: Indies Experienced Accelerated Growth in '07," *Billboard*, 22 December 2007, 38.

86. Chris Anderson, "The Long Tail," *Wired,* October 2004. http://www.wired.com/wired/archive/12.10/tail.html.

87. Ibid.

88. Ibid.

89. Ray Waddell, "Rise of the Super-Manager: As Labels Stumble, Managers Become the Industry's Force to Be Reckoned With," *Billboard*, 20 December 2008, 10.

Bibliography

Ackerman, Paul. "Gortikov Scorches Whitey Trade in NAFTRA Speech." *Billboard* (17 July 1969).

Alexander, David. "Giving the Devil More Than His Due." *The Humanist* (March–April 1990).

Allen, Harry. "Hip Hop Madness: From Def Jams to Cold Lampin', Rap Is Our Music." *Essence* (April 1989).

"American Revolution 1969." *Rolling Stone* (5 April 1969): special insert.

Anderman, Joan. "Dixie Chicks: A Brief History of an Outspoken Band." *Boston Globe* (28 July 2006), http://www.boston.com/news/globe/living/articles/2006/07/28/dixie_chicks_a_brief_history_of_an_outspoken_band/.

———. "The Female Fans Say They're in It for the Catharsis." *Boston Globe* (16 July 2000).

———. "Hip-Hop Setting the Beat." *Boston Globe* (4 October 2003), http://www.boston.com/news/local/articles/2003/10/04/hip_hop_setting_the_beat/.

———. "Shut Up." *Boston Globe* (3 December 2000).

Anderson, Chris. "The Long Tail," *Wired* (October 2004), http://www.wired.com/wired/archive/12.10/tail.html.

Ansen, David. "Rock Tycoon." *Newsweek* (31 July 1978).

Archer, Gleason L. *History of Radio to 1926.* New York: American Historical Society, 1938.

"ASCAP Defied." *Business Week* (16 November 1940).

Bangs, Lester. "The White Noise Supremacists." *Village Voice* (30 April 1979).

Barlow, William. "Cashing In." In Jannette L. Dates and William Barlow, eds., *Split Image: African Americans in the Mass Media*, 2d ed. Washington, D.C.: Howard University Press, 1993.

Barnouw, Erik. *The Golden Web: A History of Broadcasting in the United States, 1933–1953.* New York: Oxford University Press, 1968.

Belz, Carl. *The Story of Rock*, 2d ed. New York: Harper Colophon, 1971.

Bennett, Tony, Simon Firth, Lawrence Grossberg, John Shepard, and Graeme Turner, eds. *Rock and Popular Music: Politics, Policies, Institutions.* New York: Routledge, 1993.

Berry, Robert J. "Satanism: The Law Enforcement Response." *The National Sheriff* (February–March, 1987).

Biafra, Jello. "The Far Right and the Censorship of Music." *Harvard Law Record* (17 April 1987).

Binelli, Mark. "The Accidental Superstar." *Rolling Stone* (18 March 2004).

"The Birth of Our Popular Songs." *Literary Digest* (7 October 1916).

Bloomberg News. "FTC Slams Record Labels on CD Sales Practice" (10 May 2000), http://news.cnet.com/2100-1023-240383.html.

Blow, Charles M. "Swan Songs?" *New York Times* (1 August 2009), http://www.nytimes.com/2009/08/01/opinion/01blow.html.

Bondi, Vic. "Feeding Noise Back into the System: Hardcore, Hip Hop, and Heavy Metal." Paper presented at the New England American Studies Association Conference, Brandeis University, Boston, Mass., 1 May 1993.

Borland, John. "Judge: File-Swapping Tools Are Legal." CNET News.com (25 April 2003), http://news.com.com/2100-1027-998363.html.

———. "Napster Lawyer Turns Antitrust Experience on RIAA." CNET News.com (20 July 2000), http://news.cnet.com/news/0-1005-200-2295301.html.

———. "Napster Says 30,000 Metallica Fans Appeal Ban," CNET, 16 May 2000, http://news.cnet.com/Napster-says-30,000-Metallica-fans-appeal-ban/2100-1023_3-240611.html.

———. "Tech Giants Slam Napster Injunction." CNET News.com (25 August 2000), http://news.cnet.com/news/0-1005-200-2612001.html.

———. "U.S. Sides with RIAA Against Napster." CNET News.com (8 September 2000), http://news.cnet.com/news/0-1005-200-2731198.html.

Bozza, Anthony. "NSynchronicity." *Rolling Stone* (30 March 2000).

Brack, Ray. "James Brown." *Rolling Stone* (21 January 1970).

Brackett, David. "The Politics and Practice of 'Crossover' in American Popular Music, 1963 to 1965." *The Musical Quarterly* (Winter, 1994).

Bray, Hiawatha. "Hackers Go One Up." *Boston Globe* (26 October 2000).

Breskin, David. "Bob Geldof: The Rolling Stone Interview." *Rolling Stone* (5 December 1985).

Bricker, Rebecca. "Take One." *People* (4 April 1983).

Broven, John. *Rhythm and Blues in New Orleans.* Gretna, La.: Pelican Publishing Co., 1988.

Brown, Janelle. "Crack SDMI? No Thanks!" Salon.com (14 September 2000), http://www.salon.com/tech/log/2000/09/14/hack_sdmi/index.html.

Browne, David. "Turn That @#!% Down: The Complete Idiot's Guide to the Future of Rock & Roll." *Entertainment Weekly* (21 August 1992).

Bry, David. "The Song of the South." *Vibe* (June 2002).

Caramanica, Jon. "Grow Dem Bow." *Village Voice* (12 January 2006), http://www.villagevoice.com/music/0603,caramanica,71722,22.html.

Carr, Tim. "Talk That Talk, Walk That Walk." *Rolling Stone* (26 May 1983).

Carter, Bill. "How a Hit Almost Failed Its Own Audition." *New York Times* (30 April 2006).

"To Censor Popular Songs." *Literary Digest* (24 May 1913).

Chambers, Iain. *Urban Rhythms: Popular Music and Popular Culture*. New York: Macmillan, 1985.

Chang, Jeff, "Is Protest Music Dead?" CounterPunch (2 April 2002), http://www.counterpunch.org/changprotestmusic.html.

Chapple, Steve, and Reebee Garofalo. *Rock 'n' Roll Is Here to Pay: The History and Politics of the Music Industry*. Chicago: Nelson-Hall, 1977.

Christgau, Georgia. "Disco! Disco! Disco! Four Critics Address the Musical Question." *In These Times* (6–12 June 1979).

Christgau, Robert. *Any Old Way You Choose It: Rock and Other Pop Music, 1967–1973*. Baltimore, Md.: Penguin Books, 1973.

———. "A Cult Explodes—and a Movement Is Born." *Village Voice* (24 October 1977).

Clarke, Donald, ed. *The Penguin Encyclopedia of Popular Music*. New York: Viking, 1989.

Cobo, Leila. "Radio Flips for Reggaeton." *Billboard* (10 September 2005).

———. "Reggaton Broke Out but Regional Mexican Acts Drove Latin Biz." *Billboard*, (24 December 2005); special section.

———. "Reggaeton Rules." *Billboard* (30 July 2005).

Cockrell, Dale. *Demons of Disorder: Early Blackface Minstrels and Their World* (New York: Cambridge University Press, 1997).

Cohen, Kenneth, Tom Brown, Jim Gibson, Paul Hofer, Vanessa Locke, Sharon Long, Cynthia Matthews, and Courtney Semisch. "No Electronic Theft Act: Policy Development Team Report." Washington, D.C.: United States Sentencing Commission, February 1999.

Cohen, Rich. "Southern Comfort." *Rolling Stone* (10 August 1995).

Coleman, Mark. "The Revival of Conscience." *Rolling Stone* (15 November 1990).

Collin, Matthew. *Altered States: The Story of Ecstasy Culture and Acid House*. New York: Serpent's Tail, 1997.

Considine, J. D. "Led Zeppelin." *Rolling Stone* (20 September 1990).

———. "Metal Mania." *Rolling Stone* (15 November 1990).

Cotts, Cynthia. "Telecom for Dummies." *Village Voice* (5–11 September 2001), http://www.villagevoice.com/2001-09-04/news/telecom-for-dummies/.

Cripps, Thomas. "Film." In Jannette L. Dates and William Barlow, eds., *Split Image: African Americans in the Mass Media*, 2d ed. Washington, D.C.: Howard University Press, 1993.

Cross, Brian. *It's Not About a Salary: Rap, Race and Resistance in Los Angeles*. New York: Verso, 1993.

Cummings, Sue. "Road Warriors." *Spin* (August 1986).

Daly, Steven. "Britney Spears: Inside the Heart and Mind (and Bedroom) of America's New Teen Queen." *Rolling Stone* (15 April 1999).

Dates, Jannette L., and William Barlow, eds. *Split Image: African Americans in the Mass Media*, 2d ed. Washington, D.C.: Howard University Press, 1993.

Dawson, Jim, and Steve Propes. *What Was the First Rock 'n' Roll Record?* Boston: Faber and Faber, 1992.

DeCurtis, Anthony. "The Eagles." *Rolling Stone* (20 September 1990).

———. "Kurt Cobain, 1967–1994." *Rolling Stone* (2 June 1994).

———. "Ropin' the Whirl Wind." *Rolling Stone* (1 April 1993).

———. "The Year in Music." *Rolling Stone* (10–24 December 1992).

DeCurtis, Anthony, and James Henke, eds. *The Rolling Stone Illustrated History of Rock & Roll*. New York: Random House, 1992.

de Forest, Lee. *Father of Radio*. Chicago: Wilcox and Follett, 1950.

Denisoff, R. Serge, and Richard A. Peterson, eds. *The Sounds of Social Change: Studies in Popular Culture*. New York: Rand McNally, 1972.

Denselow, Robin. *When the Music's Over: The Story of Political Pop*. Boston: Faber and Faber, 1989.

Dexter, D. "1935–1945, Disk Jockey: Origin of the Species." *Billboard* (27 December 1969).

Draper, Robert. *Rolling Stone Magazine*. New York: Harper and Row, 1990.

Eisen, Jonathan, ed. *The Age of Rock*. New York: Vintage Books, 1969.

Elavsky, C. Michael. "United as ONE: Live 8 and the Politics of the Global Music Media Spectacle." *Journal of Popular Music Studies* (December 2009).

Eliscu, Jenny. "Chicks Triumph." *Rolling Stone* (29 May 2003).

Ennis, Philip. *The Seventh Stream: The Emergence of Rock 'n' Roll in American Popular Music*. Hanover, N.H.: Wesleyan University Press/University Press of New England, 1992.

Erlewine, Michael, et al., eds. *All Music Guide to Rock*. San Francisco: Miller Freeman Books, 1997.

Farrar, Richard. "Da Doo Ron Ron." *Rolling Stone* (11 May 1968).

Feld, Steven. "Notes on World Beat." *Public Culture Bulletin* (Fall, 1988).

Felder, Rachel. *Manic Pop Thrill*. Hopewell, N.J.: Echo Press, 1993.

Fikentscher, Kai. *You Better Work: Underground Dance Music in New York City*. Hanover, N.H.: University Press of New England, 2000.

Fisher, William. "Theories of Intellectual Property." In Stephen Munzer, ed., *New Essays in the Legal and Political Theory of Property*. Cambridge University Press, 2001. http://cyber.law.harvard.edu/people/tfisher/iptheory.pdf.

Flick, Larry. "Declining Sales in 2002 Trigger Desire for Less Hype, Better Records, Fresh Blood." *Billboard* (28 December 2002).

Flores, Juan. *From Bomba to Hip Hop: Puerto Rican Culture and Latino Identity*. New York: Columbia University Press, 2000.

Fong-Torres, Ben, ed. *The Rolling Stone Interviews*. 2 vols. New York: Warner Books, 1973.

———. "The Rolling Stone Interview: Ray Charles." *Rolling Stone* (18 January 1973).

Forman, Murray. "'Represent': Race, Space and Place in Rap Music." *Popular Music* (January 2000).

———. "Soundtrack to a Crisis: Music, Context, Discourse." *Television and New Media* (May 2002).

Fox, Ted. *In the Groove.* New York: St. Martin's Press, 1986.

———. *Showtime at the Apollo.* New York: Holt, Rinehart and Winston, 1983.

Fricke, David. "Imagine." *Rolling Stone* (27 December 2001–3 January 2002).

———. "Kurt Cobain." *Rolling Stone* (27 January 1994).

———. "Red Hot Chili Peppers' Naked Truth." *Rolling Stone* (25 June 1992).

Frith, Simon. "Beyond the Dole Queue: The Politics of Punk." *Village Voice* (24 October 1977).

———. "Crappy Birthday to Punk." *In These Times* (23–29 April 1986).

———, ed. *Facing the Music.* New York: Pantheon Books, 1988.

———. *Sound Effects: Youth, Leisure and the Politics of Rock 'n' Roll.* New York: Pantheon Books, 1981.

Frith, Simon, and Andrew Goodwin, eds. *On Record: Rock, Pop, and the Written Word.* New York: Pantheon Books, 1990.

Frith, Simon, and Howard Horne. *Art into Pop.* New York: Methuen, 1987.

Frith, Simon, and John Street. "Party Music." *Marxism Today* (June 1986).

Gaar, Gillian G. *She's a Rebel: The History of Women in Rock & Roll.* Seattle, Wash.: Seal Press, 1992.

Gain, Bruce. "RIAA Takes Shotgun to Traders." *Wired News* (4 October 2005), http://www.wired.com/news/digiwood/0,1412,68951,00.html.

Gaines, Donna. "Suicidal Tendencies: Kurt Did Not Die for You." *Rolling Stone* (2 June 1994).

Garofalo, Reebee. "Crossing Over, 1939–1992." In Jannette L. Dates and William Barlow, eds., *Split Image: African Americans in the Mass Media,* 2d ed. Washington, D.C.: Howard University Press, 1993.

———. "The Impact of the Civil Rights Movement on Popular Music." *Radical America.* March 1989.

———. "I Want My MP3: Who Owns Internet Music?" In Martin Cloonan and Reebee Garofalo, eds., *Policing Pop.* Philadelphia, Pa.: Temple University Press, 2003.

———. "Nelson Mandela, the Concert: Mass Culture as a Contested Terrain." In Mark O'Brien and Craig Little, eds., *Reimaging America: The Arts of Social Change.* Philadelphia, Pa.: New Society Publishers, 1990.

———. "Pop Goes to War, 2001–2004: U.S. Popular Music After 9/11." In J. Martin Daughtry and Jonathan Ritter, eds., *Music in the Post-9/11 World.* New York: Routledge, 2007.

———, ed. *Rockin' the Boat: Mass Music and Mass Movements.* Boston: South End Press, 1992.

———. "Setting the Record Straight: Censorship and Social Responsibility in Popular Music." *Journal of Popular Music Studies,* Vol. 6, 1994.

———. "Understanding Mega-Events: If We Are the World, Then How Do We Change It?" In Constance Penley and Andrew Ross, eds., *Technoculture.* Minneapolis: University of Minnesota Press, 1991.

Garrity, Brian. "Anticipated Boom Was a Bust." *Billboard* (24 December 2005).

———. "Grokster Blasts RIAA Anti-Piracy Tactics." BillBoard.com (27 June 2003). Posted on FreeRepublic.com. http://209.157.64.200/focus/f-news/936821/posts.

———. "Music Biz Gets a Makeover." *Billboard* (25 December 2004).

George, Nelson. *Buppies, B-Boys, Baps and Bohos: Notes on Post-Soul Black Culture,* New York: HarperCollins, 1992.

———. *The Death of Rhythm & Blues.* New York: Pantheon Books, 1988.

Gett, Steve. "Rock '86." *Billboard* (27 December 1986).

Gillen, Marilyn. "The Year in Business: Ups, Downs, and Rebounds." *Billboard* (27 December 1999).

Gillett, Charlie. *The Sound of the City: The Rise of Rock and Roll.* New York: Outerbridge and Dienstfrey, 1970.

Gilmore, Mikal. "Disco." *Rolling Stone* (19 April 1979).

———. "The Year in Music." *Rolling Stone* (13–27 December 1990).

Gitlin, Todd, *The Sixties: Years of Hope, Days of Rage.* New York: Bantam Books, 1993.

Glasser, Ruth. *My Music Is My Flag: Puerto Rican Musicians and Their New York Communities, 1917–1940* (Los Angeles: University of California Press, 1995).

Gleason, Ralph. "Perspectives: Changing with the Money Changers." *Rolling Stone* (20 January 1968).

———. "Stop This Shuck Mike Bloomfield." *Rolling Stone* (11 May 1968).

Goldberg, Michael. "Bill Graham: The Rolling Stone Interview." *Rolling Stone* (19 December 1985).

———. "The Spending Begins." *Rolling Stone* (24 October 1985).

Goodman, Fred. "Big Deals: How Money Fever Is Changing the Music Business." *Musician* (January 1992).

———. "Will Rock Trounce Teen Pop." *Rolling Stone* (28 February 2002).

Goodwin, Andrew. *Dancing in the Distraction Factory: Music Television and Popular Culture.* Minneapolis: University of Minnesota Press, 1992.

Graham, Renée. "Is Some Hatred More Acceptable Than Others?" *Boston Globe* (5 January 2001).

Graustark, Barbara. "Disco Takes Over." *Newsweek* (2 April 1979).

Gray, Herman. "Popular Music as a Social Problem: A Social History of Claims Against Popular Music." In Joel Best, ed., *Images of Issues.* Hawthorne, N.Y.: De Gruyter, 1989.

———. "Rate the Records: Symbolic Conflict, Popular Music, and Social Problems." *Popular Music and Society* (Fall, 1989).

Green, Heather, "Does She Look Like a Music Pirate?" *Business Week* (5 May 2008), http://www.businessweek.com/magazine/content/08_18/b4082042959954.htm.

Green, Tony. "The Dirty South." In *The VIBE History of Hip Hop,* ed. Alan Light. New York: Three Rivers Press, 1999.

Grein, Paul. "AOR Programmers Plan More Variety." *Billboard* (14 January 1984).

———. "Charts '86." *Billboard* (27 December 1986).

———. "'83 RIAA Tally: Fewer Biggies." *Billboard* (14 January 1984).

———. "Unemployment Lines: LA Industrial Personnel Face Major Challenges to Rebuild Their Careers." *Billboard* (19 May 1979).

———. "The Year in Charts." *Billboard* (26 December 1987).

Grossberg, Lawrence. "The Framing of Rock: Rock and the New Conservatism." In Tony Bennett et al., eds., *Rock and Popular Music: Politics, Policies, Institutions.* New York: Routledge, 1993.

———. *We Gotta Get Out of This Place: Popular Conservatism and Postmodern Culture.* New York: Routledge, 1992.

Grossman, Jay. "Let There Be Dancing in the Streets." *Rolling Stone* (23 May 1974).

Gundersen, Edna. "For Springsteen, 'Seeger Sessions' Sends a Message." *USA Today* (7 June 2006).

Guralnick, Peter. *Feel Like Going Home: Portraits in Blues and Rock 'n' Roll.* New York: E. P. Dutton, 1971.

———. *The Listener's Guide to the Blues.* New York: Facts on File, 1982.

———. *Sweet Soul Music: Rhythm and Blues and the Southern Dream of Freedom.* New York: Harper and Row, 1986.

Gurza, Agustin. "The Reggaeton Craze Saw a Quick Burnout with Fans and Radio." *Los Angeles Times* (19 April 2006), http://www.chicagotribune.com/features/lifestyle/chi-0604190022apr19,1,3467652.story?coll=chi-leisuretempo-hed&ctrack=1&cset=true.

Guzman, Pablo. "On the Radio, Part Two." *Rock & Roll Confidential* (January 1984).

Hager, Steven. *Hip Hop: The Illustrated History of Break Dancing, Rap Music, and Graffiti.* New York: St. Martin's Press, 1984.

Hamill, Pete. "A Day to Remember." *Rolling Stone* (29 August 1985).

Hamm, Charles. *Yesterdays: Popular Song in America.* New York: W. W. Norton, 1983.

Hammond, John. *On Record.* New York: Penguin Books, 1981.

Harding, Cortney. "Bigger Bytes: Indies Experienced Accelerated Growth in '07," *Billboard* (22 December 2007).

Harmon, Amy. "Music Industry in Global Fight on Web Copies." *New York Times* (7 October 2002), http://www.nytimes.com/2002/10/07/technology/07SWAP.html.

Harris, Ron. "Metallica to Napster: Cut Users." *Boston Globe*, (4 May 2000).

Heath, Chris. "Creed's Stairway to Heaven." *Rolling Stone* (28 February 2002).

———. "The Epic Life of Carlos Santana." *Rolling Stone* (16 March 2000).

———. "Has Anyone Seen Christina." *Rolling Stone* (14 November 2001).

Heilbut, Tony. *The Gospel Sound: Good News and Bad Times.* New York: Simon and Schuster, 1971.

Heilemann, John. "David Boies: The Wired Interview." *Wired* (October 2000). http://www.wired.com/wired/archive/8.10/boies_pr.html.

Heins, Marjorie. *Sex, Sin, and Blasphemy: A Guide to America's Censorship Wars.* New York: The New Press, 1993.

Henderson, Alex. "Active Indies." *Billboard* (24 December 1988).

Henke, James. "Record Companies Dancing to a Billion Dollar Tune." *Rolling Stone* (19 April 1979).

Hersey, Gerri. *Nowhere to Run: The Story of Soul Music.* New York: Penguin Books, 1984.

Heylin, Clinton. *From the Velvets to the Voidoids: A Pre-Punk History for a Post-Punk World.* New York: Penguin Books, 1993.

Hilburn, Robert. "Musical Lessons from 1983's First Half." *Cape Cod Times* (16 July 1983).

Hill, Trent. "The Enemy Within: Censorship in Rock Music in the 1950s." *South Atlantic Quarterly* (Fall, 1991).

"The Hip-Hop 50." *Rolling Stone* (29 October 1998).

Holden, Stephen. "The Evolution of a Dance Craze." *Rolling Stone* (19 April 1979).

———. "Musical Odyssey." *New York Times* (9 December 1987).

———. "Pop Records Turn to Hip Hop." *New York Times* (23 September 1984).

Holland, Bill. "Senate Hearing Examines Gangsta Lyrics." *Billboard* (5 March 1994).

Holloway, Joseph E., ed. *Africanisms in American Culture.* Bloomington: Indiana University Press, 1990.

Hu, Jim. "Web, Music Giants March to Different Tunes." CNET News.com (13 July 2001), http://news.cnet.com/news/0-1005-200-6561339.html.

Huffstutter, P. J. "Music Makers at Wits' End in Battle with Internet Takers." *Los Angeles Times* (29 May 2000).

Hung, Michèle, and Esteban Garcia Morencos. *World Record Sales 1969–1990: A Statistical History of the World Recording Industry.* London: International Federation of the Phonogram Industry, 1990.

"I Heard the News Today . . . " *Rolling Stone* (25 October 2001).

Jacobs, Norman, ed. *Culture for the Millions? Mass Media in Modern Society.* Princeton, N.J.: D. Van Nostrand, 1959.

Jones, Hettie. *Big Star, Fallin' Mama.* New York: Viking Press, 1974.

Jones, Kristin V. "Rocking the Hip Hop Vote." *The Nation* (1 December 2003).

Jones, Leroi [Amiri Baraka]. *Blues People.* New York: William Morrow, 1963.

Jones, Steve. "Ban(ned) in the USA: Popular Music and Censorship." *Journal of Communication Inquiry* (Winter, 1991).

Jones, Tim. "Media Giant's Rally Sponsorship Raises Questions." *Chicago Tribune* (19 March 2003), http://www.chicagotribune.com/news/showcase/chi-0303190157mar19.story.

Jones, Vanessa E. "Whose Word Is It Anyway?" *Boston Globe* (7 July 1999).

Kafka, Peter. "The Queen of Teen." *Forbes* (20 March 2000).

Kahn, Joseph P. "Musical Chairs Coming Up for the White House." *Boston Globe* (20 January 2001).

Kaplan, E. Ann. *Rocking Around the Clock: Music Television, Postmodernism, and Consumer Culture.* New York: Routledge, 1987.

Kleinfeld, N. R. "FM's Success Is Loud and Clear." *New York Times* (26 October 1979).

Konrad, Rachel. "Napster Among Fastest-Growing Net Technologies." CNET News.com (5 October 2000), http://news.cnet.com/news/0-1005-200-2938703.html.

Kopkind, Andrew. "The Dialectic of Disco." *Village Voice* (12 February 1979).

Kot, Greg. "What's Wrong with Radio." *Rolling Stone* (16 August 2001).

Krugman, Paul. "Channels of Influence," *New York Times* (25 March 2003), http://www.nytimes.com/2003/03/25/opinion/25KRUG.html.

Lamb, Bill. "How to Read the Billboard Charts." About.Com (26 August 2006), http://top40.about.com/od/popmusic101/a/billboardcharts.htm.

LaMonica, Paul R. "No False "Idol" for Fox." CNN Money.com (24 May 2006). http://money.cnn.com/2006/05/22/news/companies/idol_fox/index.htm

Landau, Jon. "The Motown Story." *Rolling Stone* (13 May 1971).
———. "Soul." *Rolling Stone* (24 February 1968).

Latonero, Mark. "Survey of MP3 Usage: Report on a University Consumption Community." The Norman Lear Center, Annenberg School for Communication, University of Southern California (June 2000).

Lax, Roger, and Frederick Smith. *The Great Song Thesaurus.* New York: Oxford University Press, 1989.

Lederman, Minna. "Music and Monopoly." *The Nation* (28 December 1940).

Levinson, Nan. "Shut Up." *Boston Globe* (20 February 1994).

Levy, Steven. "Ad Nauseum: How MTV Sells Out Rock & Roll." *Rolling Stone* (8 December 1983).

Lewis, L. *Gender Politics and MTV: Voicing the Difference.* Philadelphia, Pa.: Temple University Press, 1990.

Light, Alan. "Ice." *Rolling Stone* (20 August 1992).

Lipsitz, George. *Class and Culture in Cold War America: "A Rainbow at Midnight."* South Hadley, Mass.: J. F. Bergin, 1982.
———. *Time Passages: Collective Memory and American Popular Culture.* Minneapolis: University of Minnesota Press, 1990.

Lombardi, John. "Kenny Gamble and Leon Huff and the Resurrection of Jerry Butler and Philly Soul." *Rolling Stone* (30 April 1970).

Lont, Cynthia M. "Women's Music: No Longer a Small Private Party." In Reebee Garofalo, ed., *Rockin' the Boat: Mass Music and Mass Movements.* Boston: South End Press, 1992.

Lopez, Ana M. "Are All Latins from Manhattan: Hollywood, Ethnography, and Cultural Colonialism." In Alan Williams, ed., *Film and Nationalism.* Philadelphia, PA: Rutgers University Press, 2002.

Lott, Eric. "Love and Theft: The Racial Unconscious of Blackface Minstrelsy." *Representations* (Summer 1992).

Lydon, Michael, ed. *The Age of Rock 2: Sights and Sounds of the American Cultural Revolution.* New York: Vintage Books, 1970.
———. "The High Cost of Music and Love: Where's the Money from Monterey?" *Rolling Stone* (9 November 1967).
———. *Rock Folk: Portraits from the Rock 'n' Roll Pantheon.* New York: Dell, 1968.
———. "Smokey Robinson." *Rolling Stone* (28 September 1968).

Lyman, Rick. "New Data Shows Immigrants' Growth and Reach." *New York Times* (August 15, 2006).

Malone, Bill C. *Country Music U.S.A.*, rev. ed. Austin: University of Texas Press, 1985.

Marcus, Greil. "Is This the Woman Who Invented Rock & Roll? The Deborah Chessler Story." *Rolling Stone* (24 June 1993).
———. *Mystery Train: Images of America in Rock 'n' Roll.* New York: Dutton, 1975.
———. "Rock for Ethiopia." Panel presentation at the Third International Conference on Popular Music Studies, Montreal, Quebec, Canada (July 1985).

Marsh, Dave. "The Flip Sides of 1979." *Rolling Stone* (27 December 1979).
———. "What's Being Sold in Country?" *New York Times* (24 May 1992).

Marshall, Wayne. "The Rise of Reggaeton." *Boston Phoenix* (19 January 2006), http://www.thephoenix.com/article_ektid1595.aspx.

Martin, Linda, and Kerry Segrave. *Anti-Rock: The Opposition to Rock 'n' Roll.* New York: DeCapo Press, 1993.

Maultsby, Portia K. "Africanisms in African-American Popular Music." In Joseph E. Holloway, ed., *Africanisms in American Culture.* Bloomington: Indiana University Press, 1990.

McClary, Susan. *Feminine Endings: Music, Gender, and Sexuality.* Minneapolis: University of Minnesota Press, 1991.

McClary, Susan, and Robert Walser. "Start Making Sense: Musicology Wrestles with Rock." In Simon Frith and Andrew Goodwin, eds., *On Record: Rock, Pop, and the Written Word.* New York: Pantheon Books, 1990.

McGuinn, Roger (Statement of). Senate Judiciary Committee Hearing on "The Future of Digital Music: Is There an Upside to Downloading?" (11 July 2000), http://www.senate.gov/~judiciary/7112000_rm.htm.

McLeese, Don. "Anatomy of an Anti-Disco Riot." *In These Times* (29 August–4 September 1979).

McLeod, Kembrew. "Genres, Sub-Genres, Sub-Sub-Genres and More: Musical and Social Differentiation Within Electronic-Dance Music Communities." *Journal of Popular Music Studies* (Spring 2001).

Merritt, Jay. "Disco Station Number One in New York." *Rolling Stone* (22 March 1979).

Metzger, John. "Neil Young Are You Passionate?" *The Music Box*, 9, no. 5 (May 2002), http://www.musicbox-online.com/ny-pass.html.

Miller, Jim. "It's Not Only Rock 'n' Roll." *Boston Globe* (23 August 1991).
———, ed. *The Rolling Stone Illustrated History of Rock 'n' Roll.* New York: Rolling Stone Press, 1976.
———. "State of the Art." *Newsweek* (18 April 1983).

Mills, David. "Rap as Politics: The Sayings of Sister Souljah." *Essence* (September 1992).

Minton, Lynn. "Is Heavy Metal Dangerous?" *Parade* (20 September 1992).

Monson, Ingrid. "Jazz Chronological Overview." In Mellonee V, Burnim and Portia K. Maultsby, eds., *African American Music: An Introduction*. New York: Routlegde, 2006.

Mooney, H. F. "Popular Music Since the 1920s: The Significance of Shifting Taste." In Jonathan Eisen, ed., *The Age of Rock*. New York: Vintage Books, 1969.

Moore, Jerrold Northrop. *A Matter of Records: Fred Gaisberg and the Golden Era of the Gramophone*. New York: Taplinger Publishing Co., 1976.

Morse, Dave. *Motown*. London: Vista, 1971.

Morse, Steve. "Can American Bands Beat the British Blitz?" *Boston Globe* (1 January 1984).

———. "Napster Strikes Dissonant Chords." *Boston Globe* (5 May 2000).

———. "In Pop, Women Took New Ground All Over." *Boston Globe* (29 December 1996).

"Music Industry Counts the Cost of Online Piracy." *The Guardian* (4 April 2006), http://arts.guardian.co.uk/netmusic/story/0,,1746741,00.html.

Nathan, David. "Rap." *Billboard* (24 December 1988).

Neely, Kim. "Into the Unknown." *Rolling Stone* (16 June 1994).

Negus, Keith. *Music Genres and Corporate Cultures*. New York: Routledge, 1999.

Nelson, Havelock. "Music and Violence: Does Crime Pay?" *Billboard* (13 November 1993).

"New Black Hope." *Billboard* (17 May 1969).

"N.J. Rock Station Won't Play Jethro Tull," Associated Press (13 November 2003), http://apnews.excite.com/article/20031113/D7UPO1981.html.

Newman, Melinda. "The Good, Bad, and Mostly Ugly of 2002 Remembered." *Billboard* (28 December 2002).

"New p2p file sharing stats." p2pnet.net News (22 October 2004), http://p2pnet.net/story/2797.

Noveck, Jocelyn. "Whole Lotta Love for 'Idol' Lambert," *Boston Globe* (16 May 2009), http://www.boston.com/ae/tv/articles/2009/05/16/whole_lotta_love_for_idol_lambert/.

Nunziata, Susan. "'90 Label Tally: Units Up 7.3%, $ Jump 14.6%." *Billboard* (6 April 1991).

Odum, Howard W., and Guy B. Johnson. *Negro Workaday Songs*. Chapel Hill: University of North Carolina Press, 1926.

"Of Hard-Rock Demons: A Cardinal Speaks Out." *Boston Globe* (6 March 1990).

Ogunnaike, Lola. "Caught in the Act." *Vibe* (May 2002).

O'Neil, Thomas. *The Grammys for the Record*. New York: Penguin Books, 1993.

Orloff, Katherine. *Rock 'n' Roll Woman*. Los Angeles: Nash Publishing, 1974.

Orr, Charlene, et al. "Texas Police Pursue 'Cop Killer.'" *Billboard* (27 June 1992).

Ostling, Richard N. "No Sympathy for the Devil." *Time* (19 March 1990).

Pacini Hernandez, Deborah. "Dominicans in the Mix: Reflections on Dominicans and Reggaeton." In Raquel Z. Rivera, Deborah Pacini Hernandez and Wayne Marshall, eds., *Reggaeton*. Raleigh, NC: Duke University Press, 2009.

———. *Oye Como Va!: Hybridity and Identity in Latino Popular Music*. Philadelphia, PA: Temple University Press, 2010.

———. "Race, Ethnicity and the Production of Latin/o Popular Music." In Andreas Gabesmair and Alfred Smudits, eds., *Global Repertoires: Popular Music Within and Beyond the Transnational Music Industry*. Burlington, VT: Ashgate Publishing Ltd., 2001.

Palmer, Robert. "The Church of the Sonic Guitar." *South Atlantic Quarterly* 90, no. 4 (Fall, 1991).

———. *Deep Blues*. New York: Viking Press, 1981.

———. "The Fifties." *Rolling Stone* (19 April 1990).

———. "New Rock from the Suburbs." *New York Times* (23 September 1984).

Pareles, Jon. "Howls of Rage, Nine Hours Worth, at Waterloo Village. *New York Times* (13 August 1991).

———. "Music; So Sweet, So Sensitive, So Self-Absorbed, So 70's." *New York Times* (18 May 2003), http://www.nytimes.com/2003/05/18/arts/music-so-sweet-so-sensitive-so-self-absorbed-so-70-s.html.

———. "There's a New Sound in Pop Music: Bigotry." *New York Times* (10 September 1989).

Passman, Arnold. *The Deejays*. New York: Macmillan, 1971.

Patterson, L. Ray, and Stanley W. Lindberg. *The Nature of Copyright: A Law of User's Rights*. Athens, GA: University of Georgia Press, 1991.

Peck, Abe. "Disco! Disco! Disco! Four Critics Address the Musical Question." *In These Times* (6–12 June 1979).

Peraino, Vito. "The Law of Increasing Returns." *Wired* (August 1999).

Pérez Firmat, Gustavo. "Latunes: An Introduction." *Latin American Research Review,* December 2008).

Perry, Steve. "Ain't No Mountain High Enough: The Politics of Crossover." In Simon Frith, ed., *Facing the Music*. New York: Pantheon Books, 1988.

Peterbaugh, Parke. "Anglomania: America Surrenders to the Brits—But Who Really Wins?" *Rolling Stone* (10 November 1983).

Peterson, Richard A. "Why 1955? Explaining the Advent of Rock Music." *Popular Music* (January 1990).

Peterson, Richard A., and David C. Berger. "Cycles in Symbol Production: The Case of Popular Music." *American Sociological Review* (April 1975).

Pietroluongo, Silvio Minal Patel, and Wade Jessen, "Singles Minded: Hot 100 Adds Digital Sales; Pop 100 Debuts." *Billboard* (12 February 2005).

"Playboy Poll: Napster Users Buy CD's." MP3 Newswire (17 August 2000), http://www.mp3newswire.net/stories/2000/playboy.html.

Pond, Steve. "The Seventies." *Rolling Stone* (20 September 1990).

———. "The Trick Is to Be Loved but Not Embraced." *New York Times* (26 June 1994).

Potier, Beth. "File Sharing May Boost CD Sales: Study Defies Traditional Beliefs About Internet Use." *Harvard Gazette Archives* (15 April 2004), http://www.news.harvard.edu/gazette/2004/04.15/09-filesharing.html.

Pruter, Robert. *Chicago Soul*. Urbana: University of Illinois Press, 1992.

Ptacek, Greg. "Majors Return to Nuts and Bolts of Pre-MTV Metal Marketing Days." *Billboard* (27 April 1985).

"Readers Poll." *Rolling Stone* (20 January 2000).

Reagon, Bernice Johnson. "Songs That Moved the Movement." *Civil Rights Quarterly* (Summer, 1983).

"Record Business Sees Light Ahead—On Video Screen." *Chicago Tribune* (26 April 1983).

Recording Industry Association of America. *Inside the Recording Industry: A Statistical Overview, Update '86*. New York: Recording Industry Association of America, 1986.

Reuters. "BMG Says It Discussed Business Models with Napster." CNET News.com (3 October 2000), http://news.cnet.com/news/0-1005-200-2927330.html.

———. "Music Industry Still in First Gear Online." (7 January 2002), http://news.com.com/2100-1023-802359.html.

———. "Prince Voices Support for Napster." CNET News.com (9 August 2000), http://news.cnet.com/news/0-1005-200-2482624.html.

Reynolds, Simon. *Generation Ecstasy: Into the World of Techno and Rave Culture*. New York: Routledge, 1999.

RIAA. "Record Industry Announces 2000 Midyear Shipment Data" (press release). Washington, D.C. (25 August 2000), http://www.riaa.com/newsitem.php?news_month_filter=8&news_year_filter=2000&resultpage=&id=3525ABBC-B110-C3F5-8B63-AC4D3802C9C2.

RIAA v. The People: Two Years Later. Electronic Frontier Foundation, 2005, http://w2.eff.org/IP/P2P/RIAAatTWO_FINAL.pdf.

Rietveld, Hillegonda C. *This Is Our House: House Music, Cultural Spaces and Technologies*. Brookfield, VT: Ashgate, 1998.

Rijven, Stan. "Rock for Ethiopia." Panel presentation at the Third International Conference on Popular Music Studies, Montreal, Quebec, Canada (July 1985).

Roberts, John Storm. *The Latin Tinge: The Impact of Latin American Music on the United States*. Tivoli, NY.: Original Music, 1985.

Rock & Roll Confidential, the editors of. *You've Got a Right to Rock*. Los Angeles: Duke and Duchess Ventures, Inc., 1990.

Rockwell, John. "Atwater's Other Hat: Stealing an Inaugural Show." *New York Times* (23 January 1989).

———. "Leftist Causes? Rock Seconds Those Emotions." *New York Times* (11 December 1988).

Rodman, Sarah. "Music Lovers Pack Halls, Drown the Money Blues," *Boston Globe*, 20 May 2009, http://www.boston.com/news/local/massachusetts/articles/2009/05/20/music_lovers_pack_halls_drown_the_money_blues/

Rose, Tricia. *Black Noise: Rap Music and Black Culture in Contemporary America*. Hanover, N.H.: University Press of New England, 1994.

"Roxio Buys Pressplay, to Relaunch Napster," Salon.com (19 May 2003), http://www.salon.com/tech/wire/2003/05/19/roxio_pressplay/index.html.

Roxon, Lillian. *Lillian Roxon's Rock Encyclopedia*. New York: Grosset and Dunlap, 1971.

Sanjek, David. "Can a Fujiyama Mama Be the Female Elvis? The Wild Wild Women of Rockabilly." In Sheila Whitely, ed., *Sexing the Groove*. New York: Routledge, 1996.

Sanjek, Russell. *American Popular Music and Its Business*. 3 vols. New York: Oxford University Press, 1988.

———. "The War on Rock." In *Downbeat Music '72 Yearbook*. Chicago: Maher Publications, 1972.

Saunders, Michael. "Getting Hip to Pop." *Boston Globe* (9 May 1993).

Savage, Jon. *England's Dreaming: Anarchy, Sex Pistols, Punk Rock, and Beyond*. New York: St. Martin's Press, 1992.

Scaduto, Anthony. *Bob Dylan*. New York: Signet Books, 1973.

Scaggs, Austin. "Why Is Nelly Furtado's New Album So Loud?" *Rolling Stone* (19 June 2006), http://www.rollingstone.com/news/story/10603268/ why_is_nelly_furtados_new_album_so_loud.

Schechter, Danny. "Why We Didn't See Wembley." *Africa Report* (July–August 1990).

Schicke, C. A. *Revolution in Sound: A Biography of the Recording Industry*. Boston: Little, Brown and Co., 1974.

Schipper, Henry. "Dick Clark." *Rolling Stone* (19 April 1990).

Schruers, Fred. "Master P." *Rolling Stone* (29 October 1998).

Schuller, Gunther. *Early Jazz: Its Roots and Musical Development*. New York: Oxford University Press, 1968.

Schumacher, Joseph. "Is Protest music as Dead as Disco?" *Peace and Conflict Monitor* (12 May 2003), http://www.monitor.upeace.org/innerpg.cfm?id_article=5.

Schwartz, John. "A Heretical View of File Sharing." *New York Times* (5 April 2004), http://www.nytimes.com/2004/04/05/technology/05music.html.

Seldes, Gilbert. *The Seven Lively Arts*. 1924. Reprint, New York: A. S. Barnes, 1957.

"Senator: Trash Illegal Downloaders' PCs." CNN.com (18 June 2003), http://www.cnn.com/2003/TECH/internet/06/18/download.music.ap/index.html.

Shapiro, Nat. *Popular Music: An Annotated Index of American Popular Songs: 1940–1949*. Vol. 2. New York: Adrian Press, 1965.

Shaw, Arnold. *Black Popular Music in America*. New York: Schirmer Books, 1986.

———. *Honkers and Shouters: The Golden Years of Rhythm and Blues*. New York: Collier Books, 1978.

———. *The Rockin' '50s*. New York: Hawthorne Books, 1974.

Sheffield, Rob. "Rage Against the Latrines." *Rolling Stone* (2 September 1999).

Shore, Laurence Kenneth. "The Crossroads of Business and Music: A Study of the Music Industry in the United States and Internationally." PhD diss. Stanford University, 1983.

Shore, Michael. *The Rolling Stone Book of Rock Video*. London: Sidgwick and Jackson, 1985.

Sicko, Dan. *Techno Rebels: The Renegades of Electronic Funk*. New York: Billboard Books, 1999.

Small, Christopher. *Music of the Common Tongue: Survival and Celebration in Afro-American Music*. New York: Riverrun Press, 1987.

Smith, Ethan. "Organization Moby." *Wired* (May 2002).

Smith, Joe. *Off the Record: An Oral History of Popular Music.* New York: Warner Books, 1988.

"The Sound of Lawsuits." Editorial, *Mercury News* (9 September 2003), http://www.bayarea.com/mld/mercurynews/news/opinion/6727444.htm.

Souter, Justice David. "MGM v. Grokster." Supreme Court of the United States, No. 04-480 (27 June 2005).

Southern, Eileen. *The Music of Black Americans: A History.* New York: W. W. Norton, 1971.

Stambler, Irwin. *Encyclopedia of Pop, Rock & Soul.* New York: St. Martin's Press, 1977.

Staples, Brent. "The Trouble with Corporate Radio: The Day the Protest Music Died." *New York Times* (20 February 2003), http://www.nytimes.com/2003/02/20/opinion/20THU4.html?th=&pagewanted=print&position=bottom.

Stark, Phyllis. "Gangsta Rap Under the Gun." *Billboard* (18 December 1993).

Steinfels, Peter. "Surge in Satanic Activity Alarms O'Connor." *New York Times* (6 March 1990).

Strauss, Neil. "File-Sharing Battle Leaves Musicians Caught in Middle." *New York Times* (14 September 2003), http://www.nytimes.com/2003/09/14/technology/14MUSI.html.

———. "For Record Industry, All Signs Are Gloomy." *New York Times* (4 December 1996).

———. "The Hit Girl: Christina Aguilera." *Rolling Stone* (6–20 July 2000).

Straw, Will. "Rock for Ethiopia." Panel presentation at the Third International Conference on Popular Music Studies. Montreal, Quebec, Canada (July 1985).

Stuart, Dan. "Black Radio." *Billboard* (17 June 1989).

Sullivan, Andy. "Music Firms, DJ Offer to Pay 12-Year-Old's Fine." *Reuters* (11 September 2003), http://www.reuters.com/newsArticle.jhtml;jsessionid=GJHB5ZIZY5BNACRBAEKSFFA?type=topNews&storyID=3431108.

Sullivan, James. "Three's the Charm as the Last Lilith All-Women Music Festival Loses Its Sensitive Side." *San Francisco Chronicle,* (15 July 1999), reported on Geocities.com, http://www.sfgate.com/cgi-bin/article.cgi?f=/c/a/1999/07/15/DD90915.DTL.

Sullivan, Jim. "Lollapalooza: The Sound of Success." *Boston Globe* (2 August 1992).

Thigpen, David. "Up Against the Wall." *Rolling Stone* (24 February 1994).

Thornton, Sarah. *Club Cultures: Music, Media and Subcultural Capital.* Hanover, N.H.: University Press of New England, 1995.

Toop, David. *The Rap Attack 2: African Rap to Global Hip Hop.* London: Serpent's Tail, 1991.

Tosches, Nick. *Country: Living Legends and Dying Metaphors in America's Biggest Music.* New York: Charles Scribner's Sons, 1985.

Touré. "DMX Reigns as the Dark Prince of Hip Hop." *Rolling Stone* (13 April 2000).

———. "The Life of a Hunted Man." *Rolling Stone* (3 April 2003).

———. "The Next Queen of Soul." *Rolling Stone* (8 November 2001).

———. "Snoop Dogg's Gentle Hip Hop Growl." *New York Times* (21 November 1993).

———. "True Tales of the Pop Life: 'NSync." *Rolling Stone* (16 August 2001).

Townshend, Charles R. *San Antonio Rose: The Life and Music of Bob Wills.* Urbana: University of Illinois Press, 1976.

Tyrangiel, Josh "You Can't Ignore Kanye." *Time* (29 August 2005).

Udovitch, Mim. "Pink Fights the Power." *Rolling Stone* (4–11 July 2002).

———. "Shakira." *Rolling Stone* (31 October 2002).

U.S. Census Bureau. "Table 1.1 Population by Sex, Age, Hispanic Origin, and Race: 2004," http://www.census.gov/population/socdemo/hispanic/ASEC2004/2004CPS_tab1.1a.html.

Waddell, Ray. "Burning Up, the Road: Both Dollars and Attendance Prove Touring Is Out of Its Slump." *Billboard* (23 December 2006).

———. "Rise of the Super-Manager: As Labels Stumble, Managers Become the Industry's Force to Be Reckoned With," *Billboard* (20 December 2008).

———. "Touring Strong, but Some Numbers Cause Concern." *Billboard* (28 December 2002).

Wald, Elijah. *Escaping the Delta: Robert Johnson and the Invention of the Blues.* New York: Amistad, 2004.

———. *How the Beatles Destroyed Rock 'n' Roll: An Alternative History of American Popular Music.* New York: Oxford University Press, 2009.

Walser, Robert. *Running with the Devil: Power, Gender, and Madness in Heavy Metal Music.* Hanover, N.H.: Wesleyan University Press, 1993.

Warhol, Andy, and Pat Hackett. *POPism: The Warhol '60s.* New York: Harcourt Brace Jovanovich, 1980.

Watrous, Peter. "Good Things Happen to Lollapalooza." *New York Times* (5 August 1992).

Watson, Margeaux, "The End of Outkast?" EW.com (retrieved on 24 August 2006), http://www.ew.com/ew/report/0,6115,1195670_4_0_,00.html.

Weinstein, Deena. *Heavy Metal: A Cultural Sociology.* New York: Lexington Books, 1991.

Welch, Nathaniel. "Hit Man." *Rolling Stone* (22 August 2002).

Wenner, Jann. "A Letter from the Editor." *Rolling Stone* (9 November 1967).

———. "A Letter from the Editor: On the Occasion of Our Fourth Anniversary Issue." *Rolling Stone* (11 November 1971).

———. "Musicians Reject New Political Exploiters." *Rolling Stone* (11 May 1968).

"Wexler Attributes Greater R&B Volume to Black Buyer." *Billboard* (20 November 1971).

Wharton, Dennis. "D.C. Bluebloods Want X Rating for Porn Rock." *Variety* (22 May 1985).

Whitburn, Joel. *The Billboard Book of Top 40 Albums.* New York: Billboard, 1991.

———. *The Billboard Book of Top 40 Hits*, 7th ed. New York: Billboard, 2000.

Whitcomb, Ian. *After the Ball: Popular Music from Rag to Rock.* Baltimore, Md.: Penguin Books, 1974.

Wicke, Peter. *Rock Music: Culture, Aesthetics and Sociology.* Cambridge, Eng.: Cambridge University Press, 1990.

Widgery, David. *Beating Time: Riot 'n' Race 'n' Rock 'n' Roll.* London: Chatto and Windus, 1986.

Wilkinson, Francis. "More Washington Show Talk." *Rolling Stone* (9 December 1993).

Willis, Ellen. "Beginning to See the Light: Or Rock & Roll, Feminism, and Night Blindness." *Village Voice* (27 March 1978).

Wolfe, Tom. *The Kandy-Kolored Tangerine-Flake Streamline Baby.* New York: Farrar, Straus, and Giroux, 1965.

Work, John W. *American Negro Songs.* New York: 1960.

Yi, Matthew. "One Billion Songs Sold on iTunes." *San Francisco Chronicle* (24 February 2006), http://www.sfgate.com/cgi-bin/article.cgi?f=/c/a/2006/02/24/BUG9THDRI31.DTL.

York, Peter. *Style Wars.* London: Sidgwick and Jackson, 1980.

Young, Charles M. "Rock Is Sick and Living in London: A Report on the Sex Pistols." *Rolling Stone* (20 October 1977).

Zappa, Frank. "The Porn Wars." *Penthouse* (May 1989).

Zaslow, Jeffrey. "Music and Money." *Wall Street Journal* (21 May 1985).

Zeidler, Sue. "Music Industry Sends Warning to Song Swappers." *Yahoo News* (29 April 2003), http://msl1.mit.edu/furdlog/docs/2003-04-29_yahoo_reuters_riaa_threat.pdf.

Zimmerman, K. "Priest Ruling Gives Unclear Message." *Variety* (3 September 1990).

Zook, Kristal Brent. "Reconstructions of Nationalist Thought in Black Music and Culture." In Reebee Garofalo, ed., *Rockin' the Boat.* Boston: South End Press, 1992.

Zwick, Edward. "An Interview with the Father of Hi-Fi: Dr. Peter Goldmark." *Rolling Stone* (27 September 1973).

Subject Index

Music Index

Note: Titles in italics refer to Albums